MCSE CORE REQUIRED EXAMS

IN A NUTSHELL

Other Microsoft Windows resources from O'Reilly

Related titles

Learning Windows Server 2003

Windows Server Cookbook™

Active Directory

Active Directory Cookbook™

Securing Windows Server 2003

Windows Server 2003 Security Cookbook™

Windows Server 2003 Network Administration

Windows Books Resource Center

windows.oreilly.com is a complete catalog of O'Reilly's Windows and Office books, including sample chapters and code examples.

oreillynet.com is the essential portal for developers interested in open and emerging technologies, including new platforms, programming languages, and operating systems.

Conferences

O'Reilly brings diverse innovators together to nurture the ideas that spark revolutionary industries. We specialize in documenting the latest tools and systems, translating the innovator's knowledge into useful skills for those in the trenches. Visit *conferences.oreilly.com* for our upcoming events.

Safari Bookshelf (*safari.oreilly.com*) is the premier online reference library for programmers and IT professionals. Conduct searches across more than 1,000 books. Subscribers can zero in on answers to time-critical questions in a matter of seconds. Read the books on your Bookshelf from cover to cover or simply flip to the page you need. Try it today with a free trial.

MCSE CORE REQUIRED EXAMS

IN A NUTSHELL

Third Edition

William R. Stanek

O'REILLY®

Beijing • Cambridge • Farnham • Köln • Paris • Sebastopol • Taipei • Tokyo

MCSE Core Required Exams in a Nutshell, Third Edition
by William R. Stanek

Published by O'Reilly Media, Inc., 1005 Gravenstein Highway North, Sebastopol, CA 95472.

O'Reilly books may be purchased for educational, business, or sales promotional use. Online editions are also available for most titles (*safari.oreilly.com*). For more information, contact our corporate/institutional sales department: (800) 998-9938 or *corporate@oreilly.com*.

Editor: Jeff Pepper
Production Editor: Mary Brady
Copyeditor: Mary Brady
Proofreaders: Laurel Ruma and Adam Witwer
Indexer: Ellen Troutman-Zaig
Cover Designer: Ellie Volckhausen
Interior Designer: David Futato
Illustrators: Robert Romano and Jessamyn Read

Printing History:

June 1998:	First Edition. (Originally published as *MCSE: The Core Exams in a Nutshell.*)
March 2000:	Second Edition. (Originally published as *MCSE: The Core Exams in a Nutshell.*)
May 2006:	Third Edition.

This book uses RepKover™, a durable and flexible lay-flat binding.

ISBN: 0-596-10228-3
[M]

Table of Contents

Part II. Exam 70-291

Part III. Exam 70-293

Part IV. Exam 70-294

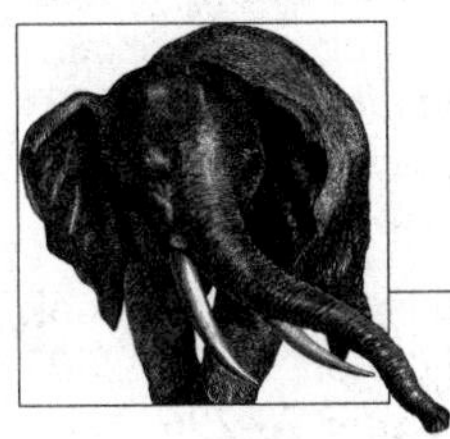

Preface

Welcome to *MCSE Core Required Exams in a Nutshell*. As the author, I designed this book for IT professionals looking to complete their Microsoft Certification. Microsoft offers multiple certification tracks and as an administrator or engineer, the tracks you'll be most interested in are:

Microsoft Certified Professional (MCP)
: Entry-level certification track. To become an MCP, you need to pass only one current Microsoft certification exam.

Microsoft Certified Systems Administrator (MCSA)
: Intermediate certification track for experienced administrators. To become an MCSA, you must pass three core exams and one elective exam.

Microsoft Certified Systems Engineer (MCSE)
: Advanced certification track for experienced administrators with strong engineering backgrounds. To become an MCSE, you must pass six core exams and one elective exam.

Taken appropriately, the certification tracks can measure the progress of your IT career from beginner to pro. Or, for those already experienced, the certification tracks can be a measure of your progress through the process of getting your professional credentials. Regardless of your certification plans, the exam I recommend studying for and taking first is *Exam 70-290: Managing and Maintaining a Microsoft Windows Server 2003 Environment*. When you pass this exam, you will get your MCP credentials.

The next exam I recommend studying for and taking is *Exam 70-291: Implementing, Managing, and Maintaining a Microsoft Windows Server 2003 Network Infrastructure*. When you pass this exam, you will have completed the two required networking systems exams for MCSA certification. To complete MCSA certification, you will need to complete a client operating system exam and an elective exam.

Exams 70-290 and 70-291 are also two of the four required networking system exams for MCSE certification. The other two required networking system exams are *Exam 70-293: Planning and Maintaining a Microsoft Windows Server 2003 Network Infrastructure* and *Exam 70-294: Planning, Implementing, and Maintaining a Microsoft Windows Server 2003 Active Directory Infrastructure*.

Exams 70-290, 70-291, 70-293, and 70-294 are covered in this book. This book also covers *Exam 70-292: Managing and Maintaining a Microsoft Server 2003 Environment for an MCSA Certified on Windows 2000* and *Exam 70-296: Planning, Implementing, and Maintaining a Microsoft Windows Server 2003 Environment for an MCSE Certified on Windows 2000*.

If you are a current MCSA on Windows 2000, you need to pass Exam 70-292 to upgrade your certification to Windows Server 2003. If you are a current MCSE on Windows 2000, you need to pass Exam 70-292 and Exam 70-296 to upgrade your certification to Windows Server 2003. These exams are designed to cover the delta (changes) between Windows 2000 and Windows Server 2003. As such, Exam 70-292 covers a subset of the objectives on Exam 70-290 and Exam 70-291. Exam 70-296 covers a subset of the objectives on Exam 70-293 and Exam 70-294.

The focus of this book is on providing the core knowledge to prepare you for the current certification exams, which include performance-based testing through simulation. This book is meant to be used as part of your final preparation—and not as your only preparation—for the exams. Think of this book as the notes you'd have written down if you were to highlight and then record every essential nugget of information related to the skills being measured in Exams 70-290, 70-291, 70-293, and 70-294 (and by association, Exams 70-292 and 70-296).

Basically, what I've done is boil down the required knowledge to its finest core. So, rather than having 500–700 pages covering each exam, there's approximately 150 pages for each. With this in mind, the best way to use this book is as part of your final review. So, after you've built sufficient hands-on expertise and studied all the relevant texts, grab this book and study it cover to cover as part of your final exam cram.

Unless you have access to a very complete test environment, I recommend employing some type of virtual machine technology as part of your exam preparation. Microsoft offers Virtual PC and Virtual Server. Virtual PC lets you configure desktops and servers and run them in a virtual network environment. Virtual Server builds on Virtual PC and offers better resource use and extended APIs for automated deployment and management. Because Virtual Server 2005 supports two-node clustering between virtual machines on the same Virtual Server host computer and uses a virtual shared SCSI bus to implement the quorum device, you can implement and test software failover between clustered virtual machines. Clustering is a skill measured in Exam 70-293.

Conventions Used in This Book

Each part in this book corresponds to a single Microsoft exam and consists of the following sections:

Exam Overview
: Provides a brief introduction to the exam's topic, a list of objectives, and a cross reference to where the objectives are covered. For those studying for Exams 70-292 or 70-296, callouts are provided to point out the related objectives.

Study Guide
: Provides a comprehensive study guide for the skills being measured on the exam. This section should be read through and studied extensively. If you encounter topics you haven't practiced and studied enough prior to reading this text, you should do more hands-on work with the related area of study and refer to an expanded discussion in a relevant text. Once you've built the real-world know-how and developed the essential background needed to succeed, you can resume your studies and move forward.

Prep and Practice
: Provides exercises and practice questions to help test your knowledge of the areas studied. Sample solutions and answers are provided with explanations where necessary.

The following font conventions are used in this book:

`Constant width`
: Used for code terms, command-line text, command-line options, and values that should be typed literally.

`Constant width italic`
: Indicates text that should be replaced with user-supplied values.

Italics
: Used for URLs, variables, filenames, and to introduce new terms.

Notes are used to provide additional information or highlight a specific point.

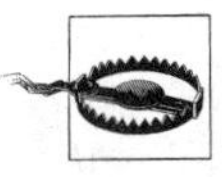

Warnings are used to provide details on potential problems.

Other Study Resources

There is no single magic bullet for passing the Microsoft Certification exams. Your current knowledge will largely determine your success with this study guide and on the exams. If you encounter topics you haven't practiced and studied extensively prior to reading this text, you need further preparation. Get the practical hands-on know-how and knowledge before continuing.

Throughout your preparations for certification, I recommend that you regularly visit the Microsoft Certifications page (*http://www.microsoft.com/certification/*). The related pages will help you keep up-to-date with the certification process and any changes that may occur.

There are a wide variety of Microsoft Certification study guides, training classes, and learning resources available. Regardless of whether these materials say they are for MCPs, MCSAs, or MCSEs, the materials should relate to specific exams. The exams are the same regardless of the certification track.

Also, a large number of practice tests and exam simulations are available for purchase and for free on the Web. These tests, like this book, are useful as part of your exam preparation.

How to Contact Us

The good folks at O'Reilly and I tested and verified the information in this book to the best of our ability, but you may find that features have changed (or even that we have made—gasp!—mistakes). To make this book better, please let us know about any errors you find, as well as your suggestions for future editions, by writing to:

O'Reilly Media, Inc.
1005 Gravenstein Highway North
Sebastopol, CA 95472
800-998-9938 (in the United States or Canada)
707-829-0515 (international or local)
707-829-0104 (fax)

O'Reilly has a web page for this book, where errata, examples, and any additional information is listed. You can access this page at:

http://www.oreilly.com/catalog/mcsecoreian

To comment or ask technical questions about this book, send email to:

bookquestions@oreilly.com

For more information about our books, conferences, Resource Centers, and the O'Reilly Network, see our web site at:

http://www.oreilly.com

For more information about the author, please visit:

http://www.williamstanek.com

Safari® Enabled

When you see a Safari® Enabled icon on the cover of your favorite technology book, it means the book is available online through the O'Reilly Network Safari Bookshelf.

Safari offers a solution that's better than e-books. It's a virtual library that lets you easily search thousands of top tech books, cut and paste code samples, download chapters, and find quick answers when you need the most accurate, current information. Try it for free at *http://safari.oreilly.com*.

Acknowledgments

Increasingly, I find myself trying to do things in fundamentally different ways than they've been done before. For this book, I had this crazy idea that I could get every essential nugget of information necessary for Exams 70-290, 70-291, 70-293, and 70-294 (and by association Exams 70-292 and 70-296) into one book and do so in a way that would give you, the reader, maximum value and learning potential. With that in mind, I started from scratch and addressed the book in an entirely different way from its predecessors. I organized the book into 4 parts and 12 chapters, creating a new approach that divides each exam study guide into three major components: an overview and a study guide followed by "prep and practice." In the overview, I tied the exam objectives directly to the sections in which those objectives are discussed and added details on the upgrade certification path for those taking the upgrade exams. In the study guide, I delved as deep as possible into every exam objective. In the "prep and practice," I created a single chapter that contains everything you need for additional review, including notes on preparing for the exam, suggested exercises, highlights from the study guide, and practice questions.

I hope the result of all the hard work is that the book you hold in your hands is something unique. This isn't a 400-page cram guide or a 600-page study guide for a single exam. This is a comprehensive 750-page guide to Exams 70-290, 70-291, 70-293, and 70-294 (and, by association, Exams 70-292 and 70-296) that contains the core knowledge to prepare you for certification.

During the many longs months of writing this book, I've worked with many different people at O'Reilly. I've enjoyed getting to know Jeff Pepper, Mary Brady, and everyone else at O'Reilly. Jeff Pepper was instrumental throughout the writing process. He was supportive of my ideas. He believed in the book and my unique approach and was really great to work with. Mary Brady headed up the production process for O'Reilly. She is a terrific person to work with, conscientious and dedicated. Her attention to detail through every step of the editing is much appreciated.

O'Reilly has an extensive editing and review process. Rodney Buike, Chris Buechler, and Pawan K. Bhardwaj were the technical reviewers of the book. Each reviewed the book from start to finish, and it was a great pleasure working with them. Of particular note is the effort Pawan put into the project to ensure the book was as accurate as it could be. In the final editing stages, the book was sent out for final comments to Ben Miller, Microsoft MVP Lead, Michael Dennis, Lead

Program Manager for Group Policy at Microsoft, and others. Al Valvano, Rob Linsky, and Lucinda Rowley of Microsoft provided extremely helpful information and support for this project. Thank you for all your help!

Thanks also to Studio B literary agency and my agents, David Rogelberg and Neil Salkind. David and Neil are great to work with.

Hopefully, I haven't forgotten anyone but if I have, it was an oversight. Honest.;-)

Exam 70-290

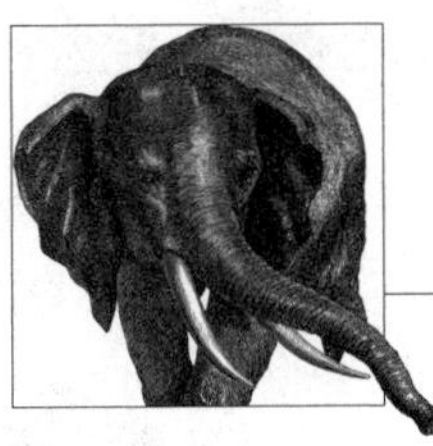

1

Exam 70-290 Overview

Exam 70-290: Managing and Maintaining a Microsoft Windows Server 2003 Environment is designed to cover the skills necessary to perform most day-to-day administration tasks. Before you begin studying for this exam, you should have extensive hands-on experience with general Windows Server 2003 administration, including management of disks, hardware devices, shared folders, and printers. You should also have a detailed understanding of configuring local, roaming, and mandatory user profiles; managing users, computers, and groups; and working with filesystem permissions and changing file ownership.

Troubleshooting and monitoring are major parts of the exam. Many troubleshooting skills are tested, including the ability to solve user and computer account issues, user authentication problems, and remote access issues. You'll need to be able to monitor server hardware using Device Manager and Control Panel utilities, and the Hardware Troubleshooting wizard. You'll also need to demonstrate skill with regard to monitoring system and application performance, server optimization, and disaster recovery.

The exam covers some not-so-routine tasks as well. For example, you'll need to be able to manage software site licensing and software update infrastructure. You'll also need to be able to resolve Terminal Services security and Terminal Services client access issues. In many large enterprises, these tasks are handled by dedicated help desk staff rather than by individual administrators.

Some of the most common problem areas for people taking the exam have to do with:

Automation
: Microsoft really wants administrators to do more with the command line. You are expected to know key command-line tools as thoroughly as you know key GUI tools.

Optimization

The ability to optimize server and application performance is a skill that's best learned through real-world practice. You need a strong understanding of the performance objects used in optimization and how to use them to resolve bottlenecks.

Access/Authentication

Many things can go wrong with user authentication and resource access, especially when Terminal Services is involved. If your organization doesn't use Terminal Services, take the time to create a test environment and work with this technology extensively.

To be prepared for Exam 70-290, you should have 12 to 18 months experience as a Windows Server 2003 administrator. You should have recently studied a Windows Server 2003 administrator's book, taken a training course, or completed a self-paced training kit that covers the related areas of study. You will then be ready to use the Exam 70-290 Study Guide in this book as your final exam preparation.

Exam 70-290 is a required exam for both MCSAs and MCSEs. If you take and pass this exam as your first exam, you will receive your MCP credentials. MCP is an entry-level certification program that requires taking and passing one Microsoft Certification exam. If you are a current MCSA on Windows 2000, you need to pass Exam 70-292 to upgrade your certification to Windows Server 2003. If you are a current MCSE on Windows 2000, you need to pass Exam 70-292 and Exam 70-296 to upgrade your certification to Windows Server 2003. Skills measured by Exam 70-292, representing a subset of Exams 70-290 and 70-291, are indicated in exam overview sections with the X symbol.

Areas of Study for Exam 70-290

Managing and Maintaining Physical and Logical Devices

- Manage basic disks and dynamic disks.
- Monitor server hardware. Tools might include Device Manager, the Hardware Troubleshooting Wizard, and appropriate Control Panel items.
- Optimize server disk performance.
  - Implement a RAID solution.
  - Defragment volumes and partitions.
- Install and configure server hardware devices.
  - Configure driver signing options.
  - Configure resource settings for a device.
  - Configure device properties and settings.

See "Managing and Maintaining Physical and Logical Devices" on page 12.

Managing Users, Computers, and Groups

- Manage local, roaming, and mandatory user profiles.
- Create and manage computer accounts in an Active Directory environment.
- Create and manage groups. X
  - Identify and modify the scope of a group. X
  - Find domain groups in which a user is a member. X
  - Manage group membership. X
  - Create and modify groups by using the Active Directory Users and Computers Microsoft Management Console (MMC) snap-in. X
  - Create and modify groups by using automation. X
- Create and manage user accounts. X
  - Create and modify user accounts by using the Active Directory Users and Computers MMC snap-in. X
  - Create and modify user accounts by using automation. X
  - Import user accounts. X
- Troubleshoot computer accounts.
  - Diagnose and resolve issues related to computer accounts by using the Active Directory Users and Computers MMC snap-in.
  - Reset computer accounts.
- Troubleshoot user accounts.
  - Diagnose and resolve account lockouts.
  - Diagnose and resolve issues related to user account properties.
- Troubleshoot user authentication issues. X

See "Managing Users, Computers, and Groups" on page 32.

Managing and Maintaining Access to Network Resources

- Configure access to shared folders.
  - Manage shared folder permissions.
- Troubleshoot Terminal Services. X
  - Diagnose and resolve issues related to Terminal Services security. X
  - Diagnose and resolve issues related to client access to Terminal Services. X
- Configure filesystem permissions.
  - Verify effective permissions when granting permissions.
  - Change ownership of files and folders.
- Troubleshoot access to files and shared folders.

See "Managing and Maintaining Access to Network Resources" on page 62.

Managing and Maintaining a Server Environment

- Monitor and analyze events. Tools might include Event Viewer and System Monitor.
- Install and configure software update infrastructure. X
  - Install and configure software update services. X
  - Install and configure automatic client update settings. X
- Configure software updates on earlier operating systems. X
- Manage software update infrastructure. X
- Manage software site licensing.
- Manage servers remotely. X
  - Manage a server by using Remote Assistance. X
  - Manage a server by using Terminal Services remote administration mode. X
  - Manage a server by using available support tools. X
- Troubleshoot print queues.
- Monitor system performance.
- Monitor file and print servers. Tools might include Task Manager, Event Viewer, and System Monitor.
  - Monitor disk quotas.
  - Monitor print queues.
  - Monitor server hardware for bottlenecks.
- Monitor and optimize a server environment for application performance.
  - Monitor memory performance objects.
  - Monitor network performance objects.
  - Monitor process performance objects.
  - Monitor disk performance objects.

- Manage a Web server. X
  - Manage Internet Information Services (IIS). X
  - Manage security for IIS. X

See "Managing and Maintaining a Server Environment" on page 84.

Managing and Implementing Disaster Recovery

- Perform system recovery for a server.
  - Implement Automated System Recovery (ASR).
  - Restore data from shadow copy volumes.
  - Back up files and System State data to media.
  - Configure security for backup operations.
- Manage backup procedures.
  - Verify the successful completion of backup jobs.
  - Manage backup storage media.
- Recover from server hardware failure.
- Restore backup data.
- Schedule backup jobs.

See "Managing and Implementing Disaster Recovery" on page 126.

2

Exam 70-290 Study Guide

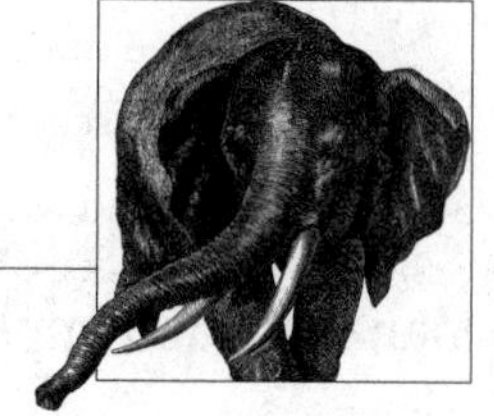

This chapter provides a study guide for *Exam 70-290: Managing and Maintaining a Microsoft Windows Server 2003 Environment*. Sections within the chapter are organized according to the exam objective they cover. Each section identifies the related exam objective, provides an overview of why the objective is important, and then discusses the key details you should know to both succeed on the test and master the objective in the real world.

The major topics covered on Exam 70-290 are:

Managing and Maintaining Physical and Logical Devices
: Designed to test your knowledge of standard disk configurations involving both basic disks and dynamic disks. Also covers hardware devices and monitoring hardware devices.

Managing Users, Computers, and Groups
: Designed to test your knowledge of the many types of accounts used on Windows networks, including user accounts, computer accounts and group accounts. Also covers user authentication and user profiles.

Managing and Maintaining Access to Network Resources
: Designed to test your knowledge of access permissions and shared folders. Also covers Terminal Services security and client access.

Managing and Maintaining a Server Environment
: Designed to test your knowledge of general administration, it is very much a catch-all objective for routine administration tasks. Also covers Internet Information Services (IIS) management and security.

Managing and Implementing Disaster Recovery
: Designed to test your knowledge of both disaster preparedness and disaster recovery procedures. Also covers shadow copies.

The sections of this chapter are designed to reinforce your knowledge of these topics. Ideally, you will review this chapter as thoroughly as you would your course notes in preparation for a college professor's final exam. That means multiple readings of the chapter, committing to memory key concepts, and performing any necessary outside readings if there are topics you have difficulty with.

As part of your preparation, I recommend installing a two-system test network, with one system acting as a workstation and the other system acting as a server. The workstation should run Windows XP Professional or later and be your primary system for management. That means you will work remotely and use the workstation to perform administration of the server as much as possible. The server should be configured to run Windows Server 2003. Both systems can be virtual machines installed as part of a virtual test environment.

Essential Administration Tools

The essential administration tools every administrator must master are:

- AdminPak
- Support Tools
- Microsoft Management Console (MMC)
- Remote Desktop for Administration
- Remote Assistance

AdminPak

The administrative tools available on your system depends on its configuration. As services are added to a system, the tools needed to manage those services are installed. If you manage systems remotely, these same tools might not be available. To ensure you have a consistent tool set, you should install the Windows Server 2003 Administration Tools (AdminPak) on systems you use for administration by completing the following steps:

1. After you log on to the system using an account with administrator privileges, insert the Windows Server 2003 CD-ROM into the CD-ROM drive.
2. When the Autorun screen appears, click Perform Additional Tasks, and then click Browse This CD to start Windows Explorer.
3. Double-click I386, and then double-click *Adminpak.msi* to install the complete set of Windows Server 2003 management tools.

The AdminPak tools can be accessed from the command line and from the Administrative Tools menu.

Support Tools

In addition to the AdminPak, you'll want to install the Windows Server 2003 Support Tools on systems you use for administration. The Windows Server 2003 Support Tools extend the core set of administration tools to include additional useful utilities and commands that can be used for administration.

To install the support tools, complete these steps:

1. Log on to the system using an account with administrator privileges and insert the Windows Server 2003 CD-ROM into the CD- ROM drive.
2. When the Autorun screen appears, click Perform Additional Tasks, and then click Browse This CD to start Windows Explorer.
3. Double-click Support, and then double-click Tools.
4. Double-click *Suptools.msi* to start the Windows Support Tools Setup Wizard.
5. Click Next. Read the End User License Agreement. Click I Agree, and then click Next.
6. Enter your user information, and then click Next.
7. Accept the default install location (*%ProgramFiles%\Support Tools*).
8. Click Install Now. Click Finish.

The Support Tools can be accessed through the Tools Management Console. To start the console, click Start → Programs → Windows Support Tools → Support Tools Help.

Microsoft Management Console

In Windows Server 2003, the primary administration tools are built using the MMC framework. At its heart are consoles and snap-ins. A *console* is a container window to which you can add functional components called snap-ins. You create custom administration tools by adding snap-ins to an empty console. Consoles can also include taskpads to create custom view tabs in the console. The custom view tabs can include shortcut links to menu items, shell commands, and Favorites links.

All consoles, including the standard administration consoles, have two basic modes:

Author
: In Author mode, administrators can make changes to the console by adding or removing snap-ins, and creating task pads. Most MMCs can be put in Author mode by right-clicking the menu option and selecting Author, or by starting the console from the command prompt using the /a parameter. This opens the console for authoring.

User
: In User mode, administrators can access the snap-in functions but cannot make changes to the console. All administrator consoles are in user mode by default. To switch from author mode to user mode in a console, click File → Options, select the desired console mode, clear Do Not Save Changes To This Console, and then click OK. You can then save the updated console to its original location by clicking File → Save or to a new location by clicking File → Save As.

By default, consoles are set to work with the local computer when started. To work with a remote computer via the console, you'll need to right-click the console root node in the left pane and then select Connect To Another Computer. This displays the Select Computer dialog box, which you can use to specify the name or IP address of the remote computer.

Remote Desktop for Administration

Windows Server 2003 Terminal Services has two operating modes: *Remote Desktop for Administration* and *Terminal Server*. One way to think of the Remote Desktop for Administration is as a limited Terminal Server mode that enables administrators to establish remote connections. Each server configured with Remote Desktop for Administration can have up to two concurrent connections.

Remote Desktop for Administration can be enabled or disabled on a per computer basis on the Remote tab of the System utility under Control Panel. To enable this feature, access the System utility's Remote tab, select Enable Remote Desktop On This Computer, and then click Select Remote Users to specify users granted remote access permission via Remote Desktop. By default, any user that is a member of the Administrators group is granted this permission. If the computer is running a firewall, TCP port 3389 must be opened to allow remote access.

Remote Desktop connections can be established using the Remote Desktop Connection client found under Programs → Accessories → Communications or by using the Remote Desktops console found on the Administrative Tools menu. Use the Remote Desktop Connection client to manage one computer remotely. Use the Remote Desktops console to manage multiple computers remotely. Both Windows XP and Windows Server 2003 support remote desktop.

With Remote Desktop Connection, establish remote connections as follows:

1. Open the Remote Desktop Connection client and then click Options.
2. In the Computer field, type the name or IP address of the remote computer.
3. Enter your username, password, and domain information.
4. Enter display, resource, and other options using the other tabs as necessary.
5. Click Connect.

Troubleshooting Remote Desktop connectivity is discussed in "Troubleshoot Terminal Services," later in this chapter.

With Remote Desktops, establish remote connections as follows:

1. Open the Remote Desktops console.
2. Right-click Remote Desktops in the console tree and select Add New Connection.
3. Type the name or IP address of the remote computer in the field provided.
4. Enter an optional Connection Name.
5. Enter your username, password, and domain information.
6. Click OK to close the Add New Connection dialog box.
7. In the left pane, expand the Remote Desktops node to show the defined connections.
8. Click a connection.

Remote Assistance

Remote Assistance allows a user to send an invitation to a more experienced user or administrator asking for troubleshooting help with a computer problem. The helper accepting the request can view the user's desktop, transfer files, and chat with the user needing help through a single interface.

Both Windows XP and Windows Server 2003 support Remote Assistance, which can be enabled or disabled using the Remote tab of the System utility under Control Panel. To enable Remote Assistance, access the System utility's Remote tab, select Turn On Remote Assistance, and then click OK. You can click the Advanced tab to set the maximum amount of time the invitations can remain open.

By default, the user or administrator accepting a remote invitation can remotely control the computer from which the invitation was sent during the remote assistance session. Typically, this is the desired behavior.

The easiest way to make a remote assistance request is to use Windows Messenger. In Windows Messenger, click Actions → Ask for Remote Assistance, and then select the helper's Windows Messenger account when prompted. The helper then receives an instant message and can click Accept to accept the remote assistance invitation. The user seeking assistance then confirms it is OK to start the remote assistance session by clicking Yes.

Another way to send a remote assistance invitation is to use Help And Support Center. Click Support on the toolbar. Under the Support heading, click Get Remote Assistance, then in the right pane, click Invite Someone To Help You.

Managing and Maintaining Physical and Logical Devices

Server systems have both physical and logical devices. Physical devices include all hardware devices connected to or configured within the server system, and include sound cards, video cards, memory, system bus, disk controllers, and physical disks. Logical devices are used to abstract the physical components of hardware devices and represent them in a way that is more manageable. The primary logical devices you'll work with are logical volumes, which are the basic unit of disk storage that you can configure and manage.

Installing and Configuring Server Hardware Devices

Hardware devices installed on a computer communicate with Windows Server 2003 using software device drivers. For a hardware device driver to work properly, the appropriate device driver variant must be installed, the resource settings for the device must be configured appropriately, and the device properties must be set correctly. In most cases, hardware manufacturers will provide a device driver for the hardware device. Windows Server 2003 includes an extensive library of device drivers.

Understanding Plug-and-Play and Non-Plug-and-Play devices

Two basic types of hardware drivers are used on Windows systems:

- Plug-and-Play (PnP)
- Non-Plug-and-Play (Non-PnP)

Most Windows-compatible devices support PnP. PnP allows Windows to detect and install a hardware device automatically either from the library of device drivers maintained by Windows or from a manufacturer-supplied device driver. If a device is detected and there is no device driver, Windows will prompt you to specify the location of the device driver.

In most cases, non-PnP devices are not detected automatically after installation and must be manually installed using the Add Hardware Wizard, which is accessible in the Control Panel and from the Hardware tab of the System utility.

Understanding signed and unsigned drivers

On Windows 2000 and later computers, all hardware device drivers are either *signed or unsigned*. If a device driver is signed, then the driver has a digital signature. The digital signature means that a driver has been authenticated by the digital signer, which typically is Microsoft Windows Publisher, and has not been altered or overwritten by other installation programs or by virus programs. If a device driver is signed by Microsoft Windows Publisher, then the device driver was included with the operating system. If a device driver is signed by Microsoft Windows Hardware Compatibility Publisher, it means the device driver has been tested in the Windows Hardware Quality Labs (WHQL) (and was probably released after the release of the operating system).

Generally speaking, you should always use a signed driver if one is available for the hardware device. Before you install hardware using an unsigned (and potentially dangerous) driver, you should test the driver on a similarly configured computer in a development or test environment.

By default, Windows Server 2003 warns you if you try to install an unsigned device driver. Windows can also be configured to allow all device drivers to be installed or prevent unsigned device drivers from being installed. These settings can be made for individual computers using Control Panel, and for all computers in a domain, site, or organizational unit (OU) through Group Policy. Group Policy can also be used to prohibit users from changing driver installation settings.

As long as you are not prohibited from doing so, you can change driver settings for individual computers by clicking the Driver Signing button on the Hardware tab of the System utility. This displays the Driver Signing Options dialog box. In this dialog box, you can choose the action you want Windows to take whenever someone tries to install an unsigned device driver. As Figure 2-1 shows, the options are:

Ignore
: Allows all device drivers to be installed without having to see and respond to a warning prompt.

Warn
Prompts with a warning message prior to installing a hardware device with an unsigned driver. The user can then continue or cancel the installation (the default).

Block
Prevents installing unsigned drivers. Windows will not install any unsigned device driver and will not display a warning prompt.

Make This Action The System Default
Select this checkbox to make this the default for all users. Clear this option to apply these options only to the current user.

Windows Server 2003 will not install drivers with known problems. If you try to install a driver with known problems, the Windows Driver Protection facility will block the installation.

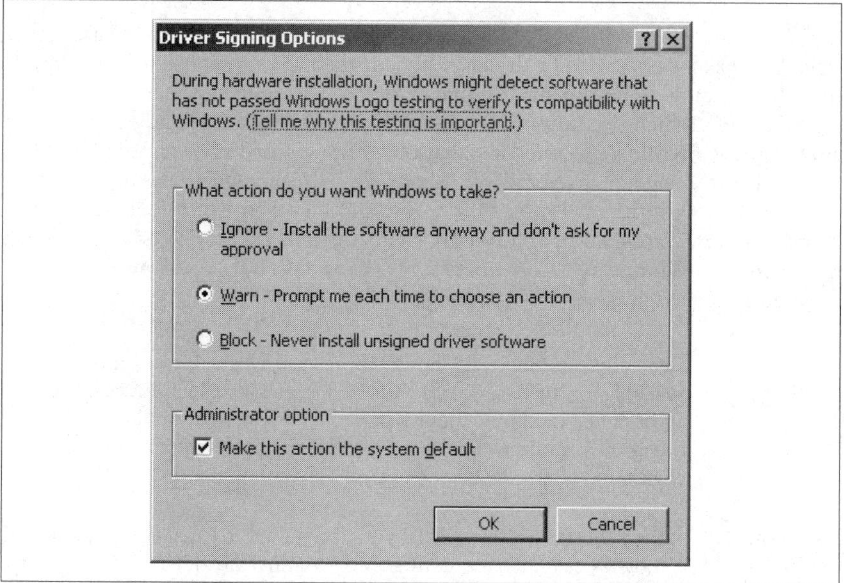

Figure 2-1. Settings in the Driver Signing Options dialog box can be used to change the way Windows handles unsigned drivers.

Installing hardware devices

Administrators can install any hardware device and its drivers, including both PnP and non-PnP devices. Users can only install PnP devices that are detected and installed automatically using signed drivers stored in Windows device driver library. If the device requires the operating system to prompt for any reason, including to specify manufacturer supplied drivers or designate configuration options, users will not be able to complete the installation. The only exception is for users who have been designated specific permission to install such devices.

For the exam, you'll definitely want to have a strong understanding of how device installation works for both administrators and users.

If a device isn't automatically installed and you have a manufacturer's installation disk, you should install the device using the disk. If this doesn't work or an installation disk isn't available, you can install it using the Add Hardware Wizard by following through these steps:

1. Open Add Hardware in Control Panel. When the wizards starts, it scans the computer for PnP devices and installs drivers for any that are found.
2. If no devices are found in Step 1, continue with the manual installation by clicking Next. Then select Yes, I Have Already Connected The Hardware, and then click Next.
3. The wizard then displays a list of all installed devices. If you select one of these devices and click Next, the wizard will quit. If you scroll down to the bottom of the installed hardware list and select Add A New Hardware Device and then click Next, you'll be able to continue with the installation.
4. Next, you can choose whether to search for and install the new hardware device, or have it presented in a list from which you can manually select a driver. If you don't already have a driver, select the search option. If you do have a driver, select the install option, and then click Next.
5. If the wizard searches and fails, or if you elect to install the hardware, you can select the hardware category of the device you are trying to install or simply accept the default to show all devices. Click Next.
6. If you have the drivers for the device, click Have Disk to specify the location of the drivers on your hard disk, floppy, or CD. Otherwise, choose the device manufacturer and device model to use a driver already available in Windows. If the device model isn't listed, the driver isn't included with the operating system.
7. Follow the remaining prompts to complete the installation. In some cases, you might be prompted to restart the computer as well.

Using Device Manager

All detected devices are listed in the Device Manager snap-in, which is installed by default in the Device Manager console (*devmgmt.msc*) and in the Computer Management console (*compmgmt.msc*) (see Figure 2-2). Devices that have been detected but are not installed or properly configured are shown with a yellow warning icon. Devices that have been disabled have a red warning icon.

Device Manager can be used to manage devices on local computers only. On remote computers, Device Manager has Read Only access. You can use Device Manager anytime you have a question as to whether hardware devices on a computer are working properly. Common tasks include:

Viewing hardware device status
: Using options of the View menu, you can view devices by type or by connection. A yellow warning icon indicates improper installation or configuration, and, as such, can indicate that a device is detected but not installed or that a device has a resource conflict with another device.

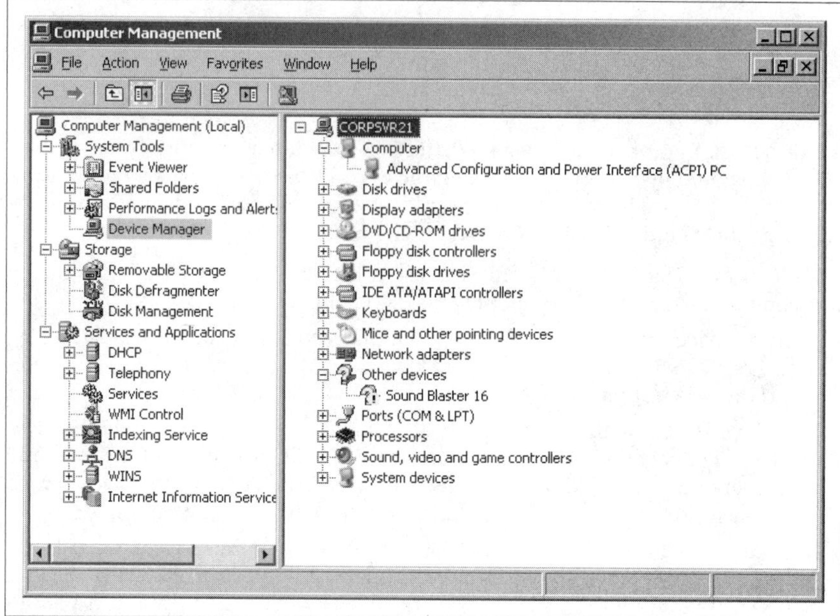

Figure 2-2. Device Manager is used to view and manage installed hardware devices.

Scanning for hardware changes
: If you've made hardware configuration changes that aren't shown in Device Manager, you can select Action → Scan For Hardware Changes.

Changing hardware configuration settings
: Right-click the device and select Properties. You can then view the properties and settings for the device. If the device allows manual configuration through Windows, you'll be able to change resource usage on the Resources tab.

Printing summaries of installed devices
: Select Action → Print. In the Print dialog box, you can then select the report type as "System summary," "Selected class or device," or "All devices and system summary." Similar reports can be obtained from the command line using `Driverquery`. Type `Driverquery /?` for details.

Configuring hardware devices

In Device Manager, you can view and configure hardware devices by right-clicking a device and selecting Properties. Most devices have a dialog box with General, Driver, Details, and Resources tabs. Depending on device type, some devices have fewer or additional tabs.

Figure 2-3 shows the three most common tabs you'll refer to when working with devices:

General

The General tab provides basic details on the device type, manufacturer, and installation location. It also lists the device status and provides a Troubleshoot button for troubleshooting device issues. Clicking Troubleshoot starts the Hardware Troubleshooter in the Help and Support Center. You can also enable or disable a device from the General tab.

Driver

The Driver tab lists the driver provider, date, version, and digital signer (if any). Clicking the Driver Details button shows the files associated with the driver as well as the standard driver details. Clicking the Update Driver buttons allows you to specify a new or updated driver for the device using a process that is similar to the manual driver installation process described previously in "Installing hardware devices." If a driver update fails or the updated driver proves to be faulty, you can go back to the previously installed driver by clicking Roll Back Driver. Drivers can be uninstalled by clicking Uninstall. An uninstalled PnP device is removed from Device Manager. An uninstalled non-PnP device is listed in Device Manager but not configured with a driver.

Resources

The Resources tab shows the resources being used by the device and lists whether there are any conflicts for in-use resources with other devices. If a device can be manually configured through Windows, you'll be able to clear Use Automatic Settings and then click Change Setting to define new resource settings. Typically, you won't need to manually configure device resource assignment. If you manually assign resources, both the device and the resource will be unavailable for automatic configuration.

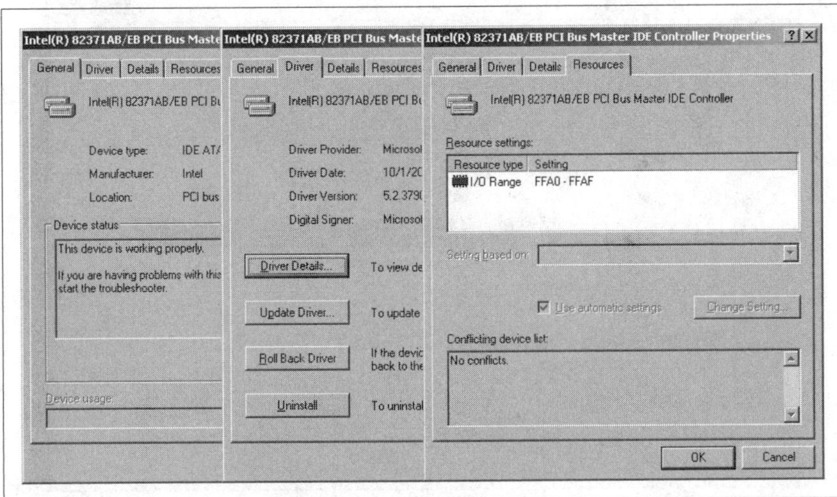

Figure 2-3. The General, Driver, and Resource tabs.

Troubleshooting hardware devices

Windows Server 2003 has fewer problems with hardware devices than previous versions of the operating system. That said, if something goes wrong with a device, it will more typically be a non-PnP device than a PnP device. You may also experience problems with a device after updating its drivers.

In Device Manager, the device is listed with a yellow warning icon if there is a problem with its configuration or it has been detected but there is no driver installed. If you've recently updated the driver for the device, you can try rolling back to the previous version to correct the problem. To do this, open Device Manager and access the device's properties dialog box. On the Driver tab, click Rollback Driver to start the rollback process and follow the prompts.

Other device problems can be resolved using the Hardware Update Wizard or the Hardware Troubleshooter. To start the Hardware Update Wizard, follow these steps:

1. Open Add Hardware in Control Panel. Click Next, select Yes, I Have Already Connected The Hardware, and then click Next again.
2. Select the hardware device you are having trouble with, as shown in Figure 2-4, and then click Next.
3. Click Finish to start the Hardware Update Wizard and then follow the instructions.

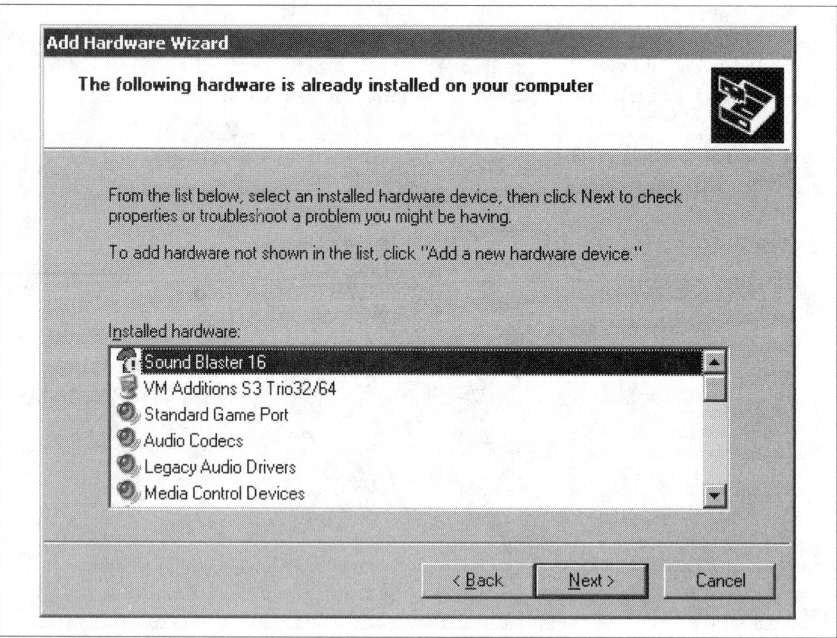

Figure 2-4. Begin troubleshooting with the Add Hardware Wizard.

For a device whose drivers are not installed, you can start the Hardware Update Wizard from Device Manager as well. In Device Manager, right-click the device and then select Properties. On the General tab, click Reinstall Driver to start the Hardware Update Wizard. If a device driver is installed, the General tab of the driver properties dialog box will have a Troubleshoot button instead of a Reinstall Driver button. Clicking the Troubleshoot button starts the Hardware Troubleshooter, which offers a series of prompts with questions and answers that can be used to troubleshoot.

If the driver has been provided by Windows Update, you don't need administrator rights on the local machine to install the driver.

Faulty drivers can also cause the operating system to crash or fail to start. Use the following technique to resolve the problem:

- If you had to restart the operating system after installing a driver and the operating system fails to start, press F8 as the system starts and then specify that you want to use the Last Known Good Configuration as the boot option. Selecting this startup option restores the registry key HKLM\System\CurrentControlSet with the previous driver information.
- If you had to restart the operating system after installing a driver and you successfully log on before a problem occurs, which could happen with an updated video driver, you will not be able to use the Last Known Good Configuration. The Last Known Good Configuration is overwritten when you successfully log on. In this case, you may need to start the computer in Safe Mode. When the computer is starting, press F8, and then choose Safe Mode as the boot option. After you log on, use Device Manager to correct the device problem by rolling back to the previous driver or disabling the device.
- If both the Last Known Good Configuration and Safe Mode do not work, you can attempt to recover the system using the Recovery Console. If Recovery Console is not available as a boot option when you press F8, it has not been installed and must be started from the operating system CD. Find it in the Windows Server 2003 CD, and then restart the system. When Setup starts, follow the onscreen instructions and then press R to choose Repair Or Recover. Next, press C to start the Recovery Console. After you provide the local computer administrator password, you'll see a command prompt. Type `help` to get a list of available commands. When you are finished, type `exit` to exit the console and restart the computer.

Managing Basic and Dynamic Disks

Physical disk drives are a type of hardware device that can be installed or attached to a computer. Although hot swappable disk drives can be installed or attached without powering down a computer, most other types of drives require that you power down a computer prior to installing or attaching the drive. Windows should automatically detect any drive you install or attach.

The primary tools you use to manage disks are the Disk Management snap-in and the DiskPart command-line utility. You must be a member of the local

Administrators group, the Backup Operators group, or have been delegated permission to manage basic and dynamic disks. Only members of the local administrators group can format a disk.

Understanding partition styles

To allow files and file structures to be written on disks, you partition them. Two partition styles are used:

- Master Boot Record (MBR)
- GUID Partition Table (GPT)

The partition styles available on a particular computer depend on the chip architecture:

- x86-based computers use the MBR partition style.
- Itanium-based computers running 64-bit Windows use MBR and GPT partition styles.
- X64-based computers running 64-bit Extended Systems versions of Windows use the MBR partition style.

The partition style provides the underlying methodology for partitioning disks. Windows structures disks and their contents according to storage type. Windows Server 2003 supports two storage types:

Basic disk
: With basic disks, Windows uses partitions to map out the disk structure and the areas of the disk available for storage.

Dynamic disk
: With dynamic disks, the unit of storage is the volume. All volumes on dynamic disks are known as dynamic volumes.

Basic disks are the industry standard and are accessible on just about every operating system. Dynamic disks, on the other hand, are specific to Windows 2000 and later. Dynamic disks are not supported for removable media, on portable computers, such as laptops and tablet PCs, or with disks connected via FireWire/USB.

Some computers ship with disks configured as dynamic disks. Any basic disk can be easily converted to a dynamic disk. However, dynamic disk volumes must be deleted before dynamic disks can be converted to basic disks—a process that destroys the data on the disk.

Understanding special drive sections

Regardless of whether they are basic or dynamic, all disks have three special drive sections:

System
: The system volume contains the hardware-specific files needed to load Windows.

Boot

The boot volume contains the operating system and operating system–related files.

Active

The active volume is the drive section from which the operating system starts.

One and only one of the primary partitions on the disk must be marked as active. Typically, the system, boot, and active partitions are the same—i.e., most computers have one active partition, which is also the system partition and the boot partition.

Using basic disks

The way basic disks are used depends on the partition style:

MBR partition style

With MBR disk partitions on basic disks, logical volumes are represented using primary partitions and extended partitions containing logical drives. A basic disk can have up to four primary partitions, or up to three primary partitions and one extended partition. Each primary partition is represented with one logical volume. Each extended partition is represented by one or more logical drives. A logical drive is a logical volume that is used to represent all of or part of an extended partition.

GPT partition style

With GPT disk partitions on basic disks, multiple partitions are created during setup and installation of the operating system, including an EFI system partition (ESP), a Microsoft Reserved (MSR) partition, and a primary partition. The disk may also contain OEM partitions. GPT disks support up to 128 partitions, any number of which can be primary partitions. Only Itanium-based computers running 64-bit Windows use GPT disks.

MBR is the partition style you'll work with the most. Partitions and logical drives are used only on basic disks. You can extend a partition using the DiskPart command-line utility, provided that the partition is formatted using NTFS and is followed by a contiguous block of unallocated space on the same physical disk.

Under Windows NT 4.0, basic disks supported all the fault tolerant features of dynamic disks. When a computer is upgraded from Windows NT 4.0 to Windows Server 2003, you will have limited management capabilities for these fault tolerant features, such as the ability to repair a damaged volume set or to delete a volume set. You will also be able to upgrade the disks containing the volume set from basic disks to dynamic disks.

Using dynamic disks

Dynamic disks were introduced with Windows 2000 and provide improved manageability by requiring fewer restarts after configuration changes and by allowing disks to be combined or to create fault-tolerant disk sets. With dynamic disks, the unit of storage is the volume. All volumes on dynamic disks are known as dynamic volumes.

Although you can create up to 2,000 volumes on a dynamic disk, the recommended maximum number of volumes is 32. When a computer has multiple dynamic disks, you have additional options for combining disks and creating fault tolerant volumes. The difference between a non-fault tolerant volume and a fault tolerant volume is an important one:

Non-fault tolerant volumes
: Provide no data redundancy or failure protection beyond that offered by the underlying filesystem. If a non-fault tolerant drive fails, you may not be able to rebuild the volume without recovering the data from backup.

Fault tolerant volumes
: Provide data redundancy and failure protection beyond that offered by the underlying filesystem. If a fault tolerant drive fails, you can often rebuild the volume without having to recover data from backup.

Windows supports disk performance and fault tolerance options at the operating system level using redundant array of independent disk (RAID) technology. Another term for Windows-supported RAID is *software RAID*.

> RAID can be implemented using hardware RAID controllers. Because hardware RAID operates at the hardware level, hardware RAID offers better performance than software RAID. Windows sees disks configured with hardware RAID as standard disks, which allows you to set the storage type and the partitioning separately from the underlying hardware implementation. You can format the disks as either basic disks or dynamic disks, and you can also apply software RAID.

As with basic disks, one and only one of the volumes on a dynamic disk must be marked as active, and the volume also is the system volume and the boot volume. With dynamic disks, the types of non-fault-tolerant and fault-tolerant volumes available are as follows:

Simple volume
: The most basic type of volume on a dynamic disk, a simple volume, is the equivalent to a basic disk partition. Simple volumes can span space only on a single disk and are represented as single logical volumes. You can extend simple volumes to unallocated space on the same disk. Simple volumes are not fault tolerant and, as such, provide no redundancy.

Spanned volume
: A spanned volume is used to combine unallocated space on multiple physical disks. Unallocated space on up to 32 physical disks can be combined to create a single spanned volume. The amount of space used on each disk can be different, and data is written to each volume in sequence, starting with the first volume. When space on the first volume fills, space on the next volume is used, and so on. You can extend spanned volumes to unallocated space as necessary to provide additional storage capacity. Spanned volumes provide no fault tolerance. If one of the disks of which the spanned volume consists fails, the entire volume fails and data must be recovered from backup.

Because of how data is written to spanned volumes, they offer poor performance and no fault tolerance. You cannot extend or span the system volume. Nor will Windows allow you to install the operating system on a spanned volume.

Striped volume

A RAID-0 or striped volume is used to combine unallocated space on multiple physical disks. As with spanned volumes, unallocated space on up to 32 physical disks can be combined to create a single striped volume. Unlike spanned volumes, the amount of space allocated to the volume on each disk must be identical, and data is written to all the physical disks in the volume at the same rate (through a technique called *striping*). Writing data to multiple disks increases write performance significantly. It also allows data to be read from multiple disks, which significantly improves read performance.

Although striped volumes offer improved read/write performance over spanned volumes, striped volumes provide no fault tolerance. If one of the disks of which the striped volume consists fails, then the entire volume fails and data must be recovered from backup. It should also be noted that you cannot extend striped volumes, nor can you stripe the system volume.

Mirrored volume

A RAID-1 or mirrored volume is used to create two identical copies of a volume. The amount of space allocated to the volume on each disk must be identical, and data is written to both disks through a technique called *mirroring* (if one disk controller is involved) or *duplexing* (if two disk controllers are involved). With standard mirroring, two independent writes are needed—one to each disk—which affects write performance. With duplexing, the two writes can be performed simultaneously using separate disk controllers, so write performance is the same as if one disk was being used.

Mirrored volumes provide fault tolerance. If one of the drives in the set fails, the other disk can continue to operate and there is no data loss. The failed drive must be replaced or another drive must be specified as the mirror partner to restore fault tolerance. Boot and system volumes can be mirrored.

Striped with parity volume

A RAID-5 or striped with parity volume is used to combine unallocated space on three or more physical disks. As with striped volumes, unallocated space on up to 32 physical disks can be combined to create a single striped volume, the amount of space allocated to the volume on each disk must be identical, and data is written to all the physical disks in the volume at the same rate (via striping). Unlike striping alone, RAID-5 writes the data with checksum information, called *parity*, which provides fault tolerance.

If one of the drives in a RAID-5 set fails, data on the failed disk can be regenerated using the parity information. The failed drive must be replaced or another drive must be specified as part of the volume to restore fault tolerance. System volumes cannot use RAID-5. If two disks in a RAID-5 set fail simultaneously, all data is lost and must be restored from backup.

Table 2-1 summarizes the volume types. Only Windows servers support fault-tolerant software RAID. Although Windows 2000 Professional and Windows XP Professional support disk spanning and disk striping, they do not support disk mirroring (RAID-1) or disk striping with parity (RAID-5). Microsoft recommends that you implement RAID-1 and RAID-5 only on identical disks.

Table 2-1. Volume types on dynamic disks

Volume type	Number of disks	Fault tolerance/performance
Simple	1	No, single disk read/write.
Spanned	2–32	No, possible read/write over multiple disks might mean poor performance.
Striped	2–32	No, striping to multiple disks can offer improved read/write performance.
Mirrored	2	Yes, supports single-drive failure, using two disk controllers (duplexing) gives better write performance than mirroring with a single disk controller.
Striped with parity	3–32	Yes, supports single-drive failure. Striping to multiple disks can offer improved read/write performance.

Table 2-2 compares the terms used with basic and dynamic disks. The most important thing to remember is the following: basic disks have partitions and within extended partitions there are logical drives. Dynamic disks have volumes and only server editions support fault-tolerant RAID.

Table 2-2. Terms used with basic and dynamic disks

Basic disks	Dynamic disks
Active, boot, system partition	Active, boot, system volume
Logical drive	Simple volume
Mirror set	Mirrored volume (RAID-1 volume)
Partition	Simple volume
Primary partition	Simple volume
Stripe set	Striped volume (RAID-0 volume)
Stripe set with parity	Striped set with parity volume (RAID-5 volume)
Volume set	Spanned volume

Understanding volume formatting

Primary partitions, logical drives on extended partitions, and volumes are formatted to create logical volumes. A logical volume must be formatted with a specific filesystem. Windows 2000 and later computers support three filesystems on basic and dynamic disks:

FAT (FAT16)
: Uses 16-bit file allocation tables with maximum volume size of 4 GB.

FAT32

Uses 32-bit file allocation tables with maximum volume size of 2 TB; limited on Windows to 32 GB.

NTFS

Uses a master file table that contains a record for each file and volume as well as metadata on the volume itself. On Windows 2000 and later, NTFS supports 2 TB volumes on basic MBR disks.

NTFS supports advanced file permissions, disk quotas, remote storage, sparse files, file-based compression, and encryption. Because NTFS provides so many security, management, and resiliency features, usually you will want to format logical volumes using NTFS. The only time you wouldn't want to do this is if you have a specific performance reason or other issue.

Understanding volume mounting

When working with logical volumes, it is important to keep in mind that a logical volume may include more than one physical disk and it may also be used to present part of a disk with a single physical disk having multiple logical volumes. In Windows Server 2003, logical volumes are represented by:

- A single drive letter
- A mount point

Table 2-3 summarizes how drive letters and mount points are used. Generally, the drive letters E to Z are available for use with driver letters A and B being used with floppy/Zip drives, drive C for the primary disk, and drive D for the computer's CD/DVD-ROM drive. Logical volumes can be mounted to empty folders on NTFS volumes as well.

Table 2-3. Drive letter and mount point usage

Drive designator	Typical usage
A:, B:	Removable media drives, floppy/Zip
C:	Primary disk
D:	Primary CD/DVD-ROM drive
E:...Z:	Secondary disk, CD/DVD-ROM drive
Folder name	Mount point (NTFS only)

Using Disk Management

The Disk Management snap-in is installed by default in the Disk Management console (*diskmgmt.msc*) and in the Computer Management console (*compmgmt.msc*). Disk Management can be used to manage disk storage on both local and remote computers. Computer Management can be accessed from the Administrative Tools menu or by right-clicking My Computer on the Start Menu and then selecting Manage.

By default, Computer Management connects to the local computer. To connect to a remote computer, right-click the Computer Management node and select

Connect To Another Computer. Then use the Select Computer dialog box to specify the name or IP address of the computer to which you want to connect.

Configuring disks and volumes using Disk Management is a five-step process:

1. Install or attach the disk with the system powered off if required. The disk should be automatically installed and listed when you access Disk Management. If it isn't, right-click the Disk Management node and select Rescan Disks.
2. Initialize the disk to make it available for use. When you start Disk Management after installing a disk, the Initialize Disk Wizard should appear automatically. If it doesn't, you can manually initialize the disk by right-clicking it in Disk Management and selecting Initialize Disk.
3. New disks are initialized as basic disks by default and can be converted to dynamic disks if desired.
    - If you want to use the disk as a basic disk, you can then partition the disk by right-clicking the disk and selecting New Partition. If you create a primary partition, the primary partition becomes a logical volume. If you create an extended partition, you can create logical drives in the partition. Right-click an area of unallocated space in the extended partition and select New Logical Drive.
    - If you want to use the disk as a dynamic disk, you must convert the disk type. Right-click the disk's status box and select Convert To Dynamic Disk. After you convert the disk, you can add volumes by right-clicking an area of unallocated space on the disk and selecting New Volume.
4. Format the volumes you've created as FAT, FAT32, or NTFS. You can do this as part of the volume creation process or afterward by right-clicking the volume and selecting Format.
5. Assign drive letter or mount points. You can do this as part of the volume creation process or afterward by right-clicking the volume and selecting Change Drive Letters And Paths. Volumes can be mounted only to empty folders on existing NTFS volumes.

Using DiskPart

DiskPart is a command-line utility for managing disks. DiskPart can be used interactively or it can call a script to obtain a list of commands to execute. When you type `diskpart` at a command prompt and press Enter, you invoke the DiskPart interpreter, and the `DISKPART>` command prompt appears. You can obtain help at anytime be entering ?. DiskPart has commands for listing and selecting disks, partitions, and volumes. You should always select the specific disk, partition, or volume you want to work with before performing management tasks.

Configuring disks and volumes using DiskPart is a four-step process:

1. Install or attach the disk with the system powered off if required. Invoke DiskPart by typing `diskpart` at a command prompt. Type `list disk` to list the available disks. The disk should be automatically installed and listed when you access DiskPart. If it isn't, type `rescan`.

2. New disks are initialized as basic disks by default and can be converted to dynamic disks if desired. Type `list disk` to determine the number of the disk, and its size and status. Select the disk to specify that you want to work with by typing `select disk` *n*, where *n* is the number of the disk.
   - If you want to use the disk as a basic disk, you can create partitions using `create partition primary`, `create partition extended`, and `create partition logical`.
   - If you want to use the disk as a dynamic disk, you must convert the disk type. Type `convert dynamic`. After you convert the disk, you can add volumes using `create volume raid`, `create volume simple`, and `create volume stripe`.
3. Format the volumes you've created as FAT, FAT32, or NTFS. You cannot do this in DiskPart. To format volumes, you must exit DiskPart by typing `exit` and then run the FORMAT command. Type `format /?` for details on formatting volumes.
4. After you format volumes, you can assign drive letter or mount points using DiskPart. Invoke DiskPart by typing `diskpart` at a command prompt. Type `list disk` to list the available disks. Select the disk you want to work with by typing `select disk` *n*, where *n* is the number of the disk. Type `list partition` or `list volume` to list the available partitions or volumes as appropriate. Select the partition or volume you want to work with by typing `select partition` *n*, where *n* is the number of the partition or typing `select volume` *n*, where *n* is the number of the volume. Assign the drive letter or mount point by typing `assign letter=`*x*, where *x* is the drive letter or `assign mount=`*folderpath*, where *folderpath* is the path to the empty NTFS folder on which to mount.

Extending volumes

You can extend simple or spanned volumes on dynamic disks using Disk Management or DiskPart. In Disk Management, right-click the volume and select Extend Volume. In DiskPart, select the disk and volume you want to work with, then type `extend size=`*n*, where *n* is the size in megabytes to extend the volume. If a partition is formatted using NTFS and is followed by a contiguous block of unallocated space on the same physical disk, you can extend a partition on a basic disk using the same technique.

Implementing RAID Solutions

RAID can be configured using hardware and software implementations. With hardware solutions, a controller card creates and maintains the RAID configuration, which typically is set up using vendor-provided software. With software solutions, Windows Server 2003 creates and maintains the RAID configuration at some cost to performance. As discussed previously, Windows supports:

- Striping (RAID-0)
- Mirroring (RAID-1)
- Striping with parity (RAID-5)

Managing and maintaining striped volumes

Striping (RAID-0) uses unallocated space on 2 to 32 dynamic disks and writes data to all disks at the same rate. To create a striped volume, follow these steps:

1. Open Disk Management, right-click an area of unallocated space on one of the disks, and then choose New Volume. This starts the New Volume wizard.
2. In the New Volume wizard, click Next, and then select Striped.
3. Click Next, and then follow the onscreen instructions for selecting disks and sizing the volume.

Striped volumes must be formatted using NTFS and can be assigned a drive letter or a mount point. Boot and system volumes cannot be striped. If any disk that is part of the striped volume fails, the entire volume will fail and be unusable. To recover the striped volume you must:

1. Delete the volume.
2. Replace the failed disk.
3. Recreate the volume.
4. Restore the data from backup.

Managing and maintaining mirrored volumes

Mirroring (RAID-1) uses an identical amount of space on two disks to create a fault tolerant volume. Since all data is written to both volumes, single-drive write performance can be achieved using two disk controllers (a process called *duplexing*). To create a new mirrored volume from unallocated space, follow these steps:

1. Open Disk Management, right-click an area of unallocated space on one of the disks, and then choose New Volume. This starts the New Volume wizard.
2. In the New Volume wizard, click Next, and then select Mirrored.
3. Click Next, and then follow the onscreen instructions for selecting disks and sizing the volume.

Mirrored volumes must be formatted using NTFS and can be assigned a drive letter or a mount point. Unlike striped volumes, boot and system volumes can be mirrored. To mirror an existing volume, follow these steps:

1. Open Disk Management, right-click an existing volume on a dynamic disk, and select Add Mirror.
2. In the Add Mirror dialog box, select one of the available dynamic disks on which to create the mirror, and then click Add Mirror.

Mirrored volumes can fail in several ways. The way you repair the mirror depends on the error status shown in Disk Management for the disk and volume:

- If data is not written to both volumes, which may occur if there are I/O errors during write operations, the mirrored volume is said to have failed redundancy. To correct a Failed Redundancy status, open Disk Management, right-click one of the volumes in the set, and choose Resynchronize Mirror. This forces Windows to resynchronize the data.

- If one of the drives in the mirrored volume has a status of Failed, Online (Errors), or Unreadable, open Disk Management, right-click the failed or missing drive, and then choose Rescan Disks. When this process finishes, right-click the drive and choose Reactivate. If the Healthy status isn't restored, right-click the volume and choose Resynchronize Mirror.

If you are unable to recover the mirror, which may occur if a disk is bad, you will need to rebuild the mirror by following these steps:

1. Replace the failed disk or have an alternate disk for use in mirroring.
2. Right-click the failed volume and then select Remove Mirror.
3. Right-click the remaining volume from the original mirror and select Add Mirror.
4. In the Add Mirror dialog box, select one of the available dynamic disks on which to create the mirror and then click Add Mirror.

Managing and maintaining striped with parity volumes

Striping with parity (RAID-5) uses an identical amount of space on 3 to 32 disks to create a fault tolerant volume. Data is written to all the physical disks in the volume at the same rate using striping. Checksum information in the form of parity is written with the data to provide fault tolerance. To create a new RAID-5 volume from unallocated space on three or more disks, follow these steps:

1. Open Disk Management, right-click an area of unallocated space on one of the disks, and then choose New Volume. This starts the New Volume wizard.
2. In the New Volume wizard, click Next, and then select RAID-5.
3. Click Next, and then follow the onscreen instructions for selecting disks and sizing the volume.

RAID-5 volumes must be formatted using NTFS and can be assigned a drive letter or a mount point. Like striped volumes, system volumes cannot use RAID-5.

Like mirrored volumes, RAID-5 volumes can fail in several ways. The way you repair the volume depends on the error status shown in Disk Management for the disk and volume:

- If one of the disks in the volume is missing or offline, right-click the failed or missing drive, and then choose Rescan Disks. When this process finishes, right-click the drive and choose Reactivate. If the Healthy status isn't restored, right-click the volume and choose Regenerate Parity.
- If parity is not written correctly to all volumes, which may occur if there are I/O errors during write operations, the RAID-5 volume is said to have failed redundancy. As before, you should try rescanning and then reactivating the problem drive. If the Healthy status isn't restored, right-click the volume and choose Regenerate Parity.

If one of the disks in the volume won't come back online, which may occur if a disk is bad, you will need to rebuild the volume by following these steps:

1. Replace the failed disk or have an alternate disk available for use.
2. Right-click the failed volume and then select Remove Volume.

3. Find an area of unallocated space on a dynamic disk not used by the volume that is at least as large as the region to repair in size. Note the disk number.
4. Right-click the RAID-5 volume and select Repair Volume. When prompted to specify where the missing volume should be recreated, select Disk Previously Located.

Maintaining Disks

Several tools are provided for maintaining disks, including Check Disk (*CHKDSK.EXE*) and Disk Defragmenter (*DFRG.MSC*). You use Check Disk to check for and repair disk errors. You use Disk Defragmenter to reorganize a disk's files and folders to optimize performance.

Using Check Disk

Check Disk (*CHKDSK.EXE*) scans the surface of disks, checking the integrity of files and folders while looking for and correcting errors, such as lost clusters and invalid file indexes. Check Disk can be run interactively or from the command prompt.

To run Check Disk interactively, open Disk Management or My Computer, right-click the volume, and then select Properties. On the Tools tab of the disk's properties dialog box, click Check Now. By default, Check Disk looks for errors only. If you want Check Disk to search for and correct errors, you should select Automatically Fix File System Errors and Scan For And Attempt Recovery Of Bad Sectors before clicking Start, as shown in Figure 2-5.

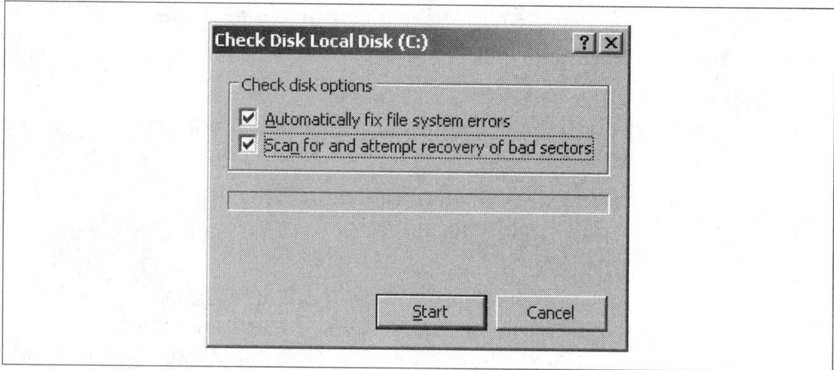

Figure 2-5. Use Check Disk to search for and correct errors.

To run Check Disk from the command line, type `chkdsk` followed by the drive designator, such as `chkdsk c:`. Use the optional parameter `/f` to automatically fix filesystem errors and `/r` to scan for and attempt recovery of bad sectors. All parameters available can be listed by typing `chkdsk /?`.

Without any switches, the `chkdsk` utility works in error-checking only mode on the drive you are working on. `chkdsk` moves the data found on a bad sector to a good sector only if this is supported based on the volume type. Otherwise, `chkdsk` cannot recover data on bad sectors and data may have to be recovered from backup.

Whether working interactively or from the command prompt, keep in mind Check Disk may need exclusive disk access to some files to fix errors. If exclusive access to files isn't available, you'll be prompted to schedule the disk check to occur next time you restart the computer. Adding the `/x` parameter at the command line can force the nonsystem volumes to dismount before checking the disk. System volumes cannot be dismounted in this way.

Using Disk Defragmenter

Disk Defragmenter (*DFRG.MSC*) checks for and corrects fragmentation problems on disks. Fragmentation can occur in a disk's Master File Table (MFT) or paging file, as well as in the files and folders stored on the volume.

Disk Defragmenter works only on local computers. For defragmenting remote computers, you'll need a third-party utility. You must have at least 15 percent free space on the disk where you want to run Disk Defragmenter.

On FAT, FAT32, and NTFS volumes, files, folders, and related disk structures are stored in units called *clusters*. Only one file can be written to a particular cluster. The default cluster size for NTFS is 4 KB. When this cluster size is used, files that are 4 KB or smaller are written to a single cluster on the disk, and files larger than 4 KB are written to multiple clusters.

For read/write operations, the operating system can write and read files faster when clusters are written in sequential or nearly sequential clusters. If there are large gaps between the file clusters, the disk controller must seek across the disk for clusters, which reduces read/write performance.

To run Disk Defragmenter interactively, open Disk Management or My Computer, right-click the volume, and then select Properties. On the Tools tab of the disk's properties dialog box, click Defragment Now. Using Disk Defragmenter is a two-part process—you must click Analyze to analyze the disk and determine the level of fragmentation. Disk Defragmenter will prompt to defragment the disk if this is recommended based on the current disk usage. Click View Report to see a detailed report of the disk usage. Begin defragmenting the disk by clicking Defragment.

To run Disk Defragmenter from the command line, type `defrag`, followed by the drive designator, such as `defrag c:`. Disk Defragmenter will then analyze the disk and begin defragmenting the disk if this is required. If you want only to analyze the volume, use the `-a` parameter. Other parameters available include `-v` for verbose output and `-f` to force defragmentation to occur even if the disk has low free space.

Whether working interactively or from the command prompt, Disk Defragmenter resolves fragmentation problems by attempting to rearrange files so they use consecutive clusters and by consolidating free space.

Managing Users, Computers, and Groups

Windows computers can be organized into the following:

Domains

Active Directory is used to provide directory services for computers and resources, such as users, computers, and groups. They are all represented as objects that are stored in the directory on domain controllers. The primary tool for working with users, computers, and groups in domains is Active Directory Users And Computers.

Workgroups

Each local computer stores details on users and groups in the Security Accounts Manager (SAM) database. The primary tool for working with local users and local groups in workgroups is the Local Users And Groups snap-in, which is installed by default in the Local Users And Groups console (*lusrmgr.msc*) and in the Computer Management console (*compmgmt.msc*).

Managing domain accounts for users, computers, and accounts is a key part of most administrator's job and an important part of the 70-290 exam. Knowing troubleshooting techniques for accounts is also essential.

Exams 70-290, 70-291, 70-293, and 70-294 (and by association Exams 70-292 and 70-296) all expect you to have familiarity with Active Directory. Exam 70-294 (70-296 for those upgrading their certification) is where the detailed knowledge of Active Directory is tested. If you are unfamiliar with the concepts of domains, domain trees, domain forests, and how objects are stored within Active Directory, you should review the introductory materials provided at the beginning of the Exam 70-294 study guide in this book before continuing.

Understanding User, Computer, and Group Naming

Names assigned to users, computers, and groups are used for assignment and reference purposes. You assign access permissions to a user, computer, or group using the associated account name. You make references to a user, computer, or group using the associated account name.

In a workgroup, each computer must have a unique name, and other names are maintained on a per-machine basis. This means each local user and local group defined on a computer must be unique.

In Active Directory, all user, computer, and group names must be unique on a per-domain basis. There is a specific set of rules that must be adhered to, which require that:

- User, computer, and group names are unique within each domain and can contain no more than 256 characters. However, an associated display name can only have up to 64 characters.

- User, computer, and group names have an associated pre-Windows 2000 name. This name is used for backward compatibility with Windows NT and must also be unique in the domain. By default, the pre-Windows 2000 name is the first 20 characters of the standard name.
- User, computer, and group names are permitted to contain spaces, periods, dashes, and underscores, but cannot contain the following special characters: " / \ [ ] ; | = , + * ? < >.

Managing Computer Accounts in an Active Directory Environment

Before a user can log on to a computer with a domain account, the computer must be a member of the domain, which means the computer must have a domain account and be joined to the domain using that account. Computer accounts, like user accounts, have an account name, password, and security identifier (SID). In Active Directory, these properties of computer accounts are stored along with many other properties in the related objects, and these objects in turn are stored in the directory itself.

Creating computer accounts

Computer accounts can be created in several ways:

- If you create an account for a computer before joining it to the domain, you are prestaging the computer account, which makes it easier for other users and administrators to join the computer to the domain.
- If you do not create an account before joining a computer to a domain, Active Directory will create the computer account for you provided you have appropriate permissions or can provide appropriate permissions when prompted.

The key advantage of prestaging computer accounts is that you can specify the Active Directory container within which the computer account will be stored. If you do not prestage the computer account, Active Directory creates the computer account in the default container for computer objects. Typically, this is the computer's organizational unit (OU). If a Windows Server 2003 computer is later made a domain controller (using DCPROMO), the computer object is moved to the default container for domain controllers, which typically is the Domain Controllers OU.

Permissions for who can prestage computer accounts and who can join computers to a domain are somewhat convoluted:

- Administrators and account operators can create computer accounts for prestaging and join computers to domains.
- Users can be delegated permission to create computer accounts or to join a specific computer with a prestaged account to a domain. Delegated users must also have local administrator permissions on the local computer.
- Authenticated users can join up to 10 computers to the domain, and Active Directory will create necessary computer objects for these computers automatically. Authenticated users must also have local administrator permissions on the local computer.

Computer accounts can be created using a variety of tools. The two you'll use the most are:

- Active Directory Users And Computers (*dsa.msc*)
- DSADD (*dsadd.exe*)

Regardless of which tool you are using, you should think about which container or OU the computer account will be placed in before creating the account. Ideally, you'll place the computer account in the container or OU where it can best be managed in terms of administration, delegation, and policy application. To create a computer account using Active Directory Users And Computers (*dsa.msc*), follow these steps:

1. Right-click the container in which you want to store the computer account.
2. On the shortcut menu, select New → Computer. This starts the New Object – Computer wizard as shown in Figure 2-6.

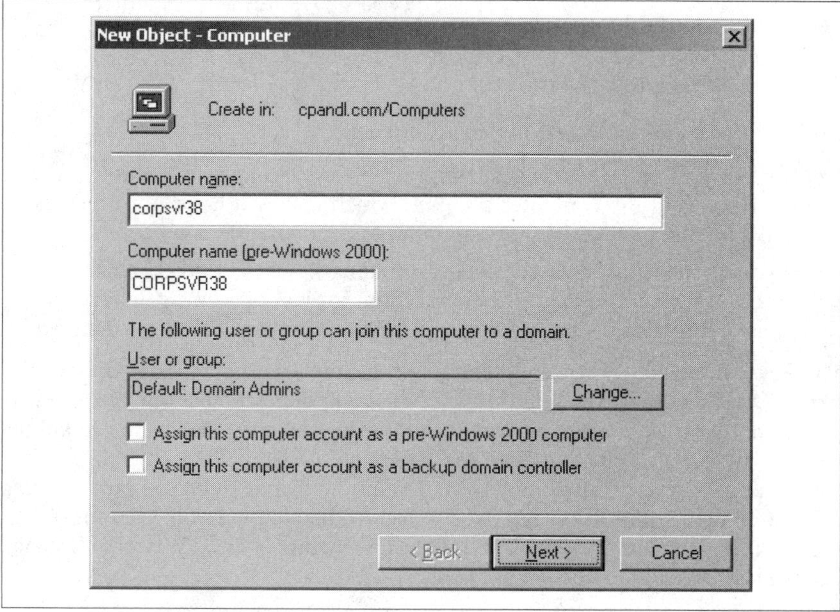

Figure 2-6. The New Object – Computer wizard is used to create computer accounts.

3. Type the computer name in the Computer Name field.
4. By default, only members of the Domain Admins group will be able to join this computer to the domain. If you want to delegate this permission to a specific user or group, click Change, and then select the user or group using the dialog box provided.
5. If the computer account is for a Windows NT computer or Windows NT backup domain controller, select the appropriate checkbox before clicking Next. Otherwise, just click Next.

6. If the computer is being prestaged for later Remote Installation Services (RIS) installation of the operating system, select This Is A Managed Computer and type in the computer's unique identifier (it's GUID or UUID). When you click Next, you will then need to specify which remote installation server can be used.
7. Click Next and then click Finish.

To create a computer account using DSADD, you'll need to have a strong understanding of Active Directory service path strings. Essentially, path strings describe the computer object's location in the directory from its most basic component, the computer name, to its most widely scoped components, the actual containers in which it is stored. Consider the following example:

- You want to create a computer account called CorpSvr32 in the Computers container for the *williamstanek.com* domain. The full path to this computer object is `CN=CorpSvr32,CN=Computers,DC=williamstanek,DC=com`. When creating the computer object using DSADD, you must specify this path as follows:

```
dsadd computer "CN=CorpSvr32,CN=Computers,DC=williamstanek,DC=com"
```

Although quotation marks are only required if the path string contains a space, it is a good idea to use them whenever specifying path strings. This way, you will remember to use them when they are required and won't get an error.

In this example, `CN=` is used to specify the common name of an object and `DC=` is used to specify a domain component. With Active Directory path strings, you will also see `OU=`, which is used to specify the name of an organizational unit object. For the full syntax and usage, type `dsadd computer /?` at a command prompt.

Joining computer accounts to domains

Any authenticated user can join a computer to a domain, provided the account for the computer hasn't been prestaged. If it has been prestaged, only a user specifically delegated permission or an administrator can join a computer to a domain. Users must also have local administrator permissions on the computer.

Computer can be joined to a domain using:

- Active Directory Users And Computers (*dsa.msc*)
- NETDOM (*netdom.exe*)

Before joining a computer to a domain, I recommend that you check the computer's network configuration. In Control Panel, access Network Connections → Local Area Connection. In the Local Area Connection Status dialog box, click Details located on the Support tab. Ensure that the TCP/IP settings for IP address, default gateway, and DNS are configured properly. If these settings are obtained from DHCP, make sure the lease is current. If the TCP/IP configuration is not correct, you will need to modify the settings before attempting to join the computer to the domain. Access the General tab of the Local Area Connection Status dialog box and click Properties. In the Local Area Connection Properties dialog box, select Internet Protocol (TCP/IP), and then click Properties. Use the options of the Internet Protocol (TCP/IP) Properties dialog box to configure the TCP/IP settings.

Typing `ipconfig /all` at a command prompt is the fastest way to check a computer's network configuration.

To join the computer to the domain, follow these steps:

1. Open the System utility in Control Panel.
2. On the Computer Name tab, click Change. This displays the Computer Name Changes dialog box (see Figure 2-7).

If the Change button is dimmed, you are not logged on using a user account that has local administrator permission. Log out and then log on again using an account with local administrator permission.

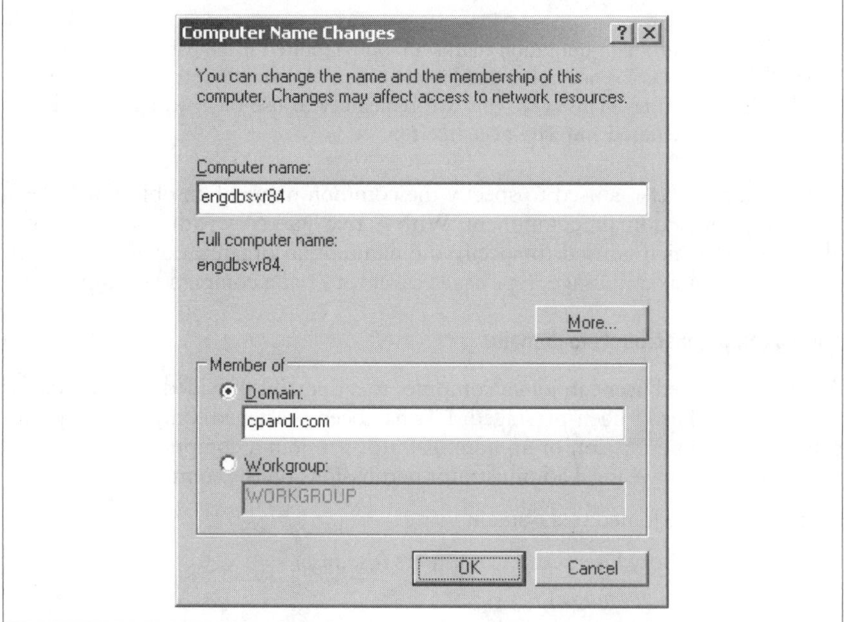

Figure 2-7. Change the computer name and domain information as necessary.

3. Note the full name of the computer. If the computer is a member of another domain already, this is listed as part of the computer's full name.
4. You can change the computer's name and domain membership. To change the computer name, type a new name in the Computer Name field. To specify that the computer should be a member of a domain, select Domain, and then type the name of the Active Directory domain.
5. Click OK.

6. When prompted, type in the name and password of a user account in the domain that has appropriate permissions for joining the computer to the domain (and creating the related account if necessary). Click OK.
7. A welcome message will confirm that the computer has joined the domain. Click OK.
8. When prompted to restart the computer, click OK. After the computer restarts, you'll see the logon screen. Click Options so you can set the logon domain using the Log On To selection list. Next type a domain user account name and password, then click OK to logon to the domain using the specified user account.

When a computer joins a domain, the computer establishes a trust relationship with the domain. The computer's SID is changed to match that of the related computer account in Active Directory, and the computer is made a member of the appropriate groups in Active Directory. Typically, this means the computer is made a member of the Domain Computers group. If the computer is later made a domain controller, the computer will be made a member of the Domain Controllers group instead.

A command-line tool for joining computers to a domain is NETDOM. NETDOM is available when the Windows Support tools are installed on a computer. You can use NETDOM to simultaneously join a computer to a domain and create a computer account in the domain. Use the following command syntax:

```
netdom add ComputerName /domain:DomainName /userD:DomainUser
/password:UserPassword
```

where *`ComputerName`* is the name of the computer, *`DomainName`* is the name of the Active Directory domain to join, *`DomainUser`* is the name of a domain user account authorized to join the computer to the domain (and create the related computer account if necessary), and *`UserPassword`* is the password for the user account. Optionally, you can use the `/ou` switch to specify the distinguished name of the OU into which the computer account should be placed.

Consider the following example:

- You want to join a computer account called CorpSvr32 in the Engineering OU for the *williamstanek.com* domain. The full path to this computer object is `CN=CorpSvr32,OU=Engineering,DC=williamstanek,DC=com`. When creating the computer object and joining the computer to the domain using NETDOM, you would type:

  ```
  netdom add corpsvr32 /ou:OU=Engineering,DC=williamstanek,DC=com
  ```

Maintaining computer accounts

In Active Directory, computer accounts are stored by default in the Computers container, and domain controller accounts are stored in the Domain Controllers OU. When you create computer accounts, you can place them in a specific container. All computer accounts have manageable properties and passwords, and there is a trust between computers and the domain in which they are located.

You can maintain computer accounts and manage related properties in several ways. Use Active Directory Users And Computers by right-clicking the account name, you'll see a shortcut menu with the following options:

Properties
: Select Properties to view and manage computer account properties, including group membership.

Delete
: Select Delete to delete the computer account from the domain.

Disable Account
: Select Disable Account to disable the account and prevent users on that computer from logging on to the domain.

Move
: Select Move to move the computer account to a new container or OU within the current domain.

Reset Account
: Select Reset Account to reset the computer password for the account. If you reset the computer account, the computer must be removed from the domain (by placing it in a workgroup or other domain) and then rejoined to the domain.

The directory services commands can also be used to perform these tasks. Use the commands as described here:

DSMOD COMPUTER
: Use to set properties, disable accounts, and reset accounts.

DSMOVE COMPUTER
: Use to move computer accounts to a new container or OU.

DSRM COMPUTER
: Use to remove the computer account.

On the exam, you'll need to know how to resolve computer account problems by:

1. Resetting the computer account.
2. Removing the computer account from the domain by joining a workgroup.
3. Rejoining the computer to the domain.

However, the Reset Account feature is not the best technique to use with member servers and domain controllers. With member servers and domain controllers, you should use NETDOM RESETPWD. You can reset the computer account password of a member server or domain controller by completing the following steps:

1. Log on locally to the computer. If you are resetting the password of a domain controller, you must stop the Kerberos Key Distribution Center service and set its startup type to Manual.
2. Open a command prompt.

3. Type `netdom resetpwd /s:`*`ComputerName`* `/ud:`*`domain\user`* `/pd:*`, where *`ComputerName`* is the name of a domain controller in the computer account's logon domain, *`domain\user`* is the name of an administrator account with the authority to change the computer account password, and * tells NETDOM to prompt you for the account password before continuing.
4. When you enter your password, NETDOM will change the computer account password locally and on the domain controller. The domain controller will then distribute the password change to other domain controllers.
5. When NETDOM completes this task, restart the computer and verify that the password has been successfully reset. If you reset a domain controller's password, restart the Kerberos Key Distribution Center service and set its startup type to Automatic.

Troubleshooting computer accounts

As an administrator, you'll see a variety of problems related to computer accounts. When you are joining a computer to a domain, you may experience problems due to:

Incorrect network settings
: The computer joining the domain must be able to communicate with the domain controller in the domain. Resolve connectivity problems by accessing Network Connections → Local Area Connection from Control Panel as discussed previously.

Insufficient permissions
: The user joining the computer to the domain must have appropriate permissions in the domain. Use an account with appropriate permissions to join the domain.

Once a computer is joined to a domain, you may occasionally see problems with the computer password or trust between the computer and the domain. A password/trust problem can be diagnosed easily: if you try to access or browse resources in the domain and are prompted for a username and password when you normally are not, you may have a password/trust issue with the computer account. For example, if you are trying to connect to a remote computer in Computer Management, and you are prompted for a username and password where you weren't previously, the computer account password should probably be reset.

You can verify a password/trust problem by checking the System event log. Look for an error with event ID 3210 generated by the NETLOGON service. The related error message should read:

> This computer could not authenticate with RESOURCENAME, a Windows domain controller for domain DOMAINNAME, and therefore this computer might deny logon requests. This inability to authenticate might be caused by another computer on the same network using the same name or the password for this computer account is not recognized. If this message appears again, contact your system administrator.

If the related computer account is disabled or deleted, you will be denied access to remote resources when connecting to those resources from this computer. For example, if you are trying to access CorpSvr23 from CorpPc18, you will be denied access if the computer account is disabled or deleted. The system event log on the remote computer (CorpSvr23) should log related NETLOGON errors specifically related to the computer account, such as the following with event ID 5722:

> The session setup from the computer CORPPC18 failed to authenticate. The name(s) of the account(s) referenced in the security database is CORPPC18$. The following error occurred: Access is denied.

Because of this, you should always check the status of the account in Active Directory Users And Computers as part of the troubleshooting process. A disabled account has a red warning icon. A deleted account will no longer be listed and you won't be able to search for and find it in the directory. If a user is trying to connect to a resource on a remote computer, the computer to which she is connecting should have a related error or warning event in the event logs.

Check the storage location of the computer and its group membership as well. Computer accounts, like user accounts, are placed in a specific container in Active Directory and can be made members of specific groups:

- The container in which a computer is placed determines how Active Directory policy settings (Group Policy) are applied to the computer. Moving a computer to a different container or OU can significantly affect the way policy settings are applied.
- The group membership of a computer determines many permissions with regard to security and resource access. Changing a computer's group membership can significantly affect security and resource access.

With Kerberos authentication, a computer's system time can affect authentication. If a computer's system time deviates outside the permitted norms set in group policy, the computer will fail authentication.

Managing Groups in an Active Directory Environment

Group accounts are used in both workgroups and domains to help manage access to resources. Depending on the group type and scope, a group can have as its members other groups, computers, users, or any permitted combination of the three. By designating Group A as a member of Group B, you grant all users and computers in Group A the permissions of Group B. By making a user or computer a member of Group A, you grant the user or computer all the permissions of Group A.

Understanding group types and scopes

In workgroups, computers have only one type of group: *local groups*. These are used to help manage local machine permissions and access to local machine resources. You manage local groups using the Local Users And Groups snap-in, which is installed by default in the Local Users And Groups console (*lusrmgr.msc*) and in the Computer Management console (*compmgmt.msc*).

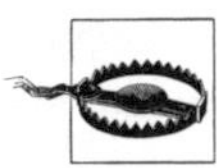

You cannot manage local users or local groups on domain controllers. Domain controllers do not have local users or local groups.

In Active Directory domains, computers have local groups as well. As with workgroups, local groups are used to help manage local machine permissions and access to local machine resources. However, that being said, the primary types of groups you'll work with in domains are:

Distribution groups
: Distribution groups are used for email distribution lists. Distribution groups do not have security descriptors.

Security groups
: Security groups are used to assign access permissions for network resources, such as shared folders and printers. All security groups have security descriptors.

Distribution groups are designed to make email services and server management easier by allowing administrators to add existing user accounts to email distribution lists. Although security groups can be used for email distribution purposes, distribution groups cannot be used to manage access to network resources.

When you create a distribution group or security group, you assign the group a specific scope: either *domain local*, *global*, or *universal*. As Table 2-4 shows, the scope determines how the group can be used and what members it can include.

Table 2-4. Group usage in Active Directory domains

Group scope	How used	Can include
Domain local	Primarily to assign access permissions to resources within a single domain.	Members from any domain in the forest and from trusted domains in other forests. Typically, global and universal groups are members of domain local groups.
Global	Primarily to define sets of users or computers in the same domain that share a similar role, function, or job.	Only accounts and groups from the domain in which it is defined, including other global groups.
Universal	Primarily to define sets of users or computers that should have wide permissions throughout a domain or forest.	Accounts and groups from any domain in the forest, including other universal groups and global groups.

Active Directory domains also have built-in local groups. These groups are created during setup of the operating system and installation of Active Directory. Built-in local groups are a special scope. Because they are managed in the same way as domain local groups, they are often included in the definition of domain local groups. However, you cannot create or delete built-in local groups.

Domain functional level affects which group scopes are available and how group scopes are used. Specifically, when the domain functional level is set to Windows 2000 Mixed or Windows Server 2003 interim, universal groups are not available and domain local groups function as local groups. In any other domain functional level, universal groups are available and domain local groups have domain-wide scope.

Table 2-5 summarizes the modifications to how groups can be used based on the domain functional level. Note that only in Windows 2000 Native or Windows Server 2003 mode can the same type of group be nested within a group. In Windows 2000 Native or Windows Server 2003 mode, domain local groups can contain other domain local groups, global groups can contain other global groups, and universal groups can contain other universal groups.

Table 2-5. Modifications to group membership based on domain functional level

Domain functional level	Domain local	Global	Universal
Windows 2000 Mixed, Windows Server 2003 Interim	Can contain accounts and global groups from any domain.	Accounts from the same domain only.	Security universal groups can't be created.
Windows 2000 Native, Windows Server 2003	Accounts and global groups are from any domain; domain local groups are from the same domain only.	Accounts and other global groups from the same domain only.	Accounts are from any domain; global and universal groups are from any domain.

Group scope is set when you create a group. Although you cannot change the scope of built-in local groups, you can change the scope of domain local groups, global groups, and universal groups. The following rules apply:

Domain local groups
: Can be changed to universal groups when the domain functional level is set to Windows 2000 Native or Windows Server 2003. However, no member of the group can have domain local scope for the scope to change to universal.

Global groups
: Can be changed to universal groups when the domain functional level is set to Windows 2000 Native or Windows Server 2003. However, no member of the group can have global scope for the scope to change to universal.

Universal groups
: Can be changed to domain local or global groups. However, no member of the group can have global scope for the scope to change to global. Universal groups are available only in Windows 2000 Native and Windows 2003 domain functional levels.

Creating groups

Groups can be created using a variety of tools. The two you'll use the most are:

- Active Directory Users And Computers (*dsa.msc*)
- DSADD (*dsadd.exe*)

Regardless of which tool you are using, you should think about which container or OU the group will be placed in before creating the group. Ideally, you'll place the group in the container or OU where it can best be managed. You must either be a member of the Enterprise Admins, Domain Admins, or Account Operators groups to create groups, or you must have been delegated this permission.

To create a group using Active Directory Users And Computers (*dsa.msc*), follow these steps:

1. Right-click the container in which you want to store the group.
2. On the shortcut menu, select New → Group. This opens the New Object – Group dialog box shown in Figure 2-8.
3. Type the group name in the Group Name field.
4. Select the appropriate group scope and group type.
5. Click OK to create the group.

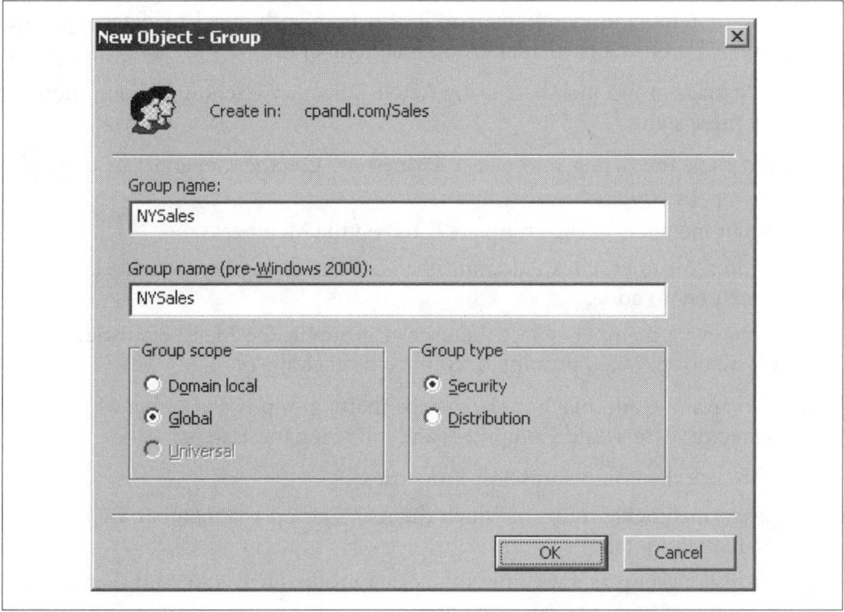

Figure 2-8. Use the New Object – Group dialog box to create group accounts.

To create a group using DSADD, you'll need to be able to set the Active Directory service path string for the group. For groups, path strings describe the group's location in the directory from the group name to the actual containers in which it is stored. You specify whether the group is a security group using `-secgrp yes` or that a group is a distribution group using `-secgrp no`. Specify the scope of the group using `-scope u` for universal, `-scope g` for global, and `-scope l` for domain local.

Consider the following example: you want to create a global security group called NYSales in the Sales OU for the *williamstanek.com* domain. The full path to this group object is CN=NYSales,OU=Sales,DC=williamstanek,DC=com. When creating the group object using DSADD, you must specify this path as follows:

```
dsadd group "CN=NYSales,OU=Sales,DC=williamstanek,DC=com" -secgrp yes
-scope g
```

Although quotation marks are only required if the path string contains a space, it is a good idea to use them whenever specifying path strings. This way you will remember to use them when they are required and won't get an error.

For the full syntax and usage, type `dsadd group /?` at a command prompt.

Setting and determining group membership

Depending on type and scope, a group can have accounts, groups, or both as its members. When you work with groups, you'll often need to manage membership by adding or removing members. You'll also frequently need to determine and manage which groups a particular group is a member of.

You can manage group members using Active Directory Users And Computers by following these steps:

1. Right-click the group and select Properties. On the General tab, note the group scope and type.
2. Current members of the group are listed on the Members tab.
3. To add a member, click Add, and then use the dialog box provided to select the member to add.
4. To remove a member, select the user or group in the Members list and then click Remove. When prompted, confirm by clicking Yes.

You can determine and manage the groups that a group is a member of by using Active Directory Users And Computers and following these steps:

1. Right-click the group and select Properties.
2. Current members groups of which the select group is a member are listed on the Member Of tab.
3. To add the group as a member of another group, click Add, and then use the dialog box provided to select the group.
4. To remove the group as a member of a particular group, select the group in the Member Of list, and then click Remove. When prompted, confirm by clicking Yes.

These tasks can also be performed using the directory services commands, including DSGET GROUP and DSMOD GROUP. By using DSGET GROUP at a command prompt, you can:

- Determine the members of a group by typing `dsget group GroupDN -members`, where `GroupDN` is the distinguished name of the group.
- Determine the groups of which a group is a member by typing `dsget group GroupDN -memberof`. The `-expand` option can be added to display the recursively expand list of groups of which a group is a member.

- Determine whether a group is a security group by typing `dsget group GroupDN -secgrp`.
- Determine group scope by typing `dsget group GroupDN -scope`.

By using DSMOD GROUP at a command prompt, you can:

- Add members by typing `dsmod group GroupDN -addmbr MemberDN`, where `GroupDN` is the distinguished name of the group and `MemberDN` is the distinguished name of the account or group you want to add to the designated group.
- Remove members by typing `dsmod group GroupDN -rmmbr MemberDN`.
- Change group scope using `dsmod group GroupDN -scope u` for universal, `-scope g` for global, and `-scope l` for domain local.
- Convert the group to a security group using `dsmod group GroupDN -secgrp yes` or convert it to a distribution group using `dsmod group GroupDN -secgrp no`.

All the previously discussed rules for changing group type and scope apply. See "Understanding group types and scopes," earlier in this chapter for details.

Maintaining groups

In Active Directory, groups are stored in a particular container, such as Users, or in a particular organizational unit. When you create groups, you can place them in a specific container and mmove them later if necessary. Using Active Directory Users And Computers, you can maintain groups by right-clicking the group name. A shortcut menu will appear with the following options:

Properties
: Select Properties to view or manage group properties, including group membership.

Delete
: Select Delete to delete the group from the domain.

Rename
: Select Rename to rename the group.

Move
: Select Move to move the group to a new container or OU within the current domain.

The directory services commands can also be used to perform these tasks. Use DSMOD GROUP to set properties and manage membership. Use DSMOVE GROUP to move groups to a new container or OU. Use DSRM GROUP to remove the group.

Understanding implicit groups and special identities

As discussed previously, built-in groups are a special type of group. I*mplicit built-in groups* are another special type of group. As the name implies, membership in implicit groups is implicitly applied according to a particular situation or circumstance. Implicit groups cannot be created or deleted. Group scopes do not apply to implicit groups, nor can you change the membership of implicit groups. You can, however, apply user rights and assign security permissions to implicit groups. Another term for an implicit group is *special identity group*, or simply, *special identity*.

Although most special identities, such as Authenticated User, Creator Owner, and Everyone, are visible in Active Directory Users And Computers and in other computer management tools, some others are not.

Special identities include:

Anonymous Logon
: Encompasses any user accessing the system through anonymous logon. This identity can be used to manage anonymous access to resources. This group bypasses the authentication process.

Authenticated Users
: Encompasses any user accessing the system through a logon process. This identity can be used to manage authenticated access to shared resources within a domain.

Batch
: Encompasses any user or process accessing the system as a batch job. This identity can be used to allow batch jobs to run scheduled tasks.

Creator Owner
: Represents the creator and owner of objects. This identity is used to automatically grant access permissions to object owners.

Dial-Up
: Encompasses any user accessing the system through a dial-up connection. This identity can be used to distinguish dial-up users from other types of authenticated users.

Everyone
: Encompasses all interactive, network, dial-up, and authenticated users. This identity can be used to grant wide access to a resource. Includes Guests and Anonymous users.

Interactive
: Encompasses any user logged on to a system locally and can include users logged on via remote desktop connections. This identity can be used to allow only local users to access a resource.

Network
: Encompasses any user accessing a resource remotely through a network. This identity can be used to allow only remote users to access a resource.

Service
: Represents any accounts logged on to the computer as a service. This identity grants access to processes being run by Windows Server 2003 services.

System
: Represents processes being run by the operating system itself. This identity is used when the operating system needs to perform system-level functions.

Terminal Server User
: Encompasses any user accessing the system through Terminal Services. This identity can be used to allow terminal server users to access terminal server applications and to perform remote tasks.

Managing User Accounts in an Active Directory Environment

Named user accounts are used to control access to resources. In Windows environments, there are two types of user accounts:

Local machine user accounts
: Users log on to computers and access local resources using local machine accounts. In workgroups, users can only log on to a local machine.

Domain user accounts
: Users log on to a domain and access network resources using domain accounts. In domains, both local machine and domain user accounts can be used, whether a user is logging on to the local machine or the domain can be set in the logon dialog box using the Log On To selection list. If this selection list is not displayed in the dialog box, clicking the Options button will display it.

User accounts have account names, passwords, and security identifiers (SIDs) associated with them. In workgroups, these properties are stored in the Security Accounts Manager (SAM) database on a per account basis. In Active Directory, these properties of user accounts are stored along with many other properties in the related objects, and these objects in turn are stored in the directory itself.

Creating user accounts

User accounts have display names and logon names associated with them. The display or full name is the name displayed in the graphical interface. The logon name is used for logging on to the domain. A standard logon name and a pre-Windows 2000 logon name are required for each user account, and either can be specified at logon.

Regardless of which tool you are using, you should think about which container or OU the user account will be placed in before creating the account. Ideally, you'll place the user account in the container or OU where it can best be managed in terms of administration, delegation, and policy application. You must be a member of the Enterprise Admins, Domain Admins, or Account Operators groups to create user accounts. Or you must have been delegated this permission.

You can create a user account using Active Directory Users And Computers (*dsa.msc*) by following these steps:

1. Right-click the container in which you want to store the user account.
2. On the shortcut menu, select New → User. This starts the New Object – User ... in Figure 2-9.
3. ... name, initials, and last name for the user. These fields are

4. The full name for display is generated based on the information you typed. You can change this as necessary.
5. Enter the standard logon name and the pre-Windows 2000 logon name. These names must be unique in the domain.
6. After you click Next, you can specify and confirm the password for the account. The password provided must meet policy requirements regarding minimum length and complexity.
7. Set account flags as appropriate using the additional checkboxes provided. Only the User Must Change Password At Next Logon flag is selected by default.
8. Click Next and then click Finish to create the account.

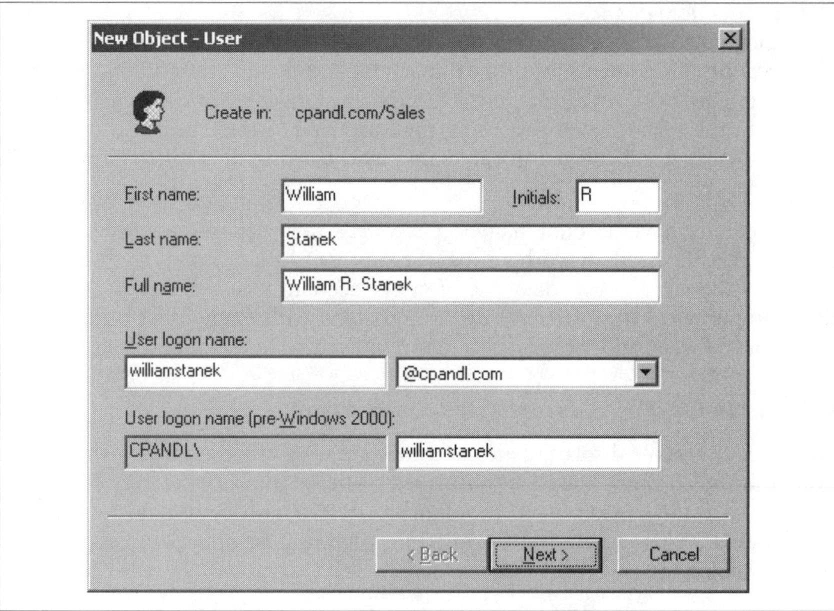

Figure 2-9. Use the New Object – User wizard to create domain user accounts.

You can create a user account using DSADD USER as well. When you do this, the DN for the account is used to set the account's full name. For example, suppose you want to create a user account with the display name "William Stanek" in the Engineering OU for the *domain.local* domain. When creating the user object using DSADD, you must specify the path as follows:

```
dsadd user "CN=William Stanek,OU=Engineering,DC=domain,DC=local"
```

If you create an account in this manner, the other properties of the account are set automatically, and the account is configured so that it is disabled. To resolve this, you need to create a password for the account and then enable the account.

In most cases, rather than have some properties set automatically, you'll want to define them. This gives you more control and allows you to create the account so that it is enabled for use. Use the following parameters:

- -FN to set the first name
- -MI to set the middle initials
- -LN to set the last name
- -Display to set the display name
- -samid to set the logon name
- -pwd to set the password

Thus, a better way to define the previous account would be to use the following command line:

```
dsadd user "CN=William Stanek,OU=Engineering,DC=domain,DC=local" -fn William
-mi R -ln stanek -Display "William Stanek" -samid williamstanek -pwd
R496Stra@$!
```

Quotation marks are only required if a path or value string contains a space.

For the full syntax and usage, type dsadd user /? at a command prompt.

Maintaining user accounts

In Active Directory, user accounts are stored in a particular container, such as Users, or in a particular organizational unit. When you create users, you can place them in a specific container and move them later if necessary. Using Active Directory Users And Computers, you can maintain user accounts by right-clicking the user name, which displays a shortcut menu with the following options:

Add To A Group
: Select this to quickly make the user a member of a particular group.

Copy
: Select this to create a new user with the same settings as the currently selected user.

Properties
: Select this to view or manage account properties, including group membership.

Disable Account
: Select this to disable the account so the user cannot log on to the domain.

Delete
: Select this to delete the user account from the domain.

Enable Account
: Select this to enable a previously disabled account.

Rename
: Select this to rename the user account. You should also modify the properties for other name components as necessary, such as the logon name and full name.

Reset Password

Select this to change the password for the account.

Move

Select this to move the user account to a new container or OU within the current domain.

When you right-click a user account and select Properties in Active Directory Users And Computers, you'll see a properties dialog box similar to the one shown in Figure 2-10.

Multiple accounts can be selected for editing by holding Shift or Ctrl when selecting account names before right-clicking and selecting Properties. Only a select subset of properties can be managed simultaneously for multiple users. On the General tab, you can modify Description, Office, Telephone Number, Fax, Web Page, and E-mail. On the Account tab, you can modify UPN Suffix, Logon Hours, Computer Restrictions, Account Options, and Account Expires. On the Profile tab, you can modify Profile Path, Logon Script, and Home Folder.

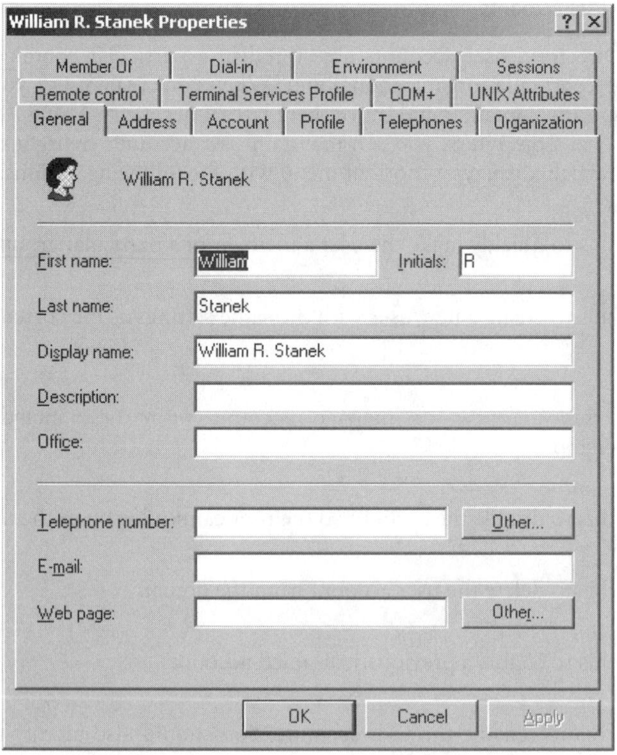

Figure 2-10. Use the user account properties dialog to configure a user's account.

Although the exact number and type of tabs available will depend on the configuration of your Windows environment, the most common tabs and their uses are summarized in Table 2-6.

Table 2-6. Common account tabs for user properties dialog boxes

Tab name	Used to manage
Account	Logon name, account options, logon times, account lock out, and account expiration
Address	Geographical address information
COM+	User's COM+ partition set
Dial-in	User's dial-in or VPN access controls
Environment	Terminal services startup environment
General	Account name, display name, email address, telephone number, and web page
Member Of	Group membership; allows you to determine all groups of which a user is a member
Organization	User's title, department, manager, and direct reports
Profile	Profile path, logon script, and home folder
Published Certificates	User's X.509 certificates
Remote Control	Remote control settings for Terminal Services
Sessions	Terminal services timeout and reconnection settings
Telephones	Home phone, pager, fax, IP phone, and cell phone numbers
Terminal Services Profile	User profile for Terminal Services
Unix Attributes	Access for Unix clients

The tab you'll work with the most is the Account tab. For the exam, you'll be expected to know how to configure logon hours, account expiration, and more. Here's an overview the main Account tab options:

Logon Hours
: Click this to configure when a user can log on to the domain. By default, users can log on at any time on any day of the week.

Log On To
: Click this to restrict which computers a user can log on from. The NetBIOS protocol is required for this functionality, as well as a pre-Windows 2000 computer name. The default setting allows users to log on from all computers.

User Must Change Password At Next Logon
: Click this to require the user to change his password the first time he logs on.

User Cannot Change Password
: Click this to prevent the user from changing his password, as may be necessary for application or service accounts.

Password Never Expires
: Click this to prevent passwords from ever expiring, which may be necessary for application or service accounts.

Store Password Using Reversible Encryption
: Click this to save the user password as encrypted clear text. Required for MAC clients using the AppleTalk protocol.

Account Is Disabled
: Click this to prevent the user from logging on to his account.

Smart Card Is Required For Interactive Logon
: Click this to require the use of a smart card and reader for logon and authentication. This option resets the Password Never Expires option to be enabled.

The directory services commands can also be used to perform these tasks. Use DSMOD USER to set properties, including passwords and group membership. Use DSMOVE USER to move users to a new container or OU. Use DSRM USER to remove user accounts.

Common user management tasks that you may want to perform from the command line include:

- Determining all the groups of which a user is a member by typing `dsget user UserDN -memberof` and using the optional `-expand` parameter to determine all the inferred group memberships based on the group of which other groups are members.
- Searching the entire domain for users with disabled accounts by typing `dsquery user -disabled`.
- Using `dsmod user UserDN` to set account flags `-mustchpwd (yes |no)`, `-canchpwd (yes |no)`, `-pwdneverexpires (yes |no)`, and `-disabled (yes |no)`.
- Determining all users who have not changed their passwords in a specified number of days by typing `dsquery user -stalepwd` *`NumDays`*, where *`NumDays`* is the number of days.
- Determining all users who have not logged on in a specified number of weeks by typing `dsquery user -inactive` *`NumWeeks`*, where *`NumWeeks`* is the number of weeks.

Importing and exporting user accounts

Microsoft provides the Comma-Separated Value Directory Exchange (CSVDE) command-line utility for importing and exporting Active Directory objects. For imports, CSVDE uses a comma-delimited text file as the import source, and you can run it using these general parameters:

-i
: To set CSVDE to import (rather than export which is the default mode)

-f filename
: To specify the source or output file

-s servername
: To set the server to which (rather than the default DC for the domain)

-v
: To turn on verbose mode.

-u
: To use Unicode (if the source or output format should be/are in Unicode format)

For imports, the source file's first row defines the list of LDAP attributes for each object defined. Each successive data line provides the details for a specific object to import, and must contain exactly the attributes listed. Here is an example:

```
DN,objectClass,sAMAccoutName,sn,givenName,userPrincipalName
"CN=WilliamStanek,OU=Eng,DC=domain,DC=local",
user,williams,William,Stanek,williams@domain.local
```


Given this listing, if the import source file is named *current.csv*, you could import the file into Active Directory using:

```
csvde -i -f current.csv
```

For exports, CSVDE writes the exported objects to a comma-delimited text file. You can run CSVDE using the general parameters listed previously as well as by using export-specific parameters, which include:

`-d RootDN`
: To set the starting point for the export, such as `-d "OU=Sales,DC=domain,DC=local"`. The default is the current naming context.

`-l list`
: To provide a comma separated list of attributes to output.

`-r Filter`
: To set the LDAP search filter, such as `-r "(objectClass=user)"`.

`-m`
: To output for Security Accounts Manager (SAM) rather than Active Directory.

To create an export file for the current naming context (the default domain), you could type:

```
csvde -f current.csv
```

However, this could result in a very large export dump. Thus, in most cases, you'll want to specify at a minimum, the RootDN and an object filter, such as:

```
csvde -f current.csv -d "OU=Sales,DC=domain,DC=local" -r
"(objectClass=user)"
```

Managing Local, Roaming, and Mandatory User Profiles

Every time a user logs on to a local machine or the domain, a profile is created or retrieved for use during the user's logon session. User profiles are meant to provide a consistent environment for users.

Understanding local user profiles

Profiles track user environment settings. Settings tracked include:

- Program-specific settings and user security settings.
- Cookies, favorites, history, and temporary files for the user's web browser.
- Settings for the user's desktop, including any files, folders, and shortcuts he has placed on the desktop.

- Shortcuts to the documents the user has recently opened.
- Shortcuts to My Network Places, Printers, Start Menu, and SendTo.
- Application templates and other user data.

Every computer has a default profile stored locally in the *%SystemDrive%\Documents and Settings\Default User* folder. By default, if a user logs on to a system and doesn't have an existing profile on that system, Windows creates a copy of the default profile and stores it as the user's new profile in the *%SystemDrive%\Documents and Settings\%UserName%* folder on that computer.

A user's environment settings are extended by the All Users profile on the local computer. The All Users profile contains system-specific settings, such as common Start Menu and desktop shortcuts, application data, and Network Places. Settings from the All Users profile are combined with a user's profile to create the user's environment. By default, only administrators can modify the All Users profile.

The profile path for Windows NT is *%Windir%\Profiles\%UserName%*. If a computer was upgraded from Windows NT, the profile path will remain in this location.

For a user that logs on to a single computer, the standard local user profile works well. However, if a user logs on to multiple machines, the standard local profile doesn't work so well. Local machine profiles are separate from domain profiles, so a user who logs in to the local machine and to the domain would have separate profiles for each. If a user logs on to multiple machines, she would have different local machine and domain profiles on each machine.

Working with local user profiles

Windows computers have Default User, All Users, and user-specific local profiles. The Default User profile is the template from which new user profiles are created when needed. The All Users profile extends the user's environment based on the local configuration and applications installed. The user profile itself provides the base environment settings for the user's logon session.

You can view the contents of any user profile by right-clicking Start on the taskbar and selecting Explore All Users. This opens Windows Explorer with the folder path opened to the Start Menu for the All Users profile. Using the folders provided, you can then browse the settings associated with the All Users profile. Typically, you would not change any settings, since any changes you make would affect all users who log on to the computer. To browse default user settings, access *%SystemDrive%\Documents and Settings\Default User*. Don't make changes to the *Default User* folders. Instead, you should preconfigure the user environment by creating a local user profile and then copying this profile to the Default User profile.

To create a preconfigured local user profile, follow these steps:

1. Log on to the computer you want to preconfigure using a nonadministrator user account. Be sure to use an account that has a local user profile rather than a roaming user profile.

2. Install and configure programs that users require.
3. Configure the desktop and start environment.
4. Log off the computer.
5. Log on to the computer using an account that is a member of the Administrators group.
6. Right-click My Computer and select Properties to display the System utility's Properties dialog box.
7. Select the Advanced tab, then under User Profiles, click the Settings button. This opens the User Profiles dialog box.
8. Select the User profile you just created, and click the Copy To button. This opens the Copy To dialog box.
9. In the Copy To dialog box, type the local profile path to the default user folder: *%SystemDrive%\Documents and Setting\Default User*.
10. In the Copy To dialog box, click Change under Permitted To Use, and then in the Select User Or Group dialog box, type "Everyone," or the name of the specific user or group that should have access to the profile. Click OK.
11. Click OK twice to close the open dialog boxes.

Now that you've preconfigured the user environment, any user logging on to the computer will get the default environment, providing he has a local user profile rather than a roaming user profile.

Working with roaming user profiles

Having a different profile for each logon machine makes it difficult to ensure a user has a consistent environment. To help mitigate problems that a user may experience when logging on to multiple machines, Windows allows administrators to configure a user's account with a roaming profile. Unlike a standard local profile, a roaming profile allows user settings to move with a user from computer to computer.

When a user has a roaming profile, the profile is stored on a server and downloaded to a computer upon logon. When a user with a roaming user profile logs on to a new system for the first time, the system does not create a copy of the default profile for the user. Instead, the computer downloads the user's roaming profile from the server on which it is stored.

Changes to roaming user profiles are tracked on a per-file basis. When a user logs off, any changes to the user's environment settings are uploaded to the server. Thus, rather than downloading the entire profile data on subsequent logons to a computer, only changes to the user profile are downloaded.

You can specify that a user should have a roaming user profile using Active Directory Users And Computers or DSMOD USER. Before you set the path, however, you should configure the shared folder on a server that will be used to host the profiles. This folder should be configured so that the group Everyone has at least Change access to the shared folder. You do not need to create the individual profile folders for each user. Windows will create a user's profile folder for this when a user logs on for the first time after you've configured his account to use a roaming profile. The permissions on this folder will be set so that only the user has access.

The best time to specify which users should have a roaming profile is when you create the user account. This makes configuring a roaming user profile very easy. In this case, with Active Directory Users And Computers, you can just as easily set the profile path for a group of users as you can for an individual user. To set the profile path for an individual user, follow these steps:

1. Open Active Directory Users And Computers.
2. Right-click the user account you want to manage and then select Properties.
3. On the Profile tab, use the Profile Path field to set the UNC path to the profile in the form *\\ServerName\ShareName\UserName*, such as *\\FileSvr08\Profiles\williams*. See Figure 2-11.
4. Click OK.

As part of standard account configuration, you can also specify logon scripts and home folders for users on the Profile tab. Logon scripts can contain a series of commands that should be executed whenever a user logs on. Home folders set the folder the user should use for storing files.

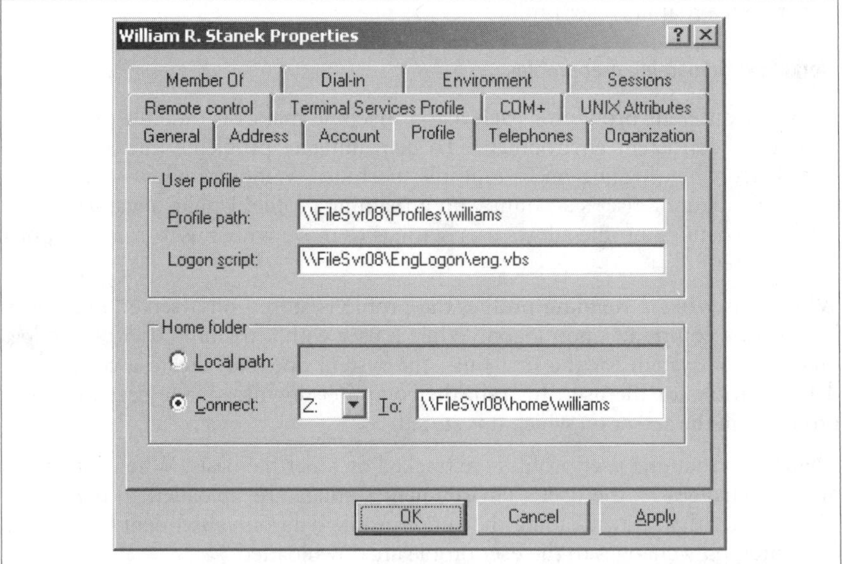

Figure 2-11. Set the profile path using the UNC path to the profile share.

To set the profile path for multiple users, follow these steps:

1. Open Active Directory Users And Computers.
2. Select more than one user, using Shift+click or Ctrl+click.
3. Right-click, and then select Properties.

4. On the Profile tab, select the Profile Path checkbox and then use the associated field to set the UNC path to the profile in the form *\\ServerName\ShareName\%UserName%*, such as *\\FileSvr08\Profiles\%UserName%*. See Figure 2-12.
5. Click OK.

In this procedure, *%UserName%* is an environment variable for the user's logon name. This lets Windows create the profile folder using the logon name as the folder name.

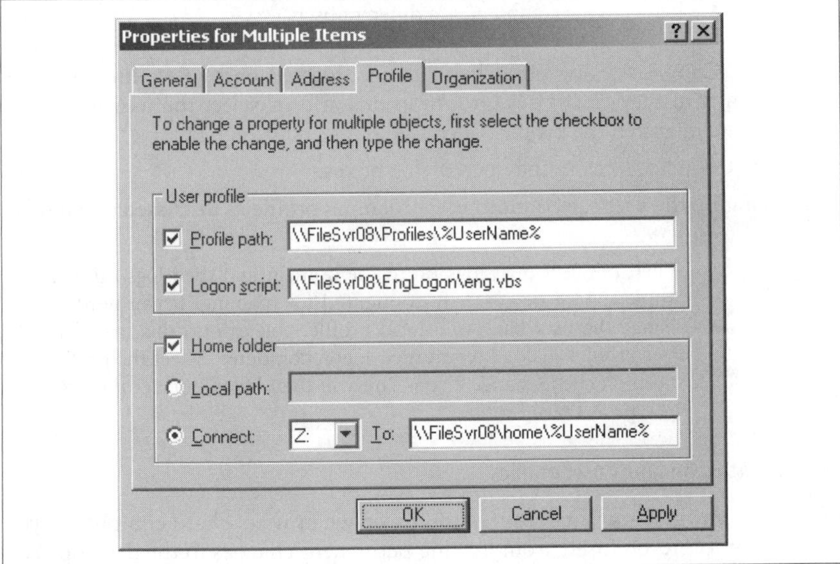

Figure 2-12. Setting the profile path for multiple users using the %UserName% environment variable.

You can use DSMOD USER to specify the profile path for a user or group of users as well. Use the syntax:

```
dsmod user UserDN -profile ProfilePath
```

For example:

```
dsmod user "CN=William Stanek,OU=Engineering,DC=domain,DC=local" -profile -b
\\FileSvr08\Profiles\williams
```

When a user already has an existing local user profile, and you need to move her to a roaming user profile, you should copy her existing local profile to the profile share prior to configuring her account to have a roaming profile by following these steps:

1. Log on the computer using an account that is a member of the Administrators group.
2. Right-click My Computer and select Properties to display the System utility's Properties dialog box.

3. Select the Advanced tab, then under User Profiles, click the Settings button. This opens the User Profiles dialog box.
4. Select the user's profile, and click the Copy To button. This opens the Copy To dialog box.
5. In the Copy To dialog box, set the UNC path to the profile in the form *-b \\ServerName\ShareName\UserName*, such as *\\FileSvr08\Profiles\williams*.

If you are unable to copy the profile, it could be because the user is logged on and the profile is locked for access. The best way to clear this is to have the user log off, restart the user's computer, and then log on to the computer as a different user.

6. In the Copy To dialog box, click Change, located under Permitted To Use, and then in the Select User Or Group dialog box, select the user for whom you've configured the profile. Click OK.
7. Click OK twice to close the open dialog boxes.
8. Configure the user's account to use a roaming profile as discussed previously.

When the user next logs on to the domain and then logs off, the profile should be correctly configured for roaming. If you need to change the user back to a local profile, you can do this from the User Profiles dialog box on their logon computer. Select the profile and then click Change Type. You will then be able to set the profile type as Local Profile.

Working with mandatory user profiles

In some environments, such as classrooms or when users share computers, you might want to prevent users from making permanent changes to the desktop. You can do this using a mandatory user profile. When a user has a mandatory profile, they can log on to different computers and get the same desktop settings and change desktop settings as permitted by policy on the local computer. However, changes are not saved to in the profile and thus are lost when a user logs off.

To configure a mandatory user profile, you simply change the name of the user's primary profile data file from *Ntuser.dat* to *Ntuser.man*. The *Ntuser.dat* file is stored in the root of the user's profile folder: either on the local machine for local profiles or on a server for roaming profiles.

As profiles are hidden system files, *Ntuser.dat* isn't automatically displayed in Windows Explorer. To display hidden files, you must choose Tools → Folder Options, and then click the View tab. Under Advanced Settings, select Show Hidden Files And Folders.

Mandatory profiles must be available for a user to log on. If for some reason the user profile becomes unavailable, the user will not be able to log on.

Managing User Access and Authentication

A key part of managing user access and authentication is to ensure that user accounts are properly configured and have valid passwords. NTFS permissions and policy settings must also be properly managed to ensure that the appropriate level access to resources is granted and that authentication works as expected.

Understanding user access and authentication

A user's access to a local computer, the domain, and the network is dependent on her logon and the policies in place to safeguard access. Authentication is the key to access. Whenever a user attempts to log on or access resources, the user's credentials are authenticated. If the user's credentials are invalid, the user will be denied logon or access to resources. If the user's credentials are valid and the user has sufficient permissions, the user will be granted logon and access to resources as appropriate for the level of permissions the user has been assigned.

The most basic components of access and authentication are the user's credentials, which include the user's account configuration and the user's password. If the user's account is misconfigured, disabled, or locked out, the user will not be authenticated and will not be able to access to the computer, the domain, or network resources. Similarly, if the user's password has expired, the user will not be authenticated and will not be able to access to the computer, the domain, or network resources.

The most advanced components of access and authentication are the NTFS permissions set on resources and the policy settings set in Active Directory. Managing resource access using NTFS permissions is discussed in "Managing and Maintaining Access to Network Resources," later in this chapter. The primary policy settings that affect user access and authentication are:

Password policy
: Controls how passwords are managed, whether they expire, and when they expire.

Account lockout policy
: Controls whether and how accounts are locked out if successive invalid passwords are provided.

Unlike most other areas of Group Policy, you should manage password policy, account lockout policy, and Kerberos policy using the highest precedence Group Policy Object (GPO) linked to a domain. By default, the highest precedent GPO linked to a domain is the Default Domain Policy GPO.

Setting password policy

Password policies control how passwords are managed, whether they expire, and when they expire. Table 2-7 provides an overview of available password policies. In Group Policy, you'll find password policies under *Computer Configuration\Windows Settings\Security Settings\Account Policies\Password Policy*.

Table 2-7. Account policies for passwords

Policy	Description
Enforce password history	Determines how many previously used passwords will be maintained in the user's password history. Since the user cannot use a password that is in the history, the user cannot reuse a recently used password. The maximum value is 24. If this value is set to zero, no password history is maintained and the user is able to reuse old passwords, which can be a security concern.
Maximum password age	Determines when the user is required to change a password. The maximum value is 999 days. If this value is set to zero, the password never expires, which can be a security concern.
Minimum password age	Requires that a specific number of days must pass before a user can change his password. This setting must be configured to be less than the maximum password age policy. If this value is set to zero, the user can change his password immediately.
Minimum password length	Determines the minimum number of characters requirement for the length of the password. Longer passwords are more secure than shorter ones.
Passwords must meet complexity requirements	Determines whether the password must meet specific complexity requirements. If this policy is defined, a password cannot contain the user account name, must contain at least six characters, and must have characters that have uppercase letters, lowercase letters, Arabic numerals, and nonalphanumeric characters.
Store passwords using reversible encryption	Determines whether passwords use plain-text encryption of passwords. Basically the same as storing passwords as plain text, and is only to be used when applications use protocols that require information about the user's password. Required for MAC clients using the AppleTalk protocol.

Setting account locking policy

Account lockout policy controls whether and how accounts are locked out if successive invalid passwords are provided. Table 2-8 provides an overview of available account lockout policies. In Group Policy, you'll find password policies under *Computer Configuration\Windows Settings\Security Settings\Account Policies\Account Lockout Policy*.

Table 2-8. Account lockout policies

Policy	Description
Account lockout duration	Determines the period of time that must elapse before Active Directory will unlock an account that has been locked out due to Account Lockout Policy. This setting is dependent on the account lockout threshold setting. The value range is 0–99,999 minutes. If this value is set to zero, the account will be locked out indefinitely and must be unlocked by an administrator.
Account lockout threshold	Determines how many failed logon attempts trigger an automatic lockout. The valid range is 0–999. If the value is set to zero, the account will never be locked out due to Account Lockout Policy.
Reset account lockout counter after	Determines the number of minutes after a failed logon attempt before the lockout counter is reset to zero. The valid ranges is 1–99,999 minutes. This must be less than or equal to the account lockout duration setting if the account lockout threshold policy is enabled.

Diagnosing and resolving user account problems

Accounts can be disabled by administrators or locked out due to Account Lockout Policy. When a user tries to log on using an account that is disabled or locked out, a prompt will notify her that she cannot log on because her account is disabled or locked out. The prompt also tells her to contact an administrator.

Active Directory Users And Computers shows disabled accounts with a red warning icon next to the account name. To enable a disabled account, right-click the account in Active Directory Users And Computers, and then select Enable Account.

You can also search the entire domain for users with disabled accounts by typing `dsquery user -disabled` at a command prompt.

To enable a disabled account from the command line, type `dsmod user UserDN -disabled no`.

Once a user account has been locked out by the Account Lockout Policy, the account cannot be used for logging on until the lockout duration has elapsed or the account is reset by an administrator. If the account lockout duration is indefinite, the only way to unlock the account is to have an administrator reset it.

You can unlock an account by completing the following steps:

1. Open Active Directory Users And Computers.
2. Right-click the locked account, and then select Properties.
3. On the Account tab of the properties dialog box, clear the Account Is Locked Out checkbox.
4. Click OK.

Logon success and failure can be recorded through auditing. When account logon failure auditing is enabled, logon failure is recorded in the security log on the login domain controller. Auditing policies for a site, domain, or OU GPO are stored under *Computer Configuration\Windows Settings\Security Settings\Local Policies\Audit Policy*.

Diagnosing and resolving user authentication problems

When a user logs on to the network using his domain user account, the account credentials are validated by a domain controller. By default, a user can log on using his domain user accounts even if the network connection is down or there is no domain controller available to authenticate the user's logon.

The user must have previously logged on to the computer and have valid, cached credentials. If the user has no cached credentials on the computer and network connection is down, or there is no domain controller available, the user will not be able to log on. Each member computer in a domain can cache up to 10 credentials by default.

When a domain is operating in Windows 2000 native or Windows Server 2003 mode, authentication can also fail if the system time on the member computer deviates from the logon domain controller's system time more than is allowed in the Kerberos Policy: Maximum Tolerance For Computer Clock Synchronization. The default tolerance is five minutes for member computers.

Managing and Maintaining Access to Network Resources

Network files and folders are one of the primary resources administrators have to manage and maintain. Files are shared over the network by configuring shared folders. Access to shared folders is managed using share permissions and filesystem permissions. While share permissions provide the top-level access controls to the files and folders being shared, filesystem permissions ultimately determine who has access to what. The two levels of permissions for shared folders can be thought of as a double set of security doors. Share permissions open the outer security doors so that specific groups of users can access a particular shared folder. Filesystem permissions determine access to the inner security doors on individual files and folders within the shared folder.

Configuring Access to Shared Folders

Users access files stored on Windows servers using shared folders. There are two general types of shares: standard and web. *Standard* shares are used to access folders over a network. *Web* shares are used to access folders over the Internet.

Configuring access to shared folders

When a user needs to access shared files and folders over the network, he uses standard shared folders. All shared folders have a folder path and a share name. The folder path sets the local file path to the shared folder. The share name sets the name of the shared folder. For example, the user might want to share the folder *C:\userdata* as *UserDirs*.

All shared folders have a specific set of permissions. Share permissions grant access directly to users by account name or according to their membership in a particular group, and are applied only when a folder is accessed remotely.

One of three levels of share permissions can be granted to a user or group:

Full Control
: Grants both Read and Change permission. Also allows the user to change file and folder permissions and take ownership of files and folders.

Change
: Grants Read permission. Also allows the user to create files and subfolders, modify files, change attributes on files and subfolders, and delete files and subfolders.

Read
: Allows the user to view file and subfolder names, access the subfolders of the share, read file data and attributes, and run program files.

Share permissions determine the maximum allowed access level. If the user has Read permission on a share, the most the user can do is perform Read operations. If a user has Change permission on a share, the most the user can do is perform Read and Change operations. If a user has Full Control permission, the user has full access to the share. However, in any case, filesystem permissions can further restrict or block access.

You can share folders using Windows Explorer and Computer Management. With Windows Explorer, you can share a folder on a local computer by right-clicking a folder, selecting Sharing And Security, and then selecting Share This Folder. The share name is set for you automatically and can be changed as desired. To set the share permissions, click the Permissions tab.

Unlike Windows NT and 2000, the default share permission for Windows Server 2003 is Everyone-Read instead of Everyone-Full Control. Further, keep in mind that with Windows Explorer, you can share only local folders but with Computer Management you can share folders on local as well as remote computers.

With Computer Management, you can share folders of any computer to which you can connect on the network. You can create a shared folder by completing these steps:

1. Start Computer Management, connect to the computer you want to work, expand System Tools and Shared Folders, and then select Shares to list the current shares on the system you are working with.
2. Right-click Shares and then select New Share. This starts the Share A Folder Wizard.
3. Click Next to display the Folder Path page. Click Browse and then use the Browse For Folder dialog box to find the folder you want to share.
4. Click Next to display the Name, Descriptions, And Settings page shown in Figure 2-13.
5. In the Share Name field, type a name for the share. Share names can be up to 80 characters in length and can contain spaces. For DOS clients, you should limit the share name to eight characters with a three-letter extension. To create a hidden administrative share, type $ as the last character of the share name.
6. Optionally, type a description of the share in the Description field. The description is displayed as a comment when the share is viewed.
7. Click Next. On the Permissions page, set the default share permissions using the options provided:

   All Users Have Read-Only Access
   Grants the Everyone group Read-only access (the default).

   Administrators Have Full Access; Other Users Have Read-Only Access
   Grants administrators Full Control and the Everyone group Read-only access.

   Administrators Have Full Access; Other Users Have Read And Write Access
   Grants administrators Full Control and the Everyone group Change access.

   Use Custom Share And Folder Permissions
   Allows you to configure access by accessing Full Control, Change, and Read access to specific users and groups (recommended).

8. Click Finish to create the share and set the initial permissions. To further restrict access, set filesystem permissions.

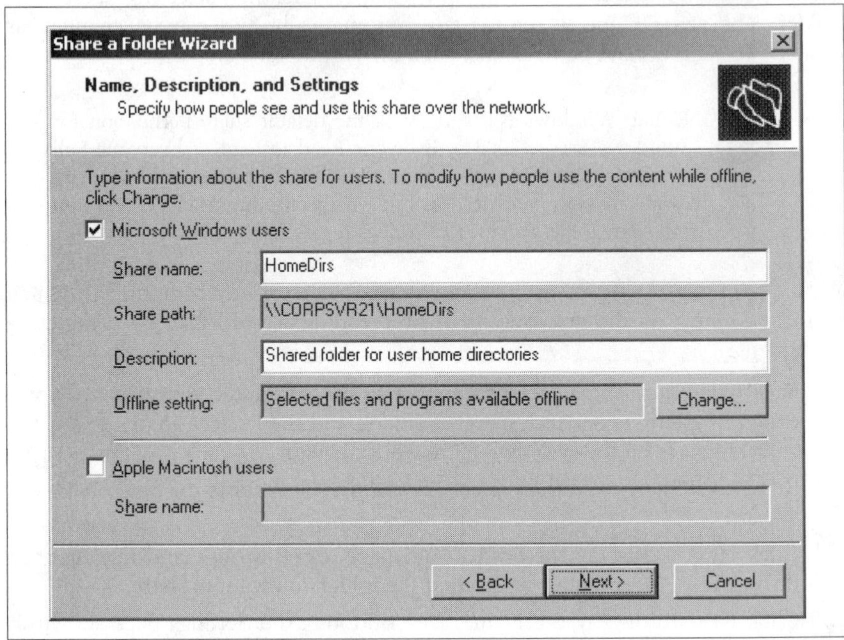

Figure 2-13. Set the share name and description.

Once you share a folder, it is available to users automatically and can be accessed using a network drive. Network drives can be mapped automatically using logon scripts. In Windows Explorer, you can map a network drive by selecting Tools → Map Network Drive. This displays the Map Network Drive dialog box shown in Figure 2-14.

You use the Drive field to select a free drive letter to use. You use the Folder field to enter the UNC path to the network share. For example, to access a server called FileServer06 and a shared folder called *HomeDirs*, type `\\FileServer06\HomeDirs`. If you don't know the name of the share, you could click Browse to search for available shares. In the Browse For Folder dialog box, expand the entry for the domain you want to work with under Microsoft Windows network, expand the entry for the file server, select the shared folder, and then click OK.

Managing shared folder properties and permissions

You can manage the properties and permissions of shared folders using Windows Explorer or Computer Management. With Computer Management, you can work with a share's properties and permissions by completing the following steps:

1. Start Computer Management, connect to the computer you want to work on, expand System Tools and Shared Folders, and then select Shares to list the current shares on the system you are working with.

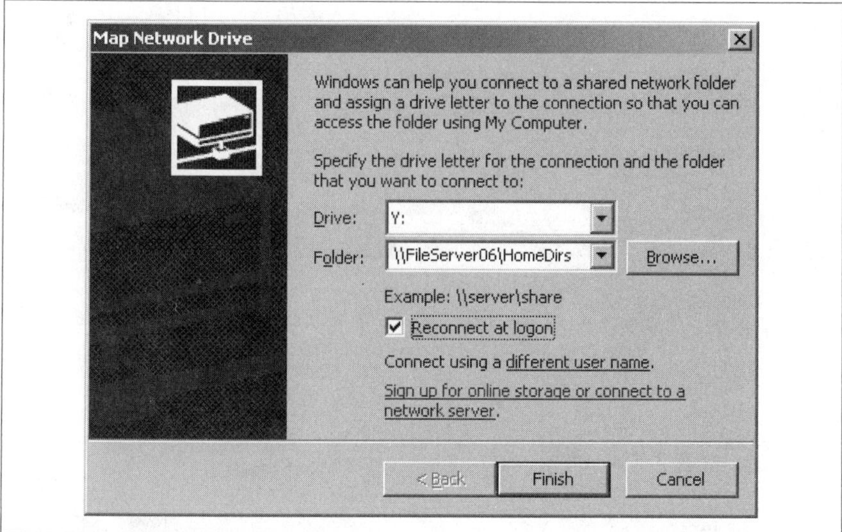

Figure 2-14. Set the drive letter and folder path.

2. Right-click the share you want to work with, and then select Properties.
3. You'll then see a dialog box similar to the one shown in Figure 2-15. The Properties dialog box has the following tabs:

   General
   : Displays the share name, description, and folder path. Use the User Limit radio buttons to control how many users can connect to the share at one time. Use the Offline Settings options to configure whether and how the contents will be available to users who are offline. To rename the share, you must stop sharing the folder, and then share it again with the new name.

   Publish
   : Allows you to publish the share in Active Directory. Select Publish This Share In Active Directory to allow users to search for the folder using Active Directory's find features. You can add keywords and owner information as well if desired.

   Share Permissions
   : Displays the current share permissions. Click a group or user in the list to view or change the related permissions. Click a group or user, and then click Remove to remove share permissions for that group or user. Click Add to specify share permissions for additional groups or users.

   Security
   : Displays the current NTFS permissions for the folder. Click a group or user in the list to view or change the related permissions. Click a group or user, and then click Remove to remove NTFS permissions for that group or user. Click Add to specify NTFS permissions for additional groups or users.

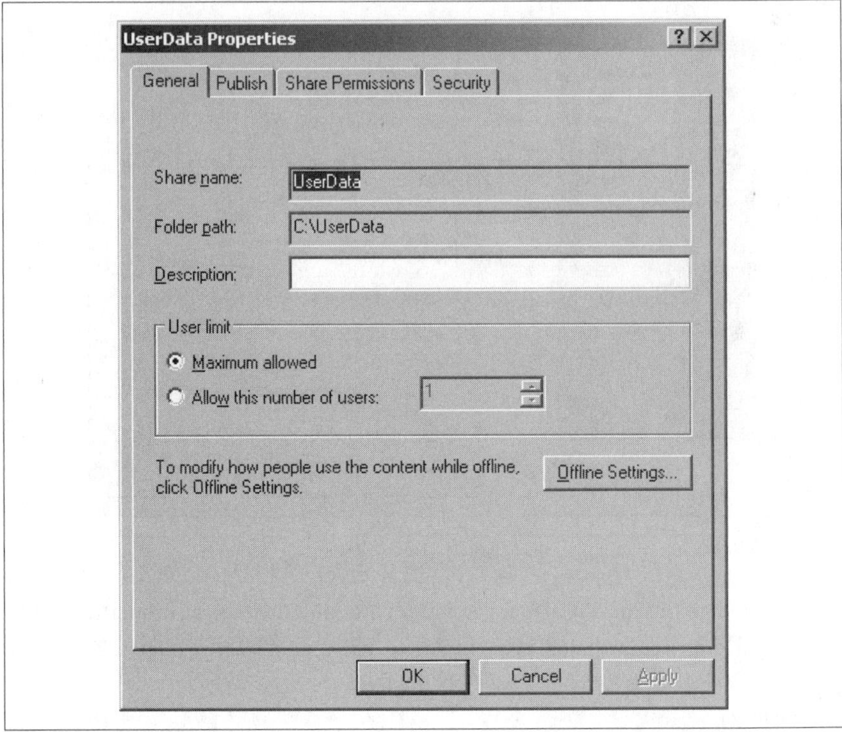

Figure 2-15. Configure share properties.

Using hidden and administrative shares

Windows Server 2003 creates several shares automatically. The shares, referred to as special or default shares, are listed when you select the Shares node in Computer Management. Shares with names ending in a dollar sign ($) are hidden. These hidden or administrative shares do not appear on the network browse list in My Network Places or elsewhere where share names would be listed normally.

The special shares that are available depend on the system configuration. Typically, you'll find one or more of the following special shares on any Windows 2000, Windows XP, or Windows Server 2003 computer:

C$, D$, E$, …
: A special share for the root of each available drive letter on the computer. Mapping a network drive to this special share provides full access to the drive.

ADMIN$
: A special share for accessing the operating system files in the *%SystemRoot%* folder.

FAXCLIENT and FXSSRVCP$
: The FAXCLIENT and FXSSRVCP$ shared are used to support network faxes.

IPC$

A special share to support named pipes and process to process communications. Named pipes can be redirected over the network to connect local and remote systems, and enable remote administration.

NETLOGON

A special share that supports the Net Logon service and is used during processing of logon requests (primarily for logon scripts).

Microsoft UAM Volume

A special share that supports Macintosh file and printer services. It is used by the File Server For Macintosh and Print Server For Macintosh services.

PRINT$

A special share that supports printer sharing by providing access to printer drivers.

SYSVOL

A special share used to support Active Directory. Domain Controllers have this share and use it to store Active Directory data, including policies and scripts.

Special shares are created each time a computer is started. If you delete a special share, it is re-created the next time the system starts.

As an administrator, you can create hidden shares by adding a dollar sign ($) to the end of a share name. Like any other share, the permissions on a hidden share determine who has access. Any user with appropriate permissions can connect to a hidden share, provided the user knows the full UNC path to the share.

Configuring web shares

To give users access to shared files and folders over the Internet, you use web shares. Web shares are accessed in a web browser using the Hypertext Transfer Protocol (HTTP). To use web shares, a system must have IIS installed. Install it using Add Or Remove Programs in the Control Panel. Click Add/Remove Windows Components, then configure the appropriate Application Server components to install and configure IIS as necessary.

All web shares have a folder path and an alias. The folder path sets the local file path to the shared folder. The alias sets the name of the web share. For example, you might want to share the folder *C:\reports* as *UserReports*.

All web shares have two sets of permissions:

Access permissions

These grant access directly to users by account name or according to their membership in a particular group, and are applied only when a folder is accessed remotely.

Application permissions
: These determine the permitted actions for programs and scripts that may be contained in the folder being shared over the Web.

Access permissions that can be granted to a user or group are as follows:

Read
: Allows web users to read files in the folder

Write
: Allows web users to write data in the folder

Script Source Access
: Allows web users to access the source code for scripts (not recommended)

Directory Browsing
: Allows web users to browse the folder and its subfolders (not recommended)

Application permissions that can be set are as follows:

None
: Disallows the execution of programs and scripts

Scripts
: Allows scripts stored in the folder to be run from the Web

Execute (Includes Scripts)
: Allows both programs and scripts stored in the folder to be executed from the Web

You can create web shares using Windows Explorer, by completing these steps:

1. Right-click the local folder you want to share, and then select Properties.
2. In the Properties dialog box, select the Web Sharing tab.
3. Use the Share On list box to select the local web site on which you want to share the selected folder.
4. Select Share This Folder and to display the Edit Alias dialog box shown in Figure 2-16.
5. In the Alias field, type an alias for the folder. This alias must be unique for the web server.
6. Use the Access Permissions checkboxes to set the access permissions. The default access permissions granted is Read.
7. Use the Application Permissions radio buttons to set the application permissions for the folder. The default application permission granted is Scripts.
8. Click OK. To further restrict access, set filesystem permissions.

Once you create a web share, it is available to users automatically and can be accessed using a web browser. The alias is the name you'll use to access the folder on the web server. On the internal network, the alias "UserReports" could be accessed on *FileServer06* using *http://fileserver06/userreports/* as the Internet address. On the Internet, the alias "UserReports" could be accessed on *williamstanek.com* using *http://williamstanek.com/userreports/* as the Internet address.

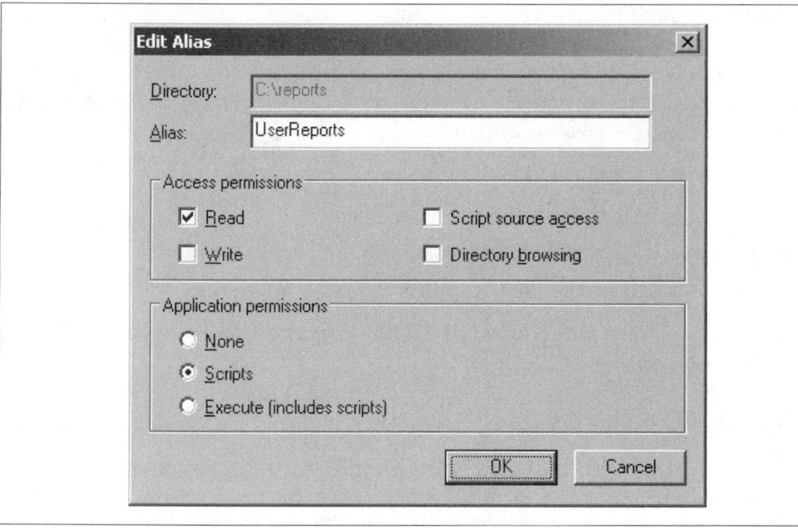

Figure 2-16. Set the web share alias and permissions.

Working with Attributes of Files and Folders

On FAT, FAT32, and NTFS volumes, all files and folders have basic attributes that allow files and folders to be marked as Hidden and Read-only. Basic attributes can be examined in Windows Explorer by right-clicking the file or folder and then selecting Properties. The Hidden attribute determines whether the file or folder is displayed in directory listings.

You can override the Hidden attribute by setting Windows Explorer to display hidden files:

1. In Windows Explorer, click Tools → Folder Options.
2. On the View tab, select Show Hidden Files And Folders.
3. Click OK.

On NTFS, the Read-only attribute is shown dimmed, meaning the attribute is in a mixed state regardless of the current state of files in the folder. To override the mixed state, select Read-only for a folder so all files in the folder will be read-only. To override the mixed state, clear the Read-only checkbox for a folder, and then all files in the folder will be writable.

Some files and folders also have extended attributes. Extended attributes come from named data streams associated with a folder or file. Many types of document files have named data streams associated with them. These define field and field values that appear on optional tabs, such as the Custom or Summary tab.

Configuring Filesystem Permissions

Filesystem permissions determine the specific set of access controls applied to a file or folder. FAT volumes have no file and folder permission capabilities. On

FAT/FAT32, share permissions provide the only access controls for shared FAT/FAT32 folders. NTFS volumes have filesystem permissions that include specific ownership permissions for files and folders. When you share folders on NTFS volumes, share permissions provide the top-level access control and NTFS permissions provide the base-level access controls.

NTFS permissions are managed according to:

- Basic or special permissions directly assigned
- Basic or special permissions inherited from higher level folders
- Ownership of the related file or folder

Together, these three components for NTFS permissions determine the effective permissions on a particular file or folder.

Working with NTFS permissions

Whether you work with files locally by logging on to a computer or remotely using shared folders, NTFS permissions provide the base access permissions. Whenever a user attempts to access a file or folder, NTFS permissions determine whether access is granted. If the user has been granted access to a file or folder, the access permissions determine the permitted actions as well, such as whether a user can change a file's contents.

On NTFS volumes, every file and folder has a security descriptor called an access control list (ACL) associated with it. Access permissions are stored within the ACL as access control entries (ACEs). The ACEs detail the specific permissions that apply to each user and group. When a user attempts to access a file or folder, the user's security access token, containing the security identifiers (SIDs) of the user's account and any groups of which the user is a member, is compared to the file or folder's security descriptor.

If the user has specific access permissions, the user will be granted access and will have the permissions assigned through the related ACE for the user. If the user is a member of a group that has specific access permissions, the user will be granted access and will have the permissions assigned through the related ACE for the group. When multiple ACEs apply, the user will have effective permissions that are a combination of the access permissions.

Generally, if a user is a member of multiple groups, her effective permissions are a combination of permissions assigned in all groups. The highest level of permissions will apply.

NTFS has both basic and special permission sets. The basic permissions represent a grouping of special permissions that together allow six commonly configured levels of access: Read, Read & Execute, Write, Modify, or Full Control. The special or advanced permissions provide granular control for when you need to fine-tune access permissions.

Managing basic permissions

You can view the basic permissions on a file or folder using Windows Explorer. Unlike Share permissions, Windows Explorer can be used to set NTFS permissions on both local and remote computers. Right-click the file or folder, select Properties, and then, in the Properties dialog box, select the Security tab. As Figure 2-17 shows, the Security tab is divided into two lists. The Groups Or Users Names list show groups and users with assigned permissions. Click a user or group name to display the allowed or denied permissions for that user or group in the Permissions For list. Dimmed permissions are inherited from a parent folder. See "Understanding and managing inherited permissions," later in this chapter for details.

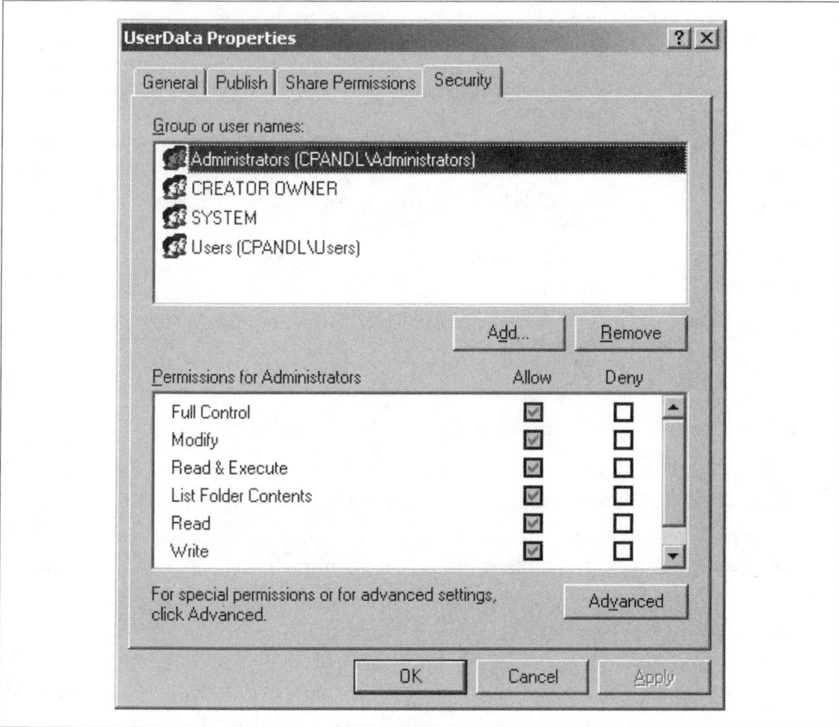

Figure 2-17. Basic access permissions are a grouping of special access permissions.

Basic file permissions differ slightly from basic folder permissions. Table 2-9 describes basic permissions for files. Table 2-10 describes basic permissions for folders.

Table 2-9. Basic permissions for files

Permission	Description
Full Control	Permits reading and listing of files; writing to files; deleting files and file contents; viewing attributes and permissions of files; changing attributes and permissions of files; taking ownership of files
Modify	Permits reading and listing of files; writing to files; deleting files and file contents; viewing attributes; setting attributes
Read & Execute	Permits executing files; reading and listing of files; viewing attributes and permissions of files

Table 2-9. Basic permissions for files (continued)

Permission	Description
Write	Permits writing to files; creating files; appending data to files; deleting files and file contents; setting attributes of files
Read	Permits reading and listing of files; viewing attributes and permissions of files

Table 2-10. Basic permissions for folders

Permission	Description
Full Control	Permits reading and listing of folders and files; writing to files; creating folders and files; deleting folders; files and file contents; viewing attributes and permissions of folders and files; changing attributes and permissions of folders and files; taking ownership of folders and files
Modify	Permits reading and listing of folders and files; writing to files; creating folders and files, deleting folders, files and file contents; viewing and setting attributes of folders and files
Read & Execute	Permits executing files; reading and listing of folders and files; viewing attributes and permissions of folders and files
List Folder Contents	Permits reading and listing of folders and files; executing files
Write	Permits creating files in folders
Read	Permits reading and listing of folders and files; viewing attributes and permissions of folders and files

To set basic permissions for files and folders, follow these steps:

1. Open Windows Explorer. Right-click the file or folder, select Properties, and then, in the Properties dialog box, select the Security tab.
2. To add a group or user to the Group Or User Names list, click Add. This displays the Select Users, Computers, Or Groups dialog box.
3. In the Enter The Object Name To Select box, type the name of a user or group account, and then click Check Names. If a match is found, the dialog box is updated as appropriate and the entry is underlined. If multiple matches are found, select one or more of the names listed, and then click OK to return to the Select Users, Computers, Or Groups dialog box. If no matches are found, try searching a different location or using a different name.
4. Click OK to close the Select Users, Computers, Or Groups dialog box. The previously selected users and groups are added to the Group Or User Name list.
5. To assign access permissions for a user and group, select an account name and then allow or deny access permissions as appropriate. To assign an access permission, select the permission in the Allow column. To deny an access permission, select the permission in the Deny column.

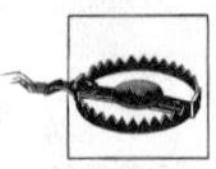

Deny overrides all other permissions. Use the Deny permission only when it is absolutely necessary.

6. To remove a group or user, select the group or user in the Group Or User Names list and then click Remove.
7. Click OK to save the settings.

Keep in mind individual file permissions override the folder permissions. You can also set NTFS folder permissions from Shared Folders snap-in of the Computer Management console. Click the Security Tab of the shared folder and set permissions as appropriate.

Managing special permissions

Special permissions allow administrators to directly edit the access control entries (ACEs) associated with a folder or file. You can view the special (advanced) permissions on a file or folder using Windows Explorer. Right-click the file or folder, and then select Properties. In the Properties dialog box, select the Security tab, and then click the Advanced button to display the Advanced Security Settings dialog box. As shown in Figure 2-18, the Permission Entries list shows the access control entry assigned to each group and user with permissions on the selected resource.

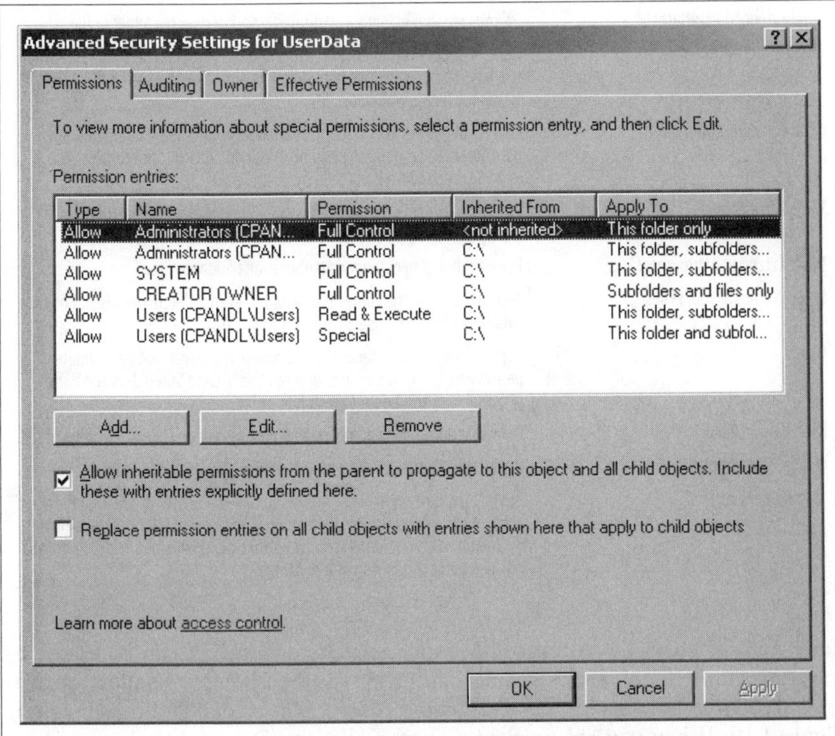

Figure 2-18. Special permissions provide granular control for fine-tuning access.

There are two general types of permissions: those that are inherited and those that are not. If a permission is inherited, the folder from which settings are inherited is listed. Typically, you'll manage inherited permissions by editing the folder from which settings are inherited. The exception is when you want to override or modify the inherited permissions for a particular user or group with respect to a specific folder or file.

As Table 2-11 shows, the special permissions are very granular in their scope. It is rare that you will need to edit the access control entry for a group or user, and more typically, you'll need to review or modify special permissions only when access controls aren't working the way you expect them to.

Table 2-11. Special permissions for folders and files

Special permission	Description
Traverse Folder/Execute File	Traverse Folder permits moving through folder to access a folder or file even if the group or user doesn't have explicit access to traversed folders; user or group must also have the Bypass Traverse Checking user right. Execute File permits running an executable file.
List Folder/Read Data	List Folder permits viewing file and folder names. Read Data permits viewing the contents of a file.
Read Attributes	Permits reading the basic attributes of a folder or file. These attributes include: Read-only, Hidden, System, and Archive.
Read Extended Attributes	Permits reading extended attributes associated with a folder or file.
Create Files/Write Data	Create Files permits adding files to a folder. Write Data permits overwriting existing data in a file (but not adding new data to an existing file since this is covered by Append Data).
Create Folders/Append Data	Create Folders permits creating subfolders within folders. Append Data permits adding data to the end of an existing file (but not to overwrite existing data, which is covered by Write Data).
Write Attributes	Permits changing basic attributes of a folder or file. These attributes include: Read-only, Hidden, System, and Archive.
Write Extended Attributes	Permits changing extended attributes of a folder or file.
Delete Subfolders and Files	Permits deleting the contents of a folder, even if Delete permission on the subfolder or file isn't specifically granted.
Delete	Permits deleting a folder or file. If a group or user doesn't have Delete permission, the group or user granted the "Delete Subfolders and Files" permission can still delete the folder or file.
Read Permissions	Permits reading all basic and special permissions assigned to a folder or file.
Change Permissions	Permits changing basic and special permissions assigned to a folder or file.
Take Ownership	Permits taking ownership of a folder or file. The owner of a folder or file can always change permissions on it, even if other permissions were removed. By default, administrators can always take ownership of a folder or file and can also grant this permission to others.

Each ACE listed in the Advanced Security Settings dialog box can be edited by selecting the ACE and then clicking Edit. You will then be able to allow or deny special permissions using the Permission Entry For... dialog box shown in Figure 2-19. When you are finished selecting Allow or Deny for each permission as appropriate, use the Apply Onto options to determine how and where these permissions are applied.

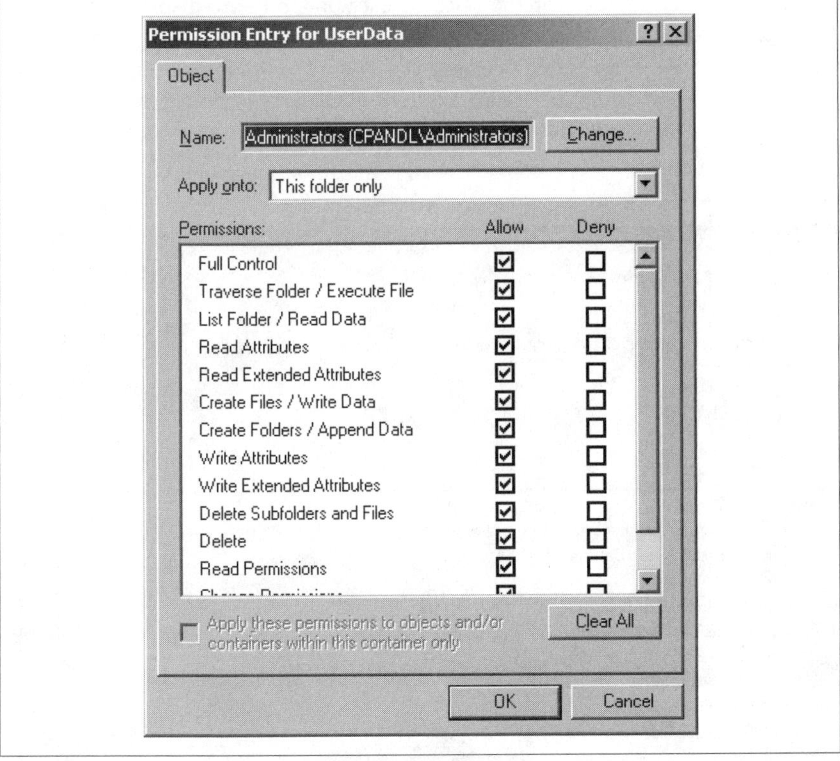

Figure 2-19. Accessing the permissions entry.

Verifying effective permissions when granting permissions

Often groups or users are members of multiple groups, and each of those groups will have separate access permission configurations. Membership in multiple groups can make it difficult if not nearly impossible to track down the exact access permissions that apply in a given situation. To resolve this problem, Windows provides the Effective Permissions tab for evaluating the access permissions that apply to a group or user with respect to a specific folder or file.

The Effective Permissions tab allows you to determine the collective set of permissions that apply based on directly assigned permissions, permissions inherited due to group membership, and permissions inherited from parent folders. Effective Permissions apply only to folder and file permissions. Share permissions are not included. To view effective permissions on a folder or file, follow these steps:

1. Open Windows Explorer. Right-click the file or folder, and then select Properties.
2. In the Properties dialog box, select the Security tab, and then click the Advanced button to display the Advanced Security Settings dialog box.
3. On the Effective Permissions tab, click Select. Type the name of the user or group, and then click OK.

The Effective Permissions for the selected user or group are displayed as shown Figure 2-20.

You cannot determine effective permissions for implicit groups or special identities. Share permissions are also not accounted for.

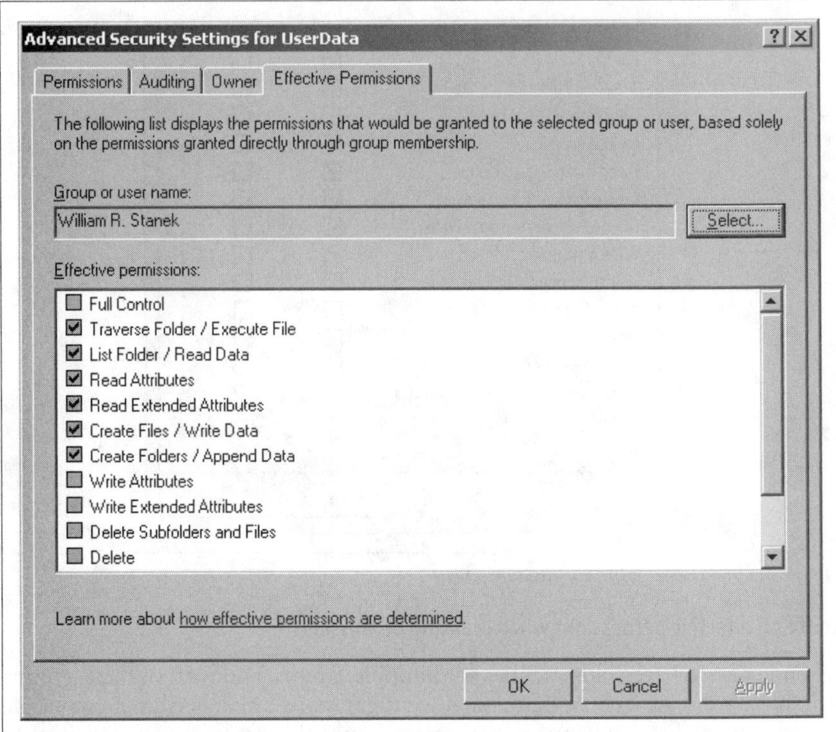

Figure 2-20. Viewing the effective permissions for a group or user.

Changing ownership of files and folders

As discussed previously in "Understanding implicit groups and special identities," Windows defines many special identities that are implicitly applied according to a particular situation or circumstance. One of these special identities is Creator Owner, which represents the creator and owner of objects and is used to grant implicit access permissions to object owners.

When a user creates a folder or file, the user is the creator and initial owner of the folder or file. If the system creates a folder or file, the default owner is the Administrators group. The owner has complete control to grant access permissions and give other users permission to take ownership of a folder or file.

Ownership can be taken or transferred in several ways:

- Users who have the right to Restore Files And Directories, such as a member of the Backup Operators group, can take ownership.
- Members of the Administrators group can take ownership because members of this group are granted this permission by default.
- Users or groups assigned with the Take Ownership permission can take ownership.
- Current owners can grant another user the Take Ownership permission.

To view or change ownership of a folder or file, follow these steps:

1. Open Windows Explorer. Right-click the file or folder, and then select Properties.
2. In the Properties dialog box, select the Security tab, and then click the Advanced button to display the Advanced Security Settings dialog box.
3. Click the Owner tab as shown in Figure 2-21. The current owner of the file or folder is listed under Current Owner Of This Item.
4. To grant Take Ownership permission, click Other Users Or Groups. Use the Select User, Computer, Or Group dialog box to select the user or group to which you want to grant Take Ownership permission.
5. To change the owner, select the new owner in the Change Owner To list box. When taking ownership of a folder, you can take ownership of all subfolders and files within the folder by selecting the Replace Owner On Subcontainers And Objects checkbox.
6. Click OK.

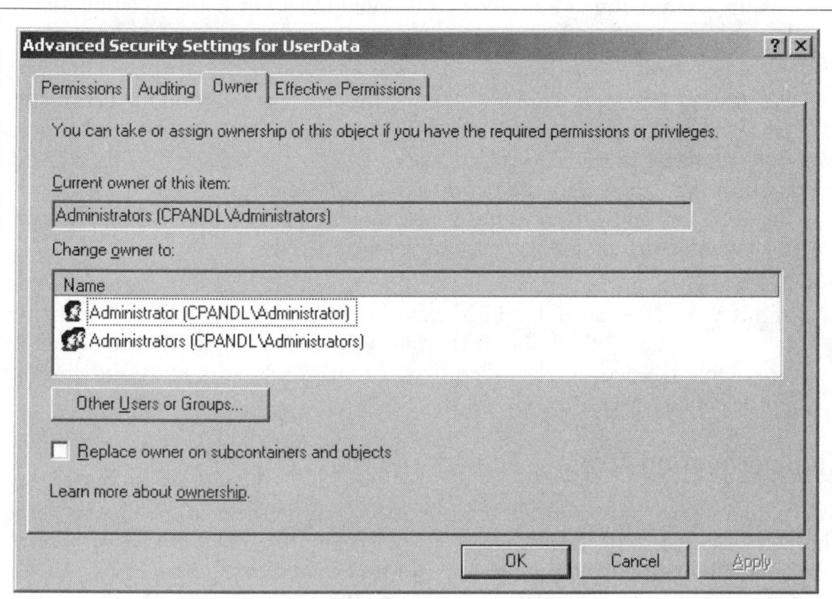

Figure 2-21. Use the Owner tab to determine and change ownership.

Understanding and managing inherited permissions

Windows Server 2003 uses inheritance so that permissions applied to a folder are, by default, applied to subfolders and files beneath that folder. If you later change the permissions of a folder, those changes, by default, affect all subfolders and files beneath that folder.

Permissions are inherited from parent folders. A file inherits its permissions from the folder in which it is stored. A subfolder inherits its permissions from the folder in which it is stored. Folders stored in the root of a drive volume inherit the permissions of the drive volume.

Permissions are inherited by default when files and folders are created. If you remove inherited permissions, any explicitly defined permissions remain. When you view the Security tab for a folder or file, inherited permissions are dimmed and are not changeable. When you view the Permission Entry for a folder or file, inherited permissions similarly are dimmed and are not changeable.

Typically, when you want to change inherited permissions, you will do so by accessing the parent folder from which the permissions are inherited and then making the desired changes. Any permission changes will then be inherited by child folders and files. The Permissions tab of the Advanced Security Settings dialog box lists the folder from which permissions are inherited. Each ACE on the folder or file has a separate entry, as shown previously in Figure 2-18.

When working with the folder or file that is inheriting permissions, you may need to override, stop, or restore inheriting:

- To override the inherited permissions, select the opposite permission. For example, if a permission is allowed through inheritance, override inheritance by explicitly denying the permission to a group or user.
- To stop inheriting permissions from a parent folder, clear Allow Inheritable Permissions From The Parent To Propagate To This Object on the Permissions tab. When prompted, you can then duplicate and apply explicitly the permissions that were previously applied, or you can elect to remove the inherited permissions and apply only the permissions that you explicitly set. Click Copy to duplicate and apply the previously inherited settings or click Remove to remove the inherited permission and use only explicit permissions.
- To restore inherited permissions to the subfolders and files within a folder and remove all explicitly defined permissions, access the folders Permissions tab, select Allow Inheritable Permissions From The Parent To Propagate To This Object, select Replace Permission Entries On All Child Objects With Entries Shown Here, and click OK.

Troubleshooting Access to Folders and Files

When it comes to folder and file access, the one truism seems to be that the larger the network, the more difficult it is to determine why a user cannot access a particular file or folder. Before you can diagnose and resolve the problem, you need to determine what type of error message the user is getting when attempting to access the folder or file. Most access errors relate to one of the following:

Network connectivity

If the user is accessing a shared folder for the first time and cannot connect to the remote server because "no network was found," the most likely culprit is that the user entered the incorrect UNC path to the shared folder. Check the folder path and the logon credentials being used. If these are correct, check network connectivity between the user's machine and the file server on which the folder or file is located.

Share permissions

If the user sees an "Access is denied" message, the most likely culprits are the share permissions on the resource. Remember, the share permissions set the top-level permissions and are the most restrictive: the user can only perform the allowed permissions regardless of the underlying access permissions. The default share permissions provide Read permission to the implicit group Everyone. If you do not change the default permissions, uses will only be able to list folder contents and read files within folders.

NTFS permissions

If the user sees an "Access is denied" message, the next most likely culprits are the NTFS permissions on the resource. Share permissions have no effect on local file access or Terminal Services remote access. With remote access via a shared folder, share permissions set the top-level permissions. NTFS permissions set the base-level permissions and can further restrict access. For example, while the Everyone group may have Full Control over the folder, a user that is not a member of a group assigned NTFS permissions will not be able to access and work with the share's folders and files. When troubleshooting, be sure to check basic permissions, special permissions, and the effective permissions.

Beyond the likely culprits, access can be affected by basic attributes as well as encryption. The Hidden basic attribute hides a folder or file from directory listings. The Read-only basic attribute makes a folder or file read-only. To determine whether basic attributes are causing access problems, right-click the folder or file and select Properties. On the General tab, as necessary, clear the Read-only, Hidden, or both checkboxes and then click OK.

NTFS volumes can contain encrypted folders and files, and encryption can limit access to folders and files. To determine whether a folder or file is encrypted, right-click the folder or file and select Properties. On the General tab, click Advanced. If the Encrypt Contents To Secure Data checkbox is selected, the resource is encrypted.

Encryption limits access to the user who encrypted the file, to the user who is granted shared access, and to the Data Recovery Agent (DRA). In domains, the default DRA is the domain Administrator user account. You can determine the exact list of users authorized to access an encrypted file by completing these steps:

1. Right-click the folder or file and select Properties.
2. On the General tab, click Advanced. If the Encrypt Contents To Secure Data checkbox is selected, the resource is encrypted.
3. Click Details to display the Encryption Details dialog box shown in Figure 2-22.

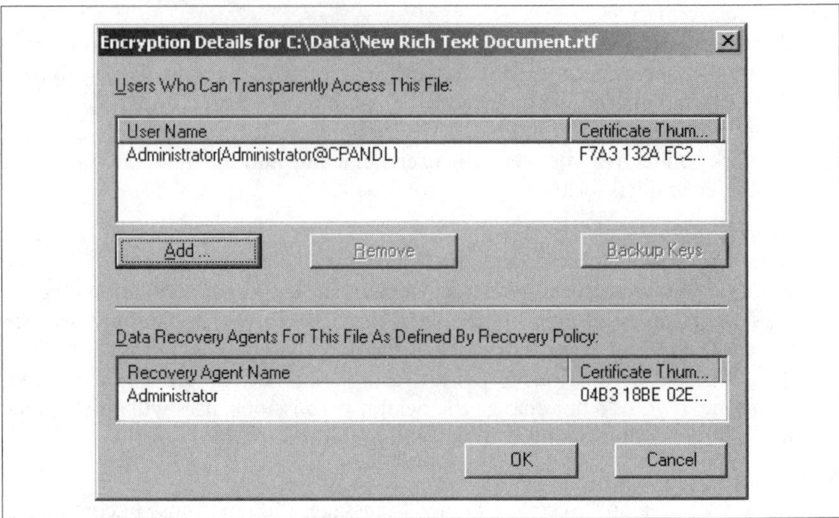

Figure 2-22. Use the Encryption Details dialog box to determine who has access to an encrypted file.

Troubleshoot Terminal Services

As discussed previously in this chapter in "Remote Desktop for Administration," Windows Server 2003 Terminal Services has two operating modes: *Remote Desktop for Administration* and *Terminal Server*. Remote Desktop for Administration is a limited Terminal Server mode that enables remote administration. When a server is configured as a Terminal Server, users establish remote sessions with the server to run Windows-based applications. In this configuration, the execution and processing takes place on the Terminal Server and the output data from the display, keyboard, and mouse are transmitted over the network to the user. A user logged in remotely to a Terminal Server is in a virtual session and any single Terminal Server can handle dozens or hundreds of such virtual sessions, depending on its configuration of course.

Exam 70-290 doesn't test your ability to install and configure Terminal Services. However, the exam does test your ability to:

- Diagnose and resolve issues related to terminal services security
- Diagnose and resolve issues related to client access to terminal services

Exam 70-290 also tests your ability to manage a server by using Terminal Services remote administration mode as discussed previously in the chapter in "Remote Desktop for Administration."

Diagnosing and resolving issues related to Terminal Services security

Windows Server 2003 provides several ways to manage security for Terminal Services. Using Active Directory Users And Computers, you can add users or group to the Remote Desktop Users group to allow users to log on to a terminal server. By adding the Domain Users group to the Remote Desktop Users group, you allow all authenticated domain users to use Terminal Services. By adding the special group Everyone to the Remote Desktop Users group, you allow anyone with access to the network to use Terminal Services.

In addition to the Remote Desktop Users group, users and groups that have access to Terminal Services by default are:

Administrators
: Any member of the Administrators group by default has Full Control access permission.

System
: By default, has Full Control access permission.

Local Server and Network Service
: Both have special access permissions.

You can manage the configuration of a designated Terminal Server using the Terminal Services Configuration tool. Click Start → Programs → Administrative Tools → Terminal Service Configuration, or type `tscc.msc` at a command prompt.

With Terminal Services and Remote Desktop for Administration, data sent between servers and clients uses Remote Desktop Protocol (RDP). You can modify the RDP settings for a server using the Terminal Services Configuration Tool. Select Connections, right-click the RDP-Tcp connection you want to work with, and select Properties. The RDP-Tcp Properties dialog box has the following tabs:

General
: Displays the RDP version and transport. Windows Server 2003 uses RDP version 5.2 over TCP by default. The encryption level in mixed environments that include Windows 2000 computers should be set to Client Compatible.

Logon Settings
: Allows you to configure logon settings. Typically, you'll use the default setting: Use Client-Provided Logon Information.

Sessions
: Allows you to configure session reconnection and timeout. These settings override the client settings.

Environment
: Allows you to use initial programs to run. These settings override the user client settings.

Remote Control
: Determines whether remote control of user sessions is enabled and sets remote control options.

Client Settings
: Determines how client screen resolution and redirection features are managed. By default, the connection settings from the clients are used and clients are limited to a maximum color depth of 16 bits.

Network Adapter
: Determines to which network adapters on the server connections can be made. The All Network Adapters option is selected by default. A maximum of two connections is the default limit.

Permissions
: Allows you to manage security permissions for the server, as discussed next.

When you want to manage Terminal Services security, you'll do so using the Permissions tab of the RDP-Tcp Properties dialog box. Similar to NTFS permissions, Terminal Services has two permission sets: *basic permissions* and *special permission*. The basic permissions represent a grouping of special permissions that together allow three commonly configured levels of access: Guest Access, User Access, and Full Control. The special permissions provide granular control for when you need to fine-tune access permissions.

The Remote Desktop Users group is granted User Access and Guest Access by default.

Terminal Services permissions set the maximum allowed permissions and are applied whenever a client connects to a Terminal Server. The basic permissions Terminal Services are:

Full Control
: Grants users full control over their sessions as well as the sessions of other users. Allows users to change session settings; view and take control of user sessions; disconnect user sessions; and establish virtual channels.

User Access
: Allows users to log on, view session settings, and connect to another session.

Guest Access
: Allows users to log on to a terminal server. Doesn't allow users to view session settings or connect to another session.

Typically, when you troubleshoot Terminal Services security, you check to see whether a user is a member of Remote Desktop Users in Active Directory Users And Computers. If groups are granted access directly through RDP-Tcp Properties, you need to examine the settings on the Permissions tab. On the Permissions tab, view the access permissions for a user or group by selecting the account name. You can then allow or deny access permissions as appropriate. Click Add to configure permissions for additional users or groups.

Diagnosing and resolving issues related to client access to Terminal Services

Users connecting to a Terminal Server will use the Remote Desktop Connection client found under Programs → Accessories → Communications. The default configuration for this client is to connect to a designated server using the user's current credentials. To connect using different credentials, start the Remote Desktop Connection client, click Options, and then enter values in the related Computer, User Name, Password, and Domain fields.

Both session and client settings are configured by default. The session settings on the server override client settings.

Session settings for display, devices, sound, start programs, experience, and security can be set through the server and the client. Most settings for sessions configured on the server override session settings configured on the client. Configure session settings on the server using the RDP-Tcp Properties dialog box. Configure session settings on the client using the options tabs.

After you click Options in the Remote Desktop Connection client, you'll see the following tabs, described here and shown in Figure 2-23:

General
: Configure logon settings. Instead of typing in settings each time, users can save and then load them when they want to make a connection. Save the current connection settings by clicking Save As, and then using the Save As dialog box to save a *.RDP* file for the connection. Load previously saved connection settings by clicking Open, and then using the Open dialog box to open the previously saved connection settings.

Display
: Configure remote desktop size and colors. The default is for 16-bit color on a full screen, but settings on the Terminal Server can override this.

Local Resources
: Configure audio redirection, keystroke combination redirection, and local device redirection.

Programs
: Configure the execution of programs when a session starts.

Experience
: Choose the connection speed to optimize performance and determine whether extras such as backgrounds and themes are allowed.

Security
: Specify whether and how authentication is used. Authentication is used to confirm the identity of the terminal server.

Most client access problems for Terminal Services have to do with the following:

Invalid credentials or connection server
: If a user is having problems connecting to a terminal server, make sure she are connecting to the appropriate server using the correct username, password, and domain settings. If the user enters the server name and then clicks Connect without setting additional options, the user's current credentials are used for the default, logon domain. If the user has recently changed her password and is using saved credentials, she will have to change the saved password and save the connection settings.

Improper group assignment
: The user must be a member of the Remote Desktop Users group in Active Directory or otherwise be assigned permissions for logon as discussed previously in "Diagnosing and resolving issues related to Terminal Services security."

Incorrect authentication mode

With authentication, the user may need to type the fully qualified domain name for the terminal server instead of the computer name. For example, the user may need to type `termserver21.williamstanek.com` instead of just `termserver21`.

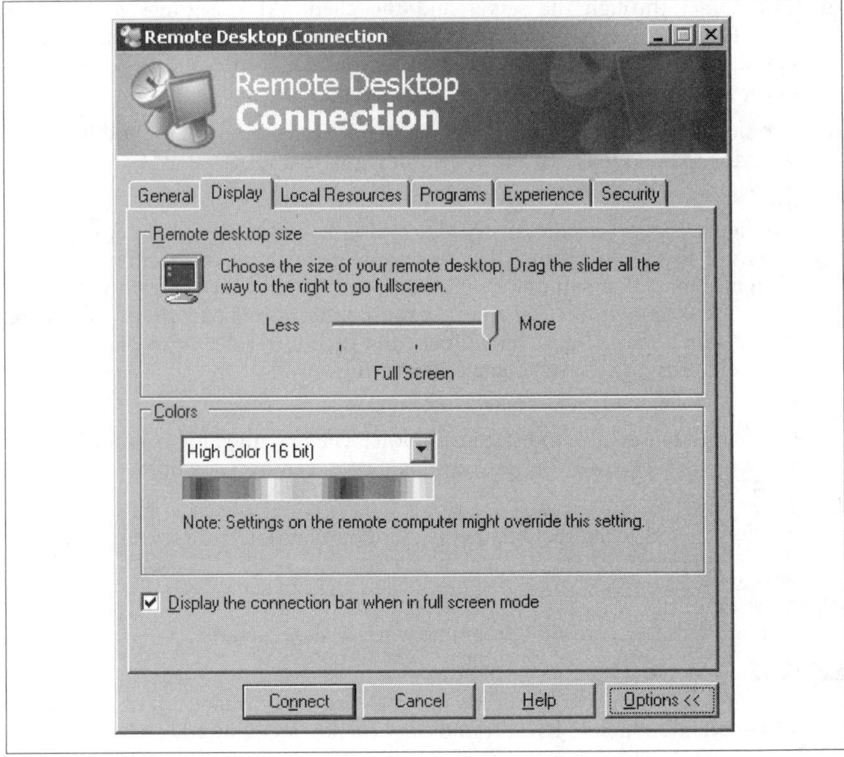

Figure 2-23. Session settings can be controlled through both client and server settings.

In a standard configuration, Terminal Services require TCP port 3389 to be open on both the client and the server. If either the client or the server is running a firewall, TCP port 3389 must be opened to allow remote access.

Managing and Maintaining a Server Environment

Managing and maintaining a server environment encompasses many aspects of administration. Because server performance can degrade over time, you need to:

- Routinely monitor events in Event Viewer
- Periodically monitor and optimize system performance
- Periodically monitor and optimize servers for application performance

Beyond the essential monitoring that may be required for maintenance, you'll also need to manage the essential infrastructure, including any web servers, print queues, software licensing, and software updates. By closely watching essential services, queues, and infrastructure, you ensure that the server environment continues to operate as expected.

Monitoring and Analyzing Events

Windows Server 2003 includes a set of logfiles that are used to record system events of various types. If you suspect a system has a problem, the event logs should be the first place you look to diagnose the problem.

Understanding the event logs

All Windows Server 2003 systems have three general purpose logs:

Application
: Contains events logged by Windows applications and printers configured on the system.

Security
: Contains events related to security auditing. Only the events configured for tracking are logged. Accessible only to administrators by default. Grant others as necessary.

System
: Contains events logged by operating system components and services. All events recorded in System category are preconfigured.

The availability of other logs depends on the system configuration. Logs you may see include:

DFS Replication
: Records DFS events if the server is configured to use DFS replication.

Directory Service
: Records events from Active Directory if the system is configured as a domain controller.

DNS Server
: Records events from DNS if the system is configured as a DNS server.

File Replication Service
: Records events from the File Replication Service if the system is configured as a domain controller.

Forwarded Events
: Records forwarded events if event forwarding is configured.

Hardware Events
: Records events from hardware subsystems on systems with this capability.

Accessing and reviewing events

Event logs are accessible in the Event Viewer (*eventvwr.exe*). In the Computer Management console (*compmgmt.msc*), you can view an event log by double-clicking System Tools, double-clicking Event Viewer, and then selecting the log you want to view as shown in Figure 2-24.

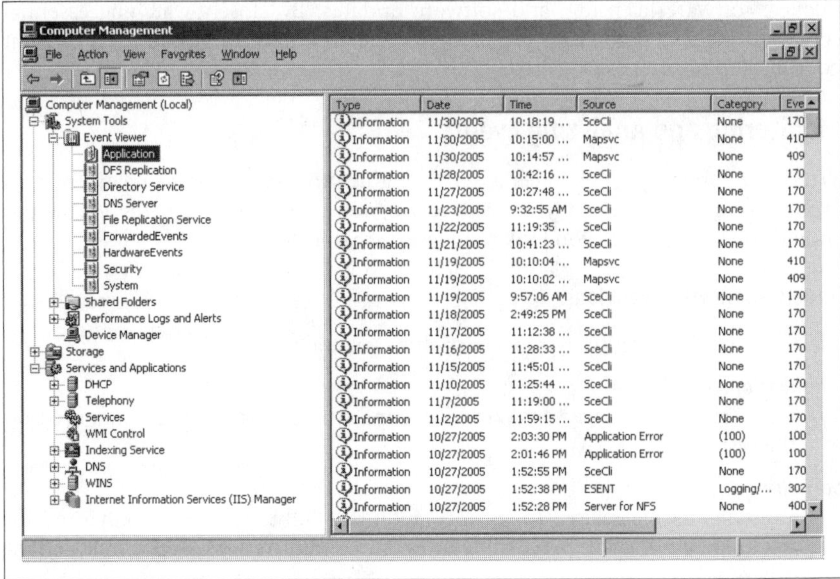

Figure 2-24. Events are listed in date/time order.

Events are recorded in date/time order with the most recent events at the start of the log and the oldest events at the end. When analyzing events, pay particular attention to the following:

Event type
: Specifies the type of event that occurred.

Event source
: Specifies the service, Windows component, or application for which the event was recorded.

Event category
: Specifies the general category of the event, if applicable.

You should use the event type designator to determine whether an event warrants further investigation. Event types you'll see include:

Information
: Routine events that typically record successful actions.

Success Audit
: When auditing is enabled, these events record successful execution of an action, such as a successful logon.

Failure Audit
: When auditing is enabled, these events record failed execution of an action, such as a failed logon.

Warning
: Notification events alerting administrators to possible problems that may need attention.

Error

Notification events alerting administrators to specific problems and errors that need attention.

When you are troubleshooting system problems, the events you'll look most closely at are warnings and errors. For security issues, the events you'll look most closely at are failure audits.

When working with a particular log, you can set properties that determine how events are recorded. You can also set filtering options so that you see only events that meet specific requirements. By default, Windows Server 2003 logs are configured to overwrite old events as needed. As a result, when a log reaches its maximum size, the operating system overwrites old events with new events.

Viewing and setting log options

You can view and set logging options on a per-log basis by completing the following steps:

1. Open Computer Management. Expand System Tools and Event Viewer.
2. Right-click the log you want to work with and then select Properties.
3. Use the options shown in Figure 2-25 to configure the maximum log size and overwrite options.

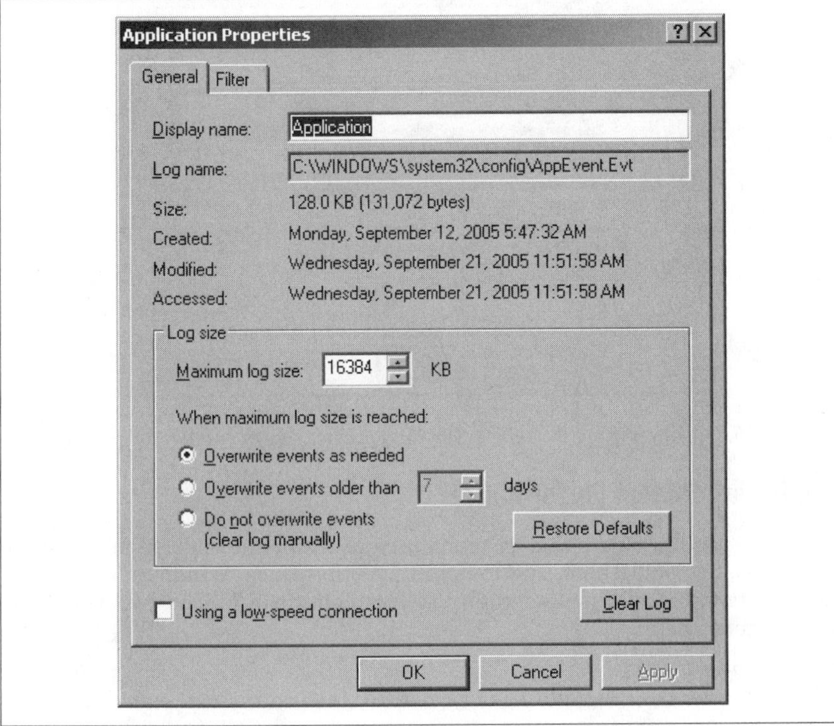

Figure 2-25. Review the logging options and change settings as necessary.

You can set filtering options for a log by completing the following steps:

1. Open Computer Management. Expand System Tools and Event Viewer.
2. Right-click the log you want to work with and then select Properties.
3. On the Filter tab, select the types of events to display and any other desired filtering options. For example, if you want to see Warning and Error events only, clear all the event type checkboxes except for Warning and Error, as shown in Figure 2-26.
4. Now when you view the selected log, you'll see only the events that meet the filter requirements. To restore the view so that all events are displayed, click Restore Defaults on the Filter tab.

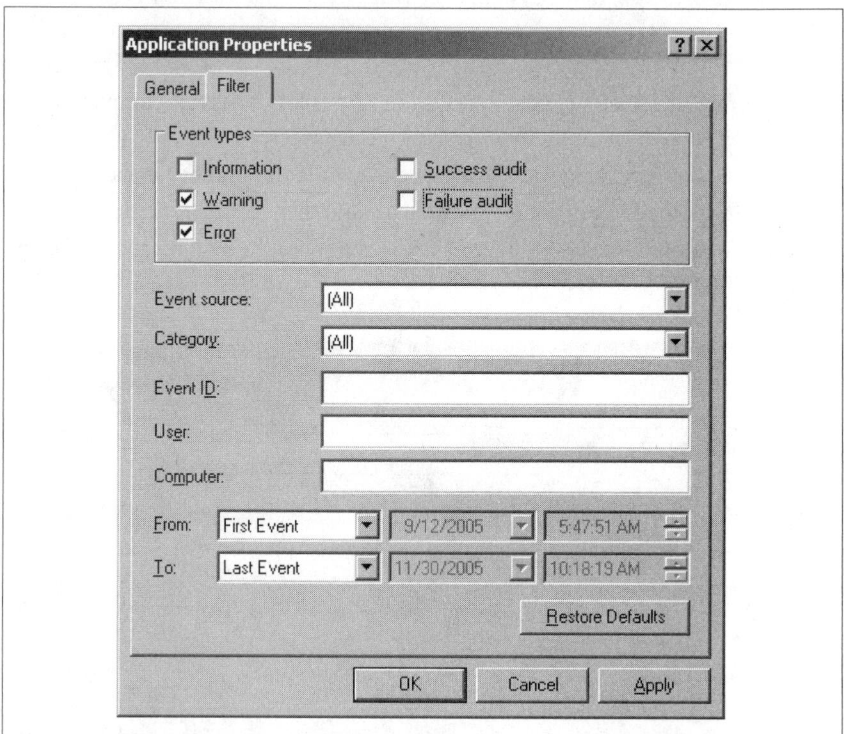

Figure 2-26. Use filtering options to help you find specific types of events.

Monitoring System Performance

Generally, you'll use performance monitoring to ensure the ongoing performance of systems, to troubleshoot, and to optimize performance. Windows Server 2003 includes several tools for monitoring system performance. The two you'll use most frequently are:

Task Manager
: Use this for basic monitoring of both application and system performance.

Performance Console
: Use this for comprehensive monitoring and analysis of ongoing performance.

Each tool has a specific use and a place in the overall system monitoring plan as well as for optimization and general troubleshooting. Task Manager can be used to diagnose non-responsive applications and identify possible problems with processors, network connections and memory. Performance Console is a power tool that can be used to pinpoint the exact origin of a performance problem and to help you optimize the system configuration.

Working with Task Manager

Task Manager displays the current status of applications, background processes, and system resources. To open Task Manager, log on to the computer you want to monitor, and then press CTRL+ALT+DEL → Task Manager or type `taskmgr` at a command prompt. When you start Task Manager, the default tab accessed is the Applications tab as shown in Figure 2-27. The Applications tab shows the status of the programs that are currently running on the system. The status can be "Running" or "Not Responding." You can stop an application that isn't responding by clicking the application name and then clicking End Task. Start a new program by selecting New Task, and then enter a command to run the application. Go to the related process in the Processes tab by right-clicking an application and then selecting Go To Process.

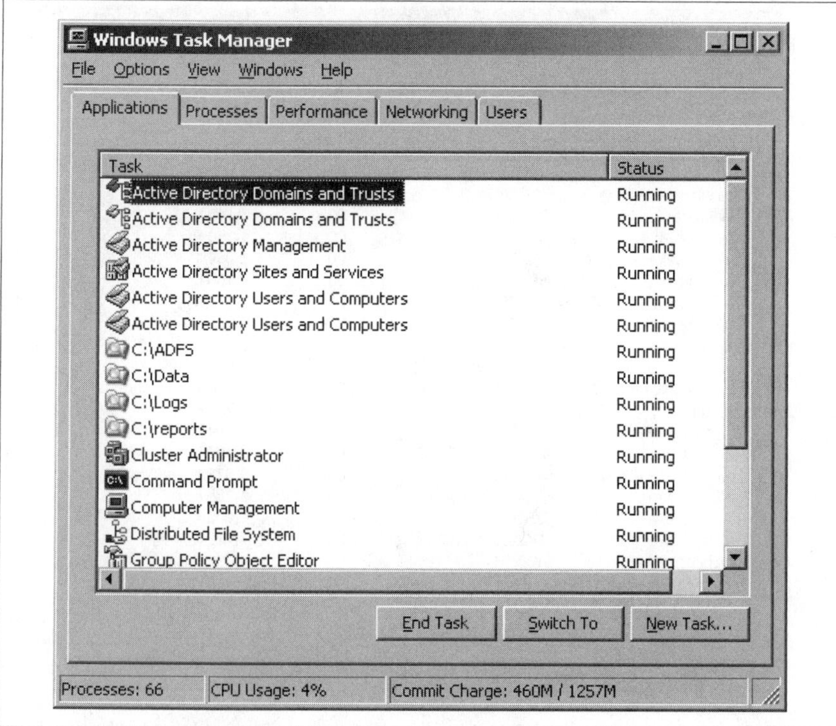

Figure 2-27. The Applications tab of Task Manager shows the status of applications.

The Processes tab (see Figure 2-28) displays detailed information about processes, which are programs running on the computer and can include foreground applications run by users and background applications run by the operating system. You can work with this tab as follows:

- By default, processes run by remote users are not displayed. Select Show Processes From All Users to display remote user processes as well as local processes.
- Right-click a process to display a list of options. Choose Set Priority to set processing priority. Most processes have Normal priority by default. Chose End Process to stop the process. Chose End Process Tree to stop the process and all child processes.
- By choosing View → Select Columns, you can change the available columns to include additional details on Base Priority (the priority of a process), CPU Time (CPU cycle time used by a process), Handle Count (the number of file handles used by a process), I/O Reads, I/O Writes (disk reads or writes since a process started), Page Faults (requests for a page in memory not found), Peak Memory Usage (highest amount of memory used by a process), Thread Count (number of threads a process is using), and more.

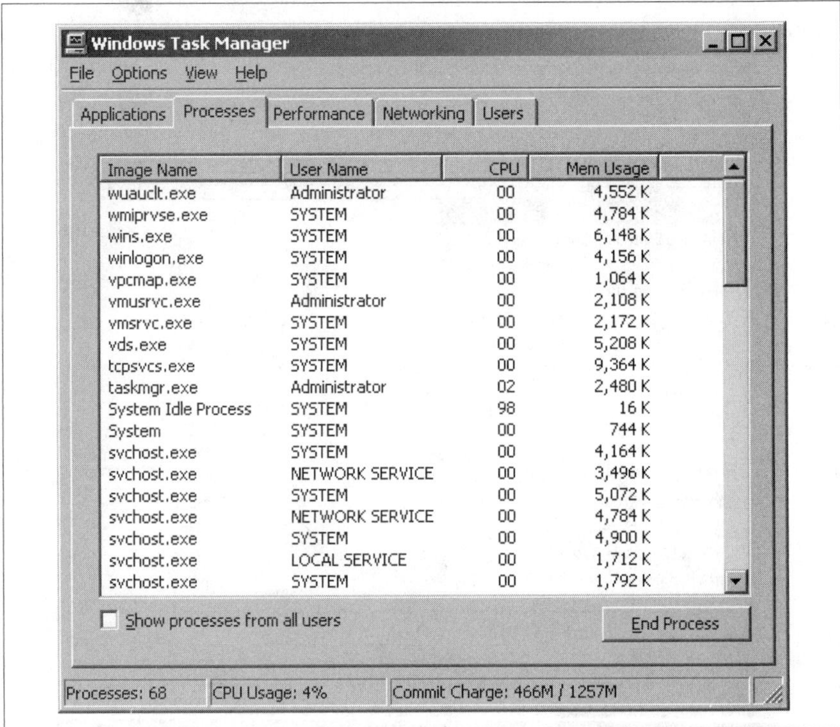

Figure 2-28. The Processes tab of Task Manager shows the foreground and background processes.

The Performance tab (see Figure 2-29) displays a real-time overview of resource usage. Graphs for each processor are provided to provide a visual summary of resource usage. CPU Usage History is a history graph of CPU usage plotted over time. Page File Usage History is a history graph of the paging file (or virtual memory) usage plotted over time. You can change the graphs using:

View → Update Speed
: Allows you to change the speed of graph updating or pause the graph.

View → CPU History
: On multiprocessor systems, allows you to specify how CPU graphs are displayed.

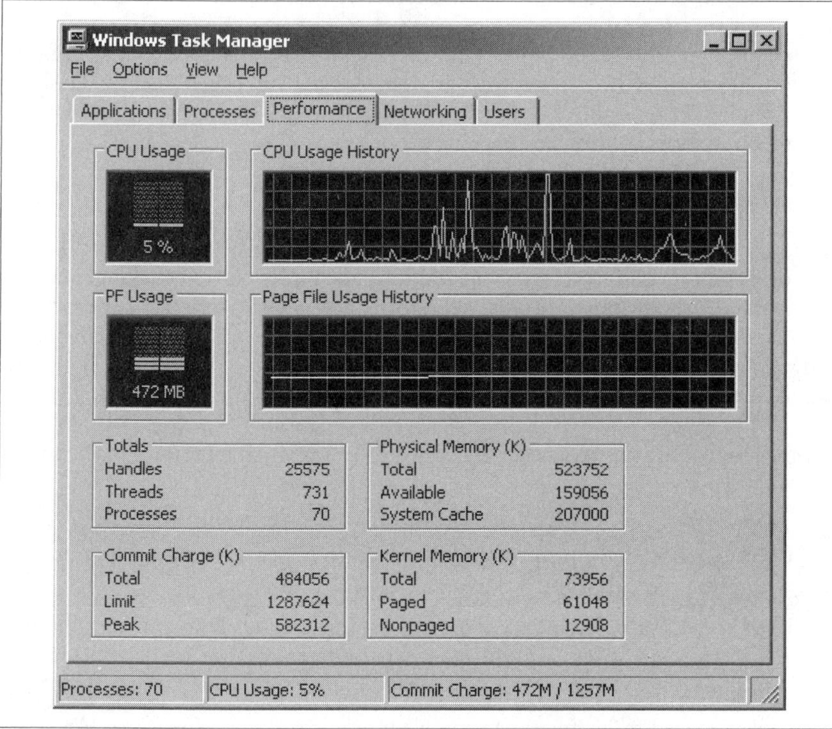

Figure 2-29. The Performance tab of Task Manager shows resource usage.

The text lists below the graphs summarize the usage of physical, kernel, and commit memory as well as the number of active handles, threads, and processes:

Physical Memory
: Summarizes RAM usage on the system: Total (the configured amount of physical RAM), Available (RAM not currently being used), and System Cache (RAM used for system caching).

Commit Charge
: Displays total memory usage: Total (current usage for physical and virtual memory), Limit (total physical and virtual memory available), and Peak (maximum memory usage since start).

Kernel Memory
: Displays memory usage by the operating system kernel: Total (current page and nonpaged kernel memory usage), Paged (kernel memory that paged to virtual memory), and Nonpaged (kernel not paged to virtual memory).

The Networking tab provides a summary for active network connections. A graph is provided to depict the percentage of utilization for each network connection. A text summary lists network connections by name, percent utilization, link speed, and operational status. By default, the graph displays network adapter history according to the total byte count. Click View → Network History to add bytes sent and bytes received.

The Users tab provides a summary of interactive user sessions for both local and remote users. Users are listed by account name, session ID, status, originating client computer, and session type. Console sessions represents users logged on to the local system. RDP-Tcp represents users logged on using Remote Desktop Protocol over TCP. Right-click user sessions to display options for disconnecting, logging off, remote control, and logging off.

Working with the Performance console

Using the Performance console, you can perform in-depth monitoring and analysis of computer activity. Start the Performance console by clicking Start → Programs → Administrative Tools → Performance or by typing `perfmon.msc` at a command prompt. The Performance console's remote monitoring capabilities allow you to track the performance of multiple computers from a single, monitoring computer.

Understanding performance monitoring. As Figure 2-30 shows, the Performance console has two snap-ins:

System Monitor
: Used to collect real-time performance data from local and remote computers.

Performance Logs and Alerts
: Used to record performance data in logs for later analysis and to configure alerts triggered when a performance parameter reaches a specific limit or threshold.

Users do not need to be administrators to monitor or log performance. Any user that is a member of the built-in group Performance Monitor Users can monitor performance counters, logs, and alerts. Any user that is a member of the built-in group Performance Log Users can schedule logging and alerting.

Whether you are monitoring system performance, configuring performance logs, or setting performance alerts, you specify the activity to track or alert by using:

Performance objects
: Represent system and application components with measurable sets of properties. Most critical system components and services have related objects. Examples of objects you can monitor include PhysicalDisk, LogicalDisk, Memory, Processor, and Paging File.

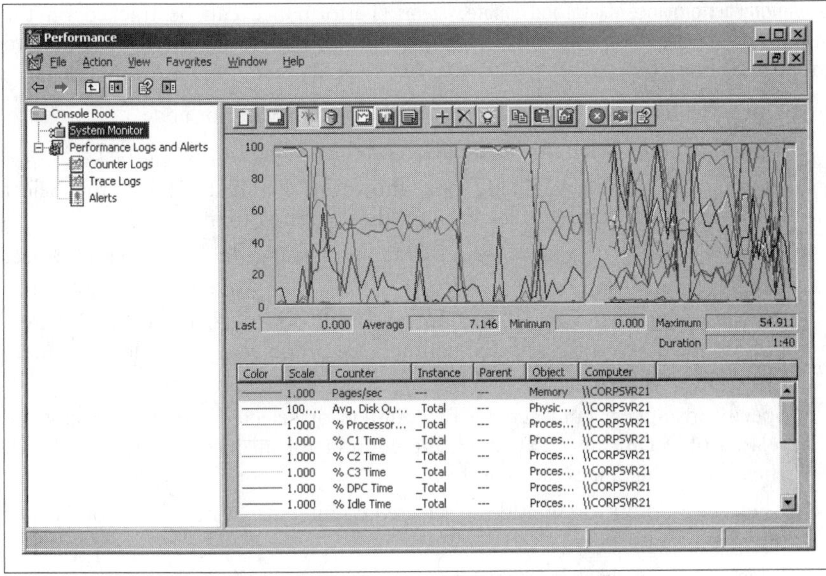

Figure 2-30. Use the Performance console to monitor and analyze computer activity.

Performance object instances
: Represent specific occurrences of performance objects. For example, if a computer has multiple processors, physical disks, and logical disks, there'll be one object instance for each and you'll be able to track the instances separately or collectively.

Performance counters
: Represent the measurable properties of performance objects. Every performance object has several performance counters associated with it. With the Process performance object, you can use the %Processor Time counter to measure processor usage. With the Memory performance object, you can use the Available MBytes counter to view the amount of physical memory available.

When working with performance objects, object counters, and object instances, you'll see various notation schemes. Typically, performance objects are referred to by name, such as the Memory object. Performance counters are referred to via the object to which they relate in the form *ObjectName\CounterName*. For example, to refer to the Committed Bytes counter of the Memory object, the notation *Memory\Committed Bytes* is used. Object instances are referred to with regard to the object and counter to which they relate in the form *ObjectName(instance_name)\CounterName*, such as *Process(dns)\Pool Paged Bytes*.

Data collected by System Monitor can be summarized in multiple formats: graphic, histogram, and report. Graph is the default format. When working with System Monitor, press Ctrl+B for histogram or Ctrl+R for report format.

Monitoring performance of local and remote systems. Performance can be tracked on the system you want to monitor or from another computer. To specify counters to monitor, follow these steps:

1. Open the Performance console. Select the System Monitor node.
2. To add counters, click the Add button on the toolbar or press Ctrl+L.
3. In the Add Counters dialog box shown in Figure 2-31, use the Select Counters From Computer list to select the computer to monitor.
4. Next, select a performance object to monitor using the Performance Object list.
5. Specify counters. To track all counters for an object, click the All Counters radio button. To track selected counters for an object, click Select Counters From List and then click a counter.
6. Specify instances. For each set of counters or selected counter, specify the related object instance. To track the counter for all instances of the object, click the All Instances radio button.
7. Click the Add button to add the selected counters to System Monitor's list of items to monitor.
8. Repeat this process for other objects, object counters, and object instances you want to monitor.
9. Click Close when you are finished adding counters.

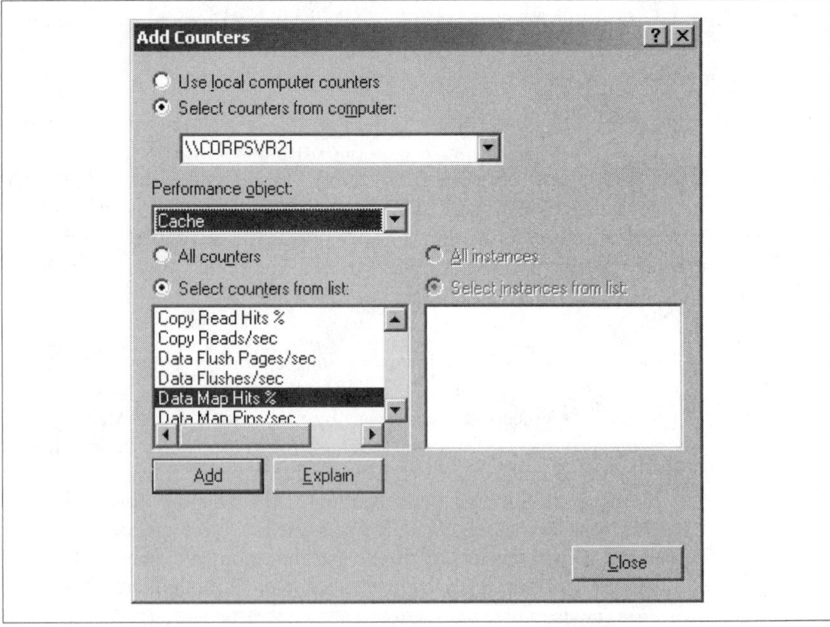

Figure 2-31. Select the counters to monitor.

When working with System Monitor, you can stop monitoring a counter by clicking a counter in the counter list and then pressing Delete.

Performance logging. Real-time monitoring in System Monitor is useful when you are diagnosing a current performance issue or problem. When you want to track performance over time, however, you'll want to use performance logging. You can configure performance logging using:

Counter logs
: Counter logs record performance data at specified intervals.

Trace logs
: Trace logs record performance data whenever tracked events occur.

To create a performance log, follow these steps:

1. Open the Performance console. Expand the Performance Logs And Alerts node and then select either Counter Logs or Trace Logs, depending on the type of log you want to create.

Any current logs are listed with a red icon to indicate logging is stopped, or with a green icon to indicate logging is active.

2. Right-click in the right pane and select New Log Settings.
3. Type a name for the log and then click OK.
4. With a counter log, you must next specify the objects, object counters, and object instances to log by clicking the Add Objects or Add Counters button. Set the sample interval. The default sample interval is 15 seconds.
5. With a trace log, you must next specify the events to track. Select the Events Logged By System Provider radio button and then use the checkboxes provided to set the tracked events. The designated events are logged whenever they occur.
6. Use the Log Files tab options to set the log file type and name. Logs are written to *C:\PerfLogs* by default.
7. Use the Schedule tab options to specify when logging starts and stops.
8. Click OK.

You can manually start or stop logging by right-clicking a log and then selecting either Start or Stop as appropriate. You can replay logged data at a later date to analyze performance by completing the following steps:

1. Open Performance Monitor. Select the System Monitor node in the left pane.
2. Click the View Log Data button on the System Monitor toolbar or press Ctrl+L.
3. With binary or text-based logfiles, click Log Files, and then click Add. Select the log file you want to analyze, and then click Open.
4. With SQL logging, click Database, and then provide the system DNS and log set details.
5. Click the Time Range button, and then drag the Total Range bar to specify the appropriate starting and ending times

6. On the Data tab, specify which of the logged counters to view. Click the Add button, and then select the counters to analyze.
7. Click OK, and then use System Monitor to review the logged data.

Performance alerting. When you want to be alerted to potential problems or track specific conditions, you'll want to use performance alerting. To configure performance alerting, specify alerts that should be triggered when a performance parameter reaches a specific limit or threshold. Alerts can be configured to start applications and performance logs as well.

To create an alert, follow these steps:

1. Open the Performance console. Expand the Performance Logs And Alerts node.

Any current alerts are listed with a red icon to indicate alerting is stopped, or with a green icon to indicate alerting is active.

2. Right-click Alerts, and then choose New Alert Settings.
3. Type a name for the alert, and then click OK.
4. Click Add to select the counters for which you want to configure alerts.
5. Click Close when you're finished.
6. Select each counter in turn and then use the Alert When Value Is... field to set the threshold for triggering the alert. For example, with %Processor Time, you might want to be alerted when value is more than 95.
7. Set the sample interval. The default sample interval is five seconds.
8. On the Action tab, choose the actions that you want the alert to perform whenever it is triggered. By default, an event is logged in the application event log. You can also send a network message, start a performance log, or run a program.
9. Use the Schedule tab options to specify when alerting starts and stops.
10. Click OK.

You can manually start or stop alerting by right-clicking a log and then selecting either Start or Stop as appropriate.

Monitoring and Optimizing a Server Environment for Performance

Monitoring Windows systems can help you establish baseline usage statistics and evaluate ongoing performance. Use baselines to determine how a system performs under various usage loads. Use performance evaluations to determine whether a system is performing as expected.

When it comes to optimization, virtual memory is as important as physical memory. In most cases, servers with 2 GB or less physical memory should have virtual memory that is at least two times physical memory. For best performance, virtual memory should have a fixed size and be located on multiple physical disks. You can set virtual memory using the System utility, under the Control Panel. In the System utility, click the Advanced Tab, then under Performance, click Settings to display the Performance Options dialog box. In the Performance Options dialog box, click the Advanced tab, and then click Change, under Virtual Memory. You can then use the available options to view and manage the virtual memory settings for the computer.

Choosing objects to monitor

The object counters you choose to monitor will vary depending on the role of the computer you are working with. With most Windows systems, you'll want to monitor the four key performance areas:

Memory usage
: Related objects include Cache, Memory, and Paging File

Processor usage
: Related objects include Processor, Job Object, Process, and Thread

Disk
: Related objects include LogicalDisk, PhysicalDisk, and System

Network
: Related objects include Network Interface, Server, and Server Work Queues

If you create performance baselines for systems, you can compare these and other performance areas in the baselines to current performance. This will help you identify potential problems and bottlenecks that might cause a system to operate at less than optimal performance levels. Table 2-12 lists various server roles and the object typically monitored for those roles and provides guidelines on additional objects to add when troubleshooting.

Table 2-12. Performance objects to monitor based on server role

Server role	Objects typically monitored	When troubleshooting, add...
Application, mail, and web server	Memory, Processor, Network Interface, System, PhysicalDisk, and LogicalDisk	Cache, Paging File; instance-specific to application Job Object, Process, and Thread as appropriate
Backup server	Processor, Network Interface, System, and Server	Memory and Server Work Queues
Database server	Memory, Processor, Network Interface, System, PhysicalDisk, and LogicalDisk	Paging File, Server, and Server Work Queues
Domain controller	Memory, Processor, Network Interface, System, PhysicalDisk, and LogicalDisk	Paging File, Server, and Server Work Queues
File and print server	Memory, Network Interface, PhysicalDisk, LogicalDisk, Print Queue, and Server	Processor, Paging File, System, and Server Work Queues

Monitoring memory performance objects

Windows systems have both physical and virtual memory. Memory bottlenecks occur when low available memory conditions cause increased usage of the paging file. Page faults occur when requests for data are not found in memory and the system must look to other areas of memory or to virtual memory on disk.

Two types of page faults are tracked:

Soft page faults
: These occur when the system must look for the necessary data in another area of memory.

Hard page faults
: These occur when the system must look for the necessary data in virtual memory on disk.

When a system is running low on memory, hard page faults can make the system appear to have a disk problem due to excessive page swapping between physical and virtual memory. You can determine physical and virtual memory usage by using *Memory\Available Kbytes* and *Memory\Committed Bytes*. *Memory\Available Kbytes* is the amount of physical memory not yet in use. *Memory\Committed Bytes* is the amount of committed virtual memory. The *Memory\PageFaults/sec* counter helps you track page faults. Specific usage of the paging file can be tracked using *Paging File\%Usage*.

If the available memory is low, consider adding physical memory, virtual memory, or both to the system. You can determine the current amount of virtual memory available to a system using *Memory\Commit Limit*. The different between the commit limit and the committed bytes is the amount of virtual memory available for use.

Table 2-13 summarizes specific indicators of memory bottlenecks and potential resolutions.

Table 2-13. Resolving memory bottlenecks

Object\Counter	Alert threshold	Solution
Memory\Available Kbytes	Consistently lower than 10 percent total physical memory.	Identify process using high amounts of memory; install additional physical memory
Memory\Nonpaged Kbytes	Increasing over time without increased workload	May indicate a memory leak; identify program that might have the memory leak and look for updated version
Memory\Page Faults/sec	Consistently 5 percent or higher	Identify process causing page faults; install additional physical memory
Memory\Pages/sec	Consistently substantially higher compared to baseline	Identify process causing excessive paging; install additional physical memory
Paging File\%Usage	Consistently higher than 90 percent	Configure additional virtual memory. If virtual memory already twice physical RAM, add physical memory as well

Monitoring processor performance objects

Systems with high processor utilization may perform poorly. If a system's processor utilization peaks to 100 percent, the processor is fully utilized and the system is likely overloaded. You can determine processor utilization using

Processor\%Processor Time. Another counter that can help you identity processor bottlenecks is *System\Processor Queue Length*, which tracks the number of threads waiting to be executed. If there are multiple threads waiting to execute, the processor isn't keeping up with the current workload. You can resolve this by shifting part of the system's workload to other computers or installing additional processors.

When programs allocate memory for use but do not fully release the allocated memory, the program may have a memory leak. Over time, a memory leak can cause a system to run low on or run out of memory. Rebooting the system can temporarily fix the problem. To help determine which specific process or processes are causing the processor bottleneck, you can use the counters of the Process object. Each running process has a separate instance of the Process object. You'll want to track *Process(process_name)\Handle Count*, *Process(process_name)\Thread Count*, *Process(process_name)\Pool Paged Bytes*, *Process(process_name)\Private Bytes*, and *Process(process_name)\Virtual Bytes* to determine how a particular process is using memory.

Table 2-14 summarizes specific indicators of processor bottlenecks and potential resolutions.

Table 2-14. Resolving processor bottlenecks

Object\Counter	Alert threshold	Solution
Process(process_name)\Pool Paged Bytes Process(process_name)\Private Bytes *Process(process_name)\Virtual Bytes*	Increasing over time without increased workload	May indicate a memory leak; may need to install updated version of the program
Processor\%Processor Time *Processor\%Privileged Time* *Processor\%User Time*	Frequently sustained at 85 percent or higher	Upgrade the CPU; install additional CPU; shift workload
Processor\Interrupts/sec	High sustained values (relative to the baseline)	May indicate problem with a hardware device; if so, find and replace the faulty hardware device
System\Processor Queue Length *Server Work Queues\Queue Length*	Sustained at 2 percent or higher	Upgrade the CPU; install additional CPU; shift workload

Monitoring network performance objects

The available network bandwidth determines how fast data is sent between clients and servers. When the network bandwidth is saturated, network performance suffers because clients and servers aren't able to communicate with each other in a timely and efficient manner. Most computers have network interfaces that operate at 100 megabits per second (100 Mbps) or at 1 gigabits per second (1 Gbps). Because most networks operate at these same speeds, the network typically would get saturated before a computer reaches maximum network utilization. That said, if you suspect the problem is with a particular computer rather than with the network itself, you can determine this using the Network Interface performance object.

The *Network Interface\Output Queue Length* counter can help you identify network saturation issues. You can use *Network Interface\Current Bandwidth* to determine the current bandwidth setting and total capacity of a particular network interface. The *Network Interface\Bytes Total/sec* provides the total bytes transferred or received per second. If the total bytes per second value is more than 50 percent of the total capacity, the system may have a network bottleneck problem. You can resolve this by shifting part of the system's workload to other computers or installing additional network interface cards.

Table 2-15 summarizes specific indicators of network bottlenecks and potential resolutions.

Table 2-15. Resolving network bottlenecks

Object\Counter	Alert threshold	Solution
Network Interface\Current Bandwidth *Network Interface\Bytes Total/sec*	Total bytes transferred more than 50 percent capacity	Upgrade network adapters; install additional network adapters
Network Interface\Output Queue Length	High sustained queue length	Decrease saturation on the network; increase network bandwidth
Network Interface\Bytes Recd/sec	Total bytes received more than 50 percent capacity	Upgrade network adapters; install additional network adapters
Network Interface\Bytes Sent/sec	Total bytes sent more than 50 percent capacity	Upgrade network adapters; install additional network adapters

Monitoring disk performance objects

Disk performance is tracked using the PhysicalDisk and LogicalDisk objects. PhysicalDisk objects are available for each physical hard disk on a system. LogicalDisk objects are available for each logical volume created on a system. To track free space on logical disks, you can use the *LogicalDisk\%Free Space* counter. To determine the level of disk I/O activity, you can use the P*hysicalDisk\Disk Writes/sec* and *Physical Disk\Disk Reads/sec* counters.

Physical Disk\Avg. DiskWrite Queue Length, *Physical Disk\Avg. DiskRead Queue Length*, and *Physical Disk\CurrentDisk Queue Length* track disk-queuing activity. The write and read queue lengths are a measure of how well disks are performing. If there are multiple requests in a write or read queue waiting to be processed, the disk isn't performing as fast as is necessary to keep up with I/O requests.

As discussed previously, this problem could be due to the excessive page swapping that may occur if physical memory is low. An indicator of this may be a consistently high PhysicalDisk\%Disk Time value. However, if physical memory is not low, the disk itself is the problem and you'll need to upgrade to faster disks or shift the disk's workload to other disks.

Table 2-16 summarizes specific indicators of disk bottlenecks and potential resolutions.

Table 2-16. Resolving disk bottlenecks

Object\Counter	Alert threshold	Solution
LogicalDisk\%Free Space	85 percent or higher	Clean up drive; move data to free space
Physical Disk\Avg. DiskWrite Queue Length *Physical Disk\Avg. DiskRead Queue Length* *Physical Disk\CurrentDisk Queue Length*	Sustained at 2 percent or higher	Install faster drives; shift workload to use additional drives
PhysicalDisk\%Disk Time	Consistently at 50 percent or higher	Determine whether excessive paging is an issue; if not, install faster drives or shift workload to use additional drives

Monitoring File and Print Servers

When you manage file and print servers, two areas you'll need to monitor closely are *disk quotas* and *print queues*. Disk quotas help you track and manage disk space usage. Print queues are where printed documents are stored as print jobs before they are printed.

Exam 70-290 has specific objectives for monitoring NTFS disk quotas and print queues. There's also an objective for troubleshooting print queues. It is important to point out that Windows now supports two types of disk quotas: NTFS disk quotas (covered on the exam) and Storage Resource Manager disk quotas (included with Windows Server 2003 R2).

Monitoring disk quotas

NTFS disk quotas are the standard type of disk quotas supported on Windows Server 2003. With NTFS disk quotas, you configure quotas on a per-user, per-volume basis. Disk quotas cannot be configured for groups.

Any NTFS volume can use disk quotas, even system volumes. FAT/FAT32 volumes, however, cannot use NTFS disk quotas.

NTFS disk quotas can be configured through Group Policy or through the Quota tab on the NTFS volume. Policy settings override Quota tab settings in most cases. Specific quota limits and quota warnings can be set on each volume:

- A quota warning is used to warn users that they've used more than a specified amount of disk space. A warning level can be exceeded.
- A quota sets a specific limit on the amount of space that can be used. Users can be prevented from exceeding a quota limit. The built-in Administrators group, however, is not affected by enforced quota limits.

The disk space usage for each user is tracked separately. Because of this, disk space used by one user doesn't affect the disk quotas for other users. Only members of the domain Administrators group or the local system Administrators group can configure disk quotas.

To enable disk quotas using the Quota tab of an NTFS volume, follow these steps:

1. Right-click the volume in Computer Management and then select Properties.
2. On the Quota tab, select Enable Quota Management as shown in Figure 2-32.

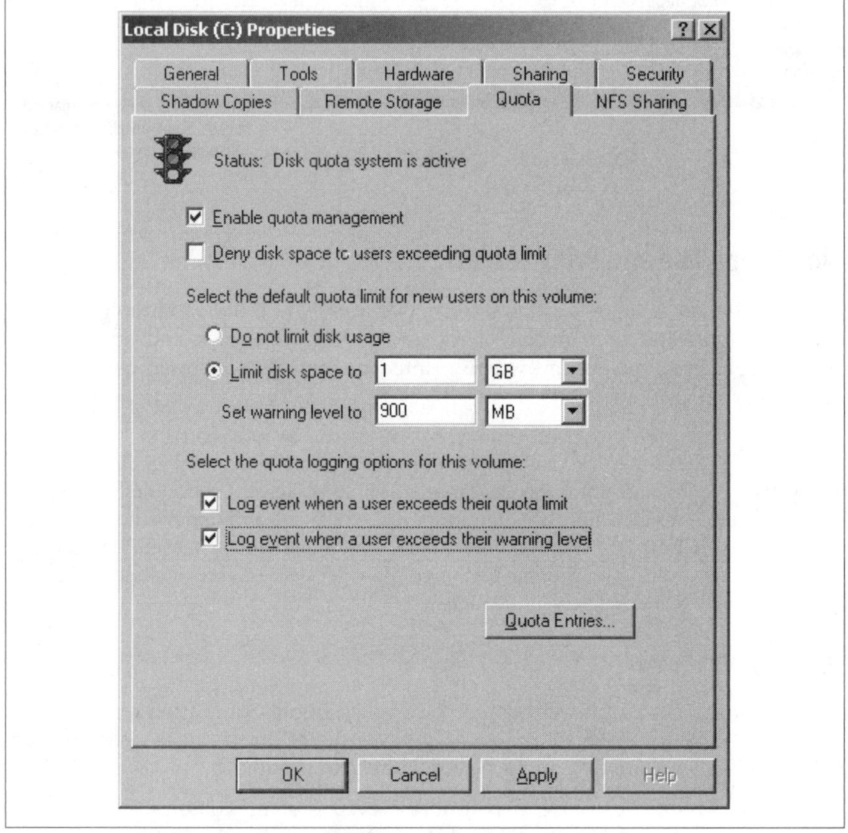

Figure 2-32. Use the Quota tab to enable and configure disk quotas.

3. Select the Limit Disk Space To radio button and then set a quota limit and warning level.
4. If you want to enforce the quota limit so that it cannot be exceeded, select the Deny Disk Space To Users Exceeding Quota Limit checkbox.
5. To enable logging when users exceed a warning limit or the quota limit, select the Log Event checkboxes.
6. Click OK. When prompted to confirm, click OK again.

After you enable quotas, users that exceed a warning or limit level will see a warning prompt. If you've enforced quota limits, the user will be prevented from exceeded the limit. If you've configured logging, administrators can determine which users have received warnings or reached limits using the Application event log.

You can view current usage on a per-user basis by viewing the disk quota entries. On the Quota tab, click the Quota Entries button. The Quota Entries For Local Disk dialog box (shown in Figure 2-33) shows the current disk space usage and quota settings for all users, including system user accounts and domain/local user accounts.

Quota Entries for Local Disk (C:)

Quota Edit View Help

Status	Name	Logon Name	Amount Used	Quota Limit	Warning Level	Percent Used
OK		BUILTIN\Administrators	2.89 GB	No Limit	No Limit	N/A
OK		\Everyone	2 KB	1 GB	900 MB	0
OK		NT AUTHORITY\SYSTEM	27 KB	1 GB	900 MB	0
OK		NT AUTHORITY\NETWORK SERVICE	547 KB	1 GB	900 MB	0
OK		NT AUTHORITY\LOCAL SERVICE	273 KB	1 GB	900 MB	0
OK		CPANDL\Administrator	653 KB	1 GB	900 MB	0
OK		CPANDL\Domain Admins	4 KB	1 GB	900 MB	0

7 total item(s), 1 selected.

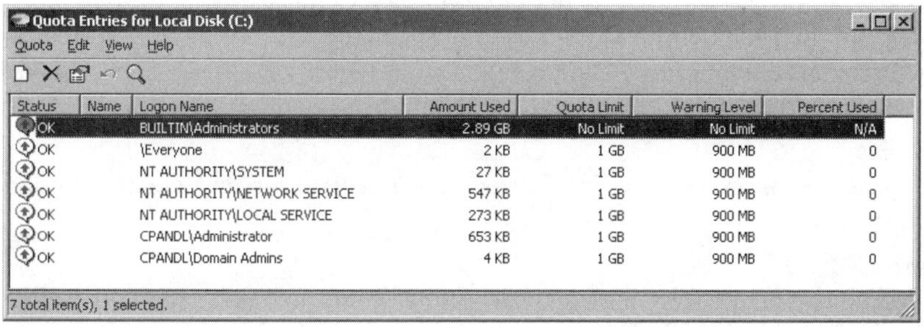

Figure 2-33. Disk quotas are tracked for system accounts, as well as user accounts.

Although quotas do not affect the built-in Administrators group, they do affect system user accounts and domain/local user accounts. Disk space used by the operating system is tracked according to the user account used during installation. Administrators can customize the disk quota entries on a per-user basis by double-clicking the entry and setting different limits and warning levels for the selected user. Administrators can also create custom quota entries for users who haven't yet saved data on a volume. To do this, click Quota → New Quota Entry.

Monitoring and troubleshooting print queues

In Windows environments, printing can be handled in two ways:

- Client computers can have their own print queues and send print jobs directly to a direct-attached or network-attached printer.
- Client computers can access shared printers and send print jobs to the print queue on a print server, which in turn sends the print job to the printer.

Although the direct client to printer approach may seem more efficient, monitoring, maintaining, and troubleshooting such a configuration can be difficult and time-consuming because every user has a separate print queue. On the other hand, with a print server, all client computers share a common print queue on the print server. This means there's a central location for monitoring and a central location to look at when users have problems with a particular printer.

Working with print servers. Any workstation or server computer running Windows can be configured to act as a print server. A print server is simply a computer that is configured to share a printer.

Install and manage printers using the Printers And Faxes folder. You can access this folder on a local system by clicking Start → Printers And Faxes. You can access this folder on a remote computer through My Network Places. In Windows Explorer, click My Network Places, click a domain, click a print server, and then double-click Printers.

When a user sends a print job to a shared printer, the print server spools the print job to the spooling folder on its local disk. Spooled print jobs are queued to be printed. Each printer has its own print queue. All printers have the same spool folder. Windows Server 2003 uses the Print Spooler service to control the spooling of print jobs. You can check the status of the Print Spooler service using Control Panel → Services utility.

Print server properties control the general settings for all shared printers on the server. In the Printers And Faxes window, click File → Server Properties to access the Print Server Properties dialog box shown in Figure 2-34. The tabs of the Print Server Properties dialog box are used as follows:

Forms
: Options allow you to view current document forms and create additional printer forms.

Ports
: Allows you to view and manage printer ports for all configured printers. Direct-attached printers use LPT, COM, or USB ports. Network-attached printers use AppleTalk, LPR, or TCP/IP ports.

Drivers
: Allows you to view and manage printer drivers for all configured printers. You can also add, remove, and reinstall drivers.

Advanced
: Allows you to view and manage spooling and notification options. You can also view and set the spool folder.

The default location for the spool folder is *%SystemRoot%\system32\spool\printers*. The default permissions on this folder grant full control to Administrators, Print Operators, Server Operators, System, and Creator Owner. Full control for Creator Owner allows users to delete and manage their own print jobs. Authenticated Users have Read & Execute permissions so that authenticated users can access the spool folder. If these permissions are changed, spooling might fail.

Working with printer properties. In the Printers And Faxes window, all printers are listed by their local name. Shared printers also have a shared name. It is through the share name that users access print queues. Print jobs are routed to printers according to the port or ports configured for use with that printer. Print jobs are processed in first-in-first-out, priority order. Generally speaking, higher priority print jobs print before lower priority jobs. When there are multiple print jobs of the same priority, jobs are processed in the order they were received, with the first job in being the first processed and printed.

You can use the printer's Properties dialog box to manage its properties. You access the Properties dialog box by completing these steps:

1. Open the Printers And Faxes window on the computer you want to work with.
2. Right-click the icon of the printer you want to configure and then select Properties.
3. Set the printer properties using the Properties dialog box shown in Figure 2-35.

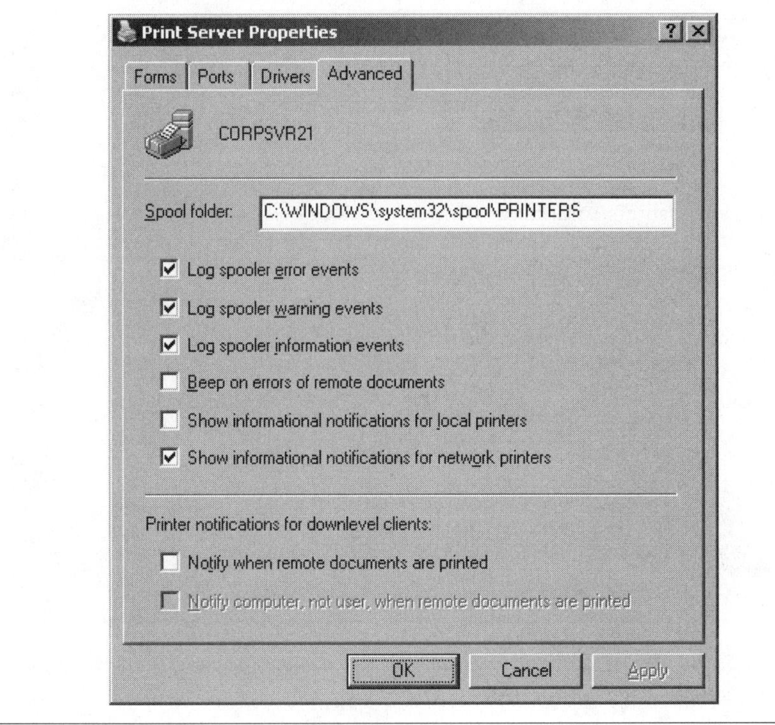

Figure 2-34. Manage general properties for all shared printers using the Print Server Properties dialog box.

The available tabs in a printer's Properties dialog box depend on the type and model of printer. Options on the most common tabs are used as follows:

General
: View or set the printer name, location, and comments. Click the Printing Preferences button to set default printing preferences for page layout, quality, etc. Click the Print Test Page button to print a test page.

Sharing
: View or set the printer share name. Select List In The Directory to list the printer in Active Directory. Click the Additional Drivers button to install additional drivers for users. By default, only x86 drivers for Windows 2000 or later computers are installed for most printers. You can add x86 drivers for pre-Windows 2000 computers, x64 printer drivers, and Itanium drivers by selecting the related checkboxes.

> If you change the printer share name, you will need to update related printer mapping on client computers so that it uses the new share name. This can be done manually by logging on to client computers or automatically through logon scripts or some other automation technique.

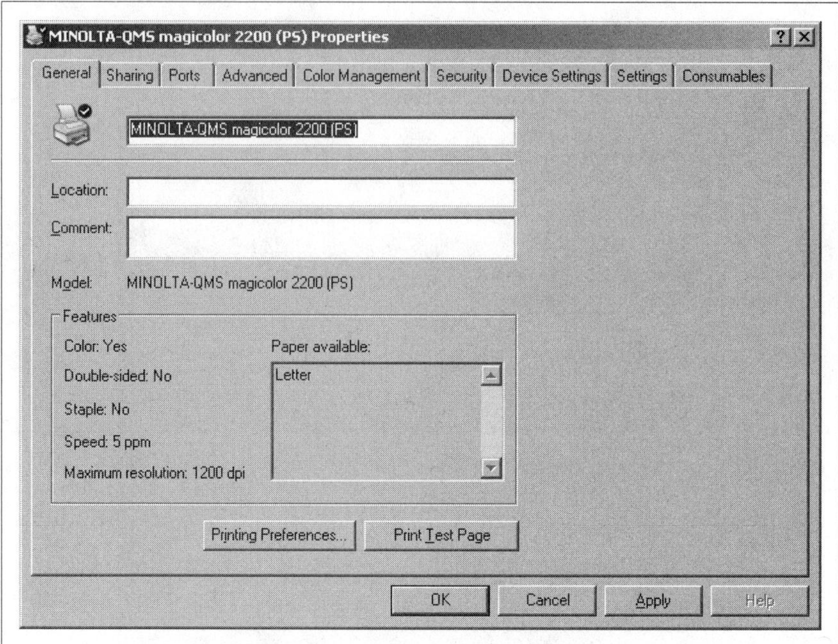

Figure 2-35. Use the printer's Properties dialog box to manage the ports, share name, and other configuration options being used.

Ports

View or set printer ports. If the hostname or IP address of a printer changes, you will need to click the current port, click Configure Port, set the new hostname or IP address, and then click OK. Printers that use TCP/IP use either a specific RAW port or a named LPR print queue. If this information is incorrectly configured, you need to click the current port, click Configure Port, modify the protocol settings as appropriate, and then click OK.

On the Ports tab, the Enable Printer Pooling checkbox should be selected only when two or more identical printers are pooled through one logical print device. In the case of pooling, there will be one configured port for each printer. If one of the printers should go offline, you need to disable the related port by clearing the associated port checkbox. If there is then only one printer online, you need to clear the Enable Printer Pooling checkbox.

Advanced

View or set availability, priority, and spooling options. Printers can be always available, or available only during specified hours. Print queues can have a default priority of 1 (low) to 99 (high). The current print driver is listed here. If you want to upgrade or reinstall the print drivers for all clients, click the New Driver button and then follow the Add Printer Driver Wizard prompts.

Security

View or set access permissions for the print queue. Print queue permissions are separate from the NTFS access permissions on the related spooling folder. By default, the special identity Everyone has permission to print. Creator Owner can manage documents and print. Administrators, Print Operators, and Server Operators can print, manage printers, and manage documents.

Working with print queues and print jobs. Manage print queues and the jobs they contain using the print management window. Double-click the printer icon in the Printers And Faxes folder. The print management window shows information about documents waiting to print, including the document name, status, owner, pages, size, and date submitted for printing.

You can manage individual print jobs by right-clicking a document and choosing to pause, restart, or cancel it. You can also right-click a document and choose Properties to view its properties.

You can manage the printer itself as well by pausing, canceling, or resuming printing. Click Printer → Pause Printing to pause printing. Click Printer → Pause Printing a second time to resume printing. To delete all print jobs queued for printing, click Printer → Cancel All Documents.

Managing Web Servers

Most network environments have web servers these days. Windows Server 2003 includes Internet Information Services (IIS) 6.0 to provide essential web services. When you install IIS on a server, you'll find there are a number of management tools that can be used. The key tool you'll use, however, is Internet Services Manager.

Installing Internet Information Services

With most versions of Windows Server 2003, IIS is not installed during the installation of the operating system. IIS is an application server component and can be installed as part of an application server configuration or separately. IIS itself includes many components that can be installed:

- Background Intelligent Transfer Service (BITS) Server Extension
- File Transfer Protocol (FTP) Server
- FrontPage Server Extensions
- Internet Services Manager
- Internet Printing
- Network News Transfer Protocol (NNTP) service
- Simple Mail Transfer Protocol (SMTP) service
- World Wide Web Server

To install and manage a web server, you need at a minimum the Internet Services Manager and World Wide Web Server components. You can install IIS by completing these steps:

1. In Control Panel, click Add Or Remove Programs.
2. Click Add/Remove Windows Components.
3. Select Application Server, making sure not to check or clear the related checkbox. Click Details.
4. Select Internet Information Services (IIS), making sure not to check or clear the related checkbox. Click Details.
5. Select IIS components to install or uninstall them.
6. Click OK twice to close all open dialog boxes and return to the Windows Component Wizard.
7. Click Next and then click Finish.

Working with the IIS Management Tools

Once you've installed IIS, you can configure and manage IIS using the Internet Services Manager (see Figure 2-36). Click Start → Programs → Administrative Tools → Internet Information Services (IIS) Manager. Internet Services Manager is also available as a snap-in that can be added to MMC.

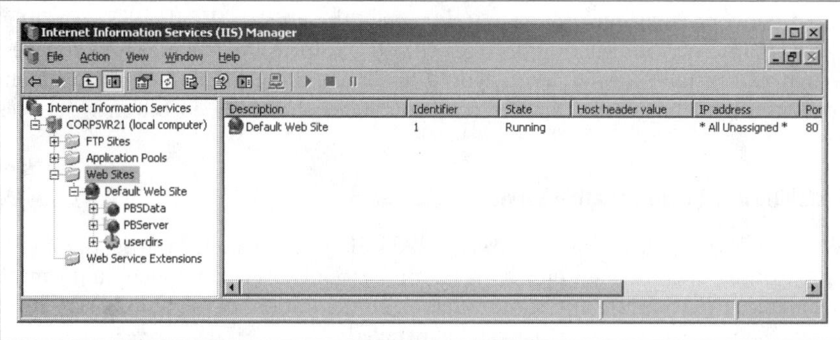

Figure 2-36. Use Internet Services Manager to configure and manage IIS.

Internet Services Manager can be used to manage both local and remote servers. When you connect to multiple computers, each computer will have a separate management node. To connect to a remote computer in Internet Services Manager, follow these steps:

1. Right-click the Internet Information Services node, and then click Connect.
2. In the Connect To Computer dialog box, type the computer name, fully qualified computer name, or IP address in the Computer Name text box.
3. If you need to use different logon credentials, select the Connect As checkbox and then type the username and password for the account.
4. Click OK.

In the default configuration, web documents are stored under *%SystemDrive%\Inetpub\wwwroot* and web server logfiles are written to *%SystemRoot%\system32\LogFiles\w3svc*. A number of management scripts are also provided under *%SystemRoot%\system32*, including:

Iisapp.vbs
: Lists application pools and worker processes. Type `iisapp /?` to obtain syntax and usage details.

Iisback.vbs
: Backs up or restores the IIS configuration. Type `iisback /?` to obtain syntax and usage details.

Iiscnfg.vbs
: Imports or exports the IIS configuration. Type `iiscnfg /?` to obtain syntax and usage details.

Iisvdir.vbs
: Manages IIS web directories. Type `iisvdir /?` to obtain syntax and usage details.

Iisweb.vbs
: Creates, queries, and manages web sites. Type `iisweb /?` to obtain syntax and usage details.

The IIS scripts must be run with the command-line scripting host, CScript, rather than the GUI script host, WScript.

IIS Reset (*iisreset.exe*), also provided in the *%SystemRoot%\system32* folder, is used to stop and then restart all IIS-related services, including IIS Admin service, FTP Publishing service, and World Wide Web Publishing Service. You can use IIS Reset to reset IIS if services become unresponsive or stop responding.

In Internet Services Manager, you can reset IIS by right-clicking the hostname of the server computer, clicking All Tasks → Restart IIS, and then clicking OK in the Stop/Start/Restart dialog box. The default "What Do You Want To Do?" option is to restart IIS.

Configuring IIS

You manage the configuration of IIS at three levels:

General IIS settings (see Figure 2-37)
: Control editing of the IIS metabase and available MIME types. In Internet Services Manager, access general settings by right-clicking the name of the server and then selecting Properties. Enable editing of the metabase while IIS is running by selecting the Enable Direct Metabase Edit checkbox. View and configure available MIME Types by clicking the MIME Types button.

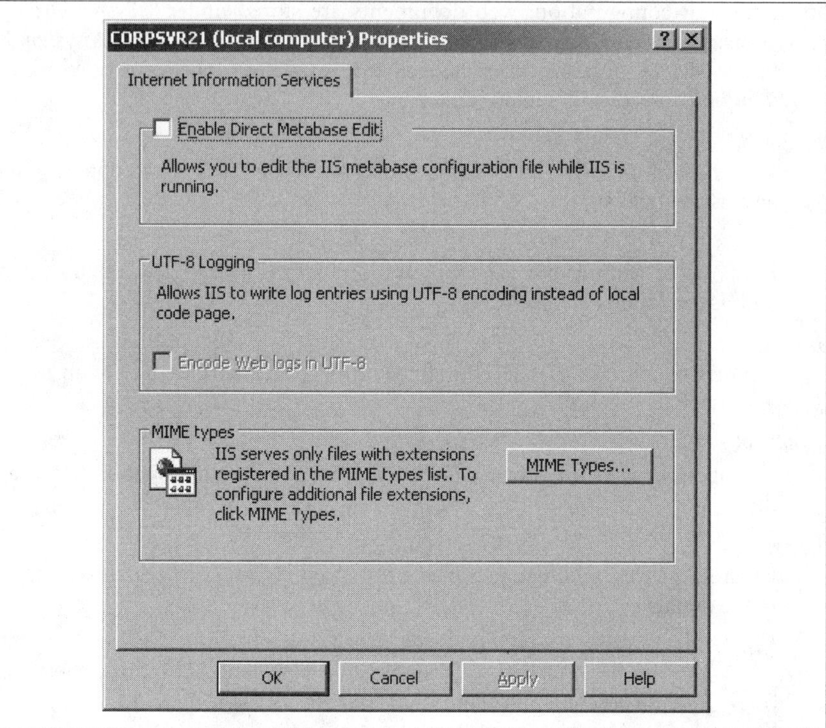

Figure 2-37. General IIS settings.

Global sites settings (see Figure 2-38)

Determine the global settings for all sites of a particular type. To manage global settings, right-click the Web Sites node and then select Properties. Use global settings to set default properties for new sites created on a server. If you change global settings, existing sites typically (but not in all cases) inherit the changes as well.

Using the options on the Service tab, you can manage the operating mode and HTTP compression settings for all web sites. The default operating mode is Worker Process Isolation Mode. By selecting Run WWW Service In IIS 5.0 Isolation Mode, you can reset the server so that IIS 5 Isolation Mode is used, as may be necessary for backward compatibility with applications created for IIS 5. However, IIS 5 Isolation Mode disables many of IIS 6's features.

Local site settings (see Figure 2-39)

Determine the effective settings for a specific site. To manage local site settings, right-click the site name and select Properties. If changes to global settings modify local settings, you can override these changes by reconfiguring the local site settings as may be necessary.

You can back up or restore the IIS configuration in its entirety using the Configuration Backup/Restore feature. In Internet Services Manager, right-click the computer name and click All Tasks → Backup/Restore Configuration. An initial

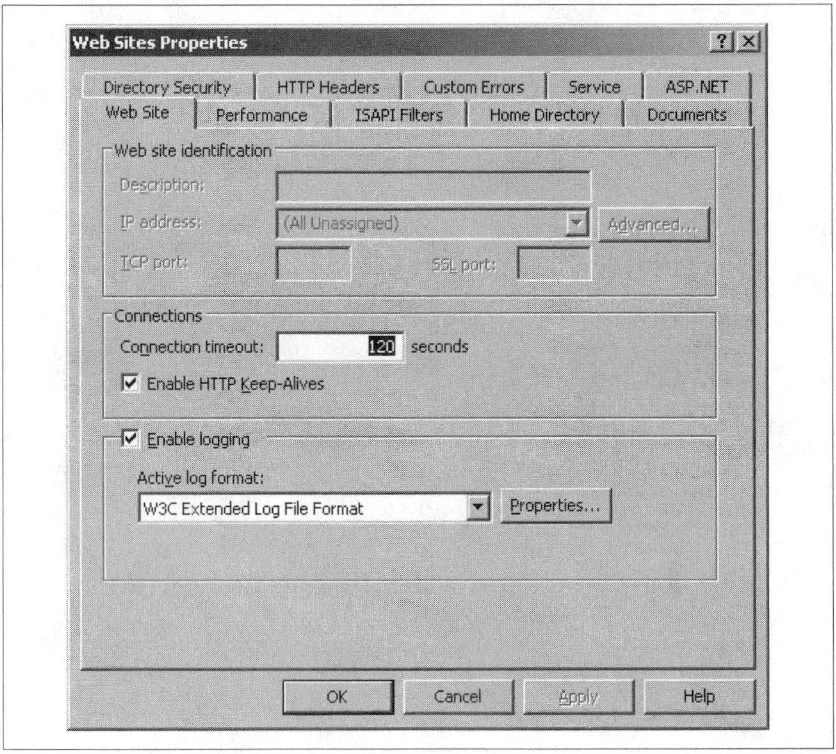

Figure 2-38. Global site settings.

backup is created automatically when IIS is installed. Automatic backups can be created in some cases as well.

With the Configuration Backup/Restore dialog box displayed, you can:

- Create a backup by clicking Create Backup.
- Restore a selected backup by clicking Restore.
- Delete a selected backup by clicking Delete.

Managing security for IIS

When users connect to web servers in a browser, two levels of security apply: IIS security and Windows security. Similar to web shares, IIS provides the top layer of security and Window provides the bottom layer. IIS security focuses on:

- Authentication controls
- Content permissions

Understanding and configuring authentication controls. All web content accessed in a browser is subject to IIS's content permissions. Two types of access are allowed:

- Anonymous access
- Authenticated access

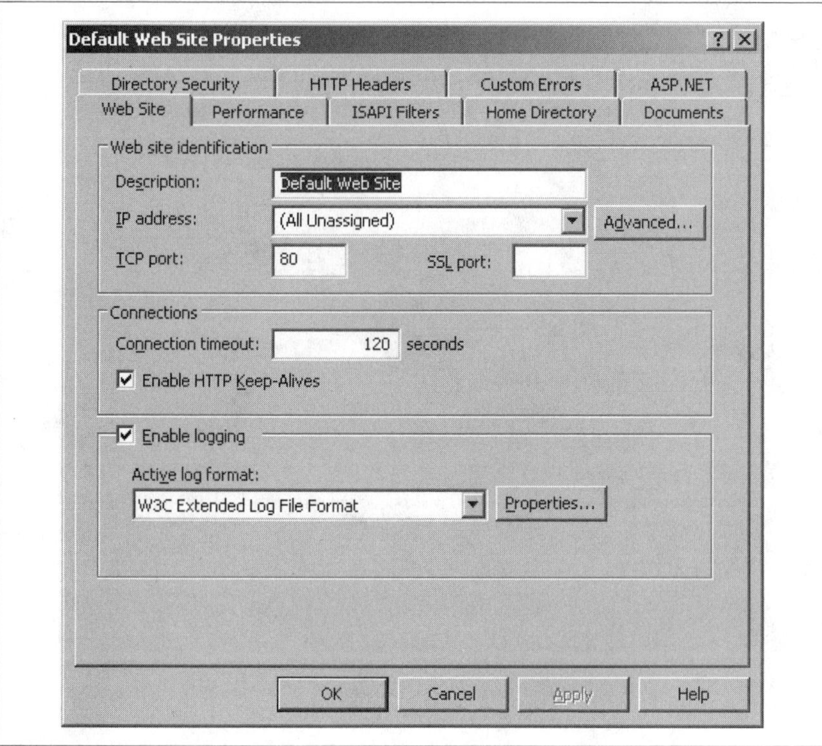

Figure 2-39. Local site settings.

Most public web sites allow users to anonymously access content pages. When a user anonymously accesses an IIS server in a browser, the Internet guest account (*IUSR_ComputerName*) determines the level and type of access granted. By default, the Internet guest account grants the user the right to log on locally or as a batch job. If this account is disabled or locked out, anonymous users won't be able to access content pages on an IIS server. If this IIS server is a member of a Windows domain, the Internet guest account is a member of the Domain Users and Guests groups by default.

With web applications, the web application account (*IWAM_ComputerName*) can be used to grant anonymous access to a web application. The web application account grants the anonymous user the right to log on as a batch job. If this account is disabled or locked out and the server is running in IIS 5 isolation mode, out-of-process applications won't be able to start. When a server is operating in IIS 6 worker process mode, this account is used only when configured for a specific application pool or pools. If the IIS server is in a domain, the web application account is a member of the Domain Users and IIS_WPG groups.

Access to IIS can be controlled using authentication. The five configurable authentication modes are:

Anonymous authentication

Allows users to access resources without being prompted for username and password information. IIS logs users on automatically using the Internet guest or web application account as appropriate.

Basic authentication

Provides the most basic authentication controls. Users are prompted for a username and password, which is passed to the IIS server as clear text unless Secure Sockets Layer (SSL) is configured and used.

Digest authentication

Uses HTTP 1.1. digest authentication to securely transmit user credentials. The user must have a valid domain account, and the IIS server must be a member of an Active Directory domain.

Integrated Windows authentication

Uses standard Windows security to validate a user's identity. Users are not prompted for logon information. Instead, the Windows logon credentials are related to the server in an encrypted format that does not require the use of SSL. Only Internet Explorer browsers support this authentication mode.

.NET Passport authentication

Uses .NET Passport authentication to validate user access and credentials. When validating the user, the server checks for a Passport Authentication ticket. If the ticket exists and the user has valid credentials, the server authenticates the user. If no valid ticket is available, the user is redirected to the Passport Logon Service.

Authentication controls can be set globally or individually for each site hosted by an IIS server. At the site level, different authentication levels can be set for the site as a whole, directories within the site, and pages without directories. This allows you to have secure directories within otherwise unsecure sites or even secure pages within unsecure directories. You can configure access and authentication for any of these levels by completing the following steps:

1. Open IIS Manager.
2. Right-click the Web Sites node, a site node, a directory node, or a file within a directory, and then select Properties.
3. Click the Directory Security or File Security tab as appropriate.
4. Under Authentication And Access Control, click Edit.
5. You can manage access and authentication using the dialog box shown in Figure 2-40 and employing the following techniques:
   - To disable anonymous access (and require authenticated access), clear the Enable Anonymous Access checkbox.
   - To change the name of the account used for anonymous access, type a username and password that should be used for anonymous access. Click Browse to select a user account.
   - To enable .NET passport authentication, select the .NET Passport Authentication checkbox. Optionally, set a default realm to specify the access level within the IIS metabase hierarchy, such as *W3SVC/1/root* for access to the root of the first web site instance.

- To enable basic authentication, select the Basic Authentication checkbox. Optionally, set a default domain that should be used if no domain information is provided.
- To enable digest authentication, select the Digest Authentication checkbox. Optionally, set a default realm.

6. Click OK twice to save and apply the changes.

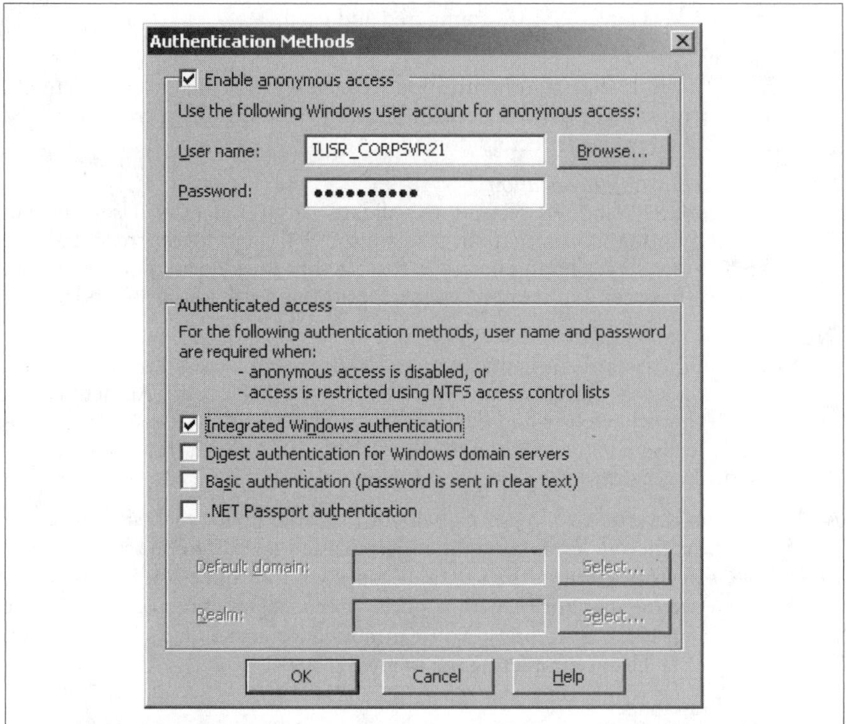

Figure 2-40. Configure access and authentication controls using the Authentication Methods dialog box.

Understanding and configuring content permissions. Content permissions provide the top level of security for IIS. Use content permissions to determine the general allowed permissions for users who are allowed access to an IIS site, directory, or file. Content permissions granted can be further restricted or completely denied by the underlying NTFS permissions. For example, if users are granted anonymous access to a site, but NTFS permissions do not grant any permissions to the Internet guest account, users will not be able to access content regardless of the content permissions.

Content permissions can be set both globally and locally. Apply global permissions using settings of the Web Sites node; these settings are in turn inherited by all the web sites, directories, and files on a server. If you set content permissions locally for a site, directory, or page, you can override the global permissions. In cases where global and local permissions conflict, you typically will see a prompt asking whether you want to apply the global settings (and in doing so override the local settings) or retain the local settings.

The content permissions are similar to those that can be applied to web shares. Content permissions include:

Read
: Allows web users to read files in the folder.

Write
: Allows web users to write data in the folder.

Script Source Access
: Allows web users to access the source code for scripts (not recommended).

Directory Browsing
: Allows web users to browse the folder and its subfolders (not recommended).

Index This Resource
: Allows the Indexing Service to index the resource so that keyword searches can be performed.

Log Visits
: Ensures access to files is recorded in the IIS logs.

As with web shares, application permissions can be set as well. The configurable application permissions are:

None
: Disallows the execution of programs and scripts.

Scripts Only
: Allows scripts to run when accessed via IIS.

Scripts and Executables
: Allows both programs and scripts to run when accessed via IIS.

You can configure global and local content permissions by completing the following steps:

1. Open IIS Manager.
2. Right-click the Web Sites node, a site node, or a directory node, and then select Properties.
3. Click the Home Directory or Directory tab as appropriate.
4. Set the content permissions using the checkboxes provided (see Figure 2-41).
5. Using the Execute Permissions list box, you can set the permission level for applications.
6. Click OK to save and apply the settings.

You can configure content permissions for individual files by completing the following steps:

1. Open IIS Manager.
2. Right-click a file and then select Properties.

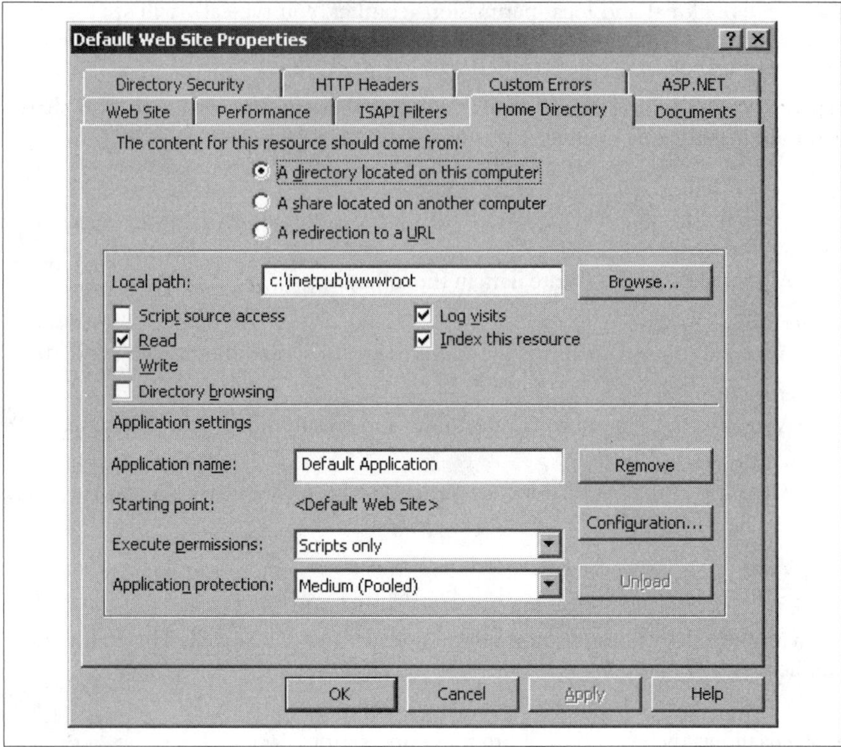

Figure 2-41. Set content and application permissions using the Home Directory or Directory tab.

3. On the File tab, set the content permissions.
4. Click OK to save and apply the settings.

Installing and Configuring Software Update Infrastructure

Maintaining the Windows operating system and software deployed throughout the organization is a critically important area of administration. Operating systems and application software that is not properly maintained will not function as expected. To help you maintain the operating system, Microsoft offers *Automatic Updates*. A system can automatically connect to Windows Update or a designated update server in your organization and obtain any necessary operating system updates.

As Automatic Updates have evolved, so have the related features:

- Automatic Updates for Windows 2000 Service Pack 3, Windows XP, and Windows Server 2003 allow you to automatically download and install critical updates.
- Automatic Updates for Windows XP Service Pack 2 and Windows Server 2003 Service Pack 1 allow you to automatically download and install critical updates, security updates, update roll-ups, and service packs.

An extension of Automatic Updates, called Microsoft Update, allows you to use the Automatic Update feature to maintain the operating system and select Microsoft products, including Office 2003 and Office XP. Microsoft Update will eventually allow you to maintain all Microsoft products using Automatic Updates.

An extension of Automatic Updates, referred to as the WSUS client, allows you to use Automatic Updates with Windows Server Update Services (WSUS). Computers running Windows XP Service Pack 2 or later and Windows Server 2003 Service Pack 1 or later already have the Automatic Updates extension for WSUS.

Microsoft Update is recommended for consumer use and for small businesses that do not have a full-time Windows administrator. In all other environments, both large and small, Microsoft recommends using WSUS in a client/server configuration. Every administrator should know how to install, configure, and maintain WSUS clients and servers.

Through the summer of 2006, Exam 70-290 objectives will cover Software Update Services (SUS). However, SUS is being phased out in favor of WSUS. SUS is no longer available for download and will be supported only through December 6, 2006. The discussion in this study guide focuses on WSUS.

Understanding Windows Server Update Services (WSUS)

WSUS (previously called Windows Update Services) is provided as a patch and an update component for Windows Server. WSUS has both a server and client component. The WSUS client can run on Windows 2000 Service Pack 3 or later, Windows XP, and Windows Server 2003. Each managed client requires a Windows Server CAL.

The WSUS server component uses a data store that runs with MSDE, WMSDE, or SQL Server. With SQL Server 2000 or SQL Server 2005, every device managed by WSUS requires a SQL Server CAL or a per-processor license.

SUS 1.0 servers can be migrated to WSUS using the *WSUSITIL.EXE* tool, which is provided in the Tools folder of the WSUS server installation.

The WSUS scanning engine is built into the Windows Update agent, which is included with Windows and is the same component that enables Automatic Updates from Windows Update. WSUS is designed to handle updates for Microsoft products, including Windows 2000, Windows XP Professional, Windows Server 2003, Office 2003, Office XP, Exchange 2003, SQL Server 2000, SQL Server 2005, and MSDE 2000. All Microsoft products will eventually be supported.

Installing Windows Software Update Services

As discussed previously, WSUS uses a client-server architecture. The WSUS server must have an NTFS-formatted system partition. The partition on which you install WSUS must likewise be formatted with NTFS. WSUS requires:

- IIS (you must install the World Wide Web Server Service at a minimum)
- Background Intelligent Transfer Service (BITS) 2.0
- Microsoft .NET Framework 1.1 Service Pack 1 for Windows Server 2003

The WSUS server component uses IIS to obtain updates over the Internet using HTTP port 80 and HTTPS port 443. WSUS also uses IIS to automatically update client computers with the necessary client software for WSUS—a WSUS-compatible version of the Automatic Updates feature. Typically, the update is installed under a virtual directory named *Selfupdate*, and accessed over HTTP port 80. During setup of WSUS, you can also create a custom web site for *Selfupdate*, which then has a port of 8530 by default.

For performance and network load balancing, large enterprises may want to have an extended WSUS environment with multiple WSUS servers. In a multiple WSUS server environment configuration, one WSUS server can be used as the central server for downloading updates, and other WSUS servers can connect to this server to obtain settings and updates.

You can install WSUS on a server by completing the following steps:

1. Download *WSUSSetup.exe* from the Microsoft web site (*http://go.microsoft.com/fwlink/?LinkId=47374*).
2. Double-click *WSUSSetup.exe* to start the installation.
3. Click Next. Click I Access The Terms Of The License Agreement, and then click Next.
4. On the Select Update Source page, specify where client computers get updates. For central download and distribution, you want WSUS to download updates and make updates available locally, so select Store Updates Locally and then specify the download folder. If you do not store updates locally, client computers connect to Microsoft Update to get approved updates. Click Next.
5. On the Database Options page, select the software used to manage the WSUS database. By default, the SQL Server Desktop Engine is used. For a more reliable and robust solution, you can use an existing database server if you'd like as well. Click Next.
6. On the Web Site Selection page, specify the web site that will be used by WSUS. If you select Use The Existing IIS Default Web Site, WSUS will use port 80. If you select Create A Microsoft Windows Server Update Services Web Site, WSUS will use port 8530. Click Next.
7. On the Mirror Update Settings page, select This Server Should Inherit The Settings From... if you have centralized control of WSUS and multiple WSUS servers. Then enter the fully qualified domain name of the central WSUS server and the port over which connections should be made. Click Next.
8. Review the settings. Click Next to begin the installation, and then click Finish.
9. The root folder of the drive on which WSUS stores updates (and folders used by WSUS) must grant read permission to the special identity NT Authority\Network Service.

Configuring Windows Software Update Services

Once you've installed the WSUS server component, you can use the WSUS console to configure the automatic client update settings. You must be a member of the local Administrators group or the WSUS Administrators group. Access the WSUS console after installation using the URL: *http://WSUSServerame:portnumber/WSUSAdmin*. On the WSUS server, you can click Start → Programs → Administrative Tools → Microsoft Windows Server Update Services.

If the network has a proxy server, you can use the WSUS console to configure WSUS to use the proxy server. This allows WSUS to access Microsoft Update on the Web. You can configure the proxy server by completing the following steps:

1. Open the WSUS console.
2. Click Options → Synchronization Options.
3. In the Proxy server box, click Use A Proxy Server When Synchronizing. Enter the proxy server name and proxy port number.
4. To connect to the proxy server using specific user credentials, click Use User Credentials To Connect To The Proxy Server. Enter the username, domain, and password of the authorized user account.
5. Click Tasks, click Save Settings, and then click OK.

Next, you should specify the products or product families that will be maintained using WSUS. To do this, follow these steps:

1. Open the WSUS console.
2. Click Options → Synchronization Options.
3. In the Products And Classifications box, under Products, click Change.
4. In the Add/Remove Products box, under Products, select the products or product families to maintain, and then click OK.
5. Under Update classifications, click Change.
6. In the Add/Remove Classifications box, under Classifications, select the update classifications for the obtained updates, and then click OK.

After you specify the products to maintain, you can synchronize WSUS. When you do this, WSUS downloads updates from Microsoft Update or another WSUS server as appropriate. Only new updates made available since the last time you synchronized are downloaded. If this is the first time you are synchronizing the WSUS server, all of the updates are made available for approval. When you approve updates, they are made available to clients for installation.

You can synchronize the WSUS server and approve updates by completing the following steps:

1. Open the WSUS console.
2. Click Options → Synchronization Options.
3. Under Tasks, click Synchronize now.
4. Click Updates to view the list of updates.
5. Select the updates you want to approve for installation.
6. Under Update Tasks, click Approve For Installation.

7. In the Approve Updates dialog box, the action for the Approve list is set to Install for the All Computers group by default. You can specify a different group if desired.
8. Click OK to approve the selected updates for the desired group.

Installing and configuring Automatic Update client settings

Once you've configured WSUS, you only need to make the client computer aware of the WSUS configuration to ensure approved updates can be downloaded and installed according to the Automatic Updates settings. Do this by configuring Automatic Updates to download and install updates, and by specifying through policy that the WSUS server should be used for obtaining updates.

The WSUS extension of Automatic Updates allows client computers to use Automatic Updates with WSUS. Computers running Windows XP Service Pack 2 or later and Windows Server 2003 Service Pack 1 or later already have the Automatic Updates extension for WSUS. Other Windows 2000, Windows XP, and Windows Server 2003 computers typically will update themselves automatically when they retrieve Automatic Updates.

On Windows XP and Windows Server 2003 computers, Automatic Updates can be managed using the options in the Automatic Updates tab of the System utility or Group Policy. Policy settings made in Group Policy always have precedence over user-defined settings.

You can enable Automatic Updates on a computer by completing the following steps:

1. Open System in Control Panel.
2. Click the Automatic Updates tab as shown in Figure 2-42.
3. Because only approved updates are made available to computers, Automatic Updates should be configured to automatically download and install updates. Select Automatic.
4. Specify the download interval and time. The download and install interval can be every day or a specific day of the week. The download time can be set to any time when the computer is on (and optimally when network activity is low).
5. Click OK.

The preferred way to configure Automatic Updates for domain computers is to use policy settings. Typically, you'll do this with the Configure Automatic Updates policy located in the applicable GPO under *Computer Configuration\Administrative Templates\Windows Components\Windows Update*. Follow these steps:

1. Open the applicable GPO for editing.
2. Expand Computer Configuration → Administrative Templates → Windows Components → Windows Update.
3. Double-click Configure Automatic Updates.

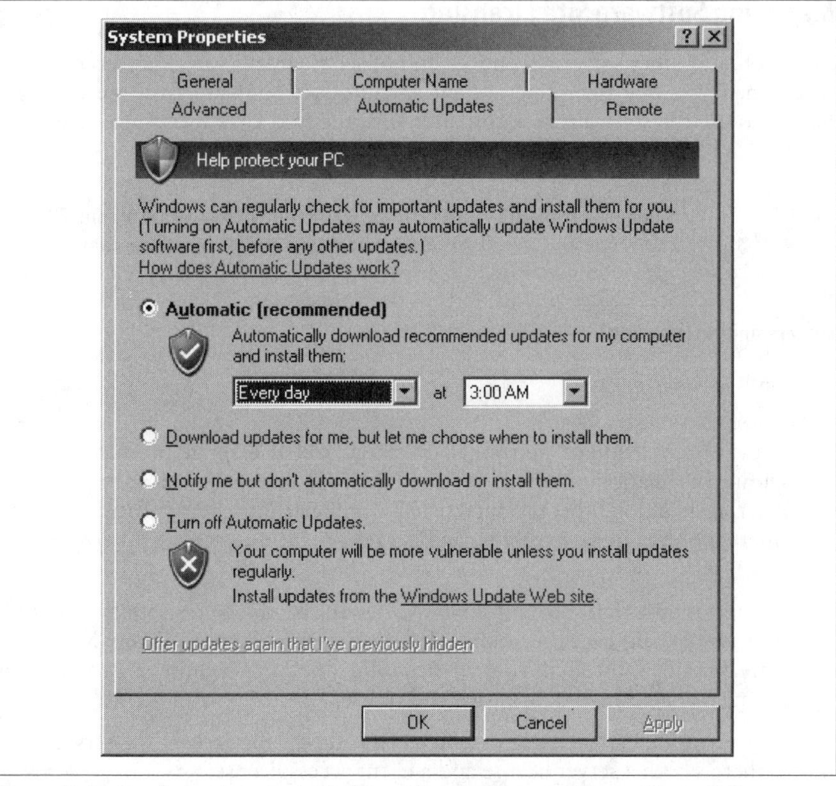

Figure 2-42. Configure Automatic Updates using the System utility or Group Policy.

4. Select the Enabled radio button.
5. Select "4 – Auto download and schedule the install."
6. Set the install day and time.
7. Click OK.

To specify the WSUS server from which updates should be obtain, follow these steps:

1. Open the applicable GPO for editing.
2. Expand Computer Configuration → Administrative Templates → Windows Components → Windows Update.
3. Double-click Specify Intranet Microsoft Update Service Location.
4. Select the Enabled radio button.
5. Type the URL of the WSUS server in both of the text boxes provided.
6. Click OK.

Once group policy is refreshed, client computers will start using the WSUS server for updates. Periodic refresh of group policy happens automatically. You can force a computer to refresh policy by typing `gpupdate /force` at a command prompt.

Managing Software Site Licensing

Microsoft and other software vendors do not sell their software; they license it for use. When you buy operating system and product software, you are buying a license to use the software in accordance with the End User Licensing Agreement (EULA) and copyright law.

Managing software site licensing is a major objective on Exam 70-290. Typically, you'll see several licensing questions on the exam.

Understanding licensing

Microsoft offers:

Retail product licenses
: Typically, individuals and small business will use retail product licenses. During installation of a retail product, a special license key must be provided. After installation, the product usually will need to be activated over the Internet or by phone so that it can be used.

Volume licensing
: Organizations that use multiple Microsoft products or require multiple licenses typically will use volume licensing to get discount pricing. Most software obtained through volume licensing does not require a product key during installation or activation prior to use.

With server products, licensing extends to the clients that access the server. This means there's both a server license and a client access license:

- Every Windows server system must have a server license for the operating system and separate licenses for any server products that are installed, such as Exchange or SQL Server.
- Every client or device that connects to a server must have a client access license (CAL).

Client access licenses can be managed:

Per server
: Each concurrent connection to a server requires a client access license. This hard limit on the number of concurrent connections cannot be exceeded. If a server has 100 CALs, the 101st connection would be denied.

: Per-server CALs are specific to a particular server. If clients connect to multiple servers, each server must have its own set of CALs, and you must purchases at least as many CALs for a given server as the maximum number of clients that might simultaneously connect to that server.

Per user or device
: Each client that connects to a server requires a client access license that allows it to connect to any server in the organization. Each client (a user or a device) must have a CAL for each type of server to which it will connect. For example, one CAL for Windows Server 2003, one CAL for Exchange Server, and one CAL for SQL Server.

Per processor

Each processor (physical or virtual) on a server must have a license. This license allows an unlimited number of clients to connect to the server and does not require a separate license for each client. SQL Server can be licensed on a per-processor basis.

Determining which licensing technique to use isn't always easy. Here are some guidelines:

- Per-server licensing may be a good option when an organization has few servers and there is limited access of these servers. If the organization has 10 servers that will each be accessed by 100 clients, each server would need 100 CALs (for a total of 1,000 CALs).
- Per-user or per-device licensing typically is the best option for an organization's internal network. With per-user or device licensing, the total number of CALs needed is determined by the number of users, devices, or mixture thereof that needs access. Allowing for a mixture of users and devices can save the organization a lot of money. If 90 shift workers use 30 computers, 30 device CALs can be used. If 30 workers each have 3 computers, 30 user CALs can be used.
- Per-processor licensing allows for an unlimited number of client connections and is most useful in large enterprises and on the Internet where thousands of users may simultaneously connect to a server.

Windows Server 2003 Terminal Services includes two CALs for remote desktop administration. This allows up to two administrators to remotely manage a server using remote desktop. For connections to applications hosted on a terminal server, all clients must have a CAL. This CAL may or may not be included with the operating system license.

Configuring server licensing

You set a server's licensing mode when you install the server. Microsoft allows you to make a one-time only switch from per-server licensing to per-user/per-device licensing. Microsoft does not permit switching from per-user/per-device licensing to per-server licensing.

After you install a Windows server, you can track CAL licensing for the server. When you install other Microsoft server products, such as Exchange Server or SQL Server, you can use CAL licensing of these products as well. To manage licensing, you must be a member of the Administrators group for the local server or for the domain. Two licensing tools are available:

Licensing utility in Control Panel

In workgroups or for individual severs, you can manage server licensing separately for each Windows server using the Licensing tool in Control Panel (see Figure 2-43). With per-server licensing, you can add licenses by selecting a product on the Product list, clicking the Add Licenses button, and then specifying the licenses to add.

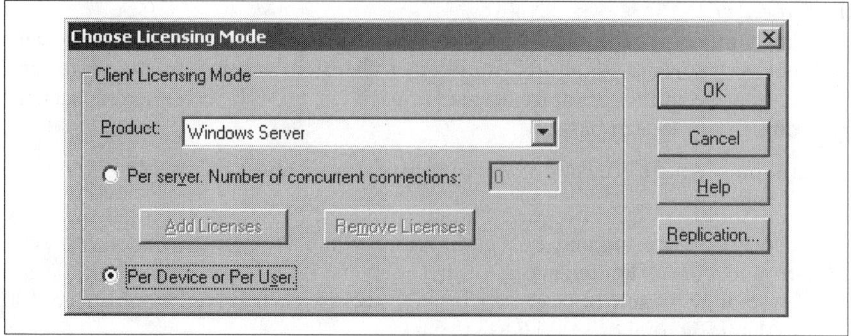

Figure 2-43. Use the Licensing utility to control licensing on individual computers.

Licensing console under Administrative Tools

In Active Directory domains, you can centralize the control of licensing on a per-site basis through a designated site-licensing server, and then replicate the licensing throughout that site. You manage site licensing using the Licensing console (see Figure 2-44). Click Start → Programs → Administrative Tools → Licensing. The License Logging service is used to manage enterprise licensing and must be running for you to assign licenses, track license usage, and manage license configurations.

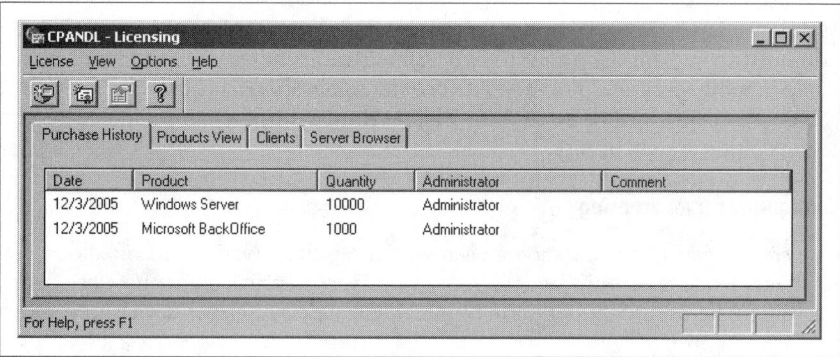

Figure 2-44. Use the Licensing console to manage enterprise site licensing.

In Active Directory domains, you must work with the proper site-licensing server to manage licensing. You can determine the site-licensing server by completing the following steps:

1. Open Active Directory Sites And Services.
2. Click the node for the site.
3. Double-click Licensing Site Settings.
4. The current site-licensing server is displayed by name and domain as shown in Figure 2-45.

By default, the license server is the first domain controller installed in a domain. Site licensing can be moved to a member server or domain controller by clicking

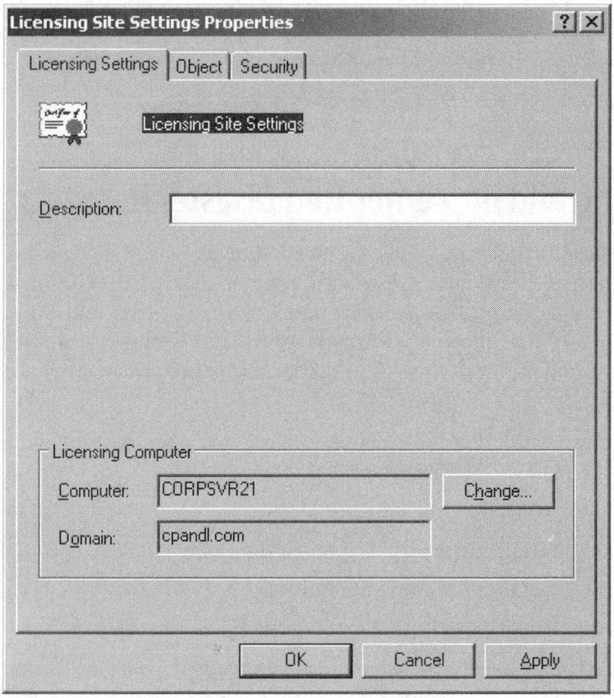

Figure 2-45. *Determining the site licensing server.*

Change on the Licensing Settings tab and selecting the member server or domain controller to which you want to move site licensing. To maintain the licensing history, you must immediately stop the License Logging service on the new site licensing server, copy licensing history from the old server to the new, and then restart the License Logging service. The files to copy are *%SystemRoot%\system32\cpl.cfg*, *%SystemRoot%\Lls\Llsuser.lls*, and *%SystemRoot%\Lls\Llsmap.lls*.

Per-device and per-user licensing require one CAL for each device. The License Logging service, however, tracks licenses by username. When multiple users share one or more devices, you must create license groups to prevent the License Logging service from incorrectly tracking license usage.

A license group is a collection of users who share one or more CALs. With a license group, the License Logging service tracks users by name, but assigns a CAL from the allocation assigned to the related license group. For example, if Alpha group in your company has 3 shifts of workers, you might create a license group with 30 users as members and assign the group 10 CALs to represent the 10 devices they share.

To create a license group, use the following technique:

1. Open the Licensing console under Administrative Tools.
2. Click Options → Advanced → New License Group.

3. Type the group name, and then use the Licenses box to set the number of licenses the group requires.
4. Using the Add button, add each user that should be a member of the license group.
5. Click OK.

Managing and Implementing Disaster Recovery

Every organization should have a comprehensive disaster recovery plan with regular system backups as an essential part of that plan. The goal of disaster recovery planning should be to help you recover systems and data in a timely manner in a way that meets the organizational needs and expectations. Without proper disaster planning, you will not be able to recovery data and systems if disaster strikes.

Every organization's disaster recovery plan will be slightly different. At a minimum, the plan should focus on:

- Using backups to protect against data loss
- Using shadow copies to protect against data loss
- Recovering from server hardware failure
- Recovering from operating system failure

Before you try to recovery a system from backup or using ASR, you should try other recovery techniques. Start by repairing or replacing failed hardware. If you are using software RAID, use the techniques discussed earlier in this chapter in "Implementing RAID Solutions" to restore RAID-1 or RAID-5 configurations. In the case of a improper configuration or invalid driver, you may be able to recover the system from hardware failure by following the techniques discussed previously in "Troubleshooting Hardware Devices." If you find that Last Known Good Configuration and Safe Mode startup do not work, you can attempt to recover the system using the Recovery Console. When these other recovery techniques fail, you can attempt to use an ASR disk or perform a complete recovery of the system from backup.

Managing Backup Procedures

The Backup utility supports five backup types:

Normal
: These back up each selected file and mark the files as backed up.

Copy
: These back up selected files but do not mark the files as backed up.

Differential
: These back up selected files only if they were created or modified since the previous backup, but does not mark them as backed up.

Incremental
These back up selected files only if they were created or modified since the previous backup, and marks them as backed up.

Daily
These contain all the files that were created or modified on a specific day.

You can protect against data loss in several ways. One is to regularly create full normal backup sets for essential systems and data. Ideally, you'll create full normal backups at least once a week, and supplement weekly full backups with incremental backups or differential backups. The difference between incremental and differential backups is important:

Incremental backups
Contain changes since the last full or incremental backup. If a system fails on a Wednesday before daily backup and the last full backup was the previous Sunday, recover the system by applying the last full backup, the Monday incremental backup, and the Tuesday incremental backup.

Differential backups
Contain changes since the last full backup. If a system fails on a Wednesday before daily backup and the last full backup was the previous Sunday, recover the system by applying the last full backup and the last differential backup (Tuesday's differential backup).

Ideally, backups should be rotated so your organization has quarterly and monthly backup sets as well as daily and weekly backups. This allows you to recover data over a longer period of time, as might be necessary if someone accidentally deletes critically important documents but the deletion isn't discovered until several weeks have passed.

As part of normal backup procedures, you should:

- Create automated system recovery (ASR) data for computers
- Back up files and system state data to media
- Configure security for backup operations

Creating Automated System Recovery (ASR) data

Having an Automated System Recovery (ASR) data for a computer can save the day when disaster strikes. ASR data stores essential boot files that can help you recover systems in case these files are missing or corrupted, as may occur if the master boot record is infected with a virus. ASR data also stores the complete System State, which includes details on the disk configuration, startup environment, and registry. The System State data can help you recover systems from many disk configuration issues, driver problems, registry corruption, and more.

You can create ASR data using the Backup utility provided with the operating system. When you do this, the primary data is stored on the backup media you choose, such as a tape backup device or hard disk drive. Secondary data needed to boot the system and access the primary data is stored on a floppy disk.

You should create an ASR disk for each essential system in your organization. To make create an ASR disk, follow these steps:

1. Click Start → Programs → Accessories → System Tools → Backup, or type `ntbackup` at a command prompt. If Backup starts in Wizard mode, click the Advanced Mode Link to switch to advanced mode.
2. Click the Automated System Recovery Wizard button on the Welcome tab.
3. Click Next. Specify the backup media type and backup media location for the primary data. On a Windows Server 2003 system, the primary data can use 1 GB or more of storage space.
4. Insert a floppy disk into the floppy disk drive. This floppy stores the secondary data.
5. Click Next and then click Finish. The ASR data is created for the computer.

If you've tried other techniques to recover the system and haven't succeeded, you can attempt to use ASR to recovery the system. ASR requires:

- The backup media with the primary ASR data
- The ASR floppy disk containing the secondary data
- The Windows Server 2003 CD-ROM

Use ASR for recovery in this way:

1. Restart the system and boot the system off the installation CD-ROM.
2. During the text portion of the setup, press F2 to perform an Automated System Recovery.

ASR then guides you through the recovery process.

Backing up files and System State data to media

You can back up workstations and servers using the Backup utility included with Windows or third-party backup programs. With the Backup utility, you can choose the data to back up. For a full backup, you should always back up the active, system, and boot volumes at a minimum. You should also include in the full backup other volumes containing essential data and the System State.

On non-DC computers, the System State includes the system registry, boot files, protected system files, and the COM+ registration database. On domain controllers, Active Directory data and system volume (SysVol) files are included in the System State data. When other services are installed, other essential data is included:

- On servers with IIS, the IIS metabase is included.
- On servers with Cluster Service, cluster configuration data is included.
- On servers with Certificate Services, the certificate services database is included.

You can back up files and the System State data using the Backup Wizard of the GUI. To use the Backup Wizard for a full backup including System State data, follow these steps:

1. Open the Backup Utility. If Backup starts in Wizard mode, click the Advanced Mode Link to switch to advanced mode.
2. On the General tab, click the Backup Wizard button. Click Next.
3. The Backup Everything On This Computer radio button is selected by default (see Figure 2-46). Click Next.

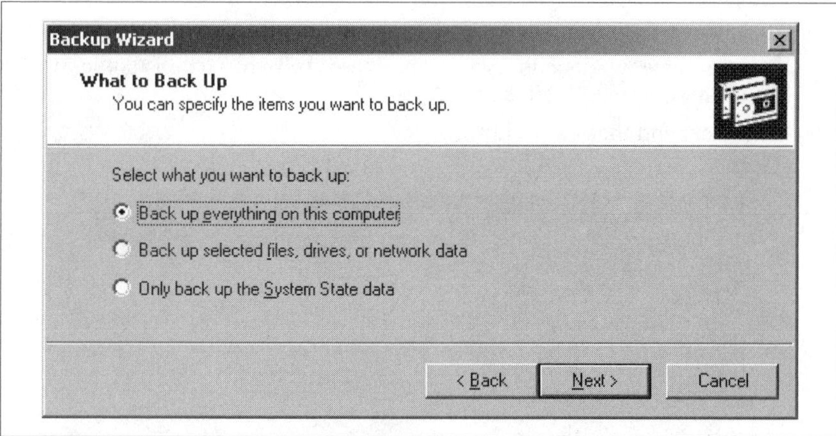

Figure 2-46. A full backup includes System State data.

4. Select the backup media type.
5. Click Browse to choose a destination for the backup file.
6. Type a name for the backup file.
7. Click Next, and then click Finish.

Although you can perform interactive backups in this manner, typically, you'll want to automate the backup process by creating backup jobs and scheduling those jobs to run periodically. For example, you might have a weekly backup job that performs a full backup including System State data, and supplement this with daily incremental or differential backups.

To create a scheduled backup job, follow these steps:

1. Open the Backup Utility. If Backup starts in Wizard mode, click the Advanced Mode Link to switch to advanced mode.
2. On the Schedule Jobs tab, click Add Job. Click Next.
3. The Backup Everything On This Computer radio button is selected by default. Click Next.
4. Select the backup media type.
5. Click Browse to choose a destination for the backup file.
6. Type a name for the backup file. Click Next.
7. Set the backup type as Normal for a full backup, Incremental for an incremental backup, or Differential for a differential backup. Click Next.
8. Select the Verify Data After Backup checkbox to ensure the backup data is verified. Click Next.

9. Set the backup option to append data to existing media or replace existing data on media. Click Next.
10. Type a job name in the Job Name text box, and then click Set Schedule.
11. Use the Schedule Task list to set the run schedule to Weekly, Daily, etc., as appropriate (see Figure 2-47).
12. Set the start time and date. Click OK.
13. When prompted, set the run as account for the backup job by entering the account name in domain\user form. Enter and then confirm the run as account password. Click OK.
14. Click Next and then click Finish.

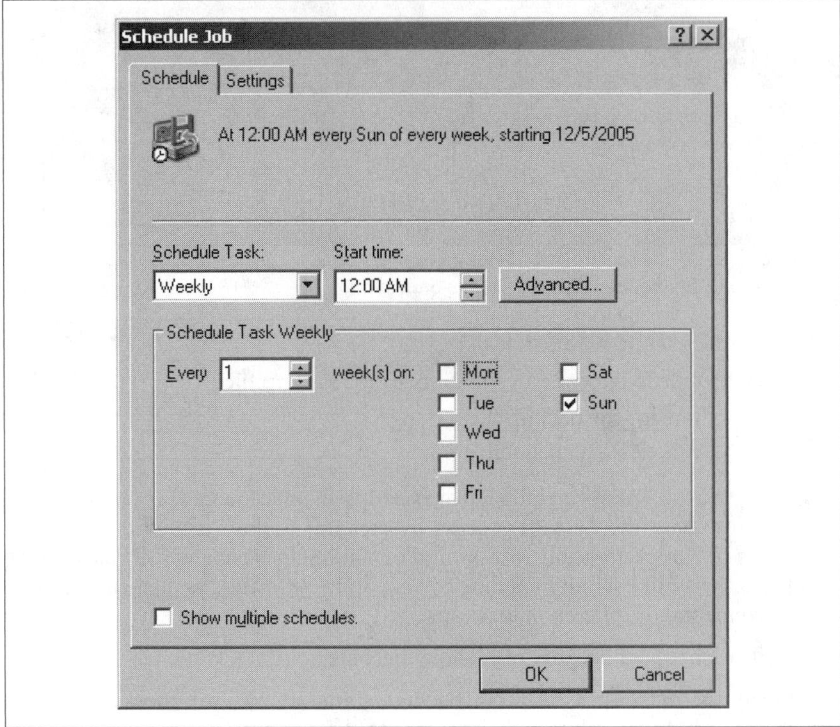

Figure 2-47. Set the run schedule for the backup job.

You can verify the successful completion of backup in several ways:

- The Backup Progress displays the status of interactive backups. If an error occurs and the backup cannot be completed, a related error is displayed.
- The Backup Progress has a Report button. Clicking this button after an interactive backup displays a detailed report on the status and progress of backups.
- For schedule backups (and any other backup), you can display the detailed run report by opening the Backup utility, clicking Tools → Report, and then double-clicking the report you want to review.

Backup reports are stored as logfiles in the user profile files of the run as account.

Managing backup storage media

The Removable Storage snap-in enables you to view and manage removable media devices, including CD and DVD drives, CD and DVD writers, tape drives, and tape library systems. Removable Storage is included by default in the Computer Management Console.

All media in Removable storage is organized by media type, media pool, and library. Media type indicates the type of media, such as tape, CD or DVD. Media pools are used to organize media. Removable Storage has media pools for:

- Unrecognized media for media that Removable Storage doesn't recognize as well as blank media.
- Free media for media that is recognized but isn't currently in use.
- Import media for media that can be imported into Removable Storage and reused.
- Application media for media that is assigned to a specific application, such as Backup.

Libraries identify removable storage devices that can be used on a system and to which media pools can be assigned. For example, you can configure application media pools to automatically draw media from free media pools.

You can work with Removable Storage in Computer Management by expanding Storage and then expanding Removable Storage. As shown in Figure 2-48, Removable Storage is organized into five nodes:

Media
: Lists media by name, type, library, media pool, and state.

Media Pools
: Lists the available media pools. Allows you to manage existing pools and create additional application pools.

Libraries
: Lists the libraries available. Each library entry is associated with a specific removable media device available and configured on the system.

Work Queue
: Lists the status of operations. Every listed operation has a specific state, such as waiting, in progress, or completed.

Operator Requests
: Lists actions that an administrator needs to perform. The state of a request is listed as submitted, refused, or completed.

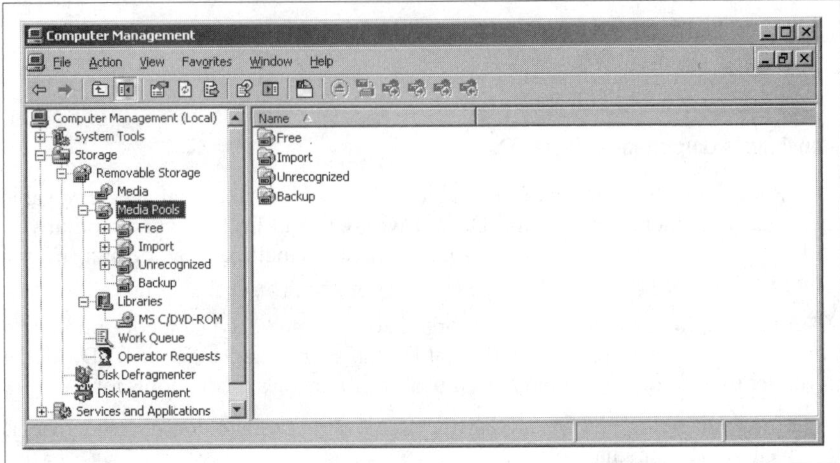

Figure 2-48. Use Removable Storage to manage removable media.

Configuring security for backup operations

By default, users can back up or restore their own folders and files but cannot back up or restore folders and files of other users. Other than this, only those granted the user rights Backup Files And Directories and Restore Files And Directories can back up and restore files. These are two separate rights, so you can assign one right or both. For example, you could create a Backup Admins group and assign this group the Backup Files And Directories user right. You could create a Restore Admins group and assign this group the Restore Files And Directories user right.

You can manage these and other user rights through local machine policy or group policy. The policy settings that control user rights are defined in *Computer Configuration\Windows Settings\Security Settings\Local Policies\User Rights Assignment*.

On Domain Controllers, members of the Backup Operators, Server Operators, and Administrators group are granted both rights. On standalone and member servers, members of the Backup Operators and Administrators group are granted both rights. Although you can edit the related user rights policy settings to specify additional groups or users that should be able to back up and restore files, you can also simply make a group or user a member of the Backup Operators group. If you later decide the group or user shouldn't be able to back up or restore files, you can remove the group or user from the Backup Operators group.

Restoring Data from Shadow Copy Volumes

To supplement (and not replace) routine backups, you should use shadow copies to help protect against data loss. Shadow copies are point-in-time backups that can be used to recover previous versions of files. Once an administrator configures shadow copying, shadow copies are created automatically according to a set schedule. Using a shadow copy client—either the Previous Version client or the Shadow Copy Client—users can recover previous versions of files without needing help from an administrator.

The Previous Version client can be used with Windows 98, Windows 2000 SP3 or later, Windows XP, and Windows Server 2003. On these systems, the installer for the Previous Version client is stored in the *%SystemRoot%\system32\clients\twclient\X86 folder* and named *twcli32.msi*.

The Shadow Copy client installer, *ShadowCopyClient.msi*, is available for download from the Microsoft web site. Computers running Windows 2000 SP3 or later, Windows XP, and Windows Server 2003 can use this client.

Shadow copying works only on NTFS volumes and only for the shared folders on these volumes. By default, the Shadow Copy service will save up to 64 versions of each file in a shared folder. However, the maximum space usage allowed to Shadow Copy on a volume is limited to 10 percent of the volume size, by default. If the maximum allowed space is reached, the oldest previous versions of files will get overwritten or deleted to make room for new versions.

On a server, you can enable shadow copying of the shared folders on an NTFS volume by completing the following steps:

1. Open Computer Management and connect to the computer you want to work with.
2. Right-click Disk Management and click All Tasks → Configure Shadow Copies.
3. In the Select A Volume list, select a volume, and then click Enable.
4. When prompted to confirm, click Yes. This enables shadow copies on the selected volume using the default settings.

Once enabled, shadow copies are created according to the defined schedule. The default schedule creates two shadow copies per day. Copies are created only for files that have been changed or deleted since the last shadow copy. You can retrieve a shadow copy following these steps:

1. In Windows Explorer, right-click the network drive that contains the shadow copies, select Properties, and then click the Previous Versions tab. In My Network Places, navigate to a server node, right-click a share, select Properties, and then click the Previous Versions tab.
2. Folders are listed by name and the time/date that the shadow copy was made. Click a folder entry, then click a button corresponding to the action to perform, from the following options:

   View
   : Click View to open the shadow copy in Windows Explorer. Although you can copy files to other locations, you cannot delete files.

   Copy
   : Click Copy to display the Copy Items dialog box, then use Copy Items to create a snapshot of the selected folder. You can then recover files from the snapshot folder.

   Restore
   : Click Restore to restore the selected folder to a previous state—the state as of the shadow copy you selected. Because this could result in losing current data, you must confirm the restore by clicking Yes when prompted.

With Windows Server 2003 R2, administrators can use Disk Management to revert an entire volume to a previous shadow copy state. Right-click Disk Management and click All Tasks → Configure Shadow Copies. Click the volume, click the shadow copy to recover, and then click the Revert button.

Recovering from Operating System Failure

As long as you have the backup media, restoring a system from backup is a fairly straightforward process. You start the recovery process using the most recent full backup. If incremental backups are made after the full backup, recover each incremental backup in order. If differential backups are made after the full backup, recover the most recent differential backup.

To restore backup data, follow these steps:

1. Open the Backup Utility. If Backup starts in Wizard mode, click the Advanced Mode Link to switch to Advanced mode.
2. On the Welcome tab, click the Restore Wizard button.
3. Click Next.
4. Under Items To Restore, expand the media item that you want to restore, and then expand the backup set that you want to restore.
5. Select the checkbox for each volume, folder, file, or data set to recover. Selecting a volume or folder selects all the related folders and files. Selecting System State allows you to recover the System State.
6. Click Next. By default, files are recovered to their original location. To change the recovery to an alternative location or folder, click the Advanced button, select the restore location, and then configure other advanced options as necessary.
7. Click Finish to begin the restore.

System State data for a domain controller includes Active Directory data and SysVol files. The System State of a domain controller can only be restored using Directory Services Restore Mode startup option. When you start a domain controller, you can enter this mode by pressing F8 during bootup and then selecting Directory Services Restore Mode as the startup option.

Active Directory must be restored in one of the following ways:

Authoritatively

You use an authoritative restore only when you need to recover Active Directory and no other domain controller has the correct data. For example, if someone accidentally deletes a large number of user accounts, you could use an authoritative restore to recover the deleted accounts.

For an authoritative restore, restore the System State, and then use NTDSUTIL to recover to determine how the authoritative restore should be implemented. Do not reboot the computer after restoring the System State.

Nonauthoritatively

You use a nonauthoritative restore to restore a domain controller and allow it to get any necessary updates for Active Directory from other domain controllers.

For a nonauthoritative restore, restore the System State and then reboot the domain controller. In this state, the domain controller will get updates of its replica of Active Directory and SysVol from other domain controllers using normal replication.

Authoritative and non-authoritative restore of Active Directory are covered in Exam 70-294 and in Exam 70-296.

3

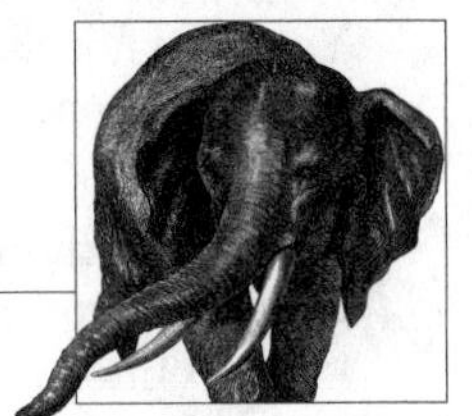

Exam 70-290 Prep and Practice

The material in this chapter is designed to help you prepare and practice for Exam 70-290. The chapter is organized into four sections:

Preparing for Exam 70-290
: This section provides an overview of the types of questions on the exam. This is useful for helping you understand how the actual exam works.

Exam 70-290 Suggested Exercises
: This section provides a numbered list of exercises that you can follow to gain experience in the exam's subject areas. This is useful for helping to ensure you have hands-on experience with all areas of the exam.

Exam 70-290 Highlighters Index
: This section compiles the facts within the exam's subject areas that you are most likely to need another look at—in other words, the areas of study that you might have highlighted while reading the Study Guide. This is useful as a final review before the exam.

Exam 70-290 Practice Questions
: This section includes a comprehensive set of practice questions to assess your knowledge of the exam. The questions are similar in format to the exam. After you've reviewed the Study Guide, performed the Suggested Exercises, and studied the Highlighters Index, read the questions and see if you can answer them correctly.

Before you take Exam 70-290, review the exam overview, perform the suggested exercises, and go through the practice questions provided. Many online sites provide practice tests for the exam. Duplicating the depth and scope of these practice exams in a printed book isn't possible. Visit Microsoft's Certification site for pointers to online practice tests (*http://www.microsoft.com/learning/mcpexams/prepare/practicetests.asp*).

Preparing for Exam 70-290

Exam 70-290 is a computer-generated exam. The exam is timed, and the amount of time remaining on the exam is displayed by an onscreen timer clock. Most questions on the exam are multiple choice. Multiple choice questions are either:

Multiple-choice, single answer
: A radio button allows you to select a single answer only.

Multiple-choice, multiple answer
: A checkbox allows you to select multiple answers. Usually the number of correct answers is indicated in the question itself.

Typically, the test environment will have Previous/Next and Mark For Review options. You can navigate through the test using the Previous/Next buttons. You can click the Mark For Review checkbox to flag a question for later review.

Prep and Practice

Other formats for questions are used as well, including:

List prioritization
: Pick the choices that answer the question and arrange the list in a specified order. Lists initially appear on the right side, and you have to click `<< ADD` to add them in the correct order to the list on the left side. For example, you might have to list system recovery steps in priority order.

Hot area
: Indicate the correct answer by clicking one or more areas of the screen or dialog box provided with the question. For example, you might see a list of users in Active Directory Users And Computers and have to click on the account or accounts that are disabled.

Select and Place
: Using drag-and-drop, pick answers from a given set of choices and place them in an appropriate spot in a dialog box or diagram.

Active screen
: Use the dialog box provided to configure the options correctly or perform the required procedure. For example, you might be asked to use the displayed dialog box to stop sharing a folder and make the appropriate selections.

Simulation
: Use the simulated desktop environment provided to perform a specific task or troubleshoot. For example, you might be asked to configure William Stanek's account with a roaming profile.

With the exception of multiple choice, single answer questions, all of the other questions can have multiple answers or multiple required procedures to obtain full credit. If all of the expected answers or procedures are not performed, you will only get partial credit for the answer.

Although many of the questions on Exam 70-290 are multiple choice, hot area, select and place, active screen, and simulation questions are being used increasingly to ensure that the testing process more accurately reflects actual hands-on knowledge rather than rote memorization. Individuals with adequate hands-on administration experience who have reviewed the study guide, performed the practice exercises, memorized the essentials, and taken practice tests should do well on this type of exam. Individuals who lack adequate hands-on experience and have not prepared appropriately will do poorly.

Exam 70-290 Suggested Exercises

Exam 70-290 expects you to know how to manage and maintain a Windows Server 2003 environment. You'll need plenty of previous hands-on experience to pass the exam. You'll need to review the study guide closely—especially any areas with which you are unfamiliar. This section provides a numbered list of exercises that you can follow to gain experience in the exam's subject areas. Performing the exercises will be useful for helping to ensure you have hands-on experience with all areas of the exam.

Although you can study for the exam using Windows Server 2003 on a single computer, I recommend setting up a test network with at least two computers: a server running Windows Server 2003 acting as a domain controller and a workstation running Windows XP Professional from which you perform most administration. Some of the exercises in this section require two computers on a network.

In addition to performing the exercises below, you should also have experience using each of the Windows Server 2003 administrative tools described in the Study Guide.

Using Remote Desktop for Administration

1. Configure a server so that it can be remotely managed using Remote Desktop.
2. Open the Remote Desktop Connection client, and then click Options.
3. Establish a remote session with the computer from a workstation or another server.

Using Remote Assistance

1. Configure a server so that it can send Remote Assistance requests.
2. While logged on to the server, ask for remote assistance.
3. Accept the remote assistance request on another computer.
4. Access the remote server and give assistance.

Examining Hardware Drivers

1. Configure a server so that it displays a warning prompt if someone attempts to install an unsigned driver.
2. Using Device Manager, check the current network adapter driver on the server to ensure it has a signed driver.
3. Print a summary of the server's installed devices.

Troubleshooting Hardware Devices

1. Using Device Manager, check a server's network adapter for possible resource conflicts.
2. Start the Hardware Troubleshooter and proceed as if the network adapter wasn't working properly.
3. Restart the server.
4. During startup, press F8.
5. Review the startup options.

Examining Disks and Volumes

1. Using Computer Management, examine a server's disks and volumes.
2. Determine the disk type, layout, and volume formatting.
3. Determine which volume is the system volume.
4. If a disk on the server has unallocated space, create, and format a new volume using NTFS.
5. Give the new volume a drive letter.
6. Remove the drive letter on the new volume.
7. Mount the new volume to an empty NTFS folder on another volume.

Create a Dynamic Disk

1. Create a dynamic disk or convert a basic disk to a dynamic disk.
2. Create a volume on the dynamic disk. Leave space so that volume can be resized.
3. Resize the dynamic volume.
4. Create a RAID-1 or RAID-5 volume.

Using DiskPart

1. Start DiskPart.
2. List the current disks.
3. Select a disk and list its volumes.
4. Exit DiskPart.

Using Check Disk

1. Check the integrity of all volumes on a server. Be sure to correct any problems found.
2. Ensure the system volume is checked and fixed as necessary.
3. Restart the server. Note the procedure Check Disk uses to examine the system volume.

Change a Server's Name

1. Determine the name of a non-DC server.
2. Change the server's name.
3. If the server is a member of a domain, remove the server from the domain.
4. Rejoin the server to the domain.

Create Security Groups

1. Create a domain local security group.
2. Add users and other groups as members of the security group.
3. Try to change the group scope.

Determining Group Membership

1. Access a group and determine its members.
2. Determine whether the group is a member of any other groups.
3. Determine the members of the same group from the command line.
4. Determine the group scope from the command line.
5. Add a user to the group using the GUI and the command line.

Creating User Accounts

1. Create a user account for a normal user.
2. Make the user a member of the appropriate groups so the user can access network resources.
3. Create a user account for an administrator.
4. Make the user a member of the appropriate groups so the user can perform domain administration.

Exporting User Accounts

1. Export user accounts from Active Directory. Be sure to get all LDAP properties.
2. Export user accounts from Active Directory getting only the following LDAP properties: `DN`, `objectClass`, `sAMAccoutName`, `sn`, `givenName`, and `userPrincipalName`.

Configuring User Profiles

1. Create a default user profile for users.
2. Create a new user account.
3. Log on as the user and ensure that the user has the default user profile.
4. Log off the user.
5. Configure the user with a roaming profile.

6. Log on as the user.
7. Confirm the roaming profile is being used.

Resolving Account Disabled and Locked Out Accounts

1. Determine whether any user accounts are locked out using the GUI and the command line.
2. If an account is locked out, clear the lockout so the user can log on.
3. Disable a user account.
4. Using the command line, confirm the account is disabled.
5. Enable the account using the command line.

Prep and Practice

Configuring Access to Shared Folders

1. Determine all the shared folders on a server.
2. Create a new share.
3. Configure permissions on the share so only Domain Users and Administrators have access.
4. Allow Domain Users to have Change access.
5. Allow Administrators to have Full Control.
6. Change the NTFS permissions on the folder so no one has access.
7. Try to access the shared folder over the network.
8. Take ownership of the folder.
9. Assign NTFS permissions on the folder so that Domain Users and Administrators have appropriate access.
10. Stop sharing the folder.
11. Try to access the shared folder over the network.

Allowing a User to Use Terminal Services

1. Determine which users currently have Terminal Services permissions.
2. Allow a user to access Terminal Services.
3. Remove a user's Terminal Services access.

Accessing the Event Logs

1. Access the event logs on a remote server.
2. Filter the application event log so that only critical and warning events are displayed.
3. Grant a user permission to access the security logs.

Using Task Manager

1. Determine the current CPU and memory usage on a server.
2. Using the System utility, configure the server so that it has two times as much virtual memory as physical memory.
3. Determine the amount of used and unused virtual memory.

Using Performance Monitoring

1. Configure performance monitoring on a server as you would for a database server.
2. Configure performance monitoring on a server as you would for a web server.
3. Configure performance logging to monitor a server according to a schedule.
4. Configure a server with performance alerts for 95 percent or higher CPU utilization and less than 10 percent free space on all essential disks.
5. Determine if a server has any performance bottlenecks.

Configuring Disk Quotas

1. Enable disk quotas on a volume.
2. Configure a quota warning of 900 MB and a quota limit of 1 GB.
3. Determine how much space each user is using on the volume.
4. Allow a user to have a quota warning of 2 GB and a quota limit of 3 GB.

Managing Print Queues

1. Create a shared printer.
2. Check the security permissions on the print queue.
3. Change the location of the printer's spool folder.
4. Check the NTFS permissions on the spool folder to ensure that they are configured properly.
5. Set the print queue priority to 50.

Managing Internet Information Services

1. Configure a server for use as a web server.
2. Allow only anonymous access to the server.
3. Configure all directories so that users can read files and run scripts and applications. Log visits but do not allow writing or directory browsing.
4. Reset the IIS services in the GUI and from the command line.

Configuring Software Update Infrastructure

1. Install an update server.
2. Configure policy so that updates are installed automatically.
3. Configure policy so that the update server is used.

Managing Software Site Licensing

1. Determine the site license server for a domain.
2. Determine whether a server uses per-server or per-user/per-device licensing.
3. Determine the current licensing for each server in a domain.

Managing and Implementing Disaster Recovery

1. Create a disaster recovery plan for a server.
2. Create an ASR disk.
3. Schedule full backups of the server on a weekly basis.
4. Schedule daily incremental backups on the server.
5. Perform a test restore to original, alternate, and single locations.

Restoring Data from Shadow Copy Volumes

1. Enable shadow copies on a volume.
2. Create shadow copies of the volume's shares.
3. Install the shadow copy client.
4. Access the shadow copy of a share.
5. Restore a corrupted or deleted file from previous version.

Exam 70-290 Highlighters Index

Here I've attempted to compile the facts within the exam's subject areas that you are most likely to need another look at—in other words, the areas of study that you might have highlighted while reading the Study Guide. The title of each highlighted element corresponds to the heading title in the Exam 70-290 Study Guide. In this way, if you have a question about a highlight, you can refer back to the corresponding section in the study guide.

For the most part, the entries under a heading are organized as term lists with a Windows Server 2003 feature, component, or administration tool as the term and the key details for this feature, component, or administration tool listed next. Here are examples:

AdminPak

- Only tools needed to manage installed components and services are installed by default.
- Install AdminPak to ensure you have a consistent tool set.
- Installed from *I386\AdminPak.msi* on the Windows Server 2003 CD.

Support Tools

- Extend the core set of administration tools.
- Include additional useful utilities and commands.
- Installed from *Support\Tools\Suptools.msi* on the Windows Server 2003 CD.

In this example, the highlights are for AdminPak and Support Tools. The entries under the listed term summarize key information that you should know about AdminPak and Support Tools—and are possibly the same details you might have highlighted as part of your exam prep. Since I've done the highlighting for you though, you don't need to get out your highlighting markers or mark up the pages (unless of course you really want to).

Essential Administration Tools

Summary of highlights from the "Essential Administration Tools" section of the Exam 70-290 Study Guide.

Microsoft Management Console (MMC)

- The primary administration tools are built using MMC.
- `Author mode` allows changes. Start with `/a` option.
- `User mode` allows access but no changes.
- Right-click the console root and then select Connect To Another Computer.

Terminal Services

- Uses Remote Desktop for Administration and Terminal Server modes.
- For administration, you'll use Remote Desktop for Administration

Remote Desktop for Administration

- TCP port 3389 must be opened to allow remote access.
- Select Remote Users to specify users granted remote access permission.
- By default, Administrators group is granted remote access permission.
- To enable, access the Remote tab of the System utility and select Enable Remote Desktop For This Computer.

Remote Assistance

- Allows a user to send remote assistance invitations.
- To enable, access the System utility's Remote tab and select Turn On Remote Assistance.
- To send a remote assistance request, in Windows Messenger, click Actions → Ask for Remote Assistance.

Managing and Maintaining Physical and Logical Devices

Summary of highlights from the "Managing and Maintaining Physical and Logical Devices" section of the Exam 70-290 Study Guide.

Hardware Devices

- PnP allows Windows to detect and install a hardware device automatically.
- Non-PnP devices are not detected automatically.
- Install devices using the Add Hardware Wizard in Control Panel.

Signed and Unsigned device drivers

- By default, Windows Server 2003 warns you if you try to install an unsigned device driver.

- To set signing options, click the Driver Signing button on the Hardware tab of the System utility.
- `Ignore` allows all device drivers to be installed without prompt.
- `Warn` prompts with a warning message prior to installing a hardware device with an unsigned driver.
- `Block` prevents installing unsigned drivers.

Device Manager

- All detected devices are listed in Device Manager.
- In Device Manager, an improperly configured device is listed with a yellow warning icon.
- On a device's Driver tab, click Update Drive to install a new driver.
- On a device's Driver tab, click Rollback Driver to go back to previous driver version.
- On the device's General tab, click Reinstall Driver to start the Hardware Update Wizard.

Bad device configuration

- Press F8 as the system starts and use the Last Known Good Configuration to restore the registry key *HKLM\System\CurrentControlSet* with the previous driver information.
- Press F8 as the system starts and use Safe Mode to try to correct a device problem.
- Start from Windows Server 2003 CD to access Recovery Console and press R to choose Repair Or Recover. Press C to start the Recovery Console.

Partition styles

- x86-based computers use the MBR partition style.
- Itanium-based computers running 64-bit Windows use MBR and GPT partition styles.
- X64-based computers use the MBR partition style.

Disk types

- Basic disks.
- Dynamic disks.

Special volumes

- The system volume contains the hardware-specific files needed to load Windows.
- The boot volume contains the operating system and operating system–related files.
- The active volume is the drive section from which the operating system starts.

Basic disks

- Use partitions to map out the disk structure.
- Accessible on just about every operating system.

- Have primary partitions and extended partitions containing logical drives.
- Have up to four primary partitions, or up to three primary partitions and one extended partition.

Basic disk partition types

- Each primary partition is represented with one logical volume.
- Each extended partition is represented by one or more logical drives.
- A logical drive is a logical volume that represents all of or part of an extended partition.

Dynamic disks

- Use volume to map out disk structure.
- Not supported for removable media, on portable computers, or with disks connected via FireWire/USB.
- Up to 2,000 volumes on a dynamic disk; the recommended maximum is 32.
- Non-fault tolerant volumes provide no data redundancy or failure protection.
- Fault tolerant volumes provide data redundancy and failure protection.

Dynamic volume types

- Simple volume is the equivalent to a basic disk partition and can be extended.
- Spanned volume is used to combine unallocated space on multiple disks and can be extended. No operating system allowed on a spanned volume.
- Striped volume (RAID-0) is used to combine unallocated space on 2–32 disks; uses efficient striping, but cannot be extended.
- Mirrored volume (RAID-1) creates two identical copies of a volume on two separate disks and is fault tolerant. Boot and system volumes can be mirrored.
- Striped with parity volume (RAID-5) is used to combine unallocated space on 3–32 disks; uses striping of parity for fault tolerance.

Volume formatting

- FAT (FAT16) uses 16-bit file allocation tables with maximum volume size of 4 GB.
- FAT32 uses 32-bit file allocation tables with maximum size of 2 TB; limited on Windows to 32 GB.
- NTFS uses a master file table that contains records for each file and metadata; up to 2 TB on basic MBR disks.

NTFS supports

- Advanced file permissions.
- Disk quotas.
- Remote storage.
- Compression.
- Encryption.

Logical volumes

- Have a drive letter or a mount point.
- Table 3-1 summarizes drive designator usage.

Table 3-1. Drive designator usage

Drive designator	Typical usage
A:, B:	Removable media drives, floppy/Zip
C:	Primary disk
D:	Primary CD/DVD-ROM drive
E: ...Z:	Secondary disk, CD/DVD-ROM drive
Folder Name	Mount point (NTFS only)

Disk Management

- Used to manage disk storage on both local and remote computers.
- Configuring disks and volumes using Disk Management is a five-step process:
    1. Install or attach the disk.
    2. Initialize the disk to make it available for use.
    3. Convert basic disks to dynamic disks as necessary.
    4. Create and format a disk's volumes.
    5. Assign drive letters or mount points.

DiskPart

- A command-line utility for managing disks.
- Can be used interactively or with scripts.
- Doesn't format; use the FORMAT command.

Check Disk

- Check disk scans disks and can correct errors.
- Type `chkdsk` followed by the drive designator and `/f` to fix errors.

Disk Defragmenter

- Disk Defragmenter checks for and corrects fragmentation problems on disks.
- Type `defrag` followed by the drive designator to analyze and defrag.

Managing Users, Computers, and Groups

Summary of highlights from the "Managing Users, Computers, and Groups" section of the Exam 70-290 Study Guide.

Domains vs. workgroups

- In domains, Active Directory is used to provide directory services.
- In workgroups, each local computer has a SAM database.

User, computer, and group naming

- Names assigned to users, computers, and groups are used for assignment and reference purposes.
- In a workgroup, each computer must have a unique name.
- In Active Directory, all user, computer, and group names must be unique on a per-domain basis.

Computer accounts

- The computer must be a member of the domain.
- Prestage by creating a computer account before joining it to the domain.
- When not prestaging, Active Directory will create the computer account.
- Manage computer accounts using Active Directory Users And Computers (*dsa.msc*).
- Create a computer account: right-click a container select New → Computer.
- Create a computer account: use DSADD COMPUTER.
- Join to a domain: open System. On the Computer Name tab, click Change.
- Join to a domain: use NETDOM ADD.

Computer properties and passwords

- Manage computer properties and passwords using Active Directory Users And Computers.
- Right-click the account name and select options.

Troubleshooting computer accounts

- To troubleshoot incorrect network settings, access Network Connections → Local Area Connection from the Control Panel.
- To resolve insufficient permissions to join, use an account with appropriate permissions to join the domain.
- To reset computer passwords, leave the domain and then rejoin or use NETDOM RESETPWD.

Groups

- Distribution groups are used for email distribution lists; they do not have security descriptors.
- Security groups are used to assign access permissions; they have security descriptors.
- Table 3-2 summarizes types of groups and Table 3-3 summarizes how domain functional level affects groups.

Table 3-2. Types of groups

Group scope	How it is used	Can include
Domain local	Primarily to assign access permissions to resources within a single domain.	Members from any domain in the forest and from trusted domains in other forests. Typically, global and universal groups are members of domain local groups.
Global	Primarily to define sets of users or computers in the same domain that share a similar role, function, or job.	Only accounts and groups from the domain in which defined, including other global groups.
Universal	Primarily to define sets of users or computers that should have wide permissions throughout a domain or forest.	Accounts and groups from any domain in the forest, including other universal groups and global groups.

Table 3-3. Domain functional level and groups

Domain functional level	Domain local	Global	Universal
Windows 2000 Mixed, Windows Server 2003 Interim	Can contain accounts and global groups from any domain.	Accounts from the same domain only.	Security universal groups can't be created.
Windows 2000 Native, Windows Server 2003	Accounts and global groups from any domain; domain local groups from the same domain only.	Accounts and other global groups from the same domain only.	Accounts from any domain; global and universal groups from any domain.

Changing group scope

- Domain local groups can be changed to universal groups; no member can have domain local scope.
- Global groups can be changed to universal groups; no member can have global scope.
- Universal groups can be changed to domain local or global groups; no member can have global scope for global.

Creating and managing groups

- Groups can be created using Active Directory Users And Computers (*dsa.msc*).
- To create a group, right-click a container and select New → Group.
- To set members, use the Member tab.
- To view where the group is a member, use the Member Of tab.
- Create a group using DSADD GROUP.
- Modify a group using DSMOD GROUP.

Implicit groups and special identities

- Membership in implicit groups is implicitly applied.
- Implicit groups cannot be created or deleted.
- No changing the membership of implicit groups.
- Apply user rights and assign security permissions as necessary.

User accounts

- With local machine user accounts, users log on locally and access local resources using local accounts.
- With domain user accounts, users log on to a domain and access network resources using domain accounts.

Creating user accounts

- Create a user account using Active Directory Users And Computers.
- To create a user, right-click a container and select New → User.
- Create a user account using DSADD USER.

Importing and exporting user accounts

- Use CSVDE for importing and exporting Active Directory objects.
- For imports, CSVDE uses a comma-delimited text file as the import source.
- For exports, CSVDE writes the exported objects to a comma-delimited text file.

User profiles

- User profiles contain user environment settings.
- Every computer has a default profile.
- A user's environment settings are extended by the All Users profile.

Roaming user profiles

- A roaming profile allows user settings to move with a user from computer to computer.
- The profile is stored on a server and downloaded to a computer upon logon.
- Changes to roaming user profiles are uploaded on logoff, and downloaded on logon.
- Set roaming profile in Active Directory Users And Computers: on the account's Profile tab, use the Profile Path field.
- Set roaming profile using DSMOD USER: use the `-profile` option.

Mandatory user profiles

- Prevent users from making permanent changes to the desktop.
- Changes are not saved in the profile and thus are lost when a user logs off.
- Configure a mandatory user profile by changing *Ntuser.dat* to *Ntuser.man*.

User access and authentication

- Password policy controls how passwords are managed.
- Account lockout policy controls whether and how accounts are locked out.
- Set Password Policy using *Computer Configuration\Windows Settings\Security Settings\Account Policies\Password Policy*.
- Set Account Locking Policy using *Computer Configuration\Windows Settings\Security Settings\Account Policies\Account Lockout Policy*.

Diagnosing and resolving user account problems

- Users cannot log on when an account being disabled or locked out.
- Active Directory Users And Computers shows disabled accounts with a red warning icon.
- Right-click the account and then select Enable Account.
- Search the entire domain for disabled accounts with `dsquery user -disabled`.
- A locked account cannot be used for logging on until the lockout duration has elapsed or the account is reset.
- Right-click the locked account and then select Properties. On the Account tab, clear Account Is Locked Out.

Diagnosing and resolving user authentication problems

- Account credentials are validated during logon by a domain controller.
- When network connection is down or there is no domain controller, cached credentials can be used.
- Each member computer in a domain can cache up to 10 credentials by default.

Managing and Maintaining Access to Network Resources

Summary of highlights from the "Managing and Maintaining Access to Network Resources" section of the Exam 70-290 Study Guide.

Shared folders

- Users access files stored on Windows servers using shared folders.
- Standard shares are used to access folders over a network.
- Web shares are used to access folders over the Internet.
- Share permissions can be granted to a user or group.
- Share permissions determine the maximum allowed access level.
- Filesystem permissions can further restrict or block access.

Share permissions

- `Full Control` grants both Read and Change. It also allows change permissions and take ownership.
- `Change` grants Read permission. It also allows create, modify, change attributes, and delete.
- `Read` allows view, read data and attributes, and run program files.

Creating shared folders

- Share a folder by right-clicking a folder, selecting Sharing And Security, and then selecting Share This Folder.
- Users access shared folders by a share name using a network drive.
- Shares with names ending in a dollar sign ($) are hidden.
- Hidden shares do not appear on the network browse list.

Web shares

- Web shares are accessed in a web browser using the Hypertext Transfer Protocol (HTTP).
- A web share is available to users in a web browser by its alias.

Web share permissions

- `Access permissions` grant access when a folder is accessed remotely.
- `Application permissions` determine the permitted actions for programs and scripts.

Access permissions for web shares

- `Read` allows web users to read files in the folder.
- `Write` allows web users to write data in the folder.

- `Script Source Access` allows web users to access the source code for scripts (not recommended).
- `Directory Browsing` allows web users to browse the folder and its subfolders (not recommended).

Application permissions for web shares

- None disallows the execution of programs and scripts.
- Scripts allows scripts to be run from the Web.
- Execute (Includes Scripts) allows both programs and scripts to be executed from the Web.
- Configure application permissions on the Web Sharing tab.

Attributes of files and folders

- All files and folders have basic attributes.
- `Hidden` determines whether files and folders are displayed in directory listings.
- `Read-only` makes the file or folder read-only.
- On NTFS, the `Read-only` attribute is shown dimmed initially.
- Some files and folders have extended attributes.
- Extended attributes come from named data streams.

Filesystem permissions

- Filesystem permissions determine access controls.
- FAT volumes have no filesystem permissions.
- Only NTFS volumes have filesystem permissions.

NTFS permissions

- Every file and folder has an access control list (ACL).
- Access permissions are stored within the ACL as access control entries (ACEs).
- ACEs detail the specific permissions that apply to each user and group.
- NTFS has both basic and special permission sets.
- Basic permissions represent a grouping of special permissions.
- Special or advanced permissions provide granular control.

Basic permissions

- In the Properties dialog box, select the Security tab.
- Tables 3-4 and 3-5 summarize basic permissions for files and folders.

Table 3-4. Basic permissions for files

Permission	Description
Full Control	Permits reading and listing of files; writing to files; deleting files and file contents; viewing attributes and permissions of files; changing attributes and permissions of files; taking ownership of files
Modify	Permits reading and listing of files; writing to files; deleting files and file contents; viewing attributes; setting attributes

Table 3-4. Basic permissions for files (continued)

Permission	Description
Read & Execute	Permits executing files; reading and listing of files; viewing attributes and permissions of files
Write	Permits writing to files; creating files; appending data to files; deleting files and file contents; setting attributes of files
Read	Permits reading and listing of files; viewing attributes and permissions of files

Table 3-5. Basic permissions for folders

Permission	Description
Full Control	Permits reading and listing of folders and files; writing to files; creating folders and files; deleting folders; files and file contents; viewing attributes and permissions of folders and files; changing attributes and permissions of folders and files; taking ownership of folders and files
Modify	Permits reading and listing of folders and files; writing to files; creating folders and files, deleting folders, files and file contents; viewing and setting attributes of folders and files
Read & Execute	Permits executing files; reading and listing of folders and files; viewing attributes and permissions of folders and files
List Folder Contents	Permits reading and listing of folders and files; executing files
Write	Permits creating files in folders
Read	Permits reading and listing of folders and files; viewing attributes and permissions of folders and files

Special permissions

- Special permissions, shown in Table 3-6, allow direct editing of the access control entries (ACEs).
- There are two general types of permissions: those that are inherited and those that are not inherited.
- The folder from which settings are inherited is listed (if applicable).
- Each ACE, listed in the Advanced Security Settings dialog box, can be edited.

Table 3-6. Special Permissions for folders and files

Special Permission	Description
Traverse Folder/Execute File	Traverse Folder permits moving through folders to access a folder or file even if the group or user doesn't have explicit access to traversed folders; user or group must also have the Bypass Traverse Checking user right. Execute File permits running an executable file.
List Folder/Read Data	List Folder permits viewing file and folder names. Read Data permits viewing the contents of a file.
Read Attributes	Permits reading the basic attributes of a folder or file. These attributes include Read-only, Hidden, System, and Archive.
Read Extended Attributes	Permits reading extended attributes associated with a folder or file.
Create Files/Write Data	Create Files permits adding files to a folder. Write Data permits overwriting existing data in a file (but not adding new data to an existing file since this is covered by Append Data).
Create Folders/Append Data	Create Folders permits creating subfolders within folders. Append Data permits adding data to the end of an existing file (but not to overwrite existing data as this is covered by Write Data).

Table 3-6. Special Permissions for folders and files (continued)

Special Permission	Description
Write Attributes	Permits changing basic attributes of a folder or file. These attributes include Read-only, Hidden, System, and Archive.
Write Extended Attributes	Permits changing extended attributes of a folder or file.
Delete Subfolders and Files	Permits deleting the contents of a folder, even if Delete permission on the subfolder or file isn't specifically granted.
Delete	Permits deleting a folder or file. If a group or user doesn't have Delete permission, the group or user granted the Delete Subfolders and Files permission can still delete the folder or file.
Read Permissions	Permits reading all basic and special permissions assigned to a folder or file.
Change Permissions	Permits changing basic and special permissions assigned to a folder or file.
Take Ownership	Permits taking ownership of a folder or file. The owner of a folder or file can always change permissions on it, even if other permissions were removed. By default, administrators can always take ownership of a folder or file and can also grant this permission to others.

Effective permissions

- Often groups or users have multiple applicable permission sets.
- The Effective Permissions tab allows you to determine the collective set of permissions that apply.
- You cannot determine effective permissions for implicit groups or special identities.
- Share permissions are also not included while calculating effective permissions.

Ownership of files and folders

- Creator Owner identity represents the creator and owner of objects.
- Owner has complete control to grant access and grant Take Ownership permission.
- Ownership can be taken or transferred on the Owner tab of the Advanced Security Settings dialog box.

Inherited permissions

- Permissions are inherited from parent folders by default.
- A file inherits its permissions from the folder in which it is stored.
- A subfolder inherits its permissions from the folder in which it is stored.
- Folders stored in the root of a drive inherit the permissions of the drive.
- Change inherited permissions by accessing the parent folder.
- Override inheritance on the Permissions tab of the Advanced Security Settings dialog box.

Troubleshooting access to folders and files

- Check the folder path and the logon credentials.
- Check the network connection and cabling.
- Check the share permissions.
- Check the NTFS permissions.

- Check the basic attributes.
- Check for restrictions based on encryption.

Terminal Services

- Remote Desktop for Administration is as a limited Terminal Server mode.
- Terminal Server users establish remote sessions with a server to run Windows-based applications.
- Add users or groups to the Remote Desktop Users group to allow users to log on a terminal server.
- Manage RDP configuration using the Terminal Services Configuration tool (*tssc.msc*).
- Right-click the RDP-Tcp connection to modify the RDP settings.
- Manage Terminal Services security using the Permissions tab of the RDP-Tcp Properties dialog box.

Terminal Services Basic permissions

- `Full Control` grants users full control over all sessions.
- `User access` allows users to log on, view session settings, and connect to another session.
- `Guest access` allows users to log on to a terminal server.

Diagnosing and resolving issues related to client access to Terminal Services

- Connect to a Terminal Server using the Remote Desktop Connection client.
- Click Options to set expanded session settings.
- Invalid credentials or connection server: make sure the clients are using the correct username, password, and domain settings.
- Improper group assignment: user must be a member of the Remote Desktop Users group in Active Directory.
- Incorrect authentication mode: user may need to type the fully qualified domain name for the terminal server.
- Use the Sessions tab to limit, disconnect, or end user sessions.

Managing and Maintaining a Server Environment

Summary of highlights from the "Managing and Maintaining a Server Environment" section of the Exam 70-290 Study Guide.

Event logs

- Application log contains events logged by Windows applications and printers configured on the system.
- Security log contains events related to security auditing. Enable auditing. Control access using the Manage Auditing and the Security Log user rights.
- System log contains events logged by operating system components and services.
- Directory Service log records events from Active Directory on DCs.
- DNS Server log records events from DNS on a name server.

Accessing and reviewing events

- Event logs are accessible in the Event Viewer (*eventvwr.exe*).
- `Event type` specifies the type of event that occurred.
- `Event source` specifies related component or service
- `Event category` specifies the general category of the event.

Event types

- `Information` events are routine events that typically record successful actions.
- `Success Audit` events indicate successful execution of an action (only when auditing enabled).
- `Failure Audit` events indicate failed execution of an action (only when auditing enabled).
- `Warning` events alert administrators to possible problems.
- `Error` events alert administrators to specific problems and errors.

Monitoring system performance

- Task Manager displays the current status of applications, background processes, and system resources.
- Performance Console is used for comprehensive monitoring and analysis.

Performance console

- Click Performance under Administrative Tools, or from the command prompt, type `perfmon.msc`.
- System Monitor is used to collect real-time performance data.
- Performance Logs record performance data in logs for later review.
- Performance alerts trigger when performance parameters are reached.
- Performance Monitor Users can monitor performance counters, logs, and alerts.
- Performance Log users can schedule logging and alerting.

Performance objects, instances, and counters

- Performance objects represent system and application components with measurable sets of properties.
- Performance object instances represent specific occurrences of performance objects.
- Performance counters represent the measurable properties of performance objects.

System Monitor

- System Monitor can use graphic, histogram, and report formats for real-time performance.
- Add counters by clicking the Add button or pressing Ctrl+L.

Performance logging

- Counter logs record performance data at specified intervals.
- Trace logs record performance data whenever tracked events occur.

Performance alerting

- Alerts are triggered when a performance parameter reaches a specific limit or threshold.
- Alerts can be configured to log an entry in the Application event log, start an application, send a network message, and/or to start a performance log.

Choosing objects to monitor

- For Memory performance monitoring, related objects include Cache, Memory, and Paging File.
- For Processor performance monitoring, related objects include Processor, Job Object, Process, and Thread.
- For Disk performance monitoring, related objects include LogicalDisk, PhysicalDisk, and System.
- For Network performance monitoring, related objects include Network Interface, Server, and Server Work Queues.

Monitoring memory performance objects

- Windows systems have both physical and virtual memory.
- Memory bottlenecks occur when low available memory causes increased paging.
- Soft page faults occur when the system must look for the necessary data in another area of memory.
- Hard faults occur when the system must look for the necessary data in virtual memory on disk.
- Hard page faults can make the system appear to have a disk problem due to excessive page swapping.
- *Memory\Available Kbytes* is the amount of physical memory not yet in use.
- *Memory\Committed Bytes* is the amount of committed virtual memory.
- *Memory\PageFaults/sec* tracks page faults per second.

Monitoring processor performance objects

- Systems with high processor utilization may perform poorly.
- Determine processor utilization using *Processor\%Processor Time*.
- *System\Processor Queue Length* tracks number of threads waiting to be executed.

Monitoring network performance objects

- Available network bandwidth determines how fast data is sent between clients and servers.
- Network interface current bandwidth determines capacity to send or receive data.
- *Network Interface\Output Queue Length* counter can help you identify network saturation issues.
- *Network Interface\Current Bandwidth* tracks current bandwidth setting.
- *Network Interface\Bytes Total/sec* provides the total bytes transferred or received per second.

Monitoring disk performance objects

- PhysicalDisk objects represent each physical hard disk.
- LogicalDisk objects represent each logical volume.
- *LogicalDisk\%Free Space* tracks free space on logical disks.
- *PhysicalDisk\Disk Writes/sec* and *Physical Disk\Disk Reads/sec* track I/O activity.
- *Physical Disk\CurrentDisk Queue Length* tracks disk-queuing activity.

Disk quotas

- Disk quotas help you track and manage disk space usage.
- NTFS disk quotas are configured on a per-user, per-volume basis.
- Disk quotas cannot be configured for groups.

NTFS disk quotas configuration

- Configured through Group Policy.
- Configured through the Quota tab on the NTFS volume.
- Policy settings override Quota tab settings in most cases.

Quota warnings and limits

- A quota warning is used to warn users on space usage.
- A quota limit sets a specific limit on space usage.
- Users see warning prompts.
- Administrators can track disk usage in the Application event log.

Quota entries

- View current usage using disk quota entries.
- On the Quota tab, click the Quota Entries button.
- Quotas do not affect the built-in Administrators group.
- Quotas affect all other system user accounts and domain/local user accounts.

Print queues

- Print queues are where printed document are stored as print jobs before they are printed.

Print servers

- A print server is a computer that is configured to share a printer.
- Install and manage printers using the Printers And Faxes folder.
- Users send print jobs to a shared printer.
- The print server spools the print job to the spooling folder on its local disk.
- By default, the print spooler folder is located in *\Windows\System32\Spool\Printers*.
- Spooled print jobs are queued to be printed.
- Each printer has its own print queue. All printers have the same spool folder.
- Check the status of the Print Spooler service using Administrative Tools → Services utility.

- In the Printers And Faxes window, click File → Server Properties to access print server properties.
- Spool folder location can be changed from the Advanced tab.

Printer Properties

- In the Printers And Faxes window, printers are listed by their local name.
- Shared printers have a shared name.
- Print jobs are routed to printers according to configured ports.
- Right-click a printer, and then select Properties.

Printer Properties dialog box tabs

- On the General tab, view or set the printer name, location, and comments.
- On the Sharing tab, view or set the printer share name. List the share in the directory. Set additional drivers for downlevel clients and printing defaults.
- On the Ports tab, view or set printer ports. Enable or disable printer pooling.
- On the Advanced tab, view or set drivers, availability, priority, and spooling options.
- On the Security tab, view or set access permissions for the print queue.

Print queues and print jobs

- Manage print queues and jobs using the print management window.
- Double-click the printer icon in the Printers And Faxes folder.
- Right-click a document and choose Properties.
- Delete all print jobs queued by clicking Printer → Cancel All Documents.

Print permissions

- Print queue permissions are separate from the NTFS access permissions on the related spooling folder.
- By default, the special identity Everyone has permission to print.
- Creator Owner can manage documents and print.
- Administrators, Print Operators, and Server Operators can print, manage printers, and manage documents.

Internet Information Services

- IIS provides essential web services.
- Install by clicking Add Or Remove Programs in Control Panel.
- Manage using the Internet Services Manager.
- Click Start → Programs → Administrative Tools → Internet Information Services (IIS) Manager.
- Web documents are stored under *%SystemDrive%\Inetpub\wwwroot*.
- Web server logfiles are written to *%SystemRoot%\system32\LogFiles\w3svc*.
- IIS Reset (*iisreset.exe*) is used to stop and then restart all IIS-related services.

Configuring IIS

- General IIS settings control editing of the IIS metabase and available MIME types.
- Global sites settings determine the global settings for all sites of a particular type.
- Local site settings determine the effective settings for a specific site.

Backup or restore the IIS configuration

- Use Configuration Backup/Restore feature of Internet Services Manager.
- Right-click the computer name and click All Tasks → Backup/Restore Configuration.

Managing security for IIS

- IIS provides the top layer of security.
- Window provides the bottom layer of security.
- IIS security focuses on authentication controls and content permissions.

IIS authentication controls

- Click the Directory Security or File Security tab.
- Anonymous authentication allows access to resources without being prompted for username and password.
- Basic authentication prompts name and password, which is passed as clear text unless SSL is used.
- Digest authentication securely transmits via HTTP 1.1 digest authentication using user credentials (Active Directory domains only).
- Integrated Windows Authentication:uses standard Windows security to validate identity (doesn't require SSL).
- .NET Passport authentication uses .NET Passport authentication to validate access and credentials.
- Authentication controls can be set globally, for the site, for directories within the site and for pages.

IIS content permissions

- Content permissions provide the top level of security for IIS.
- Content permissions can be set both globally and locally.
- Set permissions on the Home Directory, Directory, or File tab as appropriate.

Configuring IIS content permissions

- Read allows web users to read files in the folder.
- Write allows web users to write data in the folder.
- Script Source Access allows web users to access the source code for scripts (not recommended).
- Directory Browsing allows web users to browse the folder and its subfolders (not recommended).

- Index This Resource allows the Indexing Service to index for keyword searches.
- Log Visits ensures access to files is recorded in the IIS logs.

IIS application permissions

- None disallows the execution of programs and scripts.
- Scripts Only allows scripts to run when accessed via IIS.
- Scripts and Executables allows both programs and scripts to run when accessed via IIS.

Software Update infrastructure

- Automatic Updates allows a system to automatically connect to update operating system.
- Windows Update extends updates to select Microsoft products.
- Windows Server Update Services allows organizations to use their own update servers.

Windows Server Update Services (WSUS)

- WSUS has both a server and client component.
- The WSUS client is an extension of Automatic Updates and has self updating for auto install.
- The WSUS server uses a data store that runs with MSDE, WMSDE, or SQL Server.
- SUS 1.0 servers can be migrated to WSUS using *WSUSITIL.EXE*.
- WSUS is designed to handle updates for all Microsoft products.

Installing Windows Software Update Services

- WSUS requires:
  - IIS (and you must install the World Wide Web Server Service at a minimum)
  - Background Intelligent Transfer Service (BITS) 2.0
  - Microsoft .NET Framework 1.1 Service Pack 1 for Windows Server 2003
- WUS uses HTTP port 80 and HTTPS port 443.
- Custom Web site for WSUS uses port 8530 by default.
- Install WSUS on a server using *WSUSSetup.exe*.

Configuring Windows Software Update Services

- Access the WSUS console with *http://WSUSServerame:portnumber/WSUSAdmin*.
- Click Start → Programs → Administrative Tools → Microsoft Windows Server Update Services.
- To complete setup:
  1. Configure the proxy server.
  2. Specify the products or product families that will be maintained.
  3. Synchronize WSUS to download updates from Microsoft Update or another WSUS server.

Installing and configuring Automatic Client Update settings

- Make the client computer aware of the WSUS configuration.
- Configure Automatic Updates to download and install updates.
- Specify through policy that the WSUS server should be used for obtaining updates.
- In a Group Policy editor, configure Automatic Updates policy under Computer Configuration → Administrative Templates → Windows Components → Windows Update.
- In a Group Policy editor, specify Intranet Microsoft Update Service Location under Computer Configuration → Administrative Templates → Windows Components → Windows Update.

Software site licensing

- Microsoft and other software vendors license software for use according to EULA.
- Microsoft offers retail product licenses and volume licensing.

Client access licenses

- Per server: each concurrent connection to a server requires a client access license.
- Per user or per device: each client requires a client access license that allows it to connect to a Windows server.
- Per processor: each processor (physical or virtual) on a server must have a license.
- Windows Server 2003 Terminal Services includes two CALs for remote desktop administration.

Server licensing

- Microsoft allows a one-time only switch from per-server to per-user/per-device licensing.
- Microsoft does not permit switching from per-user/per-device to per-server licensing.
- To manage licensing, you must be a member of the Administrators group.
- Per-server licensing is best when there are few servers and there is limited access of these servers.
- Otherwise, use per-user or per-device licensing, which allows for a mixture of users and devices.

Managing server licensing

- The licensing utility in Control Panel is for workgroups or individual servers.
- The licensing console under Administrative Tools is for domains (centralized control on a per-site basis).
- A designated site licensing server replicates the licensing throughout a site.
- Determine the site-licensing server in Active Directory Sites And Services. Double-click Licensing Site Settings.

- By default, the license server is the first domain controller installed in a domain.
- Site licensing can be moved to a member server or domain controller.

Using license groups

- A license group is a collection of users who share one or more CALs.
- With license groups, CALs are assigned from the group allocation.

Managing and Implementing Disaster Recovery

Summary of highlights from the "Managing and Implementing Disaster Recovery" section of the Exam 70-290 Study Guide.

Managing backup procedures

- Normal (full) backups should include System State data.
- Incremental backups contain changes since the last full or incremental backup.
- Differential backups contain changes since the last full backup.
- Daily backups contain all the files changed during the day.

Creating Automated System Recovery (ASR) data

- ASR data stores essential boot files and the complete System State.
- Create ASR data using the Backup utility.
- Primary data is stored on the backup media you choose.
- Secondary data needed to boot the system and access the primary data is stored on a floppy disk.
- Click the Automated System Recovery Wizard button on the Welcome tab.

ASR Recovery

1. Restart the system and boot the system off the installation CD-ROM.
2. During the text portion of the setup, press F2 to perform an ASR.
3. ASR then guides you through the recovery process.

System State

- System State includes the system registry, boot files, protected system files, and the COM+ registration database.
- On domain controllers, System State includes Active Directory data and system volume (SysVol) files.
- System State can be backed up locally only.

Backing up files and System State data to media

- Back up workstations and servers using the Backup utility.
- Click the Backup Wizard button to start the backup process.
- Create a scheduled backup job on the Schedule Jobs tab by clicking Add Job. Make sure the Task Scheduler service is running.
- Display a detailed run report by clicking Tools → Report.

Backup Storage media

- The Removable Storage snap-in enables you to view and manage removable media devices.
- Removable Storage is included by default in the Computer Management Console.
- All media in Removable storage is organized by media type, media pool, and library.
- CDs and DVDs are not supported as storage media in Windows Server 2003.

Configuring security for backup operations

- The Backup Files And Directories user right allows users to back up files. These include encrypted files.
- Restore Files And Directories allows users to restore files.
- User rights are defined in *Computer Configuration\Windows Settings\Security Settings\Local Policies\User Rights Assignment*.
- On Domain Controllers, Backup Operators, Server Operators, and Administrators are granted both rights.
- On stand-alone and member servers, Backup Operators and Administrators are granted both rights.
- Add a user to Backup Operators group to grant the right to back up and restore data.

Shadow Copies

- Supplement but do not replace routine backups.
- Shadow Copies are point-in-time backups of previous file versions.
- They work only for shared folders on NTFS volumes.

Configuring Shadow Copy

- Shadow Copy service will save up to 64 versions, by default.
- Number of versions is limited by maximum space usage allowed.
- By default, 10 percent of volume size is set as the maximum space usage allowed.
- To configure shadow copies, right-click Disk Management and click All Tasks → Configure Shadow Copies. Alternatively, from volume properties, click the Shadow Copies tab.
- Retrieve a shadow copy after installing the Shadow Copies client on the Previous Versions tab.

Recovering from operating system failure

- Restore backup data using the Backup utility.
- Click the Restore Wizard button to get started.
- Active Directory must be restored either authoritatively or nonauthoritatively. Press F8 during system startup to access the advanced boot options and select Directory Services Restore Mode.

Exam 70-290 Practice Questions

1. Which of the following are valid modes for MMC?

   ❑ A. Edit

   ❑ B. Author

   ❑ C. Normal

   ❑ D. User

   Answers B and D are correct. Author mode allows you to create and make changes to consoles. User mode allows you to access consoles and use their features.

2. What is the default TCP port for remote administration using Remote Desktop for Administration?

   ❍ A. Port 80

   ❍ B. Port 8080

   ❍ C. Port 369

   ❍ D. Port 3389

   Answer D is correct. If the computer is running a firewall, TCP port 3389 must be opened to allow remote access.

3. How many simultaneous connections are possible using Terminal Services in Remote Desktop for Administration mode?

   ❍ A. 2 concurrent

   ❍ B. 2 but not simultaneously

   ❍ C. 4 concurrent

   ❍ D. 4 but not simultaneously

   Answer A is correct. Each server configured with Remote Desktop for Administration can have up to two concurrent connections.

4. Sarah's computer is running Windows Server 2003. Sarah, a junior administrator, frequently has difficulty performing administration tasks. Ed, as the administrator spends several hours a week helping to resolve Sarah's issues. Rather than going to Sarah's workspace to resolve problems, Ed should:

   ❑ A. Enable Remote Desktop for Administration on Sarah's computer.

   ❑ B. Enable Remote Assistance on Sarah's computer.

   ❑ C. Show Sarah how to make remote assistance requests.

   ❑ D. Use Remote Assistance to help troubleshoot.

   ❑ E. Enable Remote Desktop for Administration on his computer.

   Answers B, C, and D are correct. Remote Assistance allows a user to send an invitation to a more experienced user or administrator asking for troubleshooting help with a computer problem. The helper accepting the request can view the user's desktop, transfer files, and chat with the user needing help through a single interface.

5. Which of the following unsigned driver options are available in Windows Server 2003?

   ❑ A. PnP

   ❑ B. Non-PnP

   ❑ C. Ignore

   ❑ D. Warn

   ❑ E. Prompt

   ❑ F. Block

   Answers C, D, and F are correct. Ignore allows all device drivers to be installed without having to see and respond to a warning prompt. Warn, the default, prompts with a warning message prior to installing a hardware device with an unsigned driver. Block prevents installation of unsigned drivers.

6. Todd is a system administrator. He has completed the installation of a new server running Windows Server 2003. When he logged on, the server's display mode was 640×480. He couldn't configure the server to display at a clearer, larger display mode, so he updated the video drivers. He rebooted the server after installing the drivers and logged on successfully. However, he is unable to manage the server because the display is completely black. What is the easiest and faster way to resolve this problem?

   ❍ A. Restart the server and use the Last Known Good Configuration. Roll back the video driver to the previous version.

   ❍ B. Restart the server and use Safe Mode. Rollback the video driver to the previous version.

   ❍ C. Create a new logon user and then log on as this user.

   ❍ D. Log on locally instead of onto the domain, and then fix the problem.

   Answer B is correct. If you had to restart the operating system after installing a driver and you successfully log on before a problem occurs, which could happen with an updated video driver, you will not be able to use the Last Known Good Configuration. The Last Known Good Configuration is overwritten when you successfully log on. In this case, you may need to start the computer in Safe Mode.

7. Mary is a system administrator. One of the organization's servers has just been upgraded from Windows NT to Windows Server 2003. After the upgrade, one of the SCSI adapters on the computer fails to operate and displays a warning. According to the documentation, the adapter is non-Plug-and-play and must be manually configured to use the appropriate resources. How do you manually configure the SCSI adapter?

   ❍ A. View the driver details. If the driver is not digitally signed, you must reinstall it.

   ❍ B. Access the device's Properties dialog box. Update the driver so that it uses PnP.

   ❍ C. Uninstall the device because you can't manually configure devices.

   ❍ D. Access the device's Properties dialog box. On the Resources tab, configure the manual settings.

Answer D is correct. If a device can be manually configured through Windows, you'll be able to clear Use Automatic Settings and then click Change Setting to define new resource settings. If you manually assign resources, both the device and the resource will be unavailable for automatic configuration. You'll need to make sure the settings don't conflict with other devices.

8. Which of the following partition styles and disk types are supported by Windows Server 2003?

   ❑ A. MBR basic disks

   ❑ B. GPT dynamic disks

   ❑ C. MBR and GPT basic disks

   ❑ D. MBR and GPT dynamic disks

   Answers C and D are correct. Windows Server 2003 supports MBR and GPT partition styles, and either style can use the basic or dynamic disk type. GPT partitions are used on Itanium based 64-bit versions of Windows Server 2003.

Prep and Practice

9. Which of the following types of disks can be formatted as dynamic disks?

   ❍ A. Hard disks on desktop PCs.

   ❍ B. Hard disks on laptops.

   ❍ C. Hard disks on tablet PCs.

   ❍ D. Removable media disk drives.

   ❍ E. FireWire/USB-connected disks.

   Answer A is correct. Dynamic disks are not supported for removable media, on portable computers, such as laptops and tablet PCs, or with disks connected via FireWire/USB.

10. Which of the following disk configurations would be considered the boot volume on Windows Server 2003?

    ❑ A. Volume C:, a basic disk containing the boot files *ntldr*, *ntdetect.com*, and *boot.ini* (with the operating system files on a different volume).

    ❑ B. Volume D:, a dynamic disk where the operating system files are located.

    ❑ C. Volume C:, a basic disk where the operating system files are located.

    ❑ D. Volume C:, a basic disk containing the boot files *ntldr*, *ntdetect.com*, and *boot.ini*, and where the operating system files are located.

    Answers B, C, and D are correct. The boot volume contains the operating system and operating system–related files. The system volume contains the hardware-specific files needed to load Windows. The boot and system volume can be the same volume.

11. Which of the following are true statements regarding basic disks?

    ❑ A. Basic disks can have up to four primary partitions or up to three primary partitions and one extended partition.

    ❑ B. Basic disks can have an unlimited number of simple volumes.

❑ C. On a basic disk, each primary partition is represented with one logical volume.

❑ D. On a basic disk, each extended partition is represented by one or more logical drives.

❑ E. Basic disks can have no more than six extended logical volumes.

Answers A, C, and D are correct. With MBR disk partitions on basic disks, logical volumes are represented using primary partitions and extended partitions containing logical drives. A basic disk can have up to four primary partitions or up to three primary partitions and one extended partition. Each primary partition is represented with one logical volume. Each extended partition is represented by one or more logical drives. A logical drive is a logical volume that is used to represent all of or part of an extended partition.

12. Which RAID configurations can be used with Windows Server 2003?

❑ A. RAID-0

❑ B. RAID-1

❑ C. RAID-5

❑ D. RAID-0+1

❑ E. RAID-10

Answers, A, B, C, D, and E are correct. Windows Server 2003 can be used with hardware and software RAID. While software RAID is limited to RAID-0, RAID-1, and RAID-5, hardware RAID levels are limited only by the hardware RAID controller.

13. Which of the following dynamic volume types can be extended?

❑ A. Simple volume

❑ B. Spanned volume

❑ C. Striped volumes

❑ D. Mirrored volumes

❑ E. Striped with parity volumes

Answers A and B are correct. You can extend simple volumes to unallocated space on the disk on which they were created. You can extend spanned volumes to unallocated space on any disk as necessary to provide additional storage capacity. You cannot extend striped, mirrored, or striped with parity volumes.

14. Which of the following techniques can be used to create and format a 60 GB volume?

❍ A. Use Disk Management to create and format the volume using FAT32 or NTFS.

❍ B. Use DiskPart to create the volume and use FORMAT to format the volume using FAT32 or NTFS.

❍ C. Use Disk Management to create the volume and format the volume as FAT32 using DiskPart.

❍ D. Use Disk Management to create the volume and format the volume as NTFS using DiskPart.

❍ E. Use Disk Management to create and format the volume using NTFS.

Answer E is correct. The volume can be created only using NTFS. Although FAT32 has maximum volume size of 2TB, Disk Management and DiskPart limit this to 32 GB. Further, DiskPart cannot be used for formatting volumes. You can use Disk Management or FORMAT to format volumes.

15. How can volumes be mounted on Windows Server 2003 using Disk Management or DiskPart?

❑ A. Volumes can be mounted to a drive letter.

❑ B. Volumes can be mounted to any NTFS folder.

❑ C. Volumes can be mounted to any empty NTFS folder.

❑ D. Volumes cannot be mounted using Diskpart.

Answers A and C are correct. Volumes can be mounted to a drive letter or an empty NTFS folder. Volumes cannot be mounted to non-empty NTFS folders. Both Disk Management and DiskPart can be used to mount volumes.

16. Tom is a system administrator. He has installed a new server running Windows Server 2003. The server's C: drive has the operating system files and the files need to boot the system. He wants the C: drive to be fault tolerant. Which of the following can Tom use to configure C: to be fault tolerant?

❑ A. Use Windows Server 2003 to implement RAID-1 (disk mirroring) on C:.

❑ B. Use Windows Server 2003 to implement RAID-5 (disk striping with parity) on C:.

❑ C. Configure two hard disk controllers and use Windows Server 2003 to implement disk duplexing on C:.

❑ D. Use Windows Server 2003 to implement RAID-0 (disk striping) on C:.

Answers A and C are correct. A is correct because boot and system volumes can be mirrored. B is incorrect because system volumes cannot use RAID-5. C is correct because boot and system volumes can be duplexed; disk duplexing is a RAID-1 configuration with two hard disk controllers. D is incorrect because RAID-0 is not fault tolerant.

17. Which of the following are true regarding names assigned to users, groups, and computers in workgroups under Windows Server 2003?

❑ A. Each computer must have a unique name.

❑ B. User names must be unique, but only on a per-machine basis

❑ C. User names must be unique throughout the workgroup.

❑ D. Group names must be unique, but only on a per-machine basis.

❑ E. Group names must be unique throughout the workgroup.

Answers A, B, and D are correct. In a workgroup, each computer must have a unique name, and other names are maintained on a per-machine basis. This means each local user and local group defined on a computer must be unique.

18. Which of the following are true regarding names assigned to users, groups, and computers in Active Directory domain under Windows Server 2003?

❍ A. User, computer, and group names do not have to be unique and can be repeated.

❍ B. User, computer, and group names can contain no more than 64 characters and only 32 characters for the display name.

❍ C. User, computer, and group names must have a unique 64-character pre-Windows 2000 name.

❍ D. User, computer, and group names are permitted to contain spaces, periods, dashes, and underscores.

Answer D is correct. In Active Directory, all user, computer, and group names must be unique on a per-domain basis. Names can have up to 256 characters; display names can have up to 64 characters. By default, the pre-Windows 2000 name is the first 20 characters of the standard name. User, computer, and group names are permitted to contain spaces, periods, dashes, and underscores, but cannot contain the following special characters: " / \ [ ] ; | = , + * ? < >.

19. Which of the following methods can be used to create computer accounts in an Active Directory domain under Windows Server 2003?

❑ A. Authenticated users can join up to 10 computers to the domain and Active Directory will create necessary computer automatically.

❑ B. Only administrators can join computers to the domain. When this is done, Active Directory will create necessary computer automatically.

❑ C. Administrators can prestage a computer account using Active Directory Users And Computers. Only Domain Admins can then join the computer to the domain unless the permission is delegated.

❑ D. Administrators can prestage a computer account using DSADD COMPUTER. Any user can then join the computer to the domain.

Answers A and C are correct. Authenticated users can join up to 10 computers to the domain and Active Directory will create necessary computer objects for these computers automatically. Authenticated users must also have local administrator permissions on the local computer. With prestaging of accounts, members of the Domain Admins group only will be able to join this computer to the domain by default. If you want to delegate this permission to a specific user or group, click Change and then select the user or group using the dialog box provides.

20. Which of the following types of groups can be created by administrators in an Active Directory domain under Windows Server 2003?

❑ A. Implicit groups

❑ B. Domain local groups

❑ C. Global groups

❑ D. Universal groups

❑ E. Built-in groups

Answers B, C, and D are correct. In an Active Directory domain, administrators can create domain local, global, and universal groups. Built-in groups are created when you install Windows Server 2003 and configure the domain. Implicit built-in groups are another special type of group. Membership in implicit groups is implied, and implicit groups cannot be created by administrators.

21. Which of the following can be members of a universal group when the domain functional level is set to Windows Server 2003?

- ❑ A. Users or computer accounts from the same domain only.
- ❑ B. Users or computer accounts from any domain.
- ❑ C. Domain local groups from the same domain only.
- ❑ D. Domain local groups from any domain.
- ❑ E. Global and universal groups from any domain.
- ❑ F. Global and universal groups from the same domain only.

Prep and Practice

Answers B and E are correct. In Windows Server 2003 domain functional mode, universal groups can contains accounts from any domain. They can also contain global and universal groups from any domain. They cannot, however, contain domain local groups.

22. Joe is a system administrator at a university. He's been tasked with setting up a computer lab for the science department. Although each student who logs on to a computer in the lab will have his or her own account in the lab domain, the manager of the science department doesn't want students to be able to make permanent changes to the desktop environment settings. Profiles should not be stored on individual computers. Instead, they should be stored on the main server. How should Joe configure the student accounts in the lab domain?

- ❍ A. Use a local profile for each student.
- ❍ B. Use a roaming profile for each student.
- ❍ C. Use a mandatory local profile for each student.
- ❍ D. Use a mandatory roaming profile for each student.

Answer D is correct. When a user has a roaming profile, the profile is stored on a server. If the name of the profile is changed to *Ntuser.man*, the user is prevented from making permanent changes to his or her settings.

23. Which of the following are valid passwords when the "Passwords must meet complexity requirements" policy is enabled in an Active Directory domain under Windows Server 2003?

- ❑ A. Ilove2gotoSchool
- ❑ B. !Random56
- ❑ C. d4$#@23
- ❑ D. gottarunfaster

Answer B and C are correct. The policy determines whether the password must meet specific complexity requirements. If the policy is defined, a password cannot contain the user account name, must contain at least six characters, and must have characters that have uppercase letters, lowercase letters, Arabic numerals, and non-alphanumeric characters.

24. How can you determine whether a user's account is disabled?

❑ A. Use Active Directory Users And Computers to delete the account.

❑ B. Use Active Directory Users And Computers; if the account shows a red warning icon it has been disabled.

❑ C. Type `dsmod user UserDN -disabled` at a command prompt.

❑ D. Type `dsquery user UserDN -disabled` at a command prompt.

Answers B and D are correct. Answer A is incorrect because you don't have to delete an account to determine if it is disabled. Answer B is correct because Active Directory Users And Computers shows disabled accounts with a red warning icon next to the account name. Answer C is incorrect because you use DSMOD USER to modify user accounts. Answer D is correct because you can determine whether an account has been disabled by typing `dsquery user UserDN -disabled` at a command prompt.

25. Joe is a system administrator at a university. He's been tasked with setting up a computer lab for the science department. He's been asked to set up a shared folder that allows students to save and manage their files. Lab administrators should have full access to manage the share however necessary. Student accounts are members of the UStudents group. Lab administrators are members of the LabAdmins group. How should Joe configure the shared folder?

❍ A. Configure the share so UStudents have Change permission and LabAdmins have Full Control permission.

❍ B. Configure the share so UStudents have Change permission and LabAdmins have Change permission.

❍ C. Configure the share so UStudents have Full Control permission and LabAdmins have Change permission.

❍ D. Configure the share so UStudents have Read permission and LabAdmins have Change permission.

Answer A is correct. Full Control permission grants both Read and Change permission, and also allows a user to change file and folder permissions and take ownership of files and folders. Change allows a user to view files and folders, create files and subfolders, modify files, change attributes on files and subfolders, and delete files and subfolders.

26. Joe is a system administrator at a university. He set up a share in the computer lab but neither students nor lab administrators can access it. Joe checked the share permissions, which are configured properly. Students and lab administrators see an "Access is denied" message when they try to access the share. Joe has no problem accessing the share. What should Joe do to resolve the problem?

❍ A. Nothing; the users must be mapping to the share improperly.

❍ B. Instruct the users on the proper way to connect to the share.

❍ C. Check and modify as necessary the NTFS permissions on the folder being shared.

❍ D. Change the share permissions so that everyone has Full Control.

Answer C is correct. Share permissions determine the maximum allowed access level. NTFS permissions further restrict the access. If share permissions are correct and users see an "Access is denied" message, the NTFS permissions should be checked.

27. Joe is a system administrator at a university. In the computer lab, Joe believes someone hacked the main file server and then deleted the C$ and D$ administrative shares. What is the best way to resolve the problem?

 ❍ A. Reinstalling the file server is the only way to resolve the file server.

 ❍ B. Restart the server.

 ❍ C. Restore the file server from backup.

 ❍ D. Remove access to the security event logs.

 Answer B is correct. The special shares are created each time the operating system is started. Restarting the server will ensure the deleted shares are restored.

Prep and Practice

28. Which of the following are true about NTFS permissions?

 ❑ A. Basic permissions provide the most granular control for fine-tuning access.

 ❑ B. Special permissions provide the most granular control for fine-tuning access.

 ❑ C. Basic permissions represent a grouping of special permissions.

 ❑ D. Special permissions represent a grouping of basic permissions.

 Answers B and C are correct. Basic permissions represent a grouping of special permissions that together allow six commonly configured levels of access: Read, Read & Execute, Write, Modify, or Full Control. The special or advanced permissions provide granular control for when you need to fine-tune access permissions.

29. Which of the following are true when you view effective NTFS permissions for a user or group?

 ❑ A. Basic permissions are displayed.

 ❑ B. Directly assigned permissions are included and displayed.

 ❑ C. Permissions inherited due to group membership are included and displayed.

 ❑ D. Permissions inherited from parent folders aren't included or displayed.

 ❑ E. Share permissions are not included or displayed.

 Answers B, C, and E are correct. Effective permissions are listed using special permissions (not basic permissions). The Effective Permissions tab allows you to determine the collective set of permissions that apply based on directly assigned permissions, permissions inherited due to group membership, and permissions inherited from parent folders. Effective Permissions apply only to folder and file permissions. Share permissions are not included. You cannot determine effective permissions for implicit groups or special identities.

30. Which of the following techniques can be used to change the ownership of an NTFS folder or file?

- ❑ A. Any user who has the Restore Files And Directories user right can take ownership.
- ❑ B. Members of the Administrators group can take ownership.
- ❑ C. Any user assigned the Take Ownership permission can take ownership.
- ❑ D. Authenticated users can grant any user the Take Ownership permission.

Answers A, B, and C are correct. Users who have the right to Restore Files And Directories, such as a member of the Backup Operators group, can take ownership. Members of the Administrators group can take ownership. Users or groups assigned with the Take Ownership permission can take ownership. Current owners can grant another user the Take Ownership permission.

31. Sarah is configuring NTFS permissions and has been told that members of the TempUsers group should not have access to the *C:\Userdata\Docs* folder. Sarah checked the permissions on the Docs folder and found the TempUsers group is getting access to the *C:\Userdata\Docs* folder through permissions inherited from *C:\Userdata*. What is the best way to configure permissions so the TempUsers group cannot access the *C:\Userdata\Docs* folder?

- ❍ A. Stop inheriting permissions by clearing Allow Inheritable Permissions From The Parent To Propagate To This Object on the Permissions tab of the *C:\Userdata* folder.
- ❍ B. Stop inheriting permissions by clearing Allow Inheritable Permissions From The Parent To Propagate To This Object on the Permissions tab of the *C:\Userdata\Docs* folder.
- ❍ C. Remove the TempUsers group's permissions on the *C:\Userdata* folder.
- ❍ D. Override the inherited permissions on the *C:\Userdata* folder*\Docs* folder by explicitly denying the TempUsers group's permissions.

Answer D is correct. You can override inherited permissions by selecting the opposite permission and thereby explicitly denying the permission. You don't want to stop inheriting permissions because that could affect permissions for all users and groups. You don't want to remove TempUsers group's permissions on the *C:\Userdata* folder because the group members needs to access other folders under this folder.

32. What should you do to allow a user to log on to a terminal server?

- ❍ A. Create a local machine account for the user on the terminal server.
- ❍ B. Create a domain account for the user and configure the user's home profile so it is stored on the terminal server.
- ❍ C. Add the user to the Remote Desktop Users group in the appropriate domain.
- ❍ D. Grant the user the Logon As A Batch Job user right on the terminal server.

Answer C is correct. In a standard configuration of terminal server, you can add users or group to the Remote Desktop Users group to allow users to log on to a terminal server.

33. Tom is an administrator for a large enterprise. The organization has been using terminal servers for several months. Yesterday, one of the administrators configured the terminal servers so that authentication is required. The Remote Desktop Connection client settings were updated throughout the organization so that authentication is used. The help desk has received reports that some users can no longer connect to the terminal servers, while other users are fine. Tom and other help desk staff can connect to the terminal server without problems. What is the best way to resolve the problem while ensuring identity can be confirmed when accessing the terminal server?

   ❍ A. Nothing; everyone else is fine so the terminal server is working correctly.

   ❍ B. Remove the authentication requirement on the server.

   ❍ C. Remove the authentication requirement on both the clients and servers.

   ❍ D. Make sure all users are logging on using the proper domain, user account and password.

   ❍ E. Make sure all users are connecting using the appropriate server name.

   Answer E is correct. With authentication, the user may need to type the fully qualified domain name for the terminal server instead of the computer name.

Prep and Practice

34. Nathan is a developer. He is having problem with an application and cannot determine why authentication and logon are failing. The machine he's working with has auditing configured, but he cannot access the security logs. What needs to be done to allow Nathan to access the security logs?

   ❍ A. Only administrators can access security logs. Nathan should be made an administrator on the computer.

   ❍ B. Nathan is looking in the wrong place. Auditing events are recorded in the system logs.

   ❍ C. Nathan should be granted the Manage Auditing and the Security Log user right on the computer.

   ❍ D. Nathan should be granted the Bypass Traverse Checking user right on the computer.

   Answer C is correct. Security logs are accessible only to administrators by default. Others who need access must be granted the Manage Auditing and the Security Log user right.

35. Which of the following are not one of the standard types of events?

   ❍ A. Normal

   ❍ B. Warning

   ❍ C. Error

   ❍ D. Success Audit

   ❍ E. Failure Audit

   Answer A is correct. Normal is not one of the standard types of events. The standard event types are: Information, Warning, Error, Success Audit, and Failure Audit.

36. What tool should you use if you suspect an application is not responding?

❍ A. Computer Management

❍ B. Task Manager

❍ C. Performance

❍ D. System Monitor

❍ E. Event Viewer

Answer B is correct. The Task Manager Application's tab displays the status of running applications and can be used to stop applications that aren't responding.

37. Which of the following performance metrics do you use when specifying resources to monitor in System Monitor?

❑ A. Objects

❑ B. Counters

❑ C. Processes

❑ D. Threads

❑ E. Instances

Answers A, B, and E are correct. In System Monitor, the standard performance metrics are objects, counters, and object instances.

38. What performance metric should you track to determine whether a disk is keeping up with I/O requests?

❍ A. *Physical Disk\CurrentDisk Queue Length*

❍ B. *PhysicalDisk\%Disk Time*

❍ C. *LogicalDisk\%Free Space*

❍ D. *Logical Disk\Avg. DiskRead Queue Length*

Answer A is correct. *Physical Disk\Avg. DiskWrite Queue Length*, *Physical Disk\Avg. DiskRead Queue Length*, and *Physical Disk\CurrentDisk Queue Length* track disk-queuing activity. If there are multiple requests in any queue waiting to be processed, the disk isn't performing as fast as is necessary to keep up with I/O requests.

39. Which of the following statements are not true regarding disk quotas?

❍ A. Disk quotas apply only to NTFS volumes.

❍ B. A quota warning level can be exceeded.

❍ C. A quota limit level cannot be exceeded.

❍ D. The built-in Administrators group is not affected by quota limits.

Answer C is correct. A quota limit sets a specific limit on the amount of space that can be used. Users can be prevented from exceeding a quota limit, but only if the quota limit is enforced.

40. Sarah is a system administrator. She has moved three previously shared printers to new locations on the network and assigned each a new IP address. These printers are all hosted by a single print server. What should Sarah do to allow the printers to be used for printing?

❑ A. Modify the user profile of each user so the correct IP address is used for the printers.

❑ B. Configure user logon scripts to map to the printer share names.

❑ C. Access the Advanced tab of the Print Server Properties dialog box and configure the related TCP/IP ports.

❑ D. Access the Advanced tab of each printer's Properties dialog box and configure the related TCP/IP port.

Answers C and D are correct. The Ports tab of the each printer's Properties dialog box can be used to change port configurations. Although you also can configure ports using the Ports tab of the Print Server Properties dialog box, you cannot configure ports on the Advanced tab.

41. How do you change the location of the print spooling folder?

❍ A. Access the Advanced tab of the Print Server Properties dialog box and enter the new folder location.

❍ B. Access the Advanced tab of each printer's Properties dialog box and enter the new folder location.

❍ C. Edit the Spool Folder policy setting.

❍ D. Edit the Registry so *CurrSpoolFold* under HKLM has the correct folder location.

Answer A is correct. You can change the location of the spooling folder using the Advanced tab of the Print Server Properties dialog box. It is not possible to specify different spool folders for different folders. All printers share the same spool folder.

42. What authentication mode should you use when configuring IIS if you want users to be able to secure access and allow users to use their domain logon to access internal web servers?

❍ A. Anonymous authentication

❍ B. Basic authentication

❍ C. Digest authentication

❍ D. Integrated Windows Authentication

❍ E. .NET Passport Authentication

Answer D is correct. Integrated Windows Authentication uses standard Windows security to validate a user's identity. Users are not prompted for logon information. Instead, the Windows logon credentials are related to the server in an encrypted format that does not require the use of SSL. Only Internet Explorer browsers support this authentication mode.

43. How should you configure a server's content and application permissions so users can view files, execute scripts, but have no other permissions?

❍ A. Configure Script Source Access and Scripts Only permissions

❍ B. Configure Read, Script Source Access and Scripts Only permissions

❍ C. Configure Read and Scripts Only permissions

❍ D. Configure Read, Write, and Scripts Only permissions

Answer C is correct. Read permission allows web users to read files in the folder. Scripts Only permission allows scripts to run when accessed via IIS.

44. Amy is a systems administrator. She's configuring Automatic Updates so that all computers within the domain automatically install updates obtained from a designated internal update server. Amy installed and configured Windows Software Update Services. When she configured products to install, and synchronized the update server, updates were downloaded and she approved them for install. To complete the process, she logged on to each computer and configured Automatic Updates so updates were downloaded and installed automatically every day. However, when she checked the computers a few days later, she found no updates had been downloaded or installed. What should Amy do to correct the problem?

   ❍ A. Check the proxy settings and make sure the update server is getting current updates.

   ❍ B. Use the Configure Automatic Updates policy rather than the Control Panel.

   ❍ C. Use policy to specify the intranet Microsoft update service location.

   ❍ D. Restart the client computers.

   ❍ E. Reinstall the Windows Software Update Services.

   Answer C is correct. Answer A is incorrect because Amy was able to synchronize the update server and approved updates; the update server configuration is working properly. Answer B is correct because client computers can be configured to use Automatic Updates in policy or in Control Panel. Policy settings do take precedence, but either method works. Answers D and E are incorrect because restarting computers and reinstalling WSUS won't resolve the problem.

45. Which of the following are the licensing options permitted by Microsoft?

   ❏ A. Per server

   ❏ B. Per user or device

   ❏ C. Per workgroup

   ❏ D. Switching from per user or device to per server

   ❏ E. Switching from per server to per user or device

   Answers A, B, and E are correct. Microsoft allows per-server, per-user or device, or per-processor licensing. You can make a one-time only switch from per-server licensing to per-user or device licensing. You cannot switch from per-user or device licensing to per-server licensing.

46. Sal is a member of the Backup Operators group and has been asked to recover a server that failed Thursday evening. Sal examined the backups and discovered the last full (normal) backup was made on Sunday. Although daily differential backups were made Monday, Tuesday, and Wednesday, Thursday's differential backup was not made. What is the most efficient way for Sal to recover the server?

❍ A. Restore the last full (normal) backup.

❍ B. Restore the last full (normal) backup and the Differential backup from Wednesday.

❍ C. Restore the last full (normal) backup and the dailies from Monday, Tuesday, and Wednesday.

❍ D. Restore the last full (normal) backup and the dailies from Monday, Tuesday, and Wednesday. Restore Thursday's daily from the previous week.

Answer B is correct. Differential backups contain changes since the last full backup. If a system fails on a Thursday before daily Differential backup and the last full (normal) backup was the previous Sunday, you would recover the system by applying the last full (normal) backup, and the last differential backup (Wednesday's differential backup).

47. How can you determine whether scheduled backups completed successfully?

❍ A. Access the Backup Progress dialog box for the backup and click the Report button.

❍ B. Check the system event log for success events.

❍ C. Open the Backup utility and click Tools → Report.

❍ D. Check the size of the backup file.

Answer C is correct. For scheduled backups (and any other backup), you can display the detailed run report by opening the Backup utility, clicking Tools → Report, and then double-clicking the report you want to review.

48. Which of the following would allow a user to back up and restore files on a member server?

❑ A. Make the user a member of the Server Operators group.

❑ B. Make the user a member of the Backup Operators group.

❑ C. Grant the user the Backup Files And Directories user rights.

❑ D. Grant the user the Backup Files And Directories user rights and the Restore Files And Directories user rights.

Answers B and D are correct. On stand-alone and member servers, members of the Backup Operators and Administrators group are granted both rights. On Domain Controllers, members of the Backup Operators, Server Operators, and Administrators group are granted both rights. Other than this, only those granted the user rights Backup Files And Directories and Restore Files And Directories can back up and restore files.

II

Exam 70-291

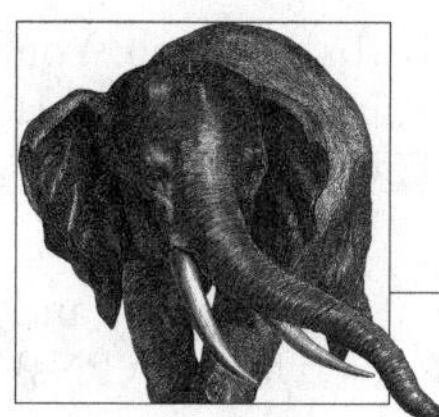

4
Exam 70-291 Overview

Exam 70-291: Implementing, Managing, and Maintaining a Microsoft Windows Server 2003 Network Infrastructure is designed to cover the skills necessary to manage the internal and external networking needs of a medium to large organization. Although you certainly do not need to be Cisco certified—i.e., a CCNA or CCNE—to pass this exam, a strong understanding of network architecture and TCP/IP networking is essential to your success. Consider these areas as the essential background details that, although not specifically tested, will make or break your exam.

The exam itself focuses on measuring your Microsoft networking skills. You need to know how to configure and troubleshoot TCP/IP addressing. You need to know DHCP and DNS in extensive detail. With DHCP, the ability to configure and manage leases, relays, reservations, and scopes are all part of the core skills measured. You'll also need to be able to diagnose and resolve issues related to incorrect configurations of TCP/IP, DHCP, and Automatic Private IP Addressing (APIPA). With DNS, everything from installation to configuration, management, and monitoring is covered. You'll need to know how to configure zones, forwarding, and server options, and be able to use monitoring to troubleshoot DNS issues.

Other areas of the exam cover network security, routing, and remote access. Both basic and advanced skills are tested, including IP connectivity, remote access management, TCP/IP routing, and IP security (IPSec).

Some of the most common problem areas for people taking the exam have to do with:

Network security
: Requires creating and working with security templates as well as monitoring security compliance. You need to have very good knowledge of how Security Configuration Management is used and what happens when security templates are applied.

Network protocol security

This is a big area of study. You must know IPSec and Kerberos very well. You must be able to use Netsh to configure and manage IPSec. You must be able to capture network traffic, use Kerberos tools, and track IPSec traffic.

Remote access

For the exam, you are expected to know how to implement, manage, and maintain remote access. Router-to-router Virtual Private Networks (VPNs) and Internet Authentication Service (IAS) aren't something administrators typically work with on a daily basis. More typically, administrators have experience with the initial setup and little experience with the actual troubleshooting, or vice versa, especially in large organizations with multiple levels of help desk support.

To be prepared for Exam 70-291, you should have 6–12 months experience working with a Microsoft network preferably as a network administrator or in a capacity where you can get equivalent experience. You should have strong familiarity with networking concepts, and a good start is getting your CompTIA Security+ certification. (You can use a CompTIA Security+ certification as an elective for MCSA certification and for MCSE certification.)

I very much recommend setting up your own test network in which you implement and put to use routing and remote access. Preferably, your test environment will involve simulated/real outside in access over multiple routers as well as inside out access. You should have recently studied a Windows Server 2003 administrator's book, taken a training course, or completed a self-paced training kit that covers the related areas of study. You will then be ready to use the Exam 70-291 Study Guide in this book as your final exam preparation.

Exam 70-291 is a required exam for both MCSAs and MCSEs. For MCSAs, it is the second of two required networking system exams. For MCSEs, it is the second of four required networking system exams. If you are a current MCSA on Windows 2000, you need to pass Exam 70-292 to upgrade your certification to Windows Server 2003. If you are a current MCSE on Windows 2000, you need to pass Exam 70-292 and Exam 70-296 to upgrade your certification to Windows Server 2003. Skills measured by Exam 70-292, representing a subset of Exams 70-290 and 70-291, are indicated in this exam overview sections by the ^{X} symbol.

Areas of Study for Exam 70-291

Implementing, Managing, and Maintaining IP Addressing

- Configure TCP/IP addressing on a server computer.
- Manage Dynamic Host Configuration Protocol (DHCP).
  - Manage DHCP clients and leases.
  - Manage DHCP Relay Agent.
  - Manage DHCP databases.
  - Manage DHCP scope options.
  - Manage reservations and reserved clients.
- Troubleshoot TCP/IP addressing.
  - Diagnose and resolve issues related to Automatic Private IP Addressing (APIPA).
  - Diagnose and resolve issues related to incorrect TCP/IP configuration.
- Troubleshoot DHCP.
  - Diagnose and resolve issues related to DHCP authorization.
  - Verify DHCP reservation configuration.
  - Examine the system event log and DHCP server audit logfiles to find related events.
  - Diagnose and resolve issues related to configuration of DHCP server and scope options.
  - Verify that the DHCP Relay Agent is working correctly.
  - Verify database integrity.

See "Implementing, Managing, and Maintaining IP Addressing" on page 189, and "Installing, Configuring, and Managing DHCP" on page 201.

Exam 70-291 Overview

Implementing, Managing, and Maintaining Name Resolution

- Install and configure the Domain Name System (DNS) Server service. X
  - Configure DNS server options. X
  - Configure DNS zone options. X
  - Configure DNS forwarding. X
- Manage DNS.
  - Manage DNS zone settings. X
  - Manage DNS record settings. X
  - Manage DNS server options. X
- Monitor DNS. Tools might include System Monitor, Event Viewer, Replication Monitor, and DNS debug logs.

See "Implementing, Managing, and Maintaining Name Resolution" on page 224.

Implementing, Managing, and Maintaining Network Security

- Implement secure network administration procedures. X
  - — Implement security baseline settings and audit security settings by using security templates. X
  - — Implement the principle of least privilege. X
- Monitor network protocol security. Tools might include the IP Security Monitor Microsoft Management Console (MMC) snap-in and Kerberos support tools.
- Troubleshoot network protocol security. Tools might include the IP Security Monitor MMC snap-in, Event Viewer, and Network Monitor.

See "Implementing, Managing, and Maintaining Network Security" on page 248.

Implementing, Managing, and Maintaining Routing and Remote Access

- Configure Routing and Remote Access user authentication.
  - — Configure remote access authentication protocols.
  - — Configure Internet Authentication Service (IAS) to provide authentication for Routing and Remote Access clients.
  - — Configure Routing and Remote Access policies to permit or deny access.
- Manage remote access.
  - — Manage packet filters.
  - — Manage Routing and Remote Access routing interfaces.
  - — Manage devices and ports.
  - — Manage routing protocols.
  - — Manage Routing and Remote Access clients.
- Manage TCP/IP routing.
  - — Manage routing protocols.
  - — Manage routing tables.
  - — Manage routing ports.
- Implement secure access between private networks.
- Troubleshoot user access to remote access services.
  - — Diagnose and resolve issues related to remote access VPNs.
  - — Diagnose and resolve issues related to establishing a remote access connection.
  - — Diagnose and resolve user access to resources beyond the remote access server.

- Troubleshoot Routing and Remote Access routing.
  - Troubleshoot demand-dial routing.
  - Troubleshoot router-to-router VPNs.

See "Implementing, Managing, and Maintaining Routing and Remote Access" on page 259.

Maintaining a Network Infrastructure

- Monitor network traffic. Tools might include Network Monitor and System Monitor.
- Troubleshoot connectivity to the Internet.
- Troubleshoot server services.
  - Diagnose and resolve issues related to service dependency.
  - Use service recovery options to diagnose and resolve service-related issues.

See "Maintaining a Network Infrastructure" on page 289.

5

Exam 70-291 Study Guide

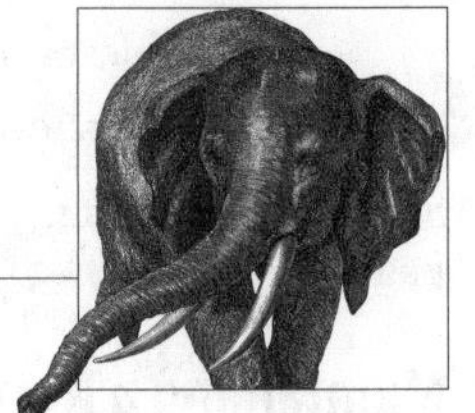

This chapter provides a study guide for *Exam 70-291: Implementing, Managing, and Maintaining a Microsoft Windows Server 2003 Network Infrastructure*. Sections within the chapter are organized according to the exam objective they cover. Each section identifies the related exam objective, provides an overview of why the objective is important, and then discusses the key details you should know about the objective to both succeed on the test and master the objective in the real world.

The major topics covered on Exam 70-291 are:

Implementing, Managing, and Maintaining IP Addressing
: Designed to test your knowledge of static, automatic private, and dynamic IP addressing. Also covers configuration and management of Dynamic Host Configuration Protocol (DHCP).

Installing, Configuring, and Managing DHCP
: Designed to test your knowledge of configuring and managing DHCP servers.

Implementing, Managing, and Maintaining Name Resolution
: Designed to test your knowledge of name resolution using Domain Name System (DNS).

Implementing, Managing, and Maintaining Network Security
: Designed to test your knowledge of network security. Focuses on using security templates and network protocol security monitoring.

Implementing, Managing, and Maintaining Routing and Remote Access
: Designed to test your knowledge of remote access, remote access authentication, and TCP/IP routing. Also covers secure access between private networks.

Maintaining a Network Infrastructure
: Designed to test your knowledge of network monitoring and network connectivity troubleshooting. Also covers troubleshooting server services.

The sections of this chapter are designed to reinforce your knowledge of these topics. Ideally, you will review this chapter as thoroughly as you would your course notes in preparation for a college professor's final exam. That means multiple readings of the chapter, committing to memory key concepts, and performing any necessary outside readings if there are topics you have difficulty with.

As part of your preparation, I recommend installing a test network with three machines:

- A domain controller running Windows Server 2003 configured with DNS, DHCP, and TCP/IP routing.
- A workstation configured as a domain member, running Windows XP Professional or later to be used as your primary system for management.
- A workstation configured as a member of a workgroup, running Windows XP Professional or later to be used for remote access testing.

These systems can be virtual machines installed as part of a virtual test environment.

Implementing, Managing, and Maintaining IP Addressing

For computers to communicate on a network, they must be configured with a communications protocol. Transmission Control Protocol/Internet Protocol (TCP/IP) is the primary communications protocol used by networked Windows computers. TCP/IP is a protocol suite, consisting of two separate protocols:

TCP
: A connection-oriented protocol for end-to-end communications.

IP
: An internetworking protocol for routing packets over a network.

During installation of Windows XP Professional or Windows Server 2003 computers, TCP/IP is automatically configured if the operating system detects a network adapter.

The default configuration for both Windows XP Professional and Windows Server 2003 computers is to automatically obtain an IP address from a DHCP server. IP addresses automatically obtained from a DHCP server are referred to as *dynamically assigned IP addresses*, or simply, *dynamic IP addresses*. Two other types of IP addresses are used:

Static IP addresses
: Addresses manually assigned to computers. Although some types of servers, including DHCP servers, require static IP addressing, most other servers can use either static or dynamic IP addressing.

Automatic private IP addresses (APIPA)
: Addresses used when a computer is configured for DHCP but no DHCP server is available. APIPA is also used when a DHCP IP address expires and cannot be renewed.

Regardless of whether IP addressing is assigned manually, dynamically, or automatically, the goal is the same: to allow a computer to communicate on a network. The sections that follow examine installing, configuring, and troubleshooting TCP/IP addressing as well as managing and troubleshooting DHCP. When computer names are used, name resolution is critical to proper functioning of TCP/IP communications. A computer must be able to look up the IP address associated with a computer name, referred to as a *forward lookup*, or determine the computer name based on an IP address, referred to as a *reverse lookup*. On Windows Server 2003 domains, DNS is the primary name resolution service.

Exam 70-291 tests knowledge of TCP/IP version 4. TCP/IP version 4 uses 32-bit IP addresses. With TCP/IP version 6, computers use 128-bit IP addresses.

Installing TCP/IP

As part of setup, TCP/IP is configured if the operating system detects a network adapter. Each network adapter installed on a computer has an associated Local Area Network connection. The default name of the first network adapter's connection is Local Area Connection. If for some reason TCP/IP isn't installed or has been uninstalled, you may need to install TCP/IP by completing the following steps:

1. Click Start → Control Panel → Network Connections → Local Area Connection.
2. Click Properties to open the Local Area Connection Properties dialog box.
3. Scroll down through the list of protocols used by the connection. If Internet Protocol (TCP/IP) is not listed, click Install.
4. Select Protocol, and then click Add.
5. In the Select Network Protocol dialog box, click Internet Protocol (TCP/IP) and then click OK.
6. Internet Protocol (TCP/IP) is installed and enabled in the default configuration.
7. Click Close.

You must be a member of the Administrators group to install TCP/IP or to configure TCP/IP properties on any computer in the domain.

Configure TCP/IP Addressing on a Server Computer

Server computers can be assigned static or dynamic IP addresses. If DHCP is configured but no DHCP server is available, the server will use APIPA. APIPA is also used when a DHCP IP address expires and cannot be renewed. Administrators have full control over how static, dynamic, and Automatic Private IP Addressing is used. In all three configurations, TCP/IP addressing can use:

An IP address

IP addresses identify computers by their associated network ID and host ID components. Address classes are used to subdivide the IP address space.

A subnet mask

Identifies which parts of the IP address belong to the network ID and which parts belong to the host ID. Subnets can be used to make more efficient use of IP address space by sizing networks appropriately for the number of nodes used.

A default gateway

Identifies the IP address of the router that will act as the computer's gateway. Proper gateway configuration is essential for communications between networks.

Preferred and alternate DNS server

Identifies the IP address of the preferred and alternate DNS servers to use for name resolution. Proper DNS configuration is essential for name resolution.

Understanding IP addressing

IP addresses are public or private. Public IP addresses are routable over the Internet and must be assigned by Internet service providers (ISPs). Private IP addresses are reserved for use on internal networks and are not routed over the public Internet. If you're connecting a computer directly to the Internet and have been assigned an IP address, you can use a public IP address. Otherwise, you should use a private IP address, preferably assigned by your organization's network administrator.

The available IP addresses are divided into network class ranges. For TCP/IP version 4, the standard classes are Class A, Class B, and Class C. These network classes are used with unicast IP addresses; which class you use is based on the anticipated number of networks and hosts per network.

TCP/IP version 4 IP addresses are comprised of sets of 32-bit numbers. When you assign IP addresses, each 8-bit section, or octet, of this 32-bit number is entered in decimal format with each set of numbers separated by periods. With Class A networks, the first octet identifies the network and the last three octets identify the computers on the network, allowing millions of hosts but a small number of networks. With Class B networks, the first and second octet identify the network and the last two octets identify the computers on the network, allowing an equal number of networks and hosts. With Class C networks, the first three octets identify the network and the last octet identifies the computers on the network, allowing many networks and relatively few hosts per network.

Table 5-1 provides an overview of private IP addresses by class. The first and last IP address of a subnet are not usable and cannot be assigned to client computers. The first IP address of a subnet is the network ID. The last IP address of a subnet is the network's broadcast address. With standard network configurations, the network ID is the .0 address of the subnet, such as 192.168.1.0, and the broadcast address is the .255 address of the subnet, such as 192.168.1.255.

Table 5-1. Private network addresses by class

Network class	Network ID	Subnet mask	Assignable IP address range
Class A	10.0.0.0	255.0.0.0	10.0.0.1–10.255.255.254
Class B	172.16.0.0	255.240.0.0	172.16.0.1–172.31.255.254
Class C	192.168.0.0	255.255.0.0	192.168.0.1–192.168.255.254

When assigning IP address ranges, you'll need to specify how many bits of an IP address to use for the network ID and how many bits to use for the host ID. Table 5-2 shows the standard bit lengths and network masks for Class A, B, and C networks.

Table 5-2. Network bit lengths and subnet masks

Network class	Bit length	Subnet mask
Class A	8	255.0.0.0
Class B	16	255.240.0.0
Class C	24	255.255.0.0

Some organizations use subnetting to subdivide networks and create additional logical networks within standard network class ranges. When you use subnetting, the standard class rules for which bits apply to the network ID and which bits apply to the host ID are determined by the subnet mask. For example, you might want to subnet so that the first 26 bits refer to the network ID and the final 6 bits refer to the host ID. This allows you to have 1,024 subnets with up to 62 hosts per subnet.

Many experienced network administrators use a prefix notation when referring to IP addresses where the network ID is followed by the number of bits in the network ID. So, for example, rather than writing or saying that the network 192.168.1.0 has a network mask of 255.255.255.0, you could say the network 192.168.1.0 is a slash 24 network. This is written in network prefix notation as:

192.168.1.0/24

Configuring static IP addressing

You can configure a static IP address by editing the TCP/IP properties for the computer's network adapter. To access the TCP/IP properties of the Local Area Connection and configure them, follow these steps:

1. Click Start → Control Panel → Network Connections → Local Area Connection.
2. Click Properties to open the Local Area Connection Properties dialog box.
3. Click Internet Protocol (TCP/IP) and then select Properties. Be careful not to clear the checkbox. Scroll down through the list of protocols used by the connection if necessary.

4. Select the Use The Following IP Address radio button, and then type the IP address in the IP Address field (see Figure 5-1). The IP address must not be used anywhere else on the network.
5. Windows inserts a default value for the subnet mask into the Subnet Mask field. As necessary, change this to what is used on your subnet.
6. Type the IP address of the default gateway.
7. Type the IP addresses of the preferred and alternate DNS servers.
8. Click OK twice to close all open dialog boxes and apply the changes.

If you use multiple gateways, custom DNS settings, WINS, or IP filtering, you may still need to configure advanced settings. Click the Advanced button on the General tab of the Internet Protocol (TCP/IP) Properties dialog box.

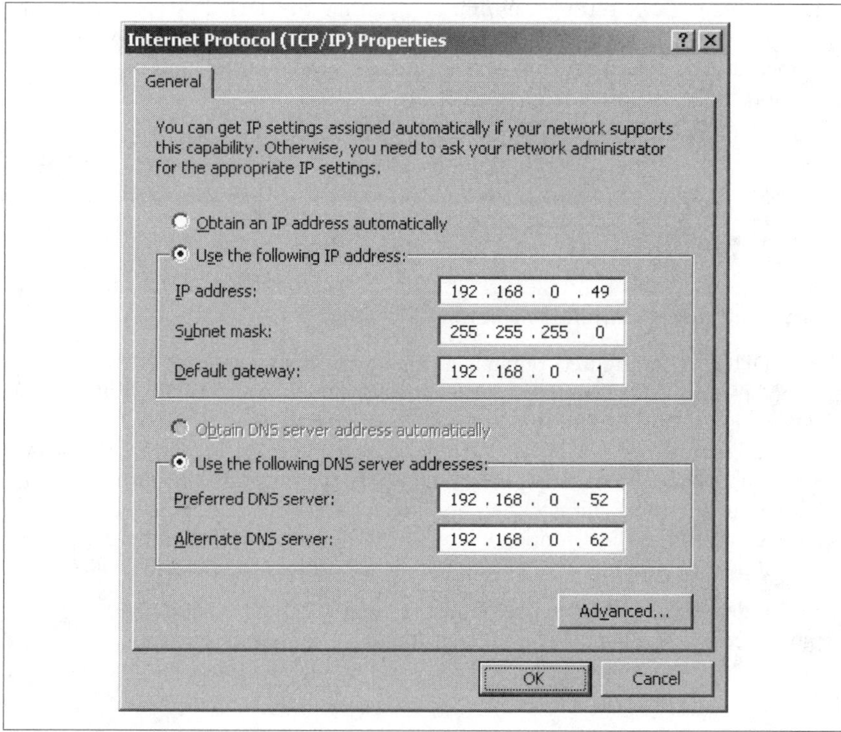

Figure 5-1. Configuring static TCP/IP settings.

Configuring dynamic IP addressing

Dynamic IP addressing is the default configuration for Windows XP Professional and Windows Server 2003. When a computer uses DHCP, the IP address settings are obtained automatically from a DHCP server. Settings for DNS can be obtained automatically as well. This is the default setting.

You can determine whether a computer is using dynamic addressing and which DHPC server is being used by typing `ipconfig /all` at a command prompt. If DHCP is enabled, the output from this command shows the current IP addressing configuration, including details on the DHCP server and IP address lease from this server.

To configure a computer to use DHCP, follow these steps:

1. Click Start → Control Panel → Network Connections → Local Area Connection.
2. Click Properties to open the Local Area Connection Properties dialog box.
3. Click Internet Protocol (TCP/IP) and then select Properties. Be careful not to clear the checkbox. Scroll down through the list of protocols used by the connection if necessary.
4. Select the Obtain An IP Address Automatically radio button (see Figure 5-2).
5. To obtain DNS settings automatically from the DHCP server, select the Obtain DNS Server Address Automatically radio button. Otherwise, select the Use The Following DNS Server Addresses radio button and provide the IP addresses of the preferred and alternate DNS servers.
6. Click OK twice to close all open dialog boxes and apply the changes.

You may still need to configure Automatic Private IP Addressing. See the next section.

Configuring Automatic Private IP Addressing

When DHCP is configured but not available or the client lease is expired and cannot be renewed, clients use Automatic Private IP Addressing. With APIPA, clients assign themselves an IP address in the range 169.254.0.1–169.254.255.254 with a subnet mask of 255.255.0.0. An IP address and subnet mask are the only IP addressing assigned to the computer, limiting its communications; through broadcasts within the local subnet, the computer periodically checks for an available DHCP server (every five minutes). You can also specify user-configured APIPA, which allows an alternate configuration to be used when DHCP isn't available.

You can determine whether a computer is using automatic private addressing by typing `ipconfig /all` at a command prompt. If DHCP is enabled and the IP address is in the range 169.254.0.1–169.254.255.254, the computer is using APIPA.

To review or set a computer's alternate configuration, follow these steps:

1. Click Start → Control Panel → Network Connections → Local Area Connection.
2. Click Properties to open the Local Area Connection Properties dialog box.
3. Click Internet Protocol (TCP/IP) and then select Properties. Be careful not to clear the checkbox. Scroll down through the list of protocols used by the connection if necessary.

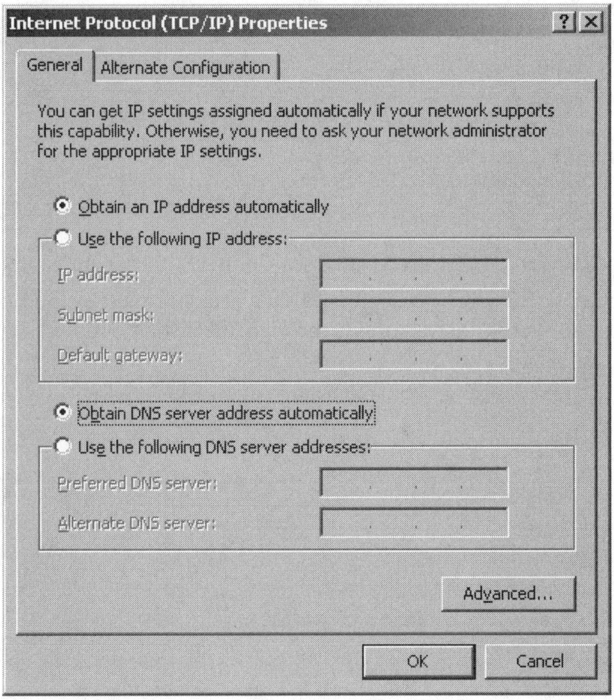

Figure 5-2. Configuring dynamic IP addressing.

4. Click the Alternate Configuration tab as shown in Figure 5-3.
5. Select the Automatic Private IP Address radio button to use the default alternate configuration.
6. Select the User Configured radio button and then provide an alternate IP address, subnet mask, default gateway, and DNS servers as necessary.
7. Click OK twice to close all open dialog boxes and apply the changes.

Troubleshooting TCP/IP Addressing

As you've seen, implementing and managing TCP/IP from a client perspective is fairly straightforward. Each computer needs to be assigned an IP address to communicate on the network. This IP address can be manually assigned, dynamically assigned by a DHCP server, or automatically assigned when DHCP is configured and not available. The subnet mask tells the computer the bounds of its environment—i.e., which bits of the IP address belong to the network ID and which bits belong to the host ID. To communicate between subnets, the computer uses a gateway. To resolve computer names, the computer uses DNS.

When computers can't connect to each other or communicate over the network, the likely culprit is the TCP/IP configuration. To successfully troubleshoot TCP/IP addressing issues, administrators need a strong understanding of the common problems and the probable resolution for those problems.

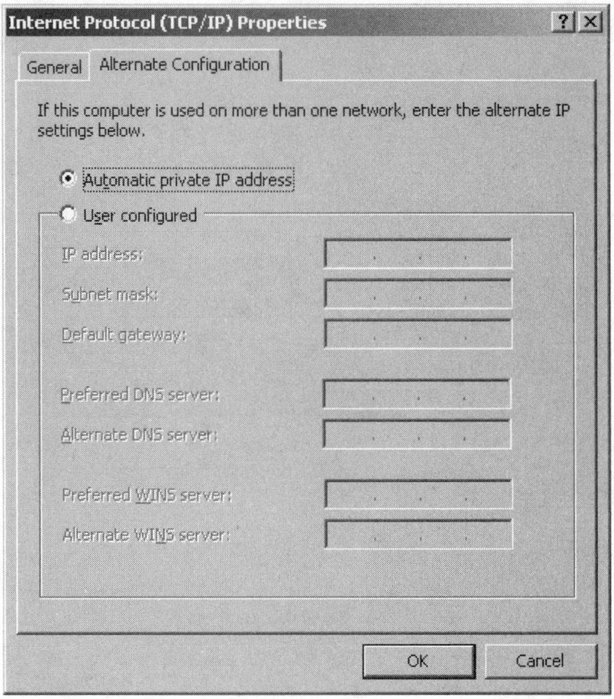

Figure 5-3. Use the default alternate configuration or define your own alternate configuration.

Diagnosing and resolving issues related to APIPA

Automatic Private IP Addressing (APIPA) is designed to ensure that computers that are configured to use dynamic IP addressing are in fact assigned an IP address when DHCP is configured but not available. The default configuration limits the computer's communications to the local subnet. This occurs because the computer is configured with an IP address and subnet mask but without a gateway.

By default, the computer will check for a DHCP server by sending a DHCP Discover message every five minutes. If the computer gets a DHCP Offer back from a DHCP server, the computer then sends a DHCP Request to the server. When the computer gets back a DHCP Acknowledgment, it will use the IP address configuration sent by the DHCP server.

When APIPA is configured and a problem occurs with networking, the computer's network connection may be left in one of three states:

- No address with or without an associated error message.
- An all zeros address.
- A nonzero IP address outside the defined APIPA range.

As odd as it may seem, APIPA requires an active network connection (in most cases) for automatic configuration to work properly. If the network cable to the computer is disconnected or improperly connected, the computer may not be assigned an IP address. When you type `ipconfig /all` at a command prompt, you may see an error stating "Media Disconnected," such as:

```
Windows IP Configuration
        Host Name . . . . . . . . . . . : engws102
        Primary Dns Suffix  . . . . . . :
        Node Type . . . . . . . . . . . : Hybrid
        IP Routing Enabled. . . . . . . : No
        WINS Proxy Enabled. . . . . . . : No
        DNS Suffix Search List. . . . . : domain.local

Ethernet adapter Local Area Connection:

        Media State . . . . . . . . . . : Media disconnected
        Description . . . . . . . . . . : Intel(R) PRO/100 VE Network
Connection
        Physical Address. . . . . . . . : 81-34-2E-4B-CD-E8
        Dhcp Enabled. . . . . . . . . . : No
        Autoconfiguration Enabled . . . : No
        IP Address. . . . . . . . . . . : 192.168.0.102
        Subnet Mask . . . . . . . . . . : 255.255.255.0
        Default Gateway . . . . . . . . : 192.168.0.1
        DNS Servers . . . . . . . . . . : 192.168.0.52
                                          192.168.0.62
```


The media may be disconnected at either end of the network cable. To resolve the problem, check the network cable connected to the computer and then type `ipconfig /all` again. If this doesn't resolve the problem, you may have a faulty cable, hub, switch, or network interface card.

If typing `ipconfig /all` doesn't provide a configuration summary, the network adapter may be disabled or faulty. If typing `ipconfig /all` shows an IP address of all zeros, the likely reason is that the dynamic IP address was released using `ipconfig /release` and was not renewed. You can attempt to renew the IP address by typing `ipconfig /renew` at a command prompt. If the all zeros address isn't cleared, then APIPA may be disabled in the Registry.

On Windows 2000 or later, you can disable APIPA by creating the IPAutoconfigurationEnabled as a DWORD value-entry under HKEY_LOCAL_MACHINE → System → CurrentControlSet → Services → Tcpip → Parameters → Interfaces → AdapterGUID, where AdapterGUID is the globally unique identifier (GUID) for the computer's network adapter. Set the value to 0x0 to disable APIPA. Set the value to 0x1 to enable APIPA. After you change this Registry entry, you must restart the computer.

If typing `ipconfig /all` shows an IP address outside the defined APIPA range, the computer may have dynamic addressing from a previous location or it may have a user-defined alternate configuration. You can resolve the incorrect dynamic IP addressing issue by typing `ipconfig /release`, and then typing `ipconfig /renew` at a command prompt. You can determine whether the computer has a user-defined alternate configuration by checking the Internet Protocol (TCP/IP) properties of the network adapter.

Diagnosing and resolving issues related to incorrect TCP/IP configuration

Although configuring TCP/IP is fairly straightforward, diagnosing and resolving issues related to incorrect configurations isn't always. The two biggest issues you'll see have to do with the computer's network cable and network configuration.

With static IP addressing, the computer is assigned the designated IP address as long as the network adapter is active. If typing `ipconfig /all` doesn't provide a configuration summary, the network adapter may be disabled or faulty. If you see an error stating "Media Disconnected," the media may be disconnected at either end of the network cable. To resolve the problem, check the network cable connected to the computer and then type `ipconfig /all` again. If this doesn't resolve the problem, you may have a faulty cable, hub, switch, or network interface card.

With any type of IP addressing configuration, improper settings will cause communications problems. Some of the problems and symptoms are as follows:

Invalid gateway configuration
: Computer may be able to communicate on local subnet but not across subnets. Computer won't be able to access resources in other subnets or connect to computers in other subnets.

Invalid IP address
: Except for broadcast communications, computer may not be able to communicate on local subnet or across subnets.

Invalid subnet mask
: Computer may not know appropriate subnet boundaries and may not route communications through a gateway when it should.

Invalid DNS configuration
: Computer may not be able to use name resolution or may fail to resolve computer names.

Invalid WINS configuration
: Windows Internet Naming Service (WINS) is used with pre-Windows 2000 computers and resources. Computer may not be able to resolve NetBIOS computer names and therefore may not be able to communicate with pre-Windows 2000 computers and resources.

You should use `ipconfig /all` to determine the computer's IP addressing configuration. If you notice incorrect settings, configure the appropriate settings using the Internet Protocol (TCP/IP) properties of the network adapter. Some problems with DNS can be caused by caching of old DNS records. You can use the following commands to diagnose and resolve DNS caching issues:

`ipconfig /displaydns`
: Displays the entries in the DNS cache.

`ipconfig /flushdns`
: Purges the entries in the DNS cache.

`ipconfig /registerdns`
: Refreshes all leased IP addresses and re-registers DNS for these entries.

Duplicate IP addressing can cause problems as well. With unicast IP addresses, only one computer on a subnet can use an IP address. Unlike earlier versions of Windows, Windows XP Professional and Windows Server 2003 display warning prompts if a computer is using the same IP address as another computer. Before assigning a computer an IP address, you can determine whether an IP address is in use by:

1. Opening a command prompt on a computer with a working and valid IP address configuration.
2. Typing `ping`, followed by the IP address, such as: `ping 192.168.1.15`.
3. If you receive a reply from the IP address, it is in use.

Provided that the `ping` requests are not being blocked by firewalls or proxy servers, `ping` can also be used to determine if a computer can connect to another computer. If you ping an IP address that is valid and should be reachable, and you get a response of "could not find host" or "request timed out," there may be a IP addressing configuration problem or there may be a problem with the physical network or cabling. Here is an example of an unsuccessful `ping`:

```
Pinging 192.169.25.2 with 32 bytes of data:

Request timed out.
Request timed out.
Request timed out.
Request timed out.

Ping statistics for 192.169.25.2:
    Packets: Sent = 4, Received = 0, Lost = 4 (100% loss),
```

Address Resolution Protocol (ARP) is used to lookup hardware MAC addresses. After TCP/IP uses ARP to determine a hardware MAC address, the client computer stores the IP-to-MAC address details in its local ARP cache. You can view the ARP cache contents by typing `arp -a` at a command prompt. You can clear the ARP cache by typing `arp -d` at a command prompt. If a computer's network adapter has just been changed, the old hardware MAC address will be stored by computers on the network. Dynamic entries in the ARP cache are automatically aged out after two minutes. However, you can clear the cache prior to this time or at any time if the cache isn't cleared for some reason.

Other commands you can use for troubleshooting include `tracert` and `pingpath`. Both tools are useful when you suspect there is a problem with the physical network between the computer you are working with and the one you are trying to reach. The results of `tracert` will indicate the specific point along the communications path where failure occurs. If the `tracert` fails at a router or gateway, this can indicate a problem with the router or gateway. The results of `pingpath` are essentially a combination of `ping` and `tracert`. Again, the results can help you identify a point of failure along the communications path.

The difference between `tracert` and `pathping` is important on the exam. Generally, you use `tracert` to quickly determine where there is a problem or break in the path of connectivity to a remote location. When you have connectivity to a remote location, but are experiencing intermittent problems, erratic pack loss, or delays, `pathping` is the command to use as it shows you exactly where packet loss occurs and the length of delays.

The Windows Support Tools include Netdiag for performing comprehensive network diagnostics and end-to-end connectivity testing. To run Netdiag, type `netdiag` at a command prompt. Netdiag will then test:

- Current configuration status
- Autoconfiguration status
- Default gateway settings
- Domain membership
- IP loopback
- DNS
- DC discovery
- DC list
- Kerberos
- LDAP
- Bindings

Test results are given as Passed, Failed, or Skipped. Some tests are skipped by default. Any test can be performed individually using the form:

```
netdiag /test:TestName
```

For example:

```
netdiag /test:dns
```

Here is an example of a failed DNS test:

```
DNS test . . . . . . . . . . . . . . : Failed
            [WARNING] Cannot find a primary authoritative DNS server for the
                 name
              'corpsvr21.cpandl.com.'. [WSAEADDRNOTAVAIL           ]
              The name 'corpsvr21.cpandl.com.' may not be registered in DNS.
            [WARNING] Cannot find a primary authoritative DNS server for the
                 name
              'corpsvr21.cpandl.com.'. [ERROR_TIMEOUT]
              The name 'corpsvr21.cpandl.com.' may not be registered in DNS.
            [WARNING] Cannot find a primary authoritative DNS server for the
                 name
              'corpsvr21.cpandl.com.'. [WSAEADDRNOTAVAIL           ]
              The name 'corpsvr21.cpandl.com.' may not be registered in DNS.
            [WARNING] Cannot find a primary authoritative DNS server for the
                 name
              'corpsvr21.cpandl.com.'. [ERROR_TIMEOUT]
```

```
        The name 'corpsvr21.cpandl.com.' may not be registered in DNS.
    [WARNING] The DNS entries for this DC are not registered correctly on
DNS server '0.0.0.0'. Please wait for 30 minutes for DNS server replication.
    [FATAL] No DNS servers have the DNS records for this DC registered.
```

As shown, the output provides sufficient detail to help you diagnose and resolve the problem. In this example, DNS is not properly configured for the domain.

Installing, Configuring, and Managing DHCP

Dynamic Host Configuration Protocol (DHCP) is an essential network infrastructure component. By default, Windows XP Professional and Windows Server 2003 computers use DHCP to obtain their network settings for TCP/IP and DNS. Through DHCP, you can manage the assignment of:

- IP addresses
- Subnet masks
- Defaults gateways
- Preferred and alternate DNS servers
- WINS servers
- Extended TCP/IP options

Not only does dynamic configuration of IP addressing and other network settings free administrators from having to perform manual configurations on each computer in the organization, it also makes long-term management of these computers easier by centralizing and automating network configuration management. Using DHCP, you can update the network configuration of any dynamically configured computer simply by making the appropriate setting changes on your organization's DHCP servers. In contrast, with manual configuration, you must change the network configuration settings on each individual machine.

Understanding DHCP

DHCP is a client/server technology. Any computer configured to dynamically obtain its network configuration settings is considered to be a DHCP client. A computer that provides DHCP services to a client is referred to as a DHCP server. DHCP servers assign IP addresses to clients for a specific period of time known as the *lease duration*. The default lease duration is eight days. Clients with active leases must renew their leases periodically.

For clients that might need to have permanent leases, you can create a reservation on a lease by specifying the IP address to reserve and the MAC address of the computer that will hold the reserved IP address. Thereafter, the client with the specified MAC address will use the IP address designated in the reservation.

When you work with DHCP servers, keep the following in mind:

- Any server that you want to configure as a DHCP server must have a static IP address.
- DHCP servers maintain a database of the IP addresses available, in use, and reserved. This database, like any other database, must be periodically maintained.

- Every DHCP server must have at least one active scope to grant leases to clients. A *scope* is simply a range of IP addresses to be leased to DHCP clients.
- Within a scope, you can define a subset of IP addresses that you do not want to be assigned to clients using exclusions. An *exclusion* is an IP address or a range of IP addresses not included in the scope and not assigned to clients.
- Using *Reservations*, you can define addresses that should always be assigned to specific clients.

On a network using Active Directory domains, you can install and configure DHCP by completing the following procedures:

1. Install the DHCP server service on your designated DHCP servers.
2. Authorize the DHCP servers in Active Directory.
3. Configure the DHCP servers so they can assign dynamic configurations to clients.
4. Activate at least one scope on each DHCP server.

Once you've completed these steps, clients in the domain will be able to obtain leases. When working with DHCP in workgroups, you do not need to perform Step 2.

Installing the DHCP Server Service

With Windows Server 2003, any server assigned a static IP address can run the DHCP Server service and act as a DHCP server. However, it is recommended that domain controllers not be configured as DHCP servers. In a standard configuration, DHCP is integrated with DNS, and DHCP clients are permitted to create, alter, and remove their own records. If you install DHCP on a DC, any client on the network might be able to alter critical service locator (SRV) records, which is an unnecessary security risk.

You must be an administrator to install windows components, including the DHCP Server service. The account you use for installing the DHCP should be a member of the global Domain Admins groups or the domain local DHCP Administrators group.

You can install the DHCP Server service by completing the following steps:

1. Open Add Or Remove Programs in the Control Panel.
2. In the Add Or Remove Programs window, click Add/Remove Windows Components.
3. Click Networking Services and then select Properties. Be careful not to clear the checkbox.
4. Select Dynamic Host Configuration Protocol (DHCP), and then click OK.
5. Click Next. Setup configures the server's components.
6. Click Finish.

You can also install the DHCP Server service using the Configure Your Server Wizard. To start the wizard, click Start → Programs → Administrative Tools → Configure Your Server Wizard. Click Next twice, and then under Server Roles, select DNS Server, and then click Next. Review the installation tasks that will be performed, and click Next again. When the wizard finishes, it will start the New Scope Wizard, which you can use to create the initial scope on the DHCP server, or you can click the Cancel button if you want to configure the initial scope later.

Working with and Authorizing the DHCP Server

Like any Windows service, the DHCP Server service can be managed using the Services utility in Administrative Tools. However, the best way to manage the DHCP Server service and DHCP itself is to use the DHCP console, which can be accessed by clicking Start → Programs → Administrative Tools → DHCP.

When you start the DHCP console on a DHCP server, the console connects automatically to DHCP on this server. If you start the DHCP console on your workstation or want to connect to a different DHCP server, you can do this by right-clicking the DHCP node, and selecting Add Server. You can then use the Add Server dialog box to select the remote server you want to work with by its fully qualified domain name or IP address. Currently authorized DHCP servers are listed as well.

As shown in Figure 5-4, the status of a DHCP server is displayed in the right pane when you select the DHCP node. A status of "Not Authorized" means the server has not yet been authorized for use in the domain of which the server is a member. Before a DHCP server can be used on an Active Directory domain, it must be authorized in Active Directory. To authorize the DHCP server, click Action → Manage Authorized Servers. In the Manage Authorized Servers dialog box, click Authorize, type the name or IP address of the DHCP server to authorize, and then click OK.

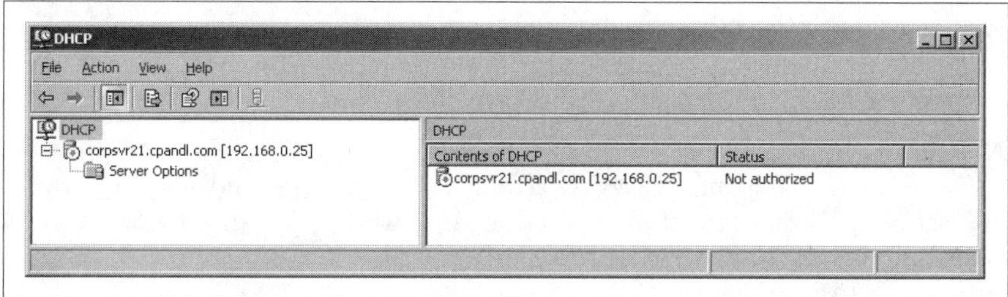

Figure 5-4. The DHCP console.

With DHCP servers configured in workgroups or standalone configurations, you do not need authorization prior to using the DHCP server—workgroups do not have domain controllers and do not use Active Directory. If your organization has workgroups that use DHCP or you plan to configure a standalone DHCP server, you must ensure the DHCP server is not on the same subnet as a domain's authorized DHCP server. With Windows 2000 or later, a workgroup or standalone DHCP server configured on the same subnet as a domain's authorized DHCP server is considered to be a rogue server. As part of a network protection process, the rogue server automatically stops its DHCP Server service and stops leasing IP addresses to clients as soon as it detects an authorized DHCP server on the local subnet.

To authorize a DHCP server for use in the domain of which the server is a member, follow these steps:

1. Open the DHCP console and connect to the server if necessary.
2. Right-click the server's entry and then select Authorize.

To authorize multiple servers, you can use the following technique:

1. Open the DHCP console.
2. Right-click the DHCP node and then select Manage Authorized Servers.
3. Click the Authorize button.
4. Type the fully qualified domain name or IP address of the DHCP server to authorize.
5. Click OK.

Once you've authorized the DHCP server, you have full access to manage the server, and clients can connect to the server to obtain IP address leases and their network configuration settings. The DHCP Server service on any DHCP server can be managed in the DHCP console by right-clicking the server entry and clicking All Tasks. You can then start, stop, pause, or restart the DHCP Server service.

As part of routine maintenance, you should periodically back up the DHCP server database and perform a manual compact of the database. See "Managing DHCP Databases," later in this chapter for details.

Creating and Configuring Scopes

Before a DHCP server can lease IP addresses and send clients their network configurations, you must create and activate the scopes that will provide these settings to clients. DHCP supports three types of scopes:

Normal scope
: A scope for assigning Class A, B, and C IP addresses and related network settings. These unicast IP address classes were summarized previously in Table 5-1.

Multicast scope
: A scope for assigning Class D IP addresses and related network settings. Class D addresses use multicasting with TCP/IP version 4 and begin with a number between 224 and 239 for the first part of the address.

Superscope
: A container for scopes that allows you to more easily work with multiple scopes. After you create a superscope, you can add to it the scopes you want to manage as a group.

Each of these scope types can be created using the DHCP console.

Creating and activating normal scopes

You should create a scope for each range of IP addresses on a logical subnet that you want to manage using DHCP. The logical subnet associated with a range of IP addresses is defined by the related subnet mask. If there are subsets of IP addresses within a range that should not be assigned to clients, you can define exclusions to block the addresses so that they aren't assigned to clients. A scope can include optional parameters to configure client TCP/IP settings for default gateways, preferred and alternate DNS servers, and more.

A single DHCP server can provide dynamic addressing and configuration for multiple subnets. However, routing and relays must be appropriately configured between the subnets. See "Managing DHCP Relay Agents," later in this chapter for details.

To create a normal scope, follow these steps:

1. Open the DHCP console and connect to the server if necessary.
2. Right-click the server's entry and then select New Scope.
3. When the New Scope Wizard starts, click Next.
4. Type a name and description for the scope. Click Next.
5. On the IP Address Range page, shown in Figure 5-5, enter the start and end IP address to use for the scope. Specify the first and last usable IP only; do not specify the network ID or broadcast address as part of the range.
6. Enter the appropriate bit length or subnet mask and then click Next.
7. If the range of IP addresses you enter crosses subnet boundaries, the New Scope Wizard will create one scope for each subnet and add these scopes to a superscope. You'll be able to set the superscope name and description on the Create Superscope page. Otherwise, this page is not displayed.
8. On the Add Exclusions page, configure any IP addresses that should be excluded from the scope, as shown in Figure 5-6. Enter separate IP addresses and then click Add. Or enter a start and end IP address range and then click Add. When you are finished defining any exclusions, click Next.
9. Set the lease duration to determine the length of time a client can use an IP address before it must be renewed. The default lease duration is eight days. Click Next.
10. On the Configure DHCP Options page, click "Yes, I want to configure these options now" and then click Next.
11. Use the Router (Default Gateway) page to configure default gateways. In the IP Address field, enter the IP address of the primary default gateway and then click Add. Repeat this process to specify other default gateways. Click Next.
12. Use the Domain Name and DNS Servers page to configure DNS name resolution options. In the Parent Domain field, type the name of the parent domain to use for DNS resolution of computer names that aren't fully qualified. In the IP Address field, type the IP address of the primary DNS server and then click Add. Repeat this process to specify additional DNS servers. Click Next.

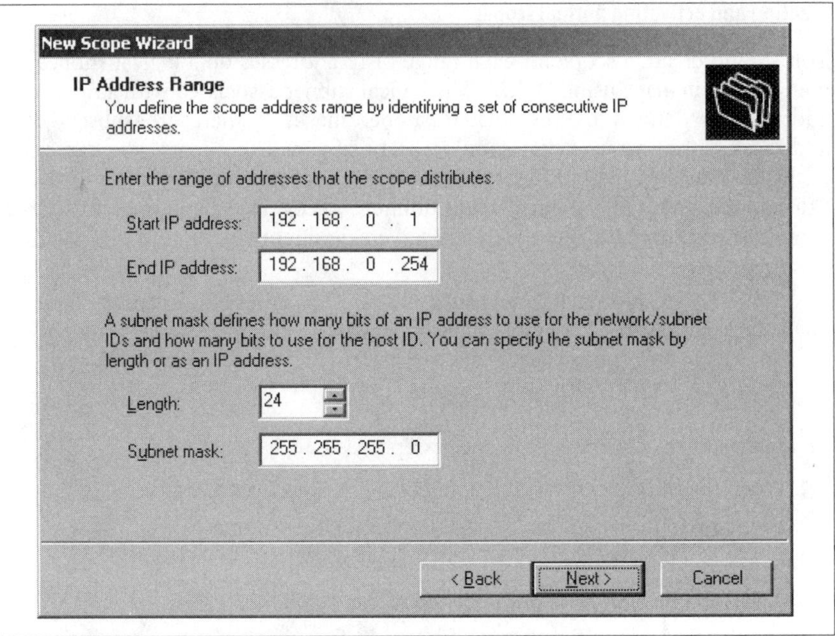

Figure 5-5. Specify the IP address range and subnet mask for the scope.

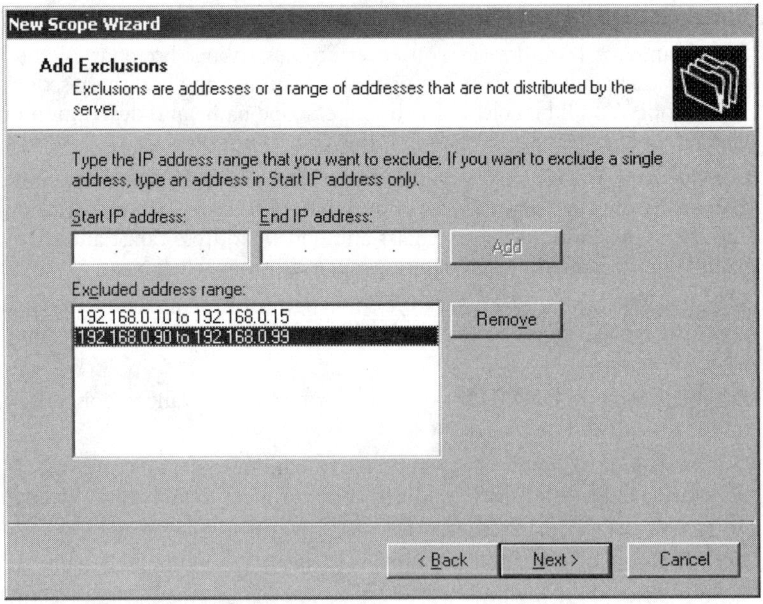

New Scope Wizard

Add Exclusions

Exclusions are addresses or a range of addresses that are not distributed by the server.

Type the IP address range that you want to exclude. If you want to exclude a single address, type an address in Start IP address only.

Start IP address: End IP address: Add

Excluded address range:

192.168.0.10 to 192.168.0.15
192.168.0.90 to 192.168.0.99

Remove

< Back Next > Cancel

Figure 5-6. Specify any IP address exclusions.

13. Use the WINS Servers page to configure NetBIOS name resolution options. In the IP Address field, type the IP address of the primary WINS server and then click Add. Repeat this process to specify additional WINS servers. Click Next.
14. Ensure the scope is activated by clicking "Yes, I want to activate this scope now." Click Next and then click Finish.

The new scope is created and listed under the DHCP server node in the DHCP console. You can activate or deactivate a scope at anytime by right-clicking it and selecting Activate or Deactivate.

Creating and activating multicast scopes

Multicast scopes are used on networks that use TCP/IP version 4 multicasting. With multicasting, multiple computers have the same destination IP address. These computers listen for packets sent to this address, allowing a single source host to send packets of information to multiple destination hosts. Class D IP addresses from 224.0.0.0 to 239.255.255.255 are used for multicasting.

To create a multicast scope, follow these steps:

1. Open the DHCP console and connect to the server if necessary.
2. Right-click the server's entry and then select New Multicast Scope.
3. When the New Multicast Scope Wizard starts, click Next.
4. Type a name and description for the multicast scope. Click Next.
5. On the IP Address Range page, enter the start and end IP address to use for the multicast scope.
6. Use the Time To Live (TTL) value to control the number of routers multicast traffic can pass through on your network. The default value is 32. Click Next.
7. On the Add Exclusions page, configure any IP addresses that should be excluded from the multicast scope. Enter separate IP addresses and then click Add. Or enter a start and end IP address range and then click Add. When you are finished defining any exclusions, click Next.
8. Set the lease duration to determine the length of time a client can use an IP address before it must be renewed. The default lease duration is 30 days. Click Next.
9. Ensure the scope is activated by clicking "Yes." Click Next and then click Finish.

The new multicast scope is created and listed under the DHCP server node in the DHCP console. You can activate or deactivate a multicast scope at anytime by right-clicking it and selecting Activate or Deactivate.

Creating and using superscopes

Superscopes allow you to group scopes for easier management. By activating or deactivating the superscope, you can activate or deactivate all the related scopes.

When you have already created one or more scopes, you can create a superscope by completing the following steps:

1. Open the DHCP console and connect to the server if necessary.
2. Right-click the server's entry and then select New Superscope.
3. When the New Superscope Wizard starts, click Next.
4. Type a name for the superscope and then click Next.
5. Select scopes to add to the superscope.
6. Click Next and then click Finish.

The new superscope is created and listed under the DHCP server node in the DHCP console. Some of the key tasks you'll want to perform with superscopes include:

Activating or deactivating scopes
: To activate or deactivate all scopes within the superscope at anytime, right-click the superscope and select Activate or Deactivate.

Adding scopes
: To add a scope to an existing superscope, right-click the scope and then select Add To Superscope. In the dialog box displayed, select a superscope and then click OK.

Removing scopes
: To remove a scope from a superscope, right-click a scope and then select Remove From Superscope. Confirm the action by clicking Yes when prompted. If this is the last scope in the superscope, the superscope is deleted automatically.

You can use superscopes to support dynamic IP addressing for multinets. A multinet is a single physical network with multiple logical subnets. To support each subnet in the multinet, you create a scope for each subnet and then add the scopes to a superscope. Because DHCP Relay Agents include details on the originating subnet, a DHCP server on a remote subnet will know which scope to use when.

When the organization has multiple DHCP servers, superscopes are useful for ensuring DHCP servers can assign the proper IP addressing to clients as well. For example, when two DHCP servers are on the same subnet and service clients on multiple subnets, you can create a superscope of both servers that includes as members all scopes defined on the physical subnet or subnets. To prevent the servers from issuing leases in each other's scopes, configure each server so that the IP address ranges of the other server are excluded.

Managing DHCP Scope Options

When you create a DHCP scope, you can define key TCP/IP options, including the default gateway, preferred and alternate DNS servers, and preferred and alternate WINS servers. These TCP/IP options, and many others, can be managed individually as well. Using the DHCP console, you can manage these options at five separate levels using:

Predefined options
You can configure preset values for TCP/IP options and to create additional TCP/IP options. To configure preset value or define additional options, right-click the server node and then select Set Predefined Options.

Server options
You can configure TCP/IP options that are assigned to all scopes created on a server. Server options can be overridden by scope, class, and reservation options. To configure server options, expand the server node, right-click Server Options, and then select Configure Options. When you select Server Options, any current server options defined are listed in the right pane.

Scope options
You can configure TCP/IP options that are assigned to all clients that use a scope. Only normal scopes have scope options; these options can be overridden by class and reservation options. To configure scope options, expand the server node, expand the scope node, right-click Scope Options, and then select Configure Options. When you select Server Options, any current scope options defined are listed in the right pane.

Class options
You can assign TCP/IP options based on membership in a particular class. Client classes can be user- or vendor-defined. Vendor classes created automatically are the "Default Routing and Remote Access Class" and the "Default BOOTP Class." User classes created automatically are "Microsoft Options" for Windows NT 4.0 computers, "Microsoft Windows 98 Options" for Windows 98 computers, and "Microsoft Windows 2000 Options" for Windows 2000 computers. These options can be overridden by reservation options. To configure class options, right-click the server node and then select Define User Classes or Define Vendor Classes as appropriate.

Reservation options
You can set TCP/IP options for individual computers with reservations. After you create a reservation for a client, you can right-click the reservation and select Configure Options to set the reservation options. Manually assigned TCP/IP settings only override reservation options (and all other options).

You'll find that user and vendor classes are particularly important when you are configured DHCP for a specific type of client. For example, you might want all Windows 2000 clients to use a specific set of options that is different from all Windows XP Professional clients. To do this, define settings for the user class Microsoft Windows 2000 Options. You may also want remote access clients to use specific settings that are different from local clients. To do this, define settings for the vendor class Default Routing and Remote Access Class.

When you are working with server and scope options, you'll see a dialog box similar to the one shown in Figure 5-7. To enable an option and configure it, select the related checkbox, and then use the Data Entry options to configure the option.

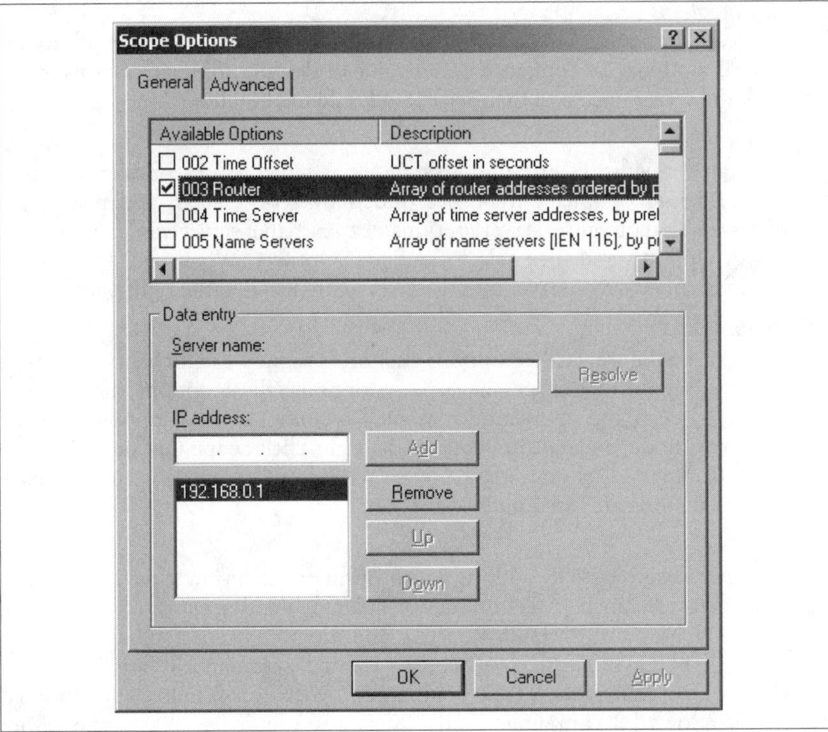

Figure 5-7. Set server and scope options.

Table 5-3 provides an overview of the TCP/IP options used on most networks. Each option is identified by its option name and associated option code. Option code 53, which cannot be configured, is included with every DHCP message and is used to set the message type as DHCP Discover, DHCP Offer, DHCP Request, or DHCP Acknowledgement. Every DHCP message header includes DCHP: Option Field as its final field, and the DHCP Message Type is listed as the first option field.

Table 5-3. Key TCP/IP options

Option name	Option code	Description
DNS Domain Name	015	Sets the DNS domain name to use when resolving unqualified host names using DNS
DNS Servers	006	Sets the primary and alternate DNS servers in preference order
Router	003	Sets the default gateways in preference order
WINS/NBNS Servers	044	Sets the primary and alternate WINS servers in preference order
WINS/NBT Node Type	046	Sets the method to use when resolving NetBIOS names

Using Dynamic DNS Updates with DHCP

DNS is the primary name service used with networks running Windows 2000 and later computers. DNS uses host (A) records to resolve computer names to IP addresses for forward lookups and pointer (PTR) records to resolve IP addresses to computer names for reverse lookups. In the standard configuration of DNS and DHCP, DHCP clients running Windows 2000 or later update their host (A) records in DNS automatically whenever an IP address is assigned or renewed, and DHCP servers update the pointer (PTR) records on behalf of clients.

In the DHCP console, you can control the default behavior by configuring the properties of the DHCP server. Right-click the server entry and then select Properties. Use the options on the DNS tab shown in Figure 5-8 to determine how dynamic DNS updating works. The configuration options available are as follows:

Enable DNS Dynamic Updates According To The Settings Below. This option is enabled by default. Select this checkbox to allow DNS dynamic updates. If you clear this option, the DHCP will not attempt to update dynamic updates on behalf of Windows 2000 or later clients.

Dynamically Update DNS A And PTR Records Only If Requested By The DHCP Clients. Allows the DHCP server to use dynamic updates if requested by Windows 2000 or later clients. By default, DHCP clients request that servers update only their PTR records.

Always Dynamically Update DNS A And PTR Records. Allows the DHCP server to use dynamic updates for A and PTR records when addresses are assigned or renewed regardless of client requests. Affects Windows 2000 or later clients only.

Discard A And PTR Records When Lease Is Deleted. This option is enabled by default. Allows the DHCP server to remove client resource records from DNS when their DHCP addresses leases expire.

Dynamically Update DNS A And PTR Records For DHCP Clients That Do Not Request Updates. Allows the DHCP server to dynamically update A and PTR records for DHCP clients not capable of requesting updates, such as Windows NT 4.0 clients.

When clients register their own A records, the method they use to create and update records is not secure. This allows any client or server, with appropriate credentials, to modify or delete the records. On the other hand, if a DHCP server dynamically updates A and PTR records on behalf of clients, the server uses secure dynamic updates. DNS records created using secure dynamic updates can only be updated by the server that created the record (the record owner). Although this improves security, this can lead to stale (old) records on the DNS server if the DHCP server that owns a record fails and a client is later assigned a lease from a second DHCP server. Consider the following scenario:

1. DHCP Server 1 performs a secure dynamic update of the A and PTR records for a client.
2. DHCP Server 1 is the owner of those records.
3. If DHCP Server 1 fails, neither the client nor DHCP Server 2 will able to update the previously created records.

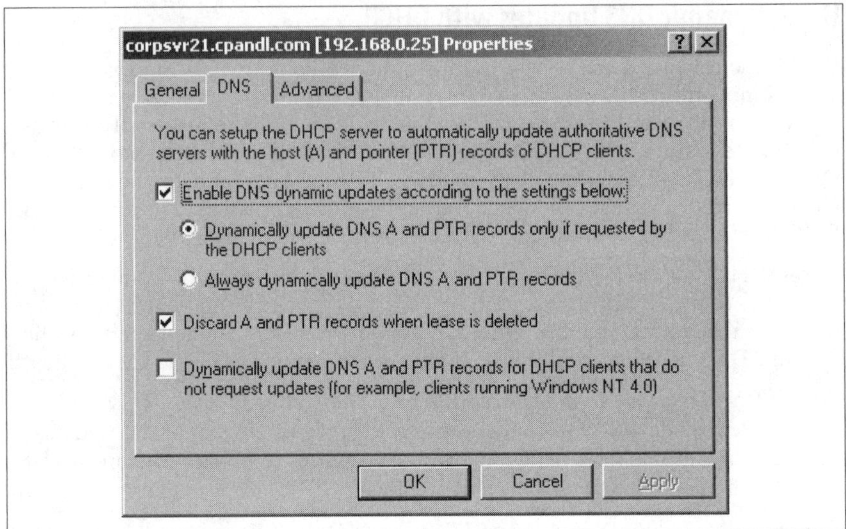

Figure 5-8. Configure dynamic DNS updating through the DHCP server properties.

When DHCP servers update both the A and PTR records, you can prevent problems due to stale records by making your organization's DHCP servers members of the DnsUpdateProxy security group. Any objects created by members of this group do not have security settings and thus have no owners. This allows any DHCP server to modify the record. However, if the DHCP server is not a member of the DnsUpdateProxy group, the DHCP server becomes the owner and no other DHCP servers can modify the record.

The DnsUpdateProxy group can be used in configurations where clients update A records and DHCP servers update PTR records. However, this can introduce additional problems and is not recommended.

In most cases, domain controllers should not be configured as DHCP servers. If DCs are configured as DHCP servers, and those servers are members of the DnsUpdateProxy group, records created by the Netlogon service for the DC are not secure.

Managing DHCP Clients and Leases

DHCP servers lease IP addresses to clients for specific periods of time. By default, for normal scopes, the lease duration is eight days. Leases are assigned initially and renewed using different techniques.

During startup of a client configured to use DHCP, a client without a current lease does the following:

1. **Discover**. Sends a DHCP Discover broadcast on the network using its MAC address and NetBIOs name. If no DHCP server responds to the initial request, the client sends the broadcast again after 2, 4, 8, and 16 seconds. If no DHCP server responds to the subsequent requests, the client assigns itself an automatic private IP address and then sends DHCP Discover broadcasts every five minutes waiting for a DHCP server response.
2. **Offer**. DHCP servers on a network that receive a DHCP Discover message respond with a DHCP Offer message, which offers the client an IP address lease.
3. **Request**. Clients accept the first offer received by broadcasting a DHCP Request message for the offered IP address.
4. **Acknowledgment**. The server accepts the request by sending the client a DHCP Acknowledgment message.

By default, DHCP discover messages are only broadcast on the client's local subnet. Before a DHCP client can contact a DHCP server on a remote subnet, you must configure a DHCP Relay Agent as discussed in "Managing DHCP Relay Agents," later in this chapter.

Clients attempt to renew their leases periodically by sending a DHCP Request to the DHCP server. The server accepts the request by sending the client a DHCP Acknowledgment message. Clients attempt to renew their leases at each restart, when the `ipconfig /renew` command is run at the client, when 50 percent of the lease time has passed, and when 87.5 percent of the lease time has expired.

When a client fails to contact a DHCP server, it pings the default gateway previously assigned, and the response (or lack of response) determines what happens next. Essentially, if the client gets a response from the default gateway, it assumes it is on the same subnet as before and continues to use the lease, attempting to renew it at the appropriate intervals (based on 50 or 87.5 percent expiration). If the client doesn't get a response from the default gateway, it assumes it is on a different subnet and configures itself to use APIPA, and then sends DHCP Discover broadcasts every five minutes.

Manage lease durations on a per-scope basis. To view or change the current lease duration, follow these steps:

1. Open the DHCP console and connect to the server if necessary.
2. Right-click the server's entry and then select Properties.
3. The Lease Duration options show the current lease settings (see Figure 5-9). Modify the settings as necessary and then click OK.

You can view and manage the current leases assigned to clients by following these steps:

1. Open the DHCP console and connect to the server if necessary.
2. Expand the associated superscope (if any) and the associated scope.

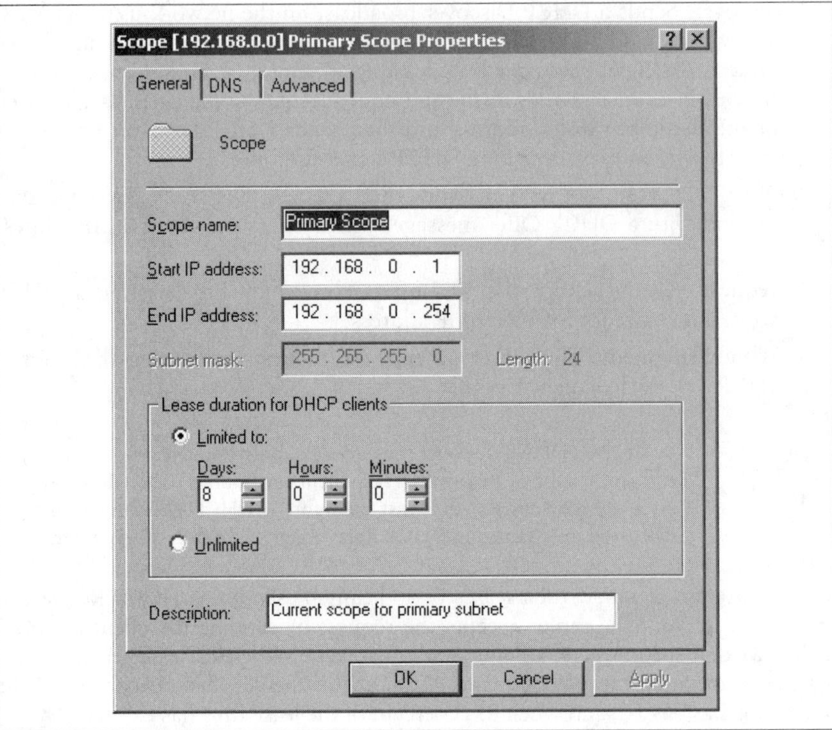

Figure 5-9. Configure the lease duration for each scope separately.

3. Select the Address Leases node. Leases are listed according to client IP address and include the client name, lease expiration, lease type, and the client's unique ID (MAC address). If a client has a reservation, the Lease Expiration entry shows the value `Reservation` followed by the status of the lease as either "active" for in-use leases or "inactive" for not-yet-in-use leases.
4. To force a client to acquire a new IP address, you can right-click the lease in the Active Leases list and then select Delete.

If you need to replace a DHCP server that failed recently and were not able to migrate an up-to-date DHCP database to this server, you may need to enable conflict detection to prevent the new DHCP server from assigning IP addresses that are already in use. With Conflict Detection enabled, the DHCP server pings an address on the network before assigning it to a client. You can enable conflict detection and specify the number of times the DHCP server should ping an IP address before assigning it by completing the following steps:

1. Open the DHCP console and connect to the server if necessary.
2. Right-click the server's entry and then select Properties.
3. On the Advanced tab, set the Conflict Detection Attempts option to the number of times to ping an IP address before assigning it. A value of zero disables conflict detection and is the default setting.

On clients, you can view and manage IP address lease details using ipconfig. As previously discussed, `ipconfig /all` lists all TCP/IP settings, `ipconfig /release` releases an IP address lease, and `ipconfig /renew` renews an IP address lease.

Managing Reservations and Reserved Clients

Use reservations to create permanent address leases assignments. For example, you might want member servers to use DHCP so they can easily be moved between or within subnets if necessary, but might not want a server's IP address to change without specific reason for such a change. In this case, you can define a reservation for the member server.

Reservation definitions must be created on each DHCP server that provides dynamic addressing on the subnet. If you don't do this, a DHCP client can potentially get assigned a different IP address by one of the other DHCP servers on the subnet.

To define a reservation for a computer, you must know the MAC address of the computer's network adapter. For a client computer with a current lease, this can be determined by locating the scope under which the lease is assigned and then finding the client lease entry. The MAC address for the client's network adapter is listed in the Unique ID column. The MAC Address is also listed as the Physical Address of the network adapter when you type `ipconfig /all` at a command prompt.

Reserved addresses cannot be part of an excluded IP address range.

Exam 70-291 Study Guide

You can reserve a DHCP address for a client by completing these steps:

1. Open the DHCP console and connect to the server if necessary.
2. Expand the associated superscope (if any) and the associated scope.
3. Select the Reservations node. Current reservations are listed by IP address and reservation name in the right pane.
4. Right-click the Reservations node, and then click New Reservation.
5. In the Reservation Name field, type a descriptive name for the reservation (see Figure 5-10).
6. In the IP Address field, type the IP address you want to reserve for the client. This IP address must be within the valid range for the currently selected scope.
7. In the MAC Address field, type the MAC Address for the client's network adapter. You can enter this as a number string with or without dashes.
8. Type an optional comment in the Description field.
9. Click Add to create the reservation.

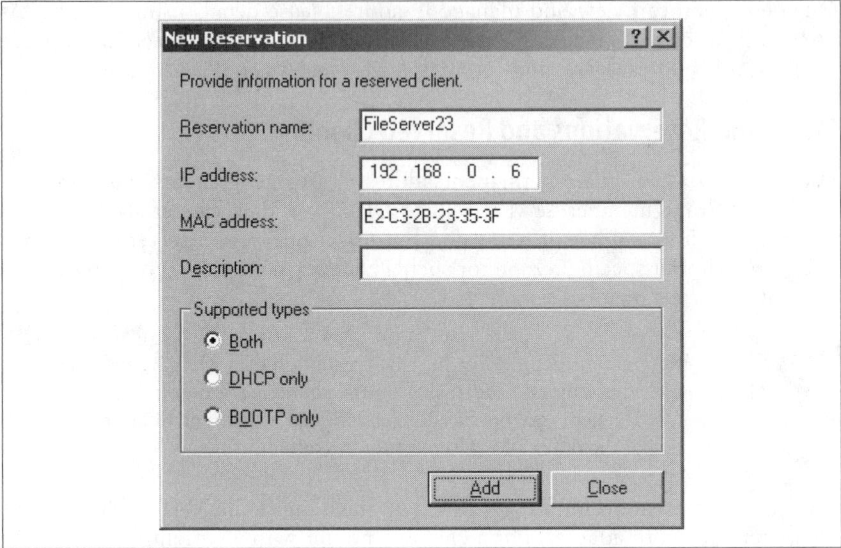

Figure 5-10. Configure the reservation using the client's MAC address.

You can edit a current reservation by right-clicking it and selecting Properties. If a client should no longer have a reservation, right-click the reservation and then select Delete. When prompt to confirm, click Yes.

Managing DHCP Databases

The DHCP database stores information about client leases, reservations, scopes, and configured options. By default, the database is located in the *%SystemRoot%\System32\DHCP* folder on a DHCP server. Windows Server 2003 automatically backs up and compacts the database periodically. Administrators can perform manual backups and compactions as well.

Automatic backups occur every 60 minutes by default and can be configured using the BackupInterval entry under the HKLM → SYSTEM → CurrentControlSet → DHCPServer → Parameters key in the Registry. If Windows Server 2003 detects that the DHCP database is corrupted, the operating system will automatically try to recover the database from the last backup. Backups are stored by default in *%SystemRoot%\System32\DHCP\backup*.

Setting the DHCP database and backup paths

The DHCP database and automatic backup folders are stored under the *%SystemRoot%* by default. If desired, you can set the database path and backup path to a different location by following these steps:

1. Open the DHCP console and connect to the server if necessary.
2. Right-click the server node and click Properties.
3. Click the Advanced tab as shown in Figure 5-11.

4. Use the Database Path and Backup Path text boxes to set the database path and backup path.
5. Click OK.

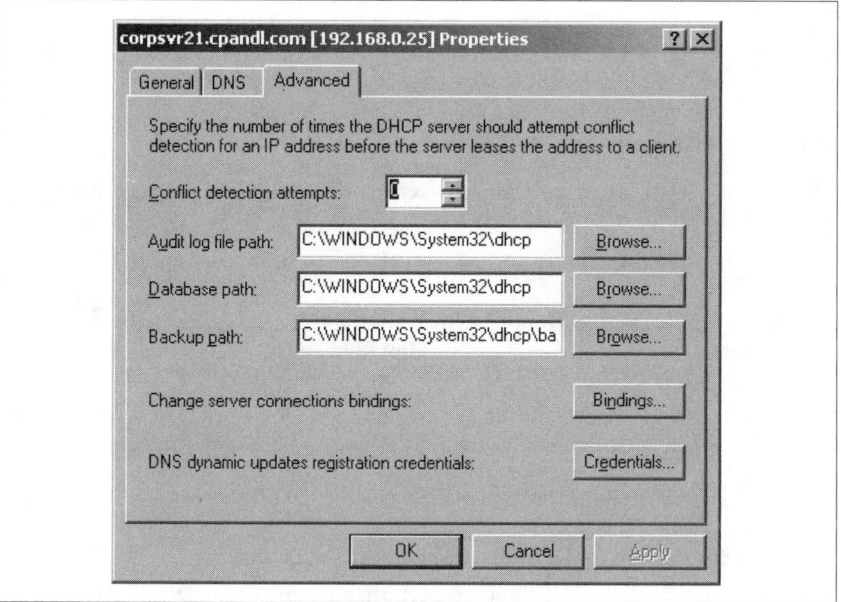

Figure 5-11. Set the database and backup paths as necessary.

Manually backing up and restoring the DHCP database

Periodic manual backups of the DHCP database are important because they allow you to manually restore the database. If you don't have a manual backup, you cannot perform a manual restore of a corrupted DHCP database. To perform a manual backup of the DHCP database, follow these steps:

1. Open the DHCP console and connect to the server if necessary.
2. Right-click the server node and click Backup.
3. Browse to the folder where the manual backup should be placed.
4. Click OK.

> You don't need to stop the DHCP server service to perform a manual backup.

To manually restore the DHCP database, follow these steps:

1. Open the DHCP console and connect to the server if necessary.
2. Right-click the server node and click Restore.
3. Browse to the folder where manual backups were placed. This must be a folder on the local machine.

4. Click OK.
5. When prompted to stop and restart the DHCP Server service, click Yes to allow the restore to complete.

Manual restores can be done using manual backups only. An automated backup cannot be used for manual restoration of the DHCP database.

Migrating a DHCP server

Moving the DHCP database from one server to another can be performed using the manual backup and restore procedure. Follow these steps:

1. On the current source DHCP server, perform a backup of the DHCP database.
2. When the backup is complete, stop the DHCP server service by typing `net stop dhcpserver` at a command prompt. This ensures clients do not connect to the DHCP server.

If necessary, disable the DHCP server service in the Services utility. This prevents the DHCP server from starting the service after the database has been migrated to another DHCP server.

3. Copy the backup folder to the destination DHCP server.
4. On the destination DHCP server, perform a restore of the DHCP database.
5. You may be prompted to stop and restart the DHCP service on the destination server.

Manually compacting the DHCP database

Periodic manual compaction of the DHCP database, in addition to automatic compaction, can help ensure that the DHCP database stays healthy in a busy network environment with many hundreds of computers using DHCP. The reason for this is that manual compaction is performed with the database offline, which allows more efficient compaction and defragmentation of the database.

To ensure DHCP works as expected, you should:

- Periodically compact the DHCP database manually whenever it grows larger than 30 MB.
- Manually compact the database if you receive error messages that the DHCP database is corrupted.

To manually compact the DHCP database, follow these steps:

1. Open a command prompt.
2. CD to the directory containing the DHCP database.
3. Type `net stop dhcpserver`.
4. Type `jetpack dhcp.mdb temp.mdb`, where `temp.mdb` is the name of the temporary file to use.
5. Type `net start dhcpserver`.

Troubleshooting DHCP

When you have problems with DHCP, the DHCP console is the first place you should look to diagnose and resolve problems. The console displays warning icons for many common problems:

- A red circle with an X through it is used if the DHCP Server service is stopped or if the DHCP server cannot otherwise be reached.
- A white circle with a red down arrow on the server node indicates the server is not authorized in Active Directory.
- A white circle with a red down arrow on the scope node indicates the scope is deactivated.
- A white circle with a green up arrow indicates the DHCP server is authorized and active.

To diagnose and resolve deeper issues with DHCP, you'll need the help of the DHCP audit logs. These logs and their use in troubleshooting are discussed in the sections that follow.

Understanding the DHCP audit logs

By default, all DHCP activity is written to the DHCP audit logs stored under *%SystemRoot%\System32\dhcp*. Audit logs are stored in a separate text files named after the day of the week, such as *DhcpSrvLog-Mon.log*, *DhcpSrvLog-Tues.log*, etc. Seven days of audit logs are maintained and old logs are overwritten when a new log of the same name is created. You can enable or disable audit logging by completing these steps:

1. Open the DHCP console and connect to the server if necessary.
2. Right-click the server node and click Properties.
3. On the General tab, select or clear the Enable DHCP Audit Logging checkbox.
4. Click OK.

You can change the location of the audit logs by following these steps:

1. Open the DHCP console and connect to the server if necessary.
2. Right-click the server node and click Properties.
3. Click the Advanced tab.
4. Use the Audit Log File Path to specify the location for the audit logs.
5. Click OK.

You can use the audit logs for troubleshooting DHCP. The audit logs contain comma-delimited, single-line entries for each audited activity. Each entry begins with an event code, the meaning of which is listed at the beginning of the audit log as shown in Figure 5-12.

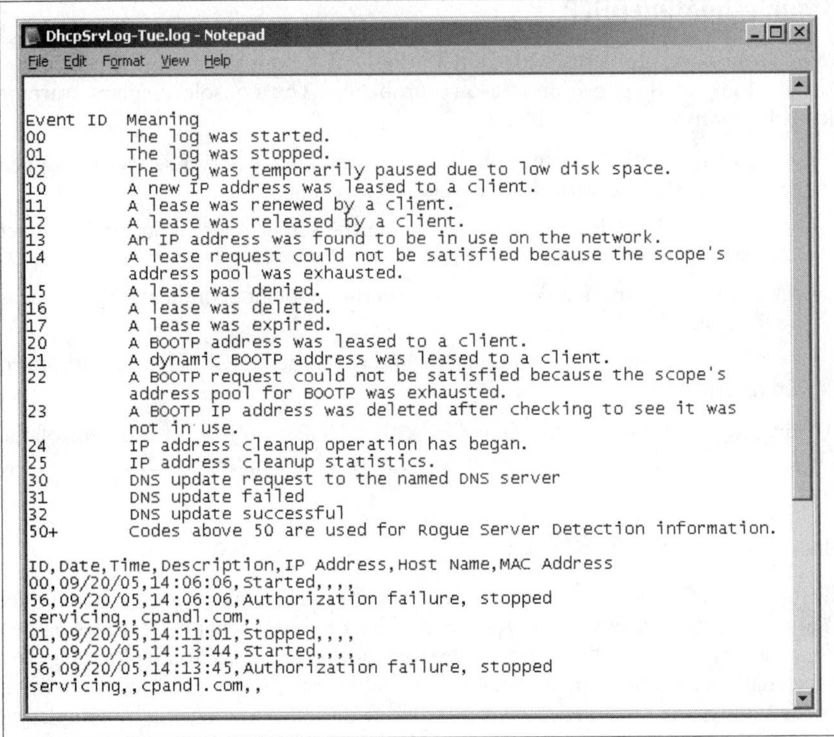

```
DhcpSrvLog-Tue.log - Notepad
File  Edit  Format  View  Help

Event ID  Meaning
00        The log was started.
01        The log was stopped.
02        The log was temporarily paused due to low disk space.
10        A new IP address was leased to a client.
11        A lease was renewed by a client.
12        A lease was released by a client.
13        An IP address was found to be in use on the network.
14        A lease request could not be satisfied because the scope's
          address pool was exhausted.
15        A lease was denied.
16        A lease was deleted.
17        A lease was expired.
20        A BOOTP address was leased to a client.
21        A dynamic BOOTP address was leased to a client.
22        A BOOTP request could not be satisfied because the scope's
          address pool for BOOTP was exhausted.
23        A BOOTP IP address was deleted after checking to see it was
          not in use.
24        IP address cleanup operation has began.
25        IP address cleanup statistics.
30        DNS update request to the named DNS server
31        DNS update failed
32        DNS update successful
50+       Codes above 50 are used for Rogue Server Detection information.

ID,Date,Time,Description,IP Address,Host Name,MAC Address
00,09/20/05,14:06:06,Started,,,,
56,09/20/05,14:06:06,Authorization failure, stopped
servicing,,cpandl.com,,
01,09/20/05,14:11:01,Stopped,,,,
00,09/20/05,14:13:44,Started,,,,
56,09/20/05,14:13:45,Authorization failure, stopped
servicing,,cpandl.com,,
```

Figure 5-12. DHCP audit logs are stored as text files with comma-delimited entries.

Diagnosing and resolving issues related to DHCP authorization

In Active Directory domains, DHCP servers must be authorized before they can assign leases to clients. Although the DHCP console shows the general status of a server as authorized or unauthorized, you'll need to look through the DHCP audit logs to perform more detailed analysis to resolve some authorization issues.

Table 5-4 provides a summary of audit log events related to authorization. Use the event text and descriptions to diagnose and resolve authorization issues. The audit code for events 50 and higher are not summarized in the header of the audit log.

Table 5-4. Audit log events related to authorization

Event ID	Event text	Description
50	Unreachable domain	The DHCP server could not locate the domain for which it is configured.
51	Authorization succeeded	The DHCP server was authorized to start on the network.
53	Cached authorization	The DHCP server was authorized to start using previously cached information. Active Directory wasn't available at the time the DHCP Server service was started on the network.
54	Authorization failed	The DHCP server was not authorized to start on the network and has stopped servicing clients. Typically, the DHCP Server service is stopped as a result.

Table 5-4. Audit log events related to authorization (continued)

Event ID	Event text	Description
55	Authorization (servicing)	The DHCP server was successfully authorized to start on the network.
56	Authorization failure, stopped servicing	The DHCP server was not authorized to start on the network and was shut down. You must authorize the server before starting it again.
57	Server found in domain	Another DHCP server exists and is authorized for the domain.
58	Server could not find domain	The DHCP server could not locate the domain for which it is configured.
59	Network failure	A network-related failure prevented the server from determining whether it is authorized.
60	No DC is DS-enabled	No domain controller was found in the domain. The DHCP server must be able to contact a DC in the domain.
61	Server found that belongs to DS domain	Another DHCP server that belongs to the domain was found.
62	Another server found	Another DHCP server was found on the network.
63	Restarting rogue detection	The DHCP server is trying to determine whether it's authorized.
64	No DHCP-enabled interfaces	The DHCP server has its service bindings or network connections configured so that the DHCP Server service is not enabled to provide services. The server may be disconnected from the network, have a dynamic IP address, or have all its static IP addresses disabled.

Verifying leases and DHCP reservation configuration

When you select a server's Active Leases node in the DHCP console, the current leases are listed. For leases, the current expiration date is listed. If a lease expires and is not renewed, the dynamically configured computer might have been moved to a different subnet or it might have obtained its configuration from another DHCP server.

With reservations, the active or inactive status of the reservation is listed. If a reservation is inactive for a dynamically configured computer that is booted and connected to the network, the reservation may be incorrectly configured. To check the reservation configuration, select a server's Reservations node in the DHCP console, right-click the reservation, and then click Properties. To determine the options used by the reservation, expand the Reservations node in the DHCP console and then in the left pane, click the entry for the lease. In the right pane, the current options are listed by name, vendor (where the options came from), and the value assigned. Verify that the reserved addresses are not simultaneously excluded.

Verifying the client configuration and examining the system event log

When DHCP clients lose access to resources or are unable to establish clients, you might have a problem with DHCP. You should start your troubleshooting by determining whether the problem originates on the client or elsewhere. On a client experiencing problems, you can view the current TCP/IP configuration by typing `ipconfig /all` at a command prompt. Issues related to TCP/IP can be resolved as discussed previously in this chapter in "Troubleshooting TCP/IP Addressing." If a client has been assigned the appropriate configuration and there is no warning message about an addressing conflict, the network problem most likely isn't a result of an addressing issue on the client.

However, if a client computer has been assigned an address in use by another computer on the network, it will have problems communicating with the network and may not be able to access network resources. A warning message regarding the address conflict will be displayed in the system tray on the client computer. Related warning events are also recorded in the System event log on the computer experiencing the problem. Typically, these warning events have the Event ID 1055 and the source as Dhcp.

If the client is assigned the IP address by DHCP, the likely issue is that another computer has been assigned a static IP address that conflicts with the range of IP addresses assigned to DHCP clients, and the IP address of the manually configured computer will need to be changed. If you locate the other computer with the same IP address and it is dynamically configured, the likely issue is that more than one DHCP server is assigning the same range of IP addresses, or the scopes assigned to a DHCP server have been modified to allow such a conflict to occur.

On the client, you can attempt to restore connectivity with the network using the Repair option on the Support tab of the Local Area Connection Status dialog box. When you use Repair, the client attempts to refresh the stored data for its connection. The client does this by:

1. Renewing the DHCP IP address lease and the related TCP/IP settings.
2. Flushing the ARP cache, the NetBIOS cache, and the DNS resolver cache.
3. Re-registering with WINS and DNS.

Although Windows 2000 and later automatically stop the DHCP Server service for unauthorized DHCP servers in a domain, other devices can be DHCP-enabled. To locate these devices, you can use the *Dhcploc.exe* utility provided in the Windows Support Tools. You can then remove any rogue DHCP servers from the network.

Diagnosing and resolving issues related to configuration of DHCP Server and scope options

TCP/IP options can be configured manually on the client and in the DHCP console. Manual configurations cannot be overridden. In the DHCP console, TCP/IP options are configured at five separate levels:

- Predefined options that set preset values and can be overridden at any other level.
- Server options that can be overridden by scope, class, and reservation options.
- Scope options that can be overridden by class and reservation options.
- Class options that can be overridden by reservation options.
- Reservation options that can be overridden only by manually assigned TCP/IP settings.

A common problem you may see is due to clients obtaining incorrect option values. If a client is getting the incorrect settings, you can resolve this by:

1. Checking the Internet Protocol (TCP/IP) properties to ensure that the client is configured to obtain settings as appropriate from DHCP.
2. Configure scope options to override other options being used, as appropriate and necessary.
3. After modifying the client configuration or the server's option settings, you would need to release and renew the client lease to ensure the client gets the correct settings.
4. Check the status of the connection from the system tray.

A less common problem you may see when troubleshooting DHCP server configuration has to do with the service binding to the server's network adapter. To provide leases for clients on the local subnet, a DHCP server must be assigned a static IP address on the local subnet. The DHCP Server service must also have a binding on one of the server's network adapters.

Verifying address scope assignment and that the DHCP Relay Agent is working correctly

Multiple scopes can be configured and active on a single DHCP server. Scopes containing IP addresses for subnets other than the subnet on which the DHCP server is located are used with remote clients. DHCP servers determine the originating subnet for remote clients by retrieving an option field inserting into DHCP Request messages by a DHCP Relay Agent. This option field identifies the originating subnet of the client, and is formatted as shown here:

```
DHCP: Relay IP Address (giaddr) = OriginatingSubnetGateway
```

In the next example, the originating subnet gateway is identified as 192.168.0.1:

```
DHCP: Relay IP Address (giaddr) = 192.168.0.1
```

You use Network Monitor to examine packets and view option fields.

If the network's DHCP Relay Agent is improperly configured or not BOOTP (RFC 1542) compliant, the originating subnet might not get attached to the DHCP Request message from the client. As a result, the client could get assigned an IP address from the wrong scope. To resolve this, you would need to verify the DHCP Relay Agent configuration. To verify the binding, follow these steps:

1. Open the DHCP console and connect to the server if necessary.
2. Right-click the server node and click Properties.
3. Click the Advanced tab.
4. Click the Bindings button.

5. In the Bindings dialog box shown in Figure 5-13, ensure that the server has a binding to a network adapter on at least one IP address. If no connections and bindings are listed, the server might not have a static IP address.
6. Click OK.

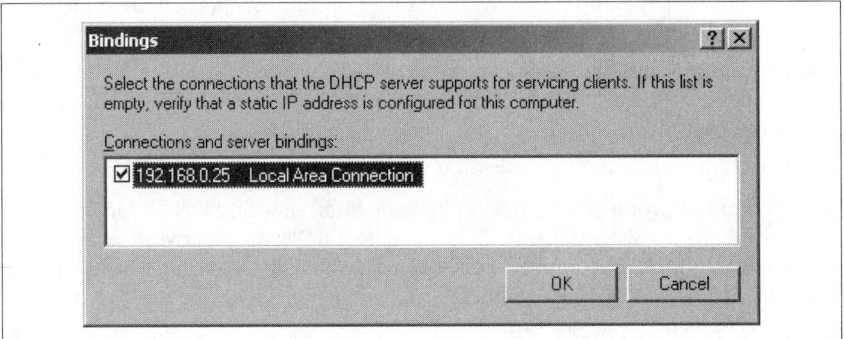

Figure 5-13. Verify the server bindings for the DHCP Server service.

Verifying database integrity

Many inconsistencies in the DHCP database can be resolved by reconciling the server's leases. When you reconcile the database, the operating system compares the information in the database to the information stored in the Registry, and uses this comparison to determine whether the DHCP database accurately reflects the current leases and reservations. To reconcile all scopes on a server, right-click the server node in the DHCP console and then select Reconcile All Scopes. When prompted to verify the action, click the Verify button. Any inconsistencies are listed. If there are no inconsistencies, you'll see a prompt stating "The database is consistent."

Implementing, Managing, and Maintaining Name Resolution

When you install a computer, you assign the computer a name, which is used as the computer's NetBIOS name and as the computer's DNS hostname. On Windows NT 4.0 networks, WINS is used to resolve NetBIOS names. On networks running Windows 2000 and later computers, DNS is used to resolve DNS hostnames. With DNS, computers are grouped by name with domains. Domains establish a hierarchical naming structure so a computer's place within the domain structure can be determined.

In a standard configuration, a computer's fully qualified domain name (FQDN) is its hostname combined with the related domain name. For example, the FQDN for the computer FileServer81 in the *WilliamStanek.com* domain is *FileServer81.WilliamStanek.com*.

Since domain structure is hierarchical, domains can have subdomains. For example, the WilliamStanek.com domain might have Tech and Eng subdomains. The computer Workstation82 in the Tech domain would have a FQDN of

Workstation82.Tech.WilliamStanek.com. The computer TestServer21 in the Eng domain would have a FQDN of *TestServer21.Eng.WilliamStanek.com*.

DNS uses client/server architecture. Any computer that uses DNS for name resolution is a DNS client. A computer that provides DNS name resolution services to a client is referred to as a DNS server. For name resolution to work properly, both DNS clients and DNS servers must be configured appropriately.

When the network is not fully configured for DNS name resolution, you might need NetBIOS name resolution. NetBIOS is also required for some applications such as the Computer Browser service. NetBIOS is enabled by default in Windows Server 2003.

Managing DNS Clients

For clients to use DNS, the client must have an appropriate computer name and a properly configured primary DNS suffix. The computer name serves as the computer's hostname. The computer's primary DNS suffix determines the domain to which it is assigned for name resolution purposes. DNS clients can dynamically update their own records and also cache query responses. The DNS Client service, also known as Resolver, is enabled by default on Windows Server 2003 and Windows XP computers.

Configuring primary and alternate DNS suffixes

By default, the primary DNS suffix is the domain in which the computer is a member. To view or modify the primary DNS suffix of a computer, follow these steps:

1. Open the System utility in Control Panel. On the Computer Name tab, click Change.
2. Click More. As shown in Figure 5-14, the computer gets its primary DNS suffix from the domain in which it is a member by default.
3. If you don't want the computer to get its primary DNS suffix from the domain in which it is a member, clear the Change Primary DNS Suffix When Domain Membership Changes checkbox, type the desired primary DNS suffix, and then click OK.

Unqualified names that are used on a computer are resolved using the primary DNS suffix. For example, you are logged on to a computer with a primary DNS suffix of Tech.WilliamStanek.com and you ping FileServer21 at a command prompt, the computer directs the query to *FileServer21.Tech.WilliamStanek.com*.

When computers have multiple IP addresses, the additional IP addresses can have different (alternate) DNS suffixes, allowing the computer to have connection-specific settings and to communicate as a local host on multiple subnets.

The way DNS suffixes are used is determined by the computer's Advanced TCP/IP Settings. You can view and modify these settings by following these steps:

1. Click Start → Control Panel → Network Connections → Local Area Connection.
2. Click Properties to open the Local Area Connection Properties dialog box.

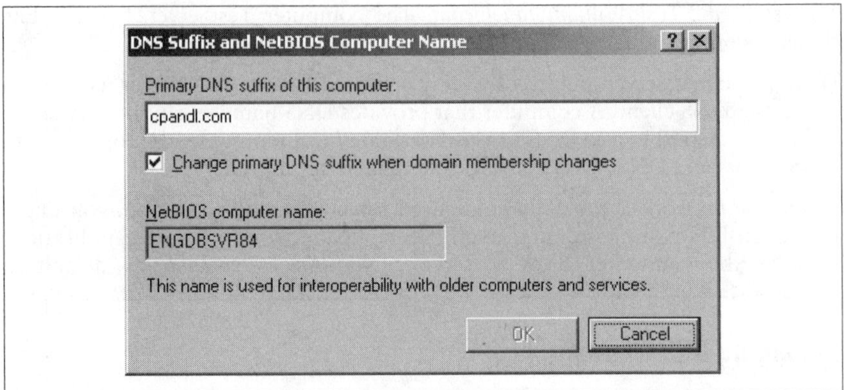

Figure 5-14. Viewing the primary DNS suffix.

3. Click Internet Protocol (TCP/IP) and then select Properties. Be careful not to clear the checkbox. Scroll down through the list of protocols used by the connection if necessary.
4. Click the Advanced Button.
5. Click the DNS tab. Figure 5-15 shows two typical configuration for DNS suffixes.
6. If the network connection you are working with uses the primary DNS suffix as configured on the computer, use the default options shown in the lefthand dialog box.
7. If the network connection you are working with uses an alternate DNS suffix that is specific to the connection, enter the alternate the DNS suffix for the connection, as shown in the righthand dialog box, and select the Use This Connection's DNS Suffix In DNS Registration checkbox.
8. Click OK.

Typically, you will use a primary or connection-specific alternate DNS suffix as discussed previously. Still, there is one other possible configuration that can be used—and that is to append specific DNS suffixes. If you select the Append These DNS Suffixes radio button, you can specify the suffixes to append and define the order in which the computer attempts to use these suffixes to resolve names.

Configuring dynamic DNS updates

In the Advanced TCP/IP Settings dialog box, the Register This Connection's Addresses In DNS checkbox is selected by default, which allows Windows 2000 and later computers to dynamically update their A and PTR records in DNS. As discussed previously, the default configuration for DHCP clients is to dynamically update their A records and allow DHCP servers to dynamically update their PTR records. This behavior is configurable.

Dynamic updates can only occur when the client is configured with a domain suffix that matches a zone name hosted by the preferred DNS server. Thus, for a computer named Workstation18 to be dynamically updated in the *eng.williamstanek.com* zone, the FDQN of the computer must be *Workstation18.eng.williamstanek.com*.

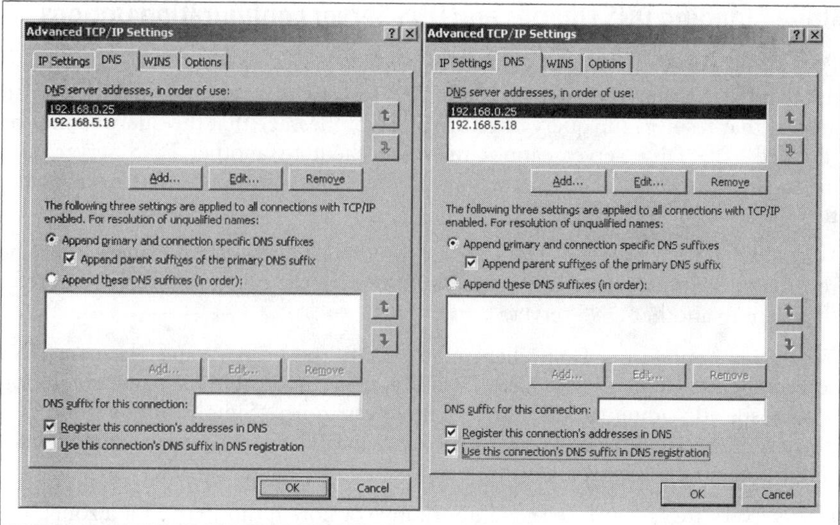

Figure 5-15. Configuring DNS suffixes.

Normally, the FQDN is the computer's name combined with the name of which the computer is a member. However, if you've modified the primary DNS suffix, the FQDN is the computer's hostname combined with the primary DNS suffix. For example, the FQDN for the computer Workstation27 with a primary DNS suffix of Tech.WilliamStanek.com is *Workstation27.Tech.WilliamStanek.com*.

If you create a connection-specific alternate DNS suffix, the FQDN is the computer's hostname combined with the DNS suffix for the connection. For example, the FQDN for the computer Workstation31 with a connection-specific DNS suffix of Eng.WilliamStanek.com is *Workstation31.Eng.WilliamStanek.com*.

Working with the resolver cache on DNS clients

You can force a client to register its DNS records by typing `ipconfig /registerdns` at a command prompt. DNS clients send name resolution queries to DNS servers using two key types of lookups: *forward lookups*, to determine the IP address of a computer from its FQDN, and *reverse lookups*, to determine a computer's FQDN from its IP address. When DNS clients receive a query response from a DNS server, the response is stored in the local DNS resolver cache. If you type `ipconfig /displaydns` at a command prompt, you can view the contents of the resolver cache.

Each stored response has a specific expiration date and time, as set for the related record on a DNS server. DNS clients display a countdown to this expiration date and time as a Time To Live (TTL) value. This value is the number of seconds until the resolver cache entry expires.

You can clear a client's resolver cache by typing `ipconfig /flushdns` at a command prompt.

Understanding DNS Queries and DNS Server Configuration Options

DNS uses both recursive and iterative queries to resolve queries. With a recursive query, the DNS client requests that the DNS server either respond directly with an answer that resolves the query or return an error message that the query cannot be resolved. The DNS server cannot refer the client to another DNS server, and instead, queries other DNS servers until it obtains a response that resolves the request or the query fails.

With an iterative query, a DNS server attempts to resolve the query from its records or from its cache. If it is unable to resolve the query, the server can refer the client to another DNS server.

When you configure a DNS client, you specify the primary and alternate DNS servers for the client to use. Each DNS server is responsible for name resolution within specific administrative areas known as zones. Simply put, a *zone* is a portion of the DNS database that is being managed. A single zone can contain a single domain or it can span multiple domains.

DNS servers are said to be either authoritative or non-authoritative for a zone:

- A DNS server that is authoritative for a zone is responsible for the related portion of the DNS database and is the primary source from which other DNS servers resolving any quests for that zone.
- A DNS server that is non-authoritative for a zone may cache information related to the zone, but ultimately, must rely on an authoritative DNS server to keep its cache up to date.

DNS servers store zone information in zone files. Zone files contain resource records that are used to resolve queries and primarily map hostnames to IP addresses. Several types of zone files are used including:

Primary
: A primary zone file is the master copy of a zone, and as such it is the only writeable copy and the one that must be updated when you want to modify or maintain records.

Secondary
: A secondary zone is a copy of a primary zone, and as such, is a read-only copy that is updated when the primary DNS server for a zone sends a copy of the zone file to a secondary server.

Stub
: A stub zone lists authoritative name servers for a zone so that DNS servers hosting a parent zone are aware of authoritative DNS servers for the related child zones.

There is a special type of DNS server known as an Active Directory–integrated primary. An Active Directory–integrated primary is a domain controller configured as a DNS server that is fully integrated with Active Directory and for which the related DNS zones information is stored in Active Directory. Both primary and stubs zones can be stored in Active Directory.

DNS servers can be configured in the following roles:

Primary
: Maintain one or more primary zone files.

Secondary
: Maintain one or more secondary copies of zone files.

Forwarding-only
: Maintain a cache of resolved queries.

A single DNS server can have multiple roles. For example, a server can be the primary for one or more zones and the secondary for other zones.

Installing, Configuring, and Managing the DNS Server Service

With Windows Server 2003, any server can run the DNS Server service and act as a DNS server. Although the server doesn't have to have a static IP address, a static IP address is recommended. However, it is also recommended that domain controllers not be configured as DHCP servers. In a standard configuration, DHCP is integrated with DNS, and DHCP clients are permitted to create, alter, and remove their own records. If you install DHCP on a DC, any client on the network might be able to alter critical service locator (SRV) records, which is an unnecessary security risk.

You must be an administrator to install windows components, including the DNS Server service. The account you use for installing DNS should be a member of the global Domain Admins groups or the DnsAdmins group.

Exam 70-291 Study Guide

You can install the DNS Server service by completing the following steps:

1. Open Add Or Remove Programs in Control Panel.
2. In the Add Or Remove Programs window, click Add/Remove Windows Components.
3. Click Networking Services and then select Properties. Be careful not to clear the checkbox.
4. Select Domain Name System (DNS), and then click OK.
5. Click Next. Setup configures the server's components.
6. Click Finish.

You can also install the DNS Server service using the Configure Your Server Wizard. To start the wizard, click Start → Programs → Administrative Tools → Configure Your Server Wizard. Click Next twice, and then under Server Roles, select DNS Server and then click Next. Review the installation tasks that will be performed and click Next again.

Installation of the DNS Server service is only the first step in the configuration of a name server. You also need to configure the name server's:

- DNS server options
- DNS zone options

- DNS resource records
- DNS forwarding

Once you've completed these steps, clients in the domain will be able to query DNS and obtain responses. If you've installed the DNS Server service on a server but have not configured DNS zones, the server acts as a caching-only server.

Configuring and managing DNS Server options

As with other Windows services, the DNS Server service can be managed using the Services utility in Control Panel. However, the best way to manage the DNS Server service and DNS itself is to use the DNS Management console, which can be accessed by clicking Start → Programs → Administrative Tools → DNS.

When you start the DNS Management console on a DNS server, the console connects automatically to DNS on this server. If you start the DNS Management console on your workstation or want to connect to a different DNS server, you can do this by right-clicking the DNS node and selecting Connect To DNS Server. You can then use the Connect To DNS Server dialog box to select the remote server you want to work with by its fully qualified domain name or IP address.

Each server to which you are connected is listed in the DNS Management console. When you select a server entry in the left pane, the DNS Management console connects to the server so that you can view and manage the server's properties and configuration. If there is a problem connecting to or communicating with a server, this is displayed as depicted in Figure 5-16. Troubleshooting can be performed by right-clicking the server entry and selecting Launch Nslookup. *NSLOOKUP.EXE* is a command-line tool for querying name servers.

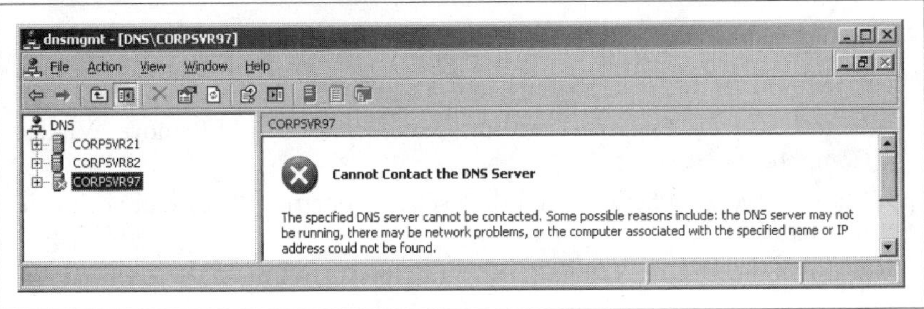

Figure 5-16. The DNS Management console.

For each Active Directory domain, there is a single primary DNS server, referred to as the domain's primary name server. This server is the holder of the primary zone file for the domain.

DNS servers have many options that can be configured using the server's Properties dialog box, which can be accessed in the DNS Management console by right-clicking the server entry and clicking Properties. As shown in Figure 5-17, the server's Properties dialog box has multiple tabs. These tabs are used as follows:

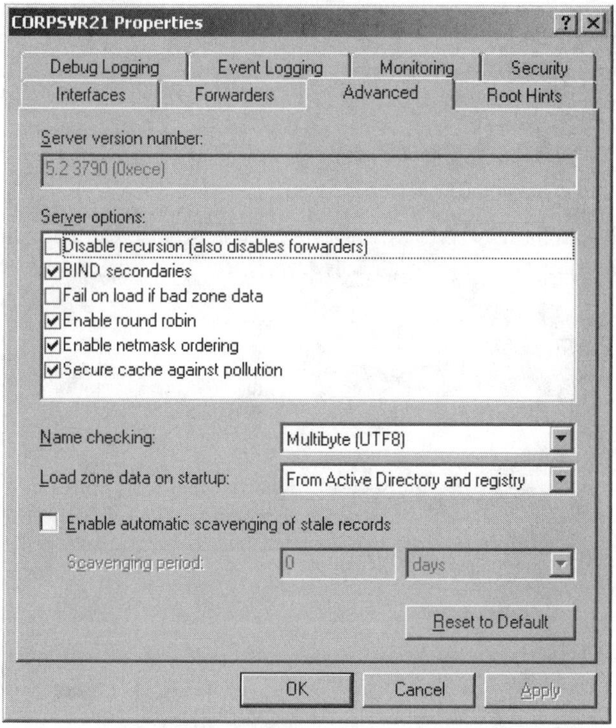

Figure 5-17. The Advanced tab.

Advanced

Using the Advanced tab shown in Figure 5-17, you can configure advanced options that determine the method of name checking, the location from which zone information is loaded, and automatic scavenging configuration.

Debug Logging

Using the Debug Logging tab shown in Figure 5-18, you can configure Debug Logging options for troubleshooting. Debugging is disabled by default. To enable Debug Logging, select the Log Packets For Debugging checkbox, configure the types of packets and packet contents to log during debugging, and then enter a log file path and name.

Event Logging

Using the Event Logging tab shown in Figure 5-19, you can configure the type of events that should be written to the DNS event logs. By default, all types of events are logged. Other logging options include No Events, to turn off event logging; Errors Only, to log only critical errors; and Errors And Warnings, to log both critical errors and warnings.

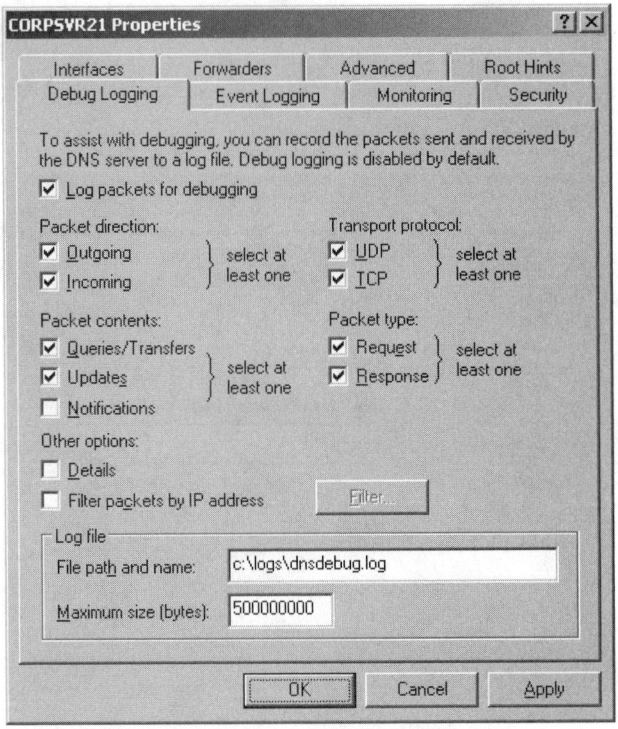

Figure 5-18. The Debug Logging tab.

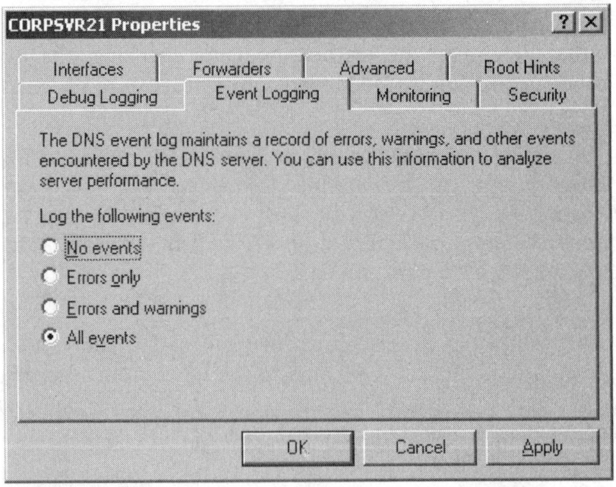

Figure 5-19. The Event Logging tab.

Forwarders

Using the Forwarders tab shown in Figure 5-20, you can configure where a DNS server can forward DNS queries that it cannot resolve. By default, a DNS server can forward queries to servers in all other DNS domains. See "Configuring and managing DNS forwarding," later in this chapter.

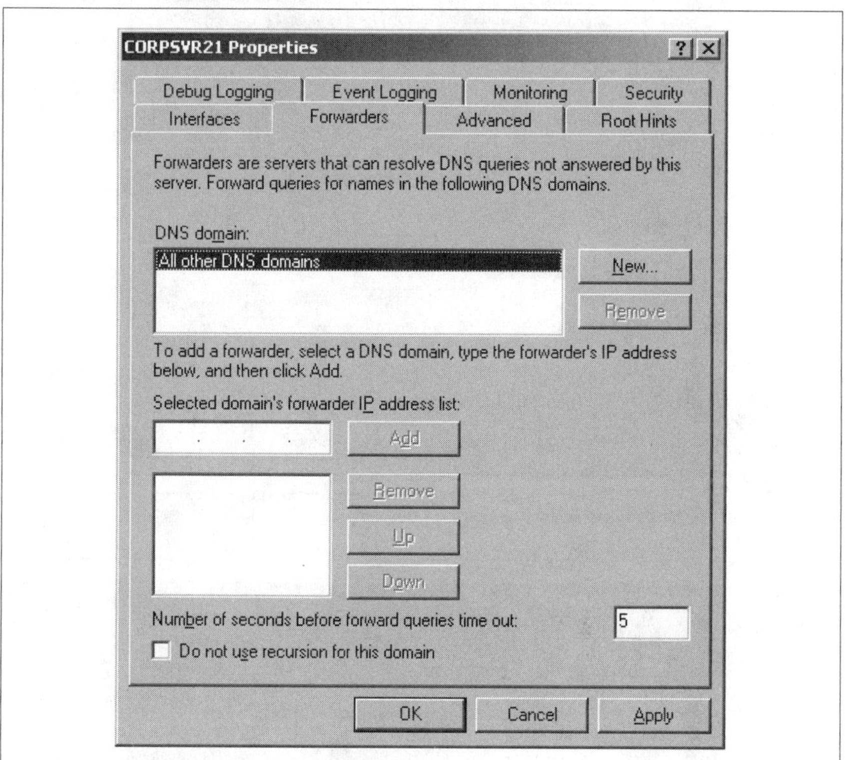

Figure 5-20. The Forwarders tab.

Interfaces

Using the Interfaces tab shown in Figure 5-21, you can configure the IP addresses on which the DNS server will listen for DNS queries. By default, a name server listens to all IP addresses defined on the computer.

Monitoring

Using the Monitoring tab shown in Figure 5-22, you can test and verify the DNS configuration by sending queries against the server. A Simply Query test uses the DNS client on the server to query the DNS service on the local machine. A Recursive Query test uses the local DNS server to query other DNS servers to resolve a query. You can perform manual monitoring for selected tests by clicking the Test Now button. To perform automatic monitoring, select the Perform Automatic Testing checkbox and then set the test interval.

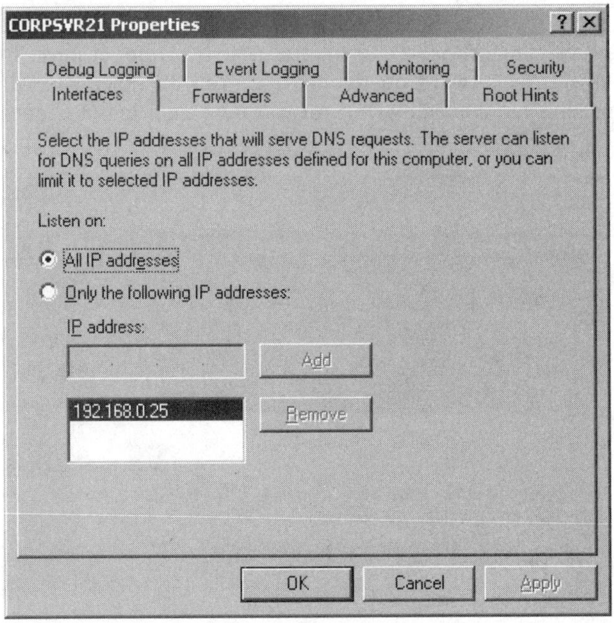

Figure 5-21. The Interfaces tab.

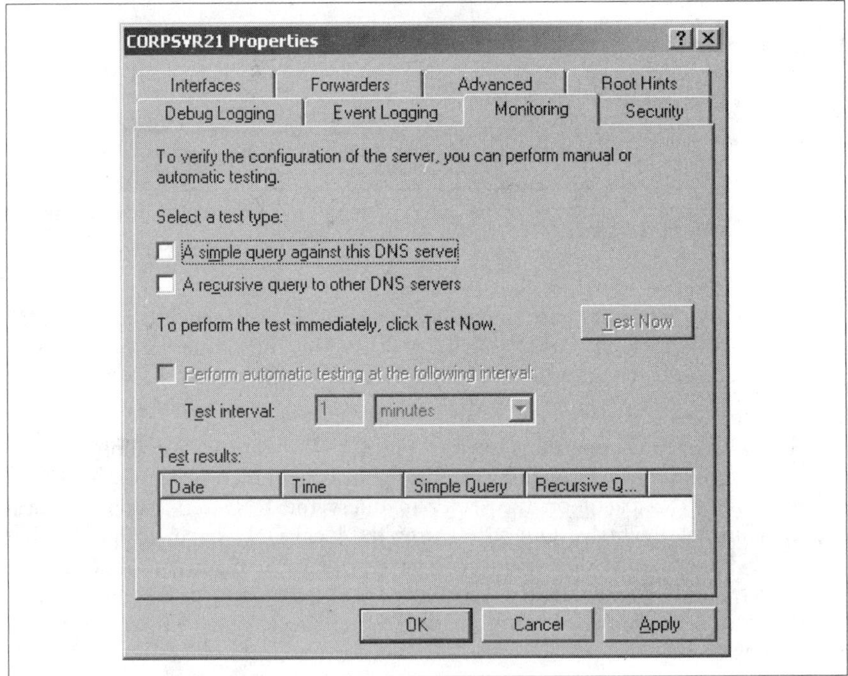

Figure 5-22. The Monitoring tab.

Root Hints

Using the Root Hints tab shown in Figure 5-23, you can configure root name servers that the DNS server can use and refer to when resolving queries. Root hints are stored in the *%SystemRoot%\System32\Dns\Cache.dns* file. For most internal DNS server, the root hints do not need to be modified. For an internal root server (name ".") on private networks, however, you should delete the *Cache.dns* file.

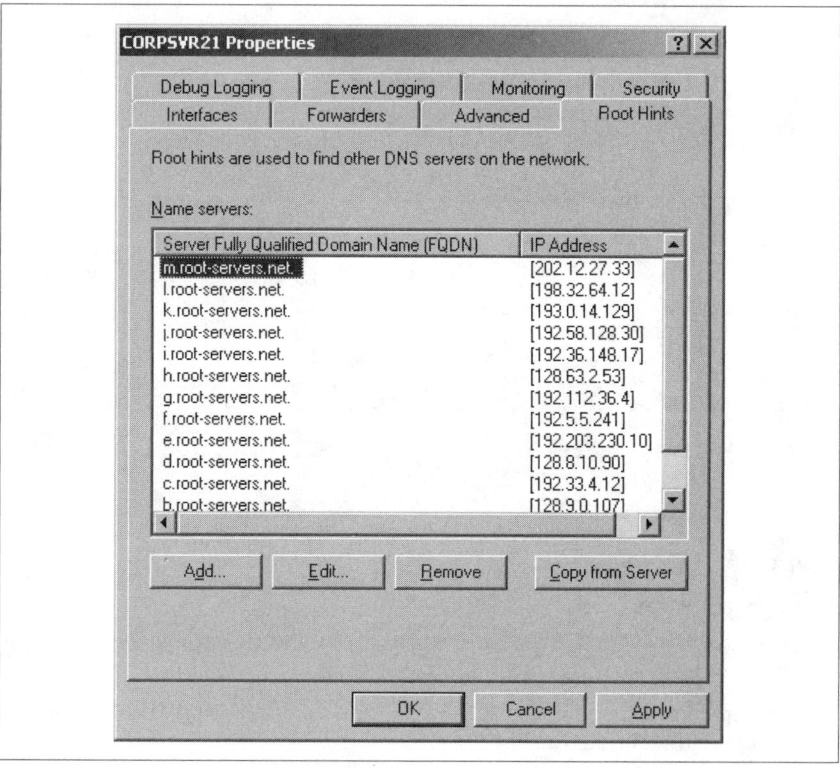

Figure 5-23. The Root Hints tab.

Security

Using the Security tab shown in Figure 5-24, you can assign permissions to users and groups for the DNS server. (Active Directory–integrated zones only.)

Configuring DNS zone options

As discussed previously, a single name server can be configured to have multiple roles in DNS. Those roles are determined by the server's configuration and by the types of zones it hosts. Zone types include: primary zones, secondary zones, and stub zones. For each type of zone, there are two related zone files:

Forward Lookup Zones

Used to resolve forward lookups, which determine the IP address of a computer from its FQDN.

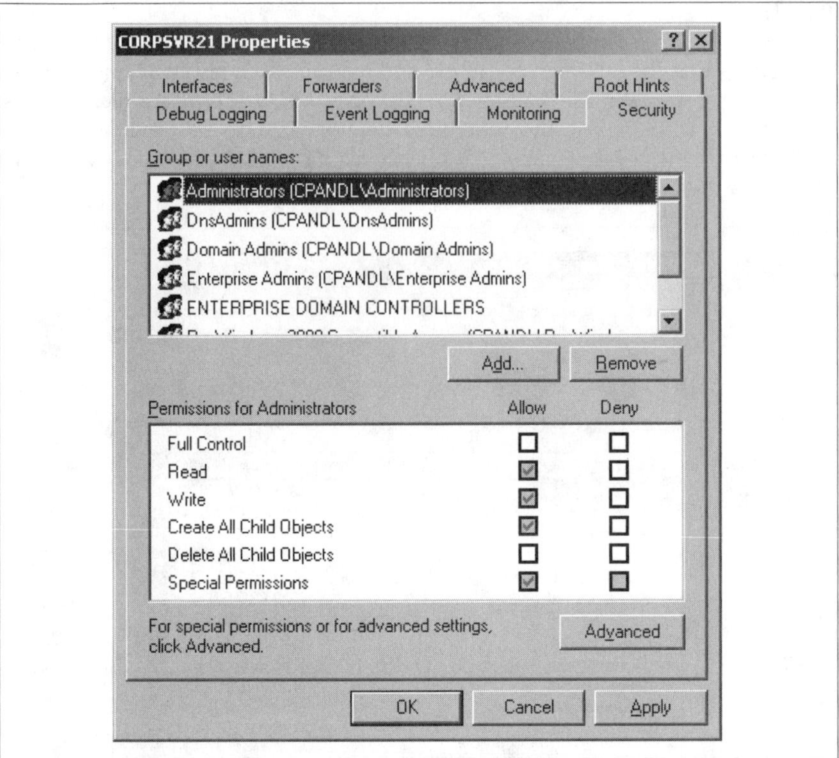

Figure 5-24. The Security tab.

Reverse Lookup Zones
Used to resolve reverse lookups, which determine a computer's FQDN from its IP address.

On domain controllers that also act as DNS servers, primary zones and secondary zones can be stored in Active Directory.

You can create a new zone by completing these steps:

1. Open the DNS Management console.
2. Right-click the DNS Server entry and click New Zone.
3. When the New Zone Wizards starts, click Next.
4. On the Zone Type page, shown in Figure 5-25, select the type of zone you want to create. If a primary or stub zones should be stored in Active Directory (and the DNS Server is also configured as a DC), select the Store The Zone In Active Directory checkbox. Click Next.
5. If you are creating an Active Directory–integrated zone, you must next specify how the zone data should be replicated. The default option is to replicate the data to all DCs in the current domain. Click Next.
6. Select the type of zone to create either a forward lookup zone or a reverse lookup zone. Click Next.

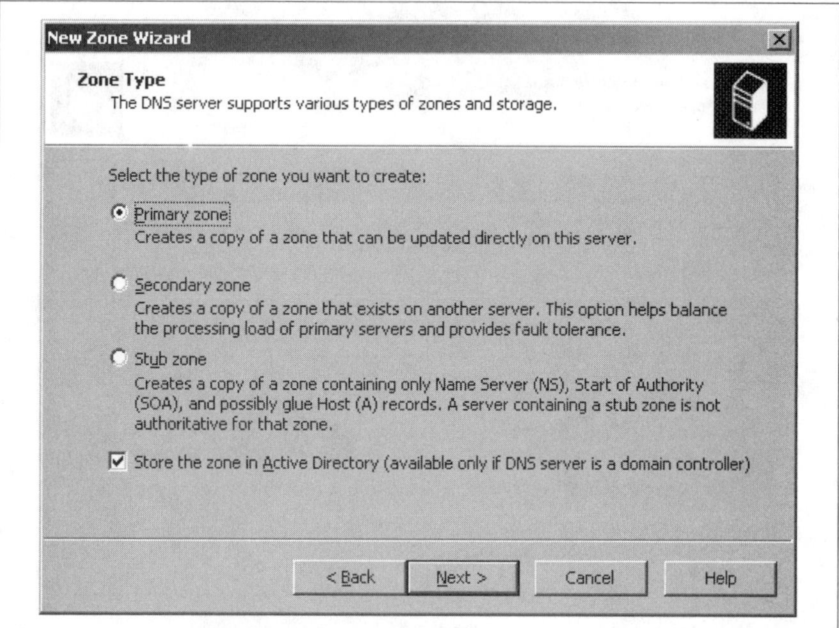

Figure 5-25. Specify the type of zone to create.

7. If you are creating a forward lookup zone, enter the portion of the DNS namespace for which the server is authoritative in the Zone Name text box, such as Tech.WilliamStanek.com. Click Next.
8. If you are creating a reverse lookup zone, identify the zone by entering its network ID (see Figure 5-26). Click Next.
9. The final wizard pages you see depend on the zone type and configuration as a forward or reverse lookup zone:
   - The Zone File Page lets you set the filename for zones files (when Active Directory–integration is not used).
   - The Master DNS Servers page lets you copy primary zone or stub data from designated primary servers (when you are configuring secondary or stub zones).
   - The Dynamic Update page lets you specify how dynamic DNS updates work. By default, dynamic DNS updates are not allowed, but you can configure the zone to allow only secure dynamic updating (in Active Directory–integrated primary zones only) or to allow both nonsecure and secure dynamic updating (in any type of zone).
10. On the final wizard page, click Finish to create the zone.

Using delegation and stub zones

In a large enterprise, you may find that you need to delegate administration of subdomains. To do this, you can create a delegated zone. When you delegate a zone, you assign authority over a portion of your DNS namespace and thereby

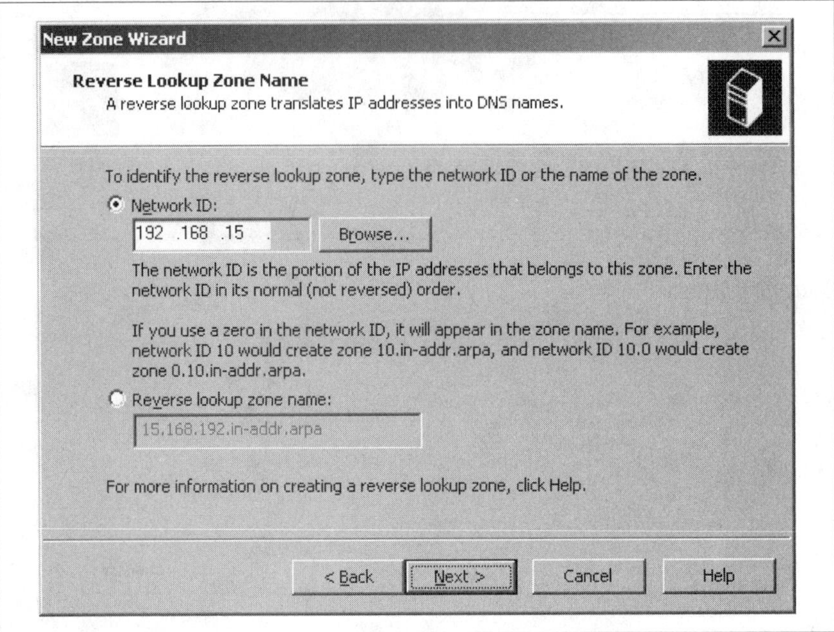

Figure 5-26. For reverse lookup zones, type the network ID.

pass control from the owner of the parent domain to the owner of a subdomain. For example, if you have *tech.domain.local* and *eng.domain.local* subdomains, you may want to delegate control over these subdomains so they can be managed separately from the organization's parent domain.

Delegation helps to ensure that branches or departments within the organization can manage their own DNS namespace. It also helps to distribute the workload so that rather than having one large DNS database, you have multiple DNS databases.

Before you can delegate a zone, you must first create the domain to be delegated on the server that will be hosting the delegated zone. Once you do this, run the New Delegation Wizard on the server hosting the parent zone to specify the zone to delegate.

To create a delegated zone, follow these steps:

1. Open the DNS Management console.
2. Right-click the parent domain and select New Delegation.
3. Follow the prompts.

Stub zones list authoritative name servers for a zone. Servers hosting stub zones do not answer queries directly, but instead direct related queries to any of the name servers specified in the stub zone's NS resource records. Stubs zones are most often used to track authoritative name servers for delegated zones—and the parent DNS servers of delegated zones are the ones to host the related stub zones.

You can create a stub zone by completing these steps:

1. Open the DNS Management console.
2. Right-click the DNS Server entry and click New Zone.
3. When the New Zone Wizards starts, click Next.
4. On the Zone Type page, select Stub Zone as the zone type. Store the stub zone in Active Directory if appropriate. Click Next.
5. Follow the prompts.

Managing DNS zone options

After you create a zone, you can manage its settings by right-clicking it and selecting Properties. The available options differ slightly based on zone type. Zone Properties dialog boxes have the following tabs:

General
: Used to configure zone type, dynamic updating, replication, and scavenging options. You can also Pause/Start the zone.

Start Of Authority (SOA)
: Used to configure the SOA record for a zone.

Names Servers
: Used to configure the name servers for a zone, as specified using NS records.

WINS/WINS-R
: The WINS tab is used with forward lookup zones and forward WINS lookups. The WINS-R tab is used with reverse lookup zones and reverse WINS lookups.

Security
: Used to configure security for the zone. (Active Directory–integrated zones only.)

Zone Transfers
: Used to configure the way a name server transfers a copy of the zone to requesting servers.

The sections that follow examine commonly configured zone options.

Configuring zone type, dynamic updating, and scavenging options. Using the General tab of the zone Properties dialog box, you can view the type and status of the zone as shown in Figure 5-27. To pause a "running" zone, click the Pause button. To change the zone type, click the Change button to the right of the Type entry, select the new zone type, and then click OK. Only one server can be designated as a primary, and thus only one server can have a primary zone. If the DNS server is also a DC, you can store the zone in Active Directory rather than in a text file. You are then able to determine how zone data is replicated by clicking the Change button to the right of the Replication entry.

Using the Dynamic Updates list, you can specify whether and how dynamic updates are used. By clicking the Aging button, you can enable aging and scavenging (see Figure 5-28). *Aging* refers to the process of placing timestamps on

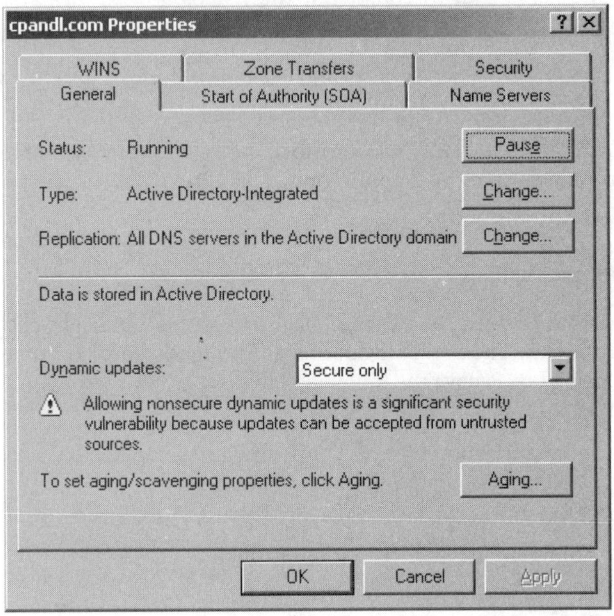

Figure 5-27. The General tab.

dynamically registered resource records and then tracking the age of the record using the TTL value. *Scavenging* refers to the process of deleting outdated (stale) resource records. Scavenging can occur when aging is enabled (because aging puts a TTL timestamp on dynamically registered resource records.

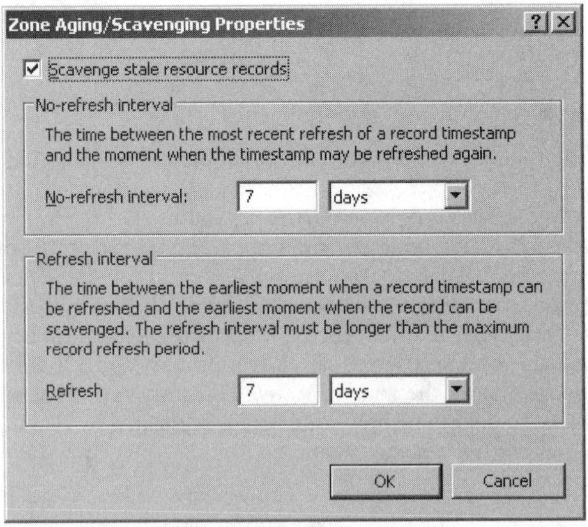

Figure 5-28. Configuring zone aging/scavenging.

To enable aging and scavenging in a zone, select the Scavenge Stale Resource Records checkbox, then set the no-refresh and refresh intervals as appropriate. The *no-refresh interval* is the period after the timestamp is set that must elapse before a resource record can be refreshed. The *refresh interval* is the period after the no-refresh interval during which the timestamp can be refreshed. If a timestamp on a resource record is not refreshed in this time, the record can be scavenged.

Manually configured resource records have no timestamp. Only dynamically created resource records do.

The default no-refresh interval is seven days. The default refresh interval is also seven days. This means dynamically registered record can be scavenged after 14 days by default.

Once aging/scavenging is enabled, scavenging can be performed manually or automatically. To manually scavenge a zone, right-click the zone entry in the DNS Management console and select Scavenge Stale Resource Records. To automatically scavenge a zone, follow these steps:

1. Right-click the server entry in the DNS Management console.
2. Click the Advanced tab.
3. Select the Enable Automatic Scavenging Of Stale Records checkbox.
4. Set the scavenging period (which is the interval between automatic scavenges).
5. Click OK.

Both Aging and Scavenging are disabled by default. Scavenging occurs only when aging is enabled. Scavenging needs to be enabled both at the DNS server properties and from the Zone properties. The Refresh interval should be more than or equal to the No-Refresh interval.

Configuring the SOA. Using the Start Of Authority (SOA) tab of the zone Properties dialog box, you can configure the SOA record for a zone (see Figure 5-29). The Serial Number field lists the revision number of the zone file. This value is incremented each time a resource record changes in the zone. Zone transfers occur only when the zone serial number on the primary (master) server is greater than the zone serial number on secondary servers. If you are troubleshooting zone transfers, you can manually increment the serial number by clicking the Increment button.

The serial number is automatically incremented whenever resources records are changed in the zone. To force DNS to think there are changes, you can manually increment the serial number.

The Primary Server text box lists the primary server for the zone. The entry must end with a period.

The Responsible Person text box lists the person responsible for administering the zone. Typically, this is listed as `hostmaster.`. The entry must end with a period.

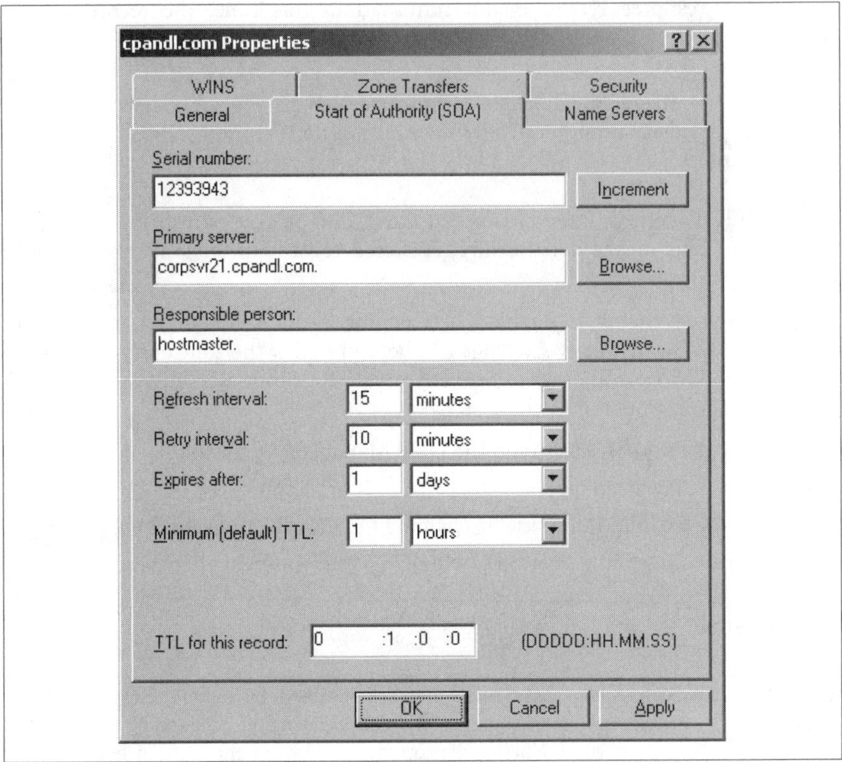

Figure 5-29. The Start Of Authority (SOA) tab.

Configuring name servers for the zone. Using the Name Servers tab of the zone Properties dialog box, you can configure NS records for the zone as shown in Figure 5-30. You use NS records to specify the authoritative servers for the zone. The NS record of the primary name server for the zone is configured automatically. Records for alternate name servers must be configured as necessary. To create a NS record, click Add. In the New Resource Record dialog box, type the FQDN and at least one IP address for the name server, then click OK.

Configuring zone transfers. Using the Zones tab of the zone Properties dialog box, you can configure zone transfers. *Zone transfers* are used to send a copy of a zone to requesting servers. By default, zone transfers are not allowed or restricted only to the DNS servers specified in the Name Servers tab. If you've configured secondary (alternate) name servers for a domain, you should enable zone transfers by selecting the Allow Zone Transfers checkbox and then specifying the servers permitted to make requests. To maintain the integrity and security of the

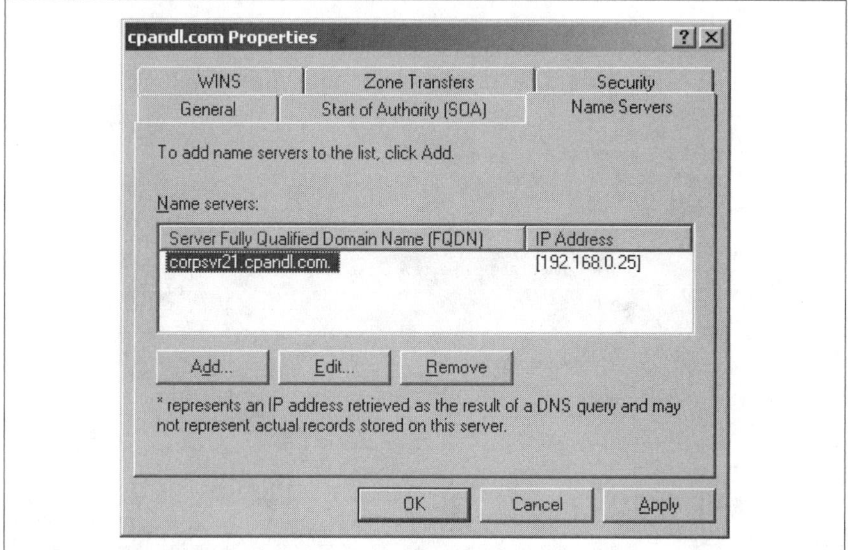

Figure 5-30. The Name Servers tab.

network, you'll usually want to limit the list of servers that can make requests to the servers listed on the Name Servers tab or to a specific list of designated name servers (see Figure 5-31).

When the zone file changes, secondary servers can be automatically notified. To configure notification, click the Notify button on the Zone Transfers tab. In the default configuration, automatic notification is enabled, but only to a designated list of name servers. You must specify the designated name servers. As shown in Figure 5-32, you can also allow automatic notification to the name servers listed on the Name Servers tab.

Configuring and managing DNS resource records

After you create a zone, you can add any necessary resource records to it. When dynamic DNS updates are allowed, DNS clients can register their own A and PTR records. With DHCP and DNS integration, DHCP servers can register records on behalf of clients as well, as discussed previously in this chapter in "Using Dynamic DNS Updates with DHCP."

The most common types of records you'll work with are:

A (address)
: An A record maps a hostname to an IP address. A computer with multiple IP addresses should have multiple address records.

CNAME (canonical name)
: A CNAME record sets an alias or alternate name for a host.

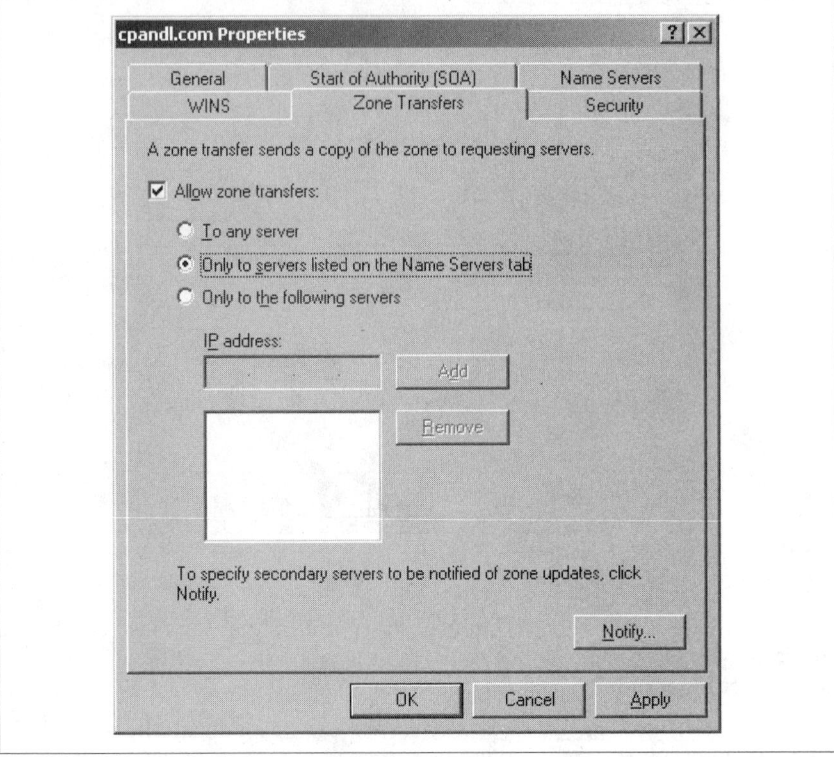

Figure 5-31. For security, limit zone transfers to authoritative Name Servers (or to a specific list of name servers).

MX (mail exchange)
: An MX record specifies a mail exchange server for the domain. A properly configured MX record is required for mail delivery in a domain.

NS (name server)
: An NS record specifies a name server for a domain. Each primary and secondary name server should be declared through this record.

PTR (pointer)
: A PTR record creates a pointer that maps an IP address to a hostname for reverse lookups.

SOA (start of authority)
: An SOA record declares the host that's the most authoritative for the zone (meaning it's the best source of DNS information for the zone).

When you first create the zone, the SOA resource record and the NS resource record for the primary DNS server are automatically created. NS resource records for secondary name servers are not created automatically.

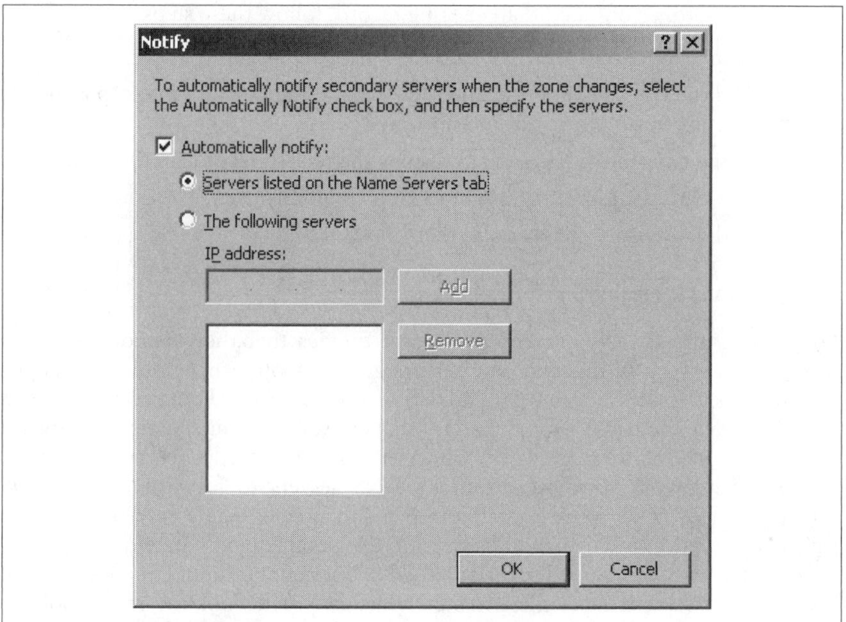

Figure 5-32. Configuring notification for servers on the Name Servers tab.

To view the records in a zone, follow these steps:

1. Open the DNS Management console.
2. Expand the DNS Server entry and then expand the Forward Lookup Zones or Reverse Lookup Zones node as appropriate.
3. Select the zone in the left pane to display the related records in the right pane.

To create resource records in a zone, follow these steps:

1. Open the DNS Management console.
2. Expand the DNS Server entry and then expand the Forward Lookup Zones or Reverse Lookup Zones node as appropriate.
3. Right-click the zone and choose the appropriate option for the type of record you want to create:
   - Choose New Host (A) to create an A record. Enter the required information and then click Add Host.
   - Choose New Alias (CNAME) to create a CNAME record. Enter the required information and then click OK.
   - Choose New Mail Exchanger (MX) to create an MX record. Enter the required information and then click OK.
   - Choose Other New Records to create other enters of records. In the Resource Record Enter dialog box, select a resource record enter and then click Create Record. Next, enter the required information and then click OK.

To view the settings of, or edit, an existing record, follow these steps:

1. Open the DNS Management console.
2. Expand the DNS Server entry and then expand the Forward Lookup Zones or Reverse Lookup Zones node as appropriate.
3. Select the zone in the left pane to display the related records in the right pane.
4. Double-click the record you want to view or modify.
5. Make the necessary changes and then click OK.

Configuring and managing DNS forwarding

Forwarding allows DNS servers to forward queries that they cannot resolve to other DNS servers; in this way, the servers get a response that resolves a client's query. In the default configuration, a DNS server can forward queries to servers in all other DNS domains. Unfortunately, this allows any name server to forward queries outside the local network, which may not be the desired configuration. Instead of allowing your organization's DNS servers to forward to any DNS server, you'll typically want them to forward to specific name servers, which in turn can forward queries inside or outside the organization's network as necessary. In this way, you control the flow of DNS queries and funnel queries through specific name servers. Since these name servers also cache lookups, many lookups can be resolved without having to look outside the network, which reduces the flow of network traffic.

A name server designated as the recipient of forwarded queries is known as a forwarder. When forwarders are used, the DNS query resolution process changes as depicted here:

1. When a DNS server receives a query, it first attempts to resolve the query using its local zone information or its local cache.
2. If the query cannot be resolved, the DNS server forwards the request to the designated forwarder.
3. The forwarder attempts to resolve the query using its local zone information or its local cache. If the forwarder is unable to resolve the query, the DNS server attempts to contact the appropriate name server (as specified in its root hints data).
4. When an answer is returned to the forwarder, the forwarder returns the response to the originating DNS server, which in turn passes the response on to the client.

In a large enterprise with multiple domains, you might want to have multiple forwarding configurations. For example, you might have designated forwarders for the enterprise domains other than those services by the zone files on a name server, and designated forwarders for all other domains.

To configure a DNS server to use a forwarder, follow these steps:

1. Open the DNS Management console.
2. Right-click the DNS Server entry and Properties.

3. Click the Forwarders tab. Under DNS Domain, the entry "All other DNS domains" is used to configure forwarding for all domains other than domains serviced by zone files on the name server.
   - To limit forwarding to all other domains and specify a designated forwarder, click All Other DNS Domains, enter the IP address of the forwarder, and then click Add.
   - To configure a forwarder for a specific domain, click New, type a domain name, and then click OK. Under DNS Domain, click the related domain entry. Afterward, enter the IP address of the forwarder, and then click Add.
4. Click OK.

To configure your designated forwarders, simply allow the forwarder query all other DNS domains and do not designate the IP address of any specific name servers to use. With this in mind, the typical configuration is achieved by completing these steps:

1. Open the DNS Management console.
2. Right-click the DNS Server entry and Properties.
3. Click the Forwarders tab.
4. Under DNS Domain, click the All Other DNS Domains entry and remove any associated IP addresses.
5. Under DNS Domain, click any other entries, each in turn, and then click Remove.
6. Click OK.

The Forwarders tab also has the option Do Not Use Recursion For This Domain. By default, a DNS server uses recursion to query other DNS servers on behalf of clients. If recursion is disabled, the client performs iterative queries using the root hints from the DNS server. Iterative queries mean that the client will make repeated queries of different DNS servers.

Recursion allows a DNS server to contact other DNS servers when it cannot resolve a query for a client. Recursion is allowed by default.

Monitoring DNS

As discussed previously in this chapter in "Configuring and managing DNS Server options," DNS Server Options can be used to monitor many aspects of DNS. A name server's Properties dialog box can be accessed in the DNS Management console by right-clicking the server entry and clicking Properties.

When you configure a new name server, you can use Monitoring tab options to perform basic tests of name resolution. The results of these tests will tell you if DNS is configured properly. You can also use recursive query tests for basic troubleshooting.

To configure event logging, you can use the Event Logging options. When logging is enabled, tracked events are written to the DNS event log. As with most other services, the key types of events you will want to examine are warnings and errors. Event logging is enabled for All Events by default. In the DNS Management console, you can access DNS event log options by expanding the server node and then clicking the Event Viewer node.

For more detailed troubleshooting, you can use Debug Logging. Debug Logging is disabled by default, and can be enabled and configured on the Debug Logging tab. The resulting logfile tracks the types of packets and packet contents that you specify, and can help you resolve many types of name resolution issues.

Using System Monitor and Performance Logging, you can monitor the overall health of DNS and the underlying server. The DNS performance object has an extensive set of performance counters that you can use to track everything from zone transfers to dynamic updates. The Secure Update Failure and Zone Transfer Failure counters can be used to track key types of failure.

One of the best tools for troubleshooting is Nslookup. In the DNS Management console, you can start Nslookup by right-clicking a server entry and selecting Launch Nslookup.

Implementing, Managing, and Maintaining Network Security

Network security is critically important to ensure the integrity and continuing operations of your organization's network. Administrators must follow standard administration procedures to ensure that network security is properly implemented, managed, and maintained. This means implementing security baseline settings on new servers, auditing security settings as appropriate, and allowing access to resources only where such access is required. As part of maintaining network security, administrators must also be proactive in monitoring network protocol security and troubleshoot problems as they occur.

Implementing Secure Network Administration Procedures

The way computers and users are authenticated on the network and authorized to access resources depends on the network security you've configured. Although authentication and authorization have a similar goal to restrict access to a network, they are used in different ways.

Authentication is used to prove user and computer identities. On networks with computers running Windows 2000 or later, the primary authentication protocol is Kerberos. Previous versions of Windows use NTLM for authentication, which can be configured for use in authentication on Windows 2000 or later networks as well.

Authorization is used to control access to resources. Authenticated users and computers will have different levels of authority, depending primarily on the groups of which they are members and the permissions they've been specifically assigned. Both Kerberos and NTLM are used for authorization.

Other aspects network security, including data integrity and confidentiality, are dependent on the secure communications and storage techniques implemented on the network. IP Security (IPSec) can be used to secure communications using encryption. Encryption can also be used to securely store data.

For nonrepudiation, when you need to determine exactly who sent and received a message, you can use Kerberos and IPSec.

For implementing and managing network security, Windows Server 2003 makes extensive use of security templates. Security templates are:

- Created and configured using the Security Templates snap-in. In addition to the standard set of security templates included with Windows Server 2003, you can create custom templates as well.
- Applied and analyzed using the Security Configuration And Analysis snap-in.

The general process for implementing network security using templates is to create and configure the templates you plan to use, and then to apply the template to implement the desired security configuration. At any time, you can analyze a computer's security settings by comparing the current settings to that of a particular security template and thereby pinpointing any discrepancies that may exist. Based on the discrepancies, you may elect to reapply a security template or modify settings as appropriate to enhance a computer's security.

Understanding security templates

To better understand how security templates are used, you need to understand how they are structured and what they contain. They contain customized sets of group policy definitions that are used to apply essential security settings. These settings can affect the following:

Account policy
: Account policy settings control security for passwords, account lockout, and Kerberos.

Local policy
: Local policy settings control security for auditing, user rights assignment, and other security options.

Event log policy
: Event log policy settings control security for event logging.

Restricted groups policy
: Restricted groups settings control security for local group membership administration.

System services policy
: System services settings control security and startup mode for local services.

Filesystem policy
: Filesystem policy settings control security for the local filesystem.

Registry policy
: Registry policy settings control the values of security-related registry keys.

Security templates are stored in the *%SystemRoot%\Security\Templates* folder and accessed using the Security Templates snap-in. All Windows Server 2003 installations include a standard set of security templates, which can be imported into any Group Policy Object (GPO). The standard templates include:

Compatws
: This template contains settings that decrease security for the purposes of compatibility with legacy applications. Settings affect file and Registry permissions.

dc security
: This template contains the default security settings for domain controllers.

Iesacls
: This template applies relaxed Registry permissions for Internet Explorer. Settings configure IE-related Registry permissions that allow Everyone Full Control and Read access.

Rootsec
: This template applies root permissions to the system drive. Settings grant Full Control to Administrators, Creator Owner, and System; Read and Execute permissions to Everyone; and Read and Change permissions to users.

setup security
: This template contains the default security settings for member servers.

securedc
: This template contains moderate security settings for domain controllers that limit account policies and apply LAN Manager restrictions.

securews
: This template contains moderate security settings for workstations that limit local account policies and apply LAN Manager restrictions.

hisecdc
: This template contains very stringent security settings that can be used to further secure domain controllers. Settings disable non-essential services, increase security for NTLM, remove members of the Power Users group, and apply addition security to the Registry and files.

hisecws
: This template contains very stringent security settings that can be used to further secure workstations. Settings increase security for NTLM, remove members of the Power Users group, and limit membership in the local machine Administrators group to Domain Admins and Administrator.

Every GPO has separate computer configuration and user configuration settings. Security templates affect only computer configuration settings, which are located under Computer Configuration in a GPO.

Accessing the security tools

When you are configuring computer security, you'll use both the Security Templates snap-in and the Security Configuration And Analysis snap-in. Use the Security Templates snap-in to view and create security templates. This snap-in can be added to an existing console or to any custom console you create.

Use the Security Configuration And Analysis snap-in to apply templates and to compare the settings in a template to the existing settings on a computer. Applying a template ensures that a computer conforms to a specific security configuration. Comparing settings pinpoints any discrepancies between what is implemented currently and what is defined in a security template. This is useful to determine whether security settings have changed over time.

To access these tools and work with the standard templates, follow these steps:

1. Click Start → Run. Type `mmc` in the Open field, and then click OK.
2. In MMC, click File, and then click Add/Remove Snap-In.
3. In the Standalone tab, click Add.
4. In the Add Standalone Snap-In dialog box, click Security Templates, and then click Add.
5. Click Security Configuration And Analysis, and then click Add.
6. Close the Add Standalone Snap-In dialog box by clicking Close, and then click OK.
7. Security Templates is added to the MMC as shown in Figure 5-33. Expand the nodes and entries under a template to determine the settings the template applies.

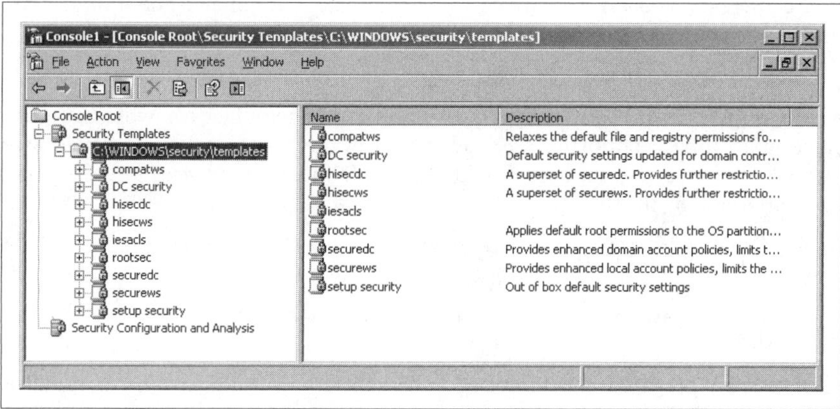

Figure 5-33. Add both security tools to an MMC to get started.

Creating security templates

The standard templates provide a solid starting point for security configurations, based on intended use. If the default security templates don't meet your needs, you can modify the settings. Generally, rather than modifying the standard templates directly, you should create a copy of the template and then modify the copy. You can create a copy of a template and then modify it by completing these steps:

1. Open the Security Templates console.
2. Right-click the template you want to copy, and then click Save As.
3. Type of new name for the template, and then click Save.

4. This creates a copy of the template with the same settings as the original template. You can then modify the settings to meet the needs of the computer role/type for which you are configuring the template.

You can create a new template without initial settings by completing the following steps:

1. Right-click the *C:\Windows\security\templates* node in the Security Templates snap-in, and then select New Template.
2. Type a name and description for the template.
3. Click OK.

Applying security template settings and analyzing security

Security Configuration And Analysis uses a working database to store template security settings and then applies the settings from this database. For analysis and comparisons, the template settings are listed as the effective database settings and the current computer settings are listed as the effective computer settings.

Prior to applying a template, you may want to create a rollback template. A *rollback template* is a reverse template that allows you to remove the settings applied with a template (except those for access control lists on files and in the Registry).

You can create a rollback template using the secedit command-line utility. Type the following:

```
secedit /generaterollback /cfg filename /rbk filename /log filename
```

where `/cfg` *`filename`* sets the name of the security template for which you are creating a rollback template, `/rbk` *`filename`* sets the name of a security template into which the reverse settings should be stored, and `/log` *`filename`* sets the name of an optional log file to use.

In the following example, you are creating a rollback template for the hisecdc security template:

```
secedit /generaterollback /cfg hisecdc.inf /rbk rev-hisecdc.inf /log
rollback.log
```

After you've prepared the template you want to use and created a rollback template as necessary, you can create a database and apply the template by completing the following steps:

1. Access the Security Configuration And Analysis snap-in.
2. Right-click the Security Configuration And Analysis node, and then click Open Database.
3. Type a new database name in the File Name field, and then click Open.
4. In the Import Template dialog box, select the security template to apply, and then click Open.
5. Right-click the Security Configuration And Analysis node and choose Configure Computer Now.
6. When prompted to set the error log path, accept the default or type a new path. Click OK.

7. View the configuration error log by right-clicking the Security Configuration And Analysis node and choosing View Log File.

If you want to compare a computer's current security settings to a particular template, complete the following steps:

1. Access the Security Configuration And Analysis snap-in.
2. Right-click the Security Configuration And Analysis node and then click Open Database.
3. Type a new database name in the File Name field and then click Open.
4. In the Import Template dialog box, select the security template to apply, and then click Open.
5. Right-click the Security Configuration And Analysis node and choose Configure Computer Now.
6. When prompted to set the error log path, accept the default or type a new path. Click OK.
7. Right-click the Security Configuration And Analysis node, and then choose Analyze Computer Now.
8. When prompted to set the error log path, type a new path or click OK to use the default path.
9. Expand nodes and select entries to pinpoint discrepancies between the template and the computer's current settings. Figure 5-34 shows an example.

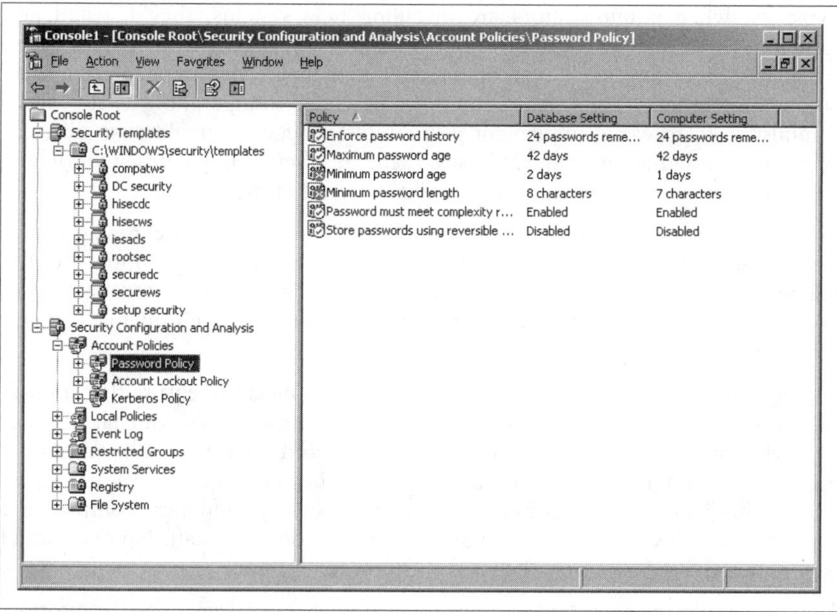

Figure 5-34. Compare the template settings stored in the working database to the computer's current settings to analyze security configurations.

Recovering from the improper application of a template

If you created a rollback template prior to applying a security template, you can recover the computer's security settings to its previous state. To apply a rollback template, follow these steps:

1. Access the Security Configuration And Analysis snap-in.
2. Right-click the Security Configuration And Analysis node and then click Import Template.
3. In the Import Template dialog box, select the rollback template.
4. Select Clear This Database Before Importing.
5. Click Open.
6. Right-click the Security Configuration And Analysis node and then click Configure Computer Now.
7. Click OK.

The only settings that cannot be recovered are the access control lists on files and in the Registry. Those settings can only be recovered to the post-installation state by applying one of the default installation templates. However, you would then need to apply the appropriate security template to the system to ensure security is set at the proper level.

Implementing the principle of least privilege

Typically, when administrators are installing new systems, they'll install and configure these systems by following a baseline configuration document or an automated procedure, such as an operating system image, that implements a baseline configuration. The idea behind a baseline configuration is to allow administrators to easily implement a common configuration. Because different computers have different intended uses, there are often multiple baselines, which are implemented depending on the intended purpose of the computer.

When implementing network security, administrators can use baselines as well to ensure standard network security configurations are applied as appropriate for the role of a computer on the network. Security baselines are implemented using security templates. Security templates can help you ensure that the Principle of Least Privilege is applied throughout your organization.

The Principle of Least Privilege is a guiding principle meant to ensure that no user has more privileges or access than they need to do their job. This principle includes modifying privileges and access as appropriate when users change jobs within the organization, and removing privileges and access when individuals leave the organization. This principle extends to cover all users, including temporary, contract, and permanent employees as well as administrators and other IT staff. No one should have more privileges or access than is required to do their job.

Security templates are a starting point to ensure least privilege access to information and resources. To ensure least privileges, administrators should be logged on using normal user accounts when performing routing tasks. When performing administrative tasks, administrators can log on under the context of a user account that has administrative privileges or use the RUNAS command.

Monitoring and Troubleshooting Network Protocol Security

To ensure that communications remain secure, administrators must make network protocol security monitoring part of the routine tasks they perform. The most important protocols to monitor are IPSec and Kerberos.

Understanding IP Security

IP Security (IPSec) is used to authenticate and encrypt traffic between two computers. IPSec is also used to block or allow traffic. With Active Directory domains, IPSec is applied using Group Policy. However, Active Directory is not required to implement IPSec.

IPSec policy is most often implemented when you need to secure communications on an internal network. For Active Directory–based Group Policy, IPSec policies are stored under *Computer Configuration\Windows Settings\Security Settings\IP Security Settings On Active Directory*. For computers in workgroups, you can configure local group policy under *Computer Configuration\Windows Settings\Security Settings\IP Security Settings On Local Computer*.

An IPSec policy defines packet filters that enforce security by blocking, allowing, or initiating secure communications. Although multiple IPSec policies can be defined, only one such policy is applied at a time. When you apply an IPSec policy to one GPO, you can edit other GPOs and assign the policy within those GPOs as well.

Active Directory has three default IPSec policies:

Server (Request Security) policy
: With this policy, servers always request security using Kerberos trust but do not require secure communications.

Client (Respond Only)
: With this policy, client communication is normally unsecure but they respond to server requests for secure communications.

Secure Server (Require Security)
: With this policy, servers always require secure communications using Kerberos trust. Servers will not respond to clients that do not or cannot use secure communications.

To assign and enforce one of these policies, follow these steps:

1. Open the GPO you want to work with for editing.
2. Access *Computer Configuration\Windows Settings\Security Settings\IP Security Settings\On Active Directory*.
3. The Policy Assigned column indicates whether a policy is assigned.
4. To assign and apply a policy, right-click it and select Assign.

To determine whether IPSec policy is applied to a computer, complete these steps:

1. Click Start → Run. Type `mmc` in the Open field, and then click OK.
2. In MMC, click File, and then click Add/Remove Snap-In.

Exam 70-291 Study Guide

3. In the Standalone tab, click Add.
4. In the Add Standalone Snap-In dialog box, click IP Security Policy Management, and then click Add.
5. In the Select Computer Or Domain window, click Local Computer to analyze the local computer's IPSec policy. Otherwise, click Another Computer and then type the name or IP address of the remote computer to analyze.
6. Click Finish
7. Click Close, and then click OK.

In the MMC, click the IP Security Policies On... node. In the right pane, you'll see a list of IPSec policies defined in the domain. Under Policy Assigned, you'll see an entry of Yes if a policy is being applied. If a policy is not applied, you'll see an entry of No in the Policy Assigned column (see Figure 5-35).

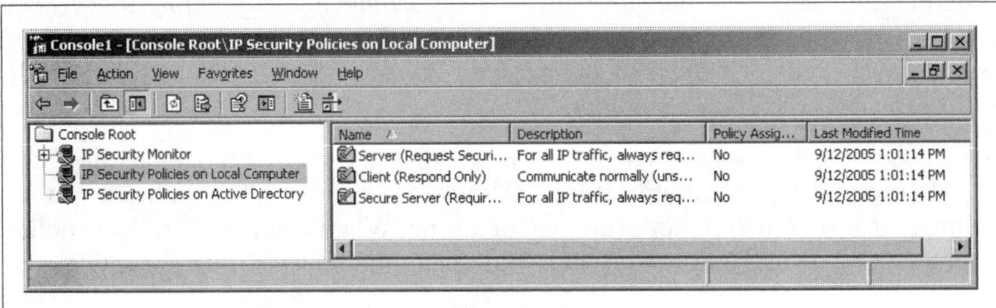

Figure 5-35. Determine whether IPSec is applied to a computer using IP Security Policy Management.

Monitoring and troubleshooting IP Security

You can monitor IPSec policy to ensure that it is working correctly using IP Security Monitor. To access this snap-in in a console, complete these steps:

1. Click Start → Run. Type `mmc` in the Open field, and then click OK.
2. In MMC, click File, and then click Add/Remove Snap-In.
3. In the Standalone tab, click Add.
4. In the Add Standalone Snap-In dialog box, click IP Security Monitor, and then click Add.
5. Click Close, and then click OK.

By default, IP Security Monitor connects to the local computer. If you want to monitor IPSec on another computer, right-click the IP Security Monitor node and then click Add Computer. Expand the computer node and then select the Active Policy entry to see the active IPSec policy on the designated computer (if any). As shown in Figure 5-36, the policy summary includes:

Policy name
: The name of the policy.

Policy description
: The description of the policy.

Policy last modified
: The last modification date of the policy.

Policy store
: The container where the policy is stored within Active Directory.

Policy path
: The LDAP path of the policy.

Organizational unit
: The organizational unit against which the policy is applied.

Group Policy Object Name
: The name of the GPO to which the policy is applied.

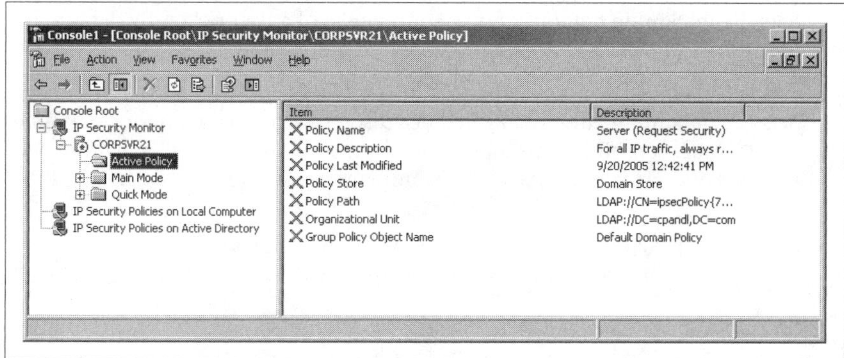

Figure 5-36. View active IPSec policies being applied using IPSec Monitor.

Nodes under Main Mode and Quick Mode show current filters, security methods, statistics, and security associations. High failure rates (relative to the level of IPSec activity) under the Statistics node can indicate IPSec configuration problems. Click the Refresh button to update the details.

Detailed IPSec information can be obtained at a command prompt by typing:

```
netsh ipsec static show all
```

If computers cannot make an IPSec connection, check to see whether the number of Authentication Failures increases. If so, authentication is the issue, and you should ensure that the computers' shared secrets match, the certificates are correct, and the computers are members of the appropriate domain.

If computers cannot make an IPSec connection, check to see whether the number of Negotiation Failures increases. If so, check the security method and authentication settings for incorrect configurations.

Monitoring and troubleshooting Kerberos

In Active Directory domains, Kerberos is the primary authentication protocol. In Group Policy, you'll find Kerberos policies under *Computer Configuration\Windows Settings\Security Settings\Account Policies\Kerberos Policy*.

Kerberos policies available are:

Enforce User Logon Restrictions
: Ensures user account restrictions, such as logon hours and logon workstations, are enforced. By default, the policy is enabled.

Maximum Lifetime For Service Ticket
: Sets the maximum duration for which a service is valid. By default, service tickets have a maximum duration of 600 minutes.

Maximum Lifetime For User Ticket
: Sets the maximum duration for which a user ticket is valid. By default, user tickets have a maximum duration of 10 hours.

Maximum Lifetime For User Ticket Renewal
: Sets the maximum amount of time for renewal of a user ticket. By default, the maximum renewal period is seven days.

Maximum Tolerance For Computer Clock Synchronization
: Sets the maximum amount of tolerance discrepancies in computer clock time. By default, computers in the domain must be synchronized within five minutes of each other. If they aren't, authentication fails.

In Active Directory domains, Windows Time services are used to automatically synchronize system clocks.

Kerberos problems can be diagnosed using Netdiag. To perform multiple diagnostic tests on Kerberos type the following at a command prompt:

```
netdiag /test:kerberos /debug
```

The results of each test are given as Passed or Failed. Of particular interest is the following line at the beginning of the output:

```
Testing Kerberos authentication... Passed
```

And the following lines at the end of the output:

```
Domain membership test . . . . . . : Passed
    Machine is a . . . . . . . . . : Primary Domain Controller Emulator
    Netbios Domain name. . . . . . : CPANDL
    Dns domain name. . . . . . . . : cpandl.com
    Dns forest name. . . . . . . . : cpandl.com
    Domain Guid. . . . . . . . . . : {3EF32F2E-C326-4343-8434-434342542543}
    Domain Sid . . . . . . . . . . : S-1-5-21-490342342-1024332424-622343242
    Logon User . . . . . . . . . . : Administrator
    Logon Domain . . . . . . . . . : CPANDL

Kerberos test. . . . . . . . . . . : Passed

    Find DC in domain 'CPANDL':
    Found this DC in domain 'CPANDL':
        DC. . . . . . . . . . . : \\corpsvr21.cpandl.com
        Address . . . . . . . . : \\192.168.0.25
        Domain Guid . . . . . . : {1C143232-C243-4234-8234-42F343243242}
```

```
        Domain Name . . . . . . : cpandl.com
        Forest Name . . . . . . : cpandl.com
        DC Site Name. . . . . . : Default-First-Site-Name
        Our Site Name . . . . . : Default-First-Site-Name
        Flags . . . . . . . . . : PDC emulator GC DS KDC TIMESERV GTIMESERV
WRIT
ABLE DNS_DC DNS_DOMAIN DNS_FOREST CLOSE_SITE 0x8
    Cached Tickets:
```

In this example, Kerberos is operating normally and has passed all the appropriate tests. If something were wrong, this would have been reported and you could pinpoint the source of the problem.

Implementing, Managing, and Maintaining Routing and Remote Access

Local area networks (LANs), wide area networks (WANs), dial-up connections, and virtual private networks (VPNs) all have increasing roles in the connected workplace, which means routing and remote access are an increasingly significant area of responsibility for today's administrators. Administrators are expected to know which of the myriad of routing and remote access options available to use when a need arises, and they are expected to know how to manage and maintain the implemented technologies.

Understanding Routing and Remote Access

Using the Routing And Remote Access Service (RRAS), Windows Server 2003 can be configured as a multipurpose remote access server and IP router for connecting LANs to LANs, LANs to WANs, dial-up to LANs, and VPNs to LANs. The key advantages of using Windows Server 2003 in this role are that it allows easier management, support, and network integration as compared to hardware routers. Ease of management, support, and integration come primarily from the fact that administrators implement access controls and permission rules using standard Windows security and group policies.

In the role as remote access server, a RRAS server can be configured for:

- Remote access over wireless, dial-up, or VPN, which enables computers to connect to the server using a dial-up or VPN connection.
- Network Address Translation (NAT), which allows internal computers to access the Internet using a public IP address from an assigned address pool.
- VPN and NAT, which allows remote clients to connect to the server through the Internet, and local clients to connect to the Internet using a public IP address from an assigned address pool.
- Secure connections between two private networks, which can be used to connect the network on which the server is located to a remote network.
- Custom configuration, which allows any combination of the available features.

Following this, a single RRAS server can handle both remote access and NAT. Remote access can also be configured for switched Ethernet connections and secure connections between private networks.

In the role as IP router, a RRAS server can be configured with static routing tables and one or more network routing protocols. Each routing protocol has a different intended purpose and function. The routing protocols you'll typically work with include:

DHCP Relay Agent routing protocol
: Allows the server to route DHCP broadcast messages between subnets. DHCP Relay Agent routing protocol is essential for organizations with centralized DHCP servers and multiple subnets.

Routing Information Protocol (RIP) Version 2 for Internet Protocol
: Allows dynamic routing between subnets. RIP is an easily managed routing protocol, but limited to a maximum hop count of 15. For successful communications, source and destination computers can have no more than 15 routing devices between them.

Open Shortest Path First (OSPF)
: Allows extended dynamic routing between subnets. With OSPF, source and destination computers can have more than 15 routing devices between them. However, OSPF is more complex to configure and maintain than RIP.

The Routing And Remote Access console is used to manage all aspects of RRAS. To access the console, click Start → Programs → Administrative Tools → Routing And Remote Access. When you start the console on a RRAS server, the console connects automatically to RRAS on this server. If you start the RRAS console on your workstation or want to connect to a different RRAS server, you can do this by right-clicking the Routing And Remote Access node and selecting Add Server. You can then use the Add Server dialog box to select the remote server you want to work with by its fully qualified domain name or IP address.

The status of all servers to which you are connected can be viewed by clicking the Server Status node. As shown in Figure 5-37, servers are listed by name, type, state, ports in use, total ports, and uptime in days:hours:minutes. To manage the underlying service, right-click a server entry, click All Tasks, and then select Start, Stop, Pause, or Restart as appropriate.

By default, the Routing And Remote Access service is installed by Windows Server 2003 Setup but is disabled. Before you can use RRAS, you must enable and preliminarily configure RRAS. Once you've done this, you must complete the configuration of each remote access and IP routing feature you plan to use. Thus, the process for completing the setup of RRAS requires the following:

1. Implementing Routing and Remote Access Service.
2. Adding and configuring necessary network interfaces.
3. Configuring Routing and Remote Access Service properties.
4. Adding and configuring necessary IP routing protocols.

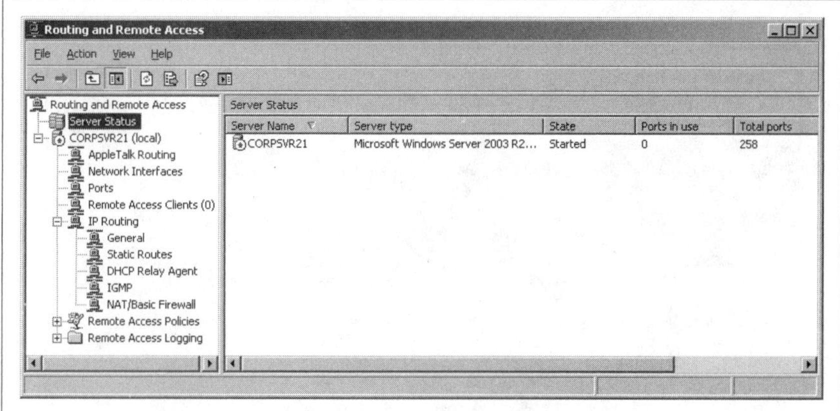

Figure 5-37. View the status of RRAS servers using the Server Status node.

Implementing Routing and Remote Access

Before you can configure a RRAS server in any role, you must configure the server for Routing And Remote Access and then enable the Routing And Remote Access Service. Routing And Remote Access servers cannot use the Windows Firewall/Internet Connection Sharing service. To disable the Windows Firewall/Internet Connection Sharing service, follow these steps:

1. Click Start → Programs → Administrative Tools → Services.
2. Right-click Windows Firewall/Internet Connection Sharing and select Stop.
3. Right-click Windows Firewall/Internet Connection Sharing and select Properties.
4. Set Startup Type to Disabled and then click OK.

The Routing And Remote Access service is installed by Windows Server 2003 Setup but is disabled. You can enable and preliminarily configure this service by completing these steps:

1. Open Routing And Remote Access. Connect to the server you want to work with (if necessary).
2. Right-click the server entry and then select Configure And Enable Routing And Remote Access.
3. When the Routing And Remote Access Server Setup wizard starts, click Next.
4. Select Custom Configuration and then click Next.
5. As shown in Figure 5-38, you can now select the services that you want to enable on the server. Select only the services you plan to configure.
6. Click Next, and then click Finish.
7. When prompted to start the Routing And Remote Access service, click Yes.

During the installation, the RRAS server is made a member of the RAS And IAS Servers security group in the local domain. This membership is required for proper working of routing and remote access.

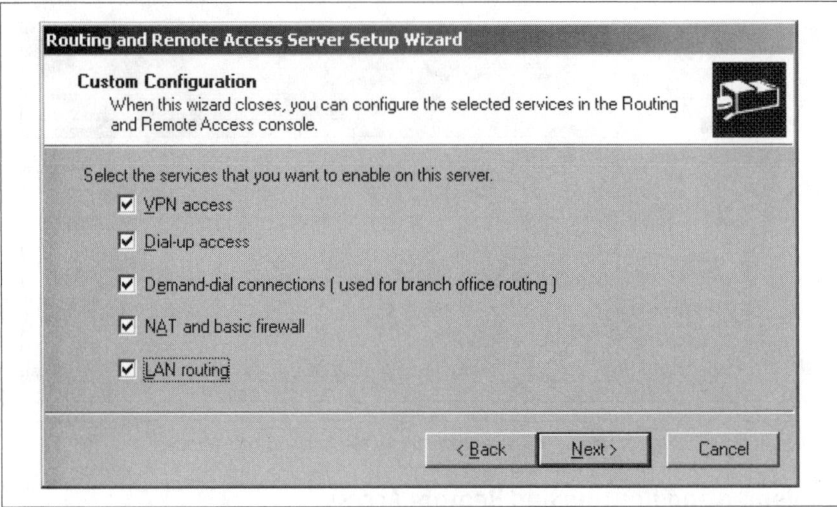

Figure 5-38. Configure a RRAS server to support the services you plan to implement.

Adding Interfaces and Implementing Secure Access Between Private Networks

Hardware routers have built-in ports that are used to connect network segments. By routing traffic from one port to another, a hardware router is able to route traffic between network segments. Generally, the number of network segments that can be connected depends on the number of built-in ports.

With RRAS, the number of network segments that can be routed is dependent on the number of network interfaces installed on the RRAS server. For example, if a RRAS server has three network cards and two modem cards, RRAS can route traffic among five networks.

The three types of network interfaces you can add and configure are:

- Network connections
- Dial-up connections
- VPN connections

These three connections are added and configured in different ways. Only VPN connections are used to implement secure access between private networks.

Adding and configuring interfaces for network connections

When you run the Routing And Remote Access Server Setup wizard, it attempts to automatically detect all installed network interfaces. The detected network interfaces are then listed on the Network Interfaces node in the Routing And Remote Access console. When you access the Network Interfaces node, you should see a local area connection for each interface card. You'll also see an interface listing for the local loopback interface and a local internal interface. If you install a new network after you configure RRAS, you'll need to manually add the interface.

To manually add a routing interface, follow these steps:

1. Open Routing And Remote Access. Connect to the server you want to work with (if necessary).
2. Expand the server node and the related IP-routing node.
3. Right-click the General node and then select New Interface.
4. In the Interfaces dialog box, click the new interface to add, and then click OK.
5. If prompted, configure the interface as appropriate.

Adding and configuring interfaces for dial-up connections

Preconfigured dial-up connections are not automatically added or configured. If you want to configure routing through on-demand or persistent dial-up connections, you must add these connections manually as demand-dial interfaces.

To add as demand-dial interfaces, follow these steps:

1. Open Routing And Remote Access. Connect to the server you want to work with (if necessary).
2. Expand the server node. Right-click the Network Interfaces node and then select New Demand-Dial Interface.
3. When the Demand-Dial Interface Wizard starts, click Next.
4. Enter a name for the interface. Click Next.
5. Select Connect Using A Modem, ISDN, Or Other Physical Device. Click Next.
6. Continue with the rest of the wizards screen.

Adding and configuring interfaces for VPN and PPPoE connections

VPN and Point-to-Point Protocol over Ethernet (PPPoE) are used for secure communications between private networks. Although the private networks can be either directly connected or connected over dial-up, VPN and PPPoE connections are configured manually as demand-dial interfaces.

To add a demand dial interface for VPN or PPPoE, follow these steps:

1. Open Routing And Remote Access. Connect to the server you want to work with (if necessary).
2. Expand the server node. Right-click the Network Interfaces node and then select New Demand-Dial Interface.
3. When the Demand-Dial Interface Wizard starts, click Next. Enter a name for the interface. Click Next.
4. Select either the Connect Using Virtual Private Networking (VPN) radio button or the Connect Using PPP Over Ethernet (PPoE) radio button as appropriate. Click Next.

5. If you are configuring VPN, choose the type of VPN interface and then click Next. Both Point-to-Point Tunneling Protocol (PPTP) and Layer 2 Tunneling Protocol (L2TP) are supported. By default, the appropriate protocol can be automatically selected when a connection is made. However, only L2TP uses IPSec for advanced encryption, making it more secure. Click Next.
6. If you are configuring PPPoE, optionally type the name of your organization's broadband connection provider. Click Next.
7. Enter the IP address of the router to which you are connecting, as shown in Figure 5-39. Click Next.

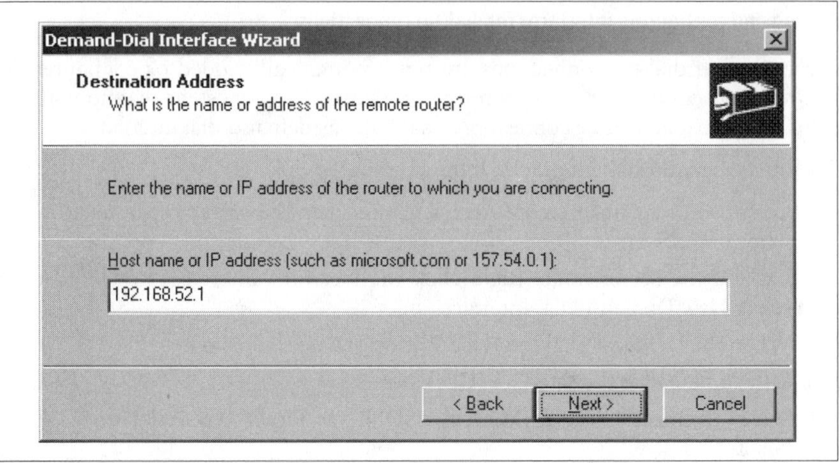

Figure 5-39. Specify the destination address for the VPN connection.

8. Select the transports and security options. The Route IP Packets On This Interface checkbox is selected by default. Click Next.
9. Specify the permanent static routes to the remote networks with which this network will communicate (see Figure 5-40). Click Add. In the Destination field, enter the network ID of the destination network. In the Network Mask field, enter the network mask of the destination network. In the Metric field, enter the relative cost of routing via this router. Click OK.
10. Repeat Step 9 to add other static routes. Click Next when you are ready to continue.
11. Click Next. Enter the user credentials to use to connect to the remote router.
12. Click Next, and then click Finish.

Configuring Remote Access Server Service Properties

RRAS server properties are used to configure many aspects of remote access, including user authentication. In the Routing And Remote Access console, access server properties by right-clicking the server node and selecting Properties. Although most changes are applied automatically, some changes, such as modification of authentication providers, require that you restart the Routing And

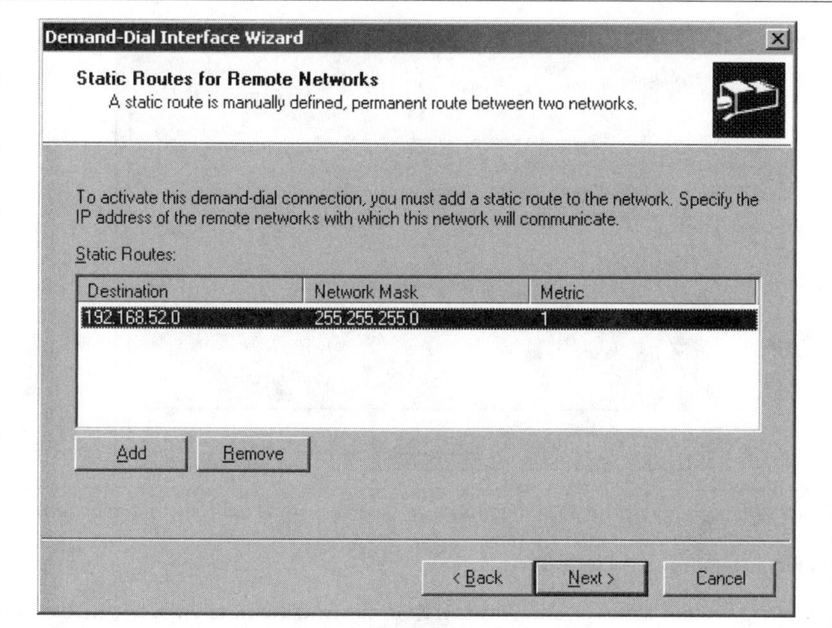

Figure 5-40. Specify static routes by the network ID, network mask, and metric.

Remote Access service. To do this, right-click a server entry, click All Tasks, and then select Restart. If you want to completely disable RRAS, right-click the server entry and then select Disable Routing And Remote Access.

Managing the Remote Access Server configuration

If you right-click a server entry in the Routing And Remote Access console and select Properties, you can use the General tab options to reconfigure RRAS (see Figure 5-41). The following list describes the options available:

Router
: Enables IP routing for use with DHCP relay agents, RIP, OSPF, etc.

Local Area Network (LAN) Routing Only
: Limits IP routing to LAN routing only, and does not allow demand-dial or VPN connections between networks.

LAN and demand-dial routing
: Allows both LAN and demand-dial routing, and supports VPN connections between networks.

Remote Access Server
: Allows the server to handle remote access connections from clients that use either dial-up or VPN.

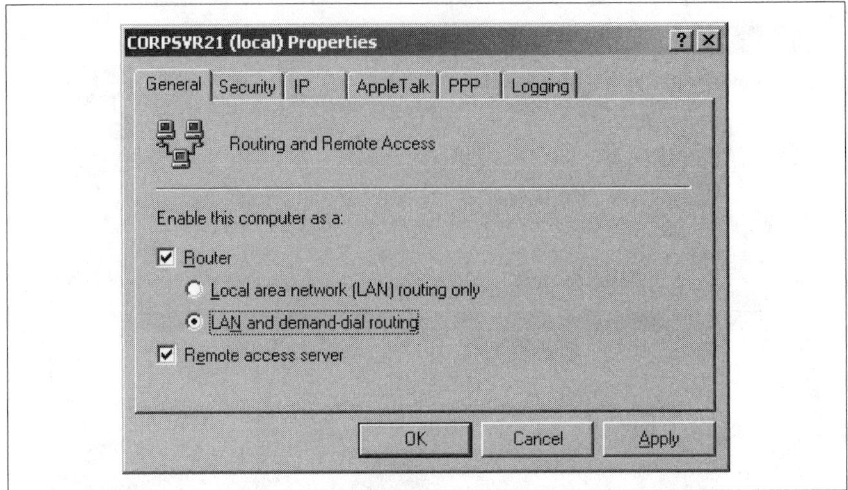

Figure 5-41. Modify the RRAS configuration as necessary using the General tab options.

Managing remote access security

If you right-click a server entry in the Routing And Remote Access console and select Properties, you can use the Security tab options to configure remote access security (see Figure 5-42). The Authentication Provider list lets you specify how remote access clients and demand-dial routers are authenticated. The authentication options are:

Windows Authentication
: The default authentication method is Windows Authentication, which lets you use standard Windows security for authentication.

RADIUS Authentication
: Remote Authentication Dial-in User Service (RADIUS) should be used only if your organization has RADIUS servers, which are used to centralize the authentication of remote access clients and the storage of accounting information.

The Accounting Provider list lets you specify whether and how connection requests and sessions are logged. The accounting options are:

None
: Turns off logging of connection requests and sessions.

Windows Accounting
: Logs connection request and sessions in logfiles stored in the Remote Access Logging folder.

RADIUS Accounting
: Sends details about connection request and sessions to the RADIUS server. The RADIUS server in turn logs this information.

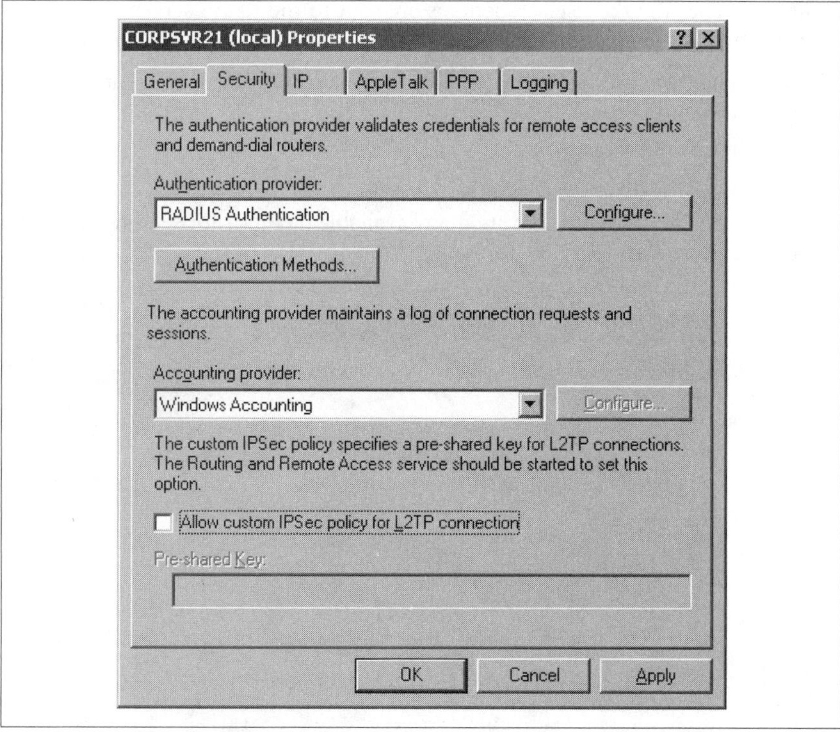

Figure 5-42. Configure RRAS server security.

The final security option you can set for an RRAS server is used with VPN. If you've configured VPN and set L2TP as the protocol type, you can use IPSec with L2TP to enhance security. To do this, you must define a custom IPSec policy and enable the related security options for your RRAS server by doing the following:

1. Right-click a server entry in the Routing And Remote Access console and select Properties.
2. Click the Security tab.
3. Select the Allow Custom IPSec Policy For L2TP Connection checkbox.
4. In the Pre-Shared Key text box, type a preshared key to use with the custom IPSec policy.
5. Each client computer that will remotely access the network over VPN and be subject to the IPSec policy must be configured with the same preshared key.

Managing user authentication

Security is a critical component of routing and remote access. In a standard configuration of RRAS, the RRAS server uses Windows authentication to authenticate remote clients and logs connection request and session details in the System event logs. The way the user credentials are sent to the RRAS server depends on the permitted authentication methods, which can be set by following these steps:

1. Right-click a server entry in the Routing And Remote Access console, and then select Properties.
2. Click the Security tab.
3. Click the Authentication Methods button.
4. As Figure 5-43 shows, there are many available methods for sending authentication credentials to a RRAS server.

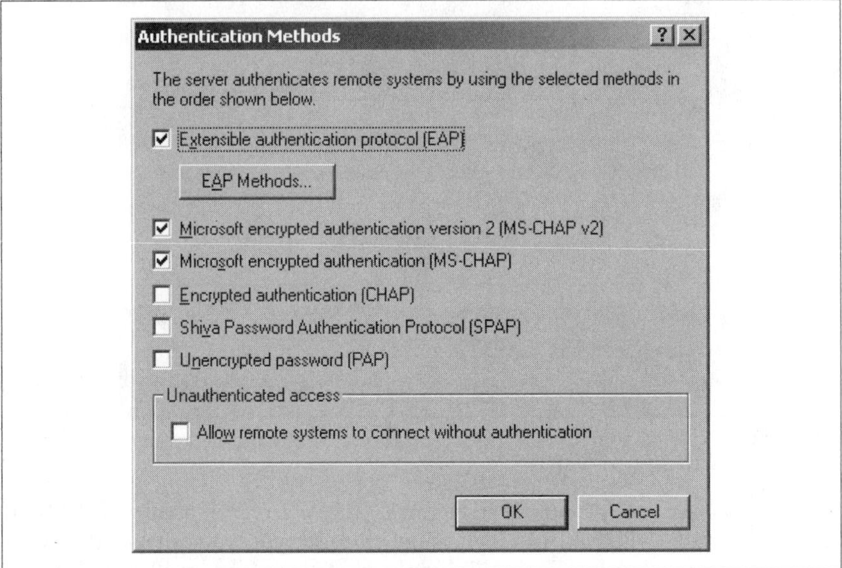

Figure 5-43. Configure the permitted user authentication methods.

When remote clients attempt to connect to the RRAS server, the server attempts to authenticate the client using the selected authentication methods. The authentication methods are used in the order shown and are essentially organized from the most secure to the least secure. The available user authentication methods are:

Extensible Authentication Protocol (EAP)
: Extensible Authentication Protocol (EAP) extends the authentication methods for PPP connections to include the EAP methods configured through remote access policies. In a standard configuration, these policies allow MD5-Challenge, Protected EAP (PEAP), Smart card, or other PKI certificate to be used.

EAP is required if you want to use smart cards with remote access clients.

Microsoft Encrypted Authentication version 2 (MS-CHAP v2)
: Microsoft Encrypted Authentication version 2 (MS-CHAP v2) uses Microsoft Challenge Handshake Authentication Protocol (MS-CHAP) version 2 to authenticate remote access and demand-dial connections using mutual authentication and strong encryption. MS-CHAP v2 is required for encrypted PPP and PPTP connections.

Microsoft Encrypted Authentication (MS-CHAP)
: Microsoft Encrypted Authentication (MS-CHAP) uses Microsoft Challenge Handshake Authentication Protocol (MS-CHAP) to authenticate remote access and demand-dial connections using encryption. MS-CHAP is required for encrypted PPP and PPTP connections.

Encrypted Authentication (CHAP)
: Encrypted Authentication (CHAP) uses MD-5 Challenge Handshake Authentication Protocol (CHAP) to authenticate remote access and demand-dial connections using encryption.

Shiva Password Authentication Protocol (SPAP)
: Shiva Password Authentication Protocol (SPAP) uses authentication with reversible encryption and is compatible with Shiva LAN Rover and Shiva clients. SPAP is not secure.

Unencrypted Password (PAP)
: Unencrypted Password (PAP) uses Password Authentication Protocol (PAP) and sends passwords in plain-text during authentication. PAP is the most unsecure authentication method.

Remote access policies for use with EAP are specified using the Remote Access Policies node in the Routing And Remote Access console. Policies are applied in priority order. The two standard policies are:

- Connections To Microsoft Routing And Remote Access Server, which applies to connections to the currently selected RRAS server.
- Connections To Other Access Servers, which applies to connections to other access servers via the current server.

These policies are extremely important when your organization uses RADIUS servers for centralizing remote access client authentication. New remote access policies can be created by right-clicking the Remote Access Policies node in the Routing And Remote Access console, selecting New Remote Access Policy, and then following the prompts by the New Remote Access Policy Wizard.

Each policy can have a dial-in profile associated with it, which is used to set access permissions. Right-click a policy, select Properties, and then click the Edit Profile button to view and modify the profile settings. Remote access settings defined in a user's profile have precedence over dial-in profile settings.

Managing IP assignment

If you right-click a server entry in the Routing And Remote Access console and select Properties, you can use the IP tab options to configure IP assignment (see Figure 5-44). IP assignment settings determine whether and how remote access clients are assigned IP addresses.

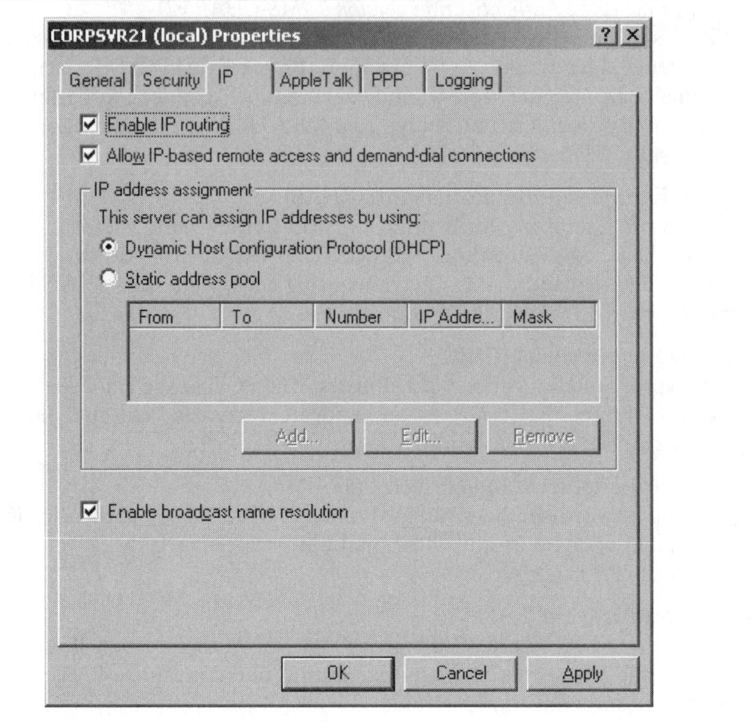

Figure 5-44. Configure IP address assignment.

The IP assignment options you can configure are:

Enable IP Routing
: IP Routing controls the forwarding of IP packets from one routing interface to another. You must select the IP Routing checkbox for LAN and demand-dial routing to occur. If you want IP-based remote access clients to be able to access the entire network to which the RRAS server is attached, select the IP Routing checkbox. If you want IP-based remote access clients to be able to access the RRAS server but not the network, clear the Enable IP Routing checkbox.

Allow IP-based Remote Access And Demand-Dial Connections
: If you select the Allow IP-based Remote Access And Demand-Dial Connections checkbox, IP-based remote access and demand-dial connections can be established using RRAS. All Point-to-Point Protocol (PPP) connections will then negotiate connections using Internet Protocol Control Protocol (IPCP). The PPP settings used are configured on the PPP tab of the Properties dialog box.

Dynamic Host Configuration Protocol (DHCP)
: If you select this option, the RRAS server assigns client IP addresses using DHCP. On your organization's DHCP servers, you can use the Default Routing And Remote Access Class to define a separate configuration for remote access clients. If you do not do this, remote access clients will use the same configuration as other DHCP clients.

On your organization's DHCP server, the scopes must be large enough so that the RRAS servers can requests blocks of 10 IP addresses. There must be at least 10 free IP addresses available on the DHCP server for the RRAS clients.

Static Address Pool
: If you select this option, the RRAS server assigns remote access clients static IP addresses from the defined IP address pools. Click the Add button to define a range of IP addresses to use as an address pool.

Enable Broadcast Name Resolution
: If you select this option, remote access clients can use broadcast messages to resolve hostnames on the local subnet to which they connect without having to use WINS or DNS. Broadcasts are not forwarded to other subnets.

Managing remote access logging

If you right-click a server entry in the Routing And Remote Access console and select Properties, you can use the Logging tab options to configure event logging and debugging. RRAS events are stored in the System event logs, and by default, only errors and warnings are recorded. You can modify the logging configuration to log errors only, to log all events, or to stop logging.

For debugging connections to RRAS, you can select the Log Additional Routing And Remote Access Information checkbox. When debugging is enabled, PPP connection events for remote access and demand-dial routing connections are written to *Ppp.log* in the *%SystemRoot%\Tracing* folder.

Managing DHCP Relay Agents

DHCP clients use broadcast messages to contact DHCP servers. Generally, broadcasts aren't routed between subnets and are limited by the logical boundaries of a subnet. Because of this, you normally need at least one DHCP server for each subnet in your organization. In large networks, it quickly can become impractical to have one DHCP server per subnet. You can work around this restriction by configuring DHCP relay agents on subnets. A relay agent is a router or a computer on the network that is configured to listen for DHCP broadcasts and forward the DHCP broadcasts between clients and servers.

Any router that supports BOOTP forwarding—i.e., routers that are RFC-1542 compliant—can be configured as a relay agent. With BOOTP forwarding, the router forwards DHCP broadcasts from DHCP clients to DHCP servers and informs the DHCP server of the originating subnet. This allows the responding DHCP server to assign addresses to remote clients from the appropriate scope.

Using Routing And Remote Access, any Windows 2000 or later server can act as a DHCP relay agent as well. The process is similar to BOOTP forwarding, and the server acting as the relay agent doesn't need to be configured as a network router between subnets. To configure a server as a DHCP relay agent, you must perform the steps that follow:

1. Install the DHCP Relay Agent routing protocol.
2. Configure the DHCP Relay Agent routing protocol.
3. Enable the DHCP Relay Agent routing protocol.

Once the DHCP Relay Agent routing protocol is installed, configured, and enabled, you can view the status by selecting the DHCP Relay Agent node in the Routing And Remote Access console.

Installing the DHCP Relay Agent routing protocol

You can install the DHCP Relay Agent routing protocol by completing these steps:

1. Open Routing And Remote Access. Connect to the server you want to work with (if necessary).
2. Expand the server node, and then expand the IP Routing node.
3. Right-click the General node, and then select New Routing Protocol.
4. Click DHCP Relay Agent, and then click OK.

Configuring the DHCP Relay Agent routing protocol

You can configure the DHCP Relay Agent routing protocol by completing these steps:

1. Open Routing And Remote Access. Connect to the server you want to work with (if necessary).
2. Expand the server node, and then expand the IP Routing node.
3. Right-click DHCP Relay Agent, and then select Properties.
4. Type the IP address of a DHCP server for the network, and then click Add. Repeat to specify additional DHCP servers.
5. Click OK.

Enabling the DHCP Relay Agent routing protocol

Once you've installed and configured the DHCP Relay Agent routing protocol, you must enable one or more of the server's network interfaces. To do this, follow these steps:

1. Open Routing And Remote Access. Connect to the server you want to work with (if necessary).
2. Expand the server node, and then expand the IP Routing node.
3. Right-click DHCP Relay Agent, and then select New Interface.
4. Click the network interface on which you want to enable the routing protocol.
5. Click OK.
6. A new dialog box is displayed with the Relay DHCP Packets checkbox selected by default.

7. Use Hop-Count Threshold to set the maximum number of routers through which DHCP broadcasts can be relayed. The default is four.
8. Use Boot Threshold (Seconds) to specify the number of seconds the relay agents waits before forwarding DHCP messages. The default is four seconds.
9. Click OK.

Managing TCP/IP Routing

When you install Routing And Remote Access and enable IP routing, you can add routing protocols. As discussed previously, the key protocols you'll work with are Routing Information Protocol (RIP) version 2 for Internet Protocol and Open Shortest Path First (OSPF). Also, as mentioned, both protocols allow you to dynamically manage routing. RIP is ideal for small networks because it is easy to set up and configure. OSPF is better for larger networks as it is more configurable and can be used on extended networks with more than 15 routers between segments.

Installing RIP and OSPF

You can install the RIP or OSPF routing protocol by completing these steps:

1. Open Routing And Remote Access. Connect to the server you want to work with (if necessary).
2. Expand the server node, and then expand the IP Routing node.
3. Right-click the General node, and then select New Routing Protocol.
4. Click Routing Information Protocol (RIP) version 2 for Internet Protocol or Open Shortest Path First (OSPF) as appropriate.
5. Click OK.

After RIP and OSPF have been installed, you can configure them as follows in "Configuring RIP" and "Configuring OSPF," respectively.

Configuring RIP

When an RIP router is initially configured, the only entries in its routing tables are for the networks to which it is physically connected. The router then starts sending announcements of its availability to other routers of the networks it services. Responses from announcements allow the router to update its routing tables.

The way announcements are made depends on the operating mode. One of two operation modes can be selected: *periodic update mode*, in which RIP announcements are sent periodically to learn of available routes, and routes are deleted automatically when the router is stopped and restarted; and *auto-static update mode*, in which RIP announcements are sent when other routers request updates, learned routes are added as static, and routes remain until they are manually deleted. When changes occur to the network topology, RIP version 2 uses triggered updates to communicate the changes to other routers.

After RIP has been installed, you must specify the network interface or interfaces through which the protocol will be used. To do this, follow these steps:

1. Open Routing And Remote Access. Connect to the server you want to work with (if necessary).
2. Expand the server node, and then expand the IP Routing node.
3. Right-click the RIP node, and then select New Interface.
4. Select one of the available network interfaces through which RIP traffic can be routed. Any available interface can be selected, and the same interface can be used by multiple IP routing protocols.
5. Click OK.

The RIP Properties dialog box is displayed. You can now configure RIP as discussed in this section. The RIP Properties dialog box can also be displayed by right-clicking the RIP node and then selecting Properties. The RIP Properties dialog box has two tabs:

General
: The General tab options control triggered update delays and event logging. By default, the maximum amount of time the router waits before it sends triggered updates is five seconds. By default, only errors are logged. You can modify these settings as necessary.

Security
: The Security tab options control how the router processes announcements. By default announcements from all routers are accepted. You can modify this so only announcements from listed routers are accepted, or so announcements from all routers except those listed are accepted.

After you set the general RIP options, set the connection properties. The connection Properties dialog box can also be displayed by clicking the RIP node in the left pane, right-clicking the network interface, and then selecting Properties. As shown in Figure 5-45, the connection Properties dialog box has four tabs:

General
: The General tab options allow you to configure the operation mode, packet protocol, and authentication. One of two operation modes can be selected: periodic update mode or auto-static update mode. The outgoing and incoming packet protocol options let you specify the required protocol compliance levels. The Activate Authentication and Password options let you enable authentication for all incoming and outgoing packets. When authentication is used, neighboring routers must be configured with identical authentication passwords. These passwords are sent in clear text.

Security
: The Security tab options allow you to configure RIP route filters. For incoming routes, the router can be configured to accept all routes, accept all routes in the ranges listed, or allow all routes except those specifically ignored. For outgoing routes, the router can be configured to announce all routes, announce all routes in the ranges listed, or to announce all routes except for those specifically ignored.

Neighbors

The Neighbors tab options allow you to configure how the router interacts with other RIP routers. By default, the router uses broadcasts or multicast only, and doesn't have defined neighbors. You can add specific neighbor routers in addition to or instead of broadcast or multicast.

Advanced

The Advanced tab options control periodic announcements, routing expiration and processing.

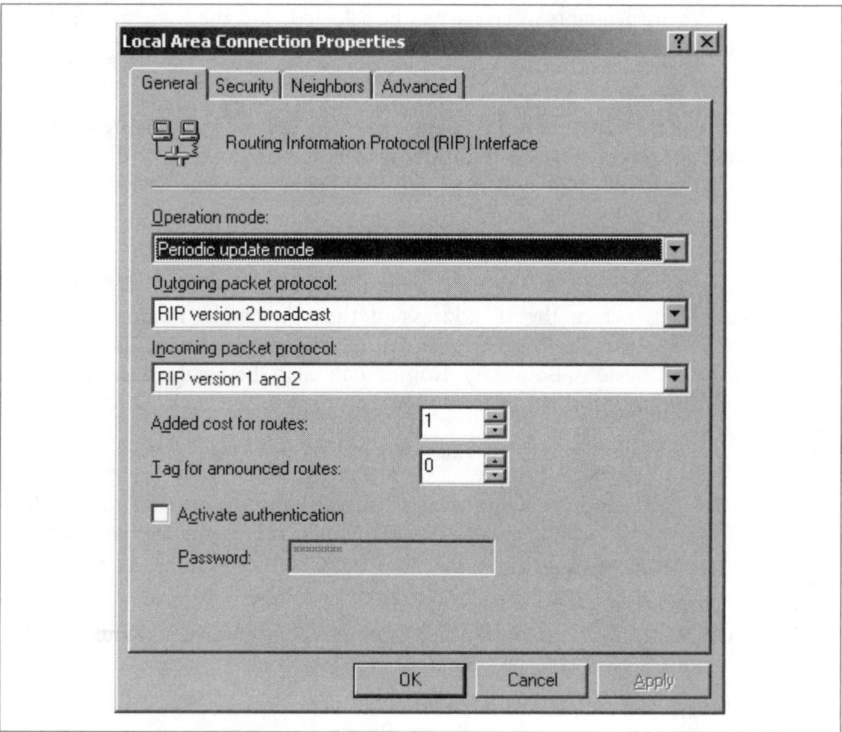

Figure 5-45. Configuring routing properties for RIP.

Configuring OSPF

OSPF uses the Shortest Path First (SPF) algorithm to calculate routes. The route with the lowest route cost is the shortest path, and the shortest path is always used first when routing. An OSPF router maintains a link-state database that it uses to track the network topology. The database is synchronized with adjacent routers or specifically defined nonbroadcast multiple access (NBMA) neighbors. When a change is made to the network topology, the first router to identify the change sends out a change notification. This change notification is used to update the link-state database so that the routing tables can be recalculated automatically.

Unlike RIP, OSPF divides the network into transit areas, which can be thought of as areas of responsibility. OSPF routers maintain link-state information only for those transit areas for which they've been configured. After OSPF has been installed, you must specify the network interface or interfaces through which the protocol will be used. To do this, follow these steps:

1. Open Routing And Remote Access. Connect to the server you want to work with (if necessary).
2. Expand the server node, and then expand the IP Routing node.
3. Right-click the OSPF node, and then select New Interface.
4. Select one of the available network interfaces through which RIP traffic can be routed. Any available interface can be selected, and the same interface can be used by multiple IP routing protocols.
5. Click OK.

The OSPF Properties dialog box is displayed. You can now configure OSPF as discussed in this section. The OSPF Properties dialog box can also be displayed by right-clicking the OSPF node and then selecting Properties. The OSPF Properties dialog box has four tabs:

General
: The General tab options set the router ID and control event logging. The network ID is set to the IP address of the connection automatically. By default, only errors are logged. You can modify these settings as necessary. Autonomous System Boundary Router can also be enabled to advertise external routing information from other route sources, such as static routes or OSPF.

Areas
: The Areas tab options can be used to subdivide the network into specific transit areas. The default area is 0.0.0.0, which represents the backbone of the current network.

Virtual Interfaces
: The Virtual Interfaces tab options allow you to configure virtual interfaces for transit areas.

External Routing
: The External Routing tab options allow you to configure Autonomous System Boundary Routing. By default, when enabled, all routes from all route sources are accepted.

After you set the general OSPF options, you should set the properties for connections, virtual connections, or both. The related Properties dialog box can also be displayed by clicking the OSPF node in the left pane, right-clicking the connection and then selecting Properties. The connection Properties dialog box includes these tabs:

General
: The General tab options allow you to configure the area ID, router priority, cost, and password. Using the Network Type options, you can specify whether the router is a broadcast interface, point-to-point interface, or nonbroadcast multiple access (NBMA) interface.

NMBA Neighbors

When the network type is an NBMA interface, the NMBA Neighbors tab options allow you to specify the IP addresses and router priority of NMBA neighbors.

Advanced

The Advanced tab options control transit delays, retransmit intervals, Hello intervals for discovery, Dead intervals for determining down routers, and poll intervals for follow-ups to dead routers. The default maximum transmission unit is 1,500 bytes. This is the standard packet size of IP networks.

Configuring routing tables

Although RIP and OSPF allow dynamic routing, you sometimes need to use static routing. *Static routes* provide a permanent mapping to a specific destination network, according to the network ID, network mask, and relative cost of the route. Routers can use this information to determine the gateway to use to forward packets so that hosts on a destination network can be reached. Static routes are not shared between routers.

You can configure static routes using the Routing And Remote Access console or the `route add` command. To view existing static routes in the Routing And Remote Access console, follow these steps:

1. Open Routing And Remote Access. Connect to the server you want to work with (if necessary).
2. Expand the server node, and then expand the IP Routing node.
3. Click the Static Routes node.
4. When no routes are configured, the default route with a destination address and subnet mask of 0.0.0.0 is shown.

To add a static route using the Routing And Remote Access console, follow these steps:

1. Open Routing And Remote Access. Connect to the server you want to work with (if necessary).
2. Expand the server node, and then expand the IP Routing node.
3. Right-click the Static Routes node, and then select New Static Route.
4. In the Static Route dialog box shown in Figure 5-46, specify the interface for which the static route will be used.
5. In the Destination and Network Mask fields, specify the destination network ID and network mask.
6. In the Gateway field, specify the IP address of the gateway for the RRAS server.
7. In the Metric field, specify the relative cost of the route.
8. Click OK.

In the Routing And Remote Access console, you can delete a static route by right-clicking it and then selecting Delete.

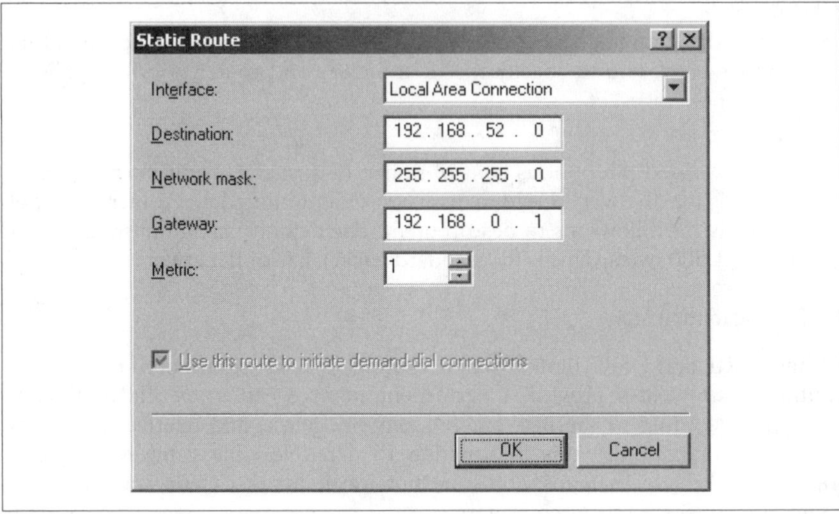

Figure 5-46. Configure the static route.

Before you work with static routes at a command prompt, you should print the currently configured static routes by entering `route print`. The output of route print shows current interfaces, static routes, and persistent routes, as shown here:

```
IPv4 Route Table
===========================================================================
Interface List
0x1 ........................... MS TCP Loopback interface
0x10003 ...00 03 ff 6b ef 12 ...... Intel 21140-Based PCI Fast Ethernet
Adapter
(Generic)
===========================================================================
===========================================================================
Active Routes:
Network Destination        Netmask          Gateway       Interface  Metric
          0.0.0.0          0.0.0.0     192.168.0.25    192.168.0.25      20
        127.0.0.0        255.0.0.0        127.0.0.1       127.0.0.1       1
      192.168.0.0    255.255.255.0     192.168.0.25    192.168.0.25      20
     192.168.0.25  255.255.255.255        127.0.0.1       127.0.0.1      20
    192.168.0.255  255.255.255.255     192.168.0.25    192.168.0.25      20
     192.168.52.0    255.255.255.0          0.0.0.0        ffffffff       1
        224.0.0.0        240.0.0.0     192.168.0.25    192.168.0.25      20
  255.255.255.255  255.255.255.255     192.168.0.25    192.168.0.25       1
Default Gateway:      192.168.0.25
===========================================================================
Persistent Routes:
  None
```

If you've configured IPv6, you'll also see IPv6 routing details. Note the hex address of the interfaces in the Interface List. You refer to interfaces by this address.

The syntax of the route add command follows:

```
route add DestinationNetworkID mask NetworkMask Gateway metric MetricCost if
Interface
```

You could configure the static route defined in Figure 5-46, using the following command:

```
route add 192.168.52.0 mask 255.255.255.0 192.168.0.1 metric 1 if 0x10003
```

The metric and interface are optional. If you do not specify them, they are selected automatically. To make a static route persistent, you can use `route add -p`. Persistent static routes are not deleted even if the router is stopped and restarted.

At the command prompt, you can delete a static route using `route delete`. The syntax is:

```
route delete DestinationNetworkID
```

For example:

```
route delete 192.168.52.0
```

Configuring routing ports

When you install RRAS, a number of routing ports are created automatically. Routing ports are used for inbound connections to the RRAS server. The types of ports available depend on the configuration of the RRAS server.

To view or reset ports, follow these steps:

1. Open Routing And Remote Access. Connect to the server you want to work with (if necessary).
2. Expand the server node.
3. Click the Ports node. Configured ports are listed by type and status in the right pane.
4. To view a port's status and statistics, double-click the port entry.
5. To reset a port, double-click the port entry, and then click the Reset button.

You can configure ports by completing the following steps:

1. Open Routing And Remote Access. Connect to the server you want to work with (if necessary).
2. Expand the server node.
3. Right-click the Ports node, and then select Properties.
4. The Ports Properties dialog box shows the types of ports configured and the number of each type of port.
5. To modify the configuration of all ports of a particular type, click the port name, and then click the Configure button.

6. Using the Configure Device dialog box shown in Figure 5-47, specify how the port should be used and set the number of ports as necessary.
    - If you've configured PPPoE, there'll be a WAN miniport for PPPoE that is used for demand-dial routing of outbound-only connections. You can disable the use of the port by clearing the Demand-Dial Routing Connections checkbox in the Configure Device dialog box.
    - If you've configured VPN using L2TP or PPTP, there'll be multiple WAN miniports for each protocol. The default configuration allows up to 128 ports. You can add ports by increasing the maximum ports option. You can configure the ports for remote access inbound use only, for inbound and outbound demand-dial routing connections, or for both.
7. Click OK.

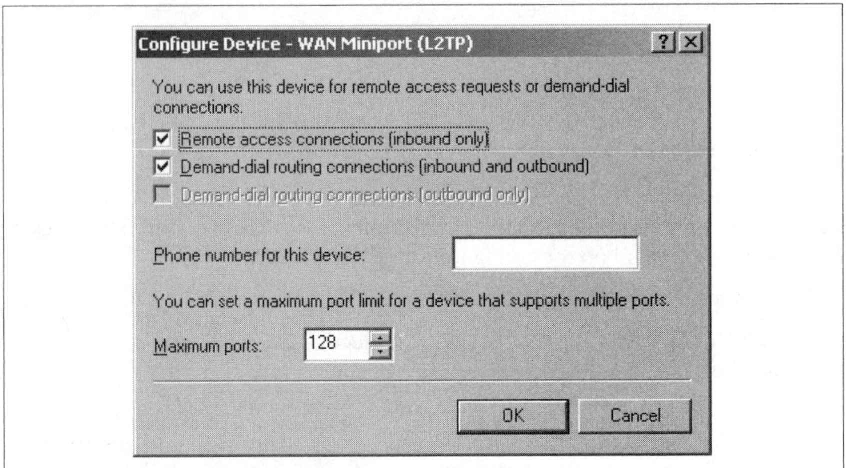

Figure 5-47. Configure the device ports.

Managing NAT and the Basic Firewall

Network Address Translation (NAT) allows multiple client computers to access the public Internet sharing a single public IP address or a pool of public IP addresses. NAT separate your organization's internal private network from the public network so that you can use private IP addresses internally and use public IP addresses when client computers need to access the Internet.

NAT provides Internet connectivity to internal clients through a single interface, which allows either a demand-dial or permanent connection. NAT includes the Basic Firewall that can be used to block external traffic from entering the internal network. In a typical secure configuration that includes a NAT server, the organization's network will use hardware firewalls as well, and the organization's network will be configured such that incoming traffic must first pass through the hardware firewall and then pass through the NAT server. This configuration is more secure and allows traffic to be blocked at the frontend hardware firewall before it reaches the NAT server.

Using Routing And Remote Access, any Windows 2000 or later server can act as a NAT server and Basic Firewall. To configure a server for NAT and the Basic Firewall, you need to:

1. Install the NAT/Basic Firewall routing protocol.
2. Specify the Network Interface to use.
3. Configure the NAT/Basic Firewall routing protocol.
4. Optionally, enable basic firewall and configure packet filtering.

Once the NAT/Basic Firewall routing protocol is installed, configured, and enabled, you can view the status by selecting the NAT/Basic Firewall node in the Routing And Remote Access console.

Installing the NAT/Basic Firewall routing protocol

You can install the NAT/Basic Firewall routing protocol by completing these steps:

1. Open Routing And Remote Access. Connect to the server you want to work with (if necessary).
2. Expand the server node, and then expand the IP Routing node.
3. Right-click the General node, and then select New Routing Protocol.
4. Click NAT/Basic Firewall, and then click OK.

Configuring the NAT/Basic Firewall routing protocol

After NAT/Basic Firewall has been installed, you must specify the network interface or interfaces through which the protocol will be used. To do this, follow these steps:

1. Open Routing And Remote Access. Connect to the server you want to work with (if necessary).
2. Expand the server node, and then expand the IP Routing node.
3. Right-click the NAT/Basic Firewall node, and then select New Interface.
4. Select the interface that is directly connect to the Internet.
5. Click OK.

You can now configure NAT and the Basic firewall as discussed in this section. The NAT/Basic Firewall Properties dialog box can also be displayed by right-clicking the NAT/Basic Firewall node, and then selecting Properties. As shown in Figure 5-48, the Network Address Translation Properties dialog box has four tabs:

General
: The options on this tab are used to configure event logging. By default, errors only are logged.

Translation
: The options on this tab are used to specify when TCP and UDP mappings are removed. By default, TCP mappings are removed after 1,440 minutes, and UDP mappings are removed after 1 minute.

Address Assignment
: The options on this tab specify whether the NAT router provides DHCP-based IP addresses to DHCP clients on the private network. When internal clients are using NAT to access the public Internet, you typically do not need to enable address assignment.

Name Resolution
: The options on this tab specify whether the NAT router relays DNS name resolution requests from hosts on the private network to the configured DNS server for the router. When internal clients are using NAT to access the public Internet, you typically do not need to enable name resolution.

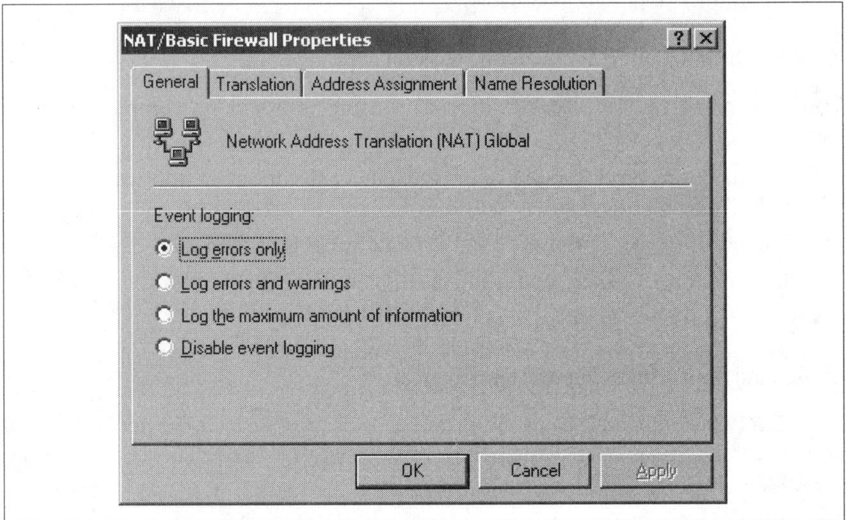

Figure 5-48. The NAT/Basic Firewall Properties dialog box.

Enabling Basic Firewall and configuring packet filtering

In the default configuration of NAT, Basic Firewall is not enabled for use with a public interface connected to the Internet. If you enable the Basic Firewall for use with a public interface connected to the Internet, the Basic Firewall accepts incoming traffic from the Internet only if it has been requested by the network. You can define packet filters to control network traffic using:

Inbound packet filters
: These control which packets are forwarded or processed by the network.

Outbound packet filters
: These control which packets are received by the network.

To enable Basic Firewall and configure packet filtering for use with a public interface connected to the Internet, follow these steps:

1. Open Routing And Remote Access. Connect to the server you want to work with (if necessary).
2. Expand the server node, and then expand the IP Routing node.

3. Click NAT/Basic Firewall and then double-click the network interface on which you want to configure.
4. On the NAT/Basic Firewall tab, select the Enable A Basic Firewall On This Interface checkbox.
5. Click the Inbound Filters button to specify which packets are forwarded or processed by the network.
6. Click the Outbound Filters button to specify which packets are received by the network.
7. Click OK.

Managing Remote Access Clients

In the Routing And Remote Access console, you can view the currently connected clients by expanding the server node and then clicking the Remote Access Clients node. Clients are listed according to the connected username, duration, and number of access ports being used. You can manage remote access clients by:

Checking status of a client
: To view a more detailed status, right-click the client entry and then select Status.

Disconnecting a client
: To disconnect a client, right-click the client entry and then select Disconnect.

Sending a message to a client
: To send a message to a client, right-click the client entry, select Send Message, type the message, and then click OK.

Sending a message to all clients
: To send a message to all clients, right-click the Remote Access Clients node, select Send To All, type the message, and then click OK.

Keep the following in mind as well:

- In Active Directory Users And Computers, you can set general remote access options on the Dial-in tab. These options are used for dial-in and VPN connections.
- In the Routing And Remote Access console, you can control remote access permissions using remote access policies.

Configuring IAS to Provide Authentication

RADIUS servers are used to centralize the authentication of remote access clients and the storage of accounting information. Centralizing authentication and accounting reduces the administrative overhead of managing multiple RRAS servers.

A Windows Server 2003 system can be configured as a RADIUS server by installing the Internet Authentication Service (IAS). To configure IAS for use in your organization, you need to:

1. Install IAS on a designated server.
2. Register the IAS server in Active Directory.

3. Configure your RRAS servers as IAS clients.
4. Configure your RRAS servers to use RADIUS.

Installing IAS

A Windows Server 2003 system can be configured as a RADIUS server by installing the IAS. Install IAS by completing the following steps:

1. Open Add Or Remove Programs in the Control Panel.
2. In the Add Or Remove Programs window, click Add/Remove Windows Components.
3. Click Networking Services and then select Properties. Be careful not to clear the checkbox.
4. Select Internet Authentication Service and then click OK.
5. Click Next. Setup configures the server's components.
6. Click Finish.

You manage Internet Authentication Service using the Internet Authentication Service console shown in Figure 5-49, which can be accessed by clicking Start → Programs → Administrative Tools → Internet Authentication Service. When you start the Internet Authentication Service console on an IAS server, the console connects automatically to IAS on this server. You cannot connect to other IAS servers.

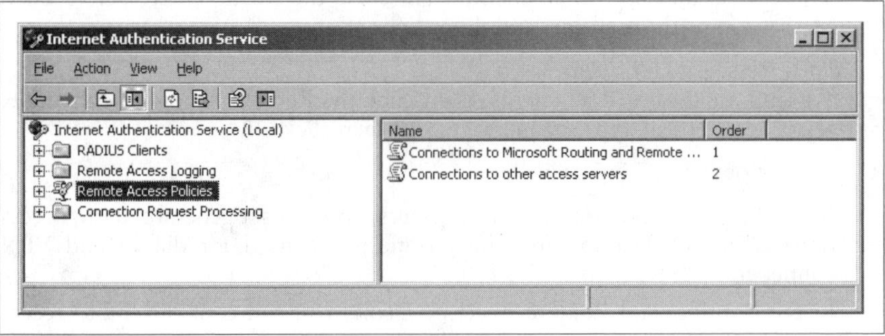

Figure 5-49. The Internet Authentication Service console.

Registering the RADIUS server and configuring clients

To complete the installation of the RADIUS server, you must register the server in Active Directory and tell RADIUS about the RRAS servers, which forwards authentication and accounting information to the RADIUS servers as clients.

You can register the RADIUS server in Active Directory by completing the following steps:

1. Open the Internet Authentication Service console.
2. Right-click the Internet Authentication Service node.
3. Select Register Server In Active Directory. If it is a domain controller, it is automatically registered in Active Directory.

Registering the server with Active Directory makes the server a member of the RAS And IAS Servers group. Members of this group are able to read remote access attributes of user accounts.

To configure your RRAS servers as clients (as is required for forwarding of authentication and accounting information), follow these steps:

1. Open the Internet Authentication Service console.
2. Right-click the RADIUS Clients node and then select New Radius Client.
3. Type the hostname of the RRAS server as the friendly name.
4. Type the IP address of FQDN of the RRAS server.
5. Click Next.
6. Access RADIUS Standard as the Client-Server type.
7. Type and then confirm the Shared Secret. This same shared secret must be set on your RRAS servers.
8. Click Finish.

Once you've configured forwarding of authentication and accounting, the Routing And Remote Access service on an RRAS server forwards remote access requests to the designated IAS server. The IAS server, acting as a RADIUS server, manages authentication and accounting.

You can also deploy the IAS service as a RADIUS proxy. In this configuration, the Routing And Remote Access service on an RRAS server forwards remote access requests to the IAS server, which is acting as a RADIUS proxy for a group of RADIUS servers. Members of the RADIUS servers group in turn manage authentication and accounting. Requests are load balanced dynamically by the IAS server acting as the RADIUS proxy. Connection request policies can be defined on the RADIUS proxy to sort access requests and send them to a specific RADIUS server.

Configure your RRAS servers to use RADIUS

After you've installed IAS on your designated server or servers, you can tell other RRAS servers about the IAS servers, by completing the following steps:

1. Right-click a server entry in the Routing And Remote Access console and select Properties.
2. Click the Security tab.
3. Specify that RADIUS should be used for authentication by selecting RADIUS Authentication as the Authentication Provider.
4. Click Configure to specify the RADIUS server to use for authentication. Add the RADIUS servers in priority order. The UDP port over which connections can be made is by default UDP port 1812 (based on RFC 2138).
5. Specify that RADIUS should be used for accounting by selecting RADIUS Accounting as the Accounting Provider.
6. Click Configure to specify the RADIUS server to use for accounting. Add the RADIUS servers in priority order. The UDP port over which connections can be made is by default UDP port 1813 (based on RFC 2138).
7. Click OK.

Troubleshooting User Access to Remote Access Services

Troubleshooting is a critically important part of any administrator's job. Users connecting to remote access services can encounter many different types of problems when connecting to the network or accessing resources. If the RRAS server is configured as a router, proper routing depends on the configuration.

Diagnosing and resolving issues related to establishing a remote access dial-up connection

Remote access clients that connect over dial-up may also use VPN. If so, you should troubleshoot the dial-up connection itself and, as necessary, the related VPN configuration.

To troubleshoot remote access dial-up connections, use the following techniques with the Routing And Remote Access console:

- On the General tab of the server's Properties dialog box, verify that Remote Access Server is enabled.
- On the IP tab of the server's Properties dialog box, verify that IP Routing is enabled if clients should have access to the network, and disabled if clients should have access to the RRAS server only.
- If static IP addresses are used, verify that the address pool configuration is correct and that there are available IP addresses.
- If dynamic IP addresses are used, verify the configuration of the DHCP server. The IP address scope must be large enough so that the RRAS server can requests blocks of 10 IP addresses.
- Using the Ports node, verify that the server has properly configured modem ports and that not all modem ports are assigned.
- Verify that the client, the RRAS server, and the remote access policy have at least one common authentication method and one common encryption method configured.
- Verify the dial-in properties of the user account in Active Directory Users And Computers.
- Verify that the client and the server permissions, credentials, and access policies are configured correctly.
- If using RADIUS for authentication, verify that the RRAS server is a member of the RAS And IAS Servers security group in the domain.

Diagnosing and resolving issues Related to remote access VPNs

Virtual Private Networks (VPNs) are used with remote access in two standard types of configurations. In the first type, remote access clients connect to the RRAS server using VPN. In the second type, RRAS servers configured as routers connect to routers in other private networks using VPN.

To troubleshoot remote access client VPN connections, use the following techniques with the Routing And Remote Access console:

- On the General tab of the server's Properties dialog box, verify that Remote Access Server is enabled.
- Using the Ports node, verify that the server has properly configured ports and that not all ports are assigned.
- On the Security tab of the server's Properties dialog box, verify that the server is using the appropriate authentication provider and that the appropriate authentication methods are selected for use.
- Verify that the remote access profile settings are correct and that they do not conflict with the server properties. Right-click a remote access policy, select Properties, and then click the Edit Profile button.
- Verify that the client, the RRAS server, and the remote access policy have at least one common authentication method and one common encryption method configured.
- Verify the RRAS server is made a member of the RAS And IAS Servers security group in the local domain. This membership is required for proper working of routing and remote access.
- Verify the underlying dial-up configuration as discussed in the previous section.

Diagnosing and resolving issues related to resources beyond the Remote Access Server

If remote access clients are able to connect to the RRAS server but not able to access resources on the network, you'll need to verify the following for troubleshooting:

- On the General tab of the server's Properties dialog box, verify that Router is enabled.
- On the General tab of the server's Properties dialog box, verify that LAN And Demand-Dial Routing is selected.
- On the IP tab of the server's Properties dialog box, verify that Enable IP Routing is selected.
- If static IP addresses are used, verify that the client's TCP/IP settings are correct.
- If dynamic IP addresses are used, verify that the client is obtaining the proper TCP/IP settings from the DHCP server.
- If your remote access clients use NetBIOS for name resolution, verify that Enable Broadcast Name Resolution is selected on the IP tab.

Troubleshooting Routing and Remote Access Routing

The Routing component of Routing And Remote Access can use demand-dial routing and router-to-router VPN configurations. The standard techniques you can use for troubleshooting depend on which type of configuration you are working with.

Troubleshooting router-to-router VPNs

To troubleshoot router-to-router VPN connections, use the following techniques with the Routing And Remote Access console:

- For the source and destination router, verify on the General tab of the server's Properties dialog box that both Router and LAN And Demand-Dial Routing are selected.
- For the source and destination router, verify on the IP tab of the server's Properties dialog box that Enable IP Routing is selected.
- For the source and destination router, verify that the servers have properly configured PPTP or L2TP ports.
- For the source and destination router, verify that the interface used for routing has Enable IP Router Manager selected on the General tab of the connection properties dialog box so that IP traffic can be routed over the connection.
- For the source and destination router, verify that the static routes are configured as appropriate to allow traffic over the appropriate interface.
- For the source and destination router, verify that permissions, credentials, and access policies are configured correctly.

Troubleshooting demand-dial routing

When troubleshooting demand-dial routing, you must check both ends of the connection—i.e., the source and destination RRAS servers. Use the following techniques for troubleshooting:

- Verify that Routing And Remote Access Services is installed.
- Verify on the General tab of the server's Properties dialog box that both Router and LAN And Demand-Dial Routing are selected.
- Verify on the IP tab of the server's Properties dialog box that both Enable IP Routing and Allow IP-Bae Remote Access And Demand Dial Connection are selected.
- Verify that the demand-dial interfaces are enabled and configured properly.
- Verify that the static routes are configured properly and that Use This Route To Initiate Demand-Dial Connections is selected in the static route properties.
- Verify that the Security tab settings of the network interfaces use a common configuration.
- Verify that the Networking tab settings of the network interfaces use a common VPN type.
- Verify that the servers use the appropriate authentication providers and that the appropriate authentication methods are selected for use. The servers must have at least one common authentication method.
- Verify that the servers have properly configured ports for demand-dial use.
- Verify that packet filters aren't blocking the routing.

Maintaining a Network Infrastructure

In the Exam 70-290 Study Guide and throughout this study guide, I've discussed techniques for maintaining network infrastructure. Rather than repeat what's already been discussed, I'll give you specific pointers you can use to extend the earlier discussions and to ensure that you understand the skills required to maintain a network infrastructure.

Monitoring Network Traffic

Windows Server 2003 includes several tools for monitoring network traffic. Some of the most basic of these tools are often the most effective:

- Using Task Manager's Networking tab, you can determine the current utilization of each network adapter installed on a server.
- Using System Monitor in the Performance console, you can view current networking activity using the Network Interface performance object. Each adapter instance can be tracked separately.
- Using Performance Logging, you can track networking activity over a period of time to determine performance bottlenecks.

With System Monitor and Performance Logging, you'll find the following counters of the Network Interface object useful in troubleshooting:

Packet Outbound Discarded
: Tracks the number of outbound packets discarded even though they did not contain errors. Packets may have been discarded to free buffer space.

Packet Outbound Errors
: Tracks the number of outbound packets that could not be transmitted because of errors.

Packet Received Discarded
: Tracks the number of inbound packets discarded even though they did not contain errors. Packets may have been discarded to free buffer space.

Packet Received Errors
: Tracks the number of inbound packets that contained errors that prevented them from being used.

Windows Server 2003 includes Network Monitor for monitoring and logging network activity. You install Network Monitor by completing the following steps:

1. Open Add Or Remove Programs in the Control Panel.
2. In the Add Or Remove Programs window, click Add/Remove Windows Components.
3. Click Management And Monitoring Tools and then select Properties. Be careful not to clear the checkbox.
4. Select Network Monitor Tools and then click OK.
5. Click Next. Setup configures the server's components.
6. Click Finish.

Network Monitor includes the Network Monitor Driver for capturing frames received by and sent to a network adapter and the Network Monitor console for viewing and analyzing data captured by the Network Monitor Driver. To open the Network Monitor console, click Start → Programs → Administrative Tools → Network Monitor. The first time you start Network Monitor, you must select the network on which you want to capture data. Click OK when prompted. In the Select A Network dialog box, expand the Local Computer node, select the network adapter that is connected to the network to monitor, and then click OK. If you need to change the monitored network, click Capture → Networks.

After you select a network, Network Monitor connects to the network but does not begin capturing data until you click Capture → Start. Once you start capturing data, Network Monitor displays captured data as shown in Figure 5-50.

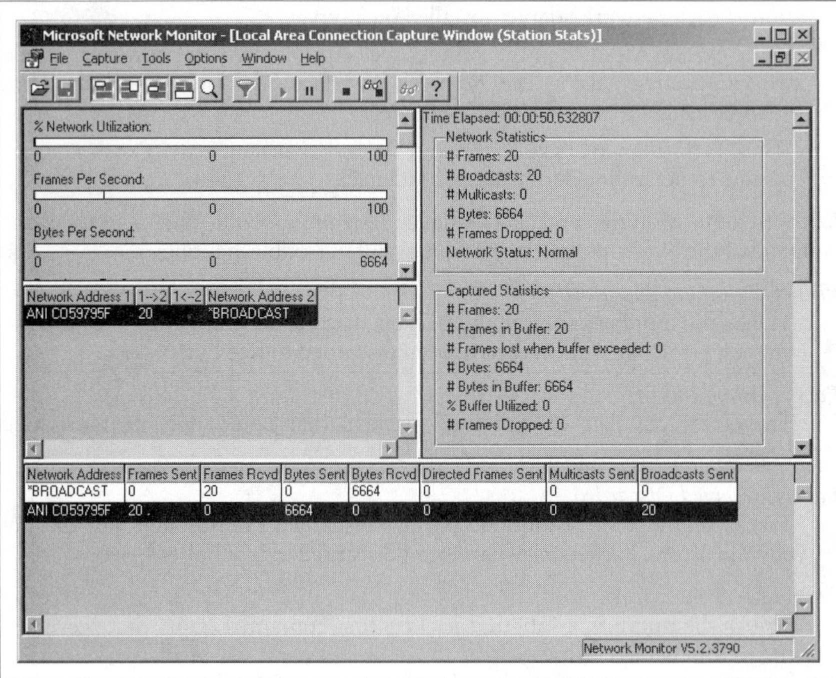

Figure 5-50. The Network Monitor.

The Network Statistics and Captured Statistics provide summary data about frames passed on the network. You can use this information to watch for excessive broadcasts and excessive packet loss as compared to the total number of frames.

Network utilization bar graphs show the percentage of network utilization as well as the number of frames, bytes, broadcasts, and multicasts per second. If the percentage network utilization is consistently more than 50 percent of the total capacity, the network may have capacity bottleneck.

To view the details of the capture data, you must click Capture → Stop And View. In View mode, Network Monitor displays all of the frames captured in a summary window. You can examine a specific frame by double-clicking the related entry. You can switch between the network window and the summary window using the options of the Window menu.

If you are looking for a specific type of frame, you can specify a capture filter. To define a capture filter, click Capture → Filter.

If you want to monitor the network traffic and receive an alert when a specific condition is met, you can use a capture trigger. To define a capture trigger, click Capture → Trigger.

Troubleshooting Connectivity to the Internet

Throughout this study guide, I've provide specific tips for troubleshooting various aspects of networking. For TCP/IP configuration issues, see "Troubleshooting TCP/IP Addressing," and or troubleshooting remote access, see "Troubleshooting User Access to Remote Access Services," both earlier in this chapter.

Troubleshooting Server Services

Windows Server 2003 includes many processes that run when you start the operating system. Each of these processes performs a specific task. Most manageable tasks run as services. Depending on the operating system components installed on a server, there can be any where from a few dozen configured services to many dozens of configured services.

Diagnosing and resolving issues related to service dependency

You can view the currently configured services using the Services utility in Administrative Tools. In Computer Management, expand the Services And Applications node and then select Services to see the configured services.

Services can be in one of three possible states: started, paused, or stopped. If the service is running, the status is listed as Started. If the service is stopped, the status is listed as blank. If a service can be paused, as indicated by the availability of the Pause option, the status is listed as Paused if you or another administrator has paused the service.

The actions you can perform depend on the run state of the service and whether a service can be paused. You can start or stop a service by clicking it, and then clicking the Start or Stop button as appropriate. You can stop and then restart a service by clicking Restart. You can pause a service by clicking Pause, and then resume the service by clicking Pause again.

The startup type of a service determines whether and how a service is started. The startup type can be set to the following:

Automatic
: The service starts automatically with the operating system.

Manual
: The service does not start automatically with the operating system. Instead, the service can be manually started if it is called by another process.

Disabled
: The service does not start automatically and also cannot be started manually until it is enabled.

Some services depend on other services in order to start. If a service depends on other services, it can only start when those services are running. Because some low-level services are the dependencies of multiple high-level services, a single low-level service that doesn't start properly can have a cascading effect on a server.

Before you stop a service, it is a good idea to determine which services depend on it. If a service isn't running and it should be, the reason might be that a dependent service isn't running. To view a service's dependencies, follow these steps:

1. Open Computer Management. Expand the Services And Applications node, and then select Services.
2. Double-click the service, and then select the Dependencies tab. Dependent services are listed as shown in Figure 5-51.
3. If the services on which the currently selected service depends in turn depend on other services, you can view those dependencies by expanding the service node in the list provided.
4. If other services depend in this service, they are listed in the lower panel.

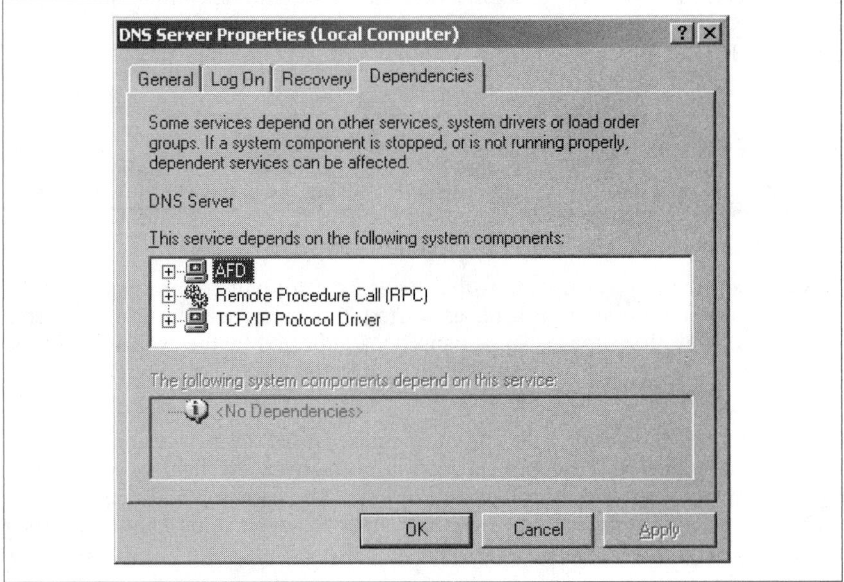

Figure 5-51. Viewing dependent services.

Using service recovery options to diagnose and resolve service-related issues

Service recovery options allow you to specify the actions that should be taken if a service fails. For example, you could attempt to restart the service or run an application.

The operating system can take one of four actions should a service fail. These actions are to:

- Take no action
- Restart the service
- Run a program
- Restart the computer

You can configure recovery options for a service by completing the following steps:

1. Open Computer Management.
2. Expand the Services And Applications node, and then click Services.
3. Right-click the service you want to configure, and then choose Properties.
4. Select the Recovery tab.
5. Configure recovery options for the first, second, and subsequent recovery attempts. If you elect to run a program, set the full file path to the program you want to run and then set any necessary command-line parameters to pass in to the program when it starts.
6. Click OK.

With Windows Server 2003, many services have recovery options set, so restart the service automatically should it fail. Event Log, Protected Storage, Plug And Play, NT LM Security Support Provider, and Security Accounts Manager service will restart the computer if the service fails, and this configuration cannot be changed.

6

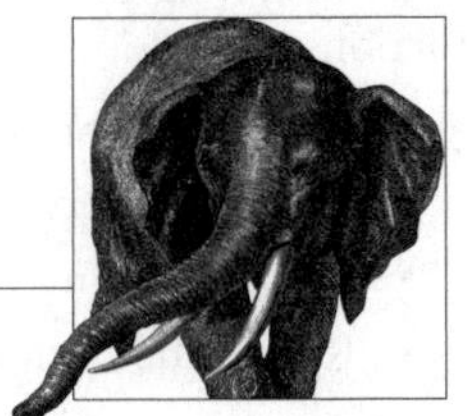

Exam 70-291 Prep and Practice

The material in this chapter is designed to help you prepare and practice for *Exam 70-291: Implementing, Managing, and Maintaining a Microsoft Windows Server 2003 Network Infrastructure*. The chapter is organized into four sections:

Preparing for Exam 70-291
: In this section, you'll find an overview of the types of questions on the exam. Reviewing this section will help you understand how the actual exam works.

Exam 70-291 Suggested Exercises
: In this section, you'll find a numbered list of exercises that you can follow to gain experience in the exam's subject areas. Performing the exercises in this section will help ensure you have hands-on experience with all areas of the exam.

Exam 70-291 Highlighters Index
: In this section, you'll find a compilation of the facts within the exam's subject areas that you are most likely to need another look at—in other words, the areas of study that you might have highlighted while reading the Study Guide. Studying the highlights is useful as a final review before the exam.

Exam 70-291 Practice Questions
: In this section, you'll find a comprehensive set of practice questions to assess your knowledge of the exam. The questions are similar in format to the exam. After you've reviewed the Study Guide, performed the Suggested Exercises, and studied the Highlighters Index, read the questions and see whether you can answer them correctly.

Before you take Exam 70-291 review the exam overview, perform the suggested exercises, and go through the practice questions provided. Many online sites provide practice tests for the exam. Duplicating the depth and scope of these practice exams in a printed book isn't possible. Visit Microsoft's Certification site for pointers to online practice tests (*http://www.microsoft.com/learning/mcpexams/prepare/practicetests.asp*).

Preparing for Exam 70-291

Exam 70-291 is a computer-generated exam. The exam is timed, and the amount of time remaining on the exam is displayed by an onscreen timer clock. Most questions on the exam are multiple choice. Multiple choice questions are either:

Multiple-choice, single answer
: A radio button allows you to select a single answer only.

Multiple-choice, multiple answer
: A checkbox allows you to select multiple answers. Usually the number of correct answers is indicated in the question itself.

Typically, the test environment will have Previous/Next and Mark For Review options. You can navigate through the test using the Previous/Next buttons. You can click the Mark For Review checkbox to flag a question for later review. At the bottom of the screen is a calculator button. You may need to use the calculator in scientific mode to calculate IP addresses, subnet masks, and subnet numbers.

Other formats for questions are used as well, including:

List prioritization
: Pick the choices that answer the question and arrange the list in a specified order. Lists initially appear on the right side, and you have to click << ADD to add them in the correct order to the list on the left side. For example, you might have to list the steps for configuring a DHCP server in priority order.

Hot area
: Indicate the correct answer by clicking one or more areas of the screen or dialog box provided with the question. For example, you might see a DHCP console window and have to click on the DHCP servers that haven't been authorized yet.

Select and Place
: Using drag-and-drop, pick answers from a given set of choices and place them in an appropriate spot in a dialog box or diagram.

Active screen
: Use the dialog box provided to configure the options correctly or perform the required procedure. For example, you might see Internet Protocol (TCP/IP) Properties dialog box and have to configure the computer for DHCP.

Simulation
: Use the simulated desktop environment provided to perform a specific task or troubleshoot. For example, you might be asked to configure a DHCP scope on the server.

With the exception of multiple-choice, single-answer questions, all of the other questions can have multiple answers or multiple required procedures to obtain full credit. If all of the expected answers or procedures are not performed, you will only get partial credit for the answer.

Although many of the questions on Exam 70-291 are multiple choice, hot area, select and place, active screen, and simulation questions are being used increasingly to ensure that the testing process more accurately reflects actual hands-on knowledge rather than rote memorization. Individuals with adequate hands-on administration experience who have reviewed the study guide, performed the practice exercises, memorized the essentials, and taken practice tests should do well on this type of exam. Individuals who lack adequate hands-on experience and have not prepared appropriately will do poorly on this type of exam.

Exam 70-291 Suggested Exercises

Exam 70-291 expects you to know how to implement, manage, and maintain network infrastructure for Windows Server 2003. You'll need plenty of hands-on previous experience to pass the exam. You'll need to review the study guide closely and review closely any areas with which you are unfamiliar. This section provides a numbered list of exercises that you can follow to gain experience in the exam's subject areas. Performing the exercises will be useful for helping to ensure that you have hands-on experience with all areas of the exam.

For this exam, I recommend setting up a three-computer test network with two servers running Windows Server 2003 and one workstation running Windows XP Professional. One of your servers should be configured as a domain controller with DNS. The other should be configured as your DHCP server and as your Routing and Remote Access Server (RRAS). The workstation will need to be used in several roles. You'll need to configure it to be a member of the domain when you test TCP/IP, DHCP, and DNS client configurations. When you test RRAS, you'll want to configure the workstation as a RRAS client.

In addition to performing the exercises below, you should also have experience using each of the Windows Server 2003 administrative tools described in the Study Guide.

Installing and Configuring TCP/IP

1. Configure a server so that it uses TCP/IP. If necessary, install TCP/IP.
2. Specify a static IP address, subnet mask, default gateway, and other appropriate TCP/IP settings for use in a domain.
3. Test the settings to ensure that the server can communicate on the network.

Installing DHCP Server Service

1. Prior to installing the DHCP Server service, confirm that a server has a static IP address.
2. Install the DHCP Server service on a server.
3. Authorize the DHCP server in Active Directory.
4. Configure the DHCP server so it can assign dynamic configurations to clients.
5. Configure and activate a scope on the DHCP server.

Configuring Dynamic Addressing for Clients

1. Configure a workstation so that it uses TCP/IP. If necessary, install TCP/IP.
2. Configure the computer to use a dynamic IP address.
3. Ensure the workstation's alternate configuration uses an Automatic Private IP address.
4. Test the settings to ensure the server can communicate on the network.

Troubleshooting TCP/IP Addressing

1. Disconnect a computer's network cable.
2. Use the command line to diagnose the problem.
3. Reconnect the computer's network cable.
4. Configure invalid settings for TCP/IP.
5. Use the command line to ping another computer on the network.
6. Use `netdiag` to test the computer's configuration.
7. Reconfigure the computer so it uses valid settings.
8. Use `netdiag` to test the computer's configuration.

Authorizing DHCP Servers

1. Open the DHCP console.
2. Determine whether your DHCP server(s) is authorized.

Creating Scopes

1. Using the DHCP console, create three normal scopes with private Class C IP addresses.
2. Add the scopes to a superscope.
3. Activate the superscope.
4. Deactivate the superscope.
5. Try to delete the superscope.
6. Remove all three normal scopes from the superscope.
7. Delete the superscope.

Configuring Scopes

1. Using the DHCP console, create a normal scope with private Class C IP addresses.
2. Exclude a range of IP addresses.
3. Configure the TCP/IP options for DNS domain name, DNS servers, and router.
4. Using the Scope Options node, modify the TCP/IP options for DNS domain name, DNS servers, and router.

Creating and Activating Multicast Scopes

1. Open the DHCP console.
2. Create a multicast scope and configure it so multicast traffic can pass through seven routers.
3. Activate the multicast scope.

Using Dynamic DNS Updates with DHCP

1. Using the DHCP console, ensure dynamic DNS updates are enabled on the DHCP server.
2. Configure dynamic updates so the DHCP server can update both A and PTR records for Windows 2000 and later clients.
3. Configure dynamic updates so the DHCP server can update both A and PTR records for Windows NT 4.0 clients.

Configuring DHCP Leases

1. Using the DHCP console, create a normal scope with private Class B IP addresses.
2. Activate the scope.
3. Change the scope's lease duration to 30 days.

Creating Reservations

1. Configure a workstation to use DHCP.
2. Ensure the workstation connects to the DHCP server and obtains a valid lease.
3. Use the client's lease entry to determine the MAC address of the workstation's network adapter.
4. Use the command line to determine the MAC address of the workstation's network adapter.
5. Create a reservation for the workstation.
6. Using the command line, release the workstation's current lease and renew its TCP/IP settings so that it obtains the reserved IP address.

Setting the DHCP Database and Backup Paths

1. Open the DHCP console.
2. Configure the DHCP server to use an alternate DHCP database and backup path.

Manually Backing Up and Restoring the DHCP Database

1. Open the DHCP console.
2. Back up the DHCP database.
3. Restore the DHCP database from backup.

Manually Compacting the DHCP Database

1. Open a command prompt.
2. Change the directory path to the directory containing the DHCP database.
3. Type `net stop dhcpserver`.
4. Type `jetpack dhcp.mdb temp.mdb`.
5. Type `net start dhcpserver`.

Auditing DHCP

1. Using the DHCP console, configure DHCP auditing to use an alternate logfile path.
2. Enable auditing on your DHCP server.
3. Examine the DHCP audit logs.
4. Review the System event logs for DHCP-related events.

Configuring Primary and Alternate DNS Suffixes

1. Using the System utility in Control Panel, determine a computer's name and domain.
2. Determine the computer's primary DNS suffix.
3. Ensure that the primary DNS suffix changes when domain membership changes.
4. Check the Advanced TCP/IP Settings for DNS.

Configuring Advanced DNS Settings

1. Ensure a computer has both a primary and an alternate DNS server configuration.
2. Modify the computer's TCP/IP settings to use a connection-specific DNS suffix.
3. Remove the connection-specific DNS suffix.
4. Ensure that the computer's primary network adapter is configured to append the primary DNS suffix, and use the standard default options.
5. Ensure that the computer is configured to use dynamic DNS updates.

Working with the Resolver Cache on DNS Clients

1. Using the command line, examine the DNS resolver cache on a computer using `ipconfig /displaydns`.
2. Clear a computer's resolver cache using `ipconfig /flushdns`.
3. Force a computer to register its DNS records using `ipconfig /registerdns`.

Installing DNS Server Service

1. Prior to installing the DNS Server service, confirm that a server has a static IP address. (Static IP addresses are not required for DNS servers, but are recommended.)
2. Install the DNS Server service on a domain controller.
3. Open the DNS Management console.
4. Ensure the server responses on the appropriate interfaces and IP addresses.
5. Configure event logging so only errors and warnings are tracked.
6. Using standard monitoring testing, test the DNS server configuration.

Configuring DNS Zone Options

1. Open the DNS Management console.
2. Create a standard forward lookup zone for the domain or a child domain of the current domain.
3. Create a standard reverse lookup zone for the domain or a child domain of the current domain.
4. Modify the forward and reverse lookup zones so they are Active Directory–integrated.
5. Configure replication so all DNS servers in the domain get updates.
6. Configure the zones to use only secure dynamic updates.

Configuring Scavenging Options

1. Using the DNS Management console, access the properties of a DNS zone.
2. Enable aging of DNS records in the zone.
3. Set the period after a timestamp that must elapse before a resource record can be refreshed to 10 days.
4. Set the period after the no-refresh interval during which the timestamp can be refreshed to 14 days.

Configuring the Start Of Authority (SOA)

1. Using the DNS Management console, access the properties of a DNS zone.
2. Review the zone's SOA record.
3. Increment the zone's serial number.

Configuring Name Servers for the Zone

1. Using the DNS Management console, access the properties of a DNS zone.
2. Review the name servers for the zone.
3. Add name servers as necessary.

Configuring Zone Transfers

1. Using the DNS Management console, access the properties of a DNS zone.
2. Configure zone transfers for listed name servers only.
3. Configure notification for listed name servers only.

Creating Records in a Zone

1. View the records on a forward lookup zone.
2. Create the A and PTR records for a host in the current domain.
3. Create an alias for a host in the current domain.

Configuring and Managing DNS Forwarding

1. Open the DNS Management console.
2. Configure a forwarder for all other domains.
3. Configure a forwarder for a specific domain.

Accessing the Security Tools

1. Open a custom MMC.
2. Add the Security Templates snap-in.
3. Add the Security Configuration And Analysis snap-in.

Creating Security Templates

1. Using the Security Templates snap-in, determine the currently available security templates.
2. Create a copy of a hisecdc and hisecws templates.
3. Review and modify the settings of your new templates.

Applying Security Template Settings and Analyzing Security

1. Access the Security Configuration And Analysis snap-in.
2. Open Database and create a database for your work.
3. Import the hisecdc template.
4. Compare the computer's current configuration to the hisecdc template.
5. Import the hisecws template.
6. Compare the computer's current configuration to the hisecws template.

Applying IP Security

1. Access the IP Security Monitor and determine whether any IPSec policies are being applied to a computer.
2. In Active Directory Group Policy, review the default IPSec policies.
3. Assign and enforce the Server (Request Security) policy.

4. Apply the new policy to the computer by typing `gpupdate /refresh` at a command prompt.
5. Access the IP Security Monitor and determine the IPSec policy applied.
6. Use the command line to determine the IPSec policy applied.

Monitoring and Troubleshooting Kerberos

1. In Active Directory Group Policy, review Kerberos policy.
2. Use the command line to determine whether Kerberos is working properly.

Implementing Routing And Remote Access

1. Prepare the computer to use Routing And Remote Access Service by disabling the Windows Firewall/Internet Connection Sharing service.
2. Enable and configure the Routing And Remote Access service for LAN and demand-dial routing as well as remote access.
3. Add a routing interface for a network connection.
4. Add a routing interface for a dial-up connection.
5. Add a routing interface for a private-network to private-network VPN connection.

Managing Remote Access Security

1. Configure the RRAS server to use Windows Authentication.
2. Configure the RRAS server to use Windows Accounting.
3. Set a preshared key for L2TP connections over IPSEC.
4. Configure user authentication so EAP and MS-CHAP V2 only are allowed.

Managing IP Assignment

1. Ensure that IP routing is enabled on the RRAS server.
2. Configure RRAS to allow IP-based remote access and demand-dial connections.
3. Configure RRAS so that IP assignment is handled by DHCP.
4. Configure RRAS so that broadcast name resolution is not allowed.

Configuring DHCP Relay Agents

1. Install the DHCP Relay Agent routing protocol.
2. Configure the DHCP Relay Agent routing protocol.
3. Enable the DHCP Relay Agent routing protocol.
4. Verify the server bindings for the DHCP Server service.

Installing and Configuring RIP

1. Install RIP as a new routing protocol.
2. Specify the network interface or interfaces to be used with RIP.
3. Configure RIP to log warnings and errors.
4. Set the connection security to accept all incoming routes for a specific range.
5. Set the connection security to accept all outgoing routes for a specific range.
6. Configure the connection to use only broadcasts and multicasts.

Configuring OSPF

1. Install OSPF as a new routing protocol.
2. Specify the network interface or interfaces to be used with OSPF.
3. Configure OSPF to log warnings and errors.
4. Configure OSPF to accept all external routes except SNMP routes.
5. Configure the connection to use NMBA as the network type.
6. Configure neighbors for the router.

Configuring Routing Tables

1. Create a static route using the Routing And Remote Access console.
2. View the current routes using the Routing And Remote Access console.
3. Create a static route using the `route add` command.
4. View the current routes using the `route print` command.

Configuring Routing Ports

1. Determine the routing ports available on a RRAS server.
2. Configure the WAN Miniport for PPTP or L2TP to use at least 256 ports.
3. Configure the WAN Miniport for PPTP or L2TP to accept remote access and demand-dial connections.

Configuring NAT and the Basic Firewall

1. Install the NAT/Basic Firewall routing protocol.
2. Specify the Network Interface to use.
3. Configure the NAT/Basic Firewall routing protocol.
4. Enable basic firewall and configure packet filtering.

Managing Remote Access Clients

1. Check the status of RRAS clients.
2. Disconnect an RRAS client.
3. Send a message to all RRAS clients.
4. Review remote access policies that might affect clients.

Configuring Internet Authentication Service (IAS) to Provide Authentication

1. Install IAS on a designated server.
2. Register the IAS server in Active Directory.
3. Configure your RRAS servers as IAS clients.
4. Configure your RRAS servers to use RADIUS.
5. Review the dial-in properties of remote access client.

Monitoring Network Traffic

1. Use Task Manager to monitor network traffic.
2. In the Performance console, use the Network Interface performance object to monitor network traffic.
3. Install the Network Monitor Tools.
4. Use the Network Monitor to analyze network traffic.

Determining Service Dependency

1. Determine which services the DNS Server service is dependent upon using the Service utility.
2. Determine which services the DHCP Server service is dependent upon.
3. Determine which services are dependent upon the Event Log service.

Configuring Services

1. Determine the run-state of the Computer Browser service.
2. Stop and restart the Computer Browser service.
3. Configure the Computer Browser service to use manual startup.
4. Stop the Computer Browser service.
5. Configure the Computer Browser service to use manual startup.
6. Configure the Computer Browser service to use automatic startup.
7. Start the Computer Browser service.

Exam 70-291 Highlighters Index

In this section, I've attempted to compile the facts within the exam's subject areas that you are most likely to need another look at—in other words, the areas of study that you might have highlighted while reading the Study Guide. The title of each highlighted element corresponds to the heading title in the Exam 70-291 Study Guide. In this way, if you have a question about a highlight, you can refer back to the corresponding section in the study guide. For the most part, the entries under a heading are organized as term lists with a Windows Server 2003 feature, component, or administration tool as the term, and the key details for this feature, component, or administration tool listed next.

Implementing, Managing, and Maintaining IP Addressing

Summary of highlights from the "Implementing, Managing, and Maintaining IP Addressing" section of the Exam 70-291 Study Guide.

Transmission Control Protocol/Internet Protocol (TCP/IP) protocol suite

- TCP is a connection-oriented protocol for end-to-end communications.
- IP is an internetworking protocol for routing packets over a network.

Three types of IP addresses

- Dynamic IP addresses are automatically obtained from a DHCP server.
- Static IP addresses are those manually assigned to computers.
- Automatic private IP addresses (APIPA) are used when a computer is configured for DHCP but no DHCP server is available.

Installing TCP/IP

- TCP/IP is configured if the operating system detects a network adapter.
- Install TCP/IP manually using the Local Area Connection Properties dialog box.

Configure TCP/IP addressing

- IP addresses identify computers by their associated network ID and host ID components.
- Subnet masks identify which parts of the IP address belong to the network ID and which parts belong to the host ID.
- Default gateways identify the IP address of the router that will act as the computer's gateway.
- Preferred and alternate DNS servers identify the IP address of the preferred and alternate DNS servers to use for name resolution.

TCP/IP version 4

- Available IP addresses are divided into network class ranges.
- Standard unicast IP address classes are Class A, Class B, and Class C.
- Private IP address classes are summarized in Table 6-1.

Prep and Practice

Table 6-1. Private network addresses by class

Network class	Network ID	Subnet mask	Assignable IP address range
Class A	10.0.0.0	255.0.0.0	10.0.0.1–10.255.255.254
Class B	172.16.0.0	255.240.0.0	172.16.0.1–172.31.255.254
Class C	192.168.0.0	255.255.0.0	192.168.0.1–192.168.255.254

Configuring static IP addressing

- Configure a static IP address by editing the TCP/IP properties.
- Select the Use The Following IP Address radio button.
- Type the IP address and network mask.

- Type the IP address of the default gateway.
- Type the IP addresses of the preferred and alternate DNS servers.

Configuring dynamic IP addressing

- Configure a dynamic IP address by editing the TCP/IP properties.
- Select Obtain An IP Address Automatically.
- Optionally, select Obtain DNS Server Address Automatically.

Configuring Automatic Private IP Addressing

- IP addresses in the range 69.254.0.1 to 169.254.255.254 with a subnet mask of 255.255.0.0.
- Determine whether a computer is using automatic private addressing by typing `ipconfig /all`.
- Configure automatic private addressing by editing the TCP/IP properties.
- Select the Automatic Private IP Address radio button to use the default alternate configuration.

Diagnosing and resolving Automatic Private IP Addressing

- An active network connection is required for automatic configuration to work properly.
- The media may be disconnected at either end of the network cable.
- Attempt to renew the IP address by typing `ipconfig /renew` at a command prompt.
- Disable APIPA using the `IPAutoconfigurationEnabled` DWORD value-entry in the Registry.

Diagnosing and resolving incorrect TCP/IP configuration

- Check for invalid gateway configuration.
- Check for invalid IP address.
- Check for invalid subnet mask.
- Check for invalid DNS configuration.
- Check for invalid WINS configuration.
- Use `ping`, `arp`, `pathping`, `tracert`, and `netdiag` for testing.

Diagnosing and resolving DNS caching issues

- Use `ipconfig /displaydns` to displays the entries in the DNS cache.
- Use `ipconfig /flushdns` to purge the entries in the DNS cache.
- Use `ipconfig /registerdns` to refresh leased IP addresses and re-registers DNS.

Installing, Configuring, and Managing DHCP

Summary of highlights from the "Installing, Configuring, and Managing DHCP" section of the Exam 70-291 Study Guide.

Understanding DHCP

- DHCP servers assign IP addresses to clients for a specific period of time known as the *lease duration*.

- Any server that you want to configure as a DHCP server must have a static IP address.
- Every DHCP server must have at least one active scope to grant leases to clients.
- A *scope* is simply a range of IP addresses to be leased to DHCP clients.
- An *exclusion* is an IP address or a IP address range not included in a scope and not assigned to clients.
- A *reservation* is an IP address that is held for use by a client with a specific hardware MAC address.

Installing and configuring DHCP is accomplished by:

1. Installing the DHCP server service on your designated DHCP servers.
2. Authorizing the DHCP servers in Active Directory.
3. Configuring the DHCP servers so they can assign dynamic configurations to clients.
4. Activating at least one scope on each DHCP server.

Installing the DHCP Server service

- Install DHCP Server service on a server assigned a static IP address.
- Do not install DHCP Server service on a DC (unless necessary).
- Use Add Or Remove Programs → Windows Components in the Control Panel to install.

Working with and authorizing the DHCP server

- Manage DHCP using the DHCP console.
- Click Start → Programs → Administrative Tools → DHCP.
- To authorize a DHCP server, right-click the server entry in the left pane and then select Authorize.

DHCP supports three types of scopes

- Normal scopes for assigning Class A, B, and C IP addresses and related network settings.
- Multicast scopes for assigning Class D IP addresses and related network settings.
- Superscopes used as containers for scopes.

Creating and activating normal scopes

- Create a new scope by right-clicking the server's entry and then selecting New Scope.
- The new scope is created and listed under the DHCP server node in the DHCP console.
- Activate the scope by right-clicking it and selecting Activate.

Creating and activating multicast scopes

- Multicast scopes are used on networks that use TCP/IP multicasting.
- Class D IP addresses from 224.0.0.0 to 239.255.255.255 are used for multicasting.

- Create a new multicast scope by right-clicking the server's entry and then selecting New Multicast Scope.
- Activate the scope by right-clicking it and selecting Activate.

Creating and using superscopes

- Superscopes allow you to group scopes for easier management.
- Verify that you have at least one scope to create the superscope.
- By activating or deactivating the superscope, you can activate or deactivate all the related scopes.
- Create a new superscope by right-clicking the server's entry and then selecting New Superscope.
- To activate or deactivate all scopes within a superscope, right-click the superscope and select Activate or Deactivate.
- To add a scope to a superscope, right-click the scope and then select Add To Superscope.
- To remove a scope from a superscope, right-click a scope and then select Remove From Superscope.

DHCP scope options

- Predefined options configure preset values and create additional TCP/IP options.
- Server options configure TCP/IP options that are assigned to all scopes created on a server.
- Scope options configure TCP/IP options that are assigned to all clients that use a scope.
- Class options assign TCP/IP options based on membership in a particular class.
- Reservation options set TCP/IP options for individual computers with reservations.
- Standard TCP/IP options used with scopes are listed in Table 6-2.

Overriding TCP/IP options

- Server options can be overridden by scope, class, and reservation options.
- Scope options can be overridden by class and reservation options.
- Class options can be overridden by reservation options.
- Reservation can be overridden only by manually assigned TCP/IP settings.

Table 6-2. Overriding TCP/IP options

Option name	Option code	Description
DNS Domain Name	015	Sets the DNS domain name to use when resolving unqualified hostnames using DNS.
DNS Servers	006	Sets the primary and alternate DNS servers in preference order.
Router	003	Sets the default gateways in preference order.

Table 6-2. Overriding TCP/IP options (continued)

Option name	Option code	Description
WINS/NBNS Servers	044	Sets the primary and alternate WINS servers in preference order.
WINS/NBT Node Type	046	Sets the method to use when resolving NetBIOS names.

Using dynamic DNS updates with DHCP

- The options on the DNS tab determine how dynamic DNS updating works.
- Clients register their A records using a nonsecure method.
- DHCP servers dynamically update A and PTR records on behalf of clients using secure updates.
- The DnsUpdateProxy security group members do not have security settings assigned to their records.

New leases are granted through a four-part process:

1. **Discover**. A client sends a DHCP Discover broadcast on the network using its MAC address and NetBIOS name.
2. **Offer**. DHCP servers on a network that receive a DHCP Discover message respond with a DHCP Offer message.
3. **Request**. Clients accept the first offer received by broadcasting a DHCP Request message for the offered IP address.
4. **Acknowledgment**. The server accepts the request by sending the client a DHCP Acknowledgment message.

Renewing leases

- Clients attempt to renew their leases:
  - At each restart.
  - When the `ipconfig /renew` command is run at the client computer.
  - When the client uses the Repair button in the connection status dialog box.
  - When 50 percent of the lease time has passed.
  - When 87.5 percent of the lease time has expired.
- On failure, use APIPA and then sends DHCP Discover broadcasts every five minutes.

Managing leases

- Using the DHCP console, you manage lease durations on a per-scope basis.
- To view or change the current lease duration, right-click the server's entry and then select Properties.
- On clients, you manage IP addressing using `ipconfig`.

Managing reservations and reserved clients

- Use reservations to create permanent address leases assignments.
- Reservation definitions must be created on each DHCP server in the subnet.

- Define a reservation using the MAC address of the computer's network adapter.
- To create a reservation, right-click the Reservations node and click New Reservation.

DHCP databases

- By default, the database is located in the *%SystemRoot%\System32\DHCP* folder.
- Automatic backups occur every 60 minutes by default.
- Set automatic backup using the BackupInterval entry in the Registry.
- Automatic backups are stored by default in *%SystemRoot%\System32\DHCP\backup*.

Manually backing up and restoring the DHCP database

- Manual backups allow you to manually restore the database.
- To back up, right-click the server node and click Backup.
- To restore, right-click the server node and click Restore.

Migrating a DHCP server

1. On the current source DHCP server, perform a backup of the DHCP database.
2. Type `net stop dhcpserver` at a command prompt.
3. Copy the backup folder to the destination DHCP server.
4. On the destination DHCP server, perform a restore of the DHCP database.

Manually compacting the DHCP database

1. Open a command prompt.
2. CD to the directory containing the DHCP database.
3. Type `net stop dhcpserver`.
4. Type `jetpack dhcp.mdb temp.mdb`.
5. Type `net start dhcpserver`.

Troubleshooting DHCP

- A red circle with an X indicates that the DHCP Server service is stopped or the DHCP server cannot be reached.
- A white circle with a red down arrow indicates that the server is not authorized in Active Directory.
- A white circle with a red down arrow on the scope node indicates that the scope is deactivated.
- A white circle with a green up arrow indicates that the DHCP server is authorized and active.

Understanding the DHCP audit logs

- By default, all DHCP activity is written to the DHCP audit logs.
- Audit logs are stored under *%SystemRoot%\System32\dhcp*.
- To configure audit logging, right-click the server node and click Properties.

- Use the audit logs for troubleshooting.
- Table 6-3 summarizes audit log events related to authorization.

Table 6-3. Audit log events related to authorization

Event ID	Event text	Description
50	Unreachable domain	The DHCP server cannot locate the domain for which it is configured.
51	Authorization succeeded	The DHCP server is authorized to start on the network.
53	Cached authorization	The DHCP server is authorized to start using previously cached information. Active Directory wasn't available at the time the DHCP Server service was started on the network.
54	Authorization failed	The DHCP server is not authorized to start on the network and has stopped servicing clients. Typically, the DHCP Server service is stopped as a result.
55	Authorization (servicing)	The DHCP server is successfully authorized to start on the network.
56	Authorization failure, stopped servicing	The DHCP server is not authorized to start on the network and is shut down. You must authorize the server before starting it again.
57	Server found in domain	Another DHCP server exists and is authorized for the domain.
58	Server could not find domain	The DHCP server cannot locate the domain for which it is configured.
59	Network failure	A network-related failure prevents the server from determining whether it is authorized.
60	No DC is DS-enabled	No domain controller is found in the domain. The DHCP server must be able to contact a DC in the domain.
61	Server found that belongs to DS domain	Another DHCP server that belongs to the domain is found.
62	Another server found	Another DHCP server is found on the network.
63	Restarting rogue detection	The DHCP server is trying to determine whether it's authorized.
64	No DHCP-enabled interfaces	The DHCP server has its service bindings or network connections configured so that the DHCP Server service is not enabled to provide services. The server may be disconnected from the network, have a dynamic IP address, or have all its static IP addresses disabled.

Verifying leases and DHCP reservation configuration

- Select a server's Active Leases node in the DHCP console.
- If a lease expires and is not renewed, the computer might have been moved.
- If a reservation is inactive, the reservation may be incorrectly configured.

Verifying the client configuration and examining the System event log

- View the current TCP/IP configuration by typing `ipconfig /all` at a command prompt.
- Warning messages regarding address conflicts are displayed in the system tray on the client computer. The System event log may have the Event ID 1055 and the source as Dhcp.

Diagnosing and resolving issues with DHCP server configuration

- Use predefined options, which set preset values and can be overridden at any other level.
- Use server options, which can be overridden by scope, class, and reservation options.
- Use scope options, which can be overridden by class and reservation options.
- Use class options, which can be overridden by reservation options.
- Use reservation options, which can be overridden only by manually assigned TCP/IP settings.

Resolve DHCP configuration problems:

1. Checking the Internet Protocol (TCP/IP) properties on the client.
2. Configuring scope options to override other options, as necessary.
3. Releasing and renewing the client lease to ensure that the client gets the correct settings.

Implementing, Managing, and Maintaining Name Resolution

Summary of highlights from the "Implementing, Managing, and Maintaining Name Resolution" section of the Exam 70-291 Study Guide.

Name resolution

- Windows Internet Naming Service (WINS) is used to resolve NetBIOS names.
- Domain Name System (DNS) is used to resolve DNS hostnames.
- With DNS, computers are grouped by name with domains.
- Domains establish a hierarchical naming structure.
- A computer's fully qualified domain name (FQDN) is its hostname combined with its domain name.

Managing DNS clients

- A computer's name serves as the computer's hostname.
- A computer's primary DNS suffix determines the domain to which it is assigned for name resolution.
- A computer gets its primary DNS suffix from the domain in which it is a member by default.
- Unqualified names that are used on a computer are resolved using the primary DNS suffix.
- Set the primary DNS suffix using the Computer Name tab of the System utility.
- Set the way DNS suffixes are used with the Advanced TCP/IP Settings dialog box.

Configuring dynamic DNS updates

- Set dynamic update options using the Advanced TCP/IP Settings dialog box.
- By default, computers dynamically update their A and PTR records in DNS.
- For updates to occur, the client must have a domain suffix that matches a zone name hosted by the preferred DNS server.

DNS queries

- With a recursive query, the DNS client requests that the DNS server respond directly.
- With an iterative query, a DNS server attempts to resolve a query or refers the client to another server.

DNS zones

- A zone is a portion of the DNS database that is being managed.
- A single zone can contain a single domain, or it can span multiple domains.
- Authoritative servers for a zone are responsible for the related portion of the DNS database.
- Nonauthoritative servers for a zone cache information related to the zone.

Types of zones

- A primary zone file is the master (writable) copy of a zone.
- A secondary zone is a read-only copy of a primary zone.
- A stub zone lists authoritative name servers for a zone.

DNS server roles

- Primary DNS servers maintain one or more primary zone files.
- Secondary DNS servers maintain one or more secondary copies of zone files.
- Forwarding-only DNS servers maintain a cache of resolved queries.
- A single DNS server can have multiple roles.
- An unconfigured DNS server acts as a caching-only server.

DNS resource records

- An A record maps a hostname to an IP address.
- A CNAME record sets an alias or alternate name for a host.
- An MX record specifies a mail exchange server for the domain.
- An NS record specifies a name server for a domain.
- A PTR record creates a pointer that maps an IP address to a hostname for reverse lookups.
- An SOA record declares the host that's the most authoritative for the zone.

Installing and configuring DNS server service

1. Install the DNS Server service using Add Or Remove Programs in the Control Panel.
2. Configure DNS server options.
3. Configure DNS zone options.
4. Configure DNS resource records.
5. Configure DNS forwarding.

Configuring and managing DNS server options

- Manage the DNS Server service using the DNS Management console.
- Click Start → Programs → Administrative Tools → DNS.
- To configure options, right-click the server entry and click Properties.

Configuring DNS zone options

- Forward Lookup Zones are used to determine the IP address of a computer from its FQDN.
- Reverse Lookup Zones are used to determine a computer's FQDN from its IP address.
- Create a zone by right-clicking the DNS Server entry and clicking New Zone.

Configuring zone type

- To configure zone type, right-click the zone and then click Properties.
- To change the zone type, click the Change button to the right of the Type entry.

Configuring dynamic updating

- To configure dynamic updating, right-click the zone, and then click Properties.
- Use Dynamic Updates list to configure update security.

Configuring scavenging

- To configure scavenging, right-click the zone and then click Properties. Click Aging.
- Aging refers to the process of placing timestamps on dynamically registered records.
- Scavenging refers to the process of deleting outdated (stale) resource records.
- The no-refresh interval is the period after the timestamp is set that must elapse before refresh can occur.
- The refresh interval is the period after the no-refresh interval during which the timestamp can be refreshed.
- Manually configured resource records have no timestamp.
- No-refresh interval should be more than or equal to refresh interval.

Configuring the Start Of Authority (SOA)

- This is set using the Start Of Authority (SOA) tab of the zone Properties dialog box.
- The Serial Number field lists the revision number of the zone file.
- The Primary Server text box lists the primary server for the zone. The entry must end with a period.
- The Responsible Person text box lists the person responsible for the zone and ends with a period.

Configuring name servers for the zone

- The Name Servers tab of the zone Properties dialog box configures NS records for the zone.
- The primary name server for the zone is configured automatically.
- Alternate name servers must be configured manually.
- To create a NS record, click Add.

Configuring zone transfers

- Zone transfers are used to send a copy of a zone to requesting servers.
- By default, zone transfers are not allowed or restricted only to the servers listed in the Name Servers tab.
- The Zones tab of the zone Properties dialog box configures zone transfers.
- When the zone file changes, secondary servers can be automatically notified.
- To configure notification, click the Notify button on the Zone Transfers tab.

DNS forwarding

- Forwarding allows DNS servers to forward queries that they cannot resolve to other DNS servers.
- By default, a DNS server can forward queries to servers in all other DNS domains.
- A name server designated as the recipient of forwarded queries is known as a forwarder.
- To use a forwarder, right-click the DNS Server entry and select Properties. Click the Forwarders tab.
- To limit forwarding, click All Other DNS Domains, enter the forwarder's IP address, and click Add.

Monitoring DNS

- DNS Server Options can be used to monitor many aspects of DNS.
- To configure monitoring, right-click the server entry and click Properties.
- Use the Monitoring tab options to perform basic tests of name resolution.
- Use the Event Logging options to configure event logging.
- Use the Debug Logging tab options for detailed troubleshooting.
- Use System Monitor and Performance Logging to monitor the overall health of DNS.

Implementing, Managing, and Maintaining Network Security

Summary of highlights from the "Implementing, Managing, and Maintaining Network Security" section of the Exam 70-291 Study Guide.

Secure network administration

- Authentication is used to prove user and computer identities.
- With Windows 2000 or later, the primary authentication protocol is Kerberos.
- Authorization is used to control access to resources.
- Authenticated users and computers authority depends primarily on group membership.
- Both Kerberos and NTLM are used for authorization.
- IP Security (IPSec) can be used to secure communications using encryption.
- Encryption can be used to securely store data.

Using security templates

- Security templates are stored in the *%SystemRoot%\Security\Templates* folder.
- Security templates can be imported into GPOs.
- Security templates contain customized group policy definitions that apply essential security settings.
- Security templates are used to implement and manage network security.
- Security templates are created and configured using the Security Templates snap-in.
- Security templates are applied and analyzed using the Security Configuration And Analysis snap-in.

Creating security templates

- Use the Security Templates snap-in to create templates.
- Create a copy of a template by right-clicking the template you want to copy and clicking Save As.
- Create a new template by right-clicking the *C:\Windows\security\templates* node and selecting New Template.

Applying security template settings and analyzing security

- Use the Security Configuration And Analysis snap-in to apply templates and to compare settings.
- Comparing settings pinpoints any discrepancies between what is implemented currently and what is defined in a security template.

Implementing the Principle of Least Privilege

- The Principle of Least Privilege is meant to ensure no user has more privileges or access than they need.
- Includes modifying privileges and access as appropriate when users change jobs.
- Removes privileges and access when individuals leave the organization.
- Extends to cover all users including administrators and other IT staff.
- No one should have more privileges or access than is required to do their job.

Understanding IP Security

- IPSec is used to authenticate and encrypt traffic between two computers.
- IPSec is also used to block traffic.
- With Active Directory domains, IPSec is applied using Group Policy.
- IPSec policy defines filters that enforce security.
- Only one IPSec policy is applied at a time.
- IP Security Policy Management determines whether IPSec policy is applied to a computer.
- To monitor IPSec, use IP Security Monitor or type `netsh ipsec static show all`.

Active Directory default IPSec policies

- With Server (Request Security) policy, servers request but do not require secure communications.

- With Client (Respond Only), clients communication is unsecure normally but respond to server requests for secure communications.
- With Secure Server (Require Security), servers require secure communications. Servers will not respond to clients that do not or cannot use secure communications.

Troubleshooting Kerberos

- In Active Directory domains, Kerberos is the primary authentication protocol.
- Kerberos policies are under *Computer Configuration\Windows Settings\Security Settings\Account Policies\Kerberos Policy*.
- To test Kerberos, type `netdiag /test:kerberos /debug`.

Implementing, Managing, and Maintaining Routing and Remote Access

Summary of highlights from the "Implementing, Managing, and Maintaining Routing and Remote Access" section of the Exam 70-291 Study Guide.

Routing And Remote Access roles

- Remote access over wireless, dial-up, or VPN, which enables computers to connect to the server using a dial-up or VPN connection.
- Network Address Translation (NAT), which allows internal computers to access the Internet using a public IP address from an assigned address pool.
- VPN and NAT, which allows remote clients to connect to the server through the Internet, and allows local clients to connect to the Internet using a public IP address from an assigned address pool.
- Secure connections between two private networks, which can be used to connect the network on which the server is located to a remote network.
- Custom configuration, which allows any combination of the available features.

Routing protocols

- DHCP Relay Agent routing protocol allows the server to route DHCP broadcast messages between subnets.
- Routing Information Protocol (RIP) version 2 for Internet Protocol allows dynamic routing between subnets and up to a maximum of 15 hops.
- Open Shortest Path First (OSPF) allows extended dynamic routing between subnets.

Managing Routing And Remote Access

- The Routing And Remote Access console is used to manage all aspects of RRAS.
- To access the console, click Start → Programs → Administrative Tools → Routing And Remote Access.

RRAS setup

1. Implement Routing and Remote Access Service
2. Add and configure necessary network interfaces.

3. Configure Routing and Remote Access Service properties.
4. Add and configure necessary IP routing protocols.

Implementing Routing And Remote Access

- Use Services utility to disable the Windows Firewall/Internet Connection Sharing service.
- Use the Routing And Remote Access console, right-click the server entry, and then select Configure And Enable Routing And Remote Access.
- Start the Routing And Remote Access service.
- During installation, the RRAS server is made a member of the RAS And IAS Servers security group.

Types of network interfaces

- Network connections
- Dial-up connections
- VPN connections

Adding and configuring interfaces for network connections

- The RRAS setup process attempts to automatically detect all installed network interfaces.
- The detected network interfaces are then listed on the Network Interfaces node.
- To manually add a routing interface, right-click the General node, and then select New Interface.

Adding and configuring interfaces for dial-up connections

- Preconfigured dial-up connections are not automatically added or configured.
- To add as demand-dial interfaces, right-click the Network Interfaces node and then select New Demand-dial Interface.

Adding and configuring interfaces for VPN and PPPoE Connections

- VPN and Point-to-Point Protocol over Ethernet (PPPoE) are used for secure communications between private networks.
- VPN and PPPoE connections are configured manually as demand-dial interfaces.
- To add a demand-dial interface for VPN or PPPoE, right-click the Network Interfaces node and then select New Demand-dial Interface.

Managing remote access security

- Right-click a server entry in the Routing And Remote Access console and select Properties.
- Use the Security tab options to configure remote access security.
- With VPN, you can use IPSec with L2TP to enhance security by using a preshared key.

Authentication options

- Windows Authentication lets you use standard Windows security for authentication.
- Remote Authentication Dial-in User Service (RADIUS) is used to centralize the authentication of remote access clients and the storage of accounting information.

Accounting options

- None turns off logging of connection requests and sessions.
- Windows Accounting logs connection request and sessions in logfiles stored in the Remote Access Logging folder.
- RADIUS Accounting sends details about connection requests and sessions to a RADIUS server.

Managing user authentication

1. Right-click a server entry in the Routing And Remote Access console and select Properties.
2. Click the Security tab.
3. Click the Authentication Methods button.

User authentication methods

- Extensible Authentication Protocol (EAP) extends the authentication methods for PPP connections.
- Microsoft Encrypted Authentication version 2 (MS-CHAP v2) authenticates remote access and demand-dial connections using mutual authentication and strong encryption. MS-CHAP v2 is required for encrypted PPP and PPTP connections.
- Microsoft Encrypted Authentication (MS-CHAP) authenticates remote access and demand-dial connections using encryption. MS-CHAP is required for encrypted PPP and PPTP connections.
- Encrypted Authentication (CHAP) authenticates remote access and demand-dial connections using encryption.
- Shiva Password Authentication Protocol (SPAP) uses authentication with reversible encryption and is compatible with Shiva LAN Rover and Shiva clients. SPAP is not secure.
- Unencrypted Password (PAP) uses Password Authentication Protocol (PAP) and sends passwords in plain-text during authentication. PAP is the most unsecure authentication method.

Remote access policies

- Remote access policies for use with EAP are specified using the Remote Access Policies node.
- Connections To Microsoft Routing And Remote Access Server applies to connections to the currently selected RRAS server.
- Connections To Other Access Servers applies to connections to other access servers via the current RRAS server.

- New remote access policies can be created by right-clicking the Remote Access Policies node and selecting New Remote Access Policy.
- Each policy can have a dial-in profile associated with it that is used to set access permissions.
- Right-click a policy, select Properties, and then click the Edit Profile button to view and modify the profile settings.
- Remote access settings defined in a user's profile have precedence over dial-in profile settings.

Managing IP assignment

- Right-click a server entry in the Routing And Remote Access console and select Properties.
- Use the IP tab options to configure IP assignment.

IP assignment options

- You must select the IP Routing checkbox for LAN and demand-dial routing to occur.
- If you select the Allow IP-based Remote Access And Demand-Dial Connections checkbox, IP-based remote access and demand-dial connections can be established using RRAS.
- Select Dynamic Host Configuration Protocol (DHCP) to use DHCP to assign client IP addresses.
- On DHCP servers, use the Default Routing And Remote Access Class to define configuration for remote access clients.
- Select Static Address Pool to assign remote access clients static IP addresses from the defined IP address pools.
- Select Enable Broadcast Name Resolution to allow remote access clients to use broadcast messages.
- Broadcasts are not forwarded to other subnets.

Managing remote access logging

- Right-click a server entry in the Routing And Remote Access console and select Properties.
- Use the Logging tab options to configure event logging and debugging.
- RRAS events are stored in the System event logs.
- For debugging connections to RRAS, select the Log Additional Routing And Remote Access Information checkbox.
- When debugging is enabled, PPP connection events are written to *Ppp.log* in the *%SystemRoot%\Tracing* folder.

DHCP Relay Agents

- DHCP clients use broadcast messages to contact DHCP servers.
- Broadcasts aren't routed between subnets and are limited by the logical boundaries of a subnet.

- You can work around this restriction by configuring DHCP Relay Agents on subnets.
- A Relay Agent listens for DHCP broadcasts and forwards the DHCP broadcasts between clients and servers.

Configuring a server as a DHCP Relay Agent

1. Install the DHCP Relay Agent routing protocol.
2. Configure the DHCP Relay Agent routing protocol.
3. Enable the DHCP Relay Agent routing protocol.

Install the DHCP Relay Agent routing protocol

- Right-click the General node, and then select New Routing Protocol.
- Click DHCP Relay Agent, and then click OK.

Configure the DHCP Relay Agent routing protocol

- Right-click DHCP Relay Agent, and then select Properties.
- Type the IP address of a DHCP server for the network and then click Add.

Enable the DHCP Relay Agent routing protocol

- Right-click DHCP Relay Agent and then select New Interface.
- Click the network interface on which you want to enable the routing protocol.

TCP/IP routing

- When you install Routing And Remote Access and enable IP routing, you can add routing protocols.
- Routing Information Protocol (RIP) version 2 for Internet Protocol is ideal for small networks.
- Open Shortest Path First (OSPF) is better for larger networks.

Understanding RIP

- Initially the only entries in routing tables are for the networks to which the router is physically connected.
- The router starts sending announcements of its availability.
- Responses from announcements allow the router to update its routing tables.
- With periodic update mode, announcements are sent periodically to learn of available routes, and routes are deleted automatically when the router is stopped and restarted.
- With auto-static update mode, announcements are sent when other routers request updates, learned routes are added as static, and routes remain until they are manually deleted.

Configuring RIP

1. Install the RIP routing protocol.
2. Specify the network interface(s) through which RIP will be used.

Installing the RIP routing protocol

- Right-click the General node, and then select New Routing Protocol.
- Click Routing Information Protocol (RIP) version 2 for Internet Protocol.

Specifying the RIP network interface

- Right-click the RIP node, and then select New Interface.
- Select one of the available network interfaces through which RIP traffic can be routed.

Configuring RIP properties

- Right-click the RIP node, and then select Properties.
- The General tab options control triggered update delays and event logging.
- The Security tab options control how the router processes announcements.

Configuring RIP connection properties

- Click the RIP node, right-click the network interface, and then select Properties.
- The General tab options allow you to configure the operation mode, packet protocol, and authentication.
- The Security tab options allow you to configure RIP route filters.
- The Neighbors tab options allow you to configure how the router interacts with other RIP routers.
- The Advanced tab options control periodic announcements, routing expiration, and processing.

Understanding OSPF

- OSPF uses the Shortest Path First (SPF) algorithm to calculate routes.
- The route with the lowest route cost is the shortest path.
- The shortest path is always used first when routing.
- An OSPF router maintains a link-state database that it uses to track the network topology.
- Data is synchronized with adjacent routers and nonbroadcast multiple access (NBMA) neighbors.
- When a change is made to the network topology, the first router to identify it sends out a change notification.
- OSPF divides the network into transit areas, which can be thought of as areas of responsibility.
- OSPF routers maintain link-state information only for those transit areas for which they've been configured.

Configuring OSPF

1. Install the OSPF routing protocol.
2. Specify the network interface(s) through which OSPF will be used.

Installing the RIP routing protocol

- Right-click the General node, and then select New Routing Protocol.
- Click Open Shortest Path First (OSPF).

Specifying the RIP network interface

- Right-click the OSPF node, and then select New Interface.
- Select one of the available network interfaces through which OSPF traffic can be routed.

Configuring RIP properties

- Right-click the RIP node, and then select Properties.
- The General tab options set the router ID and control event logging.
- The Areas tab options can be used to subdivide the network into specific transit areas.
- The Virtual Interfaces tab options allow you to configure virtual interfaces for transit areas.
- The External Routing tab options allow you to configure Autonomous System Boundary Routing.

Configuring OSPF connection properties

- Click the OSPF node, right-click the network interface, and then select Properties.
- The General tab options allow you to configure the area ID, router priority, cost, and password.
- The NMBA Neighbors tab options allow you to specify IP addresses and priority of NMBA neighbors.
- The Advanced tab options control transit delays, retransmit intervals, Hello intervals for discovery, Dead intervals for determining down routers, and poll intervals for follow-ups to dead routers.

Static routes

- Static routes provide a permanent mapping to a specific destination network.
- Static routes are set according to the network ID, network mask, and relative cost of the route.
- Routers use this information to determine the gateway to use to forward packet.
- Static routes are not shared between routers.

Configure static routes using the Routing And Remote Access console

- You can view and configure existing static routes using the Static Routes node.
- To add a static route, right-click the Static Routes node, and then select New Static Route.
- To delete a static rout, right-click it, and then select Delete.

Configure static routes using the command line

- You can view existing static routes by typing `route print`.
- You can add a static route by using `route add`.
- You can remove a static route by using `route delete`.

Routing ports

- When you install RRAS, a number of routing ports are created automatically.
- Routing ports are used for inbound connections to the RRAS server.
- The types of ports available depend on the configuration of the RRAS server.

Managing routing ports

- To view ports, click the Ports node.
- To view a port's status and statistics, double-click the port entry.
- To reset a port, double-click the port entry, and then click the Reset button.
- To configure ports, right-click the Ports node, and then select Properties. Use the options available.

Network Address Translation (NAT)

- Allows multiple client computers to access the public Internet sharing a single public IP address or a pool of public IP addresses.
- Separates your organization's internal private network from the public network.
- Allows you to use private IP addresses internally and to use public IP addresses when client computers access the Internet.

Using NAT

- NAT provides internet connectivity to internal clients through a single interface.
- NAT includes the Basic Firewall, which can block external traffic from entering the internal network.

Configuring a server for NAT and the Basic Firewall

1. Install the NAT/Basic Firewall routing protocol.
2. Specify the Network Interface to use.
3. Configure the NAT/Basic Firewall routing protocol.
4. Optionally, enable basic firewall and configure packet filtering.

Installing the NAT/Basic Firewall routing protocol

1. Use the Routing And Remote Access console.
2. Right-click the General node, and then select New Routing Protocol.
3. Click NAT/Basic Firewall, and then click OK.

Configuring the NAT/Basic Firewall routing protocol

1. Use the Routing And Remote Access console.
2. Right-click the NAT/Basic Firewall node, and then select New Interface.
3. Select the interface that is directly connect to the Internet.

Configuring NAT properties

- Right-click the NAT/Basic Firewall node, and then select Properties.
- The NAT/Basic Firewall tab options set the interface type for which NAT/Basic Firewall is being used.
- The Address Pool tab options are used to configure the public IP addresses to be used.
- The Services And Ports tab options define firewall exceptions that allow external traffic to enter the internal network.
- The ICMP tab options configure the permitted incoming and outgoing information requests.

Packet filtering

- By default, Basic Firewall is not enabled for use with a public interface connected to the Internet.
- If you enable the Basic Firewall, the Basic Firewall accepts incoming traffic from the Internet only if it has been requested by the network.
- You can define packet filters to control network traffic.
- Inbound packet filters control which packets are forwarded or processed by the network.
- Outbound packet filters control which packets are received by the network.

Enabling Basic Firewall and configuring packet filtering

- Use the Routing And Remote Access console.
- Click NAT/Basic Firewall, and then double-click the network interface on which you want to configure.
- On the NAT/Basic Firewall tab, select the Enable A Basic Firewall On This Interface checkbox.
- Click the Inbound Filters button to specify which packets are forwarded or processed by the network.
- Click the Outbound Filters button to specify which packets are received by the network.

Managing remote access clients

- View connected clients by expanding the server node and clicking the Remote Access Clients node.
- Clients are listed by connected username, duration and number of access ports being used.
- To view a more detailed status, right-click the client entry, and then select Status.
- To disconnect a client, right-click the client entry, and then select Disconnect.
- To send a message to a client, right-click the client entry, select Send Message, type the message, and then click OK.
- To send a message to all clients, right-click the Remote Access Clients node, select Send To All, type the message, and then click OK.
- Control remote access permissions using remote access policies.

Internet Authentication Service (IAS)

- RADIUS servers are used to centralize the authentication of remote access clients and the storage of accounting information.
- Centralizing authentication and accounting reduces the administrative overhead of managing multiple RRAS servers.
- Registering RADIUS servers with Active Directory makes the server a member of the RAS And IAS Servers group.
- Members of this group are able to read remote access attributes of user accounts.

Configuring a server for IAS

1. Install IAS on a designated server.
2. Register the IAS server in Active Directory.
3. Configure your RRAS servers as IAS clients.
4. Configure your RRAS servers to use RADIUS.

Installing IAS

1. Use Add Or Remove Programs in Control Panel.
2. Select Internet Authentication Service.

Managing Internet Authentication Service

- Use the Internet Authentication Service console.
- Click Start → Programs → Administrative Tools → Internet Authentication Service.

Registering the RADIUS server

1. Use the Internet Authentication Service console.
2. Right-click the Internet Authentication Service node.
3. Select Register Server In Active Directory.

Configuring RRAS servers as clients

1. Use the Internet Authentication Service console.
2. Right-click the RADIUS Clients node, and then select New Radius Client.

Configuring RRAS servers to use RADIUS

1. Use the Routing And Remote Access console.
2. Right-click a server entry and select Properties.
3. Configure the Security tab for RADIUS Authentication and RADIUS Accounting.

Diagnosing and resolving issues related to establishing a remote access dial-up connection

- On the General tab of the server's Properties dialog box, verify that Remote Access Server is enabled.
- On the IP tab of the server's Properties dialog box, verify that IP Routing is enabled if clients should have access to the network, and that it is disabled if clients should have access to the RRAS server only.
- If static IP addresses are used, verify that the address pool configuration is correct and that there are available IP addresses.
- If dynamic IP addresses are used, verify the configuration of the DHCP server. The IP address scope must be large enough so that the RRAS server can requests blocks of 10 IP addresses.
- Using the Ports node, verify that server has properly configured modem ports and that not all modem ports are assigned.
- Verify that the client, the RRAS server, and the remote access policy have at least one common authentication method configured.
- Verify the client and the server permissions, credentials, and access policies are configured correctly.

Diagnosing and resolving issues related to remote access VPNs

- On the General tab of the server's Properties dialog box, verify that Remote Access Server is enabled.
- Using the Ports node, verify that the server has properly configured ports and that not all ports are assigned.
- On the Security tab of the server's Properties dialog box, verify that the server is using the appropriate authentication provider and then the appropriate authentication methods are selected for use.
- Verify the remote access profile settings are correct and do not conflict with the server properties. Right-click a remote access policy, select Properties, and then click the Edit Profile button.
- Verify that the client, the RRAS server and the remote access policy have at least one common authentication method configured.
- Verify the RRAS server is made a member of the RAS And IAS Servers security group in the local domain. This membership is required for proper working of routing and remote access.
- Verify the underling dial-up configuration as discussed in the previous section.

Diagnosing and resolving issues related to resources beyond the Remote Access Server

- On the General tab of the server's Properties dialog box, verify that Router is enabled.
- On the General tab of the server's Properties dialog box, verify that LAN And Demand-Dial Routing is selected.
- On the IP tab of the server's Properties dialog box, verify that Enable IP Routing is selected.
- If static IP addresses are used, verify that the client's TCP/IP settings are correct.
- If dynamic IP addresses are used, verify that the client is obtaining the proper TCP/IP settings from the DHCP server.
- If your remote access clients use NetBIOS for name resolution, verify that Enable Broadcast Name Resolution is selected on the IP tab.

Troubleshooting router-to-router VPNs

- For the source and destination router, verify on the General tab of the server's Properties dialog box that both Router and LAN And Demand-Dial Routing are selected.
- For the source and destination router, verify on the IP tab of the server's Properties dialog box that Enable IP Routing is selected.
- For the source and destination router, verify that the servers have properly configured PPTP or L2TP ports.
- For the source and destination router, verify that the interface used for routing has Enable IP Router Manager selected on the General tab of the connection properties dialog box so that IP traffic can be routed over the connection.

- For the source and destination router, verify that the static routes are configured as appropriate to allow traffic over the appropriate interface.
- For the source and destination router, verify that permissions, credentials, and access policies are configured correctly.

Troubleshooting demand-dial routing

- Verify that Routing And Remote Access Services is installed.
- Verify on the General tab of the server's Properties dialog box that both Router and LAN And Demand-Dial Routing are selected.
- Verify on the IP tab of the server's Properties dialog box that Enable IP Routing is selected.
- Verify that the demand-dial interfaces are enabled and configured properly.
- Verify that the static routes are configured properly and that Use This Route To Initiate Demand-Dial Connections is selected in the static route properties.
- Verify that the Security tab settings of the network interfaces use a common configuration.
- Verify that the Networking tab settings of the network interfaces use a common VPN type.
- Verify that the servers use the appropriate authentication providers and that the appropriate authentication methods are selected for use. The servers must have at least one common authentication method.
- Verify that the servers have properly configured ports for demand-dial use.
- Verify that packet filters aren't blocking the routing.

Maintaining a Network Infrastructure

Summary of highlights from the "Maintaining a Network Infrastructure" section of the Exam 70-291 Study Guide.

Monitoring network traffic

- Use Task Manager to monitor network traffic.
- In the Performance console, use the Network Interface performance object to monitor network traffic.
- Install the Network Monitor Tools.
- Use the Network Monitor to analyze network traffic.

Network Interface object

- Use Track Packet Outbound Discarded.
- Use Track Packet Outbound Errors.
- Use Track Packet Received Discarded.
- Use Track Packet Received Errors.

Installing Network Monitor

- Use Add Or Remove Programs in Control Panel.
- Select Network Monitor Tools.

Network Monitor components

- Network Monitor Driver captures frames received by and sent to a network adapter.
- Network Monitor console is used to view and analyze data captured by the Network Monitor Driver.

Using Network Monitor

- To open, click Start → Programs → Administrative Tools → Network Monitor.
- Select the network on which you want to capture data.
- To change the monitored network, click Capture → Networks.
- Capture data by clicking Capture → Start.
- To view the details of the captured data, click Capture → Stop And View.
- To look for a specific type of frame, click Capture → Filter.
- To monitor the network traffic and alert you when a condition is met, click Capture → Trigger.

Server services

- View the currently configured services using the Services utility in Control panel.
- In Computer Management, expand the Services And Applications node, and then select Services.

Service states

- Services can be in one of three possible states: started, paused, or stopped.
- If the service is running, the status is listed as Started.
- If the service is stopped, the status is listed as blank.
- If a service can be paused, you (or another administrator) have paused the service.

Service startup type

- Automatic services start automatically with the operating system.
- Manual services do not start automatically with the operating system, but can be manually started if called by another process.
- Disabled services do not start automatically and cannot be started manually either.

Service dependency

- Some services depend on other services in order to start.
- If a service depends on other services, it can only start when those services are running.
- To view, double-click the service, and then select the Dependencies tab. Dependent services are listed.

Service recovery

- Service recovery options allow you to specify the actions that should be taken if a service fails.

- The operating system can take one of four actions should a service fail. These actions are to:
  — Take no action.
  — Restart the service.
  — Run a program.
  — Restart the computer.
- To configure recovery, double-click the service, and then select the Recovery tab.

Exam 70-291 Practice Questions

1. Alex is a network administrator. He's been asked to implement dynamic IP addressing the company's newly installed network, which has two subnets in one Active Directory domain with servers running Windows Server 2003. After Alex installs and configures the DHCP server in SubnetA, client computers in SubnetA are able to obtain DHCP leases and the proper TCP/IP configuration. However, client computers on SubnetB are unable to obtain DHCP leases. What is the most likely cause of this problem?

   ❍ A. The DHCP server is not authorized is SubnetB.

   ❍ B. The DHCP scope for SubnetB is not active.

   ❍ C. The DHCP Server service is stopped.

   ❍ D. A DHCP Relay Agent is not installed in SubnetB.

   Answer D is correct. A DHCP Relay Agent (or a BOOTP-compatible router) must be installed in SubnetB to route DHCP broadcast messages between networks.

2. Sam's computer is configured to use DHCP. When Sam logs on, he notices he can't connect to the network. The computer has no IP address according to `ipconfig`. Which of the following is most likely true?

   ❍ A. No DHCP server is on the network.

   ❍ B. The computer is using Automatic Private IP Addressing.

   ❍ C. The network cable to the computer is disconnected.

   ❍ D. The computer is using dynamic IP addressing.

   Answer C is correct. APIPA requires an active network connection (in most cases) for automatic configuration to work properly. If the network cable to a computer is disconnected or improperly connected, the computer may not be assigned an IP address. When you type `ipconfig /all` at a command prompt, you may see an error stating "Media Disconnected."

3. The company has two subnets in one Active Directory domain with servers running Windows Server 2003. On the DHCP server, Scope1 provides dynamic addressing for SubnetA, and Scope2 provides dynamic addressing for SubnetB. Clients in SubnetA are able to obtain DHCP leases, but are unable to access resources in SubnetB. What is the best way to solve the problem?

❍ A. Reconfigure the network's DHCP Relay agent.

❍ B. Activate Scope1.

❍ C. Activate Scope1 and Scope2.

❍ D. Configure the default gateway on client computers.

❍ E. Configure the TCP/IP router option for Scope1.

Answer E is correct. If client computers have an improperly configured gateway, they are not able to access resources outside of their local subnet. The best way to solve this problem is to configure the TCP/IP router option (option 003) for Scope1. Although you could configure a default gateway on client computers, this is not the best way to solve the problem, so Answer D is incorrect.

4. Which of the following is most likely true if a computer with an IP address of 169.254.0.11?

   ❍ A. No DHCP server is on the network.

   ❍ B. A DHCP server is assigning the computer's IP address.

   ❍ C. The computer has a static IP address.

   ❍ D. The network cable is disconnected.

   Answer A is correct. When DHCP is configured but not available, or the client lease is expired and cannot be renewed, clients use Automatic Private IP Addressing. With APIPA, clients assign themselves an IP address in the range of 169.254.0.1–169.254.255.254, with a subnet mask of 255.255.0.0.

5. Paula is a network administrator for an Active Directory domain with servers running Windows Server 2003. Paula recently installed a second DHCP server on the local subnet. When testing the server, she notices the DHCP Server service is being shut down and she can't get the service to stay running. What is the most likely cause of this problem?

   ❍ A. The DHCP Server service is improperly installed.

   ❍ B. The DHCP server does not have an active scope.

   ❍ C. The active scope has invalid TCP/IP options.

   ❍ D. The DHCP server has not be authorized in Active Directory.

   Answer D is correct. With Windows 2000 or later, a workgroup or standalone DHCP server configured on the same subnet as a domain's authorized DHCP server is considered to be a rogue server. As part of a network protection process, the rogue server automatically stops its DHCP Server service and stops leasing IP addresses to clients. To resolve this issue, you must authorize the DHCP server in Active Directory.

6. Tom is responsible for the managing DHCP. The organization has a single Class C subnet with 254 available IP addresses. The network ID is 192.168.10.0. Tom wants a single scope to cover all 254 IP addresses. However, he needs to ensure 14 of the IP addresses aren't used by DHCP clients and that 8 of the IP addresses are always assigned to the same member servers. Which of the following should be done to configure the scope?

❑ A. Create the scope for the IP address range 192.168.10.0–192.168.10.255.

❑ B. Create the scope for the IP address range 192.168.10.1–192.168.10.254.

❑ C. Create an exclusion range for the 8 member servers and reserve the other 14 IP addresses.

❑ D. Create an exclusion range for the 14 member servers and reserve the other 8 IP addresses.

Answers B and D are correct. With standard network configurations, the network ID is the .0 address of the subnet, such as 192.168.10.0, and the broadcast address is the .255 address of the subnet, such as 192.168.10.255. The assignable IP address for the network is 192.168.10.1 to 192.168.10.254. To ensure a client computer gets the same IP address, create a reservation on a lease. To ensure an IP address is not used, create an exclusion.

7. You want to configure multiple standard scopes so that they can be easily activated or deactivated. What should you do?

   ❍ A. Create a multicast scope and add the standard scopes to it.

   ❍ B. Create a superscope and add the standard scopes to it.

   ❍ C. Delete all the scopes except one.

   ❍ D. Configure server options instead of scope options.

   Answer B is correct. A superscope is a container for scopes that allows you to more easily work with multiple scopes. After you create a superscope, you can add to it the scopes you want to manage as a group.

8. The network has three subnets: SubnetA, SubnetB, and SubnetC. The DHCP server on SubnetA is configured with one scope for each subnet. The network administrator configured the TCP/IP settings using Server options, which works fine for Clients on SubnetA, but not for clients on SubnetB and SubnetC. What should be done to resolve this problem?

   ❍ A. Set scope options for the SubnetB and SubnetC scopes as appropriate to override server options.

   ❍ B. Remove the server options and set only scope options for the SubnetA, SubnetB, and SubnetC scopes.

   ❍ C. Remove the server options and set only class options.

   ❍ D. Set predefined options as appropriate to override server options.

   Answer A is correct. The clients on SubnetB and SubnetC are likely getting the wrong TCP/IP router option. By setting the correct TCP/IP router option as a scope option, you can override the server option for this setting.

9. What step does a DNS client perform first to resolve a DNS name?

   ❍ A. The client checks its local DNS resolver cache.

   ❍ B. The client queries its primary DNS server.

   ❍ C. The client queries its alternate DNS server.

   ❍ D. The client broadcasts on the local subnet.

   Answer A is correct. DNS clients check their local DNS resolver cache before sending queries to DNS servers.

10. Which of the following correctly describes recursive and iterative queries?

❑ A. A DNS server must respond directly to a recursive query or return an error, and queries other DNS servers on behalf of the client if unable to resolve a query from its cache/zone database.

❑ B. A DNS server must resolve an iterative query from its local cache or return an error, and is unable to contact other DNS servers on behalf of the client.

❑ C. A DNS server must resolve a recursive query from its cache if possible, and if not, must refer the client to another DNS server.

❑ D. A DNS server must resolve an iterative query from its local cache/zone database or refer the client to another DNS server.

Answers A and D are correct. With a recursive query, the DNS server must respond directly to a recursive query or return an error, and queries other DNS servers on behalf of the client if unable to resolve a query. With an iterative query, a DNS server attempts to resolve the query from its records or from its cache, and if it is unable to resolve the query, the server can refer the client to another DNS server.

11. What is the next step a forwarder takes when it is unable to resolve a query?

❍ A. The forwarder returns an error to the originating DNS server.

❍ B. The forwarder returns an error directly to the client.

❍ C. The forwarder uses the root hints *Cache.dns* file to determine the root name server to contact.

❍ D. The forwarder performs a broadcast to determine the root name server to contact.

Answer C is correct. If the forwarder is unable to resolve a query, it attempts to contact the appropriate root name server. Root name servers that the DNS server can use and refer to when resolving queries are listed in the root hints, which are stored in the *Cache.dns* file.

12. What type of zone should you create if you want to create a read-only copy of the master DNS data for the zone?

❍ A. Primary

❍ B. Secondary

❍ C. Stub

❍ D. Root Hints

Answer B is correct. A secondary zone is a copy of a zone's master data and is read-only.

13. In what role should a DNS server be configured if it should maintain a cache of resolve queries but not have zone files?

❍ A. Primary

❍ B. Secondary

❍ C. Stub

❍ D. Forwarding-only

Answer D is correct. Forwarding-only DNS servers maintain a cache of resolved queries.

14. What type of resource record must you configure to enable reverse lookups for host computers?

❍ A. Host (A) records

❍ B. Pointer (PTR) records

❍ C. Mail Exchanger (MX) records

❍ D. Name Server (NS) records

❍ E. Canonical Name (CNAME) records

Answer B is correct. DNS uses host (A) records to resolve computer names to IP addresses and pointer (PTR) records to resolve IP addresses to computer names.

15. Sarah is a network administrator. She's just installed DNS on the network, and configured a primary server and a secondary server. What must she do to specify the authoritative name servers for the zone?

❍ A. Nothing, all necessary NS records are created automatically.

❍ B. Create the NS records for the primary and secondary name server.

❍ C. Create the NS record for the primary name server.

❍ D. Create the NS record for the secondary name server.

Answer D is correct. Use NS records to specify the authoritative servers for the zone. The NS record of the primary name server for the zone is created automatically. Records for secondary name servers must be created manually.

16. Tom is a system administrator. Like Sarah, he's just configured DNS on his organization's network. He configured primary and secondary name servers. Clients are able to perform DNS lookups without any problems. However, the secondary server is not getting zone transfers from the primary server, even though zone transfers are enabled. Which of the following are possible resolutions for this problem?

❑ A. Designating a list of servers to notify.

❑ B. Allowing the DNS server to notify the servers listed on the Name Servers tab.

❑ C. Disabling automatic notification.

❑ D. Creating the NS record for the secondary name server.

Answers A and B are correct. After you enable zone transfers, the default configuration allows automatic notification, but only to a designated list of name servers. You must specify the designated name servers or allow notification of the name servers listed on the Name Servers tab.

17. You've installed DNS on a domain controller and configured a standard primary zone. To improve security, you want to ensure that only secure updates of DNS are allowed. However, when you access the zone Properties dialog box, you are not able to configure dynamic updates in the secure only mode. What should you do to resolve this problem?

❍ A. Make the server a member of the DnsUpdateProxy group.

❍ B. Log on with an account that is a member of the DnsAdmins group.

❍ C. Change the zone type so that it is Active Directory–integrated.

❍ D. Enable aging and scavenging.

Answer C is correct. By default, dynamic DNS updates are not allowed, but you can configure a zone to use secure updates. Only Active Directory–integrated primary zones can use secure-only mode. Other types of zones can be configured to allow nonsecure and secure dynamic updating.

18. Which command-line tool can you use to clear the DNS resolver cache on a DNS client?

   ❍ A. `ipconfig`

   ❍ B. `netsh`

   ❍ C. `tracert`

   ❍ D. `pathping`

   Answer A is correct. You can clear the DNS resolver cache by typing `ipconfig /flushdns`.

19. What tool should you use to configure security templates?

   ❍ A. Security Templates snap-in

   ❍ B. Security Configuration And Analysis snap-in

   ❍ C. Network Monitor

   ❍ D. Active Directory Users And Computers

   Answer A is correct. Use the Security Templates snap-in to create and configure security templates. Use the Security Configuration And Analysis snap-in to apply and analyze security templates.

20. Which of the following are true regarding authentication and authorization on Windows 2000 or later networks?

   ❑ A. The primary authentication protocol is Kerberos.

   ❑ B. Both Kerberos and NTLM are used for authorization.

   ❑ C. IPSec can be used to secure communications using encryption.

   ❑ D. Encryption can also be used to securely store data.

   Answers A, B, C, and D are correct. On networks with computers running Windows 2000 or later, the primary authentication protocol is Kerberos. Both Kerberos and NTLM are used for authorization. IPSec can be used to secure communications using encryption. Encryption can also be used to securely store data.

21. Which security template would you apply to a domain controller to implement the most stringent security settings?

   ❍ A. Rootsec

   ❍ B. Securedc

   ❍ C. Hisecdc

   ❍ D. Iesacls

   Answer A is correct. The Rootsec template applies root permissions to the system drive. The Securedc template contains moderate security settings for domain controllers. The Hisecdc template contains very stringent security settings that can be used to further secure domain controllers. The Iesacls template applies relaxed Registry permissions for Internet Explorer.

22. To whom should the Principal of Least Privilege not apply?

- ❍ A. Temporary workers
- ❍ B. Contract workers
- ❍ C. Permanent employees
- ❍ D. Administrators and other IT staff
- ❍ E. None of the above

Answer E is correct. The Principal of Least Privilege should apply to all users, including temporary, contract, and permanent employees as well as administrators and other IT staff. No one should have more privileges or access than is required to do their job.

23. Which default IPSec policy should you enable if you want to ensure that only secure communications are used?

- ❍ A. Server (Request Security) policy
- ❍ B. Client (Respond Only)
- ❍ C. Secure Server (Require Security)

Answer C is correct. With Secure Server (Require Security), servers require secure communications. Servers will not respond to clients that do not or cannot use secure communications.

24. Which of the following tools should you use to view IPSec statistics for troubleshooting?

- ❍ A. IP Security Monitor
- ❍ B. IP Security Policy Management
- ❍ C. Network Monitor
- ❍ D. Security Configuration And Analysis

Answer A is correct. In IP Security Monitor, the Main Mode and Quick Mode nodes show current filters, security methods, statistics, and security associations. The statistics can help you identify IPSec configuration problems.

25. Which command-line tool can you use to view detailed IPSec information?

- ❍ A. `ipconfig`
- ❍ B. `netsh`
- ❍ C. `tracert`
- ❍ D. `pathping`

Answer B is correct. You can view detailed IPSec information by typing `netsh ipsec static show all`.

26. Mary is a network administrator. She's been tasked with setting up a remote access server to enable remote clients to connect to the server through the Internet, and to enable local clients to connect to the Internet using a public IP address from an assigned address pool. What role or roles should the remote access server be configured for?

❍ A. Remote access over wireless, dial-up or VPN

❍ B. NAT

❍ C. VPN and NAT

❍ D. Secure network/network VPN

Answer C is correct. A remote access server configured for VPN and NAT allows remote clients to connect to the server through the Internet and allows local clients to connect to the Internet using a public IP address from an assigned address pool.

27. John configured a remote access server to use DHCP for IP address assignment. However, when clients connect to the network, they are not assigned IP addressing and instead assign themselves APIPA addresses. What are the possible causes of this problem?

❑ A. Remote Access Server is not enabled as a server option.

❑ B. Broadcast name resolution is not enabled.

❑ C. No DHCP server is available on the subnet, and a DHCP Relay Agent has not been configured.

❑ D. The DHCP server did not have 10 available IP addresses when RRAS requested its first block of IP addresses.

Answers C and D are correct. If the subnet that the RRAS server is on doesn't have a DHCP server, a DHCP Relay Agent must be configured to allow clients to be assigned dynamic IP addressing. The DHCP server must also have a block of at least 10 IP addresses available for RRAS.

28. What type of RAS connection between private networks requires a permanent static route and cannot use dynamic routing?

❍ A. Demand-dial connections

❍ B. VPN connections

❍ C. All other network connections

❍ D. All of the above

Answer B is correct. When configuring VPN between private networks, you must specify the permanent static routes to the remote networks with which the RRAS server's network will communicate.

29. Which of the following are true with regard to using IPSec with VPN?

❑ A. IPSec can be used with L2TP to enhance security.

❑ B. IPSec cannot be used with PPTP.

❑ C. PPPoE always uses IPSec.

❑ D. A custom IPSec policy for RRAS is required.

Answers A, B, and D are correct. If you've configured VPN and set L2TP as the protocol type, you can use IPSec with L2TP to enhance security. To do this, you must define a custom IPSec policy and enable the related security options on your RRAS server.

30. To improve security, you want to require that all remote access clients authenticate using smart cards. What is the only authentication protocol that should be enabled on the RRAS server?

 ❍ A. MS-CHAP

 ❍ B. MS-CHAP V2

 ❍ C. SPAP

 ❍ D. PAP

 ❍ E. EAP

 Answer E is correct. EAP extends the authentication methods for PPP connections to include the EAP methods configured through remote access policies. In a standard configuration, these policies allow MD5-Challenge, Protected EAP (PEAP), smart cards, or other PKI certificates to be used.

31. Your organization has multiple RRAS servers. Which of the following services should you install to centralize the authentication of remote access clients and the storage of accounting information?

 ❍ A. PPPoE

 ❍ B. IAS

 ❍ C. RADIUS

 ❍ D. RRAS

 ❍ E. IIS

 Answer B is correct. RADIUS servers are used to centralize the authentication of remote access clients and the storage of accounting information. A Windows Server 2003 system can be configured as a RADIUS server by installing the Internet Authentication Service (IAS). RADIUS is a protocol; IAS is the actual service.

32. Aaron is a network administrator. The organization has nine subnets connected with persistent connections and one network connected with a demand-dial connection. He doesn't want to have to maintain the routing tables manually, and is looking for the simplest solution that will also ensure that any changes to network topology are updated automatically. Which routing option should he implement?

 ❍ A. SPF

 ❍ B. OSPF

 ❍ C. RIPv2

 ❍ D. PPPoE

 Answer C is correct. RIP is ideal for small networks and can also be used with demand-dial connections. SPF is the routing algorithm used by OSPF. OSPF cannot be used with demand-dial connections. Point-to-Point Protocol over Ethernet (PPPoE) is a communications protocol used for secure communications between private networks.

33. Which of the following are valid command lines for adding a static route?

 ❍ A. `route add 192.168.52.0 mask 255.255.255.0 192.168.0.1 metric 1 if 0x10003`

- ❍ B. `route add 192.168.52.0 mask 255.255.255.0 192.168.0.1 if 0x10003`
- ❍ C. `route add 192.168.52.0 mask 255.255.255.0 192.168.0.1 metric 1`
- ❍ D. `route -p add 192.168.52.0 mask 255.255.255.0 192.168.0.1 metric 1 if 0x10003`
- ❍ E. All of the above

Answer E is correct. Answers A, B, C, and D all have valid routes. The metric and interface are optional. If you do not specify them, they are selected automatically. To make a static route persistent, you can add the `-p` option. Persistent static routes are not deleted even if the router is stopped and restarted.

34. You've configured VPN using L2TP. You know that up to 256 clients will be connecting simultaneously to the RRAS server. What modifications (if any) do you need to make to the ports on the RRAS server?

- ❍ A. None. The default configuration allows up to 256 ports per connection type.
- ❍ B. Since only 128 ports are allowed per connection type, you must configure another connection using PPTP.
- ❍ C. Since only 128 ports are allowed per connection type, you must install a second RRAS server.
- ❍ D. Since only 128 ports are preconfigured for VPN using L2TP, you must add an additional 128 ports.

Answer D is correct. The default configuration allows up to 128 ports. You can add ports by increasing the maximum ports option for L2TP connections.

35. Which of the following are true regarding IP addresses used with NAT?

- ❑ A. NAT uses public IP addresses when client computers need to access the Internet.
- ❑ B. Public IP addresses are assigned by your ISP.
- ❑ C. A pool of IP addresses is required.
- ❑ D. IP address reservations can be defined.

Answers A, B, and D are correct. NAT uses these public IP addresses, which are assigned by an ISP. Only one public IP address is required, but you can use a pool of IP addresses. You can also define reservations for IP addresses.

36. Tom is configuring NAT and the Basic Firewall. He installs and configures NAT. He enables the Basic Firewall and configures it on the LAN interface, but the Basic Firewall does not seem to be working. What is the likely problem with the configuration?

- ❍ A. Inbound packet filters must be configured.
- ❍ B. Outbound packed filters must be configured.
- ❍ C. NAT cannot be enabled with Basic Firewall.
- ❍ D. Basic Firewall is configured on the wrong interface.

Answer D is correct. The Basic Firewall must be configured for use with a public interface connected to the Internet. The Basic Firewall accepts incoming traffic from the Internet only if it has been requested by the network, and you can optionally define packet filters to control network traffic using.

37. You've installed network monitor and configured a network to monitor. What do you need to do to capture data?

   ❍ A. Click Capture → Networks

   ❍ B. Click Capture → Start

   ❍ C. Click Capture → Filter

   ❍ D. Click Capture → Trigger

   Answer B is correct. After you configure a network to monitor, you start capturing data by Capture → Start.

38. You are having trouble when connecting to the network remotely. The computer appears to make a remote access connection, but you can't access resources. Which command can you use to verify the TCP/IP configuration?

   ❍ A. `ipconfig`

   ❍ B. `pathping`

   ❍ C. `tracert`

   ❍ D. `ping`

   ❍ E. `netsh`

   Answer A is correct. Typing `ipconfig /all` shows you the current TCP/IP configuration and you can use this information for troubleshooting.

39. Amy is a network administrator. She has received numerous help desk requests about computers not being able to get an IP address. When she checks the DHCP server, she sees the DHCP Server service is not started. She attempts to start the service, but it will not start. She restarts the server, but the service still does not start. What should she do to resolve the problem?

   ❍ A. Reboot the server again.

   ❍ B. Configure the DHCP Server service to restart automatically using recovery options.

   ❍ C. Verify that dependent services are started and configured appropriately.

   ❍ D. Reinstall the DHCP Server service.

   Answer C is correct. She should verify that dependent services are started and configured appropriately. While Windows Server 2003 may restart dependent services when starting a service, attempted restarts can fail if the underlying dependent services are incorrectly configured or disabled.

40. Which of the following recovery options can you set for the Event Log service?

❍ A. Restart the service.

❍ B. Run a program.

❍ C. Restart the computer.

❍ D. None of the above.

Answer D is correct. With most services, you can configure one of four actions should a service fail: restart the service, restart the computer, run a program, or take no action. However, some critical services cannot be configured for recovery and are set so the server will restart if the service fails.

Exam 70-293

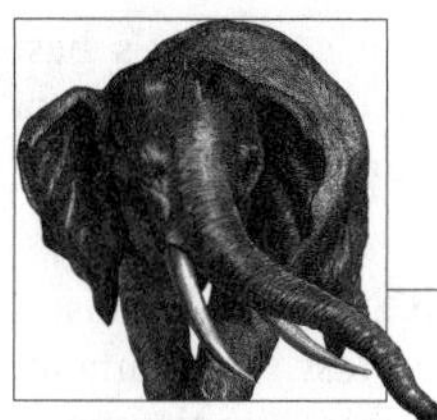

7
Exam 70-293 Overview

Exam 70-293: Planning and Maintaining a Microsoft Windows Server 2003 Network Infrastructure focuses on network infrastructure specific to Windows Server 2003 environments. At first blush, Exam 70-293 seems to measure the same or nearly the same set of skills as Exam 70-291. The difference between the two exams is one of scope and expected experience level. Many administrators have experience configuring and maintaining networking infrastructure. Fewer administrators have experience planning such infrastructure. Exam 70-293 also extends the skills measured into new and more advanced areas, including planning high availability, implementing Network Load Balancing (NLB) and clustering, and planning a Public Key Infrastructure that uses Microsoft Certificate Services.

Out of the four required MCSE exams, this one is, in my opinion, the most difficult. To pass the exam, you need the full gambit of networking infrastructure planning and implementation skills. You must be able to plan and implement everything from an organization's TCP/IP addressing scheme to its network topology to its Internet connectivity strategy. You must be able to plan and implement baseline operating system security, routing strategy, private networks, and remote access. That encompasses a lot of skills and a broad area of expertise.

Some of the most common problem areas for people taking the exam have to do with:

Server Security
: A computer's role-specific security configuration must be based on well-planned security policies and strategies. You need a strong understanding of general security policy, default security settings, and security application through templates.

Routing and Remote Access

The ability to plan and implement a routing strategy is a skill that's best learned through real-world practice. You need a strong understanding of routing protocols, remote access policies, and authentication methods.

Availability

Hands-on experience planning and implementing both NLB and Cluster Service is a must. If you don't have access to an extended test environment, you should work toward setting one up, and at the very least, implement a virtual server environment that uses these technologies.

In order to be prepared for Exam 70-293, you should have 12 to 18 months experience planning network infrastructure in support of 250 or more users. You should have recently studied a Windows Server 2003 administrator's book, taken a training course, or completed a self-paced training kit that covers the related areas of study. You will then be ready to use the Exam 70-293 Study Guide in this book as your final exam preparation.

Exam 70-293 is the third of four required networking system exams for MCSEs. If you are a current MCSE on Windows 2000, you need to pass Exam 70-292 and Exam 70-296 to upgrade your certification to Windows Server 2003. Skills measured by Exam 70-296, representing a subset of Exams 70-293 and 70-294, are indicated in this exam overview sections by the X symbol.

Areas of Study for Exam 70-293

Planning and Implementing Server Roles and Server Security

- Configure security for servers that are assigned specific roles. [X]
- Plan a secure baseline installation.
  - Plan a strategy to enforce system default security settings on new systems.
  - Identify client operating system default security settings.
  - Identify all server operating system default security settings.
- Plan security for servers that are assigned specific roles. [X]
  - Deploy the security configuration for servers that are assigned specific roles.[X]
  - Create custom security templates based on server roles. [X]
- Evaluate and select the operating system to install on computers in an enterprise.
  - Identify the minimum configuration to satisfy security requirements.

See “Planning and Implementing Server Roles and Server Security” on page 352.

Planning, Implementing, and Maintaining a Network Infrastructure

- Plan a TCP/IP network infrastructure strategy.
  - Analyze IP addressing requirements.
  - Plan an IP routing solution.
  - Create an IP subnet scheme.
- Plan and modify a network topology.
  - Plan the physical placement of network resources.
  - Identify network protocols to be used.
- Plan an Internet connectivity strategy.
- Plan network traffic monitoring.
- Troubleshoot connectivity to the Internet.
  - Diagnose and resolve issues related to Network Address Translation (NAT).
  - Diagnose and resolve issues related to name resolution cache information.
  - Diagnose and resolve issues related to client configuration.
- Troubleshoot TCP/IP addressing.
  - Diagnose and resolve issues related to client computer configuration.
  - Diagnose and resolve issues related to DHCP server address assignment.

- Plan a hostname resolution strategy. X
  - Plan a DNS namespace design. X
  - Plan zone replication requirements. X
  - Plan a forwarding configuration. X
  - Plan for DNS security. X
  - Examine the interoperability of DNS with third-party DNS solutions. X
- Plan a NetBIOS name resolution strategy.
  - Plan a WINS replication strategy.
  - Plan NetBIOS name resolution by using the *Lmhosts* file.
- Troubleshoot hostname resolution.
  - Diagnose and resolve issues related to DNS services.
  - Diagnose and resolve issues related to client computer configuration.

See "Planning, Implementing, and Maintaining a Network Infrastructure" on page 374.

Planning, Implementing, and Maintaining Routing and Remote Access

- Plan a routing strategy.
  - Identify routing protocols to use in a specified environment.
  - Plan routing for IP multicast traffic.
- Plan security for remote access users.
  - Plan remote access policies.
  - Analyze protocol security requirements.
  - Plan authentication methods for remote access clients.
- Implement secure access between private networks.
  - Create and implement an IPSec policy.
- Troubleshoot TCP/IP routing.

See "Planning, Implementing, and Maintaining Routing and Remote Access" on page 411.

Planning, Implementing, and Maintaining Server Availability

- Plan services for high availability.X
  - Plan a high-availability solution that uses clustering services. X
  - Plan a high-availability solution that uses Network Load Balancing. X
- Identify system bottlenecks, including memory, processor, disk, and network-related bottlenecks.
  - Identify system bottlenecks by using System Monitor.

- Implement a cluster server.
  - Recover from cluster node failure.
- Manage Network Load Balancing.
- Plan a backup and recovery strategy. [X]
  - Identify appropriate backup types. Methods include full, incremental, and differential. [X]
  - Plan a backup strategy that uses volume shadow copy. [X]
  - Plan system recovery that uses Automated System Recovery (ASR). [X]

See “Planning, Implementing, and Maintaining Server Availability” on page 425.

Planning and Maintaining Network Security

- Configure network protocol security.
  - Configure protocol security in a heterogeneous client computer environment.
  - Configure protocol security by using IPSec policies.
- Configure security for data transmission.
  - Configure IPSec policy settings.
- Plan for network protocol security.
  - Specify the required ports and protocols for specified services.
  - Plan an IPSec policy for secure network communications.
- Plan secure network administration methods. [X]
  - Create a plan to offer Remote Assistance to client computers. [X]
  - Plan for remote administration by using Terminal Services. [X]
- Plan security for wireless networks. [X]
- Plan security for data transmission. [X]
  - Secure data transmission between client computers to meet security requirements. [X]
  - Secure data transmission by using IPSec. [X]
- Troubleshoot security for data transmission.

See “Planning, Implementing, and Maintaining Network Security and Infrastructure” on page 435.

Planning, Implementing, and Maintaining Security Infrastructure

- Configure Active Directory directory service for certificate publication. [X]
- Plan a public key infrastructure (PKI) that uses Certificate Services. [X]
  - Identify the appropriate type of certificate authority to support certificate issuance requirements. [X]
  - Plan the enrollment and distribution of certificates. [X]
  - Plan for the use of smart cards for authentication. [X]

- Plan a framework for planning and implementing security. X
    - Plan for security monitoring. X
    - Plan a change and configuration management framework for security. X
- Plan a security update infrastructure. X

See "Planning, Implementing, and Maintaining Network Security and Infrastructure" on page 435.

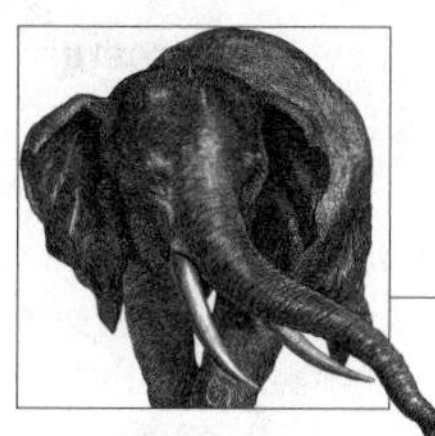

8 Exam 70-293 Study Guide

This chapter provides a study guide for *Exam 70-293: Planning and Maintaining a Microsoft Windows Server 2003 Network Infrastructure*. Sections within the chapter are organized according to the exam objective they cover. Each section identifies the related exam objective, provides an overview of why the objective is important, and then discusses the key details you should know about the objective to both succeed on the test and master the objective in the real world.

The major topics covered on Exam 70-293 are:

Planning and Implementing Server Roles and Server Security
: Designed to test your knowledge of security configuration planning for servers that are assigned specific roles. Objectives cover baseline security as well.

Planning, Implementing, and Maintaining a Network Infrastructure
: Designed to test your knowledge of network infrastructure planning for TCP/IP addressing, Internet connectivity, network traffic monitoring, and name resolution. Objectives cover both WINS and DNS naming strategies.

Planning, Implementing, and Maintaining Routing and Remote Access
: Designed to test your knowledge of remote access security planning as well as planning for IP routing. Objectives also cover implementing IPSec policy and troubleshooting TCP/IP routing.

Planning, Implementing, and Maintaining Server Availability
: Designed to test your knowledge of high-availability planning for clustering services and Network Load Balancing. Objectives also cover identifying system bottlenecks and backup and recovery planning.

Planning and Maintaining Network Security
: Designed to test your knowledge of a broad array of network security planning skills that extends to secure remote administration and network protocol security. Objectives also cover security for wireless networking.

Planning, Implementing, and Maintaining Security Infrastructure
: Designed to test your knowledge of planning for public key infrastructure (PKI) that uses Certificate Services. Objectives also cover planning security for update infrastructure.

The sections of this chapter are designed to reinforce your knowledge of these topics. Ideally, you will review this chapter as thoroughly as you would your course notes in preparation for a college professor's final exam. That means multiple readings of the chapter, committing to memory key concepts, and performing any necessary outside readings if there are topics with which you have difficulty.

As part of your preparation, I recommend using two test networks or reconfiguring a single test network as necessary to get hands-on practice for the exam. The first network/configuration can be set up as discussed for the previous exam with three machines:

- A domain controller running Windows Server 2003 configured with DNS, DHCP, and TCP/IP routing.
- A workstation configured as a domain member, running Windows XP Professional or later to be used as your primary system for management.
- A workstation configured as a member of a workgroup, running Windows XP Professional or later to be used for remote access testing.

These systems can be virtual machines installed as part of a virtual test environment and should be fresh installs to ensure that you are starting with a new environment. The second network/configuration is for planning and implementing high availability. You'll need two to three servers running Windows Server 2003, configured as part of a domain environment.

Planning and Implementing Server Roles and Server Security

The Windows operating system has workstation and server versions. Generally, computers running Windows XP Professional or other workstation operating systems are configured as clients, and computers running Windows Server 2003 are configured as servers. While computers acting as clients have general-purpose roles in the enterprise as user machines, most servers have general-purpose roles and specific roles for which they are configured, allowing the servers to act as domain controllers, name servers, file servers, print servers, etc. From the general to the specific, each role brings with it different security considerations. A computer's baseline security configuration prepares it for a general role in the enterprise. A computer's role-specific security configuration prepares it to act in a specific role.

Evaluating and Selecting the Operating System to Install on Computers in an Enterprise

Selecting the operating system to install on computers is a key decision that administrators must make. Computers should be configured with the operating system that is appropriate for the role they will fill as clients or servers. Every organization should have specific guidelines for choosing which operating system to use when; those guidelines should include specifics on hardware requirements, duty life, and upgrade frequency. Prior to purchasing or requisitioning computers, administrators should have a list of hardware requirements for each role the computers will fill and should configure the computers accordingly.

Choosing client operating systems

Before choosing an operating system for a client computer, administrators should ask themselves what is the minimum configuration to satisfy security requirements. In most cases, the answer to this question will have to do with:

- The ability of the computer to act as an Active Directory client
- The ability of the computer to have a computer account and join the domain

Why are these issues important? When a client computer can act as an Active Directory client, the computer can join a domain and take advantage of directory services. When a client computer has a computer account, administrators have better control over security and can manage the account as they manage any other type of account. For these reasons, every client configured on a Windows network should be able to act as an Active Directory client and have a computer account.

Both workstation and home user versions of the Windows operating system are available. In most cases, clients that connect directly to the network or connect through remote access should be configured with a workstation version of the Windows operating system. This ensures that the client computer can access the network as an Active Directory client and that it has a computer account, and can take advantage of all the features that are offered, including security enhancements (available only on workstation versions of Windows). Workstation versions of Windows include Windows NT Workstation, Windows 2000 Professional, and Windows XP Professional. Although Windows NT Workstation computers can be part of a domain, only Windows 2000 Professional and Windows XP Professional have all the latest capabilities. Windows Vista is the latest workstation version of the Windows operating system.

Home user versions of Windows include Windows 95, Windows 98, and Windows Me. While Windows 95, Windows 98, and Windows Me computers can be configured as Active Directory clients, they are not best suited to the task. Clients running these operating systems do not become members of the domain in the same way as computers running workstation versions of the Windows operating system, which makes it more difficult to manage security for these computers. Clients running these operating systems also cannot take advantage of many of the current security enhancements.

Windows XP Home Edition is another home user version of Windows. Unlike Windows 95, Windows 98, and Windows Me, however, Windows XP Home Edition does not have an Active Directory client and cannot join a domain. Because of this, computers that will be used in the enterprise should not use Windows XP Home Edition.

Table 8-1 provides a summary of operating system support for Active Directory.

Table 8-1. Summary of operating system support for Active Directory

Operating system	Active Directory support
Windows NT Workstation	Can join the network using a computer account as part of a Windows NT 4 domain; supports NTLM
Windows 2000 Professional, Windows XP Professional, and Windows Vista	Has an Active Directory client and can join the network using a computer account; supports Kerberos for improved security and other features
Windows 95, Windows 98, and Windows Me	Has an Active Directory client
Windows XP Home Edition	Does not have an Active Directory client

Choosing server operating systems

Windows Server 2003 is available in multiple editions, including Windows Server 2003, Web Edition; Windows Server 2003, Standard Edition; Windows Server 2003, Enterprise Edition; and Windows Server 2003, Datacenter Edition. Each edition is designed for a specific purpose.

Windows Server 2003, Web Edition is designed specifically to provide web services for enterprise Intranets and Internet web sites. While this edition includes the Microsoft .NET Framework, Microsoft Internet Information Services (IIS), ASP.NET, and network load-balancing features, it lacks many other features, including Active Directory.

Lack of Active Directory means a server running Windows Server 2003, Web Edition cannot be configured as a domain controller. It does not mean that the server cannot be a member of a domain. Servers running Windows Server 2003, Web Edition can be members of a domain.

Windows Server 2003, Standard Edition is designed specifically for small or branch office use, and is a direct replacement for Windows NT 4.0 Server and Windows 2000 Server. Servers running this edition should be used to provide the day-to-day needs of the average business, and to provide services and resources to other systems in the enterprise.

Windows Server 2003, Enterprise Edition is designed specifically for larger organizations and where functional needs surpass those of Windows Server 2003, Standard Edition. It is a direct replacement for Windows NT Server 4 Enterprise Edition and Windows 2000 Advanced Server. Servers running this edition can be used in large-scale deployments and in clustering configurations.

Windows Server 2003, Datacenter Edition is designed specifically for large-scale data centers where high availability and high scalability are requirements, and for use with business-critical and mission-critical applications that require high availability and high scalability. It is a direct replacement for Windows 2000 Datacenter Server.

Table 8-2 provides an overview and comparison of each edition of Windows Server 2003. With the exception of Web Edition, all other editions of Windows Server 2003 support both 32-bit and 64-bit computing. 32-bit versions of

Windows Server 2003 are designed for x86-based processors. 64-bit versions of Windows Server 2003 are designed for Intel Itanium (IA-64) and 64-bit extended systems.

Table 8-2. Comparison of Windows Server 2003 editions

	Windows Server 2003, Web Edition	Windows Server 2003, Standard Edition	Windows Server 2003, Enterprise Edition	Windows Server 2003, Datacenter Edition
Minimum processor speed	133 MHz	133 MHz for x86; 733 MHz for 64-bit	133 MHz for x86; 733 MHz for 64-bit	400 MHz for x86; 733 MHz for 64-bit
Minimum recommended processor speed	550 MHz	550 MHz	733 MHz	733 MHz
Multiprocessor support	Up to 2	Up to 4	Up to 8	8 to 64
Minimum RAM	128 MB	128 MB	128 MB	512 MB
Minimum recommended RAM	256 MB	256 MB	256 MB	1 GB
Maximum RAM	2 GB	4 GB	32 GB for x86; 1 TB for 64-bit	64 GB for x86; 1 TB for 64-bit
Active Directory support	Domain member only	DC or member	DC or member	DC or member

When you look beyond supported components, maximum RAM, and maximum processors, you'll find each edition of Windows Server 2003 supports the same core features and administration tools, allowing you to manage servers running the various editions using the same tools and techniques. The way in which a server is used in the enterprise largely depends on the roles for which the server is configured.

Planning and Implementing Server Roles

Servers are generally assigned to be part of a workgroup or a domain. A workgroups is a loose grouping of computers in which each individual computer is managed separately. A domain is a tight grouping of computers in which each computer can be managed collectively using Active Directory and Group Policy.

When you install a server running Windows Server 2003, you can configure the server to be:

- A member server
- A domain controller
- A standalone server

The differences between these configurations are subtle but important. Member servers are a part of a domain but don't store directory information. Domain controllers store directory information, provide authentication, and offer directory services for a domain. Standalone servers aren't part of a domain and are instead members of a workgroup. Standalone servers have their own security database for authenticating logon requests.

Like Windows 2000, Windows Server 2003 uses a multimaster replication model where any domain controller can process directory changes, and then replicate those changes to other domain controllers. This differs from the Windows NT single master replication model in which the primary domain controller stores a master copy and backup controllers store backup copies of the master. Additionally, while Windows NT distributed only the Security Account Manager (SAM) database, Windows Server 2003 distributes its entire data store of directory information.

Domains that use Active Directory are referred to as *Active Directory domains*. Although you could deploy an Active Directory domain with only one domain controller, you more typically deploy multiple domain controllers to ensure availability of directory services, should one or more of the domain controllers fail. In an Active Directory domain, any member server can be promoted to a domain controller by installing the Active Directory component on the server. Similarly, you can demote domain controllers and make them member servers, by removing the Active Directory component on the server.

You promote and demote domain controllers using the Active Directory Installation Wizard (dcpromo). To start this wizard, click Start → Run. Type `dcpromo` in the Open field, and then click OK.

DNS must be available on the network before you can install a domain controller in a new domain.

In addition to having a role as a domain controller, servers can have other roles as well. These additional roles are based on the services for which the servers are configured. Any server can support one or more of roles described in Table 8-3.

Table 8-3. Server roles for Windows Server 2003

Role	Description
Application server	A server that provides web services or hosts web applications.
DHCP server	A server that runs the DHCP Server service and can dynamically assign IP addressing to clients on the network.
Domain controller	A server that provides directory services for a domain and has a directory store. Domain controllers also manage the logon process and directory searches.
DNS server	A server that runs DNS Server service and can resolve computer names to IP addresses and vice versa.
File server	A server that hosts shared folders and manages access to files.
Mail server (POP3, SMTP)	A server that provides basic Post Office Protocol 3 (POP3) and Simple Mail Transfer Protocol (SMTP) mail services so that POP3 mail clients can send and receive mail in the domain.
Print server	A server that hosts shared printers and manages access to network printers, print queues, and printer drivers.
Remote access/VPN server	A server that routes network traffic and manages dial-up networking or virtual private networking (VPN).
Server cluster node	A server that operates as part of a group of servers working together, which is called a *cluster*. (This server role is supported by the Enterprise and Datacenter versions only.)

Table 8-3. Server roles for Windows Server 2003 (continued)

Role	Description
Streaming media server	A server that hosts streaming media content and provides it to other systems on the network or the Internet. (This server role is supported by the Standard and Enterprise versions only.)
Terminal Server	A server that hosts applications and processes tasks for multiple client computers running in terminal services mode.
WINS server	A server that runs WINS Server service and can resolve NetBIOS (Network Basic Input/Output System) names to IP addresses and vice versa.

After installing a server, you can add or remove server roles using the Manage Your Server console, the Configure Your Server wizard, or the Add/Remove Programs utility. You access Manage Your Server from the Administrative Tools menu. Click Start → Programs → Manage Your Server. When you start Manage Your Server, the currently configured roles are listed, and for each configured role, you'll find quick access links for performing related tasks. For example, if the server is configured as a file server, you'll have links for managing the file server and adding shared folders.

To add or remove a role using Manage Your Server, follow these steps:

1. Click the Add Or Remove A Role link. This starts the Configure Your Server Wizard. You can also start the Configure Your Server Wizard from the Administrative Tools menu.
2. Click Next twice. After Windows Server 2003 gathers information about the server's current roles, the Server Role page is displayed with a list of available server roles and details on whether a role is configured.
3. If a role isn't configured and you want to add the role, click the role in the Server Role column, and then click Next. Follow the prompts.
4. If a role is configured and you want to remove the role, click the role in the Server Role column, and then click Next. Follow the prompts.

Planning a Secure Baseline Installation

Security should be a primary consideration when you set up a network, add computers to a network, and configure computers. You should select clients and servers based on specific manageability, supportability, and security requirements. Prior to deploying clients and servers, you should develop a comprehensive deployment plan that includes detailed instructions for establishing a secure baseline installation for each anticipated client and server configuration. The baseline installation should provide a secure starting point for the final configuration. For clients and servers with strict/high security requirements, you may need to build on the baseline installation by modifying settings, installing additional security components, or making other such changes to strengthen security as appropriate.

Planning a strategy to enforce system default security settings on new systems

Creating a security plan for clients and servers is not something individual administrators should do alone. More typically, a security plan for clients and servers is part of larger enterprise effort and one that is designed to ensure that security settings meet or exceed a specific set of minimum security requirements. As an administrator, you need a careful understanding of the security capabilities of the Windows operating system, and you must be familiar with the default security settings so that you know what settings can and should be changed to enhance security for computers configured in specific roles as clients or servers.

When creating a security strategy for clients and servers, you'll need to determine which specific security features to use; often, you'll do this in accordance with the objectives and requirements of the organization's enterprise-wide security policy. Many organizations also have specifically assigned security teams that are responsible for security policy throughout the enterprise.

Typically, enterprise-wide security policies:

- Identify potential security risks
- Specify minimum security requirements
- Specify the minimum set of required security features
- Provide plans for meeting required security levels

If your organization doesn't have enterprise-wide security policies or specific security requirements for networked computers, you should work toward establishing such, and the effort should be managed by a designated security team. This team should include users, administrators, and manages—all of which should have a strong understanding of security, the organization's structure and resources, and how security can be implemented to meet the organization's needs.

The security policy developed by the security team should view security as an ongoing effort, and one that, like software deployment, has an ongoing life cycle. The security policy should include:

- A plan for securing the organization's infrastructure
- A plan for implementing required security features
- A plan for ongoing management and evaluation of security
- A plan for monitoring security breaches

Most security plans should cover access controls, authentication, and auditing. Access controls are used to manage access to resources and determine who has access to what. Authentication mechanisms are used to verify a user's identity prior to providing access to resources. Auditing is used to monitor access and use of privileges.

Techniques for preventing unauthorized access to the network and resources also should be covered in the security plan. Network security can be enhanced using firewalls, proxies, and Network Address Translation (NAT). Resource access can be more tightly controlled using encrypted passwords, certificates, and hardware devices such as smart card scanner. Data can be protected using NTFS security and the Encrypting File System (EFS).

After developing a plan to secure the organization's infrastructure, the security team needs to develop a plan to implement the security recommendations and requirements. As appropriate for an individual's need to know to ensure enforcement and implementation, parts of the implementation plan should be distributed throughout the organization. It is the responsibility of the security team to ensure that the implementation plan is followed and that the messaging related to security policy are expressed in ways that get maximum organizational involvement. Not everyone will adhere to the security plan. Not everyone will understand the need to implement security in a certain way. Because of this, you'll need an ongoing monitoring and management effort to ensure that security is implemented as expected. Part of the management effort should include ongoing instruction for all personnel as to the importance of and the need for security.

Identifying client and server operating system default security settings

As an administrator, you should have a strong understanding of the default security settings for Windows Server 2003 and Windows XP Professional. A strong understanding of the default security settings helps you determine what settings may need changes to enhance security when a computer is deployed in a specific role.

Windows Server 2003 and Windows XP Professional are the primary operating systems for use on networks as servers and clients. Both operating systems are designed with security in mind. Whether these computers are part of a workgroup or domain, security is largely dependent on:

- Filesystem permissions
- Share permissions
- Registry permissions
- Active Directory permissions
- Account policies
- Local policies
- Audit policies

Identifying default security for filesystem permissions. Filesystem permissions are available and applicable only when you format a computer's drives using NTFS. Under NTFS, many different levels of permissions can be set to control access to files and folders. As discussed in Chapter 2 under "Configuring Filesystem Permissions," both basic and advanced permissions can be used with NTFS, all files and folders have specific owners that can be changes, and certain permissions are inherited from parent folders. You can modify permissions, ownership, and inheritance using a file or folder's Properties dialog box, which is accessible by right-clicking the file or folder, selecting Properties, and then clicking the Security tab (see Figure 8-1).

When you install a computer running Windows Server 2003 or Windows XP Professional in an Active Directory domain and format the system drive using NTFS, the Setup program configures the computer's system drive with a specific default set of permissions. Table 8-4 summarizes the default permissions for the system drive (domains only). If the computer has other drives, Setup doesn't grant any special permissions on these additional drives. Instead, Setup grants Full Control on the entire drive to the Everyone group; it is up to the administrator to configure appropriate permissions.

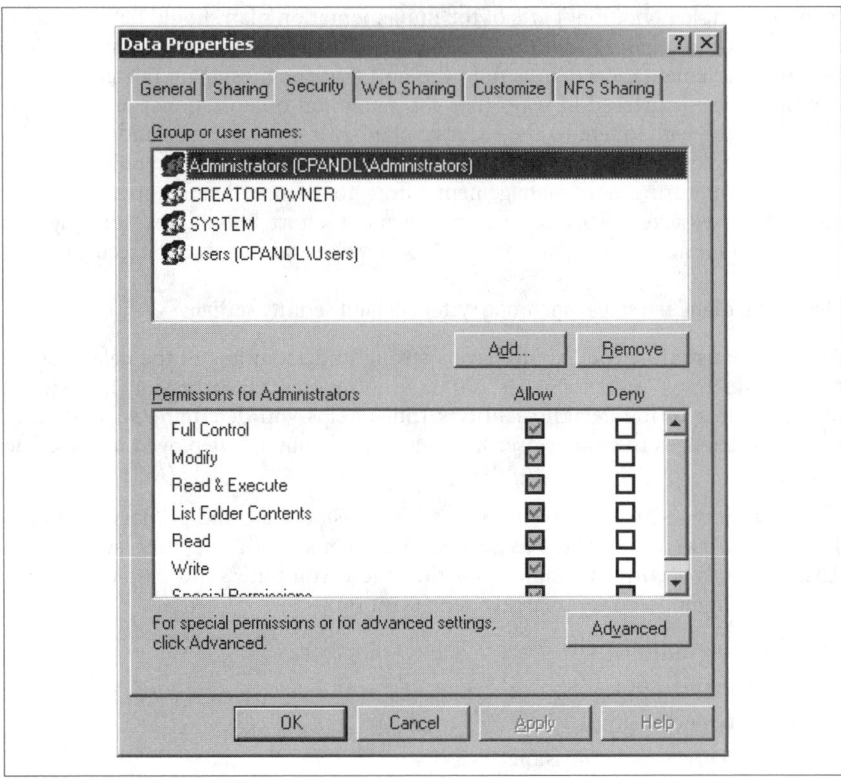

Figure 8-1. Manage permissions on the Security tab.

Table 8-4. Default permissions for the system drive

Group/User	%SystemDrive% Folder and non-Windows specific subfolders	Documents and Settings folder	Program files folder	%Windir% folder
Administrators	Full Control	Full Control	Full Control	Full Control
Users	Read & Execute, List Folder Contents, Read, Create Folders/Append Data, Create Files/ Write Data (subfolders only)	Read & Execute, List Folder Contents, Read	N/A	N/A
Everyone	Read & Execute (root only, not subfolders)	Read & Execute, List Folder Contents, Read	N/A	N/A
Authenticated Users	N/A	N/A	Read & Execute, List Folder Contents, Read, Modify	Read & Execute, List Folder Contents, Read, Modify
Server Operators	N/A	N/A	Read & Execute, List Folder Contents, Read, Write	Read & Execute, List Folder Contents, Read, Write

Table 8-4. Default permissions for the system drive (continued)

Group/User	%SystemDrive% Folder and non-Windows specific subfolders	Documents and Settings folder	Program files folder	%Windir% folder
Creator Owner	Full Control (subfolders and files only)	N/A	Full Control (subfolders and files only)	Full Control (subfolders and files only)
System	Full Control	Full Control	Full Control	Full Control

If a user's profile is stored on the computer, the user has Full Control over the *Documents and Settings/%UserName%* folder. This is the location of the user's profile and home folder. As Everyone and Authenticated Users are implicit groups, administrators cannot add or remove members from these groups.

Identifying default security for share permissions. As discussed in Chapter 2 under "Configuring Access to Shared Folders," shares are used to share folders over the network, and several administrative shares are created automatically each time the operating system is started. While the administrative shares that are available depend on the system configuration, the key ones that administrators work with are the *hidden drive shares*. These special shares for the root of each available drive letter on the computer are named with the drive letter followed by a dollar sign ($). Drive shares are available to members of the Administrators group, and the permissions for these shares cannot be modified.

When you create a new folder share on a computer running Windows Server 2003, you can configure specific permissions by choosing one of the available configuration options:

All Users Have Read-Only Access
: Grants the Everyone group Read access (the default).

Administrators Have Full Access; Other Users Have Read-Only Access
: Grants Administrators Full Control and the Everyone group Read access.

Administrators Have Full Access; Other Users Have Read And Write Access
: Grants Administrators Full Control and the Everyone group Change access.

Use Custom Share And Folder Permissions
: Allows you to configure access by accessing Full Control, Change, and Read access to specific users and groups (recommended).

Once you share a folder, it is available to users automatically and can be accessed using a network drive. You can manage the permissions on the shared folder by right-clicking the share, selecting Properties, and then using the options of the Share Permissions tab.

While under Windows Server 2003, the Everyone group has Read permissions on a share by default, and Windows 2000 (all service packs) and Windows XP computers (prior to Service Pack 2) grant the Everyone group Full Control by default. Because of this, you must modify the share permissions to properly control access.

When you share folders on NTFS volumes, share permissions provide the top-level access control and NTFS permissions provide the base-level access controls. In other words, share permissions determine the maximum allowed access level. If a user has Read permission on a share, the most the user can do is perform read operations. If a user has Change permission on a share, the most the user can do is perform Read and Change operations. If a user has Full Control permission, the user has full access to the share. However, in any case, filesystem permissions can further restrict or block access.

Identifying default security for Registry permissions. The Registry contains configuration details for system components, services, and applications. The Registry is organized into a formal grouping of keys, subkeys, and value entries. Root keys form the primary branches of the Registry. The two primary root keys are HKEY_LOCAL_MACHINE (HKLM) and HKEY_USERS (HKU). Other root keys in the Registry are logical subtrees of the two primary root keys.

When you install applications and configure Windows settings, changes are made to the Registry. Access to the Registry is controlled by a separate set of security permissions. The default security permissions for the Registry are as follows:

- Members of the Administrators group have Full Control permissions for all keys.
- The System user has Full Control permissions for all keys.
- The Everyone group has Read permission for the HKEY_LOCAL_MACHINE (HKLM) and HKEY_USERS (HKU) keys.
- The Authenticated Users group have Read permissions for HKEY_CLASSES_ROOT.
- The Server Operators group has permissions that enable members to read, create, and modify keys in HKEY_CLASSES_ROOT.
- The Users group has Read permissions for HKEY_CURRENT_CONFIG.

You can view and manage the Registry using the Registry Editor (*regedit.exe*). To start the Registry Editor, type `regedit` at a command prompt.

Identifying default security for Active Directory permissions. In Active Directory, objects are used to represent users, groups, computers, printers, and other resources. Use Active Directory permissions to specify who can access and manage the objects in the Active Directory database. As an administrator, one of your primary duties is to create and manage directory objects. Permissions for creating and managing objects can be delegated to nonadministrators as well.

Create new domains in Active Directory by running the Active Directory Installation Wizard (dcpromo) and assigning the first domain controller in the new domain. During the configuration of the domain and the domain controller, the operating system establishes default security for several key groups. The default security permissions for Active Directory are as follows:

- Members of the Enterprise Admins group have Full Control permission over the domain.
- Members of the Domain Admins and Administrators groups are assigned permissions that allow them to create and manage most Active Directory objects in the domain.
- Members of the Account Operators group are granted Full Control permission over Domain Users, Domain Computers, Domain Guests, and similar account-related groups.
- Members of the Server Operators group are granted Full Control over Domain C.
- Members of the Authenticated Users group are assigned Read permissions throughout the domain, and in some, members are assigned limited special permissions in specific instances.

Windows Server 2003 includes many other built-in groups as well, which all have a specific default set of permissions. Security groups are the primary way to manage Active Directory permissions. Typically, when individuals need to perform specific management tasks in the domain, you'll handle this by making the user a member of the appropriate security group. If no security group is available to meet a specific need, you can create additional security groups and configure permissions as appropriate for those groups. In a few special situations, you might want to delegate permissions to individuals that should be allowed to perform specific tasks in a domain or organizational unit.

Delegation is useful if you want to give someone limited administrative privileges. Delegate control to grant a user permission to manage users, groups, computers, organizational units, or other objects stored in Active Directory. To delegate administration, you can use the following technique:

1. Open Active Directory Users And Computers.
2. Right-click the domain or organizational unit for which you want to delegate administration, and then select Delegate Control.
3. When the Delegation Of Control Wizard starts, click Next.
4. On the Users Or Groups page, shown in Figure 8-2, click Add. Select the users and groups for which you want to delegate control. Click OK.
5. Click Next to continue.
6. On the Tasks To Delegate page, specify the administration tasks to delegate (see Figure 8-3) to the previously selected users or groups.
7. Click Next, and then click Finish.

On rare occasions, you may need to review or manage the specific set of Active Directory permissions assigned to an object. You can do this by using the Advanced Features view in Active Directory Users And Computers. The Advanced Features view gives you access to additional advanced properties for objects, including those for published certificates and Active Directory permissions.

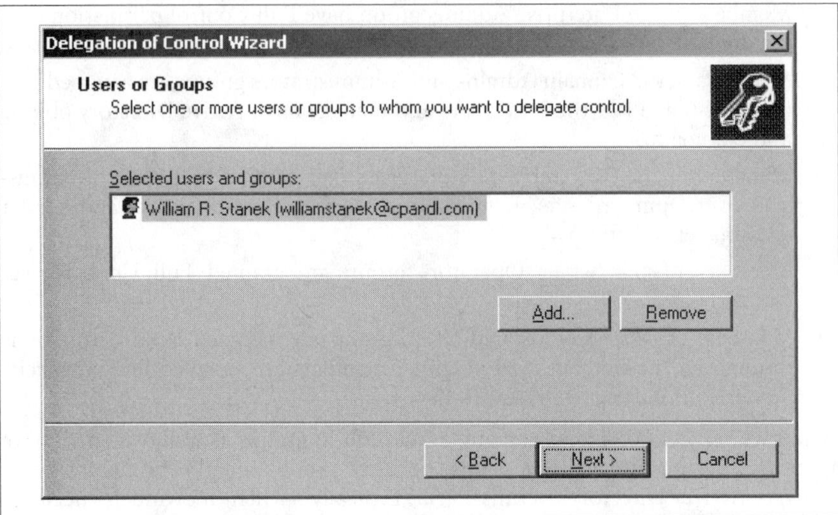

Figure 8-2. Specify the users and groups for which you want to delegate control.

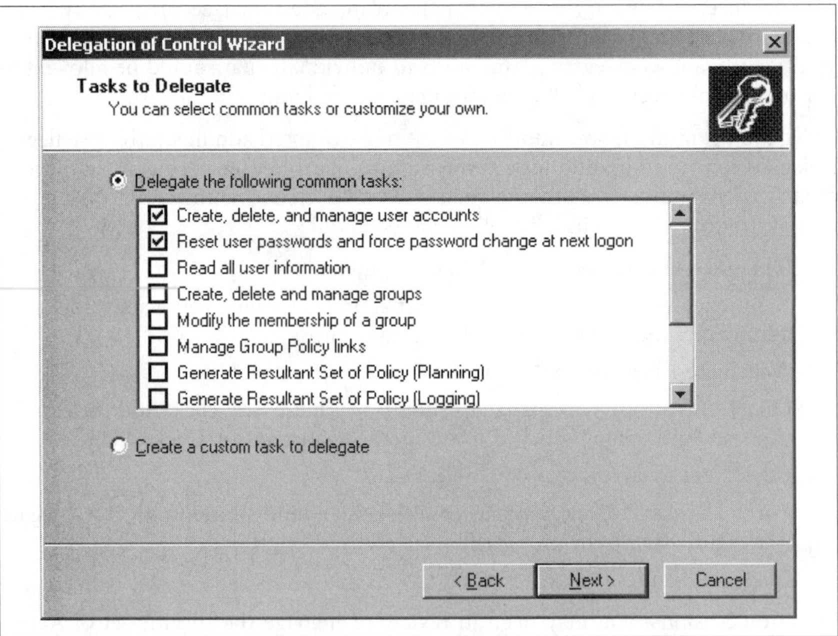

Figure 8-3. Specify the administration tasks to delegate.

To view or manage Active Directory permissions for an object, you can use the following technique:

1. Open Active Directory Users And Computers.
2. Select Advanced Features on the View menu in Active Directory Users And Computers.

3. Right-click the object, and then select Properties.
4. Use the Security tab options, shown in Figure 8-4, to view or manage Active Directory permissions for the selected object.

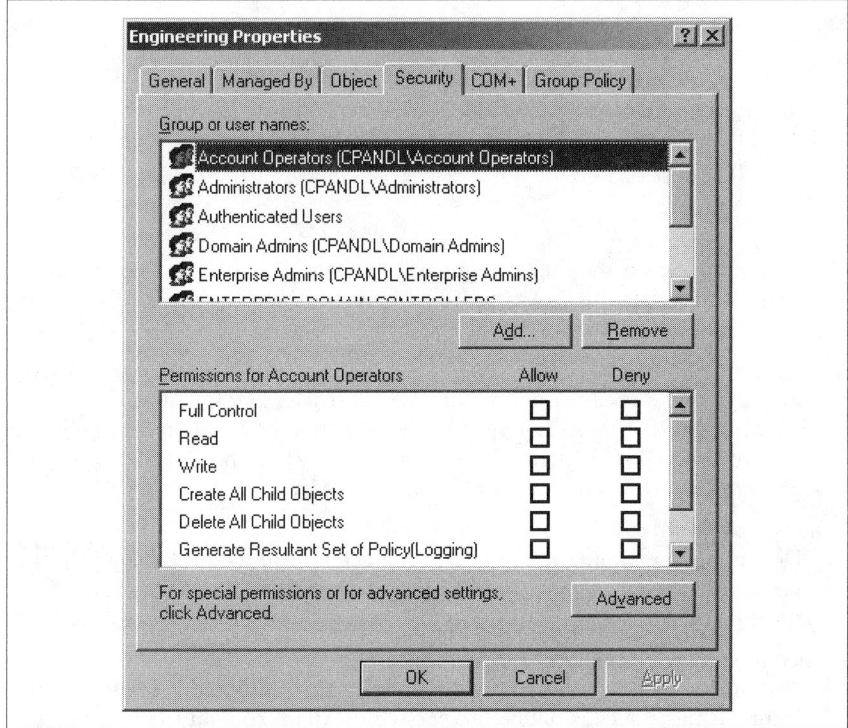

Figure 8-4. Accessing the Security tab of an Active Directory object.

Identifying default security for account policies. In Active Directory domains, Group Policy is used to manage security settings for users and computers, each of which is managed with a separate set of policies:

- User settings are managed through User Configuration policies and are applied to a user account during logon. User settings affect individual user accounts, according to groups of which a user is a member.
- Computer settings are managed through Computer Configuration policies and are applied to a computer at startup. Computer settings affect all users who log on to or access a computer.

The most important default security settings to be aware of are those for password policy, account lockout policy, and Kerberos policy that should be managed using the highest precedence Group Policy Object (GPO) linked to a domain. By default, the highest precedent GPO linked to a domain is the Default Domain Policy GPO.

While previous versions of Windows did not define specific password and account lockout policies, Windows Server 2003 does assign specific default settings to these policies.

Password policies control how passwords are managed, whether they expire, and when they expire. In Group Policy, the following password policies are stored under *Computer Configuration\Windows Settings\Security Settings\Account Policies\Password Policy*:

Enforce password history
: Determines how many previously used passwords will be maintained in the user's password history. As a user cannot use a password that is in the history, a user cannot reuse a recently used password. The maximum value is 24. If this value is set to zero, no password history is maintained and users are able to reuse old passwords, which can be a security concern. The default value is 24 passwords remembered.

Maximum password age
: Determines when the user is required to change a password. The maximum value is 999 days. If this value is set to zero, the password never expires, which can be a security concern. The default value is 42 days.

Minimum password age
: Requires that a specific number of days must pass before a user can change their password. This setting must be configured to be less than the Maximum password age policy. If this value is set to zero, the user can change their password immediately. The default value is 1 day.

Minimum password length
: Determines the minimum number of characters required for the length of the password. Longer passwords are more secure than shorter ones. The default value is seven characters.

Passwords must meet complexity requirements
: Determines whether the password must meet specific complexity requirements. If this policy is defined, a password cannot contain the user account name, must contain at least six characters, and must have characters that have upper- and lowercase letters, Arabic numerals, and nonalphanumeric characters (symbols). By default, this policy is enabled.

Store passwords using reversible encryption
: Determines whether passwords use plain-text encryption of passwords. Basically the same as storing passwords as plain text and is only to be used when applications use protocols that require information about the user's password. By default, this policy is disabled.

Account lockout policies control whether and how accounts are locked out if successive invalid passwords are provided. In Group Policy, the following password policies are stored under *Computer Configuration\Windows Settings\Security Settings\Account Policies\Account Lockout Policy*:

Account lockout duration
: Determines the period of time that must elapse before Active Directory will unlock an account that has been locked out due to Account Lockout policy. This setting is dependent on the account lockout threshold setting. The value range is from 0 through 99,999 minutes. If this value is set to zero, the account will be locked out indefinitely. By default, this policy is not defined.

Account lockout threshold
Determines how many failed logon attempts trigger an automatic lockout. The valid range is from 0 to 999. The default value is zero, which means the account will never be locked out due to Account Lockout policy, and the user will be allowed unlimited failed logon attempts.

Reset account lockout counter after
Determines the number of minutes after a failed logon attempt before the lockout counter is reset to zero. The valid range is from 1 to 99,999 minutes. This must be less than or equal to the Account lockout duration setting if the Account lockout threshold policy is enabled. By default, this policy is not defined.

Kerberos policies control the way Kerberos authentication is used in a domain. In Group Policy, the following Kerberos policies are stored under *Computer Configuration\Windows Settings\Security Settings\Account Policies\Kerberos Policy*:

Enforce User Logon Restrictions
Ensures that user account restrictions, such as logon hours and logon workstations, are enforced. By default, the policy is enabled.

Maximum Lifetime For Service Ticket
Sets the maximum duration for which a service is valid. By default, service tickets have a maximum duration of 600 minutes.

Maximum Lifetime For User Ticket
Sets the maximum duration for which a user ticket is valid. By default, user tickets have a maximum duration of 10 hours.

Maximum Lifetime For User Ticket Renewal
Sets the maximum amount of time for renewal of a user ticket. By default, the maximum renewal period is seven days.

Maximum Tolerance For Computer Clock Synchronization
Sets the maximum amount of tolerance for discrepancies in computer clock time. By default, computers in the domain must be synchronized within five minutes of each other. If they aren't, authentication fails.

You can access the Default Domain Policy GPO using the Group Policy editing tools. If you are using the Group Policy Management Console, the Default Domain Policy GPO is accessible when you click the domain name in the console tree. You then need to right-click the Default Domain Policy node and select Edit. If you want only to work with security settings in the Default Domain Policy GPO, you can use the Domain Security Policy console, which is found on the Administrative Tools menu.

Policy settings can be enabled, disabled, or not configured. Enabled policy settings are active and applied. Disabled policy settings are inactive and not applied or enforced. Not configured policy settings are not being used. Each GPO has a specific inheritance precedence. Everyone who logs on to the local machine is affected by Local Group Policy. Active Directory–based policy settings are applied in this basic order: site, domain, organizational unit (OU). By default, when policy is set at one level, the setting applies to all objects at that level and to all objects in the levels below due to inheritance.

Identifying default security for local policies. When working with Group Policy, you'll also want to carefully manage local policies. In Group Policy, the following Local policies are stored under *Computer Configuration\Windows Settings\Security Settings\Local Policies*:

Audit Policy
: Used to manage audit policy for an Active Directory domain

User Rights Assignment
: Used to manage user rights assignment for an Active Directory domain

Security Options
: Used to manage additional security options for accounts, auditing, devices, interactive logon, network access, and more

In the default configuration, all related policies are Not Defined. This means you must configure Audit Policy to enable auditing. You may also need to configure user rights assignments as well as security options.

The best way to manage local policies for a domain is to use the policies that apply to your organization's domain controllers, member servers, and workstations. For example, all domain controllers are placed in the Domain Controllers OU by default. This means any security setting applied to this OU will apply to all domain controllers automatically.

You can access the Default Domain Controllers Policy GPO using the Group Policy editing tools. If you are using the Group Policy Management Console, you'll see the Default Domain Controllers Policy GPO when you click the Domain Controllers node in the console tree. You then need to right-click the Default Domain Controllers Policy and select Edit. If you want only to work with security settings in the Default Domain Policy GPO, you can use the Domain Security Policy console, which is found on the Administrative Tools menu.

Planning Security for Servers That Are Assigned Specific Roles

Hardening servers to ensure that they are secure involves deploying specific security configuration baselines using Group Policy and creating custom security templates to enhance security as necessary to support various server roles. Creating a secure baseline provides a starting point for ensuring the security of computers on the network. Creating role-specific security templates ensures enforcement of security policy based on a computer's role on the network.

Windows Server 2003 Service Pack 1 includes the Security Configuration Wizard, which you can use to create a security policy that can be applied to any server on the network. The wizard can be used to create a new security policy, to edit or apply an existing security policy, or to rollback the last applied security policy. The wizard does not install components or set up a server to perform specific roles.

Deploying the security configuration for servers that are assigned specific roles

In an Active Directory domain, a computer's baseline security can be configured using Group Policy. During startup, a computer processes computer policy settings according to the GPOs that apply to the computer. A history of the registry-based settings that are applied to the computer are stored in *%AllUsersProfile%\Ntuser.pol*. Because of the object-based hierarchy used by Active Directory, multiple GPOs can apply. When Group Policy is set for a computer, everyone who logs on to the computer is affected by the policy settings.

When multiple policies are in place, the policies are applied in the following order:

1. Local computer group policy
2. Site group policy
3. Domain group policy
4. OU group policy

You can use the acronym *LSDO* to remember the order in which policies are applied. LSDO stands for Local, Site, Domain, and Organizational Unit.

If there are conflicts among the policy settings, the settings applied later have precedence by default, meaning they overwrite previously applied settings. The cumulative affects of policy settings in multiple GPOs are determined by inheritance- and policy-processing rules. When you apply a policy setting in a top-level GPO, the lower-level GPOs inherit the setting, unless inheritance is blocked or overridden. Because of this, a setting in a top-level GPO can affect every user and computer throughout the enterprise. The end result of inheritance and policy processing is referred to as the Resultant Set of Policy (RSoP). By determining the RSoP for a user or computer, you can determine the specific policy settings that are being applied to that user or computer.

To determine what policies apply to a computer, you must first determine where the related computer object is stored in Active Directory. By default, workstations and member servers are placed in the Computers container within Active Directory, and domain controllers are placed in the Domain Controllers OU. In this default configuration, workstations and member servers are only affected by site and domain GPOs, while domain controllers are affected by site and domain GPOs as well as any GPOs applied to the Domain Controllers OU. The highest precedence GPO applied to the Domain Controllers OU by default is the Default Domain Controllers Policy GPO.

The best way to apply a specific secure baseline to workstations and member servers is to create new organizational units in the domain, configure the appropriate policy settings for the related OU GPOs, and then move the computer objects into the OUs you've created. In this way, you associate a GPO containing your secure baseline with the computers placed in the GPO. As a rule, each type of computer that requires a different security configuration should have its own OU. Following this, you might use the following OUs to implement role-specific security configurations:

Domain Controllers
: The default OU for domain controllers.

Workstations
: An OU for general-purpose workstations.

ApplicationServers
: An OU for application servers and internal web servers.

InfrastructureServers
: An OU for member servers that provide essential services, such as DNS, DHCP, and WINS.

FilePrintServers
: An OU for file and print servers.

MailDBServers
: An OU for mail and database servers.

In Group Policy, the primary security settings you'll want to manage for computers are stored under *Computer Configuration\Windows Settings\Security Settings* and include:

Account policy
: These settings control security for passwords, account lockout, and Kerberos.

Local policy
: These settings control security for auditing, user rights assignment, and other security options.

Event log policy
: These settings control security for event logging.

Restricted groups policy
: These settings control security for local group membership administration.

System services policy
: These settings control security and startup mode for local services.

Filesystem policy
: These settings control security for the local filesystem.

Registry policy
: These settings control the values of security-related registry keys.

These are the same areas of policy that are managed using security templates.

Creating custom security templates based on server roles

To deploy security configurations, you can use security templates that contain customized sets of group policy definitions that are used to apply essential security settings. Security templates are stored as *.INF* files in the *%SystemRoot%\Security\Templates* folder.

Windows Server 2003 installations include a standard set of security templates that can be imported into any GPO. Table 8-5 summarizes the standard templates you'll work with the most.

Table 8-5. Standard security templates in Windows Server 2003

Template	Description
Compatws	Contains settings that decrease security for the purposes of compatibility with legacy applications. Settings affect file and Registry permissions.
dc security	Contains the default security settings for domain controllers.

Table 8-5. Standard security templates in Windows Server 2003 (continued)

Template	Description
Iesacls	Applies relaxed Registry permissions for Internet Explorer. Settings configure IE-related Registry permissions to allow Everyone Full Control and Read access.
Rootsec	Applies root permissions to the system drive. Settings grant Full Control to Administrators, Creator Owner, and System; Read and Execute permissions to Everyone; and Read and Change permissions to users.
setup security	Contains the default security settings for member servers.
Securedc	Contains moderate security settings for domain controllers that limit account policies and apply LAN Manager restrictions.
Securews	Contains moderate security settings for workstations that limit local account policies and apply LAN Manager restrictions.
Hisecdc	Contains very stringent security settings that can be used to further secure domain controllers. Settings disable nonessential services, increase security for NTLM, remove members of the Power Users group, and apply addition security to the Registry and files.
Hisecws	Contains very stringent security settings that can be used to further secure workstations. Settings increase security for NTLM, remove members of the Power Users group, and limit membership in the local machine Administrators group to Domain Admins and Administrator.

When you are configuring computer security, you'll use both the Security Templates snap-in and the Security Configuration And Analysis snap-in. Use the Security Templates snap-in to view and create security templates. Use the Security Configuration And Analysis snap-in to apply templates and to compare the settings in a template to the existing settings on a computer. You can use the following technique to access these tools:

1. Click Start → Run. Type `mmc` in the Open field, and then click OK.
2. In MMC, click File, and then click Add/Remove Snap-In.
3. In the Standalone tab, click Add.
4. In the Add Standalone Snap-In dialog box, click Security Templates, and then click Add.
5. Click Security Configuration And Analysis, and then click Add.
6. Close the Add Standalone Snap-In dialog box by clicking Close, and then click OK.

You should create a custom security template for each server role you've identified in the organization. Rather than starting from scratch, you should use the standard templates as a starting point for your role-specific security configurations. Do this by creating a copy of a template and then modifying it to meet the security requirements of the server role.

You can create a copy of a template and modify it by completing these steps:

1. Open the Security Templates console.
2. Right-click the template you want to copy and click Save As.
3. Type of new name for the template, and then click Save.

   This creates a copy of the template with the same settings as the original template.
4. Modify the settings to meet the needs of the computer role/type for which you are configuring the template.

You can create a new template without initial settings by completing the following steps:

1. Right-click the *C:\Windows\security\templates* node in the Security Templates snap-in, and then select New Template.
2. Type a name and description for the template.
3. Click OK.

Configuring security for servers that are assigned specific roles

Once you've created your role-specific security templates, you can deploy the security configurations. To deploy a security template through Group Policy, you import the security template into a GPO and in this way, apply the security template to every computer object in the GPO. One way to import a security template into a GPO is to follow these steps:

1. Open Active Directory Users And Computers.
2. Right-click the role-specific OU into which you want to import a security template, and then select Properties.
3. On the Group Policy tab, click the GPO you want to work with in the Group Policy Object Links list, and then click Edit.
4. Under Computer Configuration, expand Windows Settings → Security Settings.
5. Right-click Security Settings, and then select Import Policy.
6. In the Import Policy From dialog box, shown in Figure 8-5, select the security template to import, and then click Open.

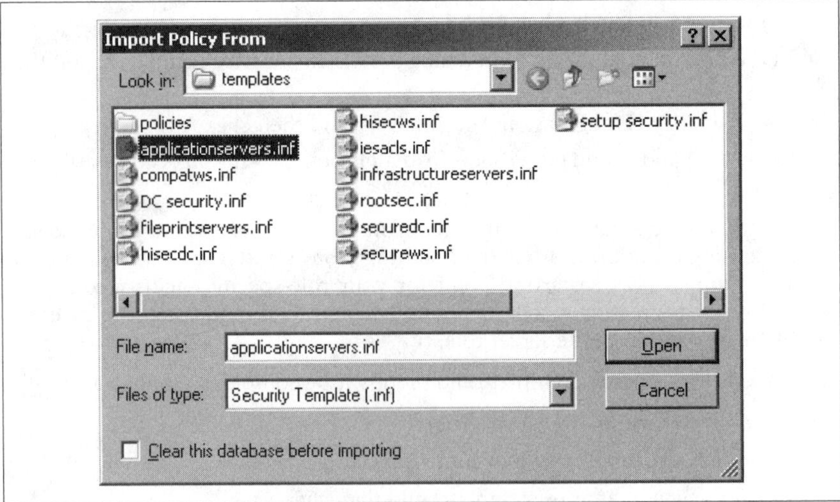

Figure 8-5. Select the security template to import.

The imported policy is applied to computers in the OU the next time Group Policy is refreshed. You can force the computer to refresh by restarting it or by running the Gpupdate command-line utility.

To apply a security template to an individual computer, you can use the Security Configuration And Analysis snap-in. This snap-in can also be used to compare the settings in a template to the effective settings on a computer. In either case, Security Configuration And Analysis uses a working database to store the settings in the template that you are applying.

You can create a database and apply a template using the following technique:

1. Open the Security Configuration And Analysis snap-in.
2. Right-click the Security Configuration And Analysis node, and then click Open Database.
3. Type a new database name in the File Name field, and then click Open.
4. In the Import Template dialog box, select the security template to apply, and then click Open.
5. Right-click the Security Configuration And Analysis node and choose Configure Computer Now.
6. When prompted to set the error log path, accept the default or type a new path. Click OK.
7. View the configuration error log by right-clicking the Security Configuration And Analysis node and choosing View Log File.

To compare a computer's current security settings to a particular template, you can use the following technique:

1. Open the Security Configuration And Analysis snap-in.
2. Right-click the Security Configuration And Analysis node, and then click Open Database.
3. Type a new database name in the File Name field, and then click Open.
4. In the Import Template dialog box, select the security template to apply, and then click Open.
5. Right-click the Security Configuration And Analysis node, and then choose Configure Computer Now.
6. When prompted to set the error log path, accept the default or type a new path. Click OK.
7. Right-click the Security Configuration And Analysis node, and then choose Analyze Computer Now.
8. When prompted to set the error log path, type a new path or click OK to use the default path.
9. Expand nodes and select entries to pinpoint discrepancies between the template and the computer's current settings.

Before you apply a template, you may want to create a rollback template. To do this, use the following syntax with the `secedit` command-line utility:

```
secedit /generaterollback /cfg filename /rbk filename /log filename
```

where `/cfg` *`filename`* sets the name of the security template for which you are creating a rollback template, `/rbk` *`filename`* sets the name of a security template

Exam 70-293 Study Guide

into which the reverse settings should be stored, and /log *filename* sets the name of an optional log file to use, such as:

```
secedit /generaterollback /cfg hisecws.inf /rbk rev-hisecws.inf /log
rollback.log
```

In the previous example, you are creating a rollback template for the *Hisecws.inf* template. While a rollback template allows you to remove the settings applied with a template, it does not recover settings for access control lists on files or the Registry. These settings must be recovered manually.

Planning, Implementing, and Maintaining a Network Infrastructure

Administrators often have to fill multiple roles in the organization. To be successful in their role as network designers, administrators must have a strong understanding of network infrastructure planning and implementation. Network infrastructure planning requires developing:

- A Network topology strategy
- A TCP/IP addressing strategy
- An Internet connectivity strategy
- A name resolution strategy

When you have a sound strategy for these four areas of network infrastructure, you can confidently implement your organization's network infrastructure.

Planning and Modifying a Network Topology

Before you can create a strategy for your organization's network topology, you must first understand what is meant by the term "network infrastructure." Knowing this, you can then identify the network protocols to be used and plan the placement of physical components.

Understanding network infrastructure

The term "network infrastructure" encompasses everything required to provide networking, connectivity, security, routing, and management on a network. Network infrastructure has physical and logical components:

- A network's *physical structure* is the physical design that defines its topology and the hardware components of which it is comprised. Common hardware components used on a network include cabling, routers, switches, workstations, and servers.
- A network's *logical structure* is the logical design that defines the abstract architecture required for communications and the software that connects, manages, and secures hosts on the network. Common abstract components include networking protocols (such as TCP/IP) and security technologies (such as IPSec). The Windows operating system provides the required software components.

Planning your organization's network infrastructure is a complex task, whether you are implementing the initial network topology or modifying the network to meet current requirements. During planning, you must select the hardware and software components required to implement the desired network infrastructure, taking into account the requirements of managers, users, and organizational policies. If your organization doesn't have specific security policies, these policies should be developed first, as discussed earlier in this chapter in the section "Planning and Implementing Server Roles and Server Security."

You must identify all required resources as part of your planning, prior to implementation. Implementing your network infrastructure plan typically requires the help of and coordination with multiple departments within the organization. You may also need to hire outside contractors to complete portions of the implementation, such as network cabling.

Exam 70-293 doesn't test your coordination and resource allocation skills. Instead, the exam focuses on your ability to select the appropriate protocols, operating systems, applications, and security configurations.

Once you've implemented the network infrastructure plan, you'll need to maintain the network by monitoring the infrastructure, troubleshooting as necessary and updating the infrastructure when required. Monitoring the network includes reviewing logs, testing components, and analyzing network traffic. Troubleshooting involves diagnosing and resolving problems that occur during day-to-day operations of the network. As requirements change or network usage change, you may need to modify or update the network infrastructure to ensure performance and security requirements are met.

Identifying network protocols to be used

The Open Systems Interconnection (OSI) reference model defines the functions that are implemented in various networking protocols. The model has seven layers:

- Application
- Presentation
- Session
- Transport
- Network
- Data-link
- Physical

Specific functions are defined for each of the seven layers defined from the lowest level (the *physical layer*) to the top level (the *application layer*). The critical layer for network communications is the *data-link layer*, which defines the interface between the network medium and the software running on a hardware device, such as a computer or router. The data-link layer is responsible for:

Packet addressing
: Allows hardware devices to direct traffic to specific destinations on networks

Media access control
: Allows multiple computers to share a single network medium

Data encapsulation
: Allows data to be formatted as data frames for transmission

The data-link layer has two sublayers:

Logical link control (LLC) sublayer
: Controls frame synchronizations, flow control, and error checking

Media access control (MAC) sublayer
: Controls the transmission of data packets from one network interface card (NIC) to another across a network medium

In the role of network designer, you must choose the data-link layer protocol to use, such as Ethernet or Token Ring, and the protocol suite, such as TCP/IP or IPX, to implement. Because of the way the OSI model works, the data-link layer protocol encompasses the physical and data-link layers in its functions. The protocol suite implements the functions of the network and transport layers. The session, presentation, and application layer functions are provided by a protocol in the protocol suite, by a separate application-layer protocol, or both.

Few current networks use Internet Package Exchange (IPX) or NetBIOS Extended User Interface (NetBEUI) as their data-link protocols. Most current networks use Transmission Control Protocol/Internet Protocol (TCP/IP). IP operates at the network layer. TCP operates at the transport layer. There is an additional transport layer protocol included in the TCP/IP protocol suite called User Datagram Protocol (UDP). TCP and UDP are very different, as described next.

TCP:

- Is a connection-oriented protocol, which ensures guaranteed delivery
- Relies on specific connections being established between two hardware devices prior to communicating
- Uses acknowledgements to ensure data is received

UDP:

- Is a connectionless protocol
- Allows two hardware devices to communicate without first establishing a connection
- Doesn't use acknowledgments, which reduces overhead but introduces the possibility of data loss

TCP should be used when reliable communications are required and when large amounts of data needs to be transmitted. UDP should be used when reliability of communications is not a requirement and for brief exchanges of data, such as a request or acknowledgement.

Most TCP/IP communications use IP at the network layer and either TCP or UDP at the transport layer. To transmit data, IP uses datagrams. A datagram includes the address of the sender and the recipient so that it can be routed to the intended recipient and so that the recipient knows from where the datagram originated.

When selecting the data-link layer protocol to use, you need to consider many criteria, including the physical distance between hardware devices and the required transmission speed. The media type you choose largely determines how far apart computers on the network can be and the supported transmission speeds. Although there are many possible media types, most current local area networks use one of three media types or a combination of these media types:

Unshielded Twisted Pair (UTP)
: Consists of four pairs of wires, each twisted together and contained inside protective shielding. Shielding protects cables from electromagnetic interface but doesn't eliminate the need to locate cables away from possible sources of electromagnetic interface.

Fiber Optic
: Consists of a strand of plastic or glass that carries signals in the form of light pulses. Using light pulses ensures that fiber optic cables are not affected by electromagnetic interference.

Wireless
: Uses wireless broadcasting and wireless transceivers instead of physical cabling. Because wireless signals are broadcast in the air, wireless signals are subject to a wide variety of environmental factors.

Each type of UTP cabling available has a category rating, which is an indicator of supported transmission speeds. With UTP cabling, a computer's network interface card uses an RJ-45 jack into which cables are connected. The two most commonly used categories are Category 3 (Cat 3) and Category 5 (Cat 5). Both categories support the Ethernet and Token Ring data-link layer protocols. The most commonly used data-link protocol is Ethernet.

Fiber optic cabling can use the same topology and data-link layer protocols as UTP cabling. Fiber optic cables use light pulses and are not affected by electromagnetic interference. With fiber optic cabling, a computer's network interface card uses a fiber optic connector into which cables are connected. Several types of fiber optic cables are available, including both single mode and multimode varieties.

Wireless networking uses wireless network adapters and wireless access points. Computer's configured with wireless network adapters transmit signals to wireless access points. Typically, the wireless access points, or base stations, are connected directly to the organization's network.

Planning the physical placement of network resources

Install UTP cabling using a star topology in which each workstation or server is connected to a central hub. Hubs can in turn be connected to each other to create a large network. On an Ethernet network using UTP cabling, the distance between workstations and hubs can be no more than 100 meters.

Ethernet has specific limitations for networks that you should be aware of:

- On a standard Ethernet running at 10 megabits per second, you can connect computers together through no more than 4 hubs on a single local area network (LAN). Another way of saying this is that a single network can have no more than five network segments connected by four repeaters.
- On a standard Ethernet running at 100 megabits per second, you can connect computers together through no more than 2 hubs on a single LAN. Another way of saying this is that a single network can have no more than three network segments connected by two repeaters.
- On a standard Ethernet running at 1,000 megabits per second (1 gigabit), you can connect computers together through no more than 1 hub on a single LAN. Another way of saying this is that a single network can have no more than two network segments connected by one repeater.

Most network designers avoid these limitations by connecting computers to hubs and in turn connecting hubs to central switches and routers. In an extended campus, the 100-meter limitation is important to keep track of. With standard Ethernet running at 10 megabits per second using repeaters, the furthest a computer could possibly be from the central switch/router is 500 meters. With standard Ethernet running at 100 megabits per second using repeaters, the furthest a computer could possibly be from the central switch/router is 300 meters. With standard Ethernet running at 1,000 megabits per second using repeaters the furthest a computer could possibly be from the central switch/router is 200 meters.

Although fiber optic cabling is much more expensive than UTP cabling, it can be used over greatest distances. The exact distance supported depends on the cable type. As an example, 50/125 and 62.5/125 multimode cables supports distances of between 500 and 550 meters. Most fiber optic cables have a transmission speed of 1,000 megabits per second. Gigabit Ethernet is available for Category 5 UTP cabling as well.

Table 8-6 summarizes the most commonly used Ethernet variants. Workstations, servers, and peripheral devices should be placed within the network environment in a way that conforms to the chosen cable type and the applicable limitations. Don't overlook the importance of planning cabling runs around possible points of interface and the need to connect hubs to your organization's network backbone routers.

Table 8-6. Overview of Ethernet variants

Ethernet type	Designation	Cable type	Cable speed	Max. segment length
Standard Ethernet	10Base-T	Category 3 UTP	10 Mbps	100 meters
Fast Ethernet	100Base-T	Category 5 UTP	100 Mbps	100 meters
Gigabit Ethernet	1000Base-T	Category 5E UTP	1,000 Mbps	100 meters
Gigabit Ethernet	1000Base-LX	50/125 or 62.5/125 multimode fiber	10,000 Mbps	550 meters
Gigabit Ethernet	1000Base-SX	50/125 multimode fiber	1,000 Mbps	500 meters

Table 8-6. Overview of Ethernet variants (continued)

Ethernet type	Designation	Cable type	Cable speed	Max. segment length
Gigabit Ethernet	1000Base-SX	62.5/125 multi-mode fiber	1,000 Mbps	220 meters
Gigabit Ethernet	1000Base-LX	9/125 single mode fiber	1,000 Mbps	3,000 meters

Most wireless network adapters and wireless access points conform to standards based on the IEEE 802.1 specification. As Table 8-7 shows, there are multiple variants of the IEEE 802.1 specification, and the variant determines effective distances and transmissions speeds. While you might want to introduce some wireless connectivity options for user workstations, most servers and peripheral devices should be connected to the network using more reliable physical cabling techniques.

Table 8-7. Overview of wireless variants

Wireless standard	Transmission speed	Transmission frequency	Effective indoor range
802.11a	Up to 54 Mbps	5 GHz	Approximately 25 to 75 feet
802.11b	Up to 11 Mbps	2.4 GHz	Approximately 100 to 150 feet
802.11g	Up to 54 Mbps	2.4 GHz	Approximately 100 to 150 feet

Planning a TCP/IP Network Infrastructure Strategy

The three essential components of every TCP/IP network infrastructure are:

- IP addressing
- IP routing
- IP subnetting

The TCP/IP protocols use IP addresses to identify computers on a network, subnet masks to determine the logical subnets within a larger network, and IP routing to route communications.

Analyzing IP addressing requirements

Windows XP Professional and Windows Server 2003 computers are configured automatically to use TCP/IP if the operating system detects a network adapter during installation. With TCP/IP, three types of IP addresses can be used:

Static IP addresses
: Static IP addresses are those manually assigned to computers. When you manually assign an IP address, you must manually assign other TCP/IP options as well, including the subnet mask and default gateway.

Dynamic IP addresses

Dynamic IP addresses are automatically obtained from a DHCP server and are the default type of IP addresses for both Windows XP Professional and Windows Server 2003. When a DHCP dynamically assigns an IP address, the server can also assign other TCP/IP options, including the subnet mask and default gateway and the addresses of DNS servers.

Automatic private IP addresses

Automatic private IP addresses (APIPA) are used when a computer is configured for DHCP but no DHCP server is available or an IP address lease expires and cannot be renewed. The default automatic addressing allows broadcasting on the local subnet, but does not allow access to remote subnets.

When determining which IP addressing type to use, keep in mind that in most cases you'll want workstations and members servers to use dynamic IP addressing. This makes it easier to manage IP addressing, since you can make changes centrally through DHCP rather than make changes on each individual computer. While some types of servers, including DHCP servers, require static IP addressing, most others can use either static or dynamic IP addressing.

The way IP addresses are used on a network depends of the version or versions of TCP/IP that are implemented. Most current networks use TCP/IP version 4. In order to determine your organization's IP addressing needs, you must consider the following:

- How many networks do you need?
- How many computers on each network?
- Will computers need to connect directly to the Internet?

The answers to these questions will determine your IP addressing needs. All IP addresses are either public or private. Public IP addresses are routable over the Internet and must be assigned by Internet Service Providers (ISPs). Private IP addresses are reserved for use on internal networks and are not routed over the public Internet. If you're connecting a computer directly to the internet and you've been assigned an IP address, you can use a public IP address. Otherwise, you should use a private IP address.

Public and private IP addresses can also be referred to as *registered* and *unregistered* IP addresses. Public (registered) IP addresses must be registered with an ISP. Private (unregistered) IP addresses do not need to be registered with an ISP.

The available IP addresses are divided into network class ranges. For TCP/IP version 4, the standard IP classes are Class A, Class B, and Class C. These network classes are used with unicast IP addresses; which class you use is based on the anticipated number of networks and hosts per network.

TCP/IP version 4 IP addresses are comprised of sets of 32-bit numbers. When you assign IP addresses, each 8-bit section, or octet, of this 32-bit number is entered in decimal format with each set of numbers separated by periods.

With Class A networks, the first octet identifies the network, and the last three octets identify the computers on the network, allowing millions of hosts but a small number of networks. Usable Class A networks have addresses that begin with a number between 1 and 126. Private Class A network addresses have a network ID of 10.0.0.0 and an assignable IP address range of 10.0.0.1 to 10.255.255.254.

The Class A address 127 has special meaning and isn't available for assignment. IP addresses with this network address are local loopback addresses. Any packets sent by a computer to this address are handled as if they've already been routed and reached their destination. In other words, any packets addressed to the 127 network are addressed to and received by a computer's local network interface.

With Class B networks, the first and second octet identify the network, and the last two octets identify the computers on the network, allowing an equal number of networks and hosts. Class B networks have addresses that begin with a number between 128 and 191. Private Class B network addresses have a network ID of 172.16.0.0 and an assignable IP address range of 172.16.0.1–172.31.255.254.

With Class C networks, the first three octets identify the network, and the last octet identifies the computers on the network, allowing many networks and relatively few hosts per network. Class C networks have addresses that begin with a number between 192 and 223. Private Class C network addresses have a network ID of 192. 168.0.0. and an assignable IP address range of 192.168.0.1–192.168.255.254.

Table 8-8 provides an overview of the standard network classes, showing the bits for the subnet mask and the network prefix of each. The table also lists the maximum number of nodes for each IP address class without subnetting. You can use this information to help you plan which IP address class to use, taking into account any possible future expansion needs.

Table 8-8. Overview of standard network classes bits and prefixes

Address class	Bits for subnet mask	Network prefix	Maximum nodes
Class A	11111111 00000000 00000000 00000000	/8	16,777,214
Class B	11111111 11111111 00000000 00000000	/16	65,534
Class C	11111111 11111111 11111111 00000000	/24	254

Table 8-9 provides an overview of IP addresses by class. The first and last IP addresses of a subnet are not usable and cannot be assigned to client computers. The first IP address of a subnet is the *network ID*. The last IP address of a subnet is the network's *broadcast address*. With standard network configurations, the network ID is the .0 address of the subnet, such as 192.168.1.0, and the broadcast address is the .255 address of the subnet, such as 192.168.1.255.

Table 8-9. Overview of private and public IP address classes

Network class	Network ID	Subnet mask
Public Class A	1.0.0.0–126.0.0.0	255.0.0.0
Private Class A	10.0.0.0	255.0.0.0

Table 8-9. Overview of private and public IP address classes (continued)

Network class	Network ID	Subnet mask
Special Class A	127.0.0.0	255.0.0.0
Public Class B	128.0.0.0–191.0.0.0	255.240.0.0
Private Class B	172.16.0.0	255.240.0.0
Public Class C	192.0.0.0.0–223.0.0.0	255.255.0.0
Private Class C	192.168.0.0	255.255.0.0

Most organizations use private IP addresses for all networking equipment, workstations, servers, and peripherals on their internal networks. If the organization has devices that connect directly to the Internet, such as routers or firewalls, those devices are assigned public IP addresses. Public IP addresses are also used for the organization's web servers and others servers accessible on the public Internet.

You'll use public IP addresses with NAT. NAT allows multiple client computers to access the public Internet, sharing a single public IP address or a pool of public IP addresses. NAT separates your organization's internal private network from the public network so that you can use private IP addresses internally and use public IP addresses when client computers need to access the Internet.

You'll also use public IP addresses with proxy servers. *Proxy servers* are used to make requests to Internet servers on behalf of internal clients. Unlike NAT, a proxy server is not a type of routing and is instead a software product that runs at the application layer. When an internal client sends a proxy server a request, the proxy server sends a request to a destination server on the public Internet. When received by the proxy server, the reply from the public Internet server is forwarded to the internal client. Each proxy server you configure must have a public IP address.

Planning an IP routing solution

On TCP/IP networks, IP routers are used to connect local area networks and can be hardware or software devices. IP routers connect networks by relaying traffic between the connected networks as necessary. Routing works like this:

- If the destination address is on the same LAN as the sender, the packet travels directly to the destination.
- If the destination address is on a different LAN than the sender, the sender transmits the packet to a router instead. This router is specified as the computer's default gateway.

As part of the standard TCP/IP configuration, every computer is assigned a default gateway to use for routing communications across subnets. The router's job is to connect network segments. When it receives a packet bound for another subnet, the router reads the destination address and compares the address to the entries in its routing table. The routing table entries tell the router where to send the packet. If the router is directly connected to the destination subnet, the router transmits the packet directly to the destination. Otherwise, the router sends the packet to another router, which in turn routes the packet.

Routers obtain their routing information using either static routing or dynamic routing. With *static routing*, an administrator manually creates routing entries. With *dynamic routing*, routers can automatically determine routes from other routers.

With Windows Server 2003, the IP routing protocols you'll work with the most are:

DHCP Relay Agent routing protocol
: Enables routing of DHCP broadcast messages between subnets. DHCP Relay Agent routing protocol is essential for organizations with centralized DHCP servers and multiple subnets.

Routing Information Protocol (RIP) version 2 for Internet Protocol
: Enables dynamic routing between subnets. RIP is an easily managed routing protocol, but limited to a maximum hop count of 15. For successful communications, source and destination computers can have no more than 15 routing devices between them.

Open Shortest Path First (OSPF)
: Enables extended dynamic routing between subnets. With OSPF, source and destination computers can have more than 15 routing devices between them, but OSPF is more complex to configure and maintain than RIP.

Network Address Translation (NAT)
: Enables internal client computers with private IP addresses to access the public Internet using a public IP address. NAT provides Internet connectivity to internal clients through a single interface and includes the Basic Firewall, which can be used to block external traffic from entering the internal network.

IP routing and subnets become increasingly important as an organization grows. Most small organizations have a single network and don't necessarily need IP routing to manage internal routing needs. Most medium and large organizations make extensive use of IP routing and have networks divided into multiple subnets. One of the primary reasons for creating multiple subnets is to help manage the traffic on the network, especially for broadcast messages.

Computers use broadcasts for all types of communications, including DHCP server discovery. All computers on the same subnet receive broadcasts transmitted by all other computers on the subnet. When any two computers on a subnet transmit a packet at the exact same time, a collision occurs and both packets are destroyed, forcing the computers to retransmit the packet. Thus, as the network grows, you can reduce the amount of broadcast traffic received and the possibility of collisions, by splitting the network into multiple subnets.

If two devices on the network try to communicate at the same time, a collision occurs. As a result of the collision, both devices must try to send their message again.

When working with broadcast and multicast traffic, it is important to understand what are broadcast domains and collision domains. A network segment in which all devices on the segment can hear broadcast and multicast traffic is a *broadcast domain*. A network segment in which all devices on the segment can hear when a collision happens is a *collision domain*. In your network planning, broadcast and collision domains are important.

Networks can use hubs, bridges, switches, and routers. In the OSI model, the Data Link Layer (Layer 2) forms the border of broadcast and collision domains. All hubs and bridges work at Layer 2. Some switches operate at Layer 2, while others operate at Layer 3. Routers are also Layer 3 devices.

Since broadcast and multicast messages are found at Layer 3, these messages pass across any device communicating at Layer 2. Thus, if network segments are connected with hubs, bridges, or Layer 2 switches, the network segments are in the same broadcast and collision domains.

To set the boundaries of network segments, use Layer 3 devices, such as a Layer 3 switch or a router. Network segments on opposite sides Layer 3 switches or routers are in different broadcast and collision domains.

Creating an IP subnet scheme

With TCP/IP, a subnet mask specifies how many bits of an IP address to use for the network ID and how many bits to use for the host ID. On a network that follows the standard class rules (also referred to as a classful network), the network ID bits are fixed. A network that doesn't follow the standard rules is referred to as a classless network.

The routing protocol you use with subnetting must support Classless Inter-Domain Routing (CIDR). Both RIP version 2 and OSPF support CIDR. However, RIP version 1 does not support CIDR.

Table 8-10 provides an overview of standard subnet masks. As the table shows, with Class A networks, the first 8 bits of the 32-bit IP address identify the network ID and the final 16 bits are the host ID. With Class B networks, the first 16 bits of the 32-bit IP address identify the network ID and the final 8 bits are the host ID. With Class C networks, the first 24 bits of the 32-bit IP address identify the network ID and the final 8 bits are the host ID.

Table 8-10. Standard subnet masks

Network class	Bit length	Subnet mask	Prefix notation
Class A	8	255.0.0.0	/8
Class B	16	255.240.0.0	/16
Class C	24	255.255.0.0	/24

Rather than writing out a network ID followed by a subnet mask, you can use a prefix notation when referring to IP addresses. In this notation, the network ID is followed by the number of bits in the network ID. Thus, rather than writing or saying that the network 10.0.0.0 has a network mask of 255.0.0.0, you could say the network 10.0.0.0 is a "slash 8" network. This is written in network prefix notation as:

10.0.0.0/8

Like IP addresses, subnet masks can be written as a 32-bit value. Bit values are assigned in a specific order, from the most significant bits to the least significant bits. From left to right the values of each bit are 128, 64, 32, 16, 8, 4, 2, and 1. Each bit that's set is noted by a 1, which means the bit is on. When you add the bits together, you get the subnet mask. For example, the binary equivalent of 255 is:

11111111

And the binary equivalent of 128 is:

10000000

Bits in the subnet mask are always set consecutively from left to right. The subnet mask 255.240.0.0 is valid because all eight bits are set in the first octet and the next four bits are set in the second octet, as shown here in the binary equivalent of the subnet mask:

11111111 11110000 00000000 00000000

The subnet mask 255.255.64.0 is invalid because it is missing a bit, as shown here in the binary equivalent of the subnet mask:

11111111 11111111 01000000 00000000

If you want to create logical networks within the standard network class ranges, you can use subnetting to subdivide the network. When you use subnetting, you determine which bits apply to the network ID and which bits apply to the host ID by the subnet mask. For example, you might want to subnet so that the first 26 bits refer to the network ID and the final 6 bits refer to the host ID.

- On a Class A network, this allows you to create up to 262,144 subnets that have up to 62 nodes each.
- On a Class B network, this allows you to create up to 1,024 subnets that have up to 62 nodes each.
- On a Class C network, this allows you to create up to 4 subnets that have up to 62 nodes each.

Class C networks are some of the most commonly subnetted network classes. Table 8-11 provides an overview of how Class C networks can be subnetted.

Table 8-11. Overview of subnetting Class C networks

Maximum subnets	Bits for subnet mask	Network prefix	Decimal	Maximum nodes
1	11111111 11111111 11111111 00000000	/24	255.255.255.0	254
2	11111111 11111111 11111111 10000000	/25	255.255.255.128	126
4	11111111 11111111 11111111 11000000	/26	255.255.255.192	62
8	11111111 11111111 11111111 11100000	/27	255.255.255.224	30
16	11111111 11111111 11111111 11110000	/28	255.255.255.240	14

Table 8-11. Overview of subnetting Class C networks (continued)

Maximum subnets	Bits for subnet mask	Network prefix	Decimal	Maximum nodes
32	11111111 11111111 11111111 11111000	/29	255.255.255.248	6
64	11111111 11111111 11111111 11111100	/30	255.255.255.252	2

Following the table, you could create eight /27 subnets for the Class C network 192.168.1.0. Excluding the subnet ID and subnet broadcast address, each of these subnets could have up to 30 nodes.

Once you've decided how you want to subnet the network, you need to calculate the network address of each subnet, and from that, determine the usable IP addresses for each subnet. The easiest way to do this is to extract the octet that contains both the subnet bits and host identifier bits and subtract it from 256. The result is the network address of the second subnet.

For example, the /27 network mask is 255.255.255.224. The result of 256 minus 224 is 32. If you are subnetting the 192.168.1.0 network, this means the second subnet ID is 192.168.1.32. To determine the network address of each successive subnet, increment the result of the previous subtraction by itself. Thus, the network IDs for the 192.168.1.0/27 network are:

192.168.1.0
192.168.1.32
192.168.1.64
192.168.1.96
192.168.1.128
192.168.1.160
192.168.1.192
192.168.1.224

You can use the formula 2^*x* to calculate the number of subnets, where *x* is the number of additional network bits in the network mask from the standard network bits in the network for the IP address class. In the previous example, you are working with Class C network addresses. With standard Class C network addresses, there are 24 bits in the network mask. You are creating a /27 network, meaning you are using three additional bits for the network ID. Using the formula (2^3 = 8), you can determine there will be eight subnets.

You can use the formula 2^*x* – 2 to calculate the number of nodes on a subnet, where *x* is the number of host bits in the network mask. For example, in the previous example, the /27 network mask means there are five bits for hosts. Using the formula (2^5 – 2 = 30), you can determine there will be 30 hosts on each subnet.

In each case, the first IP address after the network ID is the first usable IP address on the subnet, and the IP address prior to the next subnet ID address is the broadcast IP address for that subnet. Table 8-12 provides a summary of the subnets and IP addresses for the 192.168.1.0/27 network.

Table 8-12. Subnetting the 192.168.1.0/27 network

Subnet ID	First usable IP address	Last usable IP address	Broadcast IP address
192.168.1.0	192.168.1.1	192.168.1.30	192.168.1.31
192.168.1.32	192.168.1.33	192.168.1.62	192.168.1.63
192.168.1.64	192.168.1.65	192.168.1.94	192.168.1.95
192.168.1.96	192.168.1.97	192.168.1.126	192.168.1.127
192.168.1.128	192.168.1.129	192.168.1.158	192.168.1.159
192.168.1.160	192.168.1.161	192.168.1.190	192.168.1.191
192.168.1.192	192.168.1.193	192.168.1.222	192.168.1.223
192.168.1.224	192.168.1.225	192.168.1.254	192.168.1.255

Troubleshooting TCP/IP Addressing

Exam 70-293 tests your ability to troubleshoot TCP/IP addressing with respect to two specific objectives:

- Diagnosing and Resolving Issues Related to Client Computer Configuration, which was previously covered in "Troubleshooting TCP/IP Addressing" in Chapter 5.
- Diagnosing and Resolving Issues Related to DHCP Server Address Assignment, which was previously covered in "Troubleshooting DHCP" in Chapter 5.

Planning an Internet Connectivity Strategy

Just about every organization, regardless of size, will want to configure the internal network so that users can access the Internet. The Internet has a wealth of resources that users will want to access, and users will also want to be able to send and receive email. Since it is pretty much a given that administrators will need to configure Internet connectivity, the question to answer when developing an Internet strategy isn't whether Internet connectivity is needed but rather how should it be configured. The answer to this question should:

- Address the security policies and requirements of the organization
- Address the needs of users within the organization

In most cases, you'll need to balance the security policies and requirements of the organization, the needs of its users, and the costs of implementing the connectivity strategy. While some small business may be able to install a cable or DSL solution to meet connectivity requirements, most medium to large organizations will need to install a WAN connection to an ISP and share the connection with all users on the internal network. To connect the internal network with the ISP, you need a WAN router. The job of the WAN router is to forward all traffic not addressed to the internal network over the WAN connection. At the ISP, the traffic is then routed to the Internet.

NAT and firewalls provide solutions for securing your internal network and safeguarding the organization from attacks. Using NAT and firewalls, you can create a clear separation of the internal network from the Internet. NAT allows users with private IP addresses on the internal network to access the public Internet using public IP addresses. Firewalls protect the internal network from attack. Once you've planned the NAT and firewall deployment, the primary question you must answer before choosing an Internet access solution is how much bandwidth is required to meet the organization's needs.

Understanding bandwidth requirements

The bandwidth requirements of the organization will determine the type of Internet access solution you use and how much this solution will cost. Most organizations require two types of bandwidth:

- One for internal users
- One for the organization's web presence

Ideally, you'll have a strategy for connecting internal users to the Internet and a separate strategy for the organization's web presence. The connectivity strategy for users is the focus of the exam.

While most organizations centrally manage their overall Internet connectivity strategy in terms of acceptable costs, reliability objectives, and security requirements, each office or branch within the company typically has a separate Internet connectivity solution that is based on the needs of that office or branch.

To determine the bandwidth requirements for an Internet connection, you'll need to:

Determine how many users on average will simultaneously access the Internet. Regardless of the organization's size, not all users will access the Internet at the same time. To determine needs, you'll to determine how many users are working at one time and how much of that time they spend accessing the Internet. For example, in a company with 500 employees, you might find that on average, only 50 simultaneously access the Internet.

Determine when Internet bandwidth is need. Determining usage times goes hand in hand with determining the number of average users connecting to the Internet. You should plan to provide sufficient bandwidth to support peak usage times. To do that, you'll need to understand the schedule of workers at the location for which you are developing an Internet connection strategy. For example, 9 to 5 workers may only require bandwidth from 8 to 6, and use the most bandwidth just prior to, during, and just after regular business hours. On the other hand, shift workers will need bandwidth around the clock and may have peak usage periods throughout their 24-hour a day schedule.

Determine the relative importance of Internet access as compared to the cost of the access. In most organizations, cost is a key factor in choosing an Internet connectivity solution. Cost should be weighed against the relative importance of access. You'll have a different solution when 100 percent reliability and 100 percent accessibility are requirements than when reliability and accessibility are weighed equally with cost and efficiency. When cost and efficiency are determining factors, you may choose a connectivity solution that is sufficient to meet most but not all usage conditions.

Determine the categories of users relative to the types of Internet applications users run. Email, web browsers, FTP, and streaming media are all types of Internet applications. While the types of Internet applications that will be used are important, don't overlook the value of categorizing users according to how they use those applications. For example, you might classify users as low-, moderate-, and high-bandwidth consumers where: low-bandwidth users send email messages without attachments—or perhaps small text attachments—and occasionally browse the Internet; moderate-bandwidth users frequently send email messages with attachments and frequently browse the Internet; and high-bandwidth users routinely send emails with large multiple-megabyte attachments or routinely use streaming media in cases such as for teleconferencing over the Internet.

Determine where users are located. You should always carefully consider the location of the computers that will be accessing the Internet. While you may be configuring Internet access for a single remote office or division within the company, computers may be spread over many buildings, as with a corporate campus, or the computers may be on many different floors of a single building. In either case, you are working with multiple locations that may possibly need separate Internet connectivity strategies. If possible, locate the Internet connection in the same area as the computers that will be using that connection.

Choosing an Internet access solution

Every Internet access solution requires a WAN connection, a WAN router, and an ISP to provide connectivity. For security, the connection should be protected with NAT and firewall technology at a minimum and possibly proxy technology as well. Table 8-13 provides a summary of key Internet access solutions. Pay particular attention to the number of simultaneous users and applications supported for each solution. These values are based on simultaneous usage of email, web, and file transfer applications.

Cable and DSL modems offer asymmetrical solutions. The modem connections run faster downstream than upstream.

Table 8-13. Overview of Internet access solutions

Connection type	Transmission speed	Simultaneous users/application
Dial-up/Dual dial-up Modem	Up to 56 Kbps/Up to 128 Kbps	8–10 email users 2–3 web users 1–2 large files/attachments
ISDN (Basic Rate Interface)	Up to 128 Kbps	8–10 email users 2–3 web users 1–2 large files/attachments
ISDN (Primary Rate Interface)	Up to 1.544 Mbps	50–70 email users 20–30 web users 12–20 large files/attachments

Exam 70-293 Study Guide

Table 8-13. Overview of Internet access solutions (continued)

Connection type	Transmission speed	Simultaneous users/application
Cable Modem	Up to 7 Mbps downstream and 768 Kbps upstream	100–150 email users 50–75 web users 30–50 large files/attachments
DSL Modem	Up to 5 Mbps downstream and 768 Kbps* upstream	90–120 email users 40–60 web users 24–40 large files/attachments
T-1	1.544 Mbps	50–70 email users 20–30 web users 12–20 large files/attachments
Fractional T-1	Up to 1.544 Mbps in 64 Kbps increments	Varies depending on bandwidth
T-3	44.736 Mbps	1500–2500 email users 600–900 web users 360–600 large files/attachments
Fractional T-3	Up to 44.736 Mbps in 1.544 Mbps increments	Varies depending on bandwidth

It is important to point out that cable and DSL capabilities have changed considerably and are evolving—and the exam may not take these changes into consideration. When originally implemented, cable modem speeds were up to 1.544 Mbps, and DSL speeds were up to 640 Kbps, with cable modem being the more reliable solution. That is no longer the case, as the table points out. However, cable and DSL solutions typically are limited severely by their upstream capabilities, which reflect the bandwidth available for sending data.

Once you choose what the WAN technology to use, you'll need to choose a WAN router and an ISP to provide connectivity. Both hardware routers and software routers are available, and your ISP may have a preference as to which type you use. The ISP may also require you to use a specific type of router. Choose an ISP based on the services they offer, the cost of the service, and the support capabilities.

Hardware routers are standalone hardware devices that connect your network over the WAN to the ISP. Many hardware routers can be configured with components to provide NAT, DHCP, and firewall capabilities. For medium to large enterprise solutions, however, each of these components will typically be separate hardware devices.

Software routers are routers configured through software running on a computer. A computer running Windows Server 2003 can be configured as a router using Routing And Remote Access Service. When you also configure NAT and Basic Firewall, the server acting as a router can provide NAT and firewall capabilities as well.

Most WAN connections must be terminated using a separate piece of hardware. For a dial-up connection, a modem is used to terminate the WAN connection. ISDN, Cable, and DSL connections are terminated with a device that typically acts as both a terminator and a router. For a leased T-1 and T-3 line, a CSU/DSU is used to terminate the WAN connection.

Troubleshooting Connectivity to the Internet

Without a clear plan, diagnosing and resolving problems with connectivity to the Internet can be a significant challenge. When users report problems with Internet connectivity, your first task should be to determine the location and scope of the problem. Start troubleshooting with the client computer. If the problem is reproducible on other computers, it could be a problem with name resolution, NAT, firewalls, or proxies. Beyond this, the problem may be on the WAN itself.

Diagnosing and resolving issues related to client configuration and name resolution

All Internet connections use TCP/IP so TCP/IP configuration issues—as discussed in "Troubleshooting TCP/IP Addressing" in Chapter 5—may be an issue. Before you begin troubleshooting, try to determine the scope of the problem. Is this a problem with a single computer? Is this a problem with all computers in a specific location? Is this a problem with all computers in all locations?

If a specific client computer is having a problem, you can try to reproduce the problem on another computer—preferably one connected to the LAN in the same way as the computer experiencing the problem. If you are unable to reproduce the problem, it is likely isolated to a specific client's configuration and network connection. Check the computer's TCP/IP configuration and network connection. As discussed in "Troubleshooting TCP/IP Addressing" in Chapter 5, improper settings will cause communications problems. Some of the problems and symptoms are as follows:

Invalid gateway configuration
: The computer may be able to communicate on a local subnet but not across subnets. The computer won't be able to access resources in other subnets or connect to computers in other subnets.

Invalid IP address
: Except for broadcast communications, the computer may not be able to communicate on a local subnet or across subnets.

Invalid subnet mask
: The computer may not know appropriate subnet boundaries and may not route communications through a gateway when it should.

Invalid DNS configuration
: The computer may not be able to use name resolution or may fail to resolve computer names.

Invalid WINS configuration
: Windows Internet Naming Service (WINS) is used with pre-Windows 2000 computers and resources. The computer may not be able to resolve NetBIOS computer names and therefore may not be able to communicate with pre-Windows 2000 computers and resources.

You should use ipconfig /all to determine the computer's IP addressing configuration. On a client, you can attempt to restore connectivity with the network using the Repair option on Support tab of the Local Area Connection Status dialog box (see Figure 8-6).

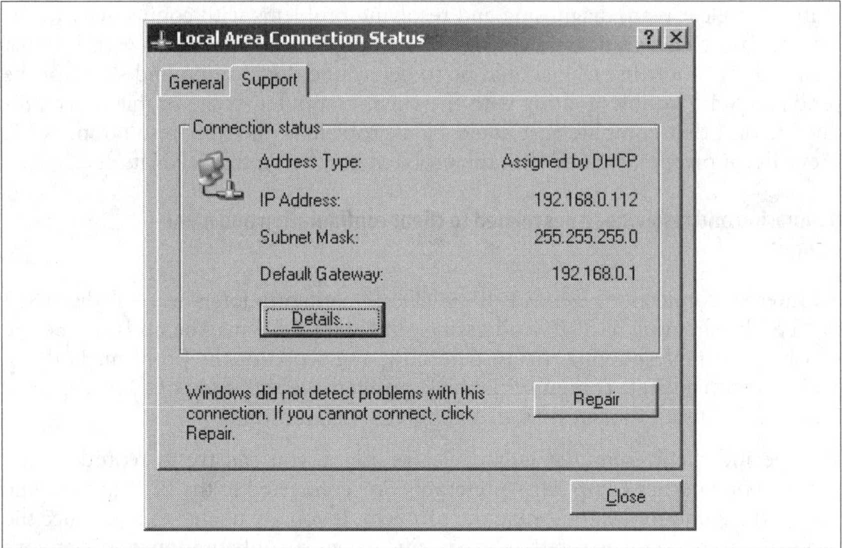

Figure 8-6. Click Repair to attempt to restore connectivity.

When you use Repair, the client attempts to refresh the stored data for its connection. The client does this by:

1. Renewing the DHCP IP address lease and the related TCP/IP settings.
2. Flushing the ARP cache, the NetBIOS cache, and the DNS resolver cache.
3. Re-registering with WINS and DNS.

Name resolution problems can cause problems with Internet connectivity as well. When name resolution fails, client computers won't be able to access Internet resources using DNS host and domain names. You can determine if name resolution is the cause of the connectivity problem by trying to access an Internet resource using an IP address instead of its DNS name. If you can successfully connect to an Internet resource by its IP address, there's a DNS configuration problem with either the client's DNS configuration or the organization's DNS server.

DNS is an integral part of Active Directory. If the DNS Server service is not running, clients may also not be able to locate Active Directory objects in the domain.

Diagnosing and resolving LAN/WAN problems

Problems experienced by all clients connected to a specific part of the network may be due to the hub or switch through which they are connected. Problems experienced by all computers on the network can be due to problems with the WAN router or the WAN connection.

If multiple clients in the same area of the network have the same problem, try to determine whether the problem affects access to all resources or access to Internet resources only. If you can access internal resources but not Internet resources, the problem is related to the components providing the Internet connection. If you have access to neither internal nor Internet resources, the problem is related to the internal network.

Internal network problems that are not due to client configurations can be diagnosed by examining the Internet infrastructure components that provide services required for accessing the Internet. This means checking for name resolution issues as well as checking for NAT, firewall, and proxy issues.

NAT routers, proxies, and firewalls must have a routing interface that connects to the WAN using a public IP address assigned by your ISP. These devices use TCP/IP as well, and like any other TCP/IP client, they must be properly configured. Check the IP address, subnet mask, default gateway, and DNS server settings to ensure that they are correct.

For NAT, the NAT router must be configured to work with computers on your internal network. For firewalls and proxies, the firewall or proxy must be configured properly, and both may be configured to block access for various reasons. If user authentication fails or there is a specific policy that is blocking access, access will fail.

WAN problems can be due to:

- A misconfigured or faulty WAN router
- A misconfigured or faulty terminus, such as a bad CSU/DSU
- A misconfigured or unavailable WAN connection
- An outage at the ISP

The `tracert`, `ping`, and `pingpath` commands can help you determine where a WAN problem originates. Try pinging the WAN router and then tracing a route to a known web site or a site set up for such purpose by your ISP. Provided that the ping/trace requests are not being blocked by firewalls or proxy servers, the failure point is the likely point of origin for the problem:

- If you can ping to the WAN router, the router is available but not necessarily configured properly. Check the routes on the router to make sure they are configured properly.
- If the route trace fails after your company's WAN router, the likely problem is the WAN connection or the ISPs WAN router. Check the terminus. If necessary, contact the ISP by phone to report the problem.
- If the route trace fails after your ISP's WAN router, the likely problem is an outage at the ISP. Contact the ISP by phone to report the problem.

WAN routers have at least two interfaces: one connected to the internal network and one connected to the WAN. These interfaces must be configured properly. In the WAN router's routing table, there should be a default gateway entry that sends all traffic not bound for the internal network through the WAN interface and over the WAN.

The CSU/DSU terminating the WAN connection may also be the source of the problem. Cycle the power on the CSU/DSU or reset the CSU/DSU.

If the WAN and CSU/DSU are working properly, the likely problem is with your ISP. The ISP may have a problem with its network infrastructure or Internet connectivity. The problem could extend to the Internet backbone as well.

For the exam, you will need strong knowledge of `ping`, `tracert`, and `pingpath`, and the differences between these commands. These commands are covered in "Troubleshooting TCP/IP Addressing" in Chapter 5.

Planning a Name Resolution Strategy

Name resolution is essential for all TCP/IP networks, and a key part of the network design process involves planning for the organization's current and future name resolution needs. As with other areas of network design, considerable planning should be performed prior to deploying a name resolution strategy. This strategy should be reviewed periodically and modified as necessary to meet changing requirements over time.

Understanding name resolution

When computer names are used, name resolution is critical to proper functioning of TCP/IP communications. A computer must be able to look up the IP address associated with a computer name, referred to as a forward lookup, or determine the computer name based on an IP address, referred to as a reverse lookup. With Windows computers, two name resolution technologies are used:

- NetBIOS (Network Basic Input/Output System)
- Domain Name System (DNS)

On Windows NT 4.0 networks, Windows Internet Naming Service (WINS) is used to resolve NetBIOS names. On networks running Windows 2000 and later computers, DNS is used to resolve DNS hostnames.

Both name resolution technologies have specific namespaces, which are used to locate computers on the network. NetBIOS uses a flat naming structure. Each computer has a single NetBIOS name of up to 16 characters, which must be unique on the network. Because Windows uses the 16th character for a reserved code that identifies the type of resource represented by the name, NetBIOS names for Windows computers can be no longer than 15 characters. Because NetBIOS uses a flat namespace, it is not very scalable and is intended for use on private networks only, and not on the public Internet.

Unlike NetBIOS, DNS uses a hierarchical namespace. With DNS, computers are grouped by name within domains. Domains establish a hierarchical naming structure so a computer's place within the domain structure can be determined.

In a standard configuration, a computer's fully qualified domain name or FQDN is its hostname combined with the related domain name. For example, the FQDN for the computer CorpSvr18 in the *WilliamStanek.com* domain is *CorpSvr18.WilliamStanek.com*.

Since DNS domain structure is hierarchical, DNS domains can have subdomains. For example, the *WilliamStanek.com* domain might have Tech and Eng subdomains. The computer Workstation41 in the Tech domain would have a FQDN of *Workstation41.Tech.WilliamStanek.com*.

When the network is not fully configured for DNS name resolution, you might need NetBIOS name resolution. NetBIOS is also required for some applications, such as the Computer Browser service. While NetBIOS and the DNS Client service are enabled by default in Windows XP Professional and in Windows Server 2003, name resolution is not fully functional unless the server components for name resolution are configured as well. This means to fully configure NetBIOS name resolution, you must install WINS servers; to fully configure DNS name resolution, you must install DNS servers.

If no WINS server is configured or available, NetBIOS name resolution uses broadcasts. These broadcasts are limited to the local subnet only.

Planning a DNS name resolution strategy

DNS is the primary name service used with networks running Windows 2000 and later computers. DNS provides name resolution for client systems by translating computer names to IP addresses and vice versa so that computers can locate each other. DNS uses host (A) records to resolve computer names to IP addresses for forward lookups, and uses pointer (PTR) records to resolve IP addresses to computer names for reverse lookups. In the standard configuration of DNS and DHCP, DHCP clients running Windows 2000 or later update their host (A) records in DNS automatically whenever an IP address is assigned or renewed, and DHCP servers update the PTR records on behalf of clients.

DNS names can be up to 255 characters.

Active Directory domains and DNS domains can, and usually do, share common naming structures. For example, the computer DataServer03 in the *williamstanek.com* Active Directory domain typically would have a fully qualified hostname in DNS as *DataServer03.williamstanek.com*. It should be noted, however, that the Active Directory and DNS naming structures can be completely different. For example, you may have an Active Directory domain structure that includes multiple subdomains, but have a DNS domain structure where all computers use the parent domain name for the purposes of name resolution.

DNS uses both iterative and recursive queries to resolve queries. With an iterative query, a DNS server attempts to resolve the query from its records or from its cache. If it is unable to resolve the query, the server refers the client, based on the server's root hints, to an authoritative server in another part of the domain namespace.

For DNS servers running Windows 2000 or later, root hints are stored in the *%SystemRoot%\System32\Dns\Cache.dns* file. For most internal DNS servers, the root hints do not need to be modified. For an internal root server (name ".") on private networks, however, you should delete the *Cache.dns* file.

With a recursive query, the DNS client requests that the DNS server respond directly an answer that resolves the query. The DNS server cannot refer the client to another DNS server and, instead, queries other DNS servers on behalf of the client. The server continues until it locates a server that is authoritative for the requested name, until an error is returned (such as "Name not found") or until the query times out.

By default, Microsoft DNS servers use recursion to query other DNS servers on behalf of clients. However, on the Forwarders tab of the DNS server's properties dialog box, shown in Figure 8-7, the option Do Not Use Recursion For This Domain can be used to disable recursion. If recursion is disabled, the client performs iterative queries using the root hints from the DNS server. Iterative queries mean that the client will make repeated queries of different DNS servers.

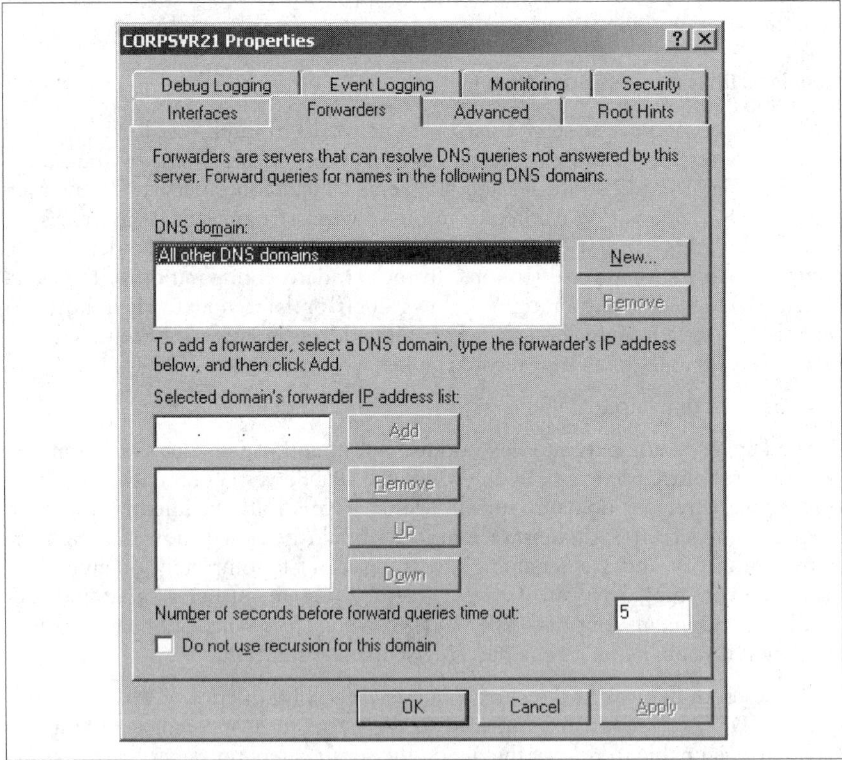

Figure 8-7. Control recursion on the Forwarders tab.

When you configure a DNS client, you specify the primary and alternate DNS servers to use. Each DNS server is responsible for name resolution within specific administrative areas known as zones. A *zone* is a portion of the DNS database that is being managed. A single zone can contain a single domain, or it can span multiple domains.

DNS servers are said to be either authoritative or nonauthoritative for a zone. An authoritative DNS server for a zone is responsible for the related portion of the DNS database and is the primary source from which other DNS servers resolving any quests for that zone. A nonauthoritative DNS server for a zone may cache information related to the zone, but ultimately, must rely on an authoritative DNS server to keep its cache up to date.

Planning a DNS namespace design. DNS servers store zone information in zone files. Zone files contain resource records that are used to resolve queries and primarily map hostnames to IP addresses. By default, zone files are created as standard text files on the DNS server. When the DNS Server service is installed on an Active Directory domain controller, the zone data can be stored in Active Directory by creating an Active Directory–integrated zone.

Zones always consist of entire domains or subdomains. While you can create a zone that contains multiple domains, those domains must be contiguous in the DNS namespace. Following this, you can create a zone that includes a parent domain and subdomains of the parent domain because the parent domain and the subdomains share a contiguous namespace. You cannot, however, create a zone containing two subdomains of a parent domain without also including the parent domain. This is because the subdomains of a parent domain are not connected and share a contiguous namespace via the parent domain only.

Subdomains of a parent domain are also referred to as child domains.

Three types of zone files are used with DNS:

Primary
: The master copy of a zone, and as such, it is the only writeable copy and the one that must be updated when you want to modify or maintain records. A primary zone can be integrated with Active Directory to create an Active Directory–integrated primary zone.

Secondary
: A copy of a primary zone, and as such, it is a read-only copy that is updated when the primary DNS server for a zone sends a copy of the zone file to a secondary server.

Stub
: Lists authoritative name servers for a zone so that DNS servers hosting a parent zone are aware of authoritative DNS servers for the related child zones. A stub zone can be integrated with Active Directory to create an Active Directory–integrated stub zone.

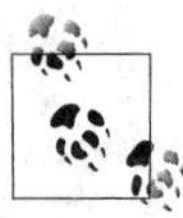

Because DNS data is replicated to domain controllers, Active Directory–integrated zones do not have any secondaries. You can, however, configure Active Directory–integrated zones to replicate zone information with third-party DNS servers.

In every DNS domain structure, you'll want to have primary and alternate name servers. All changes to zones are made in the primary zone and replicated to secondary zones. Use secondary zones to make copies of existing primary zones and to distribute the DNS name resolution workload.

Stub zones list authoritative name servers for a zone. Servers hosting stub zones do not answer queries directly, and instead direct related queries to any of the name servers specified in the stub zone's NS resource records. Stubs zones are most often used to track authoritative name servers for delegated zones—and the parent DNS servers of delegated zones are the ones to host the related stub zones.

Windows Server 2003 DNS servers can support and manage 200,000 zones on a single servers. While you can host a DNS namespace divided into multiple zones on a single DNS server, you'll usually want to create multiple zones on a server and then delegate most of the zones to other servers.

Control over zones can be delegated to make it easier to manage the DNS namespace in large enterprises. When you delegate a zone, you assign authority over a portion of the DNS namespace, and in this way, pass control from the owner of the parent domain to the owner of a subdomain. For example, if you have *hr.domain.local* and *finance.domain.local* subdomains, you may want to delegate control over these subdomains so they can be managed separately from the organization's parent domain.

Delegation allows remote offices, branches, and departments within the organization to manage their own DNS namespace. It also helps to distribute the workload so that, rather than having one large DNS database, you have multiple DNS databases. Delegating a zone is a two-part process: you must first create the domain to be delegated on the server that will be hosting the delegated zone, and then you must run the New Delegation Wizard on the server hosting the parent zone to specify the zone to delegate.

DNS servers can be configured in the following roles:

Primary
: Maintains one or more primary zone files. A DNS server acts as a primary server if you've installed the DNS Server service and created a primary zone on the server.

Secondary
: Maintains one or more secondary copies of zone files. A DNS server acts as a secondary server if you've installed the DNS Server service and created a secondary zone on the server.

Forwarding-only (caching-only)
: Maintains a cache of resolved queries; contains no zones and hosts no domains. A DNS server acts as a forwarding-only server if you've installed the DNS Server service on a server but have not configured DNS zones. Another name for a forwarding-only server is a *caching-only server*.

A single DNS server can have multiple roles. When file-based zones are used, most DNS servers act as both primaries for one or more zones and as secondaries for other zones.

Planning zone replication requirements. Most organizations will want to have multiple DNS servers to provide fault tolerance and distribute the name resolution workload. With file-based zones, this means having primary and secondary DNS servers, and replicating zone data from primary DNS servers to secondary DNS servers. With Active Directory–integrated zones, the zone database is replicated automatically.

When you configure standard primary and secondary zones, you must configure zone transfers. *Zone transfers* are used to send a copy of a zone to requesting servers. Zone transfers ensure secondary servers are kept up to date with changes in the primary zone, which enables secondary servers to perform authoritative name resolution for domains in the zone in the same way that the primary server can. You can configure zone transfers to occur when changes are made to the resource records in the primary zone or at specific intervals.

By default, zone transfers are not allowed or restricted only to the DNS servers specified in the Name Servers tab. If you've configured secondary name servers for a domain, you should enable zone transfers using the Zone Transfers tab of a zone's Properties dialog box (see Figure 8-8). Select the Allow Zone Transfers checkbox, and then specify the servers permitted to make zone transfer requests. To maintain the integrity and security of the network, you'll usually want to limit the list of servers that can make zone transfer requests to the servers listed on the Name Servers tab or to a specific list of designated name servers.

Windows Server 2003 DNS servers can use complete transfers as well as incremental transfers. Typically, complete transfers take place when you first configure secondary zones and incremental transfers take place thereafter. As the name implies, a *complete transfer* copies a complete copy of the master zone file to the secondary server, and an *incremental transfer* copies only the data that has changed since the last zone transfer.

When zone files change, secondary servers can be notified automatically. In the default configuration, automatic notification is enabled but to a designated list of name servers only. You must specify the designated name servers. To configure notification, click the Notify button on the Zone Transfers tab of the zone's properties dialog box. You can also allow automatic notification to the name servers listed on the Name Servers tab of the zone's properties dialog box.

When you install the DNS Server service on an Active Directory domain controller and select Store The Zone In Active Directory when creating a zone, the server does not use a file-based zone. Instead, zone data is stored in the Active Directory database and replicated automatically along with other data stored in Active

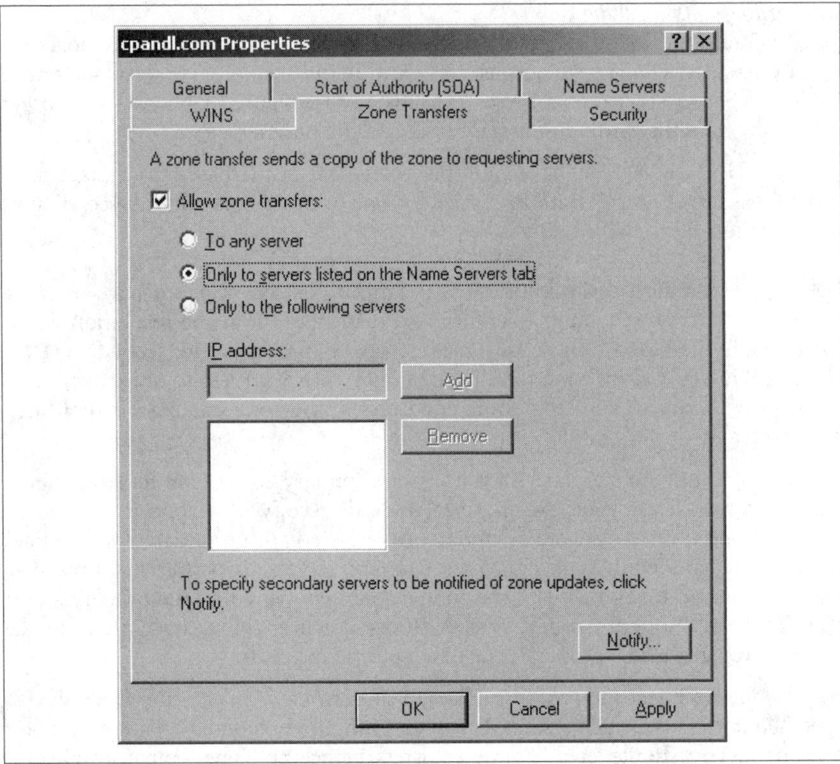

Figure 8-8. Limit zone transfers to enhance security.

Directory. The default replication technique is to replicate DNS zone data to all other domain controllers acting as DNS servers in the Active Directory domain where the primary server is located.

You can modify zone data replication in several ways. You can:

Replicate to all other domain controllers acting as DNS servers in the Active Directory forest, which replicates the data. This option replicates zone data throughout the enterprise. Any domain controller acting as a DNS server in the Active Directory forest in which the primary DNS server is located will get the zone data.

Replication to all other domain controllers in the Active Directory domain. This option replicates zone data to all domain controllers in the Active Directory domain in which the primary DNS server is located. Any domain controller, regardless of whether it is also configured as a NS server, gets the zone data.

You can configure Active Directory replication of zone data using the General tab of the zone's properties dialog box (see Figure 8-9). Click the Replication: Change... button.

Like file-based zones, Active Directory–integrated zones are replicated completely and incrementally. Typically, complete replication occurs when you first

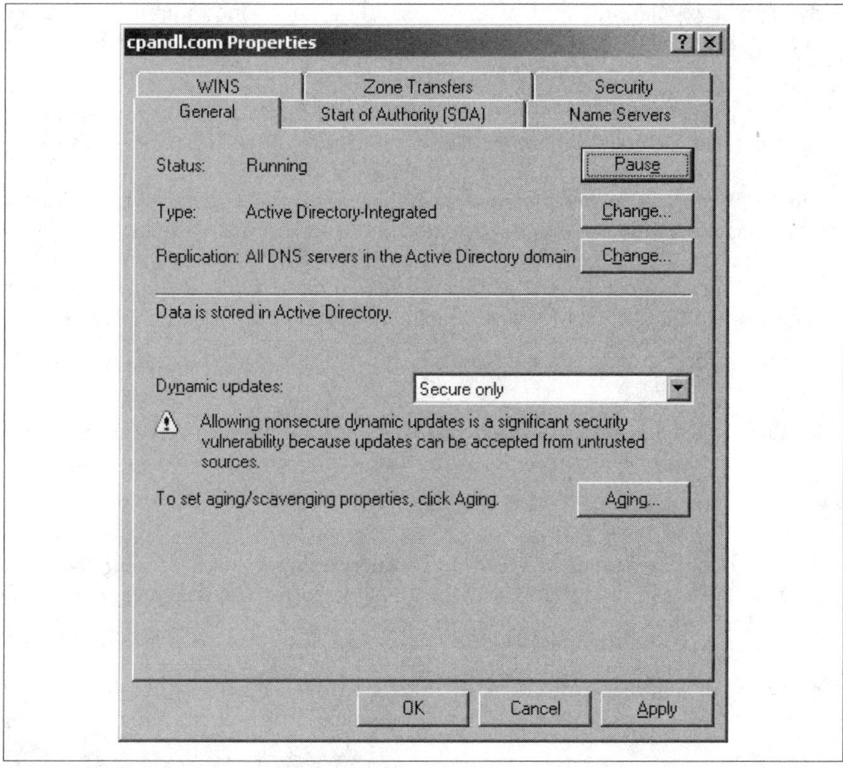

Figure 8-9. Configure replication for Active Directory–integrated zones using the replication options.

configure an Active Directory–integrated zone, and incremental replication of zone changes are replicated thereafter. Because Active Directory–integrated zones are automatically replicated, configuring secondaries is not a prerequisite for replication. There is, in fact, no such thing as an Active Directory–integrated secondary zone. That said, however, you can create file-based secondary zones for Active Directory–integrated primary zones. Situations where you might want to do this are as follows:

- If no other domain controllers are running DNS in the Active Directory domain.
- If no other domain controllers are in the Active Directory domain.
- If no other DNS servers in the organization ar running Windows Server 2003.

Once you configure secondaries, you must also configure zone transfers for the secondaries.

Planning a forwarding configuration. Most DNS servers rely on forwarders. A forwarder is not to be confused with a forwarding-only (caching-only) DNS server. A *forwarder* is a DNS server that receives queries from other DNS servers. Use forwarders to regulate the flow of name resolution traffic and to limit the number of servers that transfer name resolution queries outside the internal network.

In the default configuration of a Windows Server 2003 DNS server, a DNS server can forward queries to DNS servers in all other DNS domains and thereby allow all internal name servers to forward queries outside the local network. As this may not be the desired configuration, you'll typically want to use specifically designated forwarders, which forward queries inside or outside the organization's network as necessary. This configuration serves to control the flow of DNS queries and funnel queries through specifically designated name servers. As the designated forwarders also cache lookups, many lookups can be resolved without having to look outside the network, which reduces the flow of network traffic.

When forwarders are used, the DNS query resolution process changes as depicted here:

1. When a DNS server receives a query, it first attempts to resolve the query using its local zone information or its local cache.
2. If the query cannot be resolved, the DNS server forwards the request to the designated forwarder.
3. The forwarder attempts to resolve the query using its local zone information or its local cache. If the forwarder is unable to resolve the query, the DNS server attempts to contact the appropriate name server (as specified in its root hints data).
4. When an answer is returned to the forwarder, the forwarder returns the response to the originating DNS server, which in turn passes the response on to the client.

There are several forwarder variations that are used, including chaining forwarders and conditional forwarders. When you chain forwarders, you configure a DNS server acting as a forwarder so that it can also forward queries to another forwarder. As an example, you might configure DNS servers at remote offices to forward queries to DNS servers at the central office, and then have the central office DNS servers forward queries to the Internet through the enterprise firewalls.

Queries can also be forwarded conditionally, based on the domain name specified in the name resolution request. Conditional forwarding can allow direct forwarding of requests to an authoritative server for a domain rather than using recursive querying. In some cases, conditional forwarding can reduce network traffic for name resolution and eliminate the need for name servers to query the root name server to determine the authoritative servers for a particular domain. However, conditional forwarding typically requires more time and resources to maintain as you need to configure all DNS severs with the forwarder addresses for all the domains in the namespace and maintain those addresses as the network configuration changes.

Conditional forwarding is a new feature of Windows Server 2003. To help you prepare for the exam, you need hands on practice and should implement conditional forwarding in several different configurations.

With Windows Server 2003, DNS servers require no special configuration to act as forwarders. However, other DNS servers must be explicitly configured to send queries to the forwarder. To configure a DNS server to use a forwarder, follow these steps:

1. Open the DNS Management console.
2. Right-click the DNS Server entry, and then click Properties.
3. Click the Forwarders tab. Under DNS Domain, the entry All Other DNS Domains is used to configure forwarding for all domains other than domains serviced by zone files on the name server.
   - To limit forwarding to all other domains and specify a designated forwarder, click All Other DNS Domains, enter the IP address of the forwarder, and then click Add.
   - To configure conditional forwarding for a specific domain, click New, type a domain name, and then click OK. Under DNS Domain, click the related domain entry, enter the IP address of the forwarder, and then click Add.
4. Click OK.

To configure your designated forwarders, simply allow the forwarder query all other DNS domains and do not designate the IP address of any specific name servers to use. With this in mind, the typical configuration is achieved by completing these steps:

1. Open the DNS Management console.
2. Right-click the DNS Server entry, and then click Properties.
3. Click the Forwarders tab.
4. Under DNS Domain, click the All Other DNS Domains entry and remove any associated IP addresses.
5. Under DNS Domain, click any other entries, each in turn, and then click Remove.
6. Click OK.

Planning for DNS security. In the standard configuration of DNS and DHCP, DHCP clients running Windows 2000 or later update their host (A) records in DNS automatically whenever an IP address is assigned or renewed, and DHCP servers update the PTR records on behalf of clients. Dynamic updates can only occur when the client computer is configured with a domain suffix that matches a zone name hosted by the preferred DNS server. Thus, for a computer named Workstation93 to be dynamically updated in the *hr.williamstanek.com* zone, the FDQN of the computer must be *Workstation93.hr.williamstanek.com*.

In the DHCP console, you can control the way dynamic DNS updating works through the properties of the DHCP server. Right-click the DHCP server entry, and then select Properties. The options on the DNS tab determine how dynamic DNS updating works with DHCP. When clients register their own A records, they do not use a secure method to create and update records. This allows any client or server, with appropriate credentials, to modify or delete the records. On the other hand, if a DHCP server dynamically updates A and PTR records on behalf of clients, the server uses secure dynamic updates.

DNS records created using secure dynamic updates can only be updated by the server that created the record (the record owner). While this improves security, this can lead to stale (old) records on the DNS server if the DHCP server that owns a record fails and a client is later assigned a lease from a second DHCP server, as shown in the following scenario:

1. DHCP Server 1 performs a secure dynamic update of the A and PTR records for a client.
2. DHCP Server 1 is the owner of those records.
3. If DHCP Server 1 fails, neither the client nor DHCP Server 2 will able to update the previously created records.

When DHCP servers update both the A and PTR records, you can prevent problems due to stale records by making your organization's DHCP servers members of the DnsUpdateProxy security group. Any objects created by members of this group do not have security settings and thus have no owners. This allows any DHCP server to modify the record. However, if the DHCP server is not a member of the DnsUpdateProxy group, the DHCP server becomes the owner, and no other DHCP servers can modify the record.

The DnsUpdateProxy group should not be used in configurations where clients update A records and DHCP servers update PTR records. In most cases, domain controllers should not be configured as DHCP servers. If DCs are configured as DHCP servers and those servers are members of the DnsUpdateProxy group, records created by the Netlogon service for the DC are not secure.

In DNS, each zone has settings for dynamic updates. Configure these options on the General tab of the zone's properties dialog box. The Dynamic Updates selection list has three options:

Secure Only
: Secure DNS updates can be made. If you choose this option, you should configure DHCP so your DHCP servers update DNS records on behalf of clients.

Nonsecure and secure
: Clients can make nonsecure updates of their DNS records and DHCP servers can make secure updates of DNS records on behalf of clients.

None
: Dynamic updates are disabled. Neither clients or DHCP servers will be allowed to dynamically update DNS records.

The most secure configuration is to use the Secure Only option, which is only available with Active Directory–integrated zones. DNS is vulnerable to many other types of security threats, including denial-of-service attacks, IP spoofing, and redirecting. To help secure DNS from outside threats, you can:

Configure redundant DNS servers
: Multiple DNS servers provide fault tolerance and protection for name resolution. To ensure your internal name resolution functions properly in case one or more DNS servers fail, you should configure both primary and secondary DNS servers or configure multiple Active Directory–integrated primary servers. You may also want to place redundant DNS servers on multiple subnets or on multiple sites.

Small to medium organizations may want to configure DNS clients to use their ISP's DNS servers as alternates. This ensures that external name resolution works if internal name resolution fails. It also allows users to continue to access Internet resources if internal name resolution fails.

Limiting zone transfers
: If zone transfers are allowed, zone transfers should be limited to a specific list of name servers or to the servers listed on the Name Servers tab. This improves security for DNS by restricting the servers that have access to zone data. If you do not limit zone transfers, any DNS server can request a complete copy of your zone data. When zone transfers are allowed, you can configure zone transfers using the Zone Transfers tab of the zone's properties dialog box. Select the Only To Servers Listed On The Name Servers tab or Only To The Following Servers radio buttons to restrict zone transfer requests.

Limiting DNS interface access
: By default, DNS servers listen for DNS requests on all IP addresses for which they are configured. To prevent possible unauthorized access to DNS data, you can specify that the DNS server should listen only to selected IP addresses. On the Interfaces tab of the DNS server's properties dialog box, select the Only The Following IP Addresses radio button, and then specify the IP addresses to listen on.

Preventing cache corruption
: By default, the Secure Cache Against Pollution option is selected on the Advanced tab of the DNS server's properties dialog box. This option ensures that attackers cannot load the DNS server's name cache with incorrect data in an effort to redirect clients DNS queries and gather information about the internal network.

Table 8-14 provides a summary of the types of attacks that can be prevented using a particular configuration option.

Table 8-14. Types of attacks prevented using Secure DNS configurations

Secure DNS configuration	Type of attack prevented
Configure redundant DNS servers	Secures against denial-of-service attacks and other types of intrusion
Limiting zone transfers	Secures against footprinting and unauthorized access to DNS information
Limiting DNS interface access	Secures against IP spoofing and unauthorized access from the Internet
Preventing cache corruption	Secures against redirection and loading cache with incorrect information

Examining the interoperability of DNS with third-party DNS solutions. The DNS server included with Windows Server 2003 is compliant with most of the RFCs used to define the DNS protocol, including RFC 1034 and RFC 1035. This compliancy ensures that Windows Server 2003 DNS servers can be used with third-party DNS servers.

The DNS server included with Windows Server 2003 can be used with third-party DNS solutions in several ways:

- Windows Server 2003 DNS servers can act as primaries for secondary DNS servers using third-party solutions.
- Windows Server 2003 DNS servers can act as secondaries for primary DNS servers using third-party solutions.

In either configuration, you'll need to configure zone transfers between the primary and secondary servers. Using zone transfers, Active Directory–integrated primaries running on Windows Server 2003 DNS servers can replicate data to third-party DNS servers acting as secondaries.

Windows Server 2003 DNS servers provide basic support for the DNS Security Extensions (DNSSEC) protocol. This support ensures that Windows Server 2003 DNS servers can act as secondary DNS servers for existing DNSSEC-compliant zones.

While Windows Server 2003 DNS servers support the use of Unicode characters in UTF-8 format, this is not the standard character set used by RFC 1123–compliant DNS servers. RFC 1123, which specifies the requirements for Internet hosts, applications, and support, limits DNS names to uppercase characters (A–Z), lowercase characters (a–z), numerals (0–9), and hyphens (-). To ensure RFC 1123 compliance, you can modify the Name Checking server option on the Advanced tab of the DNS server's properties dialog box. As shown in Figure 8-10, set Name Checking to Strict RFC (ANSI) to ensure RFC 1123 compliance.

Planning a NetBIOS name resolution strategy

NetBIOS computer names are used for backward compatibility with pre-Windows 2000 computers. On networks with computers running Windows 2000 or later, WINS is primarily used to allow pre-Windows 2000 systems to browse lists of resources on the network and to allow Windows 2000, Windows XP, and Windows Server 2003 systems to locate NetBIOS resources.

Planning NetBIOS name resolution by using the LMHOSTS file. By default, computers that use NetBIOS for name resolution use broadcast messages to resolve computer names on the local subnet to IP addresses and, in this way, locate computers. Because broadcast transmissions are not routed, they are suitable for small networks with a single subnet only. For all other networks, you'll need a better solution, which is provided in the form of LMHOSTS files and WINS servers.

LMHOSTS is a text file that can be created with any standard text editor, and then stored in the *%SystemRoot%\System32\Drivers\Etc* folder of the Windows computer. Like the LMHOSTS file itself, entries in the LMHOSTS file must be manually created. A basic entry consists of an IP address followed by at least one space and the NetBIOS name associated with that IP address. Each entry must be on a separate line, and comments can be inserted using a pound (#) symbol. Everything on the line after the pound symbol is ignored. The following sample LMHOSTS file provides three commented entries:

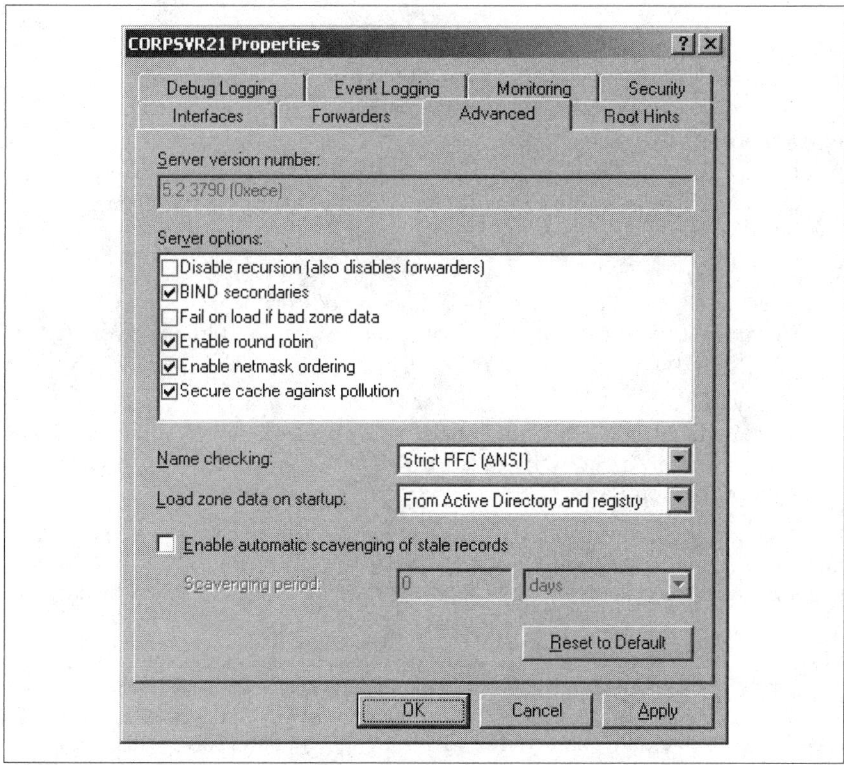

Figure 8-10. Control RFC 1123 compliance using the Name Checking selection list.

```
192.168.10.11    FileServer18     #Primary File Server
192.168.10.18    PrintServer18    #Primary Print Server
192.168.10.23    MailServer12     #Primary Mail Server
```

Because LMHOSTS files must be manually configured on each computer that needs NetBIOS for name resolution, they aren't practical for use on medium to large networks. To provide NetBIOS name resolution for medium to large networks, Windows Server 2003 includes the Windows Internet Name Service (WINS) Server service, which can be used to resolve NetBIOS names to IP addresses and vice versa.

Planning a WINS replication strategy. Enable WINS name resolution on a network by configuring WINS clients and servers. To configure WINS clients, install WINS servers and configure the clients with the IP addresses of the WINS servers. Using the WINS server IP addresses, clients can communicate with WINS servers anywhere on the network, even if the servers are on different subnets.

WINS servers require no configuration to register and resolve names. Name registration is automatic with WINS. When a WINS client starts, it transmits its NetBIOS name using the configured name resolution method. Four name resolution methods are available:

B-node (broadcast)
: Clients use broadcast messages to resolve computer names to IP addresses. When a client needs to resolve a computer name to an IP address, the client sends a broadcast message on the local subnet.

P-node (peer-to-peer)
: Clients use WINS servers to resolve computer names to IP addresses. When a client needs to resolve a computer name to an IP address, the client queries a WINS server.

M-node (mixed)
: This mode combines the b-node and p-node name resolution methods. Clients first try to use broadcasts for name resolution. If this fails, they query a WINS server.

H-node (hybrid)
: This mode is a variant of the b-node and p-node name resolution methods. Clients first query a WINS server. If this fails, they try to use broadcasts for name resolution.

If WINS servers are available on the network, Windows clients use the p-node method for name resolution by default. If no WINS servers are available on the network, Windows clients use the b-node method for name resolution by default.

When client computers are dynamically configured using DHCP, you can set the name resolution method using the DHCP option for the 046 WINS/NBT Node Type. For optimal performance, you'll typically want WINS clients to use h-node. This method also reduces broadcast traffic on the network.

When WINS clients communicate with WINS servers, they establish sessions by attempting to register their computer name and IP address in the WINS database. If the computer name and IP address aren't already in use, the WINS server accepts the request and registers the client in the WINS database. The client then has use of the name for a specified lease period and must reregister the name with the WINS server during the renewal interval. If the client can't or doesn't renew the lease, the WINS server releases the name and IP address, allowing another system on the network to use the computer name or IP address. WINS clients automatically release their names when they are shut down.

While a single WINS server can provide services for thousands of clients, you'll want to have multiple WINS servers on the network to provide fault tolerance and load balancing. When you use multiple WINS servers to provide name resolution services for the same clients, you need to configure replication so that name registration entries in one server's WINS database are replicated to other WINS servers.

WINS servers can replicate their databases using push partners, pull partners, or both. A *push partner* is a WINS server that notifies other WINS servers of changes on the network. A *pull partner* is a WINS server that requests replicas from a push partner. When a push partner notifies a pull partner regarding changes to the WINS database, the pull partner responds by requesting an update, and then the push partner sends the changes. You can configure any WINS server as a push partner, a pull partner, or both (see Figure 8-11).

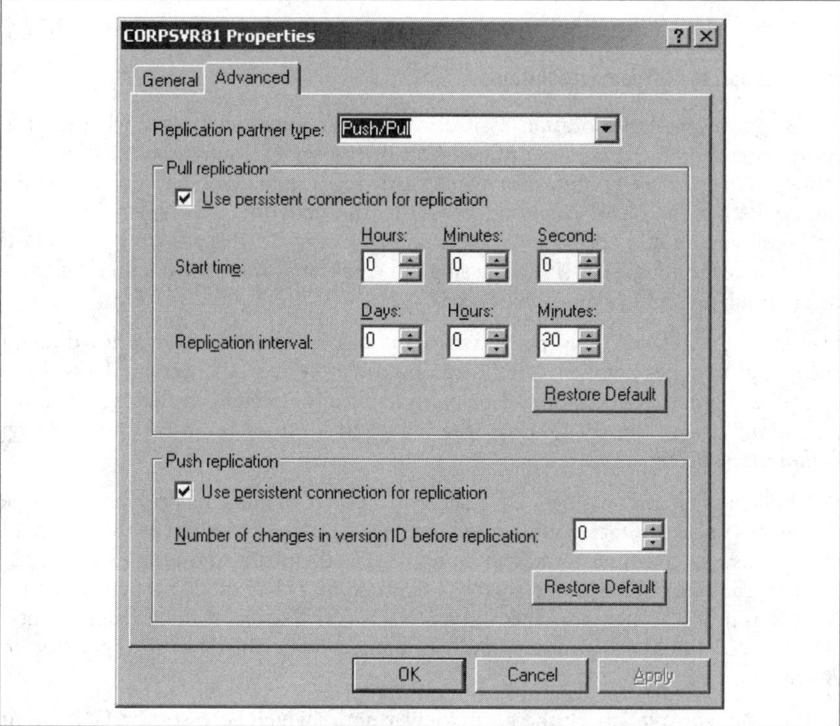

Figure 8-11. When you configure replication partner properties, you can set the replication partner type.

Pull partners pull database entries from their replication partners at a specific interval, known as the *replication interval*. By default, the replication interval for pull replication is every 30 minutes after the pull partner is started.

Push partners use the version ID on the WINS database to determine when to notify replication partners of changes. The version ID is incremented each time a change is made, and replication partners can be notified after a specific number of changes have been made. However, by default, the Number Of Changes In Version ID Before Replication option is set to zero, which specifies that no push triggers are sent to replication partners.

When WINS servers provide services for the same clients, you'll usually want the servers to be push and pull partners with each other. Because of this, the default replication partner type is push/pull, meaning both push and pull replication are to be used. Why is this important? Consider the following example: You have two WINS servers. You make each WINS server the push and pull partner of the other. This configuration ensures changes to the first server's database are replicated to the second, and changes to the second server's database are replicated to the first.

For increased replication reliability, you can configure persistent connections between replication partners. Persistent connections between replication partners are always open even when no data is being transmitted, and help to ensure quick and efficient communications.

Troubleshooting hostname resolution

To diagnose name resolution issues, you must first determine whether the problem is due to the client configuration or the server configuration. If a client reports a Name Not Found error when resolving a name, you should first determine whether the client has connectivity to the network. If connectivity isn't a problem, you should check the client's configuration. As discussed in the section of "Troubleshooting TCP/IP Addressing" in Chapter 5, there are a variety of troubleshooting techniques that can be used.

Dynamic updates can only occur when the client is configured with a domain suffix that matches a zone name hosted by the preferred DNS server. Thus, for a computer named Workstation18 to be dynamically updated in the *eng.williamstanek.com* zone, the FDQN of the computer must be *Workstation18.eng.williamstanek.com*.

If the client is unable to ping a DNS server or resolve names, the problem could be on the DNS server. Once you've ruled out the client configuration as the source of the problem, you can try to diagnose and resolve the problem on the name server. Start by making sure that the server is running and that the DNS Server service itself is running. When you check the DNS Server Service in the Services utility, the service should be running and configured with the Startup Type set to Automatic.

In the DNS console, check the event viewer node, which accesses the DNS event logs, for errors that may indicate a problem with the DNS server or its configuration. If the DNS server gets its TCP/IP configuration from a DHCP server, you should confirm that the DHCP server has a properly configured reservation for the DNS server. A reservation is required to ensure that the DNS server always uses the same IP address.

In some cases, name resolution may be working properly, but the DNS server may be providing incorrect data. Problems can occur if resources records are configured incorrectly, if dynamic updates fail, or if zone transfers fail. To resolve this problem, check the resource record for the resource the client is trying to reach. If the record was manually corrected, check the record for typos or invalid settings. If the record was dynamically created, check the dynamic DNS update configuration of DHCP and DNS. If the DNS server is incorrectly resolving names from a secondary zone, check the zone transfer configuration.

You can log detailed debugging information by enabling Debug Logging in the DNS server's properties dialog box. As Figure 8-12 shows, you enable Debug Logging on the Debug Logging tab. Select Log Packets For Debugging, and then configure the logging options.

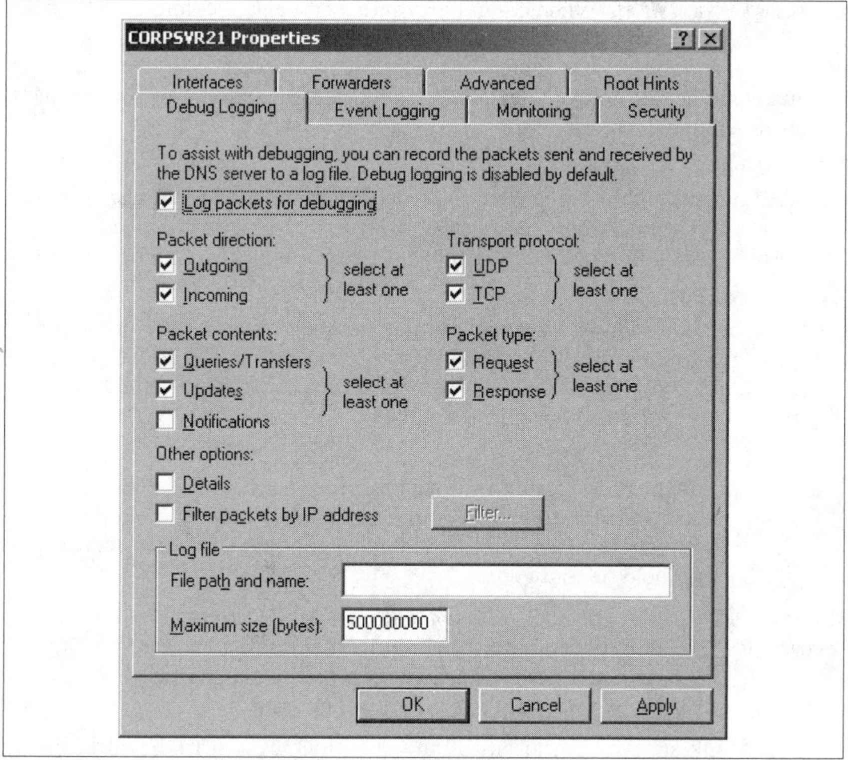

Figure 8-12. Enable Debug Logging to log details information for troubleshooting DNS.

Planning, Implementing, and Maintaining Routing and Remote Access

In Windows Server 2003, the Routing And Remote Access service (RRAS) allows a server to be configured as a multipurpose remote access server and as an IP router. As a remote access server, a Windows server can connect clients to the internal network whether they use broadband, dial-up, or VPN. As an IP router, use a Windows server to connect LANs, wide area networks (WANs), and VPNs.

Planning a Routing Strategy

Both hardware and software routers can be used to connect your organization's LANs and WANs. There are advantages and disadvantages to both hardware and software routers. Hardware routers tend to be more expensive than software routers and more complex to configure. Software routers typically are easier to configure and less expensive than hardware routers, but may not be as reliable as hardware routers. Beyond issues of cost, configurability, and reliability, the RRAS provides the same routing services as most hardware routers.

Connecting LANs and WANs. When planning a routing strategy, the difference between a LAN connection and a WAN connection is important. Most local area networks have multiple subnets over which local hosts communicate. To allow hosts to communicate across network segments, you'll need some type of routing technology. RRAS includes:

DHCP Relay Agent routing protocol
: This protocol allows the server to route DHCP broadcast messages between subnets. The maximum number of DHCP relays agents that can handle DHCP relayed traffic is 4, by default. The maximum allowed value is 16.

RIP version 2 for Internet Protocol
: This protocol allows dynamic routing between subnets. RIP is an easily managed routing protocol, but limited to a maximum hop count of 15. For successful communications, source and destination computers can have no more than 15 routing devices between them.

OSPF
: This protocol allows extended dynamic routing between subnets. With OSPF, source and destination computers can have more than 15 routing devices between them. For successful implementation, both transit areas and neighbors should be configured.

RIP is a distance vector routing protocol and uses only the number of hops for its metrics. RIP can only use broadcast or multicast transmissions for communication with other routers, both of which generate more traffic than unicast transmissions. RIP requires little planning or configuration.

OSPF is a link state routing protocol and computes its metrics based on many conditions, including network speed and congestion. OSPF can only use unicast transmissions to communicate with other routers. OSPF requires significant planning and configuration.

Neither RIP nor OSPF facilitates multicasting. Internet Group Management Protocol (IGMP) is the routing protocol that makes multicasting possible.

When these routing technologies are implemented on a LAN, you'll typically use a single LAN router to connect two subnets. This router connects the subnets by having a configured routing interface for each subnet being connected.

In contrast to tightly connected local area networks, wide area networks typically are connected over long distances. WAN connections are used to connect multiple networks at separate physical locations into a single large internetwork. With WAN connections, install a WAN router at each site and connect the routers using a WAN link. You can build in redundancy and fault tolerance using additional, redundant WAN connections.

The same routing technologies that are used on LANs can be used on WANs. It is important, however, to keep in mind the relay/routing limitations that are applicable. Common WAN configurations for multiple connections are:

- Ring topology where all sites are connected one to another in a ring and each site has two possible routes to another site. For example, if Sites 1, 2, 3, 4, 5, and 6 are in a ring, Site 1 could reach Site 3 through Site 2 or through Sites 4 and 5.
- Mesh topology where every site is connected to every other site. For example, if Sites 1, 2, 3, 4, 5, and 6 are in a mesh, each site has a direct connection to each other site and has alternate routes to a site through any of the other sites.
- Star topology where a central site is connected to remote sites. For example, the main site, Site 1, has separate connections to Sites 2, 3, 4, 5, and 6. Because the remote sites are not connected to each other, failure of the direct connection to the main site means the remote site cannot reach any other site.

When WAN connections are provided over leased lines, the connections are private and VPN technology is not need. On the other hand, if WANs are connected over the public Internet, VPN technology must be used to secure the connections.

Identifying routing protocols to use in a specified environment

To route traffic between subnets or over WAN connections, routers must be configured with the appropriate routing entries. Routers can use static or dynamic routing. With static routing, administrators must manually create routing entries and maintain those entries if the network topology changes. With dynamic routing, the router itself creates entries automatically and updates the entries as appropriate.

Whether you use static or dynamic routing will depend on your routing strategy. You must consider the number of networks, routers, and sites that are in the enterprise and determine how best to configure routing. Dynamic routing eliminates the need for administrators to create and maintain routing entries, providing an efficient and automated solution. Static routing requires administrators to create and maintain routing entries.

Static routing entries can be created and managed using either the Routing And Remote Access console or the `route` commands. Before you work with static routes at a command prompt, you should print the currently configured static routes by entering `route print`. The output of `route print` shows current interfaces, static routes, and persistent routes.

You can create static routes using the `route add` command. The syntax of the `route add` command follows:

```
route add DestinationNetworkID mask NetworkMask Gateway metric MetricCost if
    Interface
```

such as:

```
route add 192.168.11.0 mask 255.255.255.0 192.168.10.1 metric 1 if 0x10003
```

The metric and interface are optional. If you do not specify them, they are selected automatically. To make a static route persistent, you can use `route add -p`. Persistent static routes are not deleted even if the router is stopped and restarted.

Exam 70-293 Study Guide

To change a static route, you can use the route change command. The syntax of the route change command follows:

```
route change DestinationNetworkID mask NetworkMask Gateway metric MetricCost
    if Interface
```

such as:

```
route change 192.168.15.0 mask 255.255.255.0 192.168.42.1 metric 1 if
    0x10003
```

At a command prompt can delete a static route using route delete. The syntax is:

```
route delete DestinationNetworkID
```

For example:

```
route delete 192.168.11.0
```

The RIP and OSPF routing protocols use dynamic routing. When an RIP router is initially configured, the only entries in its routing tables are for the networks to which it is physically connected. The router then starts sending announcements of its availability to other routers of the networks it services. Responses from announcements allow the router to update its routing tables.

RIP announcements can be made depends using one of two operating modes:

Periodic update mode
: RIP announcements are sent periodically to learn of available routes and routes are deleted automatically when the router is stopped and restarted

Auto-static update mode
: RIP announcements are sent when other routers request updates, learned routes are added as static, and routes remain until they are manually deleted.

When changes occur to the network topology, RIP version 2 uses triggered updates to communicate the changes to other routers. To configure the version of RIP to use, you can set the Outgoing Packet Protocol and Incoming Packet Protocol on the General tab of the RIP connection's properties dialog box (see Figure 8-13).

When using RIP version 2, you can improve security by enabling authentication for your routers. On the General tab, select the Activate Authentication checkbox and enter a password in the password field. Once you enable authentication, all routers using RIP version 2 must be configured in this same way with the same password so that the routers can update each other. Otherwise, route updates fail.

On the Security tab of the RIP connection's properties dialog box (see Figure 8-14), you can configure filters to add additional security. You can set separate filter actions for incoming routes and outgoing routers. For incoming routes, you can configure filters to accept all routes, accept all routes in the ranges listed, or ignore all routes in the ranges listed. For outgoing routes, you can configure filters to announce all routes, announce all routes in the ranges listed, or not announce all routes in the ranges listed.

OSPF is a link-state protocol that uses the Shortest Path First (SPF) algorithm to calculate routes. The route with the lowest route cost is the shortest path, and the

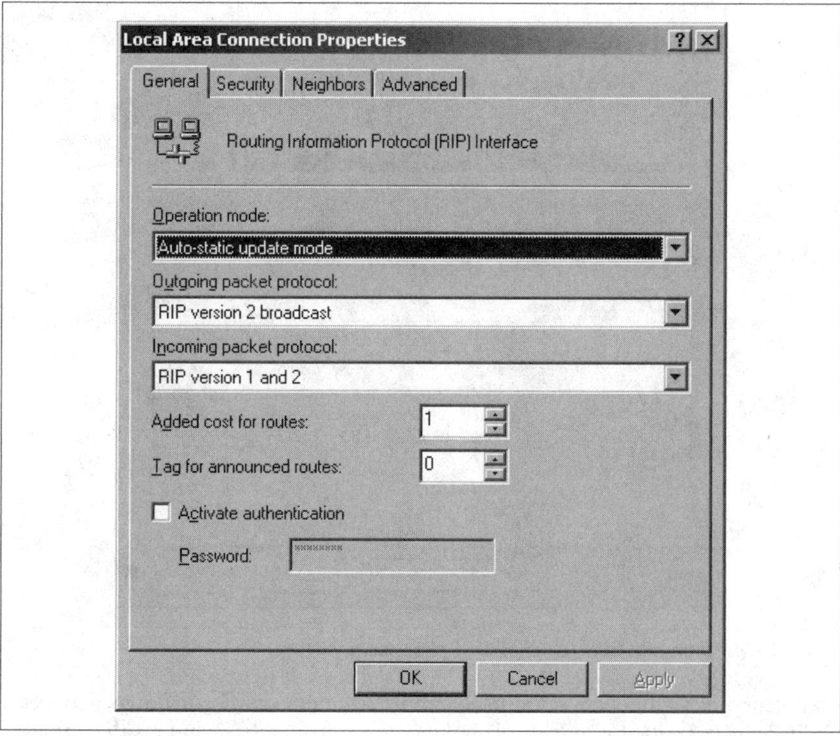

Figure 8-13. Set the RIP version for outgoing and incoming packets.

shortest path is always used first when routing. An OSPF router maintains a link-state database that it uses to track the network topology. The database is synchronized with adjacent routers or specifically defined nonbroadcast multiple access (NBMA) neighbors.

When a change is made to the network topology, the first OSPF router to identify the change sends out a change notification. This change notification is used to update the link-state database so that the routing tables can be recalculated automatically. OSPF routers divide the network into areas of responsibility called *transit areas*, and maintain link-state information only for those transit areas for which they've been configured.

Dynamic routers, such as RIP and OSPF routers, exchange information about their networks with other routers using the same dynamic routing protocols. Typically, you'll want to use RIP version 2 over RIP version 1. RIP version 1 uses broadcasts for announcements and doesn't allow for authentication. RIP version 2 uses multicast for its announcements and does allow authentication to be used. RIP version 2 is best used on medium-sized networks with 50 or less routers, and the maximum number of hops that any IP packet must be transferred over is less than 16.

On larger networks or networks with redundant paths, OSPF is a better choice than RIP. OSPF is ideally suited to networks with 50 or more routers. Where RIP

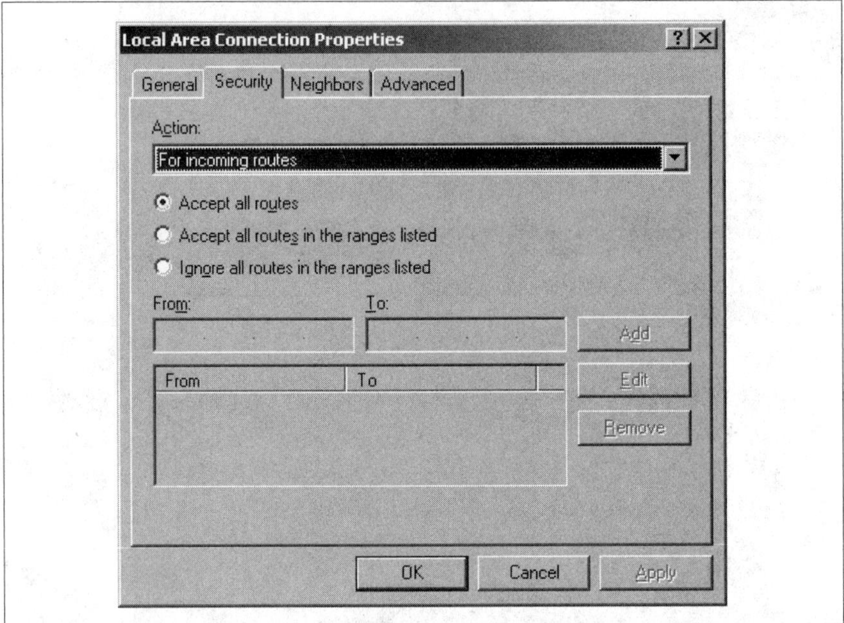

Figure 8-14. Configure filters to improve RIP security.

may generate significant amounts of announcement traffic on large networks, OSPF reduces traffic by synchronizing updates to its database and routing tables.

Planning routing for IP multicast traffic

With TCP/IP, host computers can be configured to use broadcast, unicast, and multicast message transmission. Broadcast messages are used by all computers configured to use TCP/IP. A broadcast message, as the name implies, is broadcast to every host on the network. Because broadcasts are indiscriminant and reach every system whether it is the intended recipient or not, broadcasts are limited by default to the local subnet on which the source computer is located.

With TCP version 4, Class A, B, and C IP addresses use unicast transmissions in which each computer has a separate IP address. Unicast transmissions involve only two systems: a source and a destination. To use unicast to send the same message to multiple systems, the source computer must send the message multiple times—once to each recipient.

With TCP version 4, Class D IP addresses use multicast transmissions in which a group of computers known as the host group have a single destination IP address. Because multicast transmissions identify an entire group of systems, a single source computer can send a single message to multiple recipients.

Members of the host group can be located on any LAN on the network. They can even be located in different remote locations connected via the organization's WAN. However, for the message to be transmitted across LAN and WAN connections, the routers on the network must know which hosts are members of the group. This allows the messages to be forwarded.

Computers that are members of a multicast host group must register themselves with the network routers using the Internet Group Management Protocol (IGMP). All members of the group and all routers providing access to the members of the group must support IGMP.

All Windows computers that use TCP/IP support IGMP. RRAS servers can be configured with the IGMP routing protocol.

Routers support IGMP in several ways. First, you must be able to configure the router to use the IGMP routing protocol, and then specify the routing interfaces on which IGMP traffic can be received. The interface used must support a special mode called *multicast promiscuous mode*. While most network interface adapters support this mode, you should verify that a hardware router's network interface adapters do.

To support large-scale multicasting, the router must also be able to share host group membership information with other routers. This means the router must implement a distributed multicast routing protocol, such as Distance Vector Multicast Routing Protocol (DVMRP). The RRAS does not support distributed multicast routing protocols, but can use a third-party version of one of these protocols.

Planning Security for Remote Access Users

Using RRAS, you can configure remote access so that individual users at remote locations can access the organization's network. Remote access can be used in this way for dial-up, broadband, and wireless connections from remote clients. All three types of remote access connections can use VPN as well to enhance security.

Analyzing protocol security requirements

Before you configure remote access for remote clients, you should determine how remote access security should be configured to best safeguard the internal network from attack and ensure that organizational security policies and requirements are met. You should start by determining:

- Who needs remote access
- What level of access each user requires
- What applications, if any, users need to run

One of the ways you can secure remote access is to configure the dial-in properties of the user's account. In Active Directory Users And Computers, you can configure dial-in properties for individual users. To set these for an individual user, right-click the account name, select Properties, and then click the Dial-in tab. As Figure 8-15 shows, you can set the dial-in properties thar are described next.

Remote Access Permission (Dial-in or VPN)
: Using the related options, you can allow or deny remote access to the selected user. You can also elect to control access through Remote Access Policy.

Verify Caller ID
: Using this option, you can set the user's telephone number, which can be verified prior to allowing remote access using Caller ID.

Callback Options
: Using the related options, you can configure whether callback is required to a specific number or can be set by the caller.

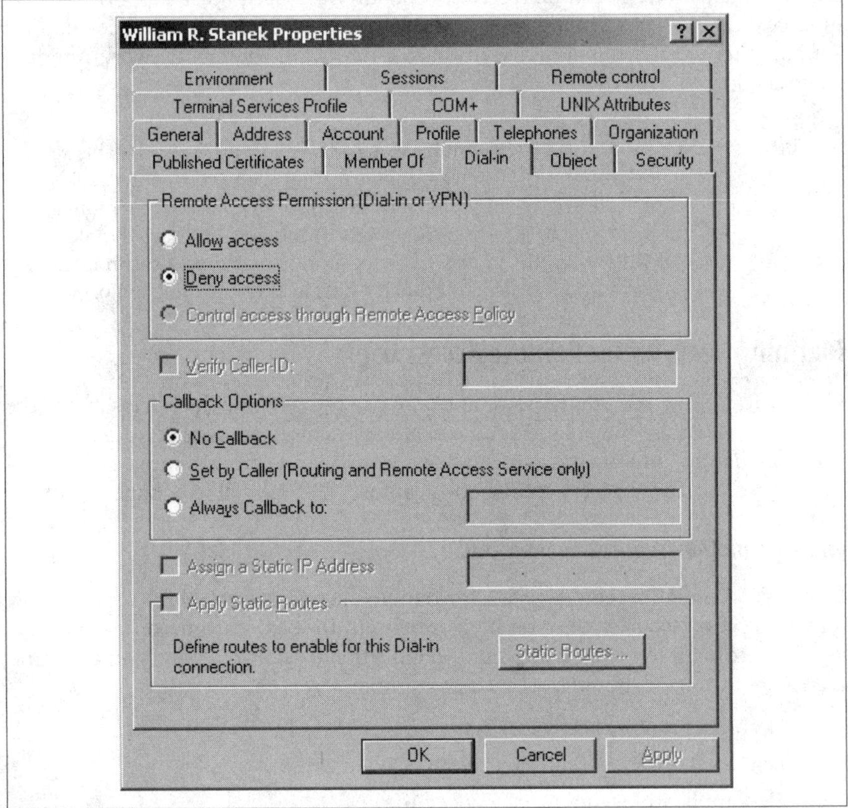

Figure 8-15. Configuring dial-in properties.

Planning authentication methods for remote access clients

RRAS enables administrators to configure Virtual Private Network (VPN) access for remote clients. With VPN connections, both Point-to-Point Tunneling Protocol (PPTP) and Layer 2 Tunneling Protocol (L2TP) are supported. By default, the appropriate protocol can be automatically selected when a connection is made. Because L2TP uses IPSec for advanced encryption, L2TP is more secure than PPTP.

RRAS supports Windows authentication and RADIUS authentication. Windows authentication is the default authentication method, and it allows you to use standard Windows security for authentication. RADIUS authentication can be used if your organization has Remote Authentication Dial-in User Service (RADIUS) servers. To configure authentication, right-click a server entry in the Routing And Remote Access console, select Properties, and then use the Authentication Provider selection list on the Security tab to configure the desired authentication method (see Figure 8-16).

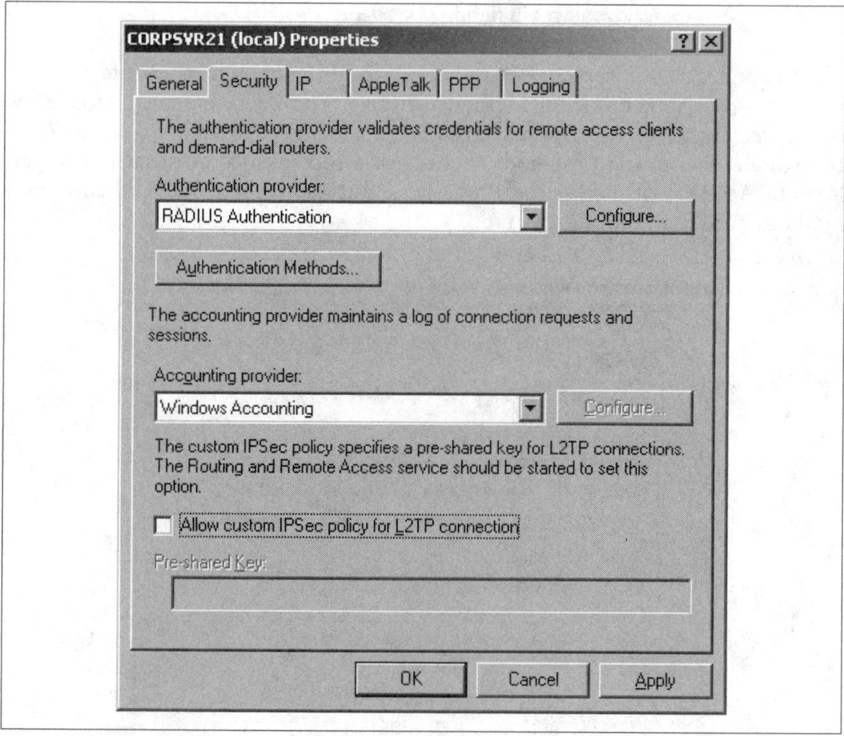

Figure 8-16. Set the desired authentication provider.

The Accounting Provider list lets you specify whether and how connection requests and sessions are logged. Windows Accounting logs connection requests and sessions in logfiles stored in the Remote Access Logging folder. RADIUS Accounting sends details about connection requests and sessions to the RADIUS server. The RADIUS server in turn logs this information.

RADIUS proxy and server support is a new feature in Windows Server 2003. You can install and use Microsoft Internet Authentication Service (IAS) to provide RADIUS proxy and server services. If you have multiple remote access servers, you can use RADIUS authentication and accounting to centralize the authentication and accounting. Do this by configuring the remote access servers to use RADIUS authentication and accounting, and then configuring a RADIUS server, such as an IAS server, to handle authentication and accounting. This allows remote access users to access any remote access server, and means you only have to maintain a single set of user accounts on the RADIUS server. When planning a remote access server deployment in a large network environment, keep these advantages in mind.

The method a RRAS server uses to authenticate remote access clients is determined by the Authentication Methods settings. You can view and manage the configured authentication methods using the dialog box shown in Figure 8-17. To configure authentication methods, right-click a server entry in the Routing And Remote Access console, select Properties, and then click the Authentication Methods button on the Security tab.

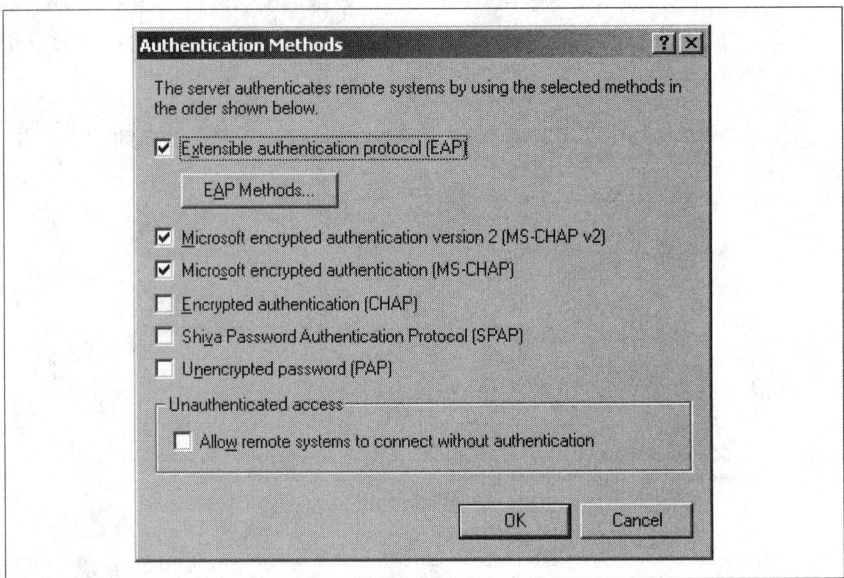

Figure 8-17. Managing RRAS authentication methods.

Table 8-15 summarizes the available user authentication methods. Before changing the settings, keep the following in mind:

- The authentication methods are used in the order shown and are essentially organized from the most secure to the least secure.

- To protect the network, remote users should be authenticated using the most secure method possible.
- To successfully establish a connection and authenticate a user, the RRAS server and the remote access client must have at least one common authentication method and one common encryption method configured.

Table 8-15. User authentication methods for RRAS

Authentication method	Authentication details	Authentication security
Extensible Authentication Protocol (EAP)	Extends the authentication methods for PPP connections to include the EAP methods configured through remote access policies. In a standard configuration, these policies allow MD5-Challenge, Protected EAP (PEAP), Smart card, or other PKI certificate to be used.	Allows use of nonpassword-based authentication. Required if you want to use smart cards with remote access clients or PKI certificates. No other authentication method used by RRAS supports smart cards or PKI certificates.
Microsoft Encrypted Authentication Version 2 (MS-CHAP v2)	Uses Microsoft Challenge Handshake Authentication Protocol (MS-CHAP) version 2 to authenticate remote access and demand-dial connections using mutual authentication and strong encryption. MS-CHAP v2 is required for encrypted PPP and PPTP connections.	Secure, encrypted, password-based authentication. Most secure encrypted password option for clients running Windows 98 or later.
Microsoft Encrypted Authentication (MS-CHAP)	Uses Microsoft Challenge Handshake Authentication Protocol (MS-CHAP) to authenticate remote access and demand-dial connections using encryption. MS-CHAP is required for encrypted PPP and PPTP connections.	Secure, encrypted, password-based authentication. Less secure than MS-CHAP v2. Supports Windows 95 and Windows NT 3.51 clients that can't use MS-CHAP v2.
Encrypted Authentication (CHAP)	Uses MD-5 Challenge Handshake Authentication Protocol (CHAP) to authenticate remote access and demand-dial connections using encryption.	Secure, reversible-encryption, password-based authentication. Supports non-Microsoft remote access clients. If required, you must specifically enable Store Passwords Using Reversible Encryption in Group Policy or user properties settings.
Shiva Password Authentication Protocol (SPAP)	Uses authentication with reversible encryption and is compatible with Shiva LAN Rover and Shiva clients.	Reversible-encryption password-based authentication. Designed for use with Shiva products. SPAP is not secure.
Unencrypted Password (PAP)	Uses Password Authentication Protocol (PAP) and sends passwords in plain-text during authentication.	Unsecured, unencrypted, password-based authentication. For clients that support no other authentication method. PAP is the most unsecure authentication method.
Allow Remote Systems To Connect Without Authentication	Allows unauthenticated remote access to the network.	Unsecured, unauthenticated access. Removes security requirements and not recommended.

When you've configured VPN and set L2TP as the protocol type, you can use IPSec with L2TP to enhance security. To do this, you must define a custom IPSec policy, and then configure L2TP security options. To configure L2TP security options, right-click a server entry in the Routing And Remote Access console, select Properties, and then click the Security tab. Select the Allow Custom IPSec Policy For L2TP Connection checkbox. In the Pre-Shared Key text box, type a preshared key to use with the custom IPSec policy. Each client computer that will remotely access the network over VPN and be subject to the IPSec policy must be configured with the same preshared key.

Planning remote access policies

After the RRAS server authenticates a remote user and verifies his identity, the server next attempts to authorize the user. Authorization determines whether the server should permit the user to connect, based on any conditions that may apply to when and how the user can remotely access the server.

Remote access policies are used to define specific conditions that users must meet before RRAS authorizes them to access the server or the network. You can:

- Create policies that limit access based on group membership, time of day, day of the week, and more.
- Specify through policies what authentication and encryption protocols must be used.
- Define different policies for different types of connections, such as dial-up, wireless, and VPN.

To view and manage remote access policies, select the Remote Access Policies node in the Routing And Remote Access console. Policies are reviewed in priority order, with the highest priority being 1. To create a policy, right-click the Remote Access Policies node, and then select New Remote Access Policy. The New Remote Access Policy Wizard, shown in Figure 8-18, walks you through the steps of creating the remote access policy and setting conditions.

When multiple policies are listed in the Remote Access Policies node as shown in Figure 8-19, you can control the order in which policies are reviewed for applicability by right-clicking a policy and using the Move Up or Move Down options as appropriate. The order of policies is important to determine how conditions are applied to a connection that has been authenticated but is not yet authorized.

Before RRAS can use remote access policies, the Control Access Through Remote Access Policy option must be set in the Dial-in tab of the user's properties dialog box. Use Active Directory Users And Computers to set this option. This option is not available in Windows 2000 Mixed Mode domains, in which the Allow Access setting is equivalent to the Control Access Through Remote Access Policy setting, when operating at the Windows Server 2003 domain functional level.

If a connection matches the conditions specified in a policy, the profile associated with the policy is applied to the connection. You can view and edit policy profiles by right-clicking the policy, and then clicking the Edit Profile button on the Settings tab. Using the Edit Dial-in Profile properties dialog box, shown in

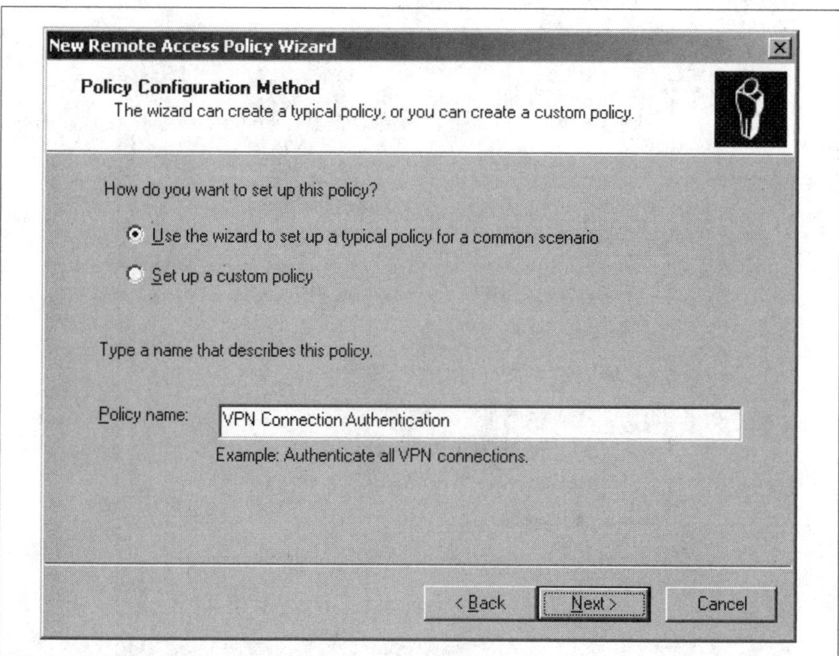

Figure 8-18. Use the New Remote Access Policy Wizard to define a remote access policy.

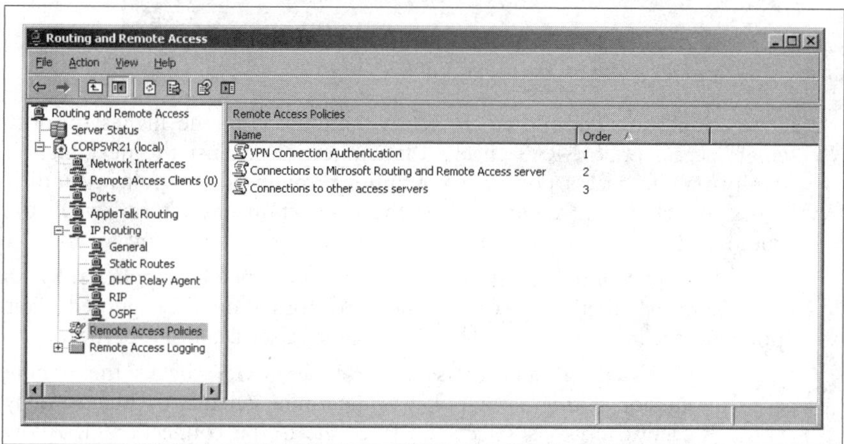

Figure 8-19. Listing remote access policies.

Figure 8-20, you can then set dial-in contracts, IP address assignment, authentication, encryption, and other options for the connection.

When remote access is controlled through policy, RRAS reviews policies using the following rules:

1. RRAS checks the connection against the highest priority remote access policy. If there are no policies listed, RRAS rejects the connection.

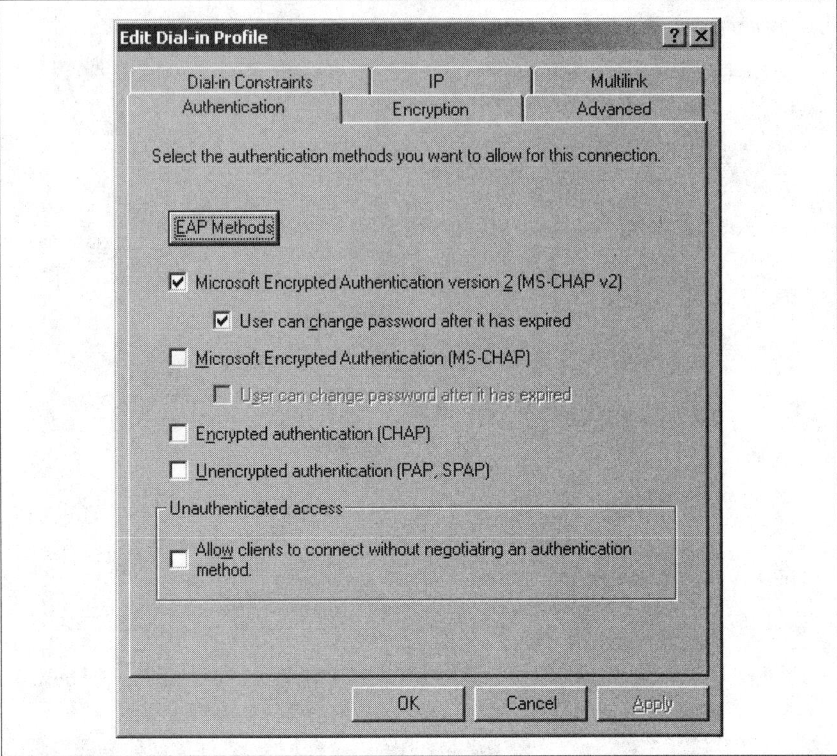

Figure 8-20. Setting options for the policy profile.

2. If the connection doesn't satisfy all the conditions in the highest priority remote access policy, RAS checks the connection against the next highest priority remote access policy. It continues through all the policies until it finds a match for all conditions. If the connection doesn't satisfy all the conditions in any one of the policies, RRAS rejects the connection.
3. When the connection satisfies all the conditions of one of the policies, RRAS next checks whether the user's dial-in properties should be ignored. This option is set using the advanced attribute Ignore-User-Dialin-Properties.
4. If Ignore-User-Dialin-Properties is set to True, RRAS checks the remote access permission setting of the policy to determine whether to grant or deny access. If Deny Access is selected, RRAS rejects the connection. If Allow Access is selected, RRAS matches the connection against the profile properties, accepting the connection if there is a match and rejecting the connection if there isn't.
5. If Ignore-User-Dialin-Properties is set to False, RRAS checks the user's dial-in properties to determine whether to grant or deny access. If Deny Access is selected, RRAS rejects the connection. If Allow Access is selected, RRAS matches the connection against the profile properties, accepting the connection if there is a match and rejecting the connection if there isn't.

Troubleshooting TCP/IP Routing

Exam 70-293 tests your ability to troubleshoot TCP/IP routing in the following areas:

- Diagnosing and resolving issues related to establishing a remote access dial-up connection, diagnosing and resolving issues related to remote access VPNs, and diagnosing and resolving issues related to resources beyond the remote access server, which were previously covered in Chapter 5 under "Troubleshooting User Access to Remote Access Services."
- Troubleshooting router-to-router VPNs and troubleshooting demand-dial routing, which were previously covered in Chapter 5 under "Troubleshooting Routing And Remote Access Routing."

Planning, Implementing, and Maintaining Server Availability

Every server deployment should be planned, implemented, and maintained with availability in mind. Availability refers to the server's ability to withstand hardware, application, or service outage. No server, application or service should be deployed in the enterprise without planning the deployment to meet a specific availability goal.

Availability goals will differ depending on how critical the server, application, or service is to the organization:

- Most noncritical systems, applications, or services have a moderate availability goal of 99 percent. This means the system, application, or service is expected to be available to users 99 percent of the time that it is needed. In a 24/7 environment with 365-days-a-year operations, this means the server can have about 88 hours of downtime a year, or about 100 minutes of downtime a week.
- Most critical systems, applications, or services have a high-availability goal of 99.9 percent. This means the system, application, or service is expected to be available to users 99.9 percent of the time that it is needed. In a 24/7 environment with 365-days-a-year operations, this means the server can have about 9 hours of downtime a year, or about 10 minutes of downtime a week.

As you can see, there's a huge difference in uptime expectations between 99 percent availability and 99.9 percent high availability. There's also a huge difference in planning, implementation, and maintenance. To meet a 99 percent availability goal, you'll need to:

- Identify the initial hardware requirements for memory, processors, disks, and networking.
- Plan a monitoring strategy that identifies potential and actual system bottlenecks.
- Plan a backup and recovery strategy that meets the availability goal in terms of recovery time.

To meet a 99.9 percent high-availability goal, you'll need to:

- Identify the initial hardware requirements for memory, processors, disks, and networking.
- Identify high-availability software solutions, such as network load balancing (NLB) or clustering, that can help you meet availability goals.
- Plan a monitoring strategy that identifies potential and actual system bottlenecks.
- Plan a backup and recovery strategy that meets the availability goal in terms of recovery time, and that also works with your chosen availability software solution.

Planning Network Traffic Monitoring and Identifying System Bottlenecks

As discussed in the exam overview, Exam 70-293 builds on the areas of study from the previous exams. With regard to server availability planning and server maintenance, you are expected to know how to monitor network traffic and identify system bottlenecks.

In "Monitoring Network Traffic" in Chapter 5, I discussed the key tools used for monitoring network traffic, including Task Manager's Networking tab, the Performance console's Network Interface performance object, and Network Monitor. As part of availability planning, you should determine current network traffic levels and how new servers and services added to the network could possibly impact network traffic levels. As part of long-term planning and maintaining server availability, you should routinely and periodically monitor network traffic.

In "Monitoring and Optimizing a Server Environment for Performance" in Chapter 2, I discussed how to use monitoring tools to identify system bottlenecks. Memory, processor, disk, and network bottlenecks can adversely affect system performance. As discussed in Chapter 2, the primary tool for detecting system bottlenecks is System Monitor. Use System Monitor to view real-time performance data or to log performance data for later review.

Planning Services for High Availability

Windows Server 2003 includes built-in functionality to support three high-availability software solutions:

Network Load Balancing (NLB)
: Provides high availability for IP-based applications and services, such as those running on a web or Internet application server.

Component Load Balancing (CLB)
: Provides high availability for COM+ application components.

Server clusters
: Provide high availability for business-critical applications and services.

Because component load balancing is primarily implemented by programmers, Exam 70-293 covers only network load balancing and server clusters.

Planning a high-availability solution that uses network load balancing

All editions of Windows Server 2003 support network load balancing, which is used to distribute incoming IP traffic across a cluster of servers that share a single virtual IP address. You can balance the load across as few as 2 systems and up to 32 systems.

Any IP-based application that uses TCP, UDP, or GRE can be used with network load balancing. This means network load balancing is ideally suited to use with web servers, Internet application servers, and media servers. Applications that are load balanced include:

- FTP over TCP/IP
- HTTP over TCP/IP
- HTTPS over TCP/IP
- IMAP4 over TCP/IP
- POP3 over TCP/IP
- SMTP over TCP/IP

Load balancing ensures that there is no single point of failure by directing client requests to a virtual IP address. If one of the load balanced servers fails, the remaining servers handle the workload of the failed server. When the failed server comes back online, the server can rejoin the group automatically and start handling requests.

Network load balancing monitors the status of each load-balanced server, referred to as a *node*, using heartbeats. If a node fails to send a heartbeat message to other nodes within a specified time, the node is considered to be unavailable, and the remaining servers take over the failed servers workload.

Clients using the failed server automatically retry the failed connection, in most cases, within several seconds, and are then redirected to another server. It is important, however, to point out that there is no shared data between the nodes, so any work that is stored only on the failed server is lost. To avoid this, clients can store data locally prior to submitting it in final form for processing and storage.

Implementing network load balancing

Use the Network Load Balancing Manager, shown in Figure 8-21, to implement and manage network load balancing. To start Network Load Balancing Manager, click Network Load Balancing Manager on the Administrative Tools menu or type `nlbmgr` at a command prompt.

To install and configure load balancing, use the following technique:

1. Open Network Load Balancing Manager.
2. Right-click Network Load Balancing Clusters, and then click New Cluster.
3. On the Cluster Parameters page, shown in Figure 8-22, type the virtual IP address and subnet mask for the cluster. The same virtual IP address is used for all NLB nodes. This IP address is fixed and cannot be a dynamic DHCP address.

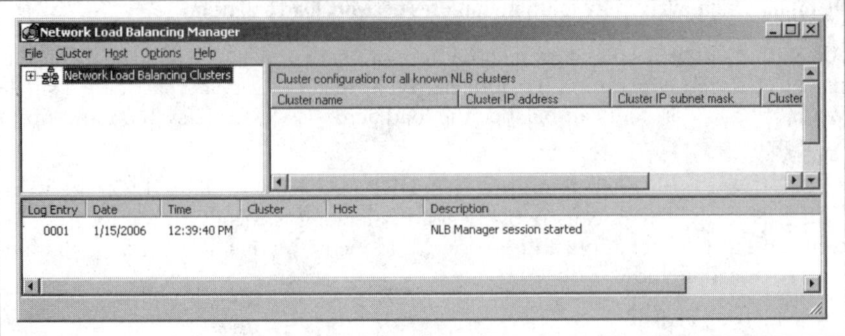

Figure 8-21. Use Network Load Balancing Manager to implement and manage network load balancing.

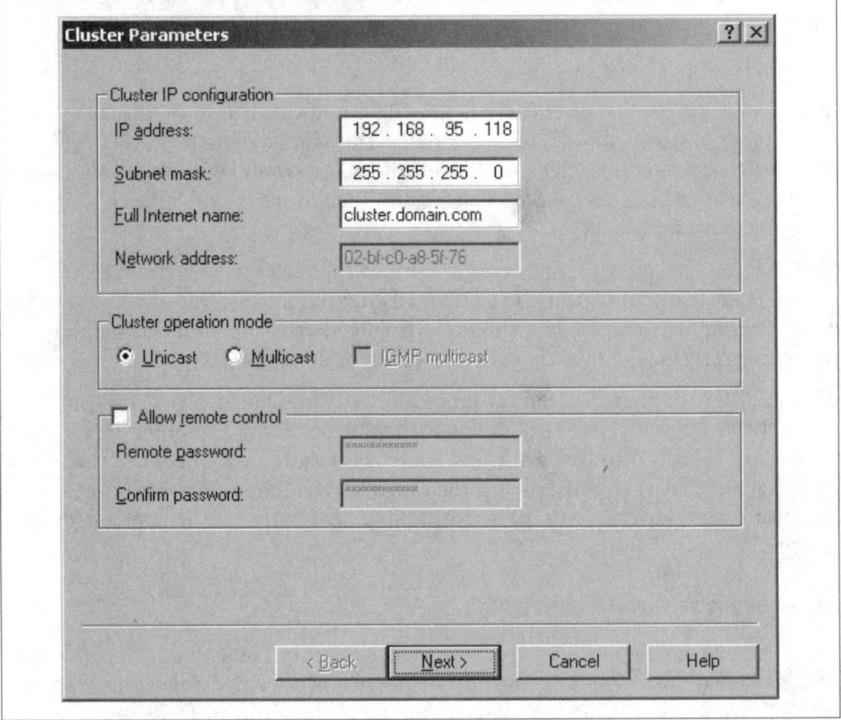

Figure 8-22. Configure the NLB cluster parameters.

4. In the Full Internet Name field, type the fully qualified domain name for the NLB cluster. Click Next.
5. If the cluster will have additional virtual IP addresses, click Add, enter the virtual IP address and subnet mask information, then click OK. Repeat this step for each additional virtual IP address that will be used, and then click Next.

6. Using the Port Rules page, shown in Figure 8-23, specify how network traffic on a port is filtered. By default, all TCP and UPD traffic is load balanced across all members of the cluster, based on the load weight of each cluster member. Click Next.

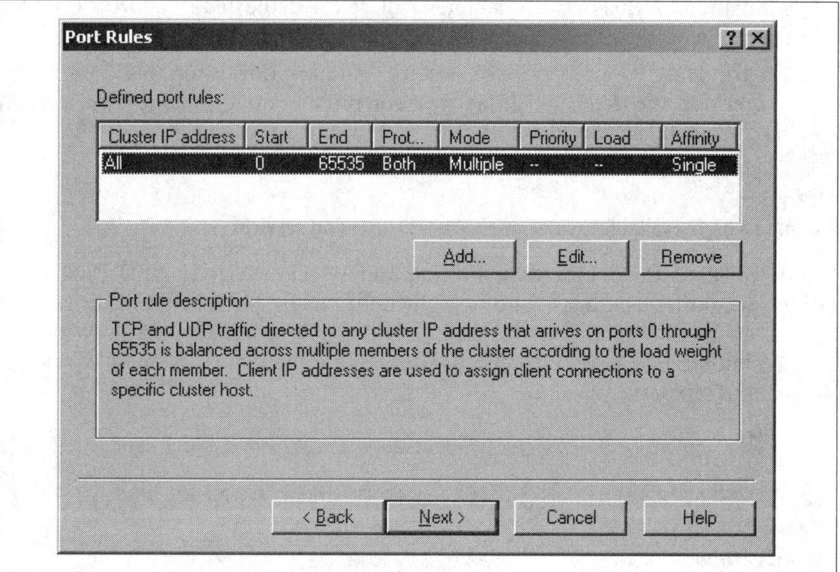

Figure 8-23. Set the port rules for NLB.

7. Enter the name or IP address of the first host that will be a member of the cluster. Click Connect to connect to the server and display a list of available network interfaces. Select the network interface to use for network load balancing, and then click Next.
8. On the Host Parameters page, set the host priority, which indicates the order in which traffic is routed among members of the cluster, and the dedicated IP address, which is used for private node-to-node traffic (as opposed to the public traffic for the cluster). Then set the default state of the host after system startup to Started.
9. Click Finish.

You can then add hosts into the cluster as appropriate. If you need to change the cluster parameters later, right-click the cluster in the left pane and select Cluster Properties. You are then able to change the cluster IP configuration, operation mode, and port rules.

After you create a cluster and add the initial host, you can add other hosts to the cluster at any time, up to a maximum of 32. Additional hosts use the cluster port rules from the initial host. To add a host to a cluster, follow these steps:

1. Open Network Load Balancing Manager. If the cluster you want to work with isn't shown, connect to it by right-clicking the Network Load Balancing Clusters node and selecting Connect To Existing. Then enter the domain name or IP address of any host in the cluster and click Connect.

2. Right-click the cluster to which you want to add a node and select Add Host To Cluster.
3. Enter the domain name or IP address of the host to add. Click Connect.
4. Select the network interface for network load balancing. The IP address configured on this network adapter will be the dedicated IP address used for the public traffic of the cluster. Click Next.
5. On the Host Parameters page, set the unique priority for this host in the cluster and the dedicated IP address for private, node-to-node traffic. Then set the default state of the host after system startup to Started.
6. Click Finish.

Planning a high-availability solution that uses clustering services

Windows Server 2003 Enterprise Edition and Windows Server 2003 Datacenter Edition support clustering for up to eight nodes using Microsoft Cluster service. As Table 8-16 shows, this is different from the clustering support in Windows 2000. All nodes in a server cluster must be running the same version of Windows. You cannot mix server versions.

Table 8-16. Support for clustering in Windows 2000 and Windows Server 2003

Operating system version	Cluster service nodes supported
Windows 2000 Advanced Server	2-nodes
Windows 2000 Datacenter Server	4-nodes
Windows Server 2003 Enterprise	8-nodes
Windows Server 2003 Datacenter	8-nodes

Server clustering with Microsoft Cluster service has many similarities and differences from clustering with Network Load Balancing. With Windows Server 2003, three types of server clusters can be used:

Single-node server clusters
: A cluster configuration with a single node that can be configured to use internal storage or an external cluster storage device. Single-node clustering allows automatic restart of applications and dependent services using Cluster service.

Single quorum device server clusters
: A cluster configuration with two or more nodes that are all connected to the same cluster storage devices. All members in the cluster use the same cluster quorum device as well. The quorum device stores cluster configuration and recovery data.

Majority node server clusters
: A cluster configuration with two or more nodes that don't have to be connected to shared storage devices. Each node can have its own cluster storage device and its own local quorum device, which means the cluster configuration and recovery data is stored on multiple disks across the cluster.

Most organizations use either single-node server clusters or single quorum device server clusters. Majority node server clusters typically are implemented for large-scale cluster deployments where cluster members of geographically separated. For example, you might use majority node server clusters to allow a backup site to handle failover from a primary site.

With server clustering, nodes can be either active or passive:

Active nodes
: Actively handle requests from clients

Passive nodes
: Wait on standby for another node to fail

With server clustering, scalability is as important as availability. Prior to deploying a cluster, you'll need to determine how many nodes you'll need, what hardware requirements must be met, and whether those nodes will be configured as active or passive nodes. Active and passive nodes are used in different ways:

- When all nodes in a cluster are active, you need to configure nodes with sufficient resources to handle the additional processing load of a failed server. For example, if you determine that each node in the cluster must have four processors and 4 GB of RAM to handle the expected workload, you need to double these resources to ensure that any single node could handle the additional processing load should one of the nodes fail. In this configuration, up to two nodes could fail and the workload would be supported.
- When a cluster includes passive nodes, you need to configure the passive node to handle the additional processing load of a failed server. For example, if you determine that each active node in the cluster must have eight processors and 32 GB of RAM to handle the expected workload, you need to configure passive nodes with this same configuration so that they can handle the processing load should one of the active nodes fail. In this configuration, up to two nodes could fail and the workload would be supported.

Microsoft Cluster Service requires that each node in a single quorum cluster be connected to the same cluster storage devices. Connecting the cluster to the same storage devices allows nodes in the cluster to share the same data. In the event of failure, the data is available to the server that assumes the failed server's workload—and the availability of data after failure is an important distinction between NLB and cluster service.

Prior to deploying clustering, you should prepare all the hard drives that the cluster will use and format all partitions appropriately using NTFS. For single quorum clusters, all nodes use the same quorum resource. With 32-bit editions of Windows Server 2003, you can use SCSI or fibre channel to share storage devices. However, fibre channel is preferred. Fibre channel is required with 64-bit editions of Windows Server 2003.

Once clustering is implemented, any cluster-aware application or service can be easily clustered using resource groups. *Resource groups* are units of failover that are configured on a single node. When any of the resources in the resource group fail, failover is initiated for the entire resource group according to the failover policy. Cluster-aware applications and services include:

- Distributed File System (DFS)
- DHCP
- Exchange Server
- Folder shares
- IIS
- Printer shares
- SMTP
- SQL Server
- WINS

Server clusters can only use TCP/IP. They cannot use AppleTalk, IPX, NWLINK, or NetBEUI. However, clients should have NetBIOS enabled so they can browse to a virtual server by name.

Cluster service tracks the status of each node in the cluster using state flags. The five possible state flags are:

Down
: Indicates a node is not active in the cluster

Joining
: Indicates the node is in the process of becoming an active participant in the cluster

Paused
: Indicates the node is active in the cluster but cannot or has not taken ownership of any resource groups

Up
: Indicates the node is active in the cluster

Unknown
: Indicates the node's state cannot be determined

Server clusters send heartbeat messages on dedicated network adapters, referred to as the *cluster adapters*. The heartbeat is used to track the availability of each node in the cluster. If a node fails to send a heartbeat message within a specified time, Cluster Service assumes the node has failed and initiates failover of resources. When failover occurs, another server takes over the workload, according to the failover policy. When the failed resource is back online, the original server is able to regain control of the resource.

Implementing a cluster server

You use the Cluster Administrator, shown in Figure 8-24, to implement and manage server clustering. To start Cluster Administrator, click Cluster Administrator on the Administrative Tools menu or type `cluadmin` at a command prompt.

To install and configure server clustering, use the following technique:

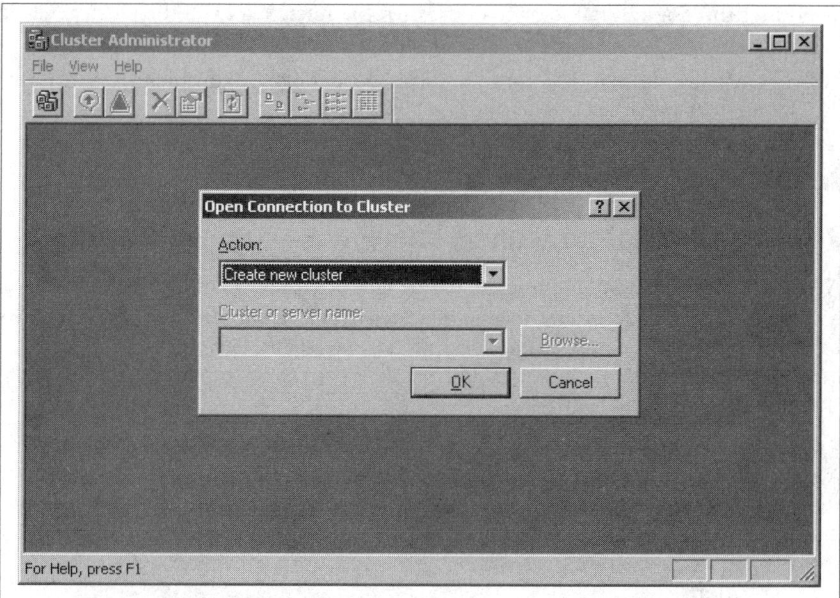

Figure 8-24. Use Cluster Administrator to create and manage server clusters.

1. Open Cluster Administrator.
2. In the Open Connection To Cluster dialog box, select Create New Cluster, and then click OK. Or click File → New → Cluster.
3. On the Cluster And Domain Name page, set the fully qualified domain name for the cluster. This is the name used for administrators of the cluster. Click Next.
4. On the Select Computer page, enter the name or IP address of the first computer in the cluster. Click Next.
5. The wizard analyzes the configuration and details any problems found. Any fatal errors must be corrected. Click Next.
6. Enter the IP address that will be used by cluster management tools to connect to the cluster. Click Next.
7. Specify the logon information for the account under which the cluster service will run. Click Next.
8. Click the Quorum button to choose the quorum type and configure the quorum device. Click Next to start configuring the cluster.

After you create a cluster and add the initial node, you can add other nodes to the cluster at any time, up to a maximum of eight. Additional nodes use the quorum and resource configuration from the initial node. To add a node to a cluster, follow these steps:

1. Open Cluster Administrator.
2. In the Open Connection To Cluster dialog box, select Add Nodes To Cluster, and then click OK.

3. Enter the domain name or IP address of the host to add to the cluster. Click Next.
4. The wizard analyzes the configuration and details any problems found. Any fatal errors must be corrected. Click Next.
5. Follow the prompts, which are very similar to those for configuring the new node.

Planning a Backup and Recovery Strategy

A key part of availability planning is ensuring that you create and then implement a comprehensive backup and recovery strategy. For Exam 70-293, you'll need to be able to identify the appropriate backup type to use in a given situation, to plan a backup strategy that includes volume shadow copy, and to plan system recovery that uses Automated System Recovery (ASR).

As part of your preparation, you should review the section "Managing and Implementing Disaster Recovery" in Chapter 2. Exam 70-293 expects you to know all the details in this section for using Backup, working with Volume Shadow Copy, and using Automated System Recovery (ASR). Additionally, the exam expects you to have a more detailed understanding of the appropriate backup types to use in a given situation.

Windows Server 2003 includes the Backup utility for backing up and recovering servers. Like most third-party backup solutions, Backup supports five backup types:

Normal backups, also called full backups
: Use normal backups to back up all selected files or folders. Normal backups do not use the archive flag to determine whether to back up files or folders. Always back up everything you've selected for backup. During a normal backup, the Backup utility clears the archive flag on all selected files and folders to indicate that the files and folders have been backed up. You should regularly perform or regularly schedule normal backups to run and supplement normal backups with other backups as necessary.

Copy backups
: Use copy backups to back up all selected files or folders. Like normal backups, copy backups do not use the archive flag to determine whether to back up files or folders, and always back up everything you've selected for backup. During a copy backup, the Backup utility does *not* clear the archive flag on all selected files and folders to indicate that the files and folders have been backed up. Copy backups should be used when you want to make a current backup of data but do not want to disrupt the backup rotation.

Daily backups
: You use daily backups to backup all selected files or folders that have changes during a particular day. Daily backups do not use or reset the archive flag. If you use daily backups with normal backups, you must create a daily backup every day thereafter until the next normal backup to be able to fully recover the system.

Differential backups

Use differential backups to back up all selected files or folders with an archive flag. During a differential backup, the Backup utility does *not* clear the archive flag. Because of this, each differential backup after a normal backup contains the full set of changes since the normal backup was created.

Incremental backups

Use incremental backups to back up all selected files or folders with an archive flag. During an incremental backup, the Backup utility clears the archive flag. Because of this, each incremental backup contains only the changes since the last incremental or full backup.

For all servers and all critical workstations, you should create normal backups at least once a week and supplement these with daily incremental backups or daily differential backups. Because incremental backups contain only changes since the last incremental or full backup, incremental backups are smaller than differential backups and can be created more quickly. However, since each differential backup contains all the changes since the last normal backup, differential backups allow you to recover a system more quickly. Therefore, the decisive factors in whether to use incremental or differential backups in addition to normal backups are the required backup time and the required recovery time.

For planning purposes, keep the following in mind:

- For recovery of a system that uses normal and incremental backups, you must apply the last normal backup and then each incremental backup in order up to the day of failure. If a system fails on a Thursday after daily incremental backup, and the last full backup was the previous Sunday, then recover the system by applying the last full backup, the Monday incremental backup, the Tuesday incremental backup, the Wednesday incremental backup, and the Thursday incremental backup.
- For recovery of a system that uses normal and differential backups, you must apply the last normal backup and then apply the last differential backup. If a system fails on a Thursday after daily differential backup, and the last full backup was the previous Sunday, then recover the system by applying the last full backup and the Thursday differential backup.

Following this, in cases where you are backing up large data sets, you may need to use daily incremental backups to ensure that all the changes can be backed up within the allotted time. In cases where speed of recovery is critically important, you may need to use daily differential backups to ensure systems can be recovered more quickly.

Planning, Implementing, and Maintaining Network Security and Infrastructure

Security is critically important to ensure the integrity of the network. The way you secure the network will depend on the organization's security policies and the configuration of the network. On a typical network, clients will send requests to servers using TCP/IP, and servers will receive and process the requests. When clients connect to the network using wireless technology or connect to the network using remote access, special considerations must be made to ensure the security of the network is not compromised.

Planning and Configuring Network Protocol Security

In addition to IP addresses, computers on TCP/IP networks use specific protocols and ports for communications. Servers configured to use a specific protocol listen on a specific TCP or UDP port for requests from clients. For example, web servers listen on TCP port 80 for Hypertext Transfer Protocol (HTTP) requests.

Specifying and configuring port and protocol security

The Internet Assigned Numbers Authority (IANA) is responsible for assigning the values used for TCP/IP protocols and ports. Commonly used protocols have permanently assigned port numbers, which are referred to as well-known ports. While clients may contact a server on a particular port, the client may in some cases use a randomly assigned port to connect to and communicate with a server. This random port is referred to as an ephemeral port.

On a server, you can type `netstat -ano` at a command prompt to list all TCP and UDP port connections to that server. The output shows, by protocol, which ports are in use, such as:

```
Proto  Local Address      Foreign Address State          PID
TCP    192.168.20.10:80   0.0.0.0:0       LISTENING      2581
```

In the example, process ID 2581 is listening on the local address 192.168.20.10 to port 80. Because this process is using port 80, another program is prevented from using this port as well. Type `tasklist /fi "pid eq` *`ProcessNumber`*`"` at the command prompt to determine which program is using the port where *`ProcessNumber`* is the PID, such as:

```
tasklist /fi "pid eq 2300"
```

Table 8-17 lists the commonly used protocols for Windows Server 2003 and the ports on which those protocols commonly are used. Keep in mind that most protocols can be configured to use different, alternate listen ports. For example, a common alternate listen port for HTTP is 8080.

Table 8-17. Commonly used protocols for Windows Server 2003

Protocol	Listen port
Domain Name System (DNS)	TCP port 53 and UDP port 53
Dynamic Host Configuration Protocol (Client)	UDP port 68
Dynamic Host Configuration Protocol (Server)	UDP port 67
File Transfer Protocol (FTP)	TCP port 20 for data; TCP port 21 for control
Global Catalog	TCP port 3268
Global Catalog with LDAP/SSL	TCP port 3269
Hypertext Transfer Protocol (HTTP)	TCP port 80
Installation Bootstrap Service	TCP ports 1067 and 1068
Internet Authentication Service (IAS)	UDP ports 1645, 1646, 1812, and 1813
Internet Security Association and Key Management (ISAKM)	UDP port 500

Table 8-17. Commonly used protocols for Windows Server 2003 (continued)

Protocol	Listen port
Kerberos change password protocol	TCP port 464
Kerberos version 5	UDP port 88
Layer 2 Tunneling Protocol (L2TP)	UDP port 1701
LDAP Secure Sockets Layer (SSL)	TCP port 686
Lightweight Directory Access Protocol (LDAP)	TCP port 389 and UDP port 389
NetBIOS Datagram protocol	UDP port 138
NetBIOS Name Server protocol	UDP port 137
NetBIOS Session Services	TCP port 139
Network News Transfer Protocol (NNTP)	TCP port 119
Point-to-Point Tunneling Protocol (PPTP)	TCP port 1723
Post Office Protocol 3 (POP3)	TCP port 110
Remote Desktop Protocol (RDP)	TCP port 3389
Remote procedure call (RPC)	TCP port 135
RPC over HTTP	TCP port 593
Secure Hypertext Transfer Protocol (HTTPS)	TCP port 443
Secure NNTP	TCP port 563
Sever Message Block (SMB) over IP	TCP port 445 and UDP port 445
Simple Mail Transfer Protocol (SMTP)	TCP port 25
Simple Network Management Protocol (SNMP)	UDP port 161
Simple Network Management Protocol trap	UDP port 162
Windows Product Activation	TCP port 80 and 443

The most common way to secure a server is to use packet filtering. *Packet filtering* is used to control the TCP/IP traffic that is permitted to reach a computer or a network, based on specific criteria, such as IP address, IP protocol, TCP port, or UDP port. Packets that do not meet the requirements of a particular filter are discarded. In this way, only packets that meet filter requirements reach a computer or network and are processed.

While packet filtering primarily is used by firewalls and routers that connect the internal network to the Internet, you can use packet filtering on your internal network as well. For example, you might want to use it to regulate the flow of traffic from one subnet to another or to limit the types of traffic that can be received by a server. In this case, you could install a firewall between the network segments or enable a software-based firewall on the server for which you want to limit traffic. You could also enable packet filtering on the router that connects the subnets or on the server for which you want to limit traffic.

Before you create packet filters, you need to determine the types of traffic that you will permit and the types of traffic that you will deny. You can then configure packet filtering to be inclusive or exclusive:

Inclusive
: You completely block all traffic and then specify the permitted traffic—i.e., the traffic to include.

Exclusive
: You open the connection completely and then specify the traffic—i.e., the traffic to exclude.

While the inclusive approach is more secure, it is much more difficult to configure as you must specifically allow all types of permitted traffic. On Windows XP Professional and Windows Server 2003, packet filtering can be configured in several ways.

Windows XP Professional and Windows Server 2003 include the Windows Firewall. To start Windows Firewall, click Windows Firewall in the Control Panel. In the default configuration, when Windows Firewall is enabled, all outside sources are blocked from connecting to the computer by default, an the exceptions specified on the Exceptions tab only are allowed.

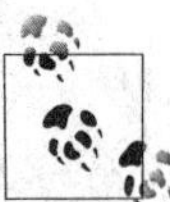

Do not use Windows Firewall on Windows Server 2003 systems configured as IP routers or for remote access servers. Instead, use the NAT/Basic Firewall features of RRAS.

Windows XP Professional and Windows Server 2003 include TCP/IP Filtering. To use TCP/IP Filtering, follow these steps:

1. Click Start → Control Panel → Network Connections → Local Area Connection.
2. Click Properties to open the Local Area Connection Properties dialog box.
3. Click Internet Protocol (TCP/IP), and then select Properties.
4. Click the Advanced Button.
5. On the Options tab, click the Properties button.
6. Use the TCP/IP Filtering dialog box, shown in Figure 8-25, to configure packet filtering. Turn on packet filtering by selecting Enable TCP/IP Filtering (All Adapters). By default, all TCP, UDP, and IP Protocols are allowed.
7. To filter TCP traffic, click Permit Only for TCP Ports. Click Add to define a permitted TCP port.
8. To filter UDP traffic, click Permit Only for UDP Ports. Click Add to define a permitted UDP port.
9. Click OK four times.

When you have configured a server as a router using Routing And Remote Access Service (RRAS), you can configure packet filtering through RRAS. Packet filtering in RRAS is more versatile and configurable than the standard Windows Server 2003 packet-filtering feature. To use packet filtering with RRAS, follow these steps:

1. Open Routing And Remote Access. Connect to the server you want to work with (if necessary).
2. Expand the server node and the related IP routing node.
3. Click the General node.
4. Right-click the WAN interface, and then select Properties.

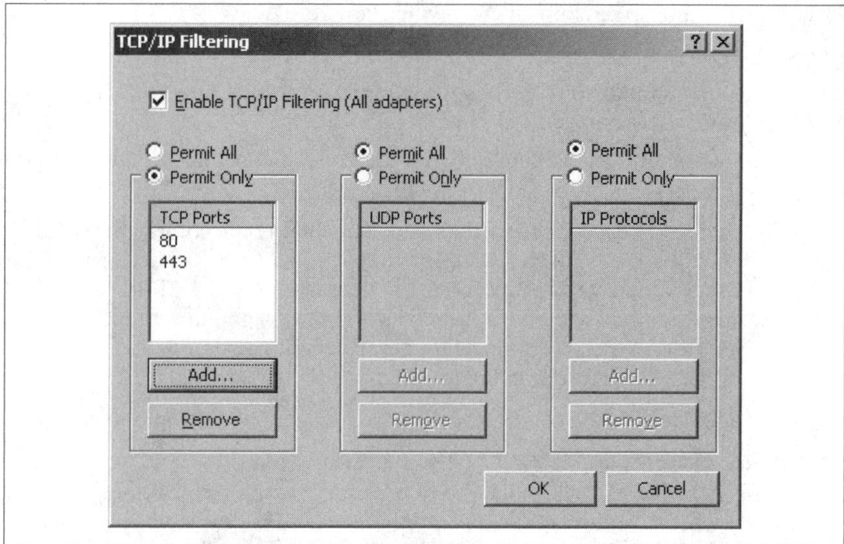

Figure 8-25. Configuring standard TCP/IP packet filtering.

5. On the General tab, click the Inbound Filters button, and then configure filters if you want to limit incoming traffic.
6. On the General tab, click the Outbound Filters button, and then configure filters if you want to limit outgoing traffic.

Planning and configuring an IPSec policy for secure network communications

To protect the data being sent between computers on the network, you can use IP Security (IPSec). IPSec is a technology for authenticating and encrypting IP traffic between computers. IPSec operates at the network layer as an extension to the IP protocol itself, and provides end-to-end encryption for IP traffic. The source computer and the intended recipient only an read the encrypted traffic.

IPSec secures traffic by encrypting it, and then encapsulating it prior to transmission. Even if packets are captured during transmission from one computer to another, the packets are protected because they can be read only by a computer that has the appropriate key needed to decrypt the data. Because the encrypted data is encapsulated in standard IP datagrams, routers, switches, and other intermediaries handle the encrypted data as they do any other packets. They do not need to be able to read the packets to forward the packets to the appropriate destination.

While there are other protocols that provide network traffic encryption, these operate at the application layer and are used to encrypt only specific types of traffic. For example, web servers can be configured to use *Secure Sockets Layer (SSL)*. SSL encrypts traffic between web clients and web servers. In contrast, IPSec can encrypt any type of traffic and is not dependent on a specific application.

IPSec policy is most often implemented when you need to:

- Secure communications on an internal network
- Secure communications between networks, especially when traffic passes over WAN connections
- Secure communications between remote access clients and the internal network

With RRAS, remote access clients that establish VPN connections with a RRAS server can use IPSec to enhance security when the Layer 2 Tunneling Protocol (L2TP) is used. When VPN connections are used to connect LANs and WANs, IPSec can also be used with L2TP to enhance security. In either configuration, IPSec is used to encrypt all traffic. Thus, regardless of the destination, all traffic passing over the VPN connection is encrypted and protected.

The IPSec standards define two protocols for securing network communications:

IP Authentication Header (AH)
: This is not used to encrypt data in IP packets. Instead, AH is used to provide authentication, anti-relay, and integrity services. AH can be used by itself or with IP Encapsulating Security Payload protocol. By itself, AH provide basic security but does not prevent unauthorized users from reading packet contents. AH does guarantee, however, that no one has modified packets enroute to its destination. It does this using relatively low overhead.

IP Encapsulating Security Payload (ESP)
: This protocol is used to encrypt data in IP packets. Encryption secures the data and prevents intruders from relaying information. ESP provides authentication, anti-relay, and integrity services. In contrast to AH, which inserts only a header into the IP packet, ESP inserts a header and a trailer to ensure that all data following the ESP header, up to and including, the ESP trailer is encrypted. As a result, anyone who captures a secured packet can only read the IP header, but cannot read any part of the rest of the packet. ESP can be used with AH; using both protocols ensures the maximum possible security for data transmission.

IPSec operates either in transport mode or tunnel mode:

Transport mode
: Two computers act as end points and communicate with each other using IPSec, but intermediaries, such as routers, do not need to use or support IPSec.

Tunnel mode
: The WAN routers on either end of a connection act as the end points and communicate with each other using IPSec, but computers transmitting packets to each other over the WAN connection do not need to use or support IPSec.

IPSec is applied using Group Policy:

- For Active Directory domains, IPSec policies are stored under *Computer Configuration\Windows Settings\Security Settings\IP Security Settings On Active Directory*.
- For computers in workgroups, you can configure local group policy under *Computer Configuration\Windows Settings\Security Settings\IP Security Settings On Local Computer*.

In Windows Server 2003, IPSec has four main components:

An IPSec Policy Agent
: This provides the services needed for end-to-end security between clients and servers. On Windows 2000 and later systems, the IPSec Policy Agent is the IPSEC Services service (*lsass.exe*). This service must be enabled and running on all systems that use IPSec.

Internet Key Exchange (IKE)
: This is the protocol used to negotiate the key exchange. The computers in the exchange must negotiate the encryption algorithm, the hashing algorithm, and the authentication method that will be used. They also exchange information about key generation.

IPSec Driver
: This enables secure communications by generating the required checksums, creating the IPSec packets, and encrypting data for transmission. The driver is also responsible for comparing each outgoing packet to the filter list obtained from the IPSec policy being used. For incoming packets, the driver calculates its own hashes and checksums, and then compares these to the hashes and checksums in the received packets.

IPSec Policy
: This defines packet filters that enforce security by blocking, allowing, or initiating secure communications. Although multiple IPSec policies can be defined, one policy only is applied at a time.

Active Directory has three default IPSec policies:

Server (Request Security) policy
: Servers always request security using Kerberos trust but do not require secure communications. This policy is intended for use when the highest levels of security are not required and servers might communicate with clients that do not support IPSec.

Client (Respond Only) policy
: Clients communicate unsecured normally but respond to server requests for secure communications. This policy is intended for computers that connect to both secured servers and unsecured servers.

Secure Server (Require Security) policy
: Servers always require secure communications using Kerberos trust. Servers will not respond to clients that do not or cannot use secure communications. This policy is intended for computers working with sensitive data that requires the highest levels of security at all times.

Only one IPSec policy can be assigned and enforced at a time. To assign and enforce one of these policies, follow these steps:

1. Open the GPO you want to work with for editing.
2. Access *Computer Configuration\Windows Settings\Security Settings\IP Security Settings On Active Directory*.
3. The Policy Assigned column indicates whether a policy is assigned.
4. To assign and apply a policy, right-click it and select Assign.

To create a new policy, follow these steps:

1. Open the GPO you want to work with for editing.
2. Access *Computer Configuration\Windows Settings\Security Settings\IP Security Settings On Active Directory*.
3. Right-click IP Security Settings On Active Directory, and then select Create IP Security Policy.
4. Follow the prompts, and the IP Security Policy Wizard guides you through the steps of creating the policy.

After you create the policy, edit its properties. The wizard automatically opens the policy's properties dialog box when you click Finish. You can display the properties dialog box by right-clicking the policy and selecting Properties (see Figure 8-26).

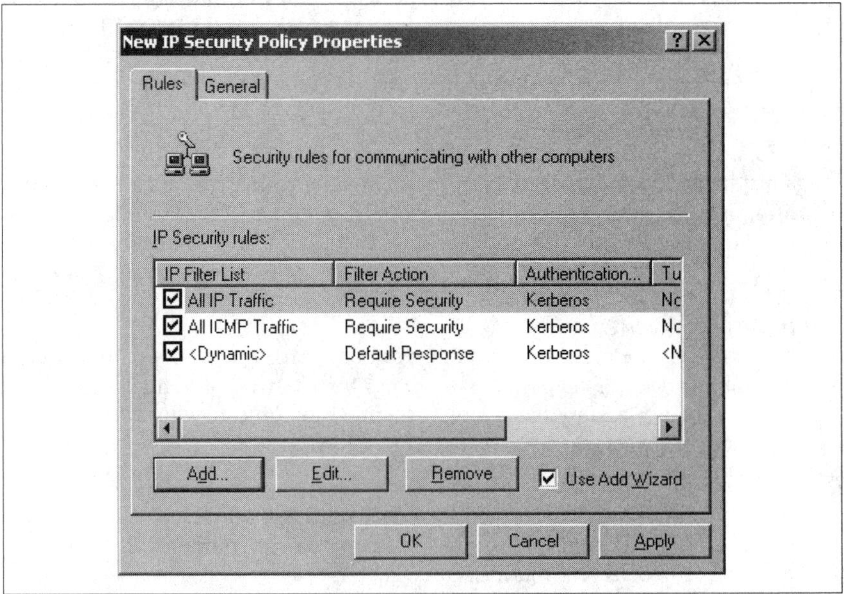

Figure 8-26. Configure rules for the IPSec policy.

IPSec policies have three components:

Rules
: These combine IP filter lists with filter actions to define whether and how computers should use IPSec. An IPSec policy can have multiple rules. Typically, there are rules for all IP traffic and all ICMP traffic, as well as a default rule. Other rules also can be defined.

IP filter lists
: These are collections of filters that specify what types of traffic a computer should secure with IPSec, such as All IP Traffic or All ICMP Traffic. Filters can be applied based on source IP address, destination IP address, protocol, source port, and destination port.

Filter actions
: These specify exactly how IPSec should secure the filtered packets. Filter actions require at least one security method. With integrity and encryption security, the data will be encrypted and authenticated. With integrity-only security, the data will be authenticated but not encrypted.

With a policy's Properties dialog box open, you can create rules that define IP filter lists and filter actions by clicking Add on the Rules tab, and then following the prompts for the Create IP Security Rule Wizard. To assign and enforce the new policy, right-click the policy and select Assign.

To determine whether IPSec policy is applied to a computer, complete these steps:

1. Click Start → Run. Type `mmc` in the Open field, and then click OK.
2. In MMC, click File, and then click Add/Remove Snap-In.
3. In the Standalone tab, click Add.
4. In the Add Standalone Snap-In dialog box, click IP Security Policy Management, and then click Add.
5. In the Select Computer Or Domain window, click Local Computer to analyze the local computer's IPSec policy. Otherwise, click Another Computer, and then type the name or IP address of the remote computer to analyze.
6. Click Finish. Click Close, and then click OK.
7. In the MMC, click the IP Security Policies On... node.
8. In the right pane, you'll see a list of IPSec policies defined in the domain. Under Policy Assigned, you'll see an entry of Yes if a policy is being applied. If a policy is not applied, you'll see an entry of No in the Policy Assigned column (see Figure 8-27).

Planning Secure Network Administration Methods

For secure network administration of remote computers, Remote Desktop for Administration and Remote Assistance are essential as they increase efficiency by allowing you to centrally and remotely manage systems, regardless of where they are located on the network. For Exam 70-293, you need to know how to configure and use Remote Desktop For Administration and Remote Assistance, as discussed in "Essential Administration Tools" in Chapter 2. Review the related sections in Chapter 2.

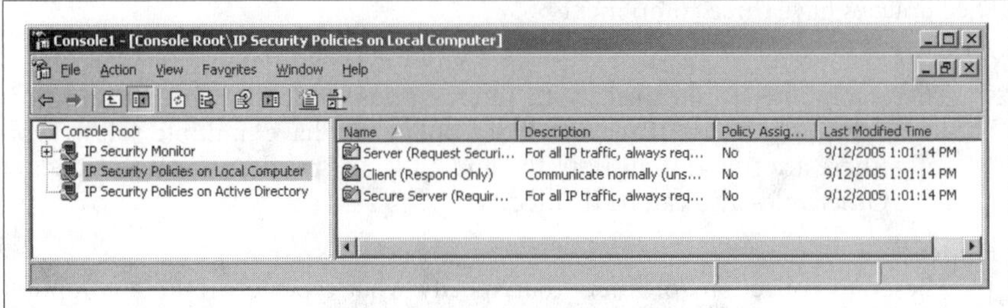

Figure 8-27. Determining whether IPSec is being applied.

As part of planning, it is important to understand the possible modes in which each can be used. Remote Desktop For Administration is one of two operating modes for Windows Server 2003 Terminal Services. Using Remote Desktop For Administration, administrators can establish remote connections to client computers. Each server configured with Remote Desktop For Administration can have up to two concurrent connections. If the feature is enabled, any user that is a member of the Administrators group can establish remote desktop connections. Additional remote desktop users can be set as well.

Using Remote Assistance, a user can send an invitation asking for troubleshooting help. The helper or expert accepting the request can view the user's desktop and transfer files, and chat with the user needing help through a single interface. Two assistance modes are possible:

- If the computer is allowed to be remotely controlled, the helper or expert can take over the computer and resolve the problem as if she is sitting in front of the computer.
- If the computer is not allowed to be remotely controlled, the helper or expert can view but not interact with the user's computer. The helper or expert can only offer guidance, and watch as the user tries to resolve the problem.

By default, remote assistance invitations are valid for 30 days. In environments where security is a high concern, 30 days typically is too long a period for invitations to remain open. In most cases, you'll want to restrict how long invitations can remain open to one day or less. You can do this through Group Policy. After you open the GPO you want to work with for editing, access *Computer Configuration\Administrative Templates\System\Remote Assistance*. You can then enable and configure the Solicited Remote Assistance policy, and in this way control how Remote Assistance is used.

Both Remote Desktop For Administration and Remote Assistance use TCP port 3389. This port should be open on the internal network to allow these features to be used. To protect your computers, this port should be blocked on external routers and firewalls to prevent users outside the organization from using these features. If you open TCP port 3389 on external routers and firewalls, you may inadvertently open the internal network to attack.

Planning Security for Wireless Networks

As discussed previously in this chapter under "Planning and Modifying a Network Topology," most wireless networks use technologies based on the IEEE 802.1

specification. Securing a wireless network is different from securing a wired network. On a wireless network, anyone who is within range of one of your wireless access points can gain access to your internal network. Unauthorized users can also intercept wireless signals being broadcast to your network and use information they've gleaned to break into the network. This makes security for wireless networks of critical importance.

To protect your internal network, all wireless transmissions should be secured and encrypted. Several technologies are available for authenticating and encrypting wireless transmissions. *Wi-Fi Protected Access (WPA)* is used for authentication. WPA has two operating modes:

Enterprise Mode
: With this mode, wireless devices have two sets of keys: session keys and group keys. *Session keys* are unique to each association between an access point and a wireless client, and are used to create a private virtual port between the access point and the client. *Group keys* are shared among all clients connected to the same access point. Both key sets are generated dynamically and rotated.

Home/Small Office Mode
: With this mode, also referred to as WPA-PSK, WPA doesn't use a changing encryption key. Instead, it uses a preshared encryption key, referred to as a group key, which is programmed into the base station and then configured on all the other wireless devices. Wireless devices use the master key as a starting point to mathematically generate session keys. Session keys are then regularly and automatically changed so that the same session key is never used twice.

Wireless Equivalency Protection (WEP) encrypts data using private key encryption. All data is encrypted using before it is transmitted, and any computer that wants to read the data must be able to decrypt it using the private key.

With *Robust Security Network (RSN)*, wireless devices dynamically negotiate the authentication and encryption algorithms to be used for communications. This allows the supported authentication and encryption algorithms to be changed as needed to address security issues. Most RSN compatible devices can use:

- Extensible Authentication Protocol (EAP) with Protected EAP (PEAP) as the encryption algorithm
- Extensible Authentication Protocol (EAP) with Smart card or other PKI certificate
- Advanced Encryption Standard (AES) as the encryption algorithm
- Temporal Key Integrity Protocol (TKIP) as the encryption algorithm

During configuration of wireless networking, you need to specify the name of the wireless network and the mode in which the wireless device will run. Signals generated by wireless devices are omnidirectional. The broadcast range of a wireless device is referred to as its *basic service area (BSA)*. All wireless devices have BSAs. Wireless devices within the same BSA are referred to as *basic service sets (BSS)*.

Wireless devices run in one of two operating modes:

Ad hoc

With Ad hoc networks, two or more wireless devices communicate directly with each other. When two wireless devices are within range of each other, they can connect to form a two-node wireless network. If additional wireless devices come within range of one of the devices in this network, they can join the network. However, ad hoc networking is not transitive. A device on the ad hoc network must be within range of another device to communicate with it—the device cannot communicate with a device outside of its own range. Ad hoc networks are most often used on home networks.

Infrastructure

With infrastructure networks, wireless adapters connect to an access point rather than to another computer directly. A *wireless access point (WAP)* acts as a bridge between the wireless adapter and the physical network, and typically is connected to the organization's internal network by Ethernet cable. A wireless device within range of the wireless access point is able to try to connect to the internal network.

You can prevent unauthorized access and secure wireless transmissions using several different authentication methods. The IEEE 802.11 defines two methods: Open System Authentication and Shared Key Authentication. Windows Server 2003 supports an additional options called IEEE 802.1X.

The default authentication method for IEEE 802.11 devices is Open System authentication. As the name implies, this authentication method essentially allows any two wireless devices to communicate with each other. Although the devices identify each other prior to communicating, there is no exchange of passwords, keys, or other security credentials, and there is, therefore, no way for devices to refuse authentication with each other.

The Shared key authentication method for IEEE 802.11 devices requires each device to authenticate using a secret key that all devices on the wireless network must have to communicate. Because all devices have the same key, this method isn't very secure. If the shared key is compromised, then the entire network is.

The IEEE 802.1X standard defines a method of authenticating and authorizing users connecting to wireless networks. With IEEE 802.1X, wireless devices act as clients of a server, such as a server running RADIUS, and the server handles authentication and authorization using any supported authentication protocols, such as Extensible Authentication Protocol (EAP), Extensible Authentication Protocol Transport Layer Security (EAP-TLS), or Protected EAP (PEAP).

By default, a Windows XP Professional computer uses an Open System configuration and can connect to any available wireless network including both ad hoc and infrastructure networks. To enhance security, you should restrict wireless connections to designated infrastructure networks. To configure the client computer directly, follow these steps:

1. Click Programs Control Panel Network Connections.
2. Right-click the wireless connection and choose Properties.
3. On the Wireless Networks tab, click Advanced.

4. Select Access Point (Infrastructure) Networks Only.
5. Click Close, and then click OK.

Group Policy can be used to configure clients to use infrastructure networks only. To configure the client computer through Group Policy, follow these steps:

1. Open the GPO you want to work with for editing.
2. Access *Computer Configuration\Windows Settings\Security Settings\Wireless Network (IEEE 802.11)*.
3. Right-click Wireless Network (IEEE 802.11), and then select Create Wireless Network Policy.
4. Follow the prompts, and the Wireless Network Policy Wizard guides you through the steps of creating the policy.
5. After you create the policy, edit its properties. The wizard automatically opens the policy's properties dialog box when you click Finish. You can display the properties dialog box by right-clicking the policy and selecting Properties.
6. On the General tab, set Networks To Access to Access Point (Infrastructure) Networks Only, as shown in Figure 8-28.

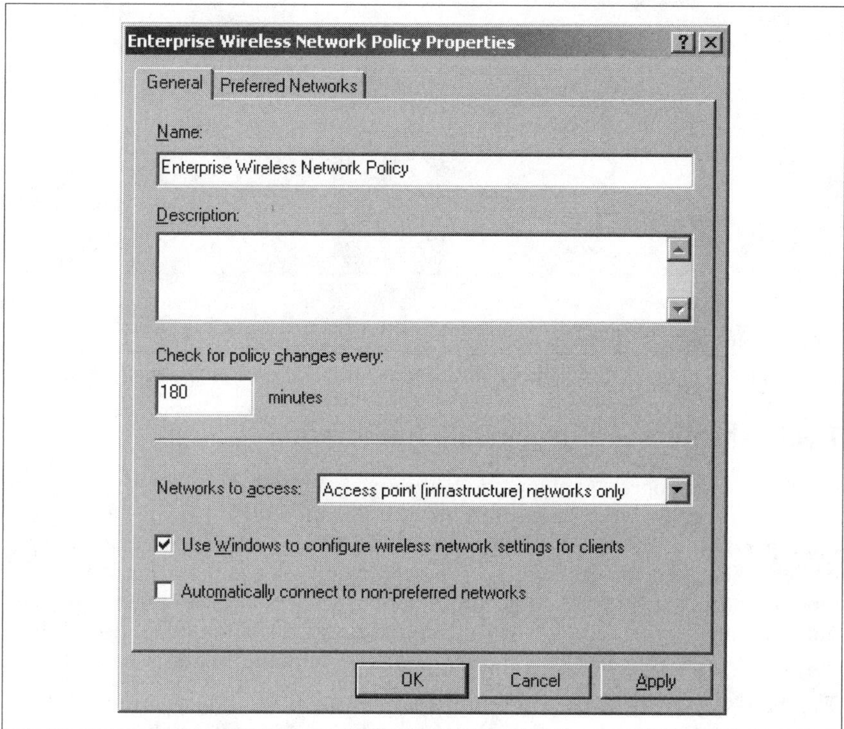

Figure 8-28. Limit clients to infrastructure networks only.

Exam 70-293 Study Guide

7. On the Preferred Networks tab, click Add to define the networks to which wireless clients subject to the GPO can connect.
8. On the Network Properties tab, type a name for the wireless network, and then set the desired network authentication and data encryption technique (see Figure 8-29).
9. Click OK.

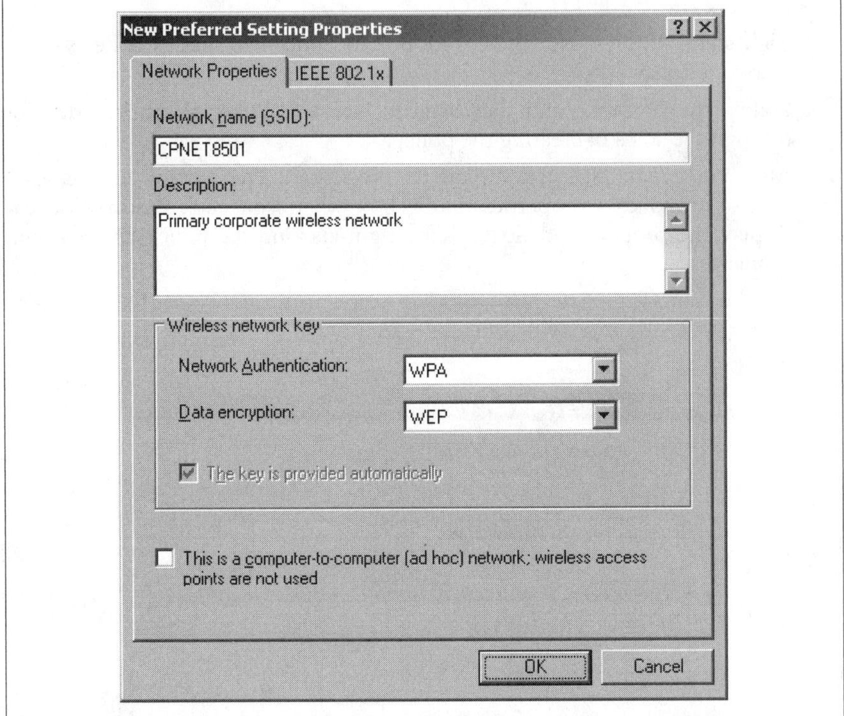

Figure 8-29. Set the network name, authentication, and data encryption details.

Troubleshooting Security for Data Transmission

If IPSec is improperly configured, network communications between secured clients and secured servers can fail. The most common reason for this failure is an improper or incompatible configuration of the IPSec components. For example, while a client and server might both be configured to use IPSec for a particular type of traffic, they may be subject to different IPSec policies and therefore, have different filter action settings for this type of traffic. Having different, incompatible settings prevents the client and server from communicating with each other.

The best way to determine whether there is an IPSec policy mismatch is to examine the Security logs of both the client and the server. The Security log should contain warning messages if the systems attempted to perform an Internet Key Exchange negotiation that failed.

Some IPSec processes are only logged when auditing is enabled. Specifically, you must enable Audit Logon Events and Audit Policy Change for Success and Failure events. The IPSec driver can be configured to log dropped packets as well. To configure logging, type the following command:

```
netsh ipsec dynamic set config ipsecdiagnostics 7
```

To disable diagnostic logging, type the following command:

```
netsh ipsec dynamic set config ipsecdiagnostics 0
```

You can monitor IPSec policy to ensure that it is working correctly using IP Security Monitor. To access this snap-in in a console, complete these steps:

1. Click Start → Run. Type `mmc` in the Open field, and then click OK.
2. In MMC, click File, and then click Add/Remove Snap-In.
3. In the Standalone tab, click Add.
4. In the Add Standalone Snap-In dialog box, click IP Security Monitor, and then click Add.
5. Click Close, and then click OK.

By default, IP Security Monitor connects to the local computer. If you want to monitor IPSec on another computer, right-click the IP Security Monitor node, and then click Add Computer. Expand the computer node, and then select the Active Policy entry to see the active IPSec policy on the designated computer (if any).

The Active Policy folder shows the IPSec policy currently assigned according to the specific GPO from which the policy was applied (see Figure 8-30). When you apply IPSec policy at multiple levels within the Active Directory structure, one IPSec policy only is applied, and by default, it is the policy processed last. Also by default, organizational unit policy has precedence over domain policy, and domain policy has precedence over site policy.

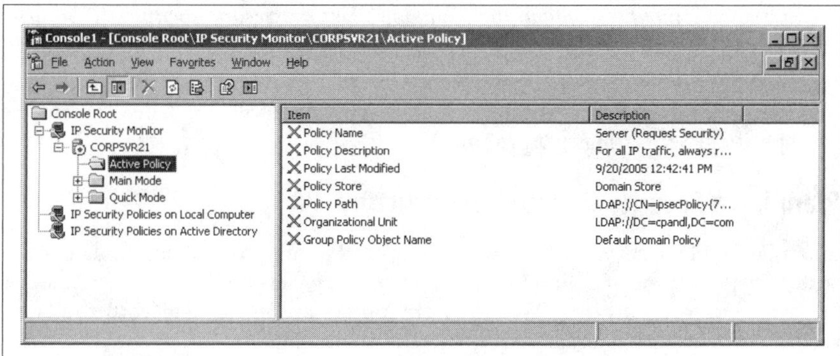

Figure 8-30. The Active Policy folder shows the IPSec policy currently assigned.

Exam 70-293 Study Guide

With the IP Security Monitor, you should use the Main Mode or Quick Mode nodes to view current filters, security methods, statistics, and security associations. High failure rates (relative to the level of IPSec activity) under the Statistics node can indicate IPSec configuration problems. If computers cannot make an IPSec connection, check to see whether the number of Authentication Failures increases. If so, authentication is the issue and you should ensure the following:

- The computers' shared secrets match
- The certificates are correct
- The computers are members of the appropriate domain

If computers cannot make an IPSec connection, check to see whether the number of Negotiation Failures increases. If so, check the security method and authentication settings for incorrect configurations.

You can view similar IPSec information at a command prompt by typing:

```
netsh ipsec static show all
```

By determining the Resultant Set of Policy for a user or computer, you can determine the specific IPSec policy settings that are being applied to that user or computer. To determine Resultant Set of Policy, follow these steps:

1. Click Start → Run. Type `mmc` in the Open field, and then click OK.
2. In MMC, click File, and then click Add/Remove Snap-In.
3. In the Standalone tab, click Add.
4. In the Add Standalone Snap-In dialog box, click Resultant Set Of Policy, and then click Add.
5. Click Close, and then click OK.
6. Right-click Resultant Set Of Policy and select Generate RSoP Data.
7. Follow the prompts for using the Resultant Set Of Policy Wizard in Logging Mode, selecting the user and computer for which you want to review the RSoP. Click Finish.
8. Expand *Computer Configuration\Windows Settings\Security Settings\IP Security Settings On Active Directory* or *Computer Configuration\Windows Settings\Security Settings\IP Security Settings On Local Computer* as appropriate.
9. The GPO from which the IPSec policy is being applied is listed, as are the specific IPSec settings being applied.

Planning a Security Update Infrastructure

Exam 70-293 expects you to know to install and configure software update infrastructure as a means of maintaining system security. Several different technologies are available to ensure that Windows computers are up to date with the latest security patches, hot fixes, and service packs, including:

- Automatic Updates
- Windows Update
- Windows Server Update Services (WSUS)

These features were discussed previously in the section "Installing and Configuring Software Update Infrastructure" in Chapter 2. Review the related sections to prepare for Exam 70-293. WSUS requires IIS, BITS, and .NET Framework 1.1. WSUS is the replacement for Software Update Services (SUS).

You can use the Microsoft Baseline Security Analyzer (MBSA) to check for common security problems on a single computer or multiple computers. MBSA is not included with Windows Server 2003, but can be downloaded from the Microsoft Downloads site (*http://download.microsoft.com*). MBSA can detect incorrect security configurations and failure to install security updates. When you run MBSA, it details:

- Account vulnerabilities
- Filesystem vulnerabilities
- Improper passwords
- Missing security updates
- Other vulnerabilities, such as those for IIS or SQL Server

Planning and Configuring a Public Key Infrastructure That Uses Certificate Services

Public Key Infrastructure (PKI) provides the components and services necessary to use public and private keys with digital certificates. You can use certificates for authentication and encryption. Two types of certificates are used:

Client certificates
: These contain identifying information about a client

Server certificates
: These contain identifying information about a server

Certificates enable clients and servers to authenticate each other prior to establishing a connection. Because certificates contain public and private encryption keys, they also are used to encrypt and decrypt data. A basic overview of public and private key encryption follows:

1. When a client wants to securely send data to a server, the client obtains the server's public key and uses it to encrypt the message. The message is then securely transmitted over the network.
2. When the server receives the encrypted message from the client, the server decrypts it using its private key.
3. When the server wants to securely reply to the client's request, the server obtains the client's public key and uses it to encrypt the reply. The reply is then securely transmitted over the network.
4. When the client receives the encrypted reply from the server, the client decrypts it using its private key.

Windows Server 2003 includes PKI components and services referred to collectively as *Microsoft Certificate Services*. Microsoft Certificate Services allow you to issue and manage digital certificates.

Identifying the appropriate type of certificate authority to support certificate issuance requirements

Certificate authorities are used to issue digital certificates. A *certificate authority (CA)* is a trusted agency responsible for confirming the identity of clients and servers, and then issuing certificates that confirm these identities. Before issuing a client certificate, CAs require you to identify the user, the user's organization, and the client application being used. Before issuing a server certificate, CAs require you to identify the organization in which the server is located and the server itself.

Certificate servers can be configured as one of four types of CAs:

Enterprise root CA
: The certificate server at the root of the hierarchy for an Active Directory domain. The enterprise root CA is the most trusted CA in the enterprise and is integrated with Active Directory.

Enterprise subordinate CA
: A certificate server that is a member of an existing CA hierarchy. The enterprise subordinate CA can issue certificates but must obtain its own CA certificate from the enterprise root CA.

Stand-alone root CA
: The certificate server at the root of a nondomain (workgroup) hierarchy. The stand-alone root CA is the most trusted CA in its hierarchy and does not use Active Directory.

Stand-alone subordinate CA
: A certificate server that is a member of an existing nonenterprise (workgroup) hierarchy. The stand-alone subordinate CA can issue certificates but must obtain its own CA certificate from the stand-alone root CA in its hierarchy.

Planning the enrollment and distribution of certificates

The enterprise root CA is at the top of the enterprise CA hierarchy. There can be only one root CA in an enterprise. All other CAs in the hierarchy must be enterprise subordinate CAs.

Enterprise CAs use certificate templates, publish their certificates and revocation lists to Active Directory, and use the information in Active Directory to determine whether to automatically approve or deny certificate enrollment requests. Clients must have access to Active Directory to receive certificates.

Enterprise CAs publish their Certificate Revocation Lists in Active Directory, making it easier to ensure that revoked certificate cannot be used.

Stand-alone CAs can use the same type of hierarchy as enterprise CAs. You can create a stand-alone root CA with all other CAs in the hierarchy created as stand-alone subordinate CAs. If you plan to use a single stand-alone CA, this CA must be configured as a stand-alone root CA.

Stand-alone CAs do not use templates and are not integrated with Active Directory. They store information locally and by default do not automatically approve or deny certificate enrollment requests. Instead, certificate enrollment requests are maintained in a queue for an administrator to manually approve or deny them.

While certificate servers don't have to be dedicated for this sole purpose, it is generally a good idea to have dedicated certificate servers. To protect the integrity of certificate services, you should create multiple levels in the CA hierarchy. In an enterprise, this means setting up an enterprise root CA, and then setting up one or more levels of enterprise subordinate CAs. Then, issue certificates through the subordinate CAs only. This safeguard should help ensure that the root CA's private key can't be easily compromised.

Planning for the use of smart cards for authentication

A *smart card* is a small card-sized device that contains memory and/or integrated circuitry. Windows can use smart cards for authentication during logon. To use smart cards for authentication, you must:

1. Install smart card reader devices on computers.
2. Set up a smart card to use for user logon.

Smart cards contain a user's digital certificate and private key, allowing the user to be authenticated when logging on the network. With smart cards, only enterprise CAs can be used. The reason for this is that smart card certificates are associated with the user's account in Active Directory, and only enterprise CAs store certificates in Active Directory.

Stand-alone CAs do not store certificates in Active Directory and should not be used to issue smart card certificates.

Once you've configured your CA infrastructure, you can set up logon for smart cards by completing the following steps:

1. Log on using an account authorized to enroll certificates for the domain where the user's account is located.
2. Open Internet Explorer. In the Address field, type the address of the CA that issues smart card certificates, and then press Enter.
3. Click Request A Certificate, and then click Advanced Certificate Request.
4. Click Request A Certificate For A Smart Card On Behalf Of Another User Using The Smart Card Certificate Enrollment Station. If you are prompted to accept the smart card signing certificate, click Yes.
5. In Certificate Template, click Smart Card Logon if you want to use the smart card for logging on to Windows only, or click Smart Card User if you want to use the smart card for secure email as well as logging on to Windows.
6. In Certification Authority, click the name of the CA that will issue the smart card certificate.

7. In Cryptographic Service Provider, select the cryptographic service provider (CSP) of the smart card's manufacturer.
8. In Administrator Signing Certificate, click the Enrollment Agent certificate that will sign the enrollment request.
9. In User To Enroll, click Select User. Select the appropriate user account, and then click Enroll.
10. When prompted, insert the smart card into the smart card reader on your computer, and then click OK. When prompted, enter the personal identification number (PIN) for the smart card.

In Active Directory Users And Computers, you can view and manage the certificates assigned to a user account using the Published Certificates tab of the user's Properties dialog box. This tab is only displayed when View → Advanced Features is selected.

Configuring Certificate Services

Microsoft Certificate Services uses IIS. You should install IIS prior to installing Certificate Services. After you install IIS, you can install Certificate Services by completing the following steps:

1. Log on to the server for which you are configuring Certificate Services. If you're creating an enterprise CA, the account must have Enterprise Admin privileges.
2. Click Start → Control Panel → Add Or Remove Programs.
3. Click the Add/Remove Windows Components button.
4. Select the Certificate Services checkbox. When prompted, click Yes, and then click Next.
5. Select the CA type. Click Next.
6. Enter the common name for the CA, such as First Root CA, and set the CA certificate's expiration date. Click Next.
7. Specify the storage location for the configuration database and log. By default, the certificate database and log are stored in the *\%SystemRoot%\System32\CertLog* folder. Click Next.
8. If IIS is running on the certificate server, Windows will need to shut down IIS before continuing. When prompted, click Yes.
9. The Windows Components Wizard begins installing and configuring Certificate Services. Click Finish when this process is completed.

When you install Certificates Services on a computer running IIS, you can manage Certificate Services using a web browser. Use the URL *http://hostname/certsrv/* where *hostname* is the name of the certificate server. The Certificate Authority console in the Administrative tools menu can also be used to manage Certificate Services. In an enterprise, the certificate server is configured for automatic enrollment by default. This means authorized users can request a certificate, and the CA automatically processes the certificate request so that the user can immediately install the certificate.

To view or change the default request processing policy, use the following technique:

1. Click Start → Programs → Administrative Tools → Certificate Authority.
2. Right-click the CA node, and then select Properties.
3. Click the Policy Module tab.
4. Click the Properties button.
5. To process requests manually, select Set The Certificate Request Status To Pending. The Administrator Must Explicitly Issue The Certificate.
6. To automatically process requests, select Follow The Settings In The Certificate Template, If Applicable. Otherwise, Automatically Issue The Certificate.
7. Click OK twice.

For manual processing of requests, you can review pending requests by selecting the Pending Requests node in the Certificate Authority console.

9

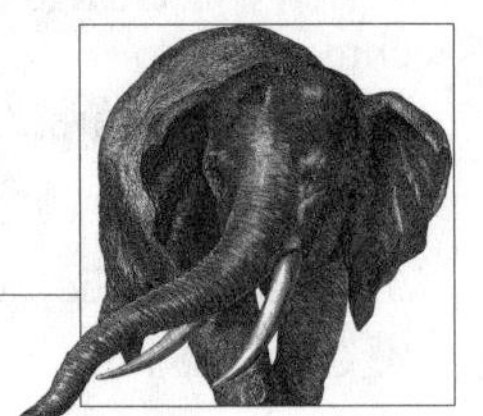

Exam 70-293 Prep and Practice

The material in this chapter is designed to help you prepare and practice for *Exam 70-293: Planning and Maintaining a Windows Server 2003 Network Infrastructure*. The chapter is organized into four sections:

Preparing for Exam 70-293
: This section provides an overview of the types of questions on the exam. Reviewing this section will help you understand how the actual exam works.

Exam 70-293 Suggested Exercises
: This section provides a numbered list of exercises that you can follow to gain experience in the exam's subject areas. Performing the exercises in this section will help ensure you have hands-on experience with all areas of the exam.

Exam 70-293 Highlighters Index
: This section compiles the facts within the exam's subject areas that you are most likely to need another look at—in other words, the areas of study that you might have highlighted while reading the Study Guide. Studying the highlights is useful as a final review before the exam.

Exam 70-293 Practice Questions
: This section includes a comprehensive set of practice questions to assess your knowledge of the exam. The questions are similar in format to the exam. After you've reviewed the Study Guide, performed the Suggested Exercises, and studied the Highlighters Index, read the questions and see whether you can answer them correctly.

Before you take Exam 70-293, review the exam overview, perform the suggested exercises, and go through the practice questions provided. Many online sites provide practice tests for the exam. Duplicating the depth and scope of these practice exams in a printed book isn't possible. Visit Microsoft's Certification site for pointers to online practice tests (*http://www.microsoft.com/learning/mcpexams/prepare/practicetests.asp*).

Preparing for Exam 70-293

Exam 70-293 is a computer-generated exam. The exam is timed, and the amount of time remaining on the exam is displayed by an onscreen timer clock. Most questions on the exam are multiple choice. Multiple choice questions are either:

Multiple-choice, single answer
: A radio button allows you to select a single answer only.

Multiple-choice, multiple answer
: A checkbox allows you to select multiple answers. Usually the number of correct answers is indicated in the question itself.

Typically, the test environment will have Previous/Next and Mark For Review options. You can navigate through the test using the Previous/Next buttons. You can click the Mark For Review checkbox to flag a question for later review. At the bottom of the screen is a calculator button. You may need to use the calculator in scientific mode to calculate IP addresses, subnet masks, and subnet numbers.

Other formats for questions are used as well, including:

List prioritization
: Pick the choices that answer the question and arrange the list in a specified order. Lists initially appear on the right side, and you have to click << ADD to add them in the correct order to the list on the left side. For example, you might have to list the steps for planning network topology in priority order.

Hot area
: Indicate the correct answer by clicking one or more areas of the screen or dialog box provided with the question. For example, you might see a TCP/IP properties dialog box and have to identify a misconfigured option by clicking it.

Select and Place
: Using drag-and-drop, pick answers from given set of choices and place them in an appropriate spot in a dialog box or diagram. For example, you might see a list of IP addresses and have to place them in the identified subnets.

Active screen
: Use the dialog box provided to configure the options correctly or perform the required procedure. For example, you might see a properties dialog box for a DNS zone and have to configure zone transfers to designated name servers.

Simulation
: Use the simulated desktop environment provided to perform a specific task or troubleshoot. For example, you might be asked to troubleshoot Internet connectivity.

With the exception of multiple choice, single answer questions, all of the other questions can have multiple answers or multiple required procedures to obtain full credit. If all of the expected answers or procedures are not performed, you will only get partial credit for the answer.

While many of the questions on Exam 70-293 are multiple choice, there are hot area, select and place, active screen, and simulation questions being used increasingly to ensure that the testing process more accurately reflects actual hands-on knowledge rather than rote memorization. Individuals with adequate hands-on administration experience who have reviewed the study guide, performed the practice exercises, memorized the essentials, and taken practice tests should do well on this type of exam. Individuals who lack adequate hands-on experience and have not prepared appropriately will do poorly.

Exam 70-293 Suggested Exercises

Exam 70-293 includes many areas of study from Exams 70-290 and 70-291, and expects you to be able to take your knowledge of the related areas of study to the next level. You are expected not only to be a good administrator in these areas, but you are also expected to have the solid planning skills of a network designer. The measured skills are extended to include many new areas of study, including WAN connectivity, WAN configurations, NetBIOS name resolution, high availability, IPSec policy, and public key infrastructure.

You'll need plenty of hands-on and design experience to pass the exam. You'll need to review the study guide closely, especially any areas with which you are unfamiliar. This section provides a numbered list of exercises that you can follow to gain experience in the exam's subject areas. Performing the exercises will be useful to help ensure that you have hands-on and design experience with all areas of the exam.

For this exam, I recommend setting up two test networks or reconfiguring a single test network as necessary to get hands-on practice for the exam. The first network/configuration should include a domain controller, a workstation for administration, and a workstation for remote access testing. The second network/configuration is for planning and implementing high availability, and should include multiple servers running Windows Server 2003, configured as part of a domain environment.

In addition to performing the exercises below, you should also have experience using each of the Windows Server 2003 administrative tools described in the Study Guide.

Choosing Client Operating Systems

1. Choose operating systems for a client deployment.
2. List preferred operating systems for Active Directory support.
3. List preferred operating systems for security.
4. List nonpreferred operating systems and detail why those operating systems should not be used.

Choosing Server Operating Systems

1. Choose operating systems for a server deployment.
2. List the preferred Windows Server 2003 edition for use as a frontend web server.
3. List the preferred Windows Server 2003 edition for use in a branch office.
4. List the preferred Windows Server 2003 edition for use two-node clustering with four CPUs.
5. List the preferred Windows Server 2003 edition for use 4-node clustering with 64 CPUs.

Planning and Implementing Server Roles

1. Plan the deployment of a new network.
2. List the server roles that need to be supported for Active Directory, dynamic addressing, name resolution with current clients and servers, and name resolution with pre-Windows 2000 clients and servers.
3. Detail how the server roles will be implemented.

Planning a Strategy to Enforce System Default Security Settings on New Systems

1. Create an outline for an enterprise-wide security plan.
2. Identify potential security risks.
3. Specify minimum security requirements.
4. Specify the minimum set of required security features.
5. Provide plans for meeting required security levels.

Developing a Security Policy

1. Outline a plan for securing the organization's infrastructure.
2. Outline a plan for implementing required security features.
3. Outline a plan for ongoing management and evaluation of security.

Identifying Client and Server Operating System Default Security Settings

1. Identify default security for filesystem permissions.
2. Identify default security for share permissions.
3. Identify default security for registry permissions.
4. Identify default security for active directory permissions.
5. Identify default security for account policies.
6. Identify default security for local policies.

Planning Security for Computers That Are Assigned Specific Roles

1. Create a plan for implementing baseline security on workstations in a high-security environment.
2. Create a plan for implementing baseline security on domain controllers in a high-security environment.
3. Create a plan for implementing baseline security for other server roles in a high-security environment.
4. Create custom security templates for workstations, domain controllers, and servers with key roles in the organization.

Planning a Network Topology

1. Plan the infrastructure for a network with multiple subnets, wireless connectivity, and a WAN connection to the Internet.
2. List the hardware and software components required to implement the desired network infrastructure.
3. Identify all required resources as part of your planning.
4. Identify the Data Link Layer protocol to use.
5. Identify the media types to use on the local subnets, wireless connections, and on the WAN connection.
6. Plan the physical placement of network resources with regard to range limitations.

Planning a TCP/IP Network Infrastructure Strategy

1. Create a plan for TCP/IP network infrastructure that supports 500 users who connect locally, wirelessly, and using remote access.
2. Analyze and list the IP Addressing requirements for workstations and servers on multiple subnets.
3. Plan an IP routing strategy to support dynamic addressing, network address translation, and remote access.

Creating an IP Subnet Scheme

1. List the subnet IDs for /28 subnets on the Class C network 192.168.10.0.
2. List the usable IP addresses in each subnet.
3. List the broadcast IP address in each subnet.

Troubleshooting TCP/IP Addressing

1. Disconnect a computer's network cable.
2. Use the command line to diagnose the problem.
3. Reconnect the computer's network cable.
4. Configure invalid settings for TCP/IP.

5. Use the command line to ping another computer on the network.
6. Use `netdiag` to test the computer's configuration.
7. Reconfigure the computer so it uses valid settings.
8. Use `netdiag` to test the computer's configuration.

Planning an Internet Connectivity Strategy

1. Create an Internet connectivity plan that ensures the security of the internal network.
2. Choose an Internet access solution to meet the needs of a small branch office with 50 users.
3. Choose an Internet access solution to meet the needs of a regional office with 500 users.
4. Choose an Internet access solution to meet the needs of a large central office with 5,000 users.

Planning a NetBIOS Name Resolution Strategy

1. Create a name resolution plan for an organization with 500 users with a mix of client types.
2. Plan the implementation of NetBIOS name resolution.
3. Choose a name resolution strategy that uses LMHOSTS and WINS as appropriate.
4. Choose a WINS replication strategy.
5. Configure replication partners.
6. Configure DHCP so DHCP clients to automatically get the correct WINS settings.

Planning a Routing Strategy

1. Create an IP-routing strategy to support multiple subnets and WAN connections.
2. Choose the appropriate routing protocols for LAN and WAN routing.
3. Create a routing plan that supports multicast traffic.

Planning Security for Remote Access Users

1. Analyze protocol security requirements.
2. Plan authentication methods for remote access clients that use smart cards.
3. Plan authentication methods for remote access clients that use Windows XP Professional.
4. Plan authentication methods for remote access clients that use Windows 95.

Planning Security for VPN

1. Create a plan for remote access using VPN with strict security requirements.
2. Implement IPSec policy.
3. Implement remote access policy.

Using Performance Monitoring

1. Configure performance monitoring on a server as you would for a database server.
2. Configure performance monitoring on a server as you would for a web server.
3. Configure performance logging to monitor a server according to a schedule.
4. Configuring a server with performance alerts for 95 percent or higher CPU utilization and less than 10 percent free space on all essential disks.
5. Determine if a server has any performance bottlenecks.

Planning Server Availability

1. Create a plan for ensuring high availability.
2. Identify applications and services that can use Network Load Balancing.
3. Identify applications and services that can use Microsoft Cluster Service.

Managing and Implementing Disaster Recovery

1. Create a disaster recovery plan for a server.
2. Create an Automated System Recovery (ASR) disk.
3. Schedule full backups of the server on a weekly basis.
4. Schedule daily differential backups on the server.
5. Perform a test restore to original, alternate, and single locations.

Restoring Data from Shadow Copy Volumes

1. Enable shadow copies on a volume.
2. Create shadow copies of the volume's shares.
3. Install the shadow copy client.
4. Access the shadow copy of a share.
5. Restore a corrupted or deleted file from previous version.

Planning and Configuring Network Protocol Security

1. Create a Network Protocol security plan.
2. Identify the ports used by DNS, WINS, DHCP, HTTP, Active Directory, and remote access.
3. Identify the ports currently being used by a server.
4. Configure TCP/IP filtering on a server running Windows Server 2003.

5. Configure packet filtering on a RRAS server.
6. Configure Windows Firewall on a workstation running Windows XP Professional.

Planning and Configuring an IPSec Policy for Secure Network Communications

1. Create an IPSec plan for the network.
2. Implement IPSec policy so IPSec is required.
3. Confirm that IPSec policy is being applied.

Using Remote Desktop for Administration

1. Configure a server so that it can be remotely managed using Remote Desktop.
2. Open the Remote Desktop Connection client, and then click Options.
3. Establish a remote session with the computer from a workstation or another server.

Using Remote Assistance

1. Configure a server so that it can send Remote Assistance requests.
2. While logged on to the server, ask for remote assistance.
3. Accept the remote assistance request on another computer.
4. Access the remote server and give assistance.

Planning Security for Wireless Networks

1. Install a wireless network adapter on a computer running Windows XP Professional.
2. Install a wireless router on the network.
3. Configure the wireless devices to use infrastructure mode.
4. Configure strict security through Wireless Policy in Active Directory.

Troubleshooting Security for Data Transmission

1. Determine if IPSec is configured properly.
2. Enable diagnostic logging for IPSec.
3. Monitor IPSec policy to ensure that it is working correctly using IP Security Monitor.
4. Determine through Resultant Set of Policy the GPO from which IPSec policy settings are being applied.

Configuring Software Update Infrastructure

1. Install an update server.
2. Configure policy so that updates are installed automatically.
3. Configure policy so that the update server is used.

Planning and Configuring a Public Key Infrastructure That Uses Certificate Services

1. Plan a Public Key Infrastructure for an Active Directory domain where smart cards will be used.
2. Identify the appropriate type of Certificate Authorities to use.
3. Plan the enrollment and distribution of certificates.
4. Install Certificate Services.

Exam 70-293 Highlighters Index

In this section, I've attempted to compile the facts within the exam's subject areas that you are most likely to need another look at—in other words, the areas of study that you might have highlighted while reading the Study Guide. The title of each highlighted element corresponds to the heading title in the Exam 70-293 Study Guide. In this way, if you have a question about a highlight, you can refer back to the corresponding section in the study guide. For the most part, the entries under a heading are organized as term lists with a Windows Server 2003 feature, component, or administration tool as the term, and the key details for this feature, component, or administration tool listed next.

Planning and Implementing Server Roles and Server Security

Summary of highlights from the "Planning and Implementing Server Roles and Server Security" section of the Exam 70-293 Study Guide.

Operating system selection

- Computers should be configured with the operating system that is appropriate for their role.
- Create specific guidelines for choosing which operating system to use when.
- Include specifics on hardware requirements, duty life, and upgrade frequency.

Client operating system selection

- Determine minimum configuration to satisfy security requirements.
- Determine preferred client operating systems.

Server operating system selection

- Windows Server 2003, Web Edition is for enterprise Intranets and Internet web sites.
- Windows Server 2003, Standard Edition is for small or branch office use.
- Windows Server 2003, Enterprise Edition is for larger organizations.

- Windows Server 2003, Datacenter Edition is for large-scale data centers.
- A comparison of each edition is provided in Table 9-1.

Table 9-1. Comparison of Windows Server 2003 operating system editions

	Windows Server 2003, Web Edition	Windows Server 2003, Standard Edition	Windows Server 2003, Enterprise Edition	Windows Server 2003, Datacenter Edition
Minimum processor speed	133 MHz	133 MHz for x86; 733 MHz for 64-bit	133 MHz for x86; 733 MHz for 64-bit	400 MHz for x86; 733 MHz for 64-bit
Minimum recommended processor speed	550 MHz	550 MHz	733 MHz	733 MHz
Multiprocessor support	Up to 2	Up to 4	Up to 8	8 to 64
Minimum RAM	128 MB	128 MB	128 MB	512 MB
Minimum recommended RAM	256 MB	256 MB	256 MB	1 GB
Maximum RAM	2 GB	4 GB	32 GB for x86; 1 TB for 64-bit	64 GB for x86; 1 TB for 64-bit
Active Directory support	Domain member only	DC or member	DC or member	DC or member

Server configurations

- Member servers are a part of a domain but don't store directory information.
- Domain controllers store directory information, provide authentication, and offer directory services.
- Standalone servers have their own security database for authenticating logon requests.

Server roles

- Servers can support multiple roles.
- You can add or remove server roles using Manage Your Server.

Secure baseline installation

- Baseline installations should provide a secure starting point for final configuration.
- Build on the baseline installation to strengthen security as appropriate.

Security plans

- Should be part of a larger enterprise security effort
- Should be created with an understanding of default security settings
- Should detail the specific security features to use
- Should meet the objectives and requirements of the enterprise security policy

Enterprise-wide security policies

- Should identify potential security risks
- Should specify minimum security requirements
- Should specify the minimum set of required security features
- Should provide plans for meeting required security levels
- Should be managed by a designated security team

Security teams

- Members should include users, administrators, and managers.
- Members should have a strong understanding of security.
- Members should develop security policy as part of an ongoing effort.
- Members are responsible for enforcement, ongoing education, and distribution as appropriate.

Security policy

- Should include a plan for securing the organization's infrastructure
- Should include a plan for implementing required security features
- Should include a plan for ongoing management and evaluation of security

Areas of security

- Access controls are used to manage access to resources and determine who has access to what.
- Authentication mechanisms are used to verify a user's identity prior to providing access to resources.
- Auditing is used to monitor access and use of privileges.

Ways to enhance security

- Network security can be enhanced using firewalls, proxies, and Network Address Translation (NAT).
- Resource access can be controlled using encrypted passwords, certificates, and hardware devices.
- Data can be protected using NTFS security and the Encrypting File System (EFS).

NTFS permissions

- Both basic and advanced permissions can be used with NTFS.
- All files and folders have specific owners, and permissions are inherited from parent folders.
- You can modify permissions, ownership, and inheritance on the Security tab.

Default NTFS permissions

- Setup grants the Everyone group Full Control on nonsystem drives.
- Setup configures default permissions on the system drive, as shown in Table 9-2.

Table 9-2. Default NTFS permissions on the system drive

	%SystemDrive% folder and non-Windows specific subfolders	Documents and Settings folder	Program Files folder	%Windir% folder
Administrators Group	Full Control	Full Control	Full Control	Full Control
Users Group	Read & Execute, List Folder Contents, Read, Create Folders/Append Data, Create Files/Write Data (subfolders only)	Read & Execute, List Folder Contents, Read	N/A	N/A
Everyone Group	Read & Execute (root only not subfolders)	Read & Execute, List Folder Contents, Read	N/A	N/A
Authenticated Users Group	N/A	N/A	Read & Execute, List Folder Contents, Read, Modify	Read & Execute, List Folder Contents, Read, Modify
Server Operators Group	N/A	N/A	Read & Execute, List Folder Contents, Read, Write	Read & Execute, List Folder Contents, Read, Write
Creator Owner	Full Control (subfolders and files only)	N/A	Full Control (subfolders and files only)	Full Control (subfolders and files only)
System	Full Control	Full Control	Full Control	Full Control

Default share permissions

- Drive shares are available to Administrators, and the permissions cannot be modified.
- Everyone group has Read permissions on a share by default on Windows Server 2003.
- Everyone group has Full Control permission on a share by default on Windows 2000.

Difference between share and NTFS permissions

- Share permissions provide the top-level access control.
- NTFS permissions provide the base-level access controls.

Default Registry permissions

- Members of the Administrators group have Full Control permissions for all keys.
- The System user has Full Control permissions for all keys.
- The Everyone group has Read permission for HKEY_LOCAL_MACHINE and HKEY_USERS keys.
- The Authenticated Users group have Read permissions for HKEY_CLASSES_ROOT.

- The Server Operators group has permissions to read, create, and modify HKEY_CLASSES_ROOT.
- The Users group has Read permissions for HKEY_CURRENT_CONFIG.

Default Active Directory permissions

- Enterprise Admins have Full Control permission over the domain.
- Domain Admins and Administrators can create and manage most objects in the domain.
- Account Operators are granted Full Control permission over account-related groups.
- Server Operators are granted Full Control over Domain Controllers.
- Authenticated Users assigned Read permissions and some limited special permissions.

Delegation of control

- Delegation is useful if you want to give someone limited administrative privileges.
- Delegate control to grant permission to manage users, groups, computers, or other objects.
- To delegate control, use the Delegation Of Control Wizard in Active Directory Users And Computers.

Active Directory object permissions

- The Advanced Features view gives you access to Active Directory object permissions.
- To view, select Advanced Features on the View menu in Active Directory Users And Computers.
- Right-click the object and then select Properties. Use the Security tab options.

Default security for password policies

- With Enforce Password History, the default value is 24 passwords remembered.
- With Maximum Password Age, the default value is 42 days.
- With Minimum Password Age, the default value is 1 day.
- With Minimum Password Length, the default value is seven characters.
- With Passwords Must Meet Complexity Requirements, the policy is enabled by default.
- With Store Passwords Using Reversible Encryption, the policy is disabled by default.

Default security for account policies

- With Account Lockout Duration, the policy is not defined by default.
- With Account Lockout Threshold, the default value is zero, meaning accounts will not be locked out due to Account Lockout policy.
- With Reset Account Lockout Counter After, the policy is not defined by default.

Default security for Kerberos policies

- With Enforce User Logon Restrictions, the policy is enabled by default.
- With Maximum Lifetime For Service Ticket, the default maximum duration is 600 minutes.
- With Maximum Lifetime For User Ticket, the maximum duration is 10 hours by default.
- With Maximum Lifetime For User Ticket Renewal, the maximum renewal period is seven days by default.
- With Maximum Tolerance For Computer Clock Synchronization, computers must be synchronized within five minutes of each other. If they aren't, authentication fails.

Local policies

- Audit Policy is used to manage audit policy for an Active Directory domain.
- User Rights Assignment is used to manage user rights assignment for an Active Directory domain.
- Security Options are used to manage additional security options.
- Manage local policies through the applicable GPOs.

Hardening servers

- Requires deploying specific security configuration baselines using Group Policy
- Requires creating custom security templates to enhance security to support server roles

Group policies are applied in the following order:

1. Local computer group policy
2. Site group policy
3. Domain group policy
4. Organizational unit (OU) group policy

Group policy settings

- Settings applied last have precedence by default, meaning they overwrite previously applied settings.
- The cumulative affects of policy settings are determined by inheritance- and policy-processing rules.
- GPOs inherit settings unless inheritance is blocked or overridden.
- The end result of inheritance- and policy-processing is referred to as the Resultant Set of Policy (RSoP).
- By determining the RSoP for a user or computer, you can determine the policy settings in affect.

Default GPOs

- Workstations and member servers are placed in the Computers container.
- Workstations and member servers are only affected by site and domain GPOs
- Domain controllers are placed in the Domain Controllers OU.
- Domain controllers are affected by site, domain, and Default Domain Controllers Policy GPOs.

Role-specific security configurations

- You can create role-specific security configurations using GPOs and OUs.
- Create role-specific OUs and configure policy settings for that role, then move computers to the appropriate OU.

Security settings

- Key security settings are stored under *Computer Configuration\Windows Settings\Security Settings*.
- These are the same areas of policy that are managed using security templates.
- Account policy settings control security for passwords, account lockout, and Kerberos.
- Local Policy settings control security for auditing, user rights assignment, and other security options.
- Event log policy settings control security for event logging.
- Restricted groups settings control security for local group membership administration.
- System services settings control security and startup mode for local services.
- Filesystem policy settings control security for the local filesystem.
- Registry policy settings control the values of security-related registry keys.

Security templates

- These are stored in the *%SystemRoot%\Security\Templates* folder.
- These can be imported into GPOs.
- These contain customized group policy definitions that apply essential security settings.
- These are used to implement and manage network security.
- These are created and configured using the Security Templates snap-in.
- These are applied and analyzed using the Security Configuration And Analysis snap-in.

Creating security templates

- Use the Security Templates snap-in to create templates.
- Create a copy of a template by right-clicking the template you want to copy and clicking Save As.
- Create a new template by right-clicking the *C:\Windows\security\templates* node and selecting New Template.

Applying security template settings and analyzing security

- Use the Security Configuration And Analysis snap-in to apply templates and to compare settings.
- Comparing settings pinpoints any discrepancies between what is implemented currently and what is defined in a security template.

Planning, Implementing, and Maintaining a Network Infrastructure

Summary of highlights from the "Planning, Implementing, and Maintaining a Network Infrastructure" section of the Exam 70-293 Study Guide.

Network infrastructure planning requires

- A Network topology strategy
- A TCP/IP addressing strategy
- An Internet connectivity strategy
- A name resolution strategy

Network infrastructure

- Encompasses networking, connectivity, security, routing, and management.
- A network's physical structure is the physical design that defines its topology and its hardware.
- A network's logical structure is the logical design that defines the abstract architecture.

Open Systems Interconnection (OSI) reference model

- Defines the functions that are implemented in various networking protocols.
- Has seven layers: Application, Presentation, Session, Transport, Network, Data-Link, and Physical.

Data-Link Layer

- This defines the interface between the network medium and the software running on a hardware device.
- This is responsible for packet addressing, media access control, and data encapsulation.

Data-Link Layer sublayers

- The logical link control (LLC) sublayer controls frame synchronizations, flow control, and error checking.
- The media access control (MAC) sublayer controls transmission of data packets.

Data-link Layer protocol

- The Data-Link Layer protocol encompasses the physical and Data-Link Layers in its functions.
- Types of Data-Link layer protocols include Ethernet and Token Ring.

Data-Link Layer protocol suite

- The protocol suite implements the functions of the network and transport layers.
- Session, presentation, and application layer functions are provided by a protocol in the protocol suite, by a separate application-layer protocol, or by both.

Types of Data Link Layer protocol suites

- Few current networks use Internet Package Exchange (IPX).
- Few current networks use NetBIOS Extended User Interface (NetBEUI).
- Most current networks use Transmission Control Protocol/Internet Protocol (TCP/IP).

TCP/IP

- IP operates at the network layer.
- TCP operates at the transport layer.
- TCP/IP includes the User Datagram Protocol (UDP) transport layer protocol.

TCP

- Is a reliable, connection-oriented protocol
- Relies on connections being established between two hardware devices prior to communicating
- Uses acknowledgements to ensure data is received

UDP

- Is a connectionless protocol
- Allows two hardware devices to communicate without first establishing a connection
- Doesn't use acknowledgments

When selecting a Data Link Layer protocol

- Consider the physical distance between hardware devices
- Consider the required transmission speed
- Consider the cost and budget

Media types include

- Unshielded Twisted Pair (UTP), which consists of four pairs of wires, each twisted together.
- Fiber optic, which consists of a strand of plastic or glass that carries signals in the form of light pulses.
- Wireless, which uses wireless broadcasting and wireless transceivers instead of physical cabling.

UTP cabling

- Uses an RJ-45 jack into which cables are connected.
- Both Cat 3 and Cat 5 support Ethernet and Token Ring.

Fiber-optic cabling

- Uses a fiber-optic connector into which cables are connected.
- Both single mode and multimode support Ethernet and Token Ring.

Wireless networking

- Uses wireless network adapters and wireless access points.
- Wireless access points, or base stations, are connected to the organization's network.

- Most wireless devices conform to standards based on the IEEE 802.1 specification.

Ethernet

- Ethernet running at 10 megabits per second can have no more than 4 hubs on a single LAN.
- Ethernet running at 100 megabits per second can have no more than 2 hubs on a single LAN.
- Ethernet running at 1,000 megabits per second can have no more than 1 hub on a single LAN.
- Common Ethernet variants are summarized in Table 9-3.

Table 9-3. Common Ethernet variants

Ethernet type	Designation	Cable type	Cable speed	Max. segment length
Standard Ethernet	10Base-T	Category 3 UTP	10 Mbps	100 meters
Fast Ethernet	100Base-T	Category 5 UTP	100 Mbps	100 meters
Gigabit Ethernet	1000Base-T	Category 5E UTP	1,000 Mbps	100 meters
Gigabit Ethernet	1000Base-LX	50/125 or 62.5/125 multimode fiber	10,000 Mbps	550 meters
Gigabit Ethernet	1000Base-SX	50/125 multimode fiber	1,000 Mbps	500 meters
Gigabit Ethernet	1000Base-SX	62.5/125 multi-mode fiber	1,000 Mbps	220 meters
Gigabit Ethernet	1000Base-LX	9/125 single mode fiber	1,000 Mbps	3,000 meters

Types of IP addresses

- Static IP addresses are those manually assigned to computers.
- Dynamic IP addresses are automatically obtained from a DHCP server.
- Automatic private IP addresses (APIPA) are used when DHCP is configured but unavailable.

Determining IP addressing needs

- How many networks do you need?
- How many computers on each network?
- Will computers need to connect directly to the Internet?

TCP/IP version 4

- Standard unicast IP classes are Class A, Class B, and Class C.
- Addresses are comprised of sets of 32-bit numbers.
- Each 8-bit section is called an octet.
- Public (registered) IP addresses must be registered with an ISP.
- Private (unregistered) IP addresses do not need to be registered with an ISP.

Class A networks

- The first octet identifies the network and the last three octets identify computers.
- Allow millions of hosts but a small number of networks.
- Have addresses that begin with a number between 1 and 126.
- Private Class A network addresses have a network ID of 10.0.0.0.

Class B networks

- The first two octets identify the network and the last two octets identify computers.
- Allow equal number of networks and hosts.
- Have addresses that begin with a number between 128 and 191.
- Private Class B network addresses have a network ID of 172.16.0.0.

Class C networks

- The first three octets identify the network and the last octet identifies computers.
- Allow many networks and relatively few hosts per network.
- Have addresses that begin with a number between 192 and 223.
- Private Class C network addresses have a network ID of 192.168.0.0.

IP routers

- IP routers are used to connect local area networks and can be hardware or software devices.
- IP routers connect networks by relaying traffic between the connected networks as necessary.

IP routing protocols

- DHCP Relay Agent routing protocol enables routing of DHCP broadcast messages between subnets.
- Routing Information Protocol (RIP) version 2 for Internet Protocol enables dynamic routing between subnets.
- Open Shortest Path First (OSPF) enables extended dynamic routing between subnets.
- Network Address Translation (NAT) provides internet connectivity and Basic Firewall functions to internal clients.

IP subnets

- The subnet mask specifies the bits to use for the network ID and the bits to use for the host ID.
- In prefix notation, the network ID is followed by the number of bits in the network ID.
- Without subnetting:
  - Class A networks are /8 networks.
  - Class B networks are /16 networks.
  - Class C networks are /24 networks.

Subnet masks

- Bits values are assigned in a specific order, from the most significant bits to the least significant bits.
- Bits in the subnet mask are always set consecutively from left to right.
- From left to right, the values of each bit are 128, 64, 32, 16, 8, 4, 2, and 1.
- Each bit that's set is noted by a 1, which means the bit is on.

Subnetting

- You can use subnetting to subdivide a network.
- You need to calculate the network address of each subnet, and from that, determine usable IP addresses.
- Extract the octet that contains both the subnet bits and host identifier bits and subtract it from 256.
- The result is the network address of the second subnet.

Diagnosing and resolving Automatic Private IP Addressing

- An active network connection is required for automatic configuration to work properly.
- The media may be disconnected at either end of the network cable.
- Attempt to renew the IP address by typing `ipconfig /renew` at a command prompt.
- Disable APIPA using the `IPAutoconfigurationEnabled` DWORD value-entry in the Registry.

Diagnosing and Resolving incorrect TCP/IP configuration

- Check for invalid gateway configuration.
- Check for invalid IP address.
- Check for invalid subnet mask.
- Check for invalid DNS configuration.
- Check for invalid WINS configuration.
- Use `ping`, `arp`, `pathping`, `tracert`, and `netdiag` for testing.

Diagnosing and resolving DNS caching issues

- Use `ipconfig /displaydns` to displays the entries in the DNS cache.
- Use `ipconfig /flushdns` to purge the entries in the DNS cache.
- Use `ipconfig /registerdns` to refresh leased IP addresses and re-register DNS.

Verifying leases and DHCP reservation configuration

- Select a server's Active Leases node in the DHCP console.
- If a lease expires and is not renewed, the computer might have been moved.
- If a reservation is inactive, the reservation may be incorrectly configured.

Verifying the client configuration and examining the System event log

- View the current TCP/IP configuration by typing `ipconfig /all` at a command prompt.
- Warning messages regarding address conflicts are displayed in the system tray on the client computer. The System event log may have the Event ID 1055 and the source as DHCP.

Diagnosing and Resolving Issues DHCP server configuration

- Set predefined options, which set preset values and can be overridden at any other level.
- Set server options, which can be overridden by scope, class, and reservation options.
- Set scope options, which can be overridden by class and reservation options.
- Set class options, which can be overridden by reservation options.
- Set reservation options, which can be overridden only by manually assigned TCP/IP settings.

Resolve DHCP configuration problems by

1. Checking the Internet Protocol (TCP/IP) properties on the client.
2. Configuring scope options to override other options, as necessary.
3. Releasing and renew the client lease to ensure the client gets the correct settings.

Internet connectivity strategy

- The strategy should address the security policies and requirements of the organization.
- The strategy should address the needs of users within the organization.
- Most organizations require bandwidth for internal users and for the organization's web presence.
- Ideally, you'll have a separate strategy for each type of bandwidth required.

Determining bandwidth requirements

- Determine how many users on average will simultaneously access the Internet.
- Determine when Internet bandwidth is needed.
- Determine the relative importance of Internet access as compared to the cost of the access.
- Determine the categories of users relative to the types of Internet applications users run.
- Determine where users are located.

Choosing an Internet access solution

- Every Internet access solution requires a WAN connection, a WAN router, and an ISP.
- The connection should be protected with NAT and firewall technology and possibly proxy technology.
- Table 9-4 provides a summary of key Internet access solutions.

Table 9-4. Summary of key Internet access solutions

Connection type	Transmission speed	Simultaneous users/application
Dial-up/Dual dial-up Modem	Up to 56 Kbps/Up to 128 Kbps	8–10 email users 2–3 web users 1–2 large files/attachments
ISDN (Basic Rate Interface)	Up to 128 Kbps	8–10 email users 2–3 web users 1–2 large files/attachments
ISDN (Primary Rate Interface)	Up to 1.544 Mbps	50–70 email users 20–30 web users 12–20 large files/attachments
Cable Modem	Up to 7 Mbps downstream and 768 Kbps upstream	100–150 email users 50–75 web users 30–50 large files/attachments
DSL Modem	Up to 5 Mbps downstream and 768 Kbps upstream	90–120 email users 40–60 web users 24–40 large files/attachments
T-1	1.544 Mbps	50–70 email users 20–30 web users 12–20 large files/attachments
Fractional T-1	Up to 1.544 Mbps in 64 Kbps increments	Varies depending on bandwidth
T-3	44.736 Mbps	1500–2500 email users 600–900 web users 360–600 large files/attachments
Fractional T-3	Up to 44.736 Mbps in 1.544 Mbps increments	Varies depending on bandwidth

WAN connections

- Most WAN connections must be terminated using a separate piece of hardware.
- For a dial-up connection, a modem is used to terminate the WAN connection.
- ISDN, Cable, and DSL connections use a combination terminator/router.
- For a leased T-1 and T-3 line, a CSU/DSU is used to terminate the WAN connection.

Diagnosing and resolving LAN/WAN problems

- Problems experienced by all clients on a subnet may be due to the hub or switch.
- Problems experienced by all clients on all subnets may be due to problems with the WAN.
- Try to determine whether the problem affects access to all resources or only Internet resources.
- For internal problems not due to client configurations, examine Internet infrastructure components.

- NAT routers, proxies, and firewalls must have a routing interface that connects to the WAN.
- NAT routers must be configured to work with computers on your internal network.
- Firewalls or proxies must be configured properly, and both may be configured to block access.

Diagnosing WAN problems

- The `tracert`, `ping`, and `pingpath` commands can help you determine where a WAN problem originates.
- WAN routers require one interface connected to the internal network and one connected to the WAN.
- The CSU/DSU terminating the WAN connection may also be the source of the problem.
- Cycle the power on the CSU/DSU or reset the CSU/DSU.
- The ISP may have a problem with its network infrastructure or Internet connectivity.
- The problem could extend to the Internet backbone.

Planning a name resolution strategy

- Name resolution is essential for all TCP/IP networks.
- Windows Internet Naming Service (WINS) is used to resolve NetBIOS names.
- NetBIOS is also required for some applications, such as the Computer Browser service.
- Domain Name System (DNS) is used to resolve DNS hostnames.
- DNS is preferred for Windows 2000 and later systems.

NetBIOS namespace

- NetBIOS uses a flat naming structure.
- Each computer has a unique NetBIOS name of up to 16 characters; 15 on Windows systems.
- Windows reserves the 16th character to identify the type of resource represented by the name.
- NetBIOS is intended for use on private networks only, and not on the public Internet.

DNS namespace

- DNS uses a hierarchical namespace.
- DNS names can be up to 255 characters in length.
- With DNS, computers are grouped by name with domains.
- Domains establish a hierarchical naming structure.
- A computer's FQDN is its hostname combined with the related domain name.

Planning DNS name resolution strategy

- DNS is the primary name service for Windows 2000 and later.
- DNS translates computer names to IP addresses and vice versa.
- Forward lookups resolve computer names to IP addresses.
- Reverse lookups resolve IP addresses to computer names.
- By default, DHCP clients running Windows 2000 or later update their host (A) records in DNS.
- By default DHCP servers update the pointer (PTR) records on behalf of clients.
- DNS uses both iterative and recursive queries to resolve queries.

DNS servers

- DNS servers are said to be either authoritative or nonauthoritative for a zone.
- An authoritative DNS server for a zone is the primary source from which other DNS servers resolve.
- A nonauthoritative DNS server relies on an authoritative DNS server to keep its cache up to date.

DNS zones

- Each DNS server is responsible for name resolution within zones.
- A zone is a portion of the DNS database that is being managed.
- A single zone can contain a single domain or it can span multiple domains.
- By default, zone files are created as standard text files on the DNS server.
- Zone data can be stored in Active Directory by creating an Active Directory–integrated zone.
- Zones always consist of entire domains or subdomains.
- Domains must be contiguous in the DNS namespace.

Types of zone files

- A primary zone file is the master copy of a zone.
- A secondary zone is a read-only copy of a primary zone.
- A stub zone lists authoritative name servers for a zone.

DNS domain structure

- You'll want to have primary and alternate name servers.
- All changes to zones are made in the primary zone and replicated to secondary zones.
- Use secondary zones to make copies of zones and to distribute workload.

Stub zones

- Stub zones list authoritative name servers for a zone.
- Servers hosting stub zones direct related queries to authoritative servers.
- Stubs zones are most often used to track authoritative name servers for delegated zones.

Using multiple zones

- Windows Server 2003 DNS servers can support and manage 200,000 zones on a single server.
- You'll usually want to create multiple zones on a server, and then delegate zones to other servers.
- Control over zones can be delegated to make it easier to manage the DNS namespace.
- When you delegate a zone, you assign authority over a portion of the DNS namespace.

DNS server roles

- A single DNS server can have multiple roles.
- Primary DNS servers maintain one or more primary zone files.
- Secondary DNS servers maintain one or more secondary copies of zone files.
- Forwarding-only (caching-only) DNS servers cache resolved queries, contain no zones, and host no domains.
- A DNS server acts as a forwarding-only server if you've installed DNS Server service but have configured no DNS zones.

Planning zone replication

- Multiple DNS servers provide fault tolerance and distribute the name resolution workload.
- With file-based zones, you need primary and secondary DNS servers, and must replicate zone data.
- With Active Directory–integrated zones, the zone database is replicated automatically.

Zone transfers

- When you configure primary and secondary zones, you must configure zone transfers.
- Zone transfers are used to send a copy of a zone to requesting servers.
- Zone transfers ensure secondary servers are kept up to date.
- By default, zone transfers are not allowed or are restricted only to specified name servers.
- Limit the list of servers that can make zone transfer requests to enhance security.
- Windows Server 2003 DNS servers use incremental transfers.

Zone transfer notification

- When zone files change, secondary servers can be notified automatically.
- By default, automatic notification is enabled but only to a designated list of name servers.
- You must specify the designated name servers.

Active Directory–integrated zones

- Zone data is stored in the Active Directory database and replicated automatically.
- Active Directory–integrated zones use incremental replication.
- By default, DNS zone data is replicated to all other DCs acting as DNS servers in the domain.
- You can also replicate to all DCs acting as DNS servers in the forest or to all DCs in the domain.

Using secondaries with Active Directory–integrated zones

- Use secondaries when no other domain controllers are running DNS in the Active Directory domain.
- Use secondaries when no other domain controllers are in the Active Directory domain.
- Use secondaries when no other DNS servers in the organization are running Windows Server 2003.

Planning a forwarding configuration

- Most DNS servers rely on forwarders; a forwarder is a DNS server that receives queries from other DNS servers.
- Use forwarders to regulate the flow of name resolution traffic and to limit transfer of queries outside the internal network.
- By default, a DNS server can forward queries to DNS servers in all other DNS domains.
- You can control forwarding using designated forwarders.

Chaining and conditional forwarders

- When you chain forwarders, you configure a DNS server acting as a forwarder so that it can also forward queries to another forwarder.
- When you conditionally forward, you do so based on the domain name specified in the name resolution request.

Configuring forwarding

- Windows DNS servers require no special configuration to act as forwarders.
- Other DNS servers must be explicitly configured to send queries to forwarders.

Planning for DNS security

- By default, DHCP clients running Windows 2000 or later update their host (A) records in DNS.
- DHCP servers update the pointer (PTR) records on behalf of clients.
- Dynamic updates occur only when the client is configured with a domain suffix that matches a zone name hosted by the preferred DNS server.
- When clients register their own A records, the method they use is not secure.
- HCP servers dynamically update A and PTR records on behalf of clients using secure dynamic updates.
- DNS records created using secure dynamic updates can only be updated by the server that created them.

DnsUpdateProxy

- Records created by DnsUpdateProxy members have no security settings and thus have no owners.
- Removal of security settings allows member DHCP servers to modify records created by their group.
- DnsUpdateProxy shouldn't be used when clients update A records and servers update PTR records.
- In most cases, domain controllers should not be configured as DHCP servers.
- If DCs are DHCP servers and are members of the DnsUpdateProxy group, records created by the Netlogon service for the DC are not secure.

Dynamic updates

- In DNS, each zone has settings for dynamic updates.
- Configure these options on the General tab of the zone's properties dialog box.

Dynamic update settings

- Dynamic updates can be set to secure only, nonsecure and secure, or none.
- With secure only, secure DNS updates only can be made.
- With nonsecure and secure, clients can make nonsecure updates and servers can make secure updates.
- With none, dynamic updates are disabled.
- Secure only is the most secure and available only with Active Directory–integrated zones.

Safeguarding DNS

- DNS is vulnerable to many types of security threats.
- Multiple DNS servers provide fault tolerance and protection for name resolution.
- If zone transfers are allowed, they should be limited.
- To prevent possible unauthorized access, have the DNS server listen only to selected IP addresses.
- Secure the cache against pollution to ensure that attackers cannot load the DNS server's name cache with incorrect data.

Using third-party DNS solutions

- Windows Server 2003 is compliant with most DNS-related RFCs.
- This compliancy ensures that Windows Server 2003 DNS servers can be used with third-party DNS servers.
- Windows Server 2003 DNS servers can act as primaries for secondary DNS servers using third-party solutions.
- Windows Server 2003 DNS servers can act as secondaries for primary DNS servers using third-party solutions.
- You'll need to configure zone transfers between the primary and secondary servers.
- To ensure RFC 1123 compliance, set Name Checking to Strict RFC (ANSI).

Planning a NetBIOS name resolution strategy

- NetBIOS computer names are used for backward compatibility.
- By default, NetBIOS uses broadcast messages to resolve computer names on the local subnet.
- These broadcast transmissions are not routed and are suitable for small networks with a single subnet.

LMHOSTS

- LMHOSTS is a text file stored in the *%SystemRoot%\System32\Drivers\Etc* folder.
- Entries in the LMHOSTS file must be manually created.
- A basic entry consists of an IP address followed by at least one space and a NetBIOS name.
- Comments can be inserted using a pound (#) symbol.

Planning a WINS replication strategy

- Enable WINS name resolution on a network by configuring WINS clients and servers.
- You must install WINS servers and configure clients with the IP addresses of the servers.
- Clients can communicate with WINS servers even if the servers are on different subnets.
- WINS servers require no configuration to register and resolve names.
- Name registration is automatic with WINS.
- Clients transmit NetBIOS names using the configured name resolution method.

WINS name resolution methods

- With B-node (broadcast) methods, clients use broadcast messages to resolve computer names to IP addresses.
- With P-node (peer-to-peer) methods, clients use WINS servers to resolve computer names to IP addresses.
- With M-node (mixed) methods, clients first try to use broadcasts for name resolution. If this fails, they query a WINS server.
- With H-node (hybrid) methods, clients first query a WINS server. If this fails, they try broadcasts.
- If WINS servers are available on the network, Windows clients use the p-node method by default.
- If no WINS servers are available on the network, Windows clients use the b-node method by default.
- In DHCP, you can set the name resolution method using the 046 WINS/NBT Node Type option.
- In DHCP, you can specify the WINS servers using the 044 WINS Server option.
- For optimal performance, you'll typically want WINS clients to use the h-node method.

Automatic WINS registration

- WINS clients attempt to register their computer name and IP address in the WINS database.
- If the name and IP address aren't in use, the server accepts the request and registers the client.
- The client uses the name for a set lease period and must reregister during the renewal interval.
- If the client can't or doesn't renew the lease, the WINS server releases the name and IP address.
- WINS clients automatically release their names when they are shut down.

Configuring WINS servers

- A single WINS server can provide services for thousands of clients.
- You'll want multiple WINS servers on the network to provide fault tolerance and load balancing.

WINS server replication

- WINS servers can replicate their databases using push partners, pull partners, or both.
- A push partner is a WINS server that notifies other WINS servers of changes on the network.
- A pull partner is a WINS server that requests replicas from a push partner.
- When a push partner notifies the server, the pull partner responds by requesting an update, and then the push partner sends the changes.
- When WINS servers provide services for the same clients, you usually want the servers to be push and pull partners with each other. This is the default configuration when you use replication partners.
- For increased reliability, you can configure persistent connections between replication partners.

Pull partners

- Pull partners pull database entries from their replication partners according to the replication interval.
- By default, the replication interval for pull replication is every 30 minutes.

Push partners

- Push partners use the version ID on the WINS database to determine when to notify of changes.
- The version ID is incremented each time a change is made.
- Replication partners can be notified after a specific number of changes have been made.
- By default, however, no push triggers are sent to replication partners.

Planning, Implementing, and Maintaining Routing and Remote Access

Summary of highlights from the "Planning, Implementing, and Maintaining Routing and Remote Access" section of the Exam 70-293 Study Guide.

Planning a routing strategy

- Both hardware and software routers can be used to connect your organization's LANs and WANs.
- Most local area networks have multiple subnets over which local hosts communicate.
- You typically use a single LAN router to connect two subnets.
- LAN routers must have a configured routing interface for each subnet being connected.
- With WAN connections, install a WAN router at each site and connect using a WAN link.
- You can build in redundancy and fault tolerance using additional, redundant WAN connections.
- The same routing technologies that are used on LANs can be used on WANs.

Common WAN configurations

- In ring topology, all sites are connected in a ring and each site has two possible routes to another site.
- In mesh topology, every site is connected to every other site.
- In star topology, a central site is connected to remote sites, and there are no redundant connections.

Identifying routing protocols to use

- To route traffic, routers must be configured with the appropriate routing entries.
- Routers can use static or dynamic routing.
- With static routing, administrators create and maintain routing entries.
- With dynamic routing, the router creates and maintains entries automatically.
- Your routing strategy will depend on the number of networks, routers, and sites.

TCP/IP routing

- When you install Routing And Remote Access and enable IP routing, you can add routing protocols.
- Routing Information Protocol (RIP) version 2 for Internet Protocol is ideal for small networks.
- Open Shortest Path First (OSPF) is better for larger networks.

Understanding RIP

- Initially the only entries in routing tables are for the networks to which the router is physically connected.
- The router starts sending announcements of its availability.

- Responses from announcements allow the router to update its routing tables.
- With periodic update mode, announcements are sent periodically to learn of available routes, and routes are deleted automatically when the router is stopped and restarted.
- With auto-static update mode, announcements are sent when other routers request updates, learned routes are added as static, and routes remain until they are manually deleted.

Understanding OSPF

- OSPF uses the Shortest Path First (SPF) algorithm to calculate routes.
- The route with the lowest route cost is the shortest path.
- The shortest path is always used first when routing.
- An OSPF router maintains a link-state database that it uses to track the changes in network topology.
- Data is synchronized with adjacent routers and nonbroadcast multiple access (NBMA) neighbors.
- When a change is made to the network topology, the first router to identify it sends out a change notification.
- OSPF divides the network into transit areas, which can be thought of as areas of responsibility.
- OSPF routers maintain link-state information only for those transit areas for which they've been configured.

Static routes

- Static routes provide a permanent mapping to a specific destination network.
- Static routes are set according to the network ID, network mask, gateway, and relative cost of the route.
- Routers use this information to determine the gateway to use to forward packet.
- Static routes are not shared between routers.

Planning routing for IP multicast traffic

- With TCP version 4, Class D IP addresses use multicast transmissions.
- With multicast transmissions, a group of computers known as the host group have a single destination IP address.
- A single source computer can send a single message to multiple recipients via the host group address.
- Members of the host group can be located on any LAN on the network or across WANs.
- LAN/WAN routers must know which hosts are members of the group.
- Members of a multicast host group must register themselves with routers using the Internet Group Management Protocol (IGMP).
- All group members and all routers providing access must support IGMP.
- All Windows computers that use TCP/IP support IGMP.
- RRAS servers can be configured with the IGMP routing protocol.

Analyzing protocol security requirements for remote access

- You should configure security to safeguard the network and meet security requirements.
- Determine who needs remote access.
- Determine what level of access each user requires.
- Determine what applications, if any, users need to run.
- Configure the dial-in properties of the user's account.
- Use Remote Access Permission (Dial-in or VPN) to allow, deny, or control access through policy.
- Use Verify Caller ID to set the user's telephone number for verification.
- Use Callback Options to configure whether callback is required.

Managing remote access security

- Right-click a server entry in the Routing And Remote Access console and select Properties.
- Use the Security tab options to configure remote access security.
- With VPN, you can use IPSec with L2TP to enhance security by using a pre-shared key.

Authentication options

- Windows Authentication lets you use standard Windows security for authentication.
- Remote Authentication Dial-in User Service (RADIUS) is used to centralize the authentication of remote access clients and the storage of accounting information.

Accounting options

- None turns off the logging of connection requests and sessions.
- Windows Accounting logs connection requests and sessions in logfiles stored in the Remote Access Logging folder.
- RADIUS Accounting sends details about connection request and sessions to a RADIUS server.

User authentication methods

- Extensible Authentication Protocol (EAP) extends the authentication methods for PPP connections.
- Microsoft Encrypted Authentication version 2 (MS-CHAP v2) authenticates remote access and demand-dial connections using mutual authentication and strong encryption. MS-CHAP v2 is required for encrypted PPP and PPTP connections.
- Microsoft Encrypted Authentication (MS-CHAP) authenticates remote access and demand-dial connections using encryption. MS-CHAP is required for encrypted PPP and PPTP connections.
- Encrypted Authentication (CHAP) authenticates remote access and demand-dial connections using encryption.

- Shiva Password Authentication Protocol (SPAP) uses authentication with reversible encryption and is compatible with Shiva LAN Rover and Shiva clients. SPAP is not secure.
- Unencrypted Password (PAP) uses Password Authentication Protocol (PAP) and sends passwords in plain text during authentication. PAP is the most unsecure authentication method.

Remote access policies

- Remote access policies for use with EAP are specified using the Remote Access Policies node.
- Connections To Microsoft Routing And Remote Access Server applies to connections to the currently selected RRAS server.
- Connections To Other Access Servers applies to connections to other access servers via the current RRAS server.
- New remote access policies can be created by right-clicking the Remote Access Policies node and selecting New Remote Access Policy.
- Each policy can have a dial-in profile associated with it, which is used to set access permissions.
- Right-click a policy, select Properties, and then click the Edit Profile button to view and modify the profile settings.
- Remote access settings defined in a user's profile have precedence over dial-in profile settings.

Planning remote access policies

- After authentication and verification, the RRAS server attempts to authorize the user.
- Authorization determines whether the server should permit the user to connect.
- Remote access policies are used to define specific conditions for authorization.
- You can create policies that limit access based on group, time of day, day of the week, and more.
- You can specify through policies what authentication and encryption protocols must be used.
- You can define different policies for different types of connections.

Remote access policy review rules

1. RRAS checks against the highest priority remote access policy. If there are no policies listed, RRAS rejects the connection.
2. If all conditions not satisfied, RAS checks the next highest-priority remote access policy, and continues through all the policies until it finds a match for all conditions. If the connection doesn't satisfy all the conditions in any one of the policies, RRAS rejects the connection.
3. When the connection satisfies all the conditions of a policy, RRAS next checks whether the user's dial-in properties should be ignored. This option is set using the advanced attribute Ignore-User-Dialin-Properties.

4. If Ignore-User-Dialin-Properties is set to True, RRAS checks the remote access permission setting of the policy to determine whether to grant or deny access.
5. If Ignore-User-Dialin-Properties is set to False, RRAS checks the user's dial-in properties to determine whether to grant or deny access.

Diagnosing and resolving issues related to establishing a remote access dial-up connection

- On the General tab of the server's Properties dialog box, verify that Remote Access Server is enabled.
- On the IP tab of the server's Properties dialog box, verify that IP Routing is enabled if clients should have access to the network, and disabled if clients should have access to the RRAS server only.
- If static IP addresses are used, verify that the address pool configuration is correct and that there are available IP addresses.
- If dynamic IP addresses are used, verify the configuration of the DHCP server. The IP address scope must be large enough so that the RRAS server can requests blocks of 10 IP addresses.
- Using the Ports node, verify that the server has properly configured modem ports and that not all modem ports are assigned.
- Verify that the client, the RRAS server, and the remote access policy have at least one common authentication method configured.
- Verify that the client and the server permissions, credentials, and access policies are configured correctly.

Diagnosing and resolving issues related to remote access VPNs

- On the General tab of the server's Properties dialog box, verify that Remote Access Server is enabled.
- Using the Ports node, verify that server has properly configured ports and that not all ports are assigned.
- On the Security tab of the server's Properties dialog box, verify that the server is using the appropriate authentication provider and then the appropriate authentication methods are selected for use.
- Verify the remote access profile settings are correct and do not conflict with the server properties. Right-click a remote access policy, select Properties, then click the Edit Profile button.
- Verify that the client, the RRAS server and the remote access policy have at least one common authentication method configured.
- Verify the RRAS server is made a member of the RAS And IAS Servers security group in the local domain. This membership is required for proper working of routing and remote access.
- Verify the underling dial-up configuration as discussed in the previous section.

Diagnosing and resolving issues related to resources beyond the remote access server

- On the General tab of the server's Properties dialog box, verify that Router is enabled.
- On the General tab of the server's Properties dialog box, verify that LAN And Demand-Dial Routing is selected.
- On the IP tab of the server's Properties dialog box, verify that Enable IP Routing is selected.
- If static IP addresses are used, verify that the client's TCP/IP settings are correct.
- If dynamic IP addresses are used, verify that the client is obtaining the proper TCP/IP settings from the DHCP server.
- If your remote access clients use NetBIOS for name resolution, verify that Enable Broadcast Name Resolution is selected on the IP tab.

Troubleshooting router-to-router VPNs

- For the source and destination router, verify on the General tab of the server's Properties dialog box that both Router and LAN And Demand-Dial Routing are selected.
- For the source and destination router, verify on the IP tab of the server's Properties dialog box that Enable IP Routing is selected.
- For the source and destination router, verify that the servers have properly configured PPTP or L2TP ports.
- For the source and destination router, verify that the interface used for routing has Enable IP Router Manager selected on the General tab of the connection properties dialog box so that IP traffic can be routed over the connection.
- For the source and destination router, verify that the static routes are configured as appropriate to allow traffic over the appropriate interface.
- For the source and destination router, verify that permissions, credentials, and access policies are configured correctly.

Troubleshooting demand-dial routing

- Verify that Routing And Remote Access Services is installed.
- Verify on the General tab of the server's Properties dialog box that both Router and LAN And Demand-Dial Routing are selected.
- Verify on the IP tab of the server's Properties dialog box that Enable IP Routing is selected.
- Verify that the demand-dial interfaces are enabled and configured properly.
- Verify that the static routes are configured properly and that Use This Route To Initiate Demand-Dial Connections is selected in the static route properties.
- Verify that the Security tab settings of the network interfaces use a common configuration.
- Verify that the Networking tab settings of the network interfaces use a common VPN type.

- Verify that the servers use the appropriate authentication providers and that the appropriate authentication methods are selected for use. The servers must have at least one common authentication method.
- Verify that the servers have properly configured ports for demand-dial use.
- Verify that packet filters aren't blocking the routing.

Planning, Implementing, and Maintaining Server Availability

Summary of highlights from the "Planning, Implementing, and Maintaining Server Availability" section of the Exam 70-293 Study Guide.

Understanding availability goals

- Every server deployment should be planned, implemented, and maintained with availability in mind.
- Availability refers to the server's ability to withstand hardware, application, or service outage.
- Most noncritical systems, applications, or services have a moderate-availability goal of 99 percent.
- Most critical systems, applications, or services have a high-availability goal of 99.9 percent.

Meeting 99 percent availability goals

- Identify the initial hardware requirements for memory, processors, disks, and networking.
- Plan a monitoring strategy that identifies potential and actual system bottlenecks.
- Plan a backup and recovery strategy that meets the availability goal in terms of recovery time.

Meeting 99.9 percent high-availability goals

- Identify the initial hardware requirements for memory, processors, disks, and networking.
- Identify high availability software solutions to meet availability goals.
- Plan a monitoring strategy that identifies potential and actual system bottlenecks.
- Plan a backup and recovery strategy that meets the availability goal in terms of recovery time and also works with your chosen availability software solution.

System Monitor

- System Monitor can use graphic, histogram, and report formats for real-time performance.
- Add counters by clicking the Add button or pressing CTL+L.

Choosing objects to monitor

- For Memory performance monitoring, related objects include Cache, Memory, and Paging File.
- For Processor performance monitoring, related objects include Processor, Job Object, Process, and Thread.

- For Disk performance monitoring, related objects include LogicalDisk, PhysicalDisk, and System.
- For Network performance monitoring, related objects include Network Interface, Server, and Server Work Queues.

Monitoring memory performance objects

- Windows systems have both physical and virtual memory.
- Memory bottlenecks occur when low available memory causes increased paging.
- Soft page faults occur when the system must look for the necessary data in another area of memory.
- Hard faults occur when the system must look for the necessary data in virtual memory on disk.
- Hard page faults can make the system appear to have a disk problem due to excessive page swapping.
- *Memory\Available Kbytes* is the amount of physical memory not yet in use.
- *Memory\Committed Bytes* is the amount of committed virtual memory.
- *Memory\PageFaults/sec* tracks page faults per second.

Monitoring processor performance objects

- Systems with high-processor utilization may perform poorly.
- Determine processor utilization using *Processor\%Processor Time*.
- *System\Processor Queue Length* tracks number of threads waiting to be executed.

Monitoring network performance objects

- The available network bandwidth determines how fast data is sent between clients and servers.
- The network interface current bandwidth determines capacity to send or receive data.
- The *Network Interface\Output Queue Length* counter can help you identify network saturation issues.
- The *Network Interface\Current Bandwidth* tracks current bandwidth setting.
- The *Network Interface\Bytes Total/sec* provides the total bytes transferred or received per second.

Monitoring disk performance objects

- PhysicalDisk objects represent each physical hard disk.
- LogicalDisk objects represent each logical volume.
- *LogicalDisk\%Free Space* tracks free space on logical disks.
- *PhysicalDisk\Disk Writes/sec* and *Physical Disk\Disk Reads/sec* track I/O activity.
- *Physical Disk\CurrentDisk Queue Length* tracks disk-queuing activity.

Planning services for high availability

- Windows supports three high-availability software solutions.
- Network Load Balancing (NLB) provides high availability for IP-based applications and services.
- Component Load Balancing (CLB) provides high availability for COM+ application components.
- Server cluster provides high availability for business-critical applications and services.

Planning a high-availability solution that uses Network Load Balancing

- All editions of Windows Server 2003 support network load balancing.
- NLB used to distribute incoming IP traffic across servers that share a single virtual IP address.
- If one of the load-balanced servers fails, the remaining servers handle the workload of the failed server.
- Clients should automatically retry the failed connection, and then be redirected to another server.
- A failed server can rejoin the group automatically and start handling requests.
- Because no data is shared between nodes, clients should store data prior to submitting for processing.

Using NLB

- You can balance the load across 2 to 32 systems.
- Any IP-based application that uses TCP, UDP, or GRE can be used with network load balancing.
- Applications that are load balanced include: FTP over TCP/IP, HTTP over TCP/IP, HTTPS over TCP/IP, IMAP4 over TCP/IP, POP3 over TCP/IP, and SMTP over TCP/IP.

Working with Network Load Balancing

- Use the Network Load Balancing Manager to implement and manage network load balancing.
- Click Network Load Balancing Manager on the Administrative Tools menu or type `nlbmgr`.

Creating an NLB cluster

- Create the NLB cluster with an initial host, and then add additional nodes.
- A virtual IP address is used for the public traffic for the cluster. This IP address is fixed and cannot be a dynamic DHCP address.
- By default, all TCP and UPD traffic is load balanced across all members of the cluster.
- Host priority sets the order in which traffic is routed among members of the cluster.

Planning a high-availability solution that uses Clustering Services

- Windows Server 2003 Enterprise Edition supports clustering for up to eight nodes.
- Windows Server 2003 Datacenter Edition supports clustering for up to eight nodes.
- Windows Server 2003 supports single node clustering, single quorum device server clusters, and majority node server clusters.
- Most organizations use either single-node server clusters or single quorum device server clusters.
- Majority node server clusters typically are used with geographically separated servers.
- With 32-bit Windows Server 2003, you can use SCSI or fibre channel to share storage devices.
- With 64-bit Windows Server 2003, fibre channel is required.
- Server clusters can only use TCP/IP. However, clients should have NetBIOS enabled so they can browse to a virtual server by name.

Single-node clustering

- A cluster configuration with a single node can be configured to use internal or external storage.
- Single-node clustering allows automatic restart of applications and dependent services.

Single quorum device server clusters

- This is a cluster configuration with two or more nodes connected to the same cluster storage devices.
- All members in the cluster use the same cluster quorum device.
- The quorum device stores cluster configuration and recovery data.

Majority node server clusters

- This is a cluster configuration with two or more nodes.
- Each node can have its own cluster storage device and its own local quorum device.
- The cluster configuration and recovery data is stored on multiple disks across the cluster.

Using server clustering

- Nodes can be either active or passive.
- Active nodes actively handle requests from clients.
- Passive nodes wait on standby for another node to fail.

Cluster resource groups

- Any cluster-aware application or service can be clustered using resource groups.
- Resource groups are units of failover that are configured on a single node.

- When any of the resources in the group fail, failover is initiated for the entire resource group.
- Cluster-aware applications and services include: Distributed File System (DFS), DHCP, Exchange Server, folder shares, IIS, printer shares, SMTP, SQL Server, and WINS.

Cluster state flags

- Track the status of each node in the cluster as part of the heartbeat monitoring.
- Down indicates that a node is not active in the cluster.
- Joining indicates that the node is in the process of becoming an active participant in the cluster.
- Paused indicates that the node is active but cannot or has not taken ownership of any resource groups.
- Up indicates that the node is active in the cluster.
- Unknown indicates that the node's state cannot be determined.

Cluster heartbeat

- Server clusters send heartbeat messages on dedicated cluster adapters.
- The heartbeat is used to track the availability of each node.
- If a node fails to send a heartbeat message within a specified time, Cluster service initiates failover.
- When failover occurs, another server takes over the workload.
- When the failed resource is back online, the original server is able to regain control of the resource.

Working with Cluster Administrator

- Use the Cluster Administrator to implement and manage server clustering.
- Click Cluster Administrator on the Administrative Tools menu or type `cluadmin`.
- Create the server cluster with an initial node, and then add additional nodes.

Managing backup procedures

- Normal (full) backups should include System State data.
- Incremental backups contain changes since the last full or incremental backup.
- Differential backups contain changes since the last full backup.
- Daily backups contain all the files changed during the day.

Creating Automated System Recovery (ASR) data

- ASR data stores essential boot files and the complete System State.
- Create ASR data using the Backup utility.
- Primary data is stored on the backup media you choose.
- Secondary data needed to boot the system and access the primary data is stored on a floppy disk.
- Click the Automated System Recovery Wizard button on the Welcome tab.

ASR recovery

1. Restart the system and boot it off the installation CD-ROM.
2. During the text portion of the setup, press F2 to perform an Automated System Recovery.
3. ASR then guides you through the recovery process.

System State

- System State includes the system registry, boot files, protected system files, and the COM+ registration database.
- On domain controllers, System State includes Active Directory data and system volume (SysVol) files.
- System State can be backed up locally only.

Shadow Copies

- Supplement but do not replace routine backups.
- Shadow Copies are point-in-time backups of previous file versions.
- They work only for shared folders on NTFS volumes.

Configuring Shadow Copy

- Shadow Copy service will save up to 64 versions, by default.
- Number of versions is limited by maximum space usage allowed.
- By default, 10 percent of volume size is set as the maximum space usage allowed.
- To configure shadow copies, right-click Disk Management and click All Tasks → Configure Shadow Copies. Alternatively, choose Volume Properties → Shadow Copies tab.
- Retrieve a shadow copy after installing the Shadow Copies client on the Previous Versions tab.

Recovering from operating system failure

- Restore backup data using the Backup utility.
- Click the Restore Wizard button to get started.
- Active Directory must be restored either authoritatively or nonauthoritatively. Press F8 during system startup to access the advanced boot options and select Directory Services Restore Mode.

Planning, Implementing, and Maintaining Network Security and Infrastructure

Summary of highlights from the "Planning, Implementing, and Maintaining Network Security and Infrastructure" section of the Exam 70-293 Study Guide.

Port and protocol security

- Computers on TCP/IP networks use specific protocols and ports for communications.
- Servers configured to use a specific protocol listen on a specific TCP or UDP port for requests.

- The Internet Assigned Numbers Authority (IANA) is responsible for assigning ports.
- Commonly used protocols have permanently assigned port numbers, referred to as well-known ports.
- Clients may in some cases use a randomly assigned port, referred to as an ephemeral port.

Listing TCP and UDP port connections

- Type `netstat -ano` at a command prompt to list all TCP and UDP port connections.
- Type `tasklist /fi "pid eq ProcessNumber"` to determine which program is using a port.
- Commonly used ports are summarized in Table 9-5.

Table 9-5. Commonly used TCP and UDP ports

Protocol	Listen port
Domain Name System (DNS)	TCP port 53 and UDP port 53
Dynamic Host Configuration Protocol (Client)	UDP port 68
Dynamic Host Configuration Protocol (Server)	UDP port 67
File Transfer Protocol (FTP)	TCP port 20 for data; TCP port 21 for control
Global Catalog	TCP port 3268
Global Catalog with LDAP/SSL	TCP port 3269
Hypertext Transfer Protocol (HTTP)	TCP port 80
Installation Bootstrap Service	TCP ports 1067 and 1068
Internet Authentication Service (IAS)	UDP ports 1645, 1646, 1812, and 1813
Internet Security Association and Key Management (ISAKM)	UDP port 500
Kerberos change password protocol	TCP port 464
Kerberos version 5	UDP port 88
Layer 2 Tunneling Protocol (L2TP)	UDP port 1701
LDAP Secure Sockets Layer (SSL)	TCP port 686
Lightweight Directory Access Protocol (LDAP)	TCP port 389 and UDP port 389
NetBIOS Datagram protocol	UDP port 138
NetBIOS Name Server protocol	UDP port 137
NetBIOS Session Services	TCP port 139
Network News Transfer Protocol (NNTP)	TCP port 119
Point-to-Point Tunneling Protocol (PPTP)	TCP port 1723
Post Office Protocol (POP)	TCP port 110
Remote Desktop Protocol (RDP)	TCP port 3389
Remote procedure call (RPC)	TCP port 135
RPC over HTTP	TCP port 593
Secure Hypertext Transfer Protocol (HTTPS)	TCP port 443
Secure NNTP	TCP port 563
Sever Message Block (SMB) over IP	TCP port 445 and UDP port 445
Simple Mail Transfer Protocol (SMTP)	TCP port 25

Table 9-5. Commonly used TCP and UDP ports (continued)

Protocol	Listen port
Simple Network Management Protocol (SNMP)	UDP port 161
Simple Network Management Protocol trap	UDP port 162
Windows Product Activation	TCP port 80 and 443

Packet filtering

- Packet filtering is the most common way to secure a server.
- Packet filtering controls the permitted TCP/IP traffic.
- Packets that do not meet the requirements of a particular filter are discarded.
- Packet filtering is used primarily by firewalls and routers connected to the Internet.

Packet-filtering techniques

- Determine the types of traffic that you will permit and the types of traffic that you will deny.
- Configure packet filtering to be inclusive or exclusive.
- With an inclusive approach, you completely block all traffic, and then specify the permitted traffic.
- With an exclusive approach, you open the connection completely, and then specify the denied traffic.
- The inclusive approach is more secure, but more difficult to configure.

Configuring packet filtering

- Use Windows Firewall
- Use TCP/IP filtering
- Use RRAS packet filtering

Windows Firewall

- Windows XP Professional and Windows Server 2003 include the Windows Firewall.
- To start Windows Firewall, click Windows Firewall in the Control Panel.
- When Windows Firewall is enabled, all outside sources are blocked by default, and only the exceptions specified on the Exceptions tab are allowed.
- Do not use Windows Firewall on Windows Server 2003 systems configured as IP routers or for remote access servers. Instead, use the NAT/Basic Firewall features of RRAS.

TCP/IP filtering

- Windows XP Professional and Windows Server 2003 include TCP/IP filtering.
- TCP/IP filtering is configured via Local Area Connection properties.
- When enabled, all TCP, UDP, and IP protocols are allowed by default.

- To filter TCP traffic, click Permit Only for TCP Ports. Click Add to define a permitted TCP port.
- To filter UDP traffic, click Permit Only for UDP Ports. Click Add to define a permitted UDP port.

RRAS packet filtering

- RRAS should use RRAS packet filtering or the Basic Firewall.
- RRAS packet filtering should be configured on the WAN interface.
- Use Inbound Filters to limit incoming traffic.
- Use Outbound Filters to limit outgoing traffic.
- On the General tab, click the Outbound Filters button, and then configure filters if you want to limit outgoing traffic.

Planning and configuring an IPSec policy

- IPSec is a technology for authenticating and encrypting IP traffic between computers.
- IPSec operates at the network layer as an extension to the IP protocol.
- IPSec secures traffic by encrypting it and then encapsulating it prior to transmission.
- IPSec is application-independent.
- Other encryption protocols operate at the application layer and are for specific types of traffic only.

Using IPSec

- With Layer 2 Tunneling Protocol (L2TP) and VPN, use IPSec to enhance security.
- Use IPSec to secure communications on an internal network.
- Use IPSec to secure communications between networks.
- Use IPSec to secure communications between remote access clients and the internal network.

Applying IPSec policies

- IPSec is applied using Group Policy.
- For Active Directory domains, IPSec policies are stored under *Computer Configuration\Windows Settings\Security Settings\IP Security Settings On Active Directory*.
- For computers in workgroups, you can configure local group policy under *Computer Configuration\Windows Settings\Security Settings\IP Security Settings On Local Computer*.

IPSec components

- IPSec has four key components: IPSec Policy Agent, Internet Key Exchange, IPSec Drive, and IPSec Policy.

IPSec Policy Agent

- The IPSec Policy Agent provides the services needed for end-to-end security.
- On Windows 2000 and later systems, the IPSec Policy Agent is the IPSEC Services service (*lsass.exe*).

Internet Key Exchange

- The Internet Key Exchange (IKE) is the protocol used to negotiate the key exchange.
- Computers negotiate encryption algorithm, hashing algorithm, and authentication method.
- Computers also exchange information about key generation.

IPSec Driver

- The IPSec Driver generates required checksums, creates IPSec packets, and encrypts data.
- The Driver compares outgoing packets to the filter list obtained from the IPSec policy being used.
- For incoming packets, the Driver calculates hashes/checksums, and compares to hashes/checksums in the received packets.

IPSec policy

- IPSec policy defines packet filters that enforce security by blocking, allowing, or initiating secure communications.
- Multiple IPSec policies can be defined; one policy only is applied at a time.
- To determine whether IPSec policy is applied to a computer, use IP Security Policy Management.
- To monitor IPSec, use IP Security Monitor or type `netsh ipsec static show all`.

Active Directory default IPSec policies

- With Server (Request Security) policy, servers request but does not require secure communications.
- With Client (Respond Only), client communication is normally unsecure but Active Directory responds to server requests for secure communications.
- With Secure Server (Require Security), servers require secure communications. Servers will not respond to clients that do not or cannot use secure communications.

IPSec policy components

- IPSec policies have three components: rules, IP filter lists, and filter actions.

IPSec policy rules

- Rules combine IP filter lists with filter actions to define whether and how computers should use IPSec
- An IPSec policy can have multiple rules.

IP filter lists

- IP filter lists are collections of filters that specify what types of traffic a computer should secure.
- Filters can be applied based on source/destination IP address, protocol, and source/destination port.

Filter actions

- Filter actions specify exactly how IPSec should secure the filtered packets.
- Filter actions require at least one security method.
- With integrity and encryption security, the data will be encrypted and authenticated.
- With integrity-only security, the data will be authenticated but not encrypted.

Terminal Services

- Uses Remote Desktop for Administration and Terminal Server modes.
- For administration, you'll use Remote Desktop For Administration.

Remote Desktop For Administration

- TCP port 3389 must be opened to allow remote access.
- Select Remote Users to specify users granted remote access permission.
- By default, the Administrators group is granted remote access permission.
- To enable, access the Remote tab of the System utility and select Enable Remote Desktop For This Computer.

Remote Assistance

- Allows a user to send remote assistance invitations.
- To enable, access the System utility's Remote tab and select Turn On Remote Assistance.
- To send a remote assistance request, in Windows Messenger, click Actions → Ask For Remote Assistance.

Planning security for wireless networks

- Wireless networks use technologies based on the IEEE 802.11 specification.
- Securing a wireless network is different from securing a wired network.
- On a wireless network, anyone within range of one of your wireless access points could gain access.
- All wireless transmissions should be secured and encrypted.

Wi-Fi Protected Access (WPA)

- WPA is used for authentication.
- WPA has two modes: enterprise mode and home/small office mode.

WPA enterprise mode

- Wireless devices have unique session keys and shared group keys.
- Session keys are unique to each association between an access point and a wireless client.
- Group keys are shared among all clients connected to the same access point.
- Both key sets are generated dynamically and rotated.

WPA home/small office mode

- Also referred to as WPA-PSK; devices don't use a changing encryption key.
- Uses a preshared encryption key, referred to as a group key, which is programmed in.
- Session keys are generated and changed automatically.

Wireless Equivalency Protection (WEP)

- WEP encrypts data using private key encryption.
- All data is encrypted using before it is transmitted.
- Data must be decrypted using the correct private key.

Robust Security Network (RSN)

- RSN devices dynamically negotiate authentication and encryption algorithms.

Encryption algorithms

- Extensible Authentication Protocol (EAP) used with Protected EAP (PEAP)
- Extensible Authentication Protocol (EAP) used with Smart card or other PKI certificate
- Advanced Encryption Standard (AES)
- Temporal Key Integrity Protocol (TKIP)

Wireless device operating modes

- With ad hoc networks, two or more wireless devices communicate directly with each other.
- With infrastructure networks, wireless adapters connect to an access point rather than to another computer directly.

Troubleshooting security for data transmission

- Determine IPSec policy mismatch by examining the Security logs on the client and the server.
- The Security log may contain warning messages related to failed Internet Key Exchange negotiation.
- Enhance logging by enabling Audit Logon Events and Audit Policy Change for Success and Failure.
- Log dropped packets using `netsh ipsec dynamic set config ipsecdiagnostics 7`.
- Disable diagnostic logging by using `netsh ipsec dynamic set config ipsecdiagnostics 0`.

Software Update Infrastructure

- Automatic Updates allows a system to automatically connect to update operating system.
- Windows Update extends updates to select Microsoft products.
- Windows Server Update Services (WSUS) allows organizations to use their own update servers.

Windows Server Update Services (WSUS)

- WSUS has both a server and client component.
- The WSUS client is an extension of Automatic Updates and has self-updating for auto-install.
- The WSUS server uses a data store that runs with MSDE, WMSDE, or SQL Server.
- SUS 1.0 servers can be migrated to WSUS using *WSUSITIL.EXE*.
- WSUS is designed to handle updates for most Microsoft products.

Planning and configuring a Public Key Infrastructure (PKI)

- PKI provides the components and services for using public and private keys with digital certificates.
- You can use certificates for authentication and encryption.
- Client certificates contain identifying information about a client.
- Server certificates contain identifying information about a server.
- Windows Server 2003 includes Microsoft Certificate Services.
- Microsoft Certificate Services allow you to issue and manage digital certificates.

Understanding public and private key encryption

1. The client obtains the server's public key and uses it to encrypt the message. The message is sent securely.
2. The server receives the encrypted message and decrypts with its private key.
3. The server obtains the client's public key and uses it to encrypt the reply. The reply is sent securely.
4. The client receives encrypted reply and decrypts with its private key.

Certificate authorities

- Certificate authorities are used to issue digital certificates.
- A certificate authority (CA) is a trusted agency responsible for confirming the identity and issuing certificates.
- Certificate servers can be configured as one enterprise or stand-alone CAs.

Enterprise CAs

- Enterprise CAs use certificate templates and publish their certificates/revocation lists to Active Directory.
- Enterprise CAs use Active Directory to determine whether to automatically approve or deny certificate enrollment requests.
- Clients must have access to Active Directory to receive certificates.

Enterprise root CA

- This is the certificate server at the root of the hierarchy for an Active Directory domain.
- The enterprise root CA is the most trusted CA in the enterprise and is integrated with Active Directory.
- The enterprise root CA is at the top of the enterprise CA hierarchy.

- There can be only one root CA in an enterprise.
- All other CAs in the hierarchy must be enterprise subordinate CAs.

Enterprise subordinate CA

- A certificate server that is a member of an existing CA hierarchy.
- The enterprise subordinate CA can issue certificates but must obtain its own CA certificate from the enterprise root CA.
- Use one or more levels of enterprise subordinate CAs to safeguard the root CA's private key.

Stand-alone CAs

- Stand-alone CAs do not use templates and are not integrated with Active Directory.
- Stand-alone CAs store information locally.
- By default, stand-alone CAs use manual enrollment.
- If you plan to use a single stand-alone CA, it must be configured as a stand-alone root CA.

Stand-alone root CA

- The certificate server at the root of a non-domain (workgroup) hierarchy.
- The stand-alone root CA is the most trusted CA in its hierarchy and does not use Active Directory.

Stand-alone subordinate CA

- A certificate server that is a member of an existing nonenterprise (workgroup) hierarchy.
- The stand-alone subordinate CA can issue certificates but must obtain its own CA certificate from the stand-alone root CA in its hierarchy.

Planning for smart cards

- A smart card is a small card-sized device that contains memory and/or integrated circuitry.
- Windows can use smart cards for authentication during logon.
- You must install smart card reader devices and set up smart cards to use for user logons.
- Stand-alone CAs do not store certificates in Active Directory and should not be used to issue smart card certificates.

Exam 70-293 Practice Questions

Planning and Implementing Server Roles and Server Security

1. Which of the following operating systems can act as an Active Directory client and join the domain using a computer account?

   ❍ A. Windows 95

   ❍ B. Windows 98

❍ C. Windows Me

❍ D. Windows 2000 Professional

❍ E. Windows XP Home Edition

Answer D is correct. Windows 2000 Professional, Windows XP Professional, and Windows Vista computers can act as Active Directory clients and join the domain using computer accounts.

2. Which editions of Windows could you use for 4-node clustering with 8 processors and 32 GB RAM?

 ❑ A. Windows Server 2003, Web Edition

 ❑ B. Windows Server 2003, Standard Edition

 ❑ C. Windows Server 2003, Enterprise Edition

 ❑ D. Windows Server 2003, Datacenter Edition

 Answers C and D are correct. Web Edition and Standard Edition do not support clustering. Enterprise Edition and Datacenter Edition support server clusters with up to eight nodes.

3. Although you can use the Configure Your Server Wizard to configure a server as domain controller, which program or utility do you use to promote or demote a domain controller?

 ❍ A. NETSH DIAG

 ❍ B. DCPROMO.EXE

 ❍ C. Active Directory Users And Computers

 ❍ D. NTDSUTIL.EXE

 ❍ E. LSASS.EXE

 Answer B is correct. Promote and demote domain controllers using the Active Directory Installation Wizard (dcpromo). To start this wizard, click Start → Run. Type `dcpromo` in the Open field, and then click OK.

4. Mary is a network administrator who has been given the task of configuration on a new file server. Windows Server 2003 Standard Edition has already been installed. The file server has three hard drives formatted with NTFS. The C drive is the system drive. Drives D and G are data drives. Assuming the default filesystem permissions are in place, which of the following tasks must be performed to ensure that only domain users have full permissions on the data drives?

 ❑ A. The Everyone group should be granted Full Control on Drives D and G.

 ❑ B. The Domain Users group should be granted Full Control on Drives D and G.

 ❑ C. Permissions for the Everyone group should be removed from Drives D and G.

 ❑ D. Permissions for the Authenticated Users group should be removed from Drives D and G.

 Answers B and C are correct. Setup doesn't grant any special permissions on additional drives. Instead, Setup grants the Everyone group Full Control on the entire drive, and it is up to the administrator to configure appropriate permissions.

5. Mary is a network administrator who has been given the task of configuration on a new file server. Windows Server 2003 Standard Edition has already been installed. The file server has three hard drives formatted with NTFS. The C drive is the system drive. Drives D and G are data drives. After configuring filesystem permissions, Mary created a shared folder on each data drive for users. What configuration option should Mary choose to ensure administrators have Full Control on the shared folders and other users have Change access?

   ❍ A. All Users Have Read-Only Access.

   ❍ B. Administrators Have Full Access; Other Users Have Read-Only Access.

   ❍ C. Administrators Have Full Access; Other Users Have Read And Write Access.

   ❍ D. None of the above; the administrator must configure custom permissions.

   Answer C is correct. Administrators Have Full Access; Other Users Have Read And Write Access grants administrators Full Control and the Everyone group Change access.

6. John is a new system administrator. He is configuring security for several new workstations running Windows XP Professional. The computers are members of the Temp OU, and he noticed that users are able to reuse old passwords whenever they are prompted to change them. Which of the following account policies can be used to prevent this behavior?

   ❍ A. Enforce Password History

   ❍ B. Maximum Password Age

   ❍ C. Minimum Password Age

   ❍ D. Store Passwords Using Reversible Encryption

   Answer A is correct. Enforce Password History determines how many previously used passwords will be maintained in the user's password history. When this policy is enabled and set to a value greater than zero, a user cannot use a password that is in the history, and thus, a user cannot reuse a recently used password.

7. While continuing to look at the domain security for the Temp OU, John noticed that a user was able to repeatedly enter a wrong password. He watched the user enter eight bad passwords in a row before finally getting the right password on the ninth attempt. Which of the following account policies can be set to ensure accounts are locked out indefinitely after 3 bad logon attempts in a 15-minute period?

   ❍ A. Account Lockout Duration

   ❍ B. Account Lockout Threshold

   ❍ C. Reset Account Lockout Counter After

   ❍ D. All of the above

Answer D is correct. All three account policies must be set to meet the requirements. In this case, Account Lockout Duration needs to be set to 0, Account Lockout Threshold needs to be set to 3, and Reset Account Lockout Counter After needs to be set to 15.

8. You've just promoted a server running Windows Server 2003 to be a domain controller. After you log on to the server, you run the Security Configuration And Analysis tool and notice security settings aren't what you expect them to be. What is the most likely reason for the security changes on the server?

   ❍ A. Domain controllers don't have local security settings, and during promotion, any previously applied security template is removed.

   ❍ B. During promotion, domain controllers are made members of the Domain Controllers OU and have the DC Security template applied during promotion.

   ❍ C. Domain controllers don't have a SAM database and use only Active Directory for security.

   ❍ D. During promotion, domain controllers are configured with default security using the Setup Security template.

   Answer B is correct. By default, computers accounts for domain controllers are stored in the Domain Controllers OU. When the server is promoted to a domain controller, the server's computer account is moved to the Domain Controllers OU. The default security for domain controllers comes from the DC Security template, which is applied when a server is promoted to be a domain controller.

9. What is the proper way to create and then apply a custom security template to a computer?

   ❍ A. Use the Security Templates snap-in to create a custom template, configure the security settings as necessary, and then apply the settings using Security Configuration And Analysis.

   ❍ B. Create a database in Security Configuration And Analysis, modify the security settings as necessary, and then apply the database to the computer.

   ❍ C. Create a database in Security Configuration And Analysis, modify the security settings as necessary, and then apply the settings using the SECEDIT utility.

   ❍ D. Create a database in the SECEDIT utility, modify the security settings as necessary in Security Configuration And Analysis, and then apply the template to the computer using the Security Templates snap-in.

   Answer A is correct. Use the Security Templates snap-in to create and manage security templates. Use Security Configuration And Analysis to analyze security and apply security templates to a computer. You could also use the SECEDIT utility to apply a security template.

10. You have created a custom template for computers in the Workstations OU. After creating a rollback template and applying the custom template, you found that the template has caused some undesirable side effects. Which of the following procedures would correct the problem by restoring the previous security settings exactly as they were?

- ❍ A. Reapply the default template using Security Configuration And Analysis, and then import this into the Workstation GPO.
- ❍ B. Use Security Configuration And Analysis to apply a rollback template and then import this into the Workstation GPO.
- ❍ C. Use Security Configuration And Analysis to apply a rollback template, import this into the Workstation GPO, and then manually modify for access control lists on files and in the Registry as necessary.
- ❍ D. Import the default template into Workstation GPO.

Answer C is correct. As discussed in the section "Applying security template settings and analyzing security" in Chapter 5, a rollback template is a reverse template that allows you to remove the settings applied with a custom template. Rollback templates, however, do not recover setting for access control lists on files or the Registry.

11. Which OSI layer is responsible for packet addressing and data encapsulation?
    - ❍ A. Application
    - ❍ B. Session
    - ❍ C. Transport
    - ❍ D. Network
    - ❍ E. Data-link

    Answer E is correct. The Data Link Layer is responsible for packet addressing, media access control, and data encapsulation.

12. Which of the following protocols are part of the TCP/IP protocol suite?
    - ❑ A. Transmission Control Protocol
    - ❑ B. Internet Protocol (TCP/IP)
    - ❑ C. User Datagram Protocol (UDP)
    - ❑ D. Internet Package Exchange (IPX)
    - ❑ E. NetBIOS Extended User Interface (NetBEUI)

    Answers A, B, and C are correct. Most current networks use Transmission Control Protocol/Internet Protocol (TCP/IP). IP operates at the network layer. TCP operates at the transport layer. There is an additional transport layer protocol included in the TCP/IP protocol suite called User Datagram Protocol (UDP).

13. You are planning the infrastructure for a new network. The data center is centrally located, and the furthest location from the data center is 400 meters. The longest cable runs are 480 meters from the central switch and your plan allows you to use up to 4 repeaters. Which of the following UTP cabling options could be used?
    - ❍ A. 10Base-T, Category 3 UTP
    - ❍ B. 100Base-T, Category 5 UTP
    - ❍ C. 1000Base-T, Category 5E UTP
    - ❍ D. None of the above

Answer A. With standard Ethernet running at 10 megabits per second using repeaters, the furthest a computer could possibly be from the central switch/router is 500 meters. With standard Ethernet running at 100 megabits per second using repeaters, the furthest a computer could possibly be from the central switch/router is 300 meters. With standard Ethernet running at 1,000 megabits per second using repeaters the furthest a computer could possibly be from the central switch/router is 200 meters.

14. You are designing a new network and plan to use Class C IP addresses. You want to be able to create 4 subnets with 60 hosts on each subnet, so you allocate 26 bits to the network ID. Which of the following subnet masks should you use for the network?

   ❍ A. 255.255.255.128

   ❍ B. 255.255.255.192

   ❍ C. 255.255.255.224

   ❍ D. 255.255.255.240

   Answer B is correct. This subnet mask allows you to create up to four subnets with up to 62 hosts on each. You can use the formula 2^*x* to calculate the number of subnets, where *x* is the number of additional network bits in the network mask from the standard network bits in the network for the IP address class. With the standard Class C network address, there are 24 bits in the network mask. You are creating a /26 network, meaning you are using two additional bits for the network ID. Using the formula (2^2 = 4), you can determine there will be four subnets.

   You can use the formula 2^*x* – 2 to calculate the number of nodes on a subnet, where *x* is the number of host bits in the network mask. The /26 network mask means there are six bits for hosts. Using the formula (2^6 – 2 = 62), you can determine there will be 62 hosts on each subnet. You have to subtract two hosts to account for the subnet ID and the broadcast IP address, which aren't assigned to hosts.

15. You are designing a network for a large branch office and have been assigned the network address 10.10.0.0/18. What are the maximum number of subnets and the maximum number of hosts on each subnet?

   ❍ A. 64 subnets; 262,142 hosts

   ❍ B. 128 subnets; 131,070 hosts

   ❍ C. 256 subnets; 65,534 hosts

   ❍ D. 512 subnets; 32,766 hosts

   ❍ E. 1024 subnets; 16,382 hosts

   Answer E is correct. You can use the formula 2^*x* to calculate the number of subnets, where *x* is the number of additional network bits in the network mask from the standard network bits in the network for the IP address class. With the standard Class A network address, there are eight bits in the network mask. You are creating a /18 network, meaning you are using 10 additional bits for the network ID. Using the formula (2^10 = 1024), you can determine there will be 1,024 subnets.

   You can use the formula 2^*x* – 2 to calculate the number of nodes on a subnet, where *x* is the number of host bits in the network mask. The /18 network mask means there are 14 bits for hosts. Using the formula (2^14 – 2 = 16,382), you can determine there will be 16,382 hosts on each subnet. You have to subtract two hosts to account for the subnet ID and the broadcast IP address, which aren't assigned to hosts.

16. You are designing a network and plan to use subnetting. You plan to use services running Routing And Remote Access Service to provide IP routing for unicast network traffic. Which routing protocols can you use?

    ❑ A. RIP version 1

    ❑ B. RIP version 2

    ❑ C. OSPF

    ❑ D. IGMP

    Answers B and C are correct; both RIP version 2 and OSPF Classless Inter-Domain Routing (CIDR). RIP version 1 does not support CIDR. IGMP is used for multicast network traffic.

17. You are installing a network in an office located above a factory floor and there is a lot of electromagnetic interference. Which of the following network media should you use?

    ❍ A. UTP cabling

    ❍ B. B Fiber optic cabling

    ❍ C. IEEE 802.11a wireless

    ❍ D. IEEE 802.11b wireless

    Answer B is correct. Fiber optic cabling uses a strand of plastic or glass that carries signals in the form of light pulses. Using light pulses ensures that fiber optic cables are not affected by electromagnetic interference.

18. You are designing an Internet connectivity strategy for a large office with 500 users. You've determined that between 50 and 100 users will be using email or browsing the Web at any given time. The amount of data downloaded is about equal to the amount of data uploaded. Which of the following Internet access solutions would provide the most reliable solution for both downstream and upstream transmissions?

    ❍ A. ISDN (Basic Rate Interface)

    ❍ B. ISDN (Primary Rate Interface)

    ❍ C. Cable/DSL Modem

    ❍ D. T-1

    Answer D is correct. While ISDN (Primary Rate Interface) and Cable/DSL modem could possibly do the job, a T-1 is a dedicated line with 1.544 Mbps transmissions speed for both downstream and upstream traffic.

19. You are a network administer at a large organization. The company has a T-1 connection to a local ISP, which is shared by all clients. Clients access the Internet using NAT. Several users have reported that they can't access the Internet. You start diagnosing the problem and find that all users reporting the problem are on the same subnet. Users on other subnets are not experiencing any problems accessing the Internet. Which of the following could be the cause of the problem?

❍ A. The NAT router is malfunctioning.

❍ B. The T-1 connection is down.

❍ C. The users' DNS Server is down.

❍ D. The users' default gateway for the subnet is malfunctioning.

❍ E. The users' DHCP server is down.

Answer D is correct. The users' default gateway for the subnet is a LAN router responsible for connecting the subnet to the rest of the network. If this router is malfunctioning, none of the users on that subnet will be able to access the other parts of the network or the Internet.

20. When clients obtain TCP/IP settings from a DHCP server, which of the following options should be configured via DHCP?

❍ A. IP Address

❍ B. Subnet Mask

❍ C. Network ID

❍ D. Router

Answer D is correct. IP Address, Subnet Mask, and Network ID are not valid TCP/IP options. Router is the DHCP option used to set the default gateway. Set the IP address and subnet mask to use through scope properties.

21. DNS servers can be configured to perform name resolution using several types of queries. With which type of query does the server return results only form its records or from its cache?

❍ A. Forward query

❍ B. Reverse query

❍ C. Iterative query

❍ D. Recursive query

Answer C is correct. With an iterative query, a DNS server attempts to resolve the query from its records or from its cache. If it is unable to resolve the query, the server refers the client, based on the server's root hints, to an authoritative server in another part of the domain namespace.

22. Tom is a network administrator. He's been asked to improve responsiveness for name resolution by configuring a local DNS server that will maintain a cache of resolved queries. What should Tom do to prepare the server?

❍ A. Install the DNS Server service.

❍ B. Install the DNS Server service, and then configure the server as a forwarder.

❍ C. Install the DNS Server service, and then configure server to maintain copies of the necessary zones.

❍ D. Install the DNS Server service, and then configure server to host the necessary zones.

Answer A is correct. A DNS server acts as a forwarding-only server if you've installed the DNS Server service on a server but have not configured DNS zones. Forwarding-only DNS servers maintain a cache of resolved queries. They contain no zones and host no domains.

23. Sarah is a network administrator. The network's domain structure has recently been reconfigured, and ever since, there are several clients that are unable to update their DNS records. She checked and all the clients having problems are in Technical resources department, which is part of the *tech.domain.local* domain. She suspects the problem has to do with the preferred DNS server the clients are using. The preferred DNS server for these clients hosts the *eng.domain.local* domain. What is the best and easiest way to resolve the problem?

   ❍ A. The computer accounts for the problem clients should be moved to the *eng.domain.local* domain.

   ❍ B. The DNS server should be moved to the *tech.domain.local* domain.

   ❍ C. The primary DNS suffix for the computers should be changed to *eng.domain.local* domain.

   ❍ D. The preferred DNS server being used for the clients should be changed.

   Answer D is correct. The preferred DNS server being used by the clients doesn't host the *tech.domain.local* zone. Dynamic updates can only occur when the client is configured with a domain suffix that matches a zone name hosted by the preferred DNS server.

24. You are a network administrator. Multiple users have reported that they can access some local resources but not all, and they have no access to resources on the Internet. You try to diagnose the problem and find that the preferred DNS server used by the clients having the problem can only resolve names for zones stored on the server. The TCP/IP settings on the DNS server are configured correctly. What is the likely cause of the problem?

   ❍ A. The DNS server has incorrect or corrupt root hints.

   ❍ B. The DNS server's resolver cache is corrupted.

   ❍ C. The DNS server is not getting zone transfers.

   ❍ D. The DNS server doesn't have any forwarders configured.

   Answer A is correct. A server is authoritative only for the zones that it stores. If a DNS server is unable to resolve a query, the server refers the client, based on the server's root hints, to an authoritative server in another part of the domain namespace. If a server can only resolve names for which it is authoritative, the server has problems sending queries to other servers, which could be caused by incorrect or corrupt root hints.

25. Which routing protocol should use to enable members of a host group to register themselves with routers?

   ❍ A. Routing Information Protocol (RIP) version 2 for Internet Protocol

   ❍ B. Open Shortest Path First (OSPF)

   ❍ C. Internet Group Management Protocol (IGMP)

   ❍ D. DHCP Relay Agent routing protocol

   Answer C is correct. Internet Group Management Protocol (IGMP) is the routing protocol that makes multicasting possible. Using IGMP, members of a host group can register themselves with routers.

26. You are planning routing for a large, congested network. Many network segments are separated by at least 12 hops. You are considering using either link state routing or distance vector routing on a computer running Windows Server 2003. Which of the following are valid reasons link state routing would be preferred in this instance?

❍ A. Link state routing uses only the number of hops for its metrics.

❍ B. Links state routing factors in conditions such as network speed and congestion.

❍ C. Link state routing requires little planning and is easy to configure.

❍ D. Link state routing supports multicast for efficient communications with multiple routers.

Answer B is correct. With link state routing protocols, such as OSPF, routers compute metrics based on many conditions, including network speed and congestion. OSPF uses only unicast transmissions to communication with other routers and requires significant planning and configuration.

27. Which of the following authentication protocols is required when you want to use digital certificates?

❍ A. Extensible Authentication Protocol (EAP)

❍ B. Microsoft Encrypted Authentication version 2 (MS-CHAP v2)

❍ C. Microsoft Encrypted Authentication (MS-CHAP)

❍ D. Encrypted Authentication (CHAP)

❍ E. Shiva Password Authentication Protocol (SPAP)

Answer A is correct. Extensible Authentication Protocol (EAP) allows use of nonpassword-based authentication and is required if you want to use smart cards with remote access clients or PKI certificates.

28. You are configuring remote access and want to limit client access to the Routing And Remote Access Service server based on group membership. Which of the following procedures can you use?

❍ A. Set the Dial-in properties for users in Active Directory Users And Computers.

❍ B. Configure clients to use VPN with IPSec and L2TP.

❍ C. Configure clients to use RADIUS servers for authentication.

❍ D. Configure the server to use remote access policies.

Answer D is correct. Using Remote Access policies you can limit access based on group membership, time of day, day of the week, and more.

29. You are configuring IPSec policy for a group of computers that you want to use IPSec encryption whenever possible. However, some of the clients in the group don't support IPSec. Which of the following IPSec policies should you use?

❍ A. Client (Respond Only) policy.

❍ B. Server (Request Security) policy.

❍ C. Secure Server (Require Security) policy.

❍ D. A custom IPSec policy must be created.

Answer B is correct. With Server (Request Security) policy, servers always request security using Kerberos trust but do not require secure communications. This policy is intended for use when the highest levels of security are not required and servers might communicate with clients that do not support IPSec.

30. You want to create a group of highly available web servers. All servers are running Windows Server 2003 and are used to provide HTTP and HTTPS services on the internal network. Which high-availability software solution should you use?

    ❍ A. Network Load Balancing

    ❍ B. Component Load Balancing

    ❍ C. Server clusters

    ❍ D. Multicasting Server Grouping

    Answer A is correct. Network Load Balancing is used to distribute incoming IP traffic across a cluster of servers. Any IP-based application that uses TCP, UDP, or GRE can be used with network load balancing. This means network load balancing is ideally suited to use with web servers, Internet application servers, and media servers.

31. Which type of clustering uses shared storage and stores the cluster configuration and recovery data on the same device?

    ❍ A. Passive-node clusters

    ❍ B. Single-node server clusters

    ❍ C. Single quorum device server clusters

    ❍ D. Majority node server clusters

    Answer C is correct. Single quorum device server clusters are all connected to the same cluster storage devices. All members in the cluster use the same cluster quorum device as well. The quorum device stores cluster configuration and recovery data.

32. You are configuring a four-node cluster on servers running Windows Server 2003 Enterprise Edition. If all four nodes are active, you've determined that at least four processors and 4 GB of RAM are required on each server to handle the expected workload. You also think you might want to use two active nodes and two passive nodes. What are the minimum configurations to handle the workload and allow for two-node failure?

    ❍ A. Configure four active nodes each with at least eight processors and 8 GB RAM.

    ❍ B. Configure two active nodes and two passive each with at least four processors and 4 GB RAM.

    ❍ C. Configure 4 active nodes each with at least 32 processors and 16 GB RAM.

    ❍ D. Configure 2 active nodes and 2 passive each with at least 16 processors and 32 GB RAM.

    Answer A is correct. If you determine that each node in the cluster must have four processors and 4 GB of RAM to handle the expected workload, you would need to double these resources to ensure that any single node could handle the additional processing load, should one of the nodes fail. In this configuration, up to two nodes could fail and the workload would be supported.

33. Which of the following performance counters could you use to determine a possible problem with memory or a memory leak?

❑ A. *Process(process_name)\Pool Paged Bytes*

❑ B. *Memory\Available Kbytes*

❑ C. *Memory\Nonpaged Kbytes*

❑ D. *Processor\%Processor Time*

Answers A, B, and C are correct. Increasing *Process(process_name)\Pool Paged Bytes and Memory\Nonpaged Kbytes* may indicate a memory leak; may need to install updated version of the program. Consistently low Memory\Available Kbytes may indicate a memory bottleneck and a need to add physical memory.

34. Which of the following features can you use to supplement backups and allow users to recover their own files?

❍ A. Volume Shadow Copy

❍ B. Automated System Recovery

❍ C. Automatic Supplemental Restore

❍ D. Normal backup

Answer A is correct. Backup and recovery strategy should include volume shadow copy to allow users to recover their own files. Volume shadow copy is not a replacement for backups.

35. Which type of backup should you use if you want to track the full set of changes since the last normal backup?

❍ A. Incremental backups

❍ B. Copy backups

❍ C. Daily backups

❍ D. Differential backups

Answer D is correct. Differential backups back up all selected files or folders with an archive flag. Each differential backup after a normal backup contains the full set of changes since the normal backup was created.

36. Which tool can you use to determine which ports a server has open?

❍ A. NETSH

❍ B. NETSTAT

❍ C. Security Configuration And Analysis

❍ D. Security Monitor

Answer B is correct. On a server, you can type `netstat -ano` at a command prompt to list all TCP and UDP port connections to that server.

37. Which of the following are assigned by the Internet Assigned Numbers Authority (IANA)?

- ❑ A. Well-known port numbers
- ❑ B. Ephermeral numbers
- ❑ C. Protocol codes
- ❑ D. Listen Pids

Answers A and C are correct. The Internet Assigned Numbers Authority (IANA) is responsible for assigning the values used for TCP/IP protocols and ports. Commonly used protocols have permanently assigned port numbers, which are referred to as well-known ports.

38. You've configured IP filter lists so IPSec encrypts email traffic. The organization uses Post Office Protocol 3 (POP3) and Simple Mail Transfer Protocol (SMTP). For which of the following well-known ports should you configure the filter list?

- ❑ A. 25
- ❑ B. 80
- ❑ C. 90
- ❑ D. 110

Answers A and D are correct. Post Office Protocol 3 (POP3) uses port 110 and Simple Mail Transfer Protocol (SMTP) uses port 25.

39. Bob, who is not an administrator, is commonly asked to help Joe with computer problems. Your manager has asked you to configure Bob's account so Bob can remotely assist Joe. Which of the following tasks must you perform to allow Bob to do this?

- ❑ A. Enable Remote Desktop for Administration on Joe's computer.
- ❑ B. Enable Remote Assistance on Joe's computer.
- ❑ C. Make Bob a member of the Remote Desktop Users group on Joe's computer.
- ❑ D. Make Bob a member of the Remote Administrators group on Joe's computer.

Answers B and C are correct. Joe's computer must have Remote Assistance enabled and Bob's user account must be made a member of the Remote Desktop Users group on Joe's computer.

40. You don't want wireless clients to be able to connect directly to other wireless clients. Which wireless operating modes should you use to ensure that clients can only connect to wireless access points?

- ❍ A. Any Available Network (Access Point Preferred)
- ❍ B. Access Point (Infrastructure) Networks Only
- ❍ C. Computer-to-Computer (Ad Hoc) Networks Only
- ❍ D. Ad Hoc Networks Only

Answer B is correct. You can restrict wireless clients to infrastructure networks only to prevent risky direct computer to computer connections.

41. Which of the following audit policies should you enable to log all IPSec events in the Security event log?

- ❑ A. Audit Logon Events
- ❑ B. Audit Policy Change
- ❑ C. Audit Security
- ❑ D. Audit IP Policy

Answers A and B are correct. Some IPSec processes are only logged when auditing is enabled. Specifically, you must enable Audit Logon Events and Audit Policy Change for Success and Failure events.

42. Which type of Certificate Authority (CA) must you use if you want to use smart card certificates?

- ❍ A. Stand-alone CA
- ❍ B. Domain CA
- ❍ C. Enterprise CA
- ❍ D. Subordinate CA

Answer C is correct. Only enterprise CAs support smart card certificates. Stand-alone CAs do not store certificates in Active Directory and should not be used to issue smart card certificates.

43. You are planning the deployment of Public Key Infrastructure (PKI). You want the CAs to publish their certificates and revocation lists to Active Directory, and you want to use autoenrollment. Which of the following is the first CA you should deploy to support your infrastructure?

- ❍ A. Enterprise root CA
- ❍ B. Enterprise subordinate CA
- ❍ C. Stand-alone root CA
- ❍ D. Stand-alone subordinate CA

Answer A is correct. The enterprise root CA is at the top of the enterprise CA hierarchy. Enterprise CAs only publish their certificates and revocation lists to Active Directory, and use the information for automatic enrollment.

44. You've implemented IPSec and now you want to check to make sure it is working. Which of the following tools can you use to monitor the network to make sure all network transmissions are using IPSec?

- ❍ A. Performance Monitor
- ❍ B. System Monitor
- ❍ C. Network Monitor
- ❍ D. IP Security Monitor

Answer D is correct. Using the IP Security Monitor, you can view the current active IPSec policy and review the IPSec activity for the entire network. While you could use Network Monitor to check network packets and see they are encrypted. This would only be for a single computer and not for all computers on the network.

45. Which Windows components must you install to use Windows Server Update Services (WSUS)?

- ❑ A. SQL Server
- ❑ B. IIS
- ❑ C. Background Intelligent Transfer Service (BITS) 2.0
- ❑ D. Microsoft .NET Framework 1.1 Service Pack 1 for Windows Server 2003
- ❑ E. SUS

Answers B, C, and D are correct. WSUS requires IIS, BITS, and .NET Framework 1.1. WSUS is the replacement for Software Update Services (SUS).

IV

Exam 70-294

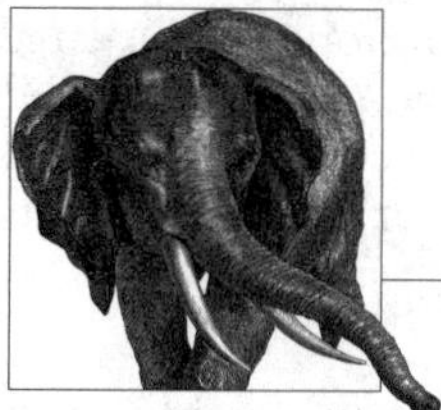

10
Exam 70-294 Overview

Exam 70-294: Planning, Implementing, and Maintaining a Microsoft Windows Serer 2003 Active Directory Infrastructure is designed to cover the skills necessary to manage the directory service needs of a medium to large organization with a specific focus on Active Directory. The planning skills required aren't as extensive as those required for network infrastructure in Exam 70-293, and mostly extend to planning the placement of Flexible Single Master Operations Roles (FSMOs) and Global Catalogs (GCs) as well as developing a Group Policy strategy. Planning also extends to Organizational Unit (OU) and security group structure.

You should be able to implement forest and domain structure including domain controller installation, site topology configuration for site links and bridgehead servers, and trust relationships. A key part of this is troubleshooting, which includes diagnosing and resolving problems as well as restoring Active Directory.

Some not so routine tasks are covered with respect to Group Policy. Not only do you need to know how to configure policy settings and obtain Resultant Set of Policy (RSoP), but you also need to know how to use Group Policy to automatically enroll computer certificates, to distribute software, and to maintain installed software.

Some of the most common problem areas for people taking the exam have to do with:

Trusts
: In an environment with multiple forests and domains, many types of trusts may exist, including internal, external, shortcut, and cross-forest trusts. Establishing and managing these isn't something you'll do every day. More often than not, you'll work only with trusts when things break. Make it a point to spend some extra time with trusts.

Sites

A small organization may not have multiple Active Directory sites. A large organization may have multiple sites but allow only the most experienced administrators to manage them. To get the hands-on expertise and essential background required, you'll probably have to experiment with the theoretical and set up an extended test environment.

Group Policy troubleshooting

Troubleshooting Group Policy requires a keen understanding of policy application, processing, and refresh. Keep in mind that all the things that can affect processing including loopback, slow links, and refresh.

In order to be prepared for Exam 70-294, you should have 12 to 18 months prior experience as a Windows Server 2003 administrator in a medium to large organization. You should have recently studied a Windows Server 2003 administrator's book, taken a training course, or completed a self-paced training kit that covers the related areas of study. You will then be ready to use the Exam 70-294 Study Guide in this book as your final exam preparation.

Exam 70-294 is the fourth of four required networking system exams for MCSEs. If you are a current MCSE on Windows 2000, you need to pass Exam 70-292 and Exam 70-296 to upgrade your certification to Windows Server 2003. Skills measured by Exam 70-296, representing a subset of Exams 70-293 and 70-294, are indicated in this exam overview sections by the ^{X} symbol.

Areas of Study for Exam 70-294

Planning and Implementing an Active Directory Infrastructure

- Plan a strategy for placing global catalog servers.[X]
  - Evaluate network traffic considerations when placing global catalog servers.[X]
  - Evaluate the need to enable universal group caching.[X]
- Plan flexible operations master role placement.
  - Plan for business continuity of operations master roles.
  - Identify operations master role dependencies.
- Implement an Active Directory directory service forest and domain structure.[X]
  - Create the forest root domain.[X]
  - Create a child domain.[X]
  - Create and configure Application Data Partitions.[X]
  - Install and configure an Active Directory domain controller.[X]
  - Set an Active Directory forest and domain functional level based on requirements.[X]
  - Establish trust relationships.[X]
- Implement an Active Directory site topology.
  - Configure site links.
  - Configure preferred bridgehead servers.
- Plan an administrative delegation strategy.
  - Plan an organizational unit (OU) structure based on delegation requirements.
  - Plan a security group hierarchy based on delegation requirements.

See pages 527 to 559.

Managing and Maintaining an Active Directory Infrastructure

- Manage an Active Directory forest and domain structure.[X]
  - Manage trust relationships.[X]
  - Manage schema modifications.[X]
  - Add or remove a UPN suffix.[X]
- Manage an Active Directory site.
  - Configure replication schedules.
  - Configure site link costs.
  - Configure site boundaries.

- Monitor Active Directory replication failures.
  - Monitor Active Directory replication.
  - Monitor File Replication service (FRS) replication.
- Restore Active Directory directory services.[X]
  - Perform an authoritative restore operation.[X]
  - Perform a nonauthoritative restore operation.[X]
- Troubleshoot Active Directory.
  - Diagnose and resolve issues related to Active Directory replication.
  - Diagnose and resolve issues related to operations master role failure.
  - Diagnose and resolve issues related to the Active Directory database.

See "Planning an Active Directory Forest and Domain Structure" on page 527, "Planning and Managing Active Directory Sites" on page 560, and "Maintaining Active Directory Infrastructure" on page 575.

Planning and Implementing User, Computer, and Group Strategies

- Plan a security group strategy.
- Plan a user authentication strategy.[X]
  - Plan a smart card authentication strategy.[X]
  - Create a password policy for domain users.[X]
- Plan an OU structure.
  - Analyze the administrative requirements for an OU.
  - Analyze the Group Policy requirements for an OU structure.
- Implement an OU structure.
  - Create an OU.
  - Delegate permissions for an OU to a user or to a security group.
  - Move objects within an OU hierarchy.

See "Planning and Implementing Computer, User, and Group Strategies" on page 593.

Planning and Implementing Group Policy

- Plan Group Policy strategy.[X]
  - Plan a Group Policy strategy by using Resultant Set of Policy (RSoP) Planning mode.[X]
  - Plan a strategy for configuring the user environment by using Group Policy.[X]
  - Plan a strategy for configuring the computer environment by using Group Policy.[X]

- Configure the user environment by using Group Policy.[X]
  - Distribute software by using Group Policy.[X]
  - Automatically enroll user certificates by using Group Policy.[X]
  - Redirect folders by using Group Policy.[X]
  - Configure user security settings by using Group Policy.[X]
- Deploy a computer environment by using Group Policy.
  - Distribute software by using Group Policy.
  - Automatically enroll computer certificates by using Group Policy.
  - Configure computer security settings by using Group Policy.

See "Planning and Implementing Computer, User, and Group Strategies" on page 593.

Managing and Maintaining Group Policy

- Troubleshoot issues related to Group Policy application deployment.[X]
- Maintain installed software by using Group Policy.
  - Distribute updates to software distributed by Group Policy.
  - Configure automatic updates for network clients by using Group Policy.
- Troubleshoot the application of Group Policy security settings.[X]

See "Planning, Implementing, and Maintaining Group Policy" on page 594.

11

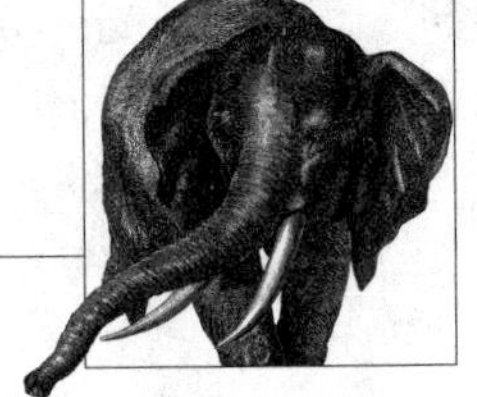

Exam 70-294 Study Guide

This chapter provides a study guide for *Exam 70-294: Planning, Implementing, and Maintaining a Microsoft Windows Server 2003 Active Directory Infrastructure*. Sections within the chapter are organized according to the exam objective they cover. Each section identifies the related exam objective, provides an overview of why the objective is important, and then discusses the key details you should know about the objective to both succeed on the test and master the objective in the real world.

The major topics covered on Exam 70-294 are:

Planning and Implementing an Active Directory Infrastructure
: Designed to test your knowledge of designing Active Directory forests, domains, and sites. Also covers placement of global catalog servers and flexible operations master roles.

Managing and Maintaining an Active Directory Infrastructure
: Designed to test your knowledge of managing and maintaining existing Active Directory forests, domains, and sites. Also covers restoring Active Directory.

Planning and Implementing User, Computer, and Group Strategies
: Designed to test your knowledge of planning security groups, user authentication, and organizational units. Also covers creating organizational units.

Planning and Implementing Group Policy
: Designed to test your knowledge of using Group Policy to configure user and computer environments. Also covers the automation features of Group Policy.

Managing and Maintaining Group Policy
: Designed to test your knowledge of troubleshooting Group Policy and using Resultant Set of Policy (RSoP). Also covers maintaining installed software using Group Policy.

The sections of this chapter are designed to reinforce your knowledge of these topics. Ideally, you will review this chapter as thoroughly as you would your course notes in preparation for a college professor's final exam. That means multiple readings of the chapter, committing to memory key concepts, and performing any necessary outside readings if there are topics you have difficulty with.

As part of your preparation, I recommend creating a test environment that creates a forest root domain and a child domain with four servers running Windows Server 2003. In the forest root domain, install two domain controllers to handle the forest and parent domain roles. In a child domain, install two domain controllers to handle child domain roles. This configuration should help ensure that you can practice all the management and maintenance tasks measured by the exam.

If you are unable to use four systems for testing, you can use two separate configurations of two systems for preparation. In the first configuration, you should install a forest root domain controller and a domain controller in a child domain. In the second configuration, you should install two domain controllers in the same domain.

Planning an Active Directory Forest and Domain Structure

Active Directory directory service is used when computers are organized into domains. The configuration of an organization's Active Directory infrastructure is critically important to ensure proper domain operations. Active Directory has physical and logical components.

Understanding Active Directory Infrastructure and Partitions

Active Directory infrastructure is built around three key structures:

Domains
: Logical groupings of objects that allow centralized management and control. Every organization has at least one domain, which is implemented when Active Directory is installed on the first domain controller in that domain.

Domain trees
: Groups of domains that share the same namespace. Every domain tree has a root domain, which is at the top of the domain tree. Domains in a domain tree have two-way transitive trusts between them.

Forests
: Groups of domain trees that are grouped together to share resources. Every forest has a forest root domain, which is the first domain created in the forest. Domain trees in a forest have two-way transitive trusts between them.

Forests and domains are considered to be the logical components of Active Directory. Use logical components to organize accounts and resources. Establish Active Directory infrastructure by creating the forest root domain, and then adding any other domains that are needed as necessary.

Active Directory represents data stored in the database as objects. Objects have several types of names associated with them:

Common name (CN)
: The name assigned when the object is created with the `CN=` designator. For example, the user account for William R. Stanek is created as a user object and has the common name of `CN=William R. Stanek`.

Distinguished name (DN)
: Describes its place in the directory according to the series of containers in which it is stored. No two objects in the directory have the same distinguished name. Most objects are contained within Organizational Unit (OU) containers or within a default container (CN). As an example, the Engineering OU in the *WilliamStanek.com* domain would have a distinguished name of `OU=engineering,DC=williamstanek,DC=com`.

All objects in the directory have parents except for the root of the directory tree, which is referred to as the `rootDSE`. The `rootDSE` represents the top of the logical namespace for a directory. Below the `rootDSE` is the root domain, which is established when you create the first domain in an Active Directory forest. Once established, the forest root domain never changes.

When you install Active Directory on the first domain controller in a new forest, three containers are created below the `rootDSE`. These containers are as follows:

Forest Root Domain container
: The container for objects in the forest root domain.

Configuration container
: The container for the default configuration and all policy information.

Schema container
: The container for all objects classes, attributes, and syntaxes.

The forest root domain, configuration, and schema containers are defined within like-named partitions:

Forest Root Domain partition
: Stores the Forest Root Domain container

Configuration partition
: Stores the Configuration container

Schema partition
: The Schema container

Active Directory uses partitions to logically divide up the directory. Partitions are the largest logical category of objects in the directory. All directory partitions are created as instances of the domainDNS object class.

Active Directory sees domains as another type of container object. When you create a new domain, you create a new container object in the directory tree which is stored in a domain directory partition for the purposes of management and replication.

Active Directory partitions are used to distribute three general types of data:

Domain-wide data
: Domain-wide data is replicated to every domain controller in a domain. Data in a domain directory partition is replicated to every domain controller in the domain as a writeable replica.

Forest-wide data
: Forest-wide data is replicated to every domain controller in a forest. The configuration partition is replicated as a writable replica. The schema partition is replicated as a read-only replica and the only writeable replica is stored on a domain controller which is designated as having the schema operations master role.

Application data
: Application partition data is replicated on a forest-wide, domain-wide, or other basis to domain controllers that have a particular application partition. Domain controllers running Windows 2000 or earlier versions of Windows do not recognize user-defined application partitions. If a domain controller doesn't have an application partition, it doesn't receive a replica of the application partition. Another name for an application data partition is an application directory partition.

All domain controllers store at least one domain directory partition and two forest-wide data partitions. If a domain controller is also a DNS server that uses Active Directory-integrated zones, the DNS data is stored in application data partitions. These application data partitions are: ForestDnsZones and DomainDnsZones.

In addition to full replicas which are distributed within domains, Active Directory distributes partial replicas of every domain in the forest to special domain controllers designated as global catalog servers. These partial replicas contain information on every object in the forest and are used to facilitate searches and queries. Because only a subset of an object's attributes are stored, the data replica is significantly less than the total size of all object data stored in all domains in the forest. Every domain must have at least one global catalog server. By default, the first domain controller installed in a domain is configured as a global catalog server. The global catalog can be changed and additional servers can be designated for hosting global catalogs as necessary.

Creating the Forest Root Domain

You create a forest root domain when you install Active Directory on the first domain controller in a new forest. Once you've established the forest root domain, you can add new domains to the forest. Any domains that are part of a different namespace as the forest root domain establish a root domain for a new domain tree.

A forest root domain can be:

A dedicated root
: Used as a placeholder to start the directory. It has no accounts associated with it other than those created when the forest root is installed, and those that are needed to manage the forest. It is not used to assign access to resources.

A nondedicated root
: Used as a normal part of the directory and has accounts associated with it. It is used to assign access to resources.

When working with forests, keep the following in mind:

- All domain controllers share the same configuration container that is used to store the default configuration and policy information.
- All domains in a forest trust all the other domains in that forest. There are two-way transitive trusts between all domains in a forest.
- All domains in a forest have the same global catalog. The global catalog stores a partial replica of all objects in the forest.
- All domain controllers in a forest have the same schema. A single schema master is designated for the forest.
- All domains in the forest have the same top-level administrators. These are the members of the Enterprise Admins and Schema Admins groups.

Creating a Child Domain

Use domains to logically group objects for central management and control. After you create the forest root domain, you can create additional domains to divide a forest into smaller components.

Domains set the replication boundary for the domain directory partition and for domain policy information. When you make changes to the domain directory partition or to domain policy information on a domain controller in a domain, the changes are replicated automatically to the other domain controllers in the domain. In contrast, forest directory partitions, like the schema and configuration partitions, are replicated throughout a forest.

Domain boundaries are also boundaries for resource access and administration. Users must be granted permission to access resources in another domain. Administrators of a domain can only manage resources in that domain by default.

Group Policy settings that apply to one domain are independent from those applied to other domains. This allows you to configure policies in different ways for different domains.

Creating Application Data Partitions

While some third-party vendors provide tools for creating application partitions that may be required by their software, you can create application partitions that may be required yourself using Active Directory Services Interfaces (ADSI): *Ldp.exe*, and *Ntdstutil.exe*. To manually create an application partition using *Ntdsutil.exe*, follow these steps:

1. Type `ntdsutil` at a command prompt.
2. At the `ntdsutil:` prompt, type `domain management`.

3. Type `create nc` *`AppPartitionName DomainController`*, where *`AppPartitionName`* is the distinguished name of the application partition to create and *`DomainController`* is the fully qualified domain name of the domain controller on which to create the partition, such as:

```
create nc dc=appdata1,dc=domain,dc=local engsvr52.domain.local
```

4. `ntdsutil` then creates the application partition.

If you need to delete an application partition, you `delete nc`. The syntax for `delete nc` is the same as for `create nc`. When you remove an application partition, any data contained in the partition is lost.

You may also need to create and remove an *application directory partition replica*. This is an instance of a partition on another domain controller, which is created for data access or redundancy. To manually create an application partition replica using *Ntdsutil.exe*, follow these steps:

1. Type `ntdsutil` at a command prompt.
2. At the `ntdsutil:` prompt, type `domain management`.
3. Type `add nc replica` *`AppPartitionName DomainController`*, where *`AppPartitionName`* is the distinguished name of the application partition for which you want to create a replica and is the fully qualified domain name of the domain controller on which to create the partition replica, such as:

```
add nc replica dc=appdata1,dc=domain,dc=local engsvr84.domain.local
```

4. `ntdsutil` then creates the application partition replica.

If you need to delete an application partition, you use `remove nc replica`. The syntax for `remove nc replica` is the same as for `add nc replica`. When you remove an application partition replica, any data contained in the replica is lost.

Installing and Configuring an Active Directory Domain Controller

Active Directory works in concert with DNS. DNS servers must be installed on the network prior to installing Active Directory and promoting servers to be domain controllers. To designate a server as a domain controller, use the Active Directory Installation Wizard (*DCPROMO.EXE*) to install the Active Directory directory service. During installation, you have the option of configuring the domain controller in a new domain or as an additional domain controller in an existing domain.

To extend Active Directory infrastructure from the first domain in a new forest to include additional domains and domain trees, you must configure the domain controller in a new domain. This allows you to create:

- A new domain in a new forest
- A child domain in an existing domain tree
- A domain tree in an existing forest.

Keep the following in mind when working with the Active Directory Installation Wizard:

- When you install a domain controller, DCPROMO deletes all local accounts, certificates and cryptographic keys. This occurs because domain controllers do not have local accounts or separate cryptographic keys. Thus, before installing Active Directory, you should determine whether the server has important local accounts or encrypted files and folders.
- When you are extending infrastructure to include new domain trees and domains, you should log on to the local machine using either the local Administrator account or an account that has administrator privileges on the local machine, and then start the installation.
- When you are creating an additional domain controller in an existing domain, you should log on to the server using a domain account that is a member of the Domain Admins group in the domain of which the domain controller will be a part, and then start the installation.

You can start an Active Directory installation using the Configure Your Server Wizard or by typing `dcpromo` at a command prompt. If you want to use the Configure Your Server wizard, click Configure Your Server Wizard on the Administrative Tools menu. When the wizard starts, click Next twice. On the Server Role page, select Domain Controller (Active Directory), and then click Next twice. Configure Your Server then starts the Active Directory Installation Wizard.

You can perform an advanced installation of Active Directory in two ways:

Active Directory Installation Wizard
: With an answer file (`DCPROMO /ANSWER:`*`answerfile`*), where *`answerfile`* is the name of an answer file that contains answers to questions that should be automated during installation. Use this technique to automate the installation. The answer file that is used to install Windows Server 2003 can also be used to install Active Directory.

Active Directory Installation Wizard
: With backup media (`DCPROMO /ADV`), where the `/ADV` option is used to start the wizard in advanced mode. You use this technique to restore Active Directory from backup media or a network share so the database for the new domain controller doesn't have to be replicated across the network in its entirety.

Before you install Active Directory, you should configure the server to use a static IP address and designate a preferred DNS server. If you are installing the first domain controller in a domain, you can allow DNS to be configured automatically during Active Directory installation by making the server a DNS server and configuring DNS for use with Active Directory.

To install an Active Directory domain controller, follow these steps:

1. Start the Active Directory Installation Wizard.
2. Click Next twice.

3. On the Domain Controller Type page, specify the role of the server as shown in Figure 11-1. You must choose to either create a domain controller in a new domain or an additional domain controller for an existing domain. Click Next.

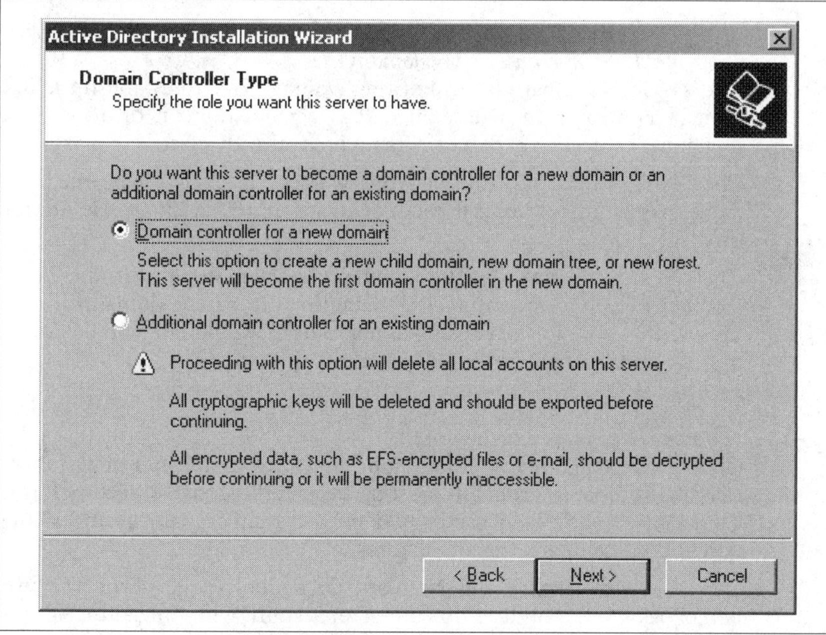

Figure 11-1. Specify the domain controller type.

4. If you choose to create an additional domain controller for an existing page, you see the Network Credentials page. On this page, type the username, password, and user domain of an account with Domain Admins privileges. When you click Next, you see the Database And Log Folders page as discussed in Step 7. Skip ahead to Step 7.
5. If you choose to create a domain controller for a new domain, you will next need to choose whether to do one of the following:

   Create a root domain in a new forest

   Choose Domain In A New Forest to establish the first domain controller in the organization or if you want to install a new forest that is completely separate from any existing forests. This establishes the forest root domain and means the domain controller will have the forest-wide operations master roles as well as the domain-wide operations master roles.

   Click Next to go directly to the New Domain Name page, skipping the Network Credentials page. You don't need specific credentials as you are establishing a new forest with its own set of security groups.

Click Next to display the New Domain Name page. Type the full DNS name for the new domain. Domain names are not case sensitive, and use the letters A to Z, the numerals 0 to 9, and the hyphen (-) character. Each component of the domain name must be separated by a dot (.) and cannot be longer than 63 characters.

Click Next.

Create a child domain in an existing domain tree

Choose Child Domain In An Existing Domain Tree to establish the first domain controller in a domain that is a child domain of an existing domain. The necessary parent domain must already exist.

Click Next to display the Network Credentials page. Type the username, password, and user domain of an account with Enterprise Admins privileges.

Click Next to display the Child Domain Installation page. In the Parent Domain field, type the full DNS name for the parent domain or click Browse to search for an existing domain. In the Child Domain field, type the name component of the child domain.

Click Next.

Create domain tree in an existing forest

Choose Domain Tree In An Existing Forest to establish a new domain tree that is separate from any existing trees in the Active Directory forest. The domain name you use should not be a subdomain of an existing parent domain in any tree of the forest.

Click Next to display the Network Credentials page. Type the user name, password, and user domain of an account with Enterprise Admins privileges.

Click Next to display the New Domain Tree page. Type the full DNS name for the new domain.

Click Next.

6. The Active Directory Installation Wizard uses the domain name you specified to set a default NetBIOS domain name. You can accept the default or type a new NetBIOS name of up to 14 characters. If there are any problems creating the default name, the wizard will display a warning prompt similar to the one shown in the following screen. The wizard displays this prompt when there is a name collision on the default name originally selected and an alternate name has to be used.
7. On the Database And Log Folders page, shown in Figure 11-2, specify the location for the Active Directory database folder and log folder. The default location for both is *%SystemRoot%\NTDS*. Click Next.
8. On the Shared System Volume page, shown in Figure 11-3, specify the location for the Sysvol folder. The default location is *%SystemRoot%\Sysvol*. In most cases, you'll want to accept the default. Click Next.

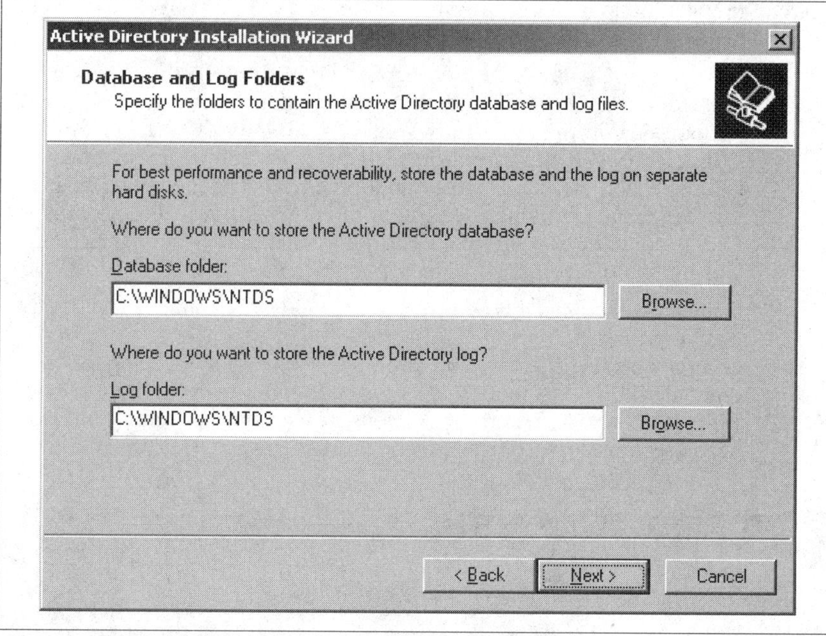

Figure 11-2. Specify the location for database files and logs.

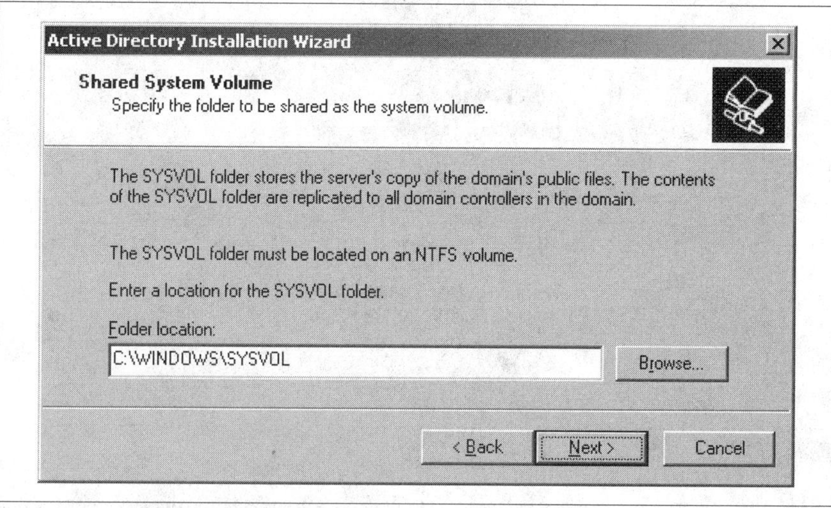

Figure 11-3. Specify the location for the Sysvol.

9. The wizard examines the network environment and attempts to register the domain and the domain controller in DNS. If it has any problems with registration, the wizard will display a diagnostics page and allow you to correct the problems. Click Next.

10. On the Permissions page, specify the default permissions for users and groups. As shown in Figure 11-4, the available options are:

Permissions Compatible With Pre-Windows 2000 Server Operating Systems
: Reduces default security and allows anonymous user logons. Select this option only if the domain will have Windows NT servers running Windows NT applications or services that require anonymous user logons. When you choose this option, the wizard adds the special groups Everyone and Anonymous Logon to the Pre-Windows 2000 Compatible Access domain local group on the server that allows anonymous logon and anonymous access to Active Directory data.

Permissions Compatible Only With Windows 2000 or Windows Server 2003 Operating Systems
: Enforces default security and prevents anonymous user logons. If the domain will have Windows 2000 or later computers running Windows 2000 or later services and applications, choose this option so only authorized users can logon to the domain and access Active Directory data.

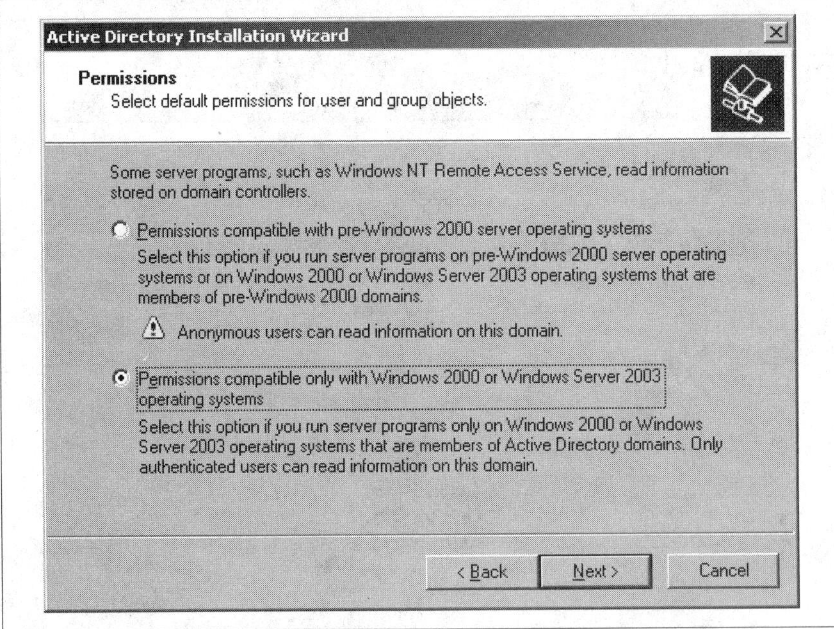

Figure 11-4. Specify the permissions type.

11. Click Next. As shown in Figure 11-5, type and then confirm the password that should be used when starting the computer in Directory Services Restore Mode. This special password is used only for restore mode and is separate from the Administrator account password.
12. Click Next. On the Summary page, review the installation options.
13. Click Next to begin the installation and configuration of Active Directory.
14. Click Finish. When prompted to restart the domain controller, click Restart Now.

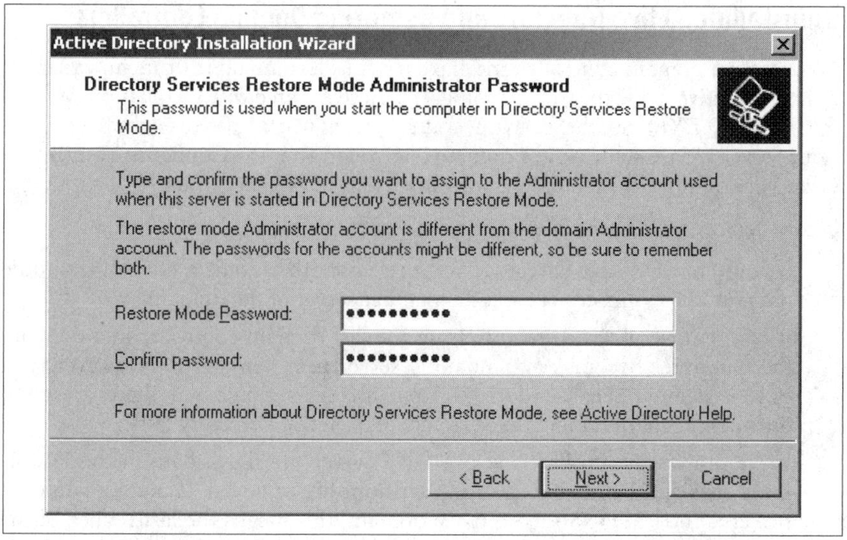

Active Directory Installation Wizard

Directory Services Restore Mode Administrator Password

This password is used when you start the computer in Directory Services Restore Mode.

Type and confirm the password you want to assign to the Administrator account used when this server is started in Directory Services Restore Mode.

The restore mode Administrator account is different from the domain Administrator account. The passwords for the accounts might be different, so be sure to remember both.

Restore Mode Password: ••••••••••

Confirm password: ••••••••••

For more information about Directory Services Restore Mode, see Active Directory Help.

< Back | Next > | Cancel

Figure 11-5. Specify the restore mode password.

After installing Active Directory, you should verify the installation. Start by reviewing the installation logs, which are stored in the *%SystemRoot%\Debug* folder. The *Dcpromo.log* file is the primary log file for recording the details on the installation or removal of Active Directory. The *Dcpromoui.log* file is used to log details on the installation or removal of Active Directory related to the graphical user interface.

After reviewing the installation logs, examine your organization's DNS servers to ensure that SRV records were created for the domain controller. The domain controller should also have NTDS and Sysvol folders.

The Windows Support Tools contain two tools you can use to troubleshoot an Active Directory installation. These tools are:

Netdiag
: Netdiag is used for network connectivity testing. Use Netdiag whenever a computer is having network problems. Type `netdiag /q` to perform network tests and return only errors. Type `netdiag /v` to display verbose output. Type `netdiag /debug` to list debugging details with reasons for success or failure.

Dcdiag
: Dcdiag is used for performing domain controller diagnostics. Type `dcdiag /s:DomainController`, where `DomainController` is the hostname or DNS name of the server on which to perform diagnostics. Use the `/v` option to display verbose output. Use the `/?` option to display help.

In the *%SystemRoot%\System32* folder, you'll find the Ntdsutil utility. This utility is used for performing Active Directory diagnostics and restores. Only experienced administrators should use Ntdsutil.

Uninstalling Active Directory and Demoting Domain Controllers

To demote a domain controller and have it act as a standalone or member server, uninstall Active Directory by running the Active Directory Installation Wizard (*DCPROMO.EXE*) on the domain controller. You can also use the Configure Your Server wizard to demote a domain controller. Run the Configure Your Server wizard and remove the Domain Controller (Active Directory) role.

Before demoting domain controllers, consider the following:

- If you remove Active Directory and there are other domain controllers in the domain, the computer becomes a member server of the domain.
- If you remove Active Directory from the last domain controller in a domain, the computer becomes a standalone server in a workgroup. However, you cannot demote the last domain controller in a domain if there are child domains. If child domains exist, removal of Active Directory fails.
- If the domain controller is also a DNS server, the DNS data in the ForestDnsZones and DomainDnsZones partitions are removed. If the domain controller is the last DNS server in the domain, this means the last replica of the DNS information is removed from the domain and all domain DNS records will be lost.
- If the domain controller has a TAPI application directory partition, you may need to use the *Tapicfg.exe* utility to remove the partition prior to demoting the domain controller. You can determine the location of any TAPI application directory partitions in the domain by typing `tapicfg show` at a command prompt.
- If you try to demote a domain controller that is also a global catalog, you will see a warning prompt. Don't remove the last global catalog from a domain. If you do this, users won't be able to log on to the domain. To determine the global catalog servers in a domain, type the following at a command prompt:

  ```
  dsquery server -domain DomainName | dsget server -isgc -dnsname
  ```

  where *`DomainName`* is the name of the domain.

You must be a member of the Domain Admins group to remove an additional domain controller in a domain, and a member of the Enterprise Admins group to remove the last domain controller from a domain.

To demote a domain controller, follow these steps:

1. Log on to the domain controller using an account with the appropriate administrator privileges.
2. Start the Active Directory Installation Wizard by typing `dcpromo` at a command prompt.
3. Click Next, and then follow the prompts. You will be prompted to type and confirm the password for the local Administrator account on the server. This is required because domain controllers don't have local accounts, but member or standalone servers do.

The Active Directory Installation Wizard demotes domain controllers by:

- Removing Active Directory and related services.
- Removing domain controller SRV records from DNS.
- Removing Group Policy security settings for domain controllers and reenabling local security settings.
- Changing the computer account type and moving the computer account from the Domain Controllers container to the Computers container.
- Transferring any operations master roles from the server to another domain controller in the domain.
- Creating a local SAM account database and a local Administrator account.

Setting Active Directory Forest and Domain Functional Levels

With Active Directory, each forest and each domain within a forest operates at a specific functional level. The functional level of forests and domains within forests are separate. The functional level for a forest is referred to as the forest functional level. The functional level for a domain within a forest is referred to as the domain functional level. While all domains in a forest have the same forest functional level, each domain in a forest can have a different domain functional level.

The functional level determines how Active Directory can be used and what features are enabled. By default, Active Directory is configured to be compatible with Windows NT domains and clients. When a domain is operating in the default mode, a domain controller running Windows 2000 or later is designated as a PDC emulator. A *PDC emulator* is a special operations master role that allows the domain controller to act as the primary domain controller for Windows NT clients in the domain. Windows NT domains have a primary domain controller and one or more backup domain controllers rather than multiple domain controllers that are all equally accountable.

The domain functional levels follow:

Windows 2000 mixed mode
: The default mode, unless you're upgrading from Windows NT 4.0. This mode supports Windows Server 2003, Windows 2000, and Windows NT domains. Domains operating in this mode can't use many Active Directory features, including group nesting, group type conversion, universal groups, easy domain controller renaming, update logon timestamps, migration of security principals, and Kerberos key distribution center (KDC) key version numbers.

Windows 2000 native mode
: This mode supports Windows Server 2003 and Windows 2000 domains only. Windows NT domains are not supported. Domains operating in this mode can use group nesting, group type conversion, universal groups, and migration of security principals. Domains operating in this mode aren't able to use easy domain controller renaming, update logon timestamps, and Kerberos KDC key version numbers.

Windows Server 2003 interim mode

This mode supports Windows Server 2003 and Windows NT domains only. Windows 2000 domains aren't supported. If you upgrade from a Windows NT domain to a Windows Server 2003 domain, this is the default mode. Only servers running Windows NT and Windows Server 2003 can be used.

Windows Server 2003 mode

This mode supports Windows Server 2003 domains only. Windows NT and Windows 2000 domains are not supported. Domains in this mode can use all Active Directory features, including group nesting, group type conversion, universal groups, easy domain controller renaming, updating logon timestamps, migration of security principals, and Kerberos KDC key version numbers.

Domain functional level can be raised, but not lowered. You can:

- Raise the domain functional level from Windows 2000 Mixed mode to Windows 2000 Native mode.
- Raise the domain functional level from Windows 2000 Native mode or Windows Server 2003 Interim mode to Windows Server 2003 mode.

To raise the domain functional level, follow these steps:

1. Start Active Directory Domains And Trusts from the Administrative Tools menu.
2. Right-click the domain, and then click All Tasks → Raise Domain Functional Level. The current domain name and functional level is displayed in the Raise Domain Functional Level dialog box.
3. To change the domain functionality, use the selection list provided to choose the new domain functional level, and then click Raise.
4. When you click OK, the new domain functional level is replicated to each domain controller in the domain. You can't reserve this action.

The forest functional levels follow:

Windows 2000

The default mode, unless you're upgrading from Windows NT 4.0. This mode supports domain controllers running Windows Server 2003, Windows 2000, and Windows NT. Forests operating in this mode can't use many Active Directory features, including extended two-way trusts between forests, domain rename, domain restructure using renaming, and global catalog replication enhancements.

Windows Server 2003 interim mode

This mode supports Windows Server 2003 and Windows NT only. Windows 2000 domain controllers aren't supported. If you upgrade from Windows NT to a Windows Server 2003, this is the default mode for the forest.

Windows Server 2003 mode

This mode supports Windows Server 2003 domain controllers only. Windows NT and Windows 2000 domain controllers are not supported. Forests operating in this mode can use many Active Directory features, including extended two-way trusts between forests, domain rename, domain restructure using renaming, and global catalog replication enhancements.

Forest functional level can be raised, but not lowered. You can:

- Raise the forest functional level from Windows 2000 mode to Windows Server 2003 mode.
- Raise the forest functional level from Windows Server 2003 Interim mode to Windows Server 2003 mode.

To raise the forest functional level, follow these steps:

1. Start Active Directory Domains And Trusts from the Administrative Tools menu.
2. Right-click the domain, and then click Raise Forest Functional Level. The current forest name and functional level is displayed in the Raise Forest Functional Level dialog box.
3. To change the forest functionality, use the selection list provided to choose the new forest functional level, and then click Raise.
4. When you click OK, the new forest functional level is replicated to each domain controller in the forest. You can't reserve this action.

Using UPN Suffixes

Every user account has a User Principal Name (UPN) that consists of the User Logon Name combined with the at symbol (@) and a UPN suffix. The names of the current domain and the root domain are set as the default UPN suffix. You can specify an alternate UPN suffix to use to simplify logon or provide additional logon security. This name is used only within the forest and does not have to be a valid DNS name. For example, if the UPN suffix for a domain is tech.domain.local, you could use an alternate UPN suffix to simplify this domain. This would allow the user Williams to log on using *williams@domain* rather than *williams@tech.domain.local*.

You can add or remove UPN suffixes for an Active Directory forest and all domains within that forest by completing the following steps:

1. Start Active Directory Domains And Trusts from the Administrative Tools menu.
2. Right-click the Active Directory Domains And Trusts node, and then click Properties.
3. To add a UPN suffix, type the alternate suffix in the box provided, and then click Add.
4. To remove a UPN suffix, click the suffix to remove in the list provided, and then click Remove.
5. Click OK.

Planning and Implementing a Strategy for Placing Global Catalog Servers

Domain controllers designated as global catalogs contain additional data stores called global catalogs. A *global catalog* contains a full copy of all objects in the directory for its host domain and a partial, read-only replica of objects in all other domains in the Active Directory forest. This configuration enables the global catalog to be used for efficient searching and faster logon.

Placing Global Catalog Servers

The global catalog:

- Enables a user to log on to a network by providing universal group membership information to a requesting domain controller during logon.
- Enables finding directory information throughout the forest.
- Helps to resolve User Principal Names for domains outside a domain controller's current domain.

If a global catalog isn't available when a user in a universal security group logs on to a domain, the logon computer may be able to use cached credentials if the user has logged on previously and the logon domain controller is running Windows Server 2003. If the user has not logged on to the domain previously, the user can log on only to the local computer.

By default, the first domain controller installed in a domain is automatically designated as a global catalog server. You can move the global catalog to another domain controller and designate additional domain controllers to be global catalog servers as well. To designate a domain controller as a global catalog, follow these steps:

1. Start Active Directory Sites And Services from the Administrative Tools menu.
2. Expand the site you want to work with, such as Default-First-Site-Name.
3. Expand the Servers node, and then select the server you want to designate as a global catalog.
4. In the right-pane, right-click NTDS Settings and then select Properties.
5. To designate the domain controller to be a global catalog, select the Global Catalog option as shown in Figure 11-6.
6. To remove the global catalog from a domain controller, clear the Global Catalog option.
7. Click OK.

Queries to global catalog servers are done over TCP port 3268 for standard communications and TCP port 3269 for secure communications. When considering where to place global catalog servers, you should examine the network's site topology. Each site should have at least one global catalog to ensure availability and optimal response time. When each site has at least one global catalog, user logon requests and queries can be resolved locally without having to go across WAN connections. To determine which domain controllers to designate as global catalogs, consider the server's ability to handle replication and query traffic. The global catalog requires more network resources than normal directory replication traffic.

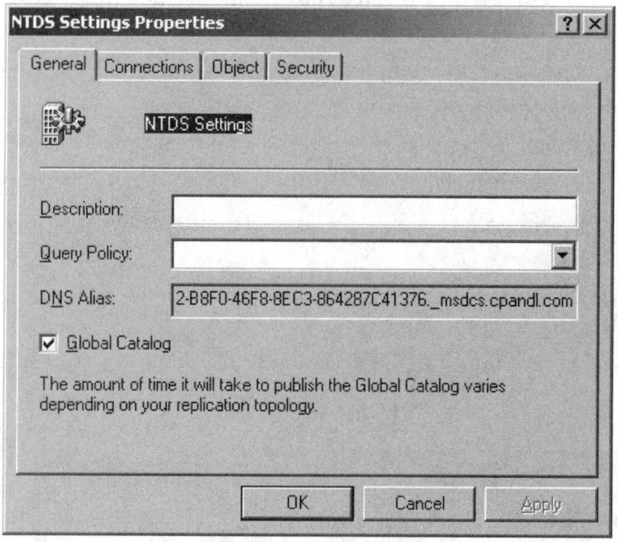

Figure 11-6. Designating global catalog servers.

Having one global catalog in each site is especially important when:

- Slow or unreliable WAN connections are used to connect to other sites.
- Users in the site belong to a domain running in Windows 2000 native mode.
- Other applications in the site use port 3268 or 3269 to resolve global catalog queries.

Exchange Server uses Active Directory as its directory service. Mailbox names are resolved through Active Directory by queries to the global catalog server.

Designating Replication Attributes

Each object class, such as User, Group, or Computer, has a set of attributes that are designated for replication. Global catalog servers use the replication details to create the partial replica of objects from other domains.

Schema administrators can designate additional attributes to be replicated. If users routinely search for an attribute that isn't replicated, you might want to add attributes to the list of replicated attributes. You shouldn't stop replication attributes that are replicated by default, however.

Members of the Schema Admins group can manage the attributes that are replicated using the Active Directory Schema snap-in. This snap-in is not available by default. You must install the Administration Tools (*ADMINPAK.MSI*). Then you must register the snap-in for use on your computer by typing the following at a command prompt:

```
regsvr32 schmmgmt.dll
```

Once you install the Administrative Tools, you can add the Active Directory Schema snap-in to a custom console by completing these steps:

1. Type `mmc` at a command prompt.
2. Click File → Add/Remove Snap-in.
3. Click Add. Click Active Directory Schema, and then click Add.
4. Click Close, and then click OK.

You can edit the schema for an object whose attribute you want to replicate using the following steps:

1. In Active Directory Schema, expand the Active Directory Schema node, and then select the Attributes node.
2. A list of the attributes for all objects in the directory is then displayed in the right pane (see Figure 11-7).

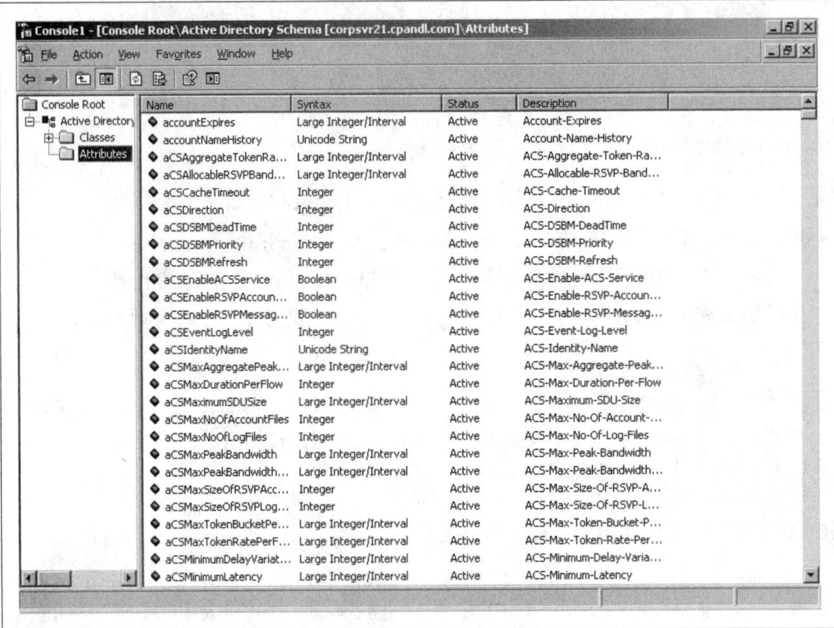

Figure 11-7. Displaying available schema attributes.

3. Double-click the attribute to replicate to the global catalog.
4. In the attribute's properties dialog box, select the Replicate This Attribute To The Global Catalog checkbox (see Figure 11-8).
5. If you want the attribute to be indexed in Active Directory for faster search and retrieval, select Index This Attribute In The Active Directory. This increases the size of the Active Directory database.
6. Click OK.

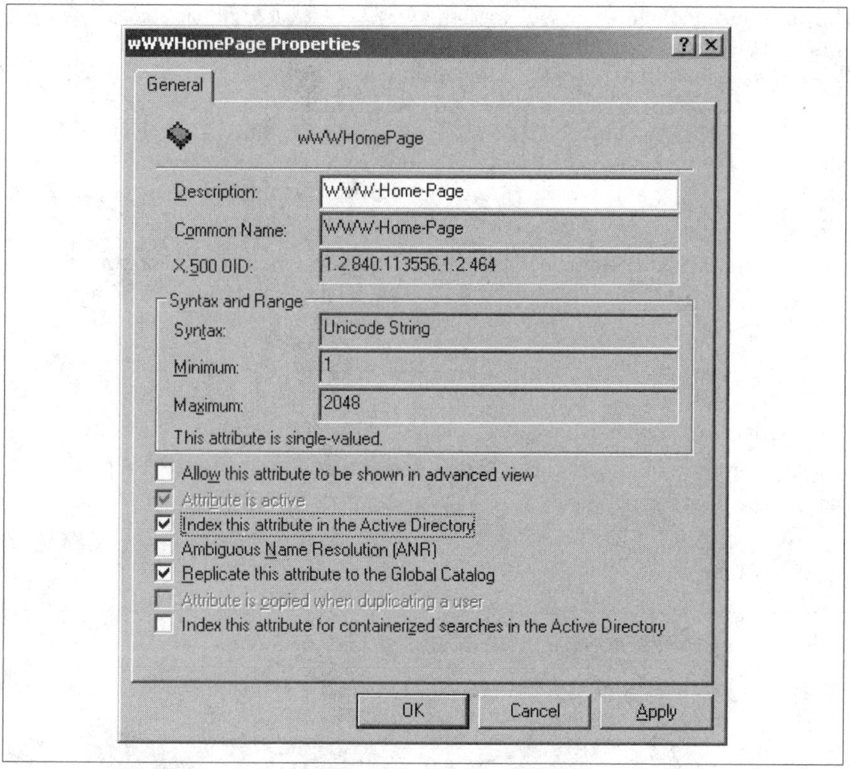

Figure 11-8. Replicate and index attributes as necessary.

Evaluating the Need to Enable Universal Group Caching

On a domain with domain controllers running Windows Server 2003, universal group membership caching can be enabled. Once caching is enabled, domain controllers store universal group membership information in a cache and use the cache for the next time the user logs on to the domain. The cache is maintained indefinitely and updated every eight hours by default to ensure its consistency. Up to 500 universal group memberships can be updated at once.

For Exam 70-294, you need a strong understanding of universal group caching. Since only 500 universal group memberships can be updated at once, it can take multiple updates to replicate all changes.

Universal group caching has the following benefits:

- Faster logon because domain controllers no longer need to access global catalogs to obtain universal group membership details.
- Reduced bandwidth usage because you can deploy fewer global catalogs and in this way reduce replication traffic.
- Reduced resource usage and possibly the requirement to update server hardware to handle the additional load of maintaining a global catalog.

Universal group caching may change the way you deploy global catalogs within your organization. With universal group caching enabled, remote sites running Windows Server 2003 domain controllers don't have to have global catalogs configured as well. While this gives you additional configuration options, you should still consider whether sites are connected over slow or unreliable WAN connections, whether users in the site belong to a domain running in Windows 2000 native mode, and whether other applications in the site use port 3268 or 3269 to resolve global catalog queries.

On a domain with controllers running Windows Server 2003, you enable universal group membership caching on a-per site basis. To enable caching, follow these steps:

1. Start Active Directory Sites And Services from the Administrative Tools menu.
2. Expand the site you want to work with, such as Default-First-Site-Name.
3. In the right-pane, right-click NTDS Site Settings and then select Properties.
4. As shown in Figure 11-9, select Enable Universal Group Membership Caching.
5. Click OK.

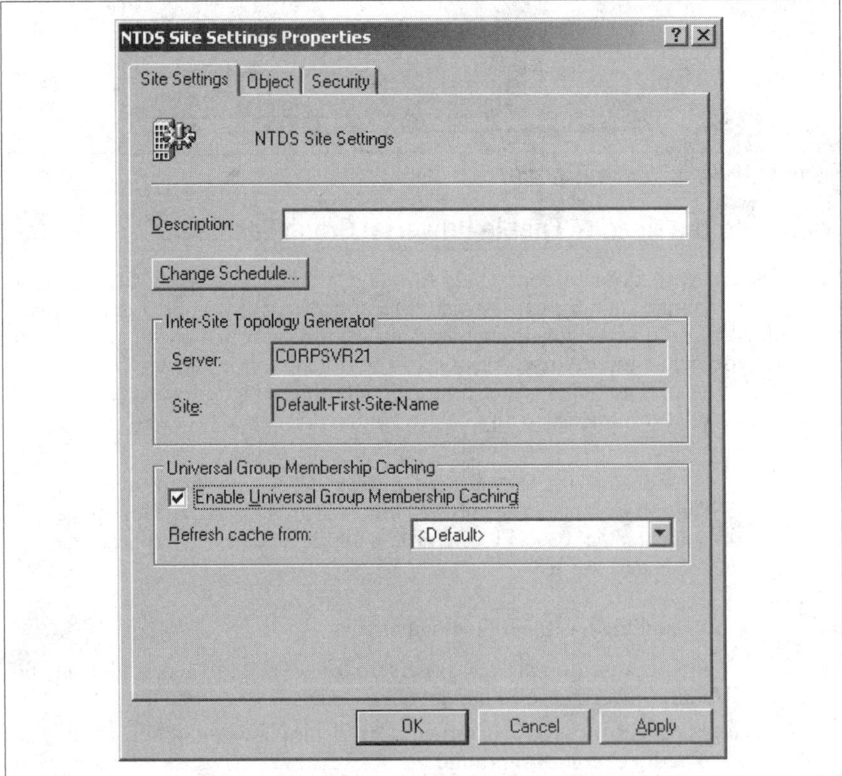

Figure 11-9. Enabling universal group membership caching for a site.

Planning Flexible Operations Master Role Placement

Unlike Windows NT domains, Active Directory domains use a multimaster replication model. In this model, there are no primary or backup domain controllers. Every domain controller in a domain has its own copy of the directory. Every domain controller is equally accountable, and any domain controller can be used to make changes to the standard directory data.

However, some Active Directory operations can only be performed by a single authoritative domain controller, called an *operations master*. A designated operations master has a flexible single-master operations (FSMO) role. Operations performed by an operations master are not permitted to occur at different places on the network at the same time.

Understanding Operations Master Roles

Five operations master roles are designated. These roles are:

- Schema master
- Domain-naming master
- Relative ID (RID) master
- PDC emulator
- Infrastructure master

The schema master and domain-naming master roles are assigned on a per-forest basis. There is only one schema master and only one domain-naming master in a forest.

The RID master, infrastructure master, and PDC emulator are assigned on a per-domain basis. Each domain in a forest has an RID master, an infrastructure master, and a PDC emulator.

The schema master and domain-naming master are critical to forest operations. The schema master maintains the only writeable copy of the schema container and is the only domain controller in the forest on which you can make changes to the schema. There can be just one schema master in the entire forest.

The domain-naming master is responsible for adding or removing domains from the forest. If the domain-naming master cannot be contacted when you are trying to add or remove a domain, you will not be able to add or remove the domain. There can be only one domain-naming master in the entire forest.

The RID master, PDC emulator, and infrastructure master are critical for domain operations. The relative ID (RID) master allocates blocks of relative IDs. Every domain controller in a domain is issued a block of relative IDs by the RID master; these IDs are used to build the security IDs, which uniquely identify security principals in a domain. If a domain controller cannot contact the RID master and runs outs of RIDs, no new objects are able to be created on the domain controller and object creation fails. There can be only one RID master in a domain.

In a domain using the Windows 2000 mixed or Windows Server 2003 interim functional level, the PDC emulator master acts as the primary domain controller

(PDC) for all Windows NT 4.0 backup domain controllers (BDCs) and is required to authenticate Windows NT logons, process password changes, and replicate domain changes to BDCs. It also runs the domain master browser service.

In a domain using the Windows 2000 native or Windows Server 2003 functional level, the PDC emulator master is responsible for processing password changes. When a user changes his password, the change is first sent to the PDC emulator, which in turn replicates the change to all of the other domain controllers in the domain. There can be only one PDC emulator master in a domain.

When a user tries to log on to the network but provides an incorrect password, the logon domain controller checks the PDC emulator to see whether there is a recent password change for the user's account. If so, the domain controller retries the logon authentication on the PDC emulator. This ensures that if a user has recently changed his password, he is not denied logon with the new password.

The infrastructure master is responsible for updating group-to-user references across domains. When you rename or move a member of a group, the infrastructure master is responsible for ensuring that changes to the common name are correctly reflected in the group membership information for groups in other domains in the forest.

The infrastructure master maintains group-to-user references by comparing its directory data with that of a global catalog. As necessary, it updates references and replicates the changes to other domain controllers in the domain. There can be only one infrastructure master in a domain.

Planning Operations Master Role Placement

When you install Active Directory and create the first domain controller in a new forest, all five roles are assigned to that domain controller. When you add domains, the first domain controller installed in a new domain is automatically designated as the RID master, infrastructure master, and PDC emulator for that domain.

As part of domain design, you should consider:

- How many domain controllers you need for each domain
- Whether you need to transfer operations master roles to other domain controllers

You should have at least two domain controllers in each domain in the forest. As you add sites and domains to the network, consider whether to transfer the operations master roles. You might want to transfer an operations master role to balance the workload or to improve performance. You might need to transfer an operations master role to accommodate maintenance or failure recovery.

Some recommendations for planning operations master roles follow:

- In most cases, you want the forest-wide roles—schema master and domain naming master—to be on the same domain controller. These roles use few resources and have little overhead. The server acting as the domain naming master should also be a global catalog server.
- In most cases, the RID master and PDC emulator master roles should be on the same domain controller. The key reason for this is that the PDC emulator uses more relative IDs than most other domain controllers. If the RID master and PDC emulator master roles aren't on the same domain controller, the domain controllers on which these roles are placed should be in the same Active Directory site with a reliable connection between them.
- Except for a single domain forest or a multidomain forest where all domain controllers are global catalog servers, the infrastructure master should not be placed on a domain controller that is also a global catalog. If the infrastructure master and the global catalog are on the same server, the infrastructure master doesn't see that group membership changes have been made and thus doesn't replicate them.

Locating and Transferring the Operations Master Roles

You can determine the current operations masters for your logon domain by typing the following at a command prompt:

```
netdom query fsmo
```

As shown here, the output lists each role owner by its fully qualified domain name:

```
Schema owner                corpsvr64.domain.local
Domain role owner           corpsvr64.domain.local
PDC role                    corpsvr21.tech.domain.local
RID pool manager            corpsvr21.tech.domain.local
Infrastructure owner        corpsvr15.tech.domain.local
```

From the output in this example, you can also determine that the forest root domain is *domain.local* and the current logon domain is *tech.domain.local*. If you want to determine the operations masters for a specific domain, use the following command:

```
netdom query fsmo /d:DomainName
```

where *DomainName* is the name of the domain, such as *eng.domain.local*.

Operations master roles can be changed in two ways:

- If the current operations master is online, you can perform a role transfer, gracefully shifting the role from one domain controller to another.
- If the current operations master has failed and will not be coming back online, you can seize the role and forcibly transfer it to another domain controller.

You can view and transfer the location of domain-wide operations master roles by completing the following steps:

1. Start Active Directory Users And Computers from the Administrative Tools menu.

2. In the console tree, right-click Active Directory Users And Computers, and then select Connect To Domain. In the Connect To Domain dialog box, type the fully qualified domain name of the domain for which you want to view or transfer roles, and then click OK.
3. In the console tree, right-click Active Directory Users And Computers, and then select Connect To Domain Controller. In the Connect To Domain Controller dialog box, select the domain controller to which you want to transfer a domain-wide operations master role, and then click OK.
4. In the console tree, right-click Active Directory Users And Computers and then click All Tasks → Operations Masters. This opens the Operations Masters dialog box as shown in Figure 11-10.
5. On the RID tab, the current RID master is listed. To change the role to the previously selected domain controller, click Change.
6. On the PDC tab, the current PDC Emulator master is listed. To change the role to the previously selected domain controller, click Change.
7. On the Infrastructure tab, the current Infrastructure master is listed. To change the role to the previously selected domain controller, click Change.
8. Click Close.

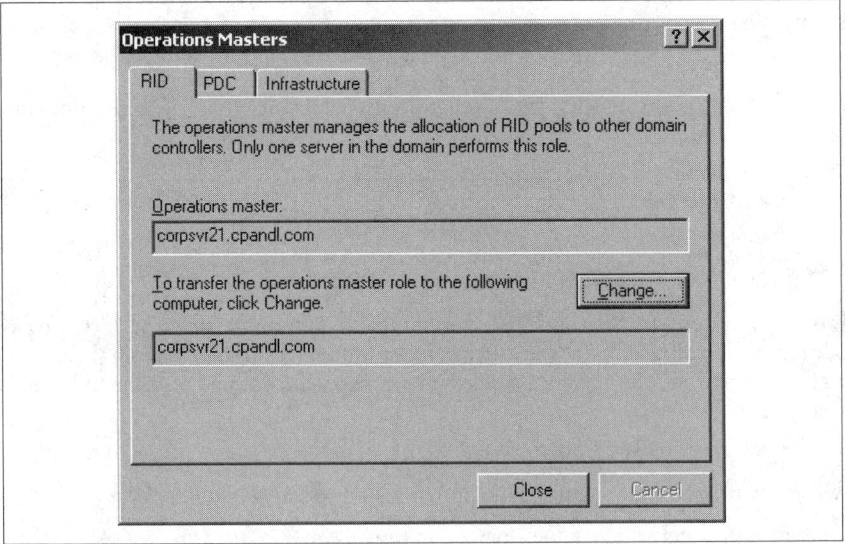

Figure 11-10. Transferring domain-wide operations master roles.

You can view or transfer the location of the domain-naming master by completing the following steps:

1. Start Active Directory Domains And Trusts from the Administrative Tools menu.
2. In the console tree, right-click Active Directory Domains And Trusts, and then select Connect To Domain. In the Connect To Domain dialog box, type the fully qualified domain name of the domain for which you want to view or transfer roles, and then click OK.

3. In the console tree, right-click Active Directory Domains And Trusts, and then select Connect To Domain Controller. In the Connect To Domain Controller dialog box, select the domain controller to which you want to transfer a domain-wide operations master role, and then click OK.
4. In the console tree, right-click Active Directory Domains And Trusts, and then click Operations Master. This opens the Change Operations Masters dialog box as shown in Figure 11-11.
5. The current domain-naming master is listed. To change the role to the previously selected domain controller, click Change.
6. Click Close.

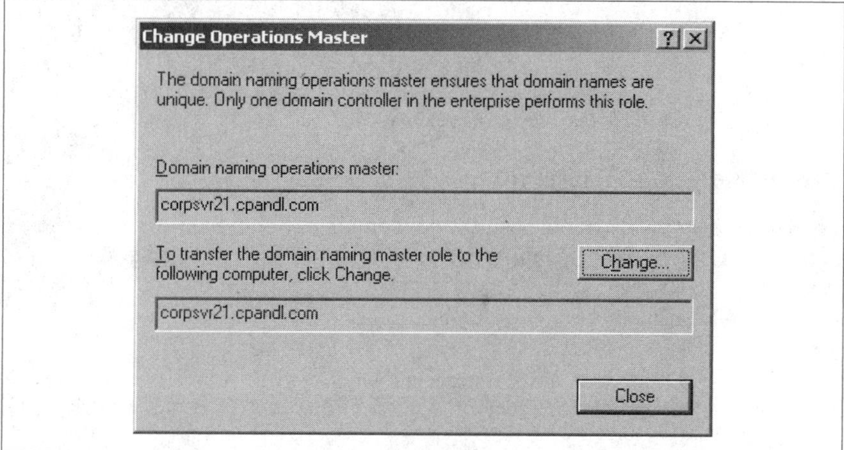

Figure 11-11. Transferring the domain-naming master role.

You can view or transfer the location of the schema master by completing the following steps:

1. Type `mmc` at a command prompt.
2. Click File → Add/Remove Snap-in.
3. Click Add. Click Active Directory Schema, and then click Add.
4. Click Close, and then click OK.
5. In Active Directory Schema, right-click the Active Directory Schema node, and then click Change Domain Controller. In the Change Domain Controller dialog box, click Specify Name, type the fully qualified domain name of the domain controller to which you want to transfer the role, and then click OK.
6. In Active Directory Schema, right-click the Active Directory Schema node and then click Operations Master. This opens the Change Schema Master dialog box as shown in Figure 11-12.
7. The current schema master is listed. To change the role to the previously selected domain controller, click Change.
8. Click Close.

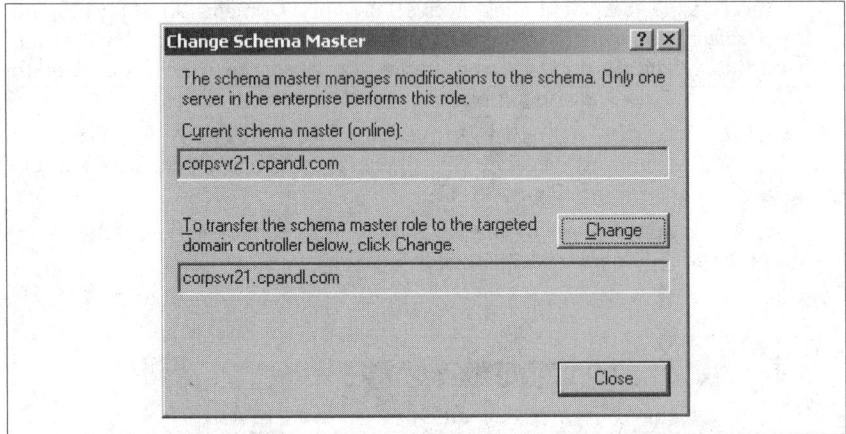

Figure 11-12. Transferring the schema master role.

Seizing Operations Master Roles

When an operations master fails and is not coming back online, you need to seize the role to forcibly transfer it to another domain controller. Seizing a role is a drastic step that should only be performed when the previous role owner will never be available again.

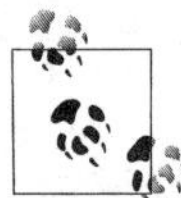

Do not seize an operations master role when you can transfer it gracefully using the normal transfer procedure. Seize only a role as a last resort.

Before you seize a role and forcibly transfer it, you should determine how up to date the domain controller that will take over the role is with respect to the previous role owner. Active Directory tracks replication changes using Update Sequence Numbers (USNs). Because of replication latency, domain controllers might not all be up to date. If you compare a domain controller's USN to that of other servers in the domain, you can determine whether the domain controller is the most up to date with respect to changes from the previous role owner. If the domain controller is up to date, you can transfer the role safely. If the domain controller isn't up to date, you can wait for replication to occur, and then transfer the role to the domain controller.

The Windows Support Tools includes Repadmin for working with Active Directory replication. To display the highest sequence number for a specified naming context on each replication partner of a designated domain controller, type the following at a command prompt:

```
repadmin /showutdvec DomainControllerName NamingContext
```

where *`DomainControllerName`* is the fully qualified domain name of the domain controller and *`NamingContext`* is the distinguished name of the domain in which the server is located, such as:

```
repadmin /showutdvec engsvr18.domain.local dc=domain,dc=local
```

The output shows the highest USN on replication partners for the domain partition:

```
Main-Site\engsvr21    @ USN    321348 @ Time 2006-06-12 21:32:32
Main-Site\engsvr32    @ USN    324113 @ Time 2006-06-12 21:34:17
```

In this example, if Engsvr21 is the previous role owner and the domain controller you are examining has an equal or larger USN for Engsvr21, the domain controller is up to date. However, if Engsvr21 is the previous role owner and the domain controller you are examining has a lower USN for Engsvr21, the domain controller is not up to date and you should wait for replication to occur before seizing the role. You could also use `Repadmin /Syncall` to force the domain controller that is the most up to date with respect to the previous role owner to replication with all of its replication partners.

To seize an operations master role, follow these steps:

1. Open a command prompt.

Microsoft recommends that you log on to the console of the server you want to assign as the new operations master locally or via Remote Desktop.

2. List current operations masters by typing `netdom query fsmo`.
3. Type `ntdsutil`.
4. At the `ntdsutil` prompt, type `roles`.
5. At the `fsmo` maintenance prompt, type `connections`.
6. At the server connections prompt, type `connect to server`, followed by the fully qualified domain name of the domain controller to which you want to assign the operations master role.
7. Once you've established a connection to the domain controller, type `quit` to exit the server connections prompt.
8. At the `fsmo maintenance` prompt, type one of the following:

```
seize pdc
seize rid master
seize infrastructure master
seize schema master
seize domain naming master
```

9. At the `fsmo maintenance` prompt, type `quit`.
10. At the `ntdsutil` prompt, type `quit`.

After seizing operations master role, you may need to remove the related data from Active Directory.

Planning and Implementing Organizational Unit Structure

The logical structure of Active Directory determines how accounts and resources are organized. In addition to forests and domains, Active Directory provides organizational units (OUs) as a way of logically organizing accounts and resources. You can think of organizational units as logical administrative units that are used to group accounts and resources together within domains.

Understanding Organizational Units

Within a domain, organizational units are used to:

- Delegate administrator privileges while limiting administrative access
- Create hierarchies that mirror business structure or functions
- Manage groups of objects as a single unit through Group Policy

Organizational units are used to contain objects within a domain and do not contain objects from other domains. Because a single domain can have many organizational units, and those organizational units can be organized into a hierarchy, you can use organizational units instead of domains to represent the structure of the organization or its business functions.

The ability to delegate administration is the primary reason for creating organizational units. To delegate administration for all objects stored in an organizational unit, grant administrators the necessary permissions on the organizational unit's access control list. In this way, you can give administrators limited or full control over only a part of a domain.

Within the Active Directory database, organizational units are represented as container objects that are part of a designated domain. For directory searches, the organizational units are referenced with the `OU=` identifier as part of their common name, such as `OU=Engineering` for an organizational unit named Engineering. The distinguished name of an organizational unit includes the full path to its parent as well as its relative name. For example, the Engineering OU in the *domain.local* domain has a DN of `OU=Engineering OU,DC=domain,DC=local`.

Organizational units are not a part of DNS structure. This means users don't have to reference organizational units when they log on or when they access resources. This makes organizational unit hierarchies much easier to work with than domain hierarchies. Additionally, while it is easy to change the names and structure of OUs, it is not easy to change the names of domains.

Most OU hierarchies are organized by:

Division or business unit within the company
: Use organizational units to reflect the department structure within the organization. This structure is easy to understand and one most administrators will know. However, if the company restructures, you need to change the organizational unit structure.

Geographic or business location

Use organizational units to reflect the actual physical location of units within the company. This structure makes it easy to determine where accounts and resources are physically located. However, this structure doesn't reflect the business structure of the organization.

Areas of administrative control

Use organizational units to reflect the way resources and accounts are managed. This model can also reflect business structure, business location, or both of a company. However, the focus is on administrative control of accounts and on resources with enterprise administrators having full administrative control over the top-level OUs.

Analyzing the Administrative Requirements for an OU

Organizational units allow you to delegate administrative rights over a portion of a domain. You can delegate administrative rights in two key ways:

- Assign a user full administrative control
- Assign a user a specific set of administrative permissions

The permissions assigned depend on the way you configure delegation. When you delegate full administrative control over a particular OU, a local administrator is able to manage all accounts and resources in the OU. If you decide not to give an administrator full administrative control, you can grant permissions to:

- Create, delete, and manage accounts
- Reset user passwords and force password changed at next logon
- Read user account information
- Create, delete, and manage groups
- Modify the membership of a group
- Manage Group Policy links
- Generate Resultant Set of Policy

You should plan your organizational unit structure with delegation in mind. For example, you might want Help Desk technicians to have permission to reset user passwords in an OU. Or you might want a manager to be able to read user account information in an OU. If you have branch offices, you might want to create OUs for each branch office and grant local administrators full administrative control over their OU.

Analyzing the Group Policy Requirements for an OU Structure

Every site, domain, and OU has an associated Group Policy Object (GPO). Using Group Policy, you can specify a set of rules for computer and user configuration and security settings within that site, domain, or organizational unit. Manage policy settings using either the Group Policy Object Editor or the Group Policy Management console. You can use Group Policy to:

- Define default options for configuration and security settings
- Limit options for changing configuration and security settings
- Prevent changing certain configuration and security settings

You should plan your OU structure with Group Policy in mind. Do this by grouping objects together that require the same policy settings. For example, if a group of users and computers require the same stringent security settings, you can create an OU for these users and computers, and then configure the required security settings through Group Policy.

Creating an OU

Each domain has its own OU hierarchy. If your company uses multiple domains, you can create separate OU structures within each domain. To create an OU, you must be a member of the Administrators group in the domain.

You can create an organizational unit by following these steps:

1. Start Active Directory Users And Computers from the Administrative Tools menu.

> By default, you are connected to your logon domain. To connect to another domain, right-click the Active Directory Users And Computers node, and then select Connect To Domain. In the Connect To Domain dialog box, type the fully qualified domain name of the domain in which you want to create the OU, and then click OK.

2. Right-click the location where you want to create the OU, which can be either a domain node or an OU node, point to New, and then click Organizational Unit.
3. In the New Object – Organizational Unit dialog box, type a new name for the organizational unit as shown in Figure 11-13, and then click OK.

Moving Objects Within an OU Hierarchy

Once you create organizational units, you can add objects, such as user or computer accounts, into the organizational unit. To create a new object in an OU, follow these steps:

1. Start Active Directory Users And Computers from the Administrative Tools menu.
2. Right-click the organizational unit, point to New, and then select the type of object to create, such as Computer or User.
3. Provide the necessary information or follow the prompts to create the object.

You can move existing objects from one organizational unit or container to another by completing the following steps:

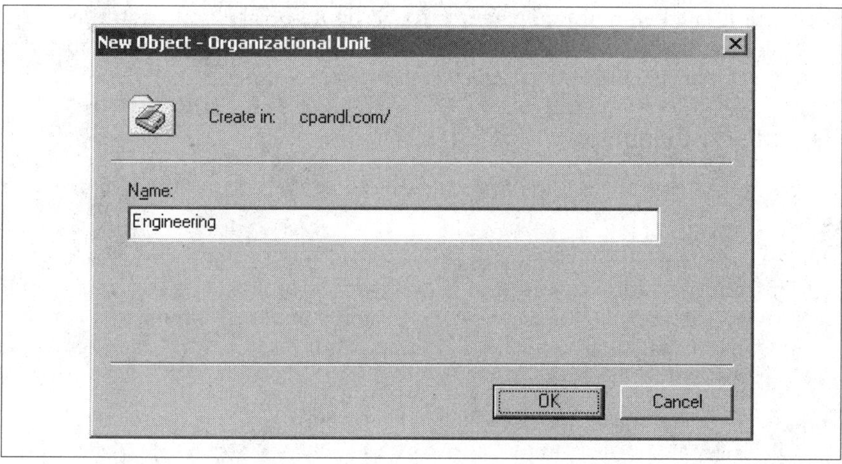

Figure 11-13. Creating an organizational unit.

1. Start Active Directory Users And Computers from the Administrative Tools menu.
2. Select the objects in its existing container by clicking and holding the left mouse button.
3. Drag the object to the desired destination organizational unit.
4. When you release the mouse button, the object is moved to the desired organizational unit.

In Active Directory Users And Computers, you can also move an object by right-clicking it and selecting Move. In the Move dialog box, select the OU or container to which you want to move the object. To move multiple objects in this way, use Ctrl+click or Shift+click to select the objects to move before right-clicking.

When you move an object from one OU to another, the settings assigned directly to the object remain the same. The object inherits the policy settings from the GPO of the new OU and any high-level GPOs as may apply. The policy settings from the GPO of the previous OU no longer apply, unless of course you move the object from a top-level OU to a lower-level OU.

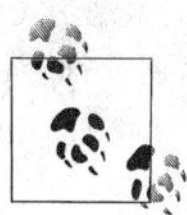

In Active Directory Users And Computers, you can only move objects within a domain. You cannot move objects between domains. To move objects between domains, you must use the *Movetree.exe* utility included in the Windows Support Tools.

Planning and Implementing an Administrative Delegation Strategy

Delegate control of Active Directory objects to grant users permission to manage specific types of objects stored in Active Directory. You want to delegate permissions in such a way that users can perform necessary tasks while preventing them from performing tasks that they should not perform. Determining the tasks that users with limited administrative permissions should be able to perform requires planning. You might need to meet with the user to discuss their job responsibilities or ask a manager about the user's responsibilities.

Planning for Delegation

Delegation can be used at the domain level and at the organizational unit level. You can:

Grant full control over an OU
: This allows a local administrator to create and manage all accounts and resources in the OU. For example, you might want local administrators to be able to manage all types of accounts and resources in their area of responsibility.

Grant full control over specific types of objects in an OU
: This allows a local administrator to create and manage a specific type of object. For example, you might want local administrators to be able to manage users and groups but not be able to manage computer accounts.

Grant full control over specific types of object in a domain
: This allows an administrator to create and manage specific types of objects in a domain. Thus, rather than adding the user as a member of the Administrators group, you grant the user full control over the specific types of objects they need to manage to perform their jobs. For example, you might have user account administrators who are allowed to create and manage user accounts throughout the domain, but are not allowed to perform other administrative tasks.

Grant rights to perform specific tasks in a domain or OU
: This allows a user to perform a specific task. For example, you might want to allow help desk staff to reset user passwords but not allow them to perform other administrative tasks on Active Directory objects.

When you delegate permissions, don't forget about inheritance. Lower level objects inherit permissions from top-level objects. In a domain, the top-level object is the domain object itself. Any user designated as an administrator for a domain automatically has full control over the domain. Any user delegated permissions at the domain level has those permissions for all organizational units in the domain. Similarly, any user delegated permissions in a top-level organizational unit has those permissions for all organizational units that are created within the top-level organizational unit.

Delegating Administration

You can delegate administration of a domain or organizational unit by completing the following steps:

1. Start Active Directory Users And Computers from the Administrative Tools menu.
2. Right-click the organizational unit for which you want to delegate administration and then select Delegate Control. This starts the Delegation Of Control Wizard starts.

3. Click Next. On the Users Or Groups page, shown in Figure 11-14, click Add to display the Select Users, Computers, Or Groups dialog box. Use the Select Users, Computers, Or Groups dialog box to select the user or group to which you are delegating permissions. Repeat this step as necessary.

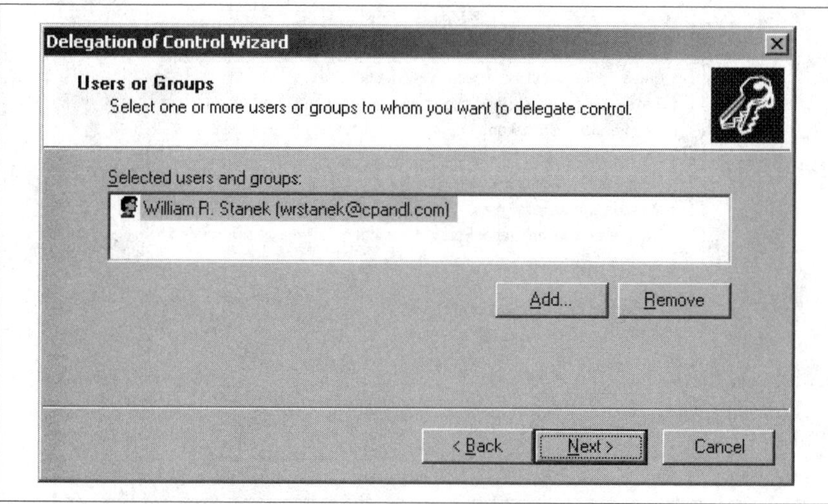

Figure 11-14. Specify the users or groups to which you are delegating permissions.

4. Click Next. On the Tasks To Delegate page, select the tasks you want to delegate, as shown in Figure 11-15. You also have the option to create a custom task, which allows you to specify permissions for various objects—such as users, groups, or computers—within the organizational unit.
5. Click Next, and then click Finish.

As with all other security permissions assigned to an object, users or groups who have been delegated permissions are listed on the Security tab in the organizational unit's properties dialog box. In most cases, a user or group delegated administration permissions will be listed as having Special Permissions. Rather than trying to edit advanced security settings, the best way to change delegated permissions is to do one of the following:

- If you want to grant the user or group additional administrative permissions while keeping current permissions, start the Delegation Of Control Wizard and use the wizard to grant the additional permissions.
- If you want to define a new set of delegated administrative permissions for a user or group, access the Security tab in the organizational unit's properties dialog box. Remove the current permissions for the user or group. Start the Delegation Of Control Wizard and use the wizard to grant the desired permissions.

The Delegation Of Control Wizard cannot be used to remove any delegated privileges. You must access the Security tab of the object's properties dialog box to do this.

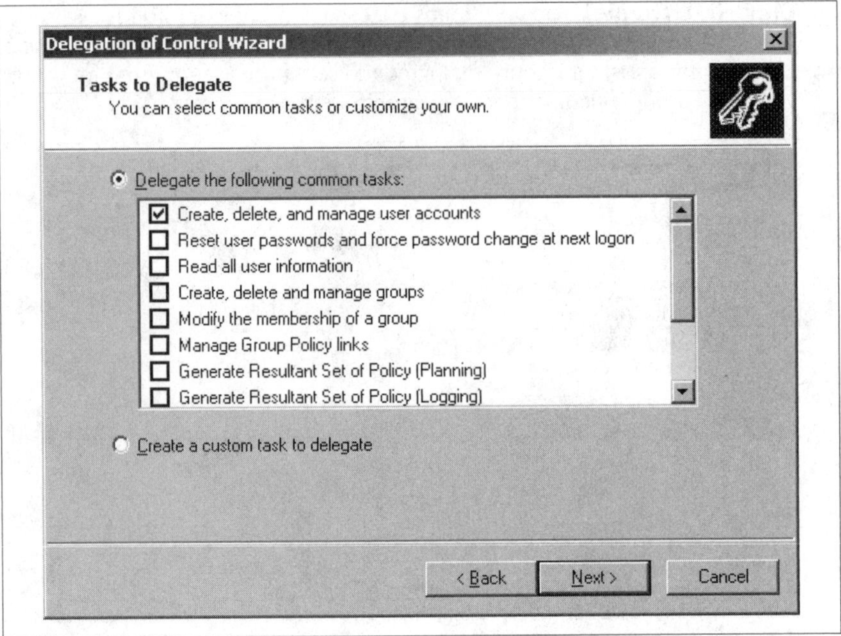

Figure 11-15. Specify the administrative tasks to delegate.

Planning and Managing Active Directory Sites

Sites and subnets are considered to be the physical components of Active Directory. Use physical components to manage network traffic and replication between physical locations or subnets.

Understanding Sites

Every Active Directory implementation has at least one site. A *site* is a group of IP subnets that are connected by reliable, high-speed links. A *subnet* is a subdivision of an IP network. Sites are connected to each other via site links. A *site link* is a logical, transitive connection between two or more sites.

Site structure reflects the physical environment and is separate from the logical representation of the network, which is represented by forests, domains, and organizational units. Sites are used to designate replication boundaries and isolate logon authentication traffic between physical network locations. Typically, individual sites represent the individual LANs within an organization, and the WAN links between business locations mark site boundaries.

Domain and site boundaries are separate. With respect to domains, a single site can contain resources from multiple domains, and a single domain can extend across multiple sites. With respect to subnets, a single site can have multiple subnets, but a single subnet can be a part of one site only.

Key reasons to create additional sites at a single physical location are as follows:

Control replication traffic
: Replication traffic between sites is automatically compressed, reducing the amount of traffic passed between sites by 85–90 percent of its original size.

Isolate logon traffic
: Network clients try to log on to network resources within their local site first, isolating logon traffic to the local site in most cases.

When designing site topology, you should keep the following in mind:

- For client logon and authentication, each site should have at least one domain controller and one global catalog.
- For name resolution and IP assignment, each site should have at least one DNS server and one DHCP server.
- For maintaining access to network resources, each site may also need local file servers, messaging servers, and certificate authorities.

This design should help reduce traffic between sites and ensure faster logon, authentication, and resource access. Use connectivity between network segments to determine where site boundaries should be located. Subnets connected with fast connections should be a part of the same site unless you have specific requirements to control replication or the logon process. Subnets connected with limited bandwidth or unreliable links should be part of different sites.

Understanding Replication

Active Directory replicates data within sites using a different technique than it uses to replicate data between sites. Replication within a site is referred to as *intrasite replication*. Replication between sites is referred to as *intersite replication*.

Sites isolate logon traffic. If a user logs in to her home domain, a domain controller within the local site authenticates the logon. If a user logs in to a domain other than her home domain, a domain controller in the local site forwards the logon request to a domain controller in the user's home domain.

Actions such as creating, deleting, modifying, and moving objects trigger replication between domain controllers. The domain controller on which a change is made replicates the changes with its replication partners.

As Table 11-1 shows, intrasite and intersite replication is very different. Intrasite replication is designed to ensure that domain controllers are notified rapidly of changes. Intersite replication is designed to reduce traffic over Wide Area Network (WAN) links.

Table 11-1. Comparing intrasite and intersite replication

Feature compared	Intrasite replication	Intersite replication
Replication compression	Replication data is not compressed, which reduces processor and memory usage.	Replication data is compressed by default to reduce network bandwidth usage. This increases the load on the domain controller.
Replication notification	Replication partners notify each other when changes need to be replicated, allowing partners to request the changes. This reduces replication latency.	Replication partners do not notify each other when changes need to be replicated. This increases replication latency.
Replication frequency	Replication partners poll each other periodically to determine whether there are updates.	Replication partners poll each other at specified intervals, but only during scheduled periods.
Transport protocol	Remote Procedure Call (RPC) is used.	RPC over IP or Simple Mail Transport Protocol (SMTP) is used.

Replication topology is dependent on domain controller availability and configuration. The Knowledge Consistency Checker (KCC) running on each domain controller monitors domain controller availability and configuration, and updates replication topology as changes occur. The Inter-Site Topology Generator (ISTG) performs similar monitoring to determine the best way to configure intersite replication.

With intrasite replication, the replication topology is automatically generated and optimized by the Knowledge Consistency Checker (KCC) running on each domain controller. The KCC maintains replication topology on a per-directory partition basis by automatically creating connection objects between domain controllers hosting a particular directory partition. These connection objects represent the inbound-only connection to a domain controller, and can be manually created as well force replication between specific domain controllers.

When the organization has multiple geographic locations connected over WAN links, it is important to keep in mind that all domain controllers in the same forest replicate information with each other. The schema and configuration partitions are replicated to all domain controllers in a forest. If you make a change to the forest-wide configuration or schema partitions, those changes are replicated to all domain controllers in all the domains of the forest. When a change is made to a domain partition, the change is replicated to all domain controllers in the domain. If an attribute of an object tracked by the global catalog was changed, the change is replicated to all global catalog servers in all domains of the forest.

When multiple sites are involved, a designated domain controller in the site where the changes were made forwards the changes to a domain controller in another site. The receiving domain controller in turn stores the changes, and then forwards the changes to all the domain controllers in its site. The domain controllers responsible for forwarding changes between sites are referred to as bridgehead servers. A *bridgehead server* is the contact point for replication between sites.

The Inter-Site Topology Generator (ISTG) automatically designates a domain controller in each site to be the bridgehead server and automatically creates connection objects between these bridgehead servers. Only one bridgehead server is designated and active in a site. If this server fails, the ISTG designates another bridgehead server automatically.

You can also designate a preferred bridgehead server. Typically, you do this if you want to ensure that a particular domain controller handles the additional intersite replication workload, which can be considerable for a large network because data compression requires processor time. Multiple preferred bridgehead servers can be specified.

Although multiple preferred bridgehead servers can be specified, as before, only one is active at any one time. If the current preferred server fails, failover to another preferred server is automatic. However, if you designate preferred servers and all preferred servers fail, replication does not occur to that site.

Configuring and Maintaining Sites

When you install Active Directory on the first domain controller in a site, the Active Directory Installation Wizard (*DCPROMO.EXE*) creates a default site and a default site link. The default site is named Default-First-Site-Name, and the default site link is called DEFAULTIPSITELINK. The default site and site link can be renamed. You must create subsequent sites and site links manually.

To configure a site, you must complete these tasks:

1. Create the site.
2. Create one or more subnets and associate them with the site.
3. Link the site to other sites using site links.
4. Associating a domain controller with a site.
5. Specify a Licensing Server for the site.

These tasks are discussed in the sections that follow.

Creating sites

You can create an additional site by completing these steps:

1. Open Active Directory Sites And Services.
2. In the console tree, right-click the Sites container and select New Site.
3. In the New Object – Site dialog box, type a name for the site (see Figure 11-16).
4. Click the site link that will be used to connect this site to other sites. If the site link you want to use doesn't exist, select the default site link and change the site link settings later.
5. Click OK. A prompt is displayed detailing the steps you must complete to finish the site configuration. Click OK again.
6. To complete site configuration, you must complete the remaining configuration tasks.

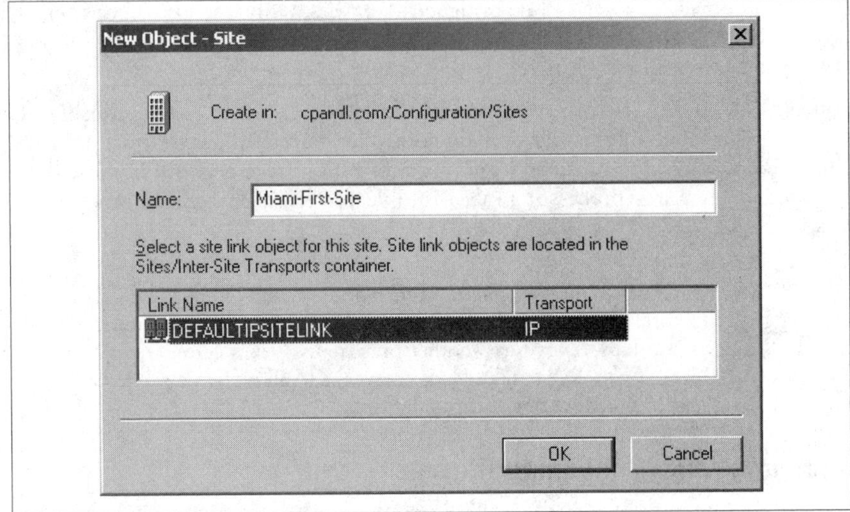

Figure 11-16. Creating a new site.

Creating subnets

After you create a site, you must tell Active Directory about the network segments that belong to the site. Do this by creating the required subnets and associating them with the site. Any computer with an IP address on a network segment associated with a site is considered to be located in the site. While a site can have multiple subnets associated with it, each subnet can be associated with one site only.

You can create a subnet and associate it with a site by completing these steps:

1. Open Active Directory Sites And Services.
2. Right-click the Subnets container in the console tree and select New Subnet.
3. In the Address field, type the network address for the subnet (see Figure 11-17).
4. In the Mask field, type the subnet mask for the network segment.
5. Select the site with which the subnet should be associated, and then click OK.

To change the site association for the subnet, double-click the subnet in the Subnets folder, and then, in the General tab, use the Site selection list to change the site association.

Associating domain controllers with sites

Each site should have at least one domain controller associated with it. If this domain controller is also a global catalog server, you can ensure that directory searches and authentication traffic are isolated to the site. To provide fault tolerance and redundancy, you should have at least two domain controllers in each site.

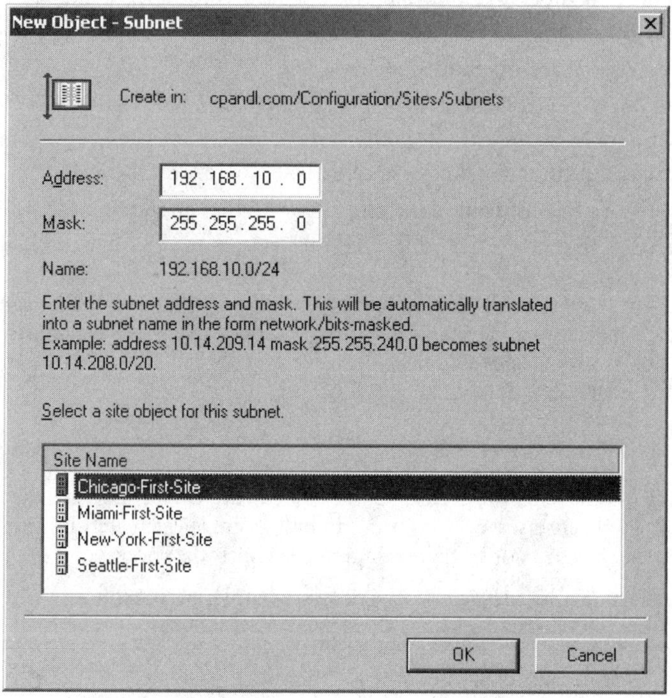

Figure 11-17. Creating a subnet.

After you associate subnets with a site, any domain controllers you install will be located in the site automatically if the domain controller's IP address is within the valid range of IP addresses for a particular subnet. However, any domain controllers installed before you establish the site and associated subnets will not be associated with the site automatically. You must manually associate any existing domain controllers with the appropriate site by moving the domain controller object into the site.

Before you can move a domain controller from one site to another, you must determine in which site the domain controller is currently located. One way to do this would be to use examine the Servers nodes for each site in Active Directory Sites And Services. Another way to do this is to type the following command at a command prompt:

```
dsquery server -s DomainControllerName | dsget server -site
```

where *DomainControllerName* is the fully qualified domain name of the domain controller, such as:

```
dsquery server -s engsvr38.domain.local | dsget server -site
```

The output of this command is the name of the site in which the designated domain controller is located.

You can move a domain controller object from one site to another site by completing the following steps:

1. Open Active Directory Sites And Services.
2. Any domain controllers associated with a site are listed in the site's Servers node.
3. Right-click the domain controller object, and then select Move.
4. In the Move Server dialog box, click the site that should contain the server, and then click OK.

Only move a domain controller to a site if it is on a subnet associated with the site. If you change subnet and site associations, you need to move domain controllers in the affected subnets to the appropriate site containers.

Specifying a site license server for a site

Every site must have a site license server associated with it. For the default site, the default site license server is the first domain controller created in the site. The site license server does not have to be a domain controller, however.

You can determine the site-licensing server by completing the following steps:

1. Open Active Directory Sites And Services.
2. In the console tree, click the node for the site.
3. In the right pane, double-click Licensing Site Settings.
4. The current site-licensing server is displayed by name and domain as shown in Figure 11-18.

You can change the site-licensing server by completing the following steps:

1. Open Active Directory Sites And Services.
2. In the console tree, click the site for which you want to change the licensing server.
3. In the right pane, double-click Licensing Site Settings.
4. On the Licensing Settings tab, click Change.
5. In the Select Computer dialog box, choose the server that you want to designate as the licensing server for the site. This server should have an IP address for a subnet located within the site.
6. To maintain the licensing history, you must immediately stop the License Logging service on the new site-licensing server, copy licensing history from the old server to the new, and then restart the License Logging service. The files to copy are *%SystemRoot%\system32\cpl.cfg*, *%SystemRoot%\Lls\Llsuser.lls*, and *%SystemRoot%\Lls\Llsmap.lls*.

Configuring and Maintaining Intersite Replication

As discussed previously, sites are groups of IP subnets that are connected by reliable, high-speed links. Typically, but not always, all subnets on a LAN will be part

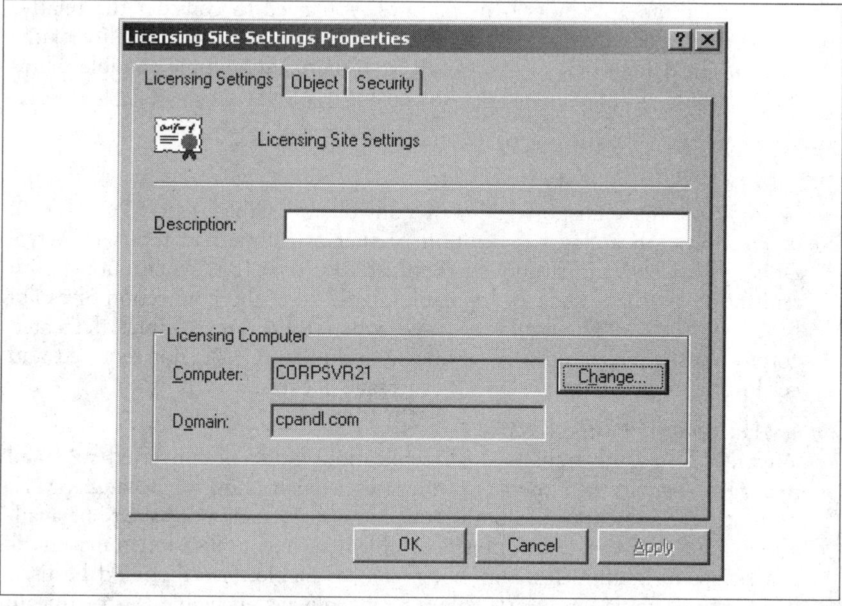

Figure 11-18. Determining the current site license server.

of the same site. On a network with multiple sites, the sites are connected via site links. Site links are logical, transitive connections between two or more sites. Each site link has a replication schedule, replication interval, a link cost, and a replication transport.

To configure and maintain intersite replication, you must complete these tasks:

1. Create the required site links.
2. Configure site link properties for replication cost, interval, and schedule as appropriate.
3. Optionally, create site link bridges.
4. Optionally, determine and monitor the Inter-Site Topology Generator.
5. Optionally, determine and monitor bridgehead servers.
6. Optionally, specify preferred bridgehead servers.
7. Optionally, create and configure connection objects.

These tasks are discussed in the sections that follow.

Creating site links

Because site links are used over WAN links, the primary consideration when configuring site links in most cases is bandwidth usage. By default, replication is scheduled to occur over the site link 24 hours a day, 7 days a week, at an interval of at least 180 minutes. If you have limited bandwidth, you may need to alter the schedule to allow user traffic to have priority during peak usage times.

When you have multiple links between sites, you need to consider the relative priority of each link. Assign priority based on availability and reliability of the connection. The default link cost is set to 100. If there are multiple possible routes to a site, the route with the lowest site link cost is used first.

With site links, you can use one of two transport protocols:

RPC over IP
: With IP as the transport, domain controllers establish an RPC over IP connection with a single replication partner at a time and replicate Active Directory changes synchronously. Because RPC over IP is synchronous, both replication partners must be available at the time the connection is established. RPC over IP should be used when there are reliable, dedicated connections between sites. A certificate authority (CA) is not required and certificates are not used to sign RPC message packets.

Simple Mail Transfer Protocol (SMTP)
: With SMTP as the transport, all replication traffic is converted to email messages that are sent between the sites asynchronously. Because SMTP replication is asynchronous, both replication partners do not have to be available at the time the connection is established, and replication transactions can be stored until a destination server is available. SMTP should be used when connections are unreliable or not always available. A certificate authority (CA) is required. Certificates from the CA are used to digitally sign and encrypt the SMTP messages sent between the sites.

The RPC and SMTP replication transport protocols are also referred to as DS-RPC and ISM-SMTP respectively. While intrasite replication uses only RPC over IP, intersite replication may use RPC over IP or SMTP. Use of SMTP is limited to DCs in different domains. DCs in same domains must use RPC over IP.

To create a site link between two or more sites, you can use the following technique:

1. Open Active Directory Sites And Services.
2. Expand the Sites container, and then expand the Inter-Site Transports container.
3. Right-click the container for the transport protocol you want to use, either IP or SMTP, and select New Site Link.
4. In the New Object – Site Link dialog box, type a name for the site link as shown in Figure 11-19.
5. In the Sites Not In This Site Link list, click the first site that should be included in the link, and then click the Add button to add the site to the Sites In This Link list. Repeat this process for each site you want to add to the link. A link must include at least two sites.
6. Click OK.

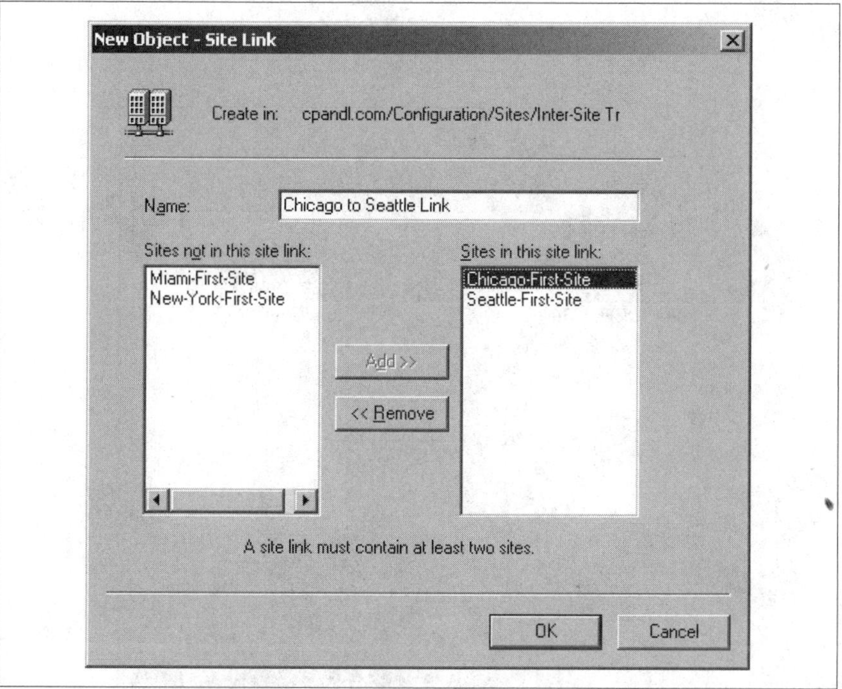

Figure 11-19. Creating a site link.

After you create a site link, you should configure the link's properties. This allows you to specify the link cost, replication schedule, and replication interval. To configure site link properties, follow these steps:

1. In Active Directory Sites And Services, site links are added to the IP or SMTP folder under Inter-Site Transports as appropriate for the type of transport used in the site link. In the console tree, click the transport protocol node, and then double-click the site link in the right pane.
2. As shown in Figure 11-20, use the Cost box to set the relative cost of the link. The default cost is 100.
3. Use the Replicate Every box to set the replication interval. The default interval is 180 minutes.
4. The default replication schedule is 24 hours a day, 7 days a week. To set a different schedule, click Change Schedule, and then use the Schedule For dialog box to set the desired replication schedule.
5. Click OK.

You can change the sites associated with a site link at any time. To do this, follow these steps:

1. In Active Directory Sites And Services, site links are added to the IP or SMTP folder under Inter-Site Transports as appropriate for the type of transport used in the site link. In the console tree, click the transport protocol node, and then double-click the site link in the right pane.

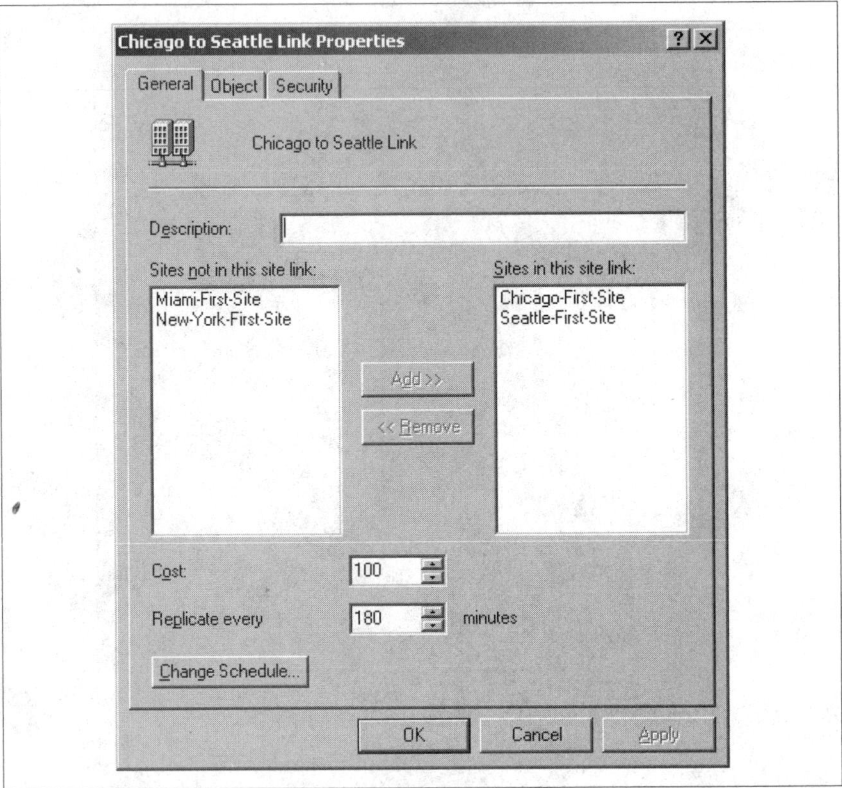

Figure 11-20. Configuring site link properties.

2. In the Sites In This Site Link list, click the first site that should not be included in the link, and then click the Remove button to remove the site from the Sites In This Link list. Repeat this process for each site you want to remove from the link.
3. In the Sites Not In This Site Link list, click the first site that should be included in the link, and then click the Add button to add the site to the Sites In This Link list. Repeat this process for each site you want to add to the link.
4. Click OK.

Configuring site link bridges

By default, site link transitivity is enabled. When more than two sites are linked for replication and use the same transport, sites links are bridged, allowing links to be transitive between sites. This means any two domain controllers can make a connection across any consecutive series of links. For example, a domain controller in Site A could connect to a domain controller in Site C through Site B.

The link path that domain controllers choose for connections across sites is largely determined by the site link bridge cost. The site link bridge cost is the sum of all the links included in the bridge, and generally the path with the lowest total site link bridge cost is used.

If you know the costs of links and link bridges, you can calculate the effects of a network link failure and determine the paths that will be used when a connection is down. For example, a domain controller in Site A would normally connect to a domain controller in Site C through Site B. However, if the connection to Site B is down, the two domain controllers would choose an alternate path automatically if one is available, such as going through Site D and Site E to establish a connection.

By default, intersite replication topology is optimized for a maximum of three hops. In large site configurations, this can have unintended consequences, such as the same replication traffic going over the same link several times. In this case, disable automatic site link bridging and manually configure site link bridges.

With an Active Directory forest, site link transitivity is enabled or disabled on a per-transport protocol basis. This means all site links that use a particular transport either use site link transitivity or they don't. You can enable or disable transitive site links for a transport protocol by completing these steps:

1. Open Active Directory Sites And Services.
2. Expand the Sites container, and then expand the Inter-Site Transports container.
3. Right-click the container for the transport protocol you want to work with, either IP or SMTP, and then select Properties.
4. To enable site link transitivity, select Bridge All Site Links, as shown in Figure 11-21, and then click OK. When site link transitivity is enabled, any site link bridges you've created for a particular transport protocol are ignored.
5. To disable site link transitivity, clear the Bridge All Site Links checkbox, and then click OK. When site link transitivity is disabled, you must configure site link bridges for the affected protocol.

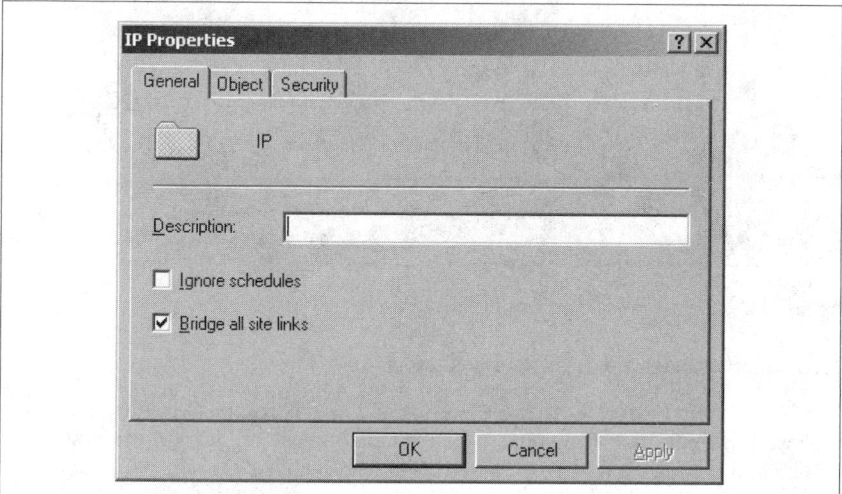

Figure 11-21. Enabling site link transitivity.

Once you've disabled transitive links, you can manually create a site link bridge between two or more sites by completing the following steps:

1. Open Active Directory Sites And Services.
2. Expand the Sites container, and then expand the Inter-Site Transports container.
3. Right-click the container for the transport protocol you want to work with, either IP or SMTP, and then select New Site Link Bridge.
4. In the New Object – Site Link Bridge dialog box, type a name for the site link bridge, as shown in Figure 11-22.
5. In the Site Links Not In This Site Link Bridge list, select a site link that should be included in the bridge, and then click Add to add the site link to the Site Links In This Site Link Bridge list. Repeat this process for each site link you want to add to the bridge. A bridge must include at least two site links.
6. Click OK.

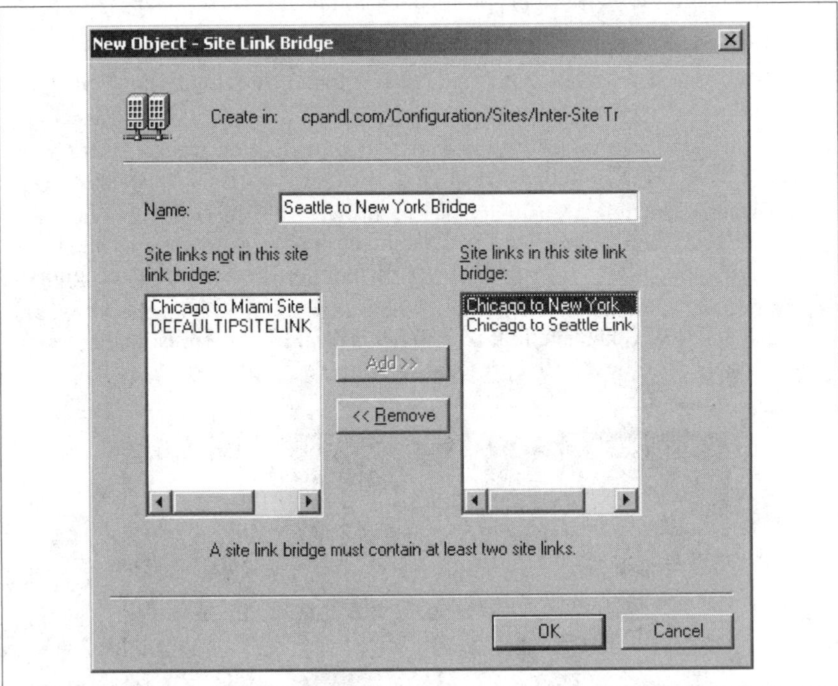

Figure 11-22. Enabling a site link bridge.

Determining the Inter-Site Topology Generator

The Inter-Site Topology Generator (ISTG) in a site is responsible for generating the intersite replication topology. When calculating the replication topology, the ISTG can use considerable processing power, especially as the size of the network grows. Because of this, you should closely monitor the ISTGs in each site to ensure they are not overloaded.

You can determine the ISTG by completing the following steps:

1. Open Active Directory Sites And Services.
2. Expand the Sites container, and then expand the site for the ISTG you want to locate in the console tree.
3. In the Details pane, double-click NTDS Site Settings.
4. In the NTDS Site Settings dialog box, the current ISTG is listed in the Inter-Site Topology Generator panel, as shown in Figure 11-23.

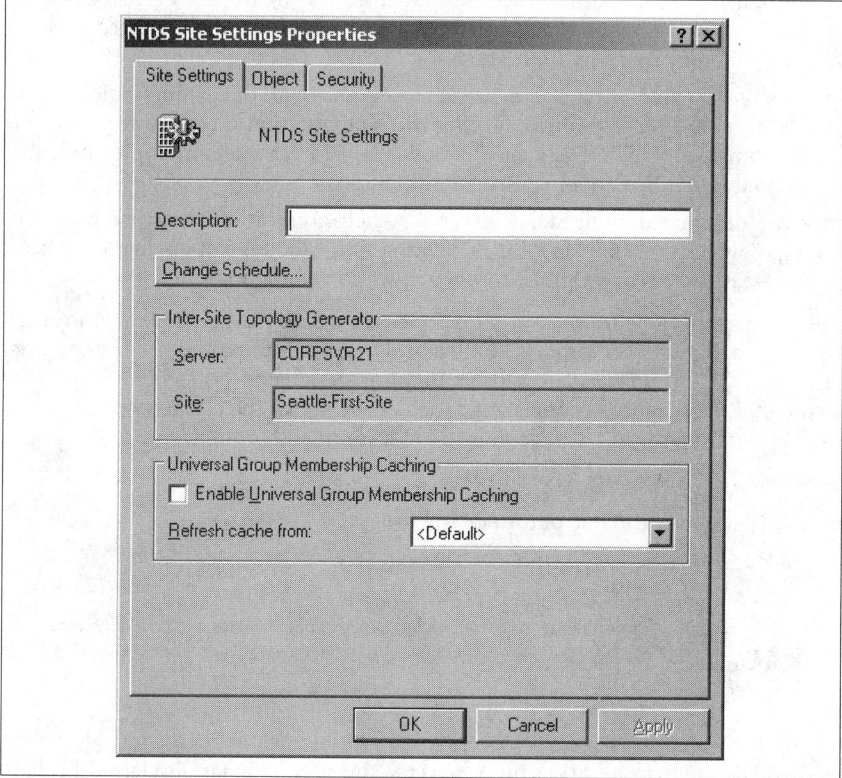

Figure 11-23. Determining a site's ISTG.

Determining and configuring site bridgehead servers

Replication between sites is performed by bridgehead servers. A *bridgehead server* is a domain controller designated by the ISTG to perform intersite replication. When two sites are connected by a site link, the ISTG selects one bridgehead server in each site and creates inbound-only connection objects between the servers. These connections are used for intersite replication.

The ISTG configures a bridgehead server for each Active Directory partition that needs to be replicated and maintains a separate replication topology for each type of partition. Although a single bridgehead server can be responsible for replicating multiple directory partitions, the replication topology for each partition is maintained separately. On a per-site basis, this means there is:

- One designated bridgehead server for each domain, which is responsible for replicating the domain directory partition for the domain of which it is a member. When a domain spans multiple sites, the related replication topology spans multiple sites.
- One designated bridgehead server for replicating the schema, which is responsible for replicating the schema directory partition for the forest of which it is a member. When a forest spans multiple sites, the related replication topology spans multiple sites.
- One designated bridgehead server for replicating the configuration data, which is responsible for replicating the configuration directory partition for the forest of which it is a member. When a forest spans multiple sites, the related replication topology spans multiple sites.
- One designated bridgehead server for each application directory partition type, which is responsible for replicating a specific type of application directory partition as appropriate for the replication configuration.

Operating as a bridgehead server adds to the workload of the domain controller. The workload increases with the number and frequency of replication changes. As with the ISTG, you'll want to closely monitor designated bridgehead servers to ensure that they do not become overloaded. You can list the bridgehead servers in a site by entering the following command at a command prompt:

```
repadmin /bridgeheads site:SiteName
```

where *SiteName* is the name of the site, such as:

```
repadmin /bridgeheads site:Seattle-First-Site
```

If you omit the `site:` option, the details for the current site are returned. Note also there should be no space between `site:` and the site name.

If current bridgehead servers are overloaded or you have domain controllers that you would prefer to be bridgehead servers, you can designate preferred bridgehead servers to use. Once you designate a preferred bridgehead server for a site, the ISTG uses only the preferred bridgehead server for intersite replication. If the preferred bridgehead server goes offline or is unable to replicate for any reason, intersite replication stops until the server is again available for replication or you change the preferred bridgehead server configuration options.

If you designate a single preferred bridgehead server in a site, you have a single point of failure. To avoid possible problems with intersite replication, you can designate multiple preferred bridgehead servers. The ISTG then chooses one of the servers you've designated as the preferred bridgehead server. If this server fails, the ISTG then chooses another server from the list of preferred bridgehead servers.

You must configure a bridgehead server for each partition that needs to be replicated. This means you must configure at least one domain controller with a replica of each directory partition as a bridgehead server. If you don't do this, replication of the partition fails and the ISTG logs an event in the Directory Services event log detailing the failure.

When you've designated preferred bridgehead servers, you can recover from replication failure by performing the following tasks:

- Remove the failed servers as preferred bridgehead servers, and then specify different preferred bridgehead servers.
- Remove all servers as preferred bridgehead servers, and then allow the ISTG to select the bridgehead servers that should be used.

You can configure a domain controller as a preferred bridgehead server by completing the following steps:

1. Open Active Directory Sites And Services.
2. Any domain controllers associated with a site are listed in the site's Servers node.
3. Right-click the server you want to designate as a preferred bridgehead, and then select Properties.
4. In the Properties dialog box, shown in Figure 11-24, select the intersite transport protocol for which the server should be a preferred bridgehead in the Transports Available For list, and then click Add. Repeat as necessary to specify both IP and SMTP.
5. Click OK.

To stop a server from being a preferred bridgehead for a particular transport protocol, select the transport protocol in the This Server Is A Preferred Bridgehead Server list, and then click Remove.

Maintaining Active Directory Infrastructure

As discussed earlier in the chapter, Active Directory has many physical and logical components, which need to be maintained to ensure proper operations. Beyond these components, Active Directory maintenance extends to managing trust relationships, monitoring Active Directory and File Replication Service, and performing Active Directory restores.

Managing Trust Relationships

As part of maintenance, you'll also need to manage Active Directory trusts periodically. Every domain in a forest has two-way transitive trusts between them. Other types of trusts can be created as well, including external, shortcut, realm, and forest trusts.

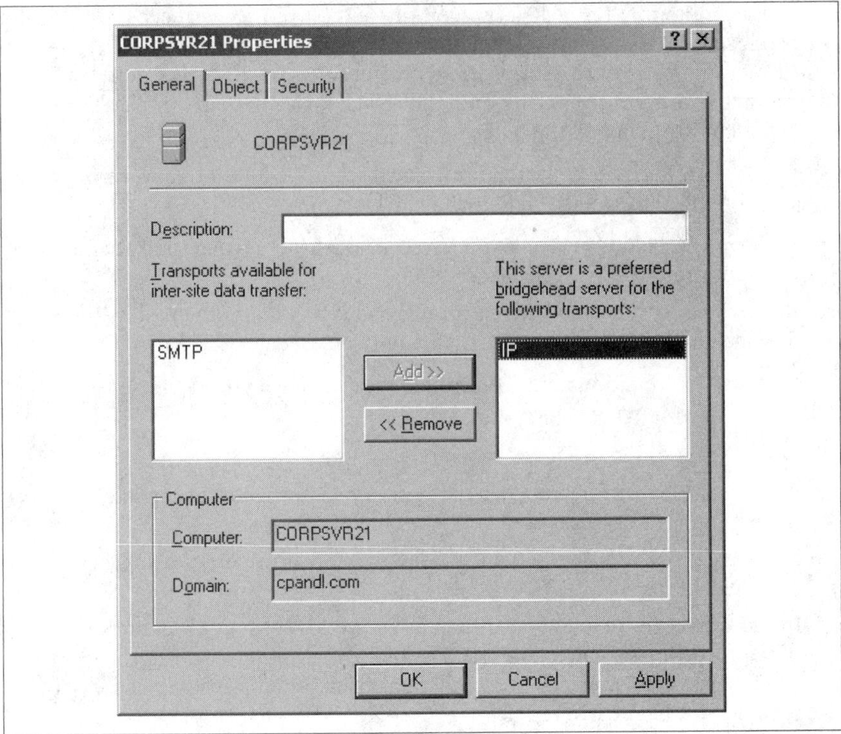

Figure 11-24. Designating a preferred bridgehead server.

Understanding trust relationships

In Windows NT 4, you created one-way trusts when you had separate account and resource domains. The establishment of the trust allowed users in the account domain to access resources in the resource domain.

In Windows 2000 and later, all domains in a forest have automatic two-way transitive trusts between parent and child domains. Because trusts are automatic, you do not need to create them. Because trusts are two-way, a user in any domain in a forest can access resources in any other domain in the forest, providing he has the appropriate access permissions. Because trusts are transitive, they are not bound by the domains in the trust relationship, and users can access resources across any consecutive series of domains in a forest. For example, a user in Domain A could access a shared folder in Domain C through Domain B.

Windows Server 2003 uses Kerberos version 5 (by default) or NT LM for authentication and establishment of trusts. Kerberos is used with Windows 2000 or later clients and servers. NT LM is used with pre-Windows 2000 clients and servers.

Within forests, trust trees are used. When a user attempts to access a resource in another domain, a trust tree is used and the user's request passes through one domain controller in each domain between the user and the resource. The request is then authenticated in the domain where the resource resides. Authentication across domain boundaries also occurs when a user with an account in one domain logs on to a computer in another domain.

When a forest has many domains and domain trees, the trust tree can grow quite large. Each domain tree in the forest has a tree-root trust, which is established when you add a new tree root domain to a forest. All authentication requests between domain trees must pass from the source domain through parent-child trusts to the tree-root, and then through parent-child trusts to the destination domain. Thus, a user's authentication request might have to pass through several domains to reach the domain tree-root where it is then passed through several additional domains to reach a domain controller in the domain where the resource the user is trying to access is located.

To avoid a lengthy referral process, you can establish an explicit shortcut trust between domains. For example, if users in a child domain of a particular domain tree frequently access resources in a child domain of another domain tree, you can establish a shortcut trust between the domains to establish an authentication shortcut between the domains. The domain controller in the first child domain is then able to forward authentication requests directly to a domain controller in the second child domain, allowing for more rapid authentication.

In addition to parent-child trusts, tree-root trusts, and shortcut trusts, Windows Server 2003 allows you to establish three additional types of trusts:

External trusts
: External trusts are non-transitive trusts that must be explicitly established by administrators. An external trust can be one-way or two-way, and is applicable only to the domains for which the trust is established. Users in other domains cannot make use of the trust because it is non-transitive. External trusts are provided for backward compatibility with Windows NT domains or for connecting to domains in other forests that could not otherwise be reached.

Forest trusts
: Forest trusts are one-way or two-way transitive trust between forest root domains that must be explicitly established by administrators. Forest trusts are used to share resources and to authenticate users between forests. Before you can use forest trusts, all domain controllers in all domains of both forests must be upgraded to Windows Server 2003. Forest trusts are transitive between two forests only.

Realm trusts
: Realm trusts are trusts between Windows domains and Kerberos realms that must be explicitly established by administrators. Realm trusts are provided for interoperability with Kerberos Version 5 realms and can be non-transitive, transitive, two-way, or one-way.

Out of these three additional trusts, the ones you'll work with the most are forest trusts. Forest trusts allows authentication across two forests for when a user account is in one forest and resources are in another trusted forest. As part of authentication across forests, administrators can select users and groups from trusted forests for inclusion in local groups. This ensures the integrity of the forest security boundary while allowing trust between forests.

When you connect two or more forests using forest trusts, the implementation is referred to as a federated forest. A federated forest is most useful when you need to join two separate Active Directory structures, such as could occur if your organization has a major restructuring or merges with another company. When forest trusts are two way, users in Forest A can access resources in Forest B and users in Forest B can access resources in Forest A.

Viewing Current Trust Relationships

Using Active Directory Domains And Trusts, you can view available domains and existing trusts. To start and work with Active Directory Domains And Trusts, follow these steps:

1. Start Active Directory Domains And Trusts from the Administrative Tools menu.
2. Available domains are listed in the console tree. To view the existing trusts for a domain, right-click the domain node and select Properties.
3. In the domain's Properties dialog box, click the Trust tab as shown in Figure 11-25. The Trust tab is organized into two panels:

   Domains Trusted By This Domain (Outgoing Trusts)
   Shows the domains that establish trust with the selected domain. Domains that establish trust with another domain are referred to as trusting domains.

   Domains That Trust This Domain (Incoming Trusts)
   Shows the domains that trust this domain. Domains that trust other domains are referred to as trusted domains.

4. To view more information about a trust, click it and then click Properties. As Figure 11-26 shows, the Properties dialog box contains the following information:

   This Domain
   Shows the domain with which you are working.

   Other Domain
   Shows the domain with which the trust is established.

   Trust Type
   Shows the type of trust.

Establishing explicit trust relationships

Windows Server 2003 uses two default trust types: Tree-Root and Parent And Child. When a new domain is added to a new domain tree within the forest, the default trust is a tree-root trust. When a new domain is a subdomain of a root domain, the default trust is a parent and child trust. All default trusts are established as two-way, transitive trusts, which allow access to indirectly trusted domains.

For all trusts there are two sides: an incoming trust and an outgoing trust. To establish a trust, you must be able to configure both sides of the trust, or you must configure one side of the trust and have another administrator configure the other side of the trust.

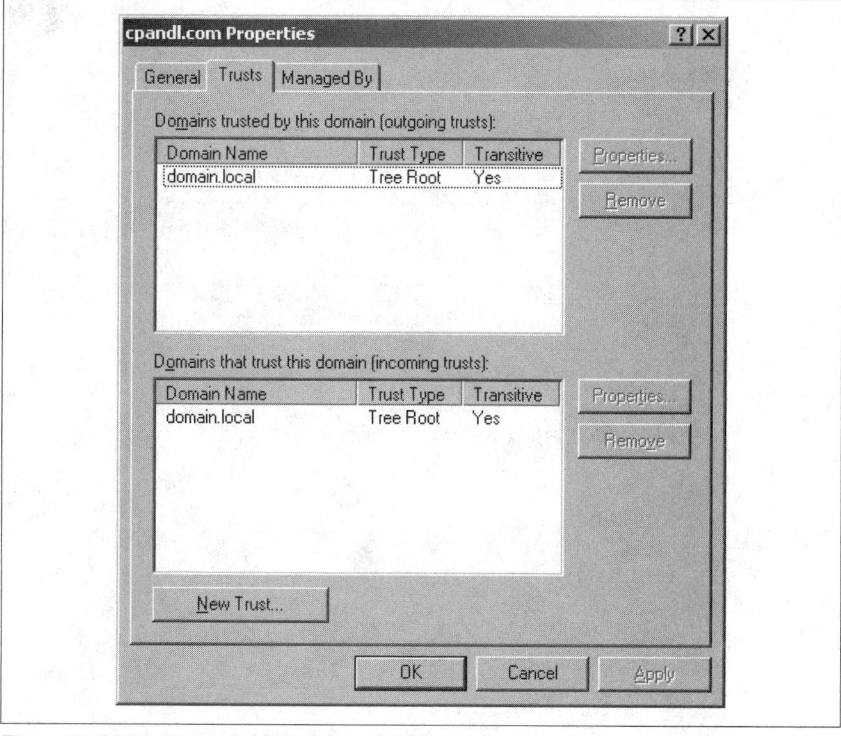

Figure 11-25. Viewing established trusts to a domain.

When establishing explicit trust relationships, keep the following in mind:

- With domain trusts, you need two accounts: one that is a member of the Domain Admins group in the first domain, and one that is a member of the Domain Admins in the second domain. If you don't have appropriate accounts in both domains, you can establish one side of the trust and allow another administrator in the other domain to establish the other side of the trust.
- With forest trusts, you need two accounts: one that is a member of the Enterprise Admins group in the first forest and one that is a member of the Enterprise Admins group in the second forest. If you don't have appropriate accounts in both forests, you can establish one side of the trust and allow another administrator in the other forest to establish the other side of the trust.
- With realm trusts, you need to establish the trust separately for the Windows domain and the Kerberos realm. If you don't have appropriate administrative access to both the Windows domain and the Kerberos realm, you can establish one side of the trust and allow another administrator to establish the other side of the trust.

When only a one-way trust is established, either incoming or outgoing, users on one side of the forest are not able to access resources on the other side of the forest.

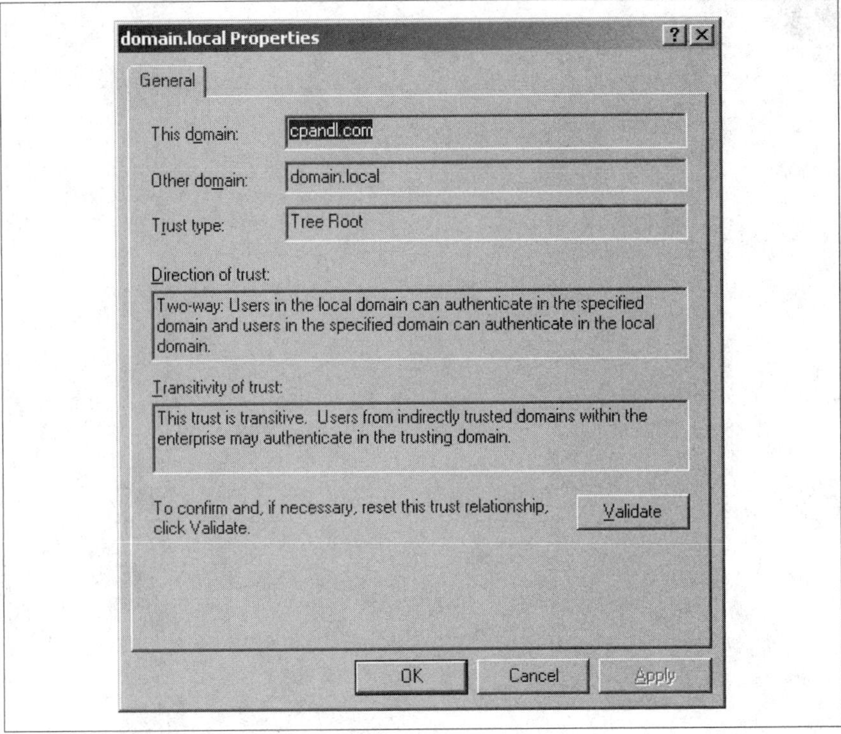

Figure 11-26. Viewing the properties of an established trust.

To establish an explicit trust relationship, follow these steps:

1. Start Active Directory Domains And Trusts from the Administrative Tools menu.
2. Right-click the domain for which you want to establish an explicit trust, and then select Properties. For a forest trust, this must be the forest root domain in one of the participating forests.
3. In the domain's Properties dialog box, click the Trust tab and click the New Trust button.
4. Click Next. On the Trust Name page, type the DNS name of the target domain (see Figure 11-27). For a forest trust, this must be the DNS name of the forest root domain in the second forest.
5. Click Next. The wizard tries to connect to the specified domain. Your options depend on the type of domain to which you are connecting:
    - If the domain is in another Windows forest, you can create an external trust that is nontransitive or a forest trust that is transitive. Choose either External Trust or Forest Trust as appropriate, and then click Next to display the Direction Of Trust page.
    - If the domain is in the same forest, it is assumed you are creating a shortcut trust, and the wizard displays the Direction Of Trust page.

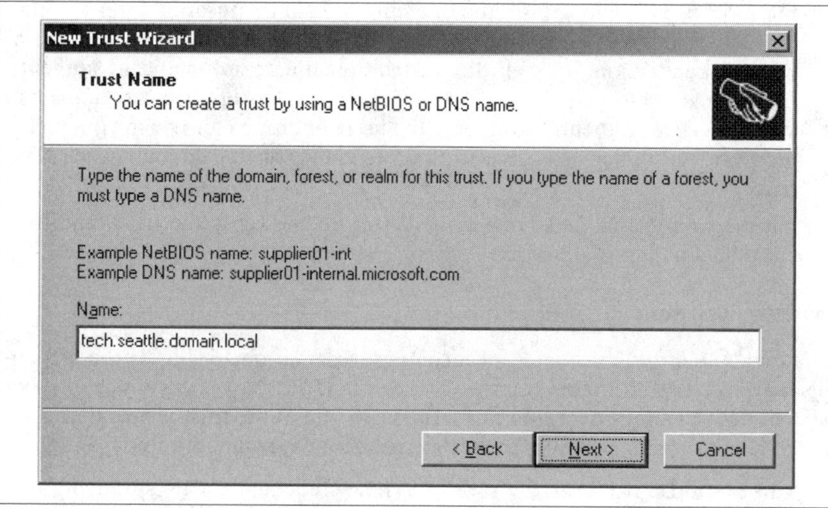

Figure 11-27. Specify the DNS name of the target domain.

- If the domain is a non-Windows domain, you can create a realm trust with a Kerberos v5 realm. Click Realm Trust and then click Next. On the Transitivity Of Trust page, select either Nontransitive or Transitive, and then click Next to display the Direction Of Trust page.

6. On the Direction Of Trust page, choose the direction of Trust as "Two-Way," "One-way: Incoming," or "One-way: Outgoing," and then click Next.
7. For shortcut or forest trusts, the Sides Of Trust page is displayed next. To begin using a trust, both sides of the trust must be created. You have the option of setting the sides of the trust for This Domain Only or for Both This Domain And The Specified Domain:
   - If you are only creating one side of the trust, select This Domain Only, and then click Next.
   - If you are setting both sides of the trust, select Both This Domain And The Specified Domain, and then click Next. When prompted, type the name and password of an appropriate account in the other domain or forest and then click OK.
8. On the Trust Password page, type and then confirm the initial password for the trust.

The initial password is arbitrary but must be at least eight characters and contain a combination of upper- and lowercase characters and also have either numerals or special characters. Once the trust is established, the password is maintained automatically.

9. For domain or realm trusts, click Next twice to begin the trust creation process.

10. For forest trusts, you can set the outgoing trust authentication level as either Domain-Wide Authentication or Selective Authentication. With domain-wide authentication, users in the trusted domain are automatically authenticated for all resources in the trusting domain (and any trusted domains). With Selective Authentication, only the users or groups for which you explicitly grant permissions can access resources in the trusting domain. Click Next twice.
11. On the Completing The New Trust Wizard page, verify the trust, and then click Finish.

Troubleshooting trusts

Windows Server 2003 validates all incoming trusts automatically. If the credentials used to establish the trust are no longer valid, the trust fails verification. For external trusts, realm trusts, and forest trusts, failure of the trust means that users are not able to access resources in the external domain, realm, or forest.

You can re-validate the trust by providing new credentials or by specifying that incoming trusts should not be validated. To re-validate and, if necessary, reset a trust relationship, follow these steps:

1. Start Active Directory Domains And Trusts from the Administrative Tools menu.
2. Right-click the domain for which you want to validate trusts.
3. In the domain's Properties dialog box, select the Trust tab and click the Validate button.
4. To stop validation of the incoming trust, click No, Do Not Validate The Incoming Trust.
5. To re-validate the incoming trust, click Yes, Validate The Incoming Trust. Type the user account and password for an administrator account in the other domain.
6. Click OK. For a two-way trust, repeat this procedure for the other domain.

If re-validating and resetting the trust doesn't resolve the issue, you may have a deeper problem. Here are some general tips for troubleshooting:

- With external trusts to Windows NT 4 domains, a PDC emulator must be available to reset and verify the external trust.
- In Windows domains, Windows 2000 domain controllers must be running Service Pack 3 or later for trust validation to work properly.
- System time on clients and servers trying to authenticate must not be more than five minutes off, which is the default maximum time difference allowed for Kerberos authentication.
- After upgrading a Windows NT 4.0 domain with existing trusts to Active Directory domains, you must delete and recreate all the preexisting trusts. These trusts are not automatically upgraded.

Monitoring and Troubleshooting Active Directory

Monitoring is a key part of maintenance. You need to monitor domain controllers, global catalog servers, bridgehead servers, and site links. When you suspect there are problems with Active Directory, one of the first areas you should examine is replication. If Active Directory data is not being replicated properly, Active Directory will have problems. By configuring monitoring of Active Directory intrasite and intersite replication, you can diagnose and resolve the problem.

Active Directory replication has several key service dependencies including:

- LDAP
- Domain Name System (DNS)
- Kerberos v5 Authentication
- Remote Procedure Call (RPC)

These Windows services must be functioning properly to allow directory updates to be replicated. Additionally, for replication of files in the System Volume (SYSVOL) shared folders on domain controllers, Active Directory uses the File Replication Service (FRS). This service must be running and properly configured to replicate System Volume files.

During replication, Active Directory relies on various TCP and UDP ports being open. Table 11-2 lists the ports and the components that use them. If servers, LAN connections, or WAN connections are protected by firewalls, these ports must be open.

Table 11-2. TCP and UDP ports used in replication

Service	TCP port	UDP port
LDAP	389	389
LDAP SSL	686	
Global Catalog (LDAP)	3268	
Kerberos v5	88	88
DNS	53	53
SMB over IP	445	445

Changes to Active Directory are tracked using Update Sequence Numbers (USNs). Anytime a change is made to the directory, the domain controller processing the change assigns the change a USN. Each domain controller maintains its own local USNs and increments the value each time a change occurs. The domain controller also assigns the local USN to the object attribute that changed. Each object has a related attributed called `uSNChanged`, which is stored with the object and identifies the highest USN that has been assigned to any of the object's attributes.

Each domain controller tracks its local USN and also the local USNs of other domain controllers. During replication, domain controllers compare the USN values received to what is stored. If the current USN value for a particular domain controller is higher than the stored value, changes associated with that domain controller need to be replicated. If the current value for a particular domain controller is the same as the stored value, changes for that domain controller do not need to be replicated.

The Windows Support Tools includes several tools for monitoring and troubleshooting replication issues. The tools you'll use the most are Replication Administrator (Repadmin) and Replication Monitor (Replmon). Both tools provide similar functionality. Repadmin is a command-line utility and Replmon is its GUI counterpart.

For Repadmin, most command-line parameters accept a list of the domain controllers that you want to work with, called DCList. The values for DCList can be specified as follows:

*
: This is used as a wildcard to include all domain controllers in the enterprise.

`PartialName*`
: *PartialName* is a partial server name that includes a wildcard to match the remainder of the server name.

Site:`SiteName`
: `SiteName` is the name of the site for which you want to include domain controllers.

Gc:
: This is used to include all global catalog servers in the enterprise.

The Repadmin commands you'll work with the most are:

`repadmin /bridgeheads DCList [/verbose]`
: Displays the bridgehead servers that match the DClist.

`repadmin /failcache DCList`
: Displays failed replication events that were detected by the Knowledge Consistency Checker (KCC).

`repadmin /kcc DCList [/async]`
: Forces the KCC to recalculate the intrasite replication topology for a specified domain controller. By default, this recalculation occurs every 15 minutes. Use `/async` to start the KCC and not wait for the calculation to complete.

`repadmin /latency DCList [/verbose]`
: Displays the amount of time between intersite replications using the ISTG Keep Alive timestamp.

`repadmin /queue DCList`
: Displays the tasks waiting in the replication queue.

`repadmin /replsummary DCList`
: Displays a summary of the replication state.

`repadmin /showcert DCList`
: Displays the server certificates loaded on the specified domain controllers.

`repadmin /showconn DCList`
: Displays the connection objects for the specified domain controllers. Defaults to the local site.

`repadmin /showctx DCList`
: Displays the computers that have opened sessions with a specified domain controller.

`repadmin /showrepl DCList`
: Displays the replication partners for each directory partition on the specified domain controller.

`repadmin /showtrust DCList`
: Displays all domains trusted by a specified domain.

`repadmin istg DCList [/verbose]`
: Displays the name of the ISTG for a specified site.

`repadmin /showoutcalls DCList`
: Displays the calls made, but not yet answered, by the specified server to other servers.

Replmon can perform many of the same tasks as Repadmin. You can start this tool by typing `replmon` at a command prompt. Once you start Replmon, you must add the domain controllers that you want to monitor.

To specify a domain controller to monitor, follow these steps:

1. Right-click the Monitored Servers node in the console tree, and then click Add Monitored Server.
2. In the Add Monitored Server Wizard, you have the option to add the server by name or search the directory. Click Search The Directory For The Server To Add as shown in Figure 11-28.

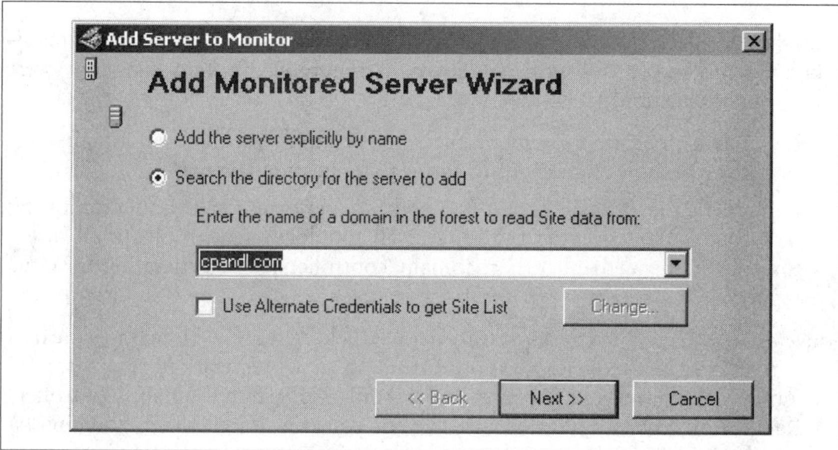

Figure 11-28. Search the directory for domain controllers to monitor.

3. On the Add Server To Monitor page, shown in Figure 11-29, a list of available sites is displayed. Expand the node for the site where the domain controllers you want to monitor are located. Click the domain controller to monitor, and then click Finish.
4. The domain controller is then added to the Replication Monitor.

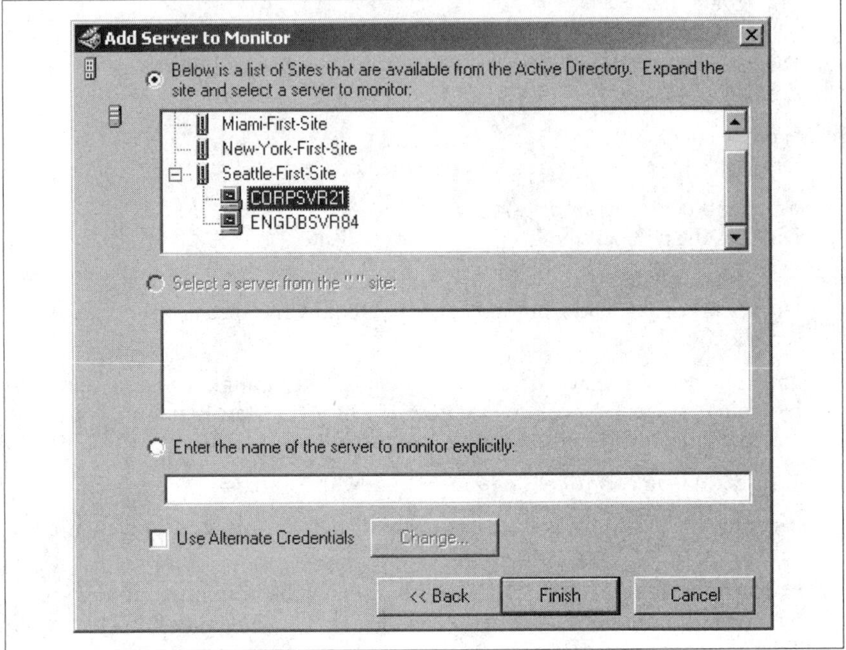

Figure 11-29. Locate and select the domain controller to monitor.

Once you've add a domain controller to monitor, each directory partition maintained by the server is listed, as shown in Figure 11-30. You can now start monitoring replication.

- Right-click a partition to synchronize the partition with all other domain controllers or to show change notifications to replication partners.
- Right-click the domain controller node to perform replication monitoring tasks, including checking the replication topology, synchronizing all directory partitions with all other domain controllers, and generating a status report.

You can also search for replication errors. Click Action → Domain → Search Domain Controllers For Replication Errors to view replication errors for all domain controllers in your logon domain. With the Search Domain Controllers For Replication Errors dialog box displayed, you can search other domains by clicking the Run Search button, typing the DNS name of the domain to search, and then clicking OK.

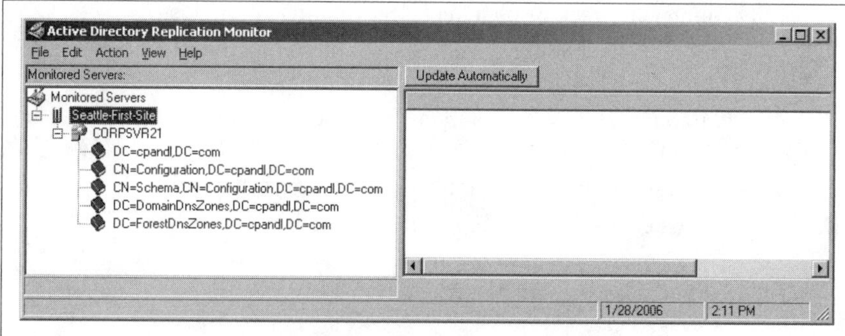

Figure 11-30. Monitor replication of the domain controller or its partitions.

Diagnosing and Resolving Active Directory and File Replication Service Issues

Using the Performance console, you can perform in-depth monitoring and analysis of Active Directory. Start the Performance console by clicking Start → Programs → Administrative Tools → Performance or by typing `perfmon.msc` at a command prompt. Using the Performance console's remote monitoring capabilities, you can track the performance of multiple domain controllers from a single, monitoring server.

NTDS is the performance object to use for monitoring Active Directory. Over 100 performance counters are available for selection. Each counter has a prefix that reflects the aspect of Active Directory to which the counter relates:

- AB counters relate to the Address Book in Active Directory.
- ATQ counters relate to the Asynchronous Thread Queue in Active Directory.
- DRA counters relate to the Directory Replication Agent in Active Directory.
- DS counters relate to the Directory Service in Active Directory.
- KDC counters relate to the Key Distribution Center in Active Directory.
- Kerberos counters relate to Kerberos in Active Directory.
- LDAP counters relate to the Lightweight Directory Access Protocol in Active Directory.
- NTLM counters relate to the NT LAN Manager in Active Directory.
- SAM counters relate to the Security Accounts Manager in Active Directory.

To specify NTDS counters to monitor, follow these steps:

1. Start the Performance console from the Administrative Tools menu.
2. Click the System Monitor node.
3. Click the Add (+) button on the toolbar or press CTL+L.
4. In the Add Counters dialog box, use the Select Counters From Computer list to select the computer to monitor (see Figure 11-31).
5. Select NTDS on the Performance Object list.

6. Specify counters to track by clicking Select Counters From List.
7. To learn more about a counter, click the counter in the Select Counters From List, and then click Explain to display a description of the counter.
8. To track a counter, click the counter in the Select Counters From List, and then click Add.
9. Repeat this process for other counters you want to monitor.
10. Click Close when you are finished adding counters.

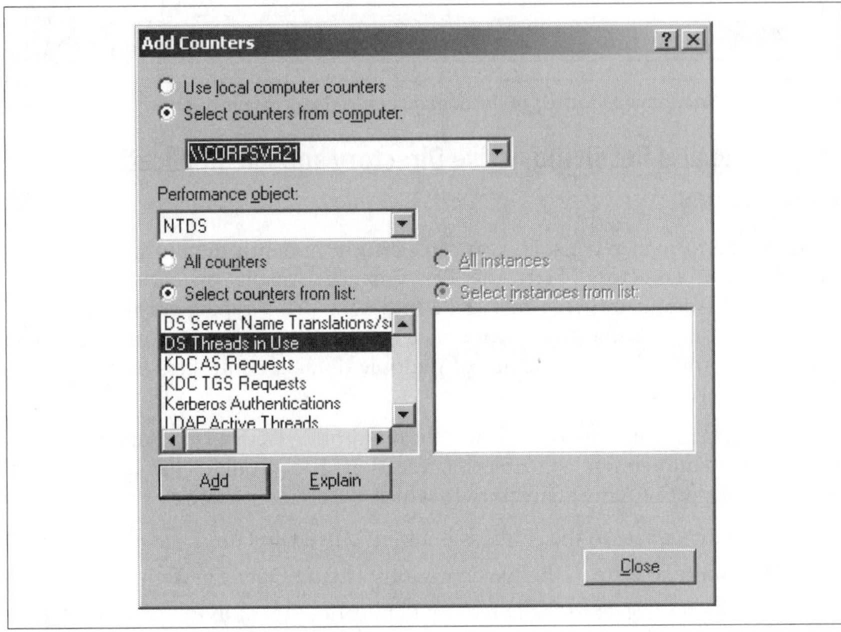

Figure 11-31. Select the computer and counters to monitor.

As with other types of monitoring, you can configure performance logging and performance alerting if desired. Events related to Active Directory are also logged in the event logs. Active Directory–related events, including NTDS replication events, are logged in the Directory Service log located on the domain controller.

File Replication Service (FRS) is used to replicate the Sysvol files between domain controllers. To monitor File Replication Service, use the `FileReplicaConn` and `FileReplicatSet` monitoring objects. Each object has a number of counters that can be used to track the status and health of FRS replication. As with Active Directory, you can configure performance logging and alerting for FRS.

To replicate the Sysvol, FRS relies on the availability of a properly configured Sysvol share. You can type `net share` at a command prompt to check the Sysvol share. The Netlogon service also uses Sysvol for obtaining scripts. NTFS permissions on the Sysvol folder and Share permissions on the Sysvol share must be configured properly.

Events related to File Replication Service (FRS), which is used for replicating the Sysvol files, are recorded in the File Replication Service log located on the domain controller. The primary source for events is NtFrs, which is the File Replication Service itself.

Restoring Active Directory

As part of your enterprise backup and recovery strategy, you should back up the system state on domain controllers whenever you perform Normal backups to ensure Active Directory data is stored in the full backup set. System State data for a domain controller includes Active Directory data and system volume (Sysvol) files. The System State of a domain controller can only be restored using the Directory Services Restore Mode startup option. When you start a domain controller, you can enter this mode by pressing F8 during boot up, and then selecting Directory Services Restore Mode as the startup option.

As a part of the planning process, the administrator should make a decision about how often the System State is to be backed up. Typically, you back up the System State as part of every normal (full) backup.

When you have multiple domain controllers in a domain and one fails, the other domain controllers automatically detect the failure and change their replication topology accordingly. You can restore the failed domain controller from backup if necessary. However, the restore doesn't recover Active Directory information stored on the domain controller.

To restore Active Directory on the failed domain controller, you must do so using either of the following:

Authoritative restore

Use an authoritative restore only when you need to recover Active Directory and no other domain controller has the correct data. For example, if someone accidentally deletes a large number of user accounts, you could use an authoritative restore to recover the deleted accounts.

For an authoritative restore, restore the System State, and then use NTDSUTIL to determine how the authoritative restore should be implemented. Do not reboot the computer after restoring the System State. Sysvol is not restored authoritatively unless you do a primary restore of the Sysvol.

Nonauthoritative restore

Use a nonauthoritative restore to restore a domain controller and allow it to get any necessary updates for Active Directory from other domain controllers.

For a nonauthoritative restore, restore the System State, and then reboot the domain controller. In this state, the domain controller gets updates in its replica of Active Directory and Sysvol from other domain controllers using normal replication. You have the option of doing a primary restore of the Sysvol.

Nonauthoritative restores, authoritative restores, and primary restores of Sysvol are discussed in the sections that follow.

Performing a nonauthoritative restore operation

To restore Active Directory on a domain controller and have the domain controller get directory updates from other domain controllers, you should repair the server, replacing an failed hardware as necessary, and then perform a nonauthoritative restore. A nonauthoritative restore allows the domain controller to come back online, and then get replication updates from other domain controllers.

You can perform a nonauthoritative restore by completing the following steps:

1. Restart the domain controller. Press F8 during startup to display the Windows Advanced Options menu.
2. Select Directory Services Restore Mode (Windows Domain Controllers Only), and then press Enter.
3. Windows then restarts in Safe Mode without loading Active Directory components. When the system starts, log on using the Administrator account with the Directory Services Restore password.
4. An operating system prompt warns you that you are running in Safe Mode. Click OK.
5. Click Start → Programs → Accessories → System Tools → Backup to start the Backup utility. If Backup starts in Wizard mode, click the Advanced Mode Link to switch to Advanced mode.
6. On the Welcome tab, click the Restore Wizard button. Click Next.
7. Under Items To Restore, expand the media item that you want to restore, and then expand the backup set that you want to restore.
8. Select the checkbox for each volume, folder, file, or data set to recover. Selecting a volume or folder selects all the related folders and files. Selecting System State allows you to recover the System State, which is required to restore Active Directory.
9. Click Next. By default, files are recovered to their original location. To change the recovery to an alternative location or folder, click the Advanced button, select the restore location, and then configure other advanced options as necessary.
10. Click Finish to begin the nonauthoritative restore. When warned that you will overwrite current system state, click OK.
11. The Restore Progress dialog box shows the progress of the restore operation. When the restore completes, click Close to complete the process or click Report to view a log report of the restore operation.
12. Restart the computer as instructed. Once the server restarts, it is able to act as a domain controller and has a directory database that is current as of the date of the backup. During its normal replication process, the domain controller obtains updates from its replication partners.

Performing an authoritative restore operation

To restore Active Directory on a domain controller and have the domain controller be the authoritative domain controller for the domain, you should repair the server, replacing failed hardware as necessary, and then perform an authoritative restore. An authoritative restore is used when you need to recover Active Directory to a specific point in time, and then replicate the restored data to all other domain controllers.

Before performing an authoritative restore, keep in mind that passwords used for computers and NTLM trusts are changed automatically every seven days. When you perform an authoritative restore of Active Directory, the restored database contains the passwords that were in use when the backup archive was made.

Computer account passwords allow computers to authenticate themselves in a domain using a computer trust. If a computer password has changed, the computer may not be able to re-authenticate itself in the domain. In this case, you may need to reset the computer account password.

Deleted objects have a default tombstone lifetime of 60 days. You won't be able to restore System State data from backups that are older than 60 days. If you try to restore data older than 60 days, the tombstone lifetime will have expired and as a result, the data is not restored.

To reset the computer account password for a workstation, you need to:

1. Right-click the computer account in Active Directory Users And Computers, and then select Reset Account.
2. Log on the problem computer and remove the computer from the domain by joining a workgroup.
3. While logged on to the problem computer, rejoin the computer to the domain.

With member servers and domain controllers, you should use NETDOM RESETPWD. You can reset the computer account password of a member server or domain controller by completing the following steps:

1. Log on locally to the computer. If you are resetting the password of a domain controller, you must stop the Kerberos Key Distribution Center service and set its startup type to Manual.
2. Open a command prompt.
3. Type `netdom resetpwd /s:`*`ComputerName`* `/ud:`*`domain\user`* `/pd:*`, where *`ComputerName`* is the name of a domain controller in the computer account's logon domain, *`domain\user`* is the name of an administrator account with the authority to change the computer account password, and * tells NETDOM to prompt you for the account password before continuing.
4. When you enter your password, NETDOM will change the computer account password locally and on the domain controller. The domain controller then distributes the password change to other domain controllers.
5. When NETDOM completes this task, restart the computer and verify that the password has been successfully reset. If you reset a domain controller's password, restart the Kerberos Key Distribution Center service and set its startup type to Automatic.

NTLM trusts are trusts between Active Directory Domains and Windows NT domains. If a trust password changes, the trust between the domains may fail. In this case, you may need to delete the trust, and then recreate it as discussed previously under "Managing Trusts."

You can perform an authoritative restore by completing the following steps:

1. Restart the domain controller. Press F8 during startup to display the Windows Advanced Options menu.
2. Select Directory Services Restore Mode (Windows Domain Controllers Only), and then press Enter.
3. Windows then restarts in Safe Mode without loading Active Directory components. When the system starts, log on using the Administrator account with the Directory Services Restore password.
4. An operating system prompt warns you that you are running in Safe Mode. Click OK.
5. Click Start → Programs → Accessories → System Tools → Backup to start the Backup utility. If Backup starts in Wizard mode, click the Advanced Mode Link to switch to Advanced mode.
6. On the Welcome tab, click the Restore Wizard button. Click Next.
7. Under Items To Restore, expand the media item that you want to restore, and then expand the backup set that you want to restore.
8. Select the checkbox for each volume, folder, file, or data set to recover. Selecting a volume or folder selects all the related folders and files. Selecting System State allows you to recover the System State, which is required to restore Active Directory.
9. Click Next. By default, files are recovered to their original location. To change the recovery to an alternative location or folder, click the Advanced button, select the restore location, and then configure other advanced options as necessary.
10. Click Finish to begin the authoritative restore. When warned that you will overwrite current system state, click OK.
11. The Restore Progress dialog box shows the progress of the restore operation. When the restore completes, click Close to complete the process or click Report to view a log report of the restore operation.
12. Do not restart the computer when prompted. Instead, open a command prompt and type `ntdsutil`. This starts the Directory Services Management Tool.
13. At the Ntdsutil prompt, type `authoritative restore`.
14. You can authoritatively restore Active Directory in several ways:
    - Restore the entire Active Directory database by typing `restore database`. Restore the entire database only if Active Directory has been corrupted or there is some other considerable reason for doing so.

- Restore a portion or subtree of the directory by typing `restore subtree` *`ObjectDN`*, where *`ObjectDN`* is the distinguished name of the container to restore. For example, you could restore the Tech OU and all the objects it contained by typing the command `restore subtree ou=tech,dc=domain,dc=local`.
- Restore an individual object by typing `restore object` *`ObjectDN`*, where *`ObjectDN`* is the distinguished name of the object to restore. For example, you could restore the Engineering security group by typing the command `restore object cn=engineering,dc=domain,dc=local`.

15. Type `quit` twice to exit Ntdsutil.
16. Restart the server.

Exam 70-294 Study Guide

Performing a primary restore operation on the Sysvol

The Sysvol folder is backed up as part of the System State. It contains critical domain information, including Group Policy Objects, group policy templates, and scripts. If you restore a domain controller, the Sysvol data on the restored domain controller is overwritten with a replica from other domain controllers. The reason this occurs is because Sysvol data is replicated using the File Replication Service (FRS).

You must perform a primary restore of the Sysvol to ensure that the restored Sysvol is replicated to all other domain controllers. To perform a primary restore of the Sysvol, use Backup to restore the System State using either an authoritative or nonauthoritative restore technique as discussed previously. There is one important change, however.

During the restore, do not accept the default restore settings. Instead, on the Completing The Restore Wizard page, click the Advanced button to access the advanced restore options. Then click Next twice. On the Advanced Restore Options page, select When Restoring Replicated Data Sets, Mark The Restored Data As The Primary Data For All Replicas. Click Next, and then click Finish.

Planning and Implementing Computer, User, and Group Strategies

In the Exam 70-290 Study Guide, I provided a detailed discussion on planning and implementing users, computers, and groups. For Exam 70-294, you are expected to be able to plan a security group strategy, which requires a strong understanding of group types, group scopes, implicit groups, creating groups, setting group membership, and maintaining groups—all of which are discussed in the section of Chapter 2 titled, "Managing Groups in an Active Directory Environment."

Exam 70-294 also expects you to be able to plan a user authentication strategy using smart cards and strict password policies. These policies are critically important for ensuring the security of the network. Smart cards are small card-sized devices that contain memory and/or integrated circuitry for storing digital certificates used in logon authentication. For remote access users, Extensible Authentication Protocol (EAP) is the only authentication protocol you can use.

Using Active Directory Users And Computers, you can require users to use smart cards for authentication by completing the following steps:

1. Right-clicking the account and then select Properties.
2. On the Account tab, select Smart Card Is Required For Interactive Logon. This ensures that use of a smart card and reader for logon and authentication is required. This option resets the Password Never Expires option to be enabled.
3. Click OK.

To use smart cards for authentication, you must install smart card reader devices on computers and set up a smart card to use for user logon. Smart cards contain a user's digital certificate and private key, allowing the user to be authenticated when logging on the network. With smart cards, only enterprise CAs can be used because they have smart card certificates in Active Directory.

As preparation for Exam 70-294, you should also review the section of Chapter 2 titled "Managing User Access and Authentication." Password policies control how passwords are managed, whether they expire, and when they expire. In Group Policy, password policies are stored under *Computer Configuration\Windows Settings\Security Settings\Account Policies\Password Policy*.

Account lockout policies control whether and how accounts are locked out if successive invalid passwords are provided. In Group Policy, password policies are stored under *Computer Configuration\Windows Settings\Security Settings\Account Policies\Account Lockout Policy*.

To configure password policy and account policy for domain users, you should configure the related policies using the Default Domain Policy GPO. If you are using the Group Policy Management Console, the Default Domain Policy GPO is accessible when you click the domain name in the console tree. You then need to right-click the Default Domain Policy node and select Edit. If you want only to work with security settings in the Default Domain Policy GPO, you can use the Domain Security Policy console, which is found on the Administrative Tools menu.

Planning, Implementing, and Maintaining Group Policy

Group Policy is critical for proper domain operations. You configure and maintain Group Policy to manage computer and user security, to configure the user environment, and to configure the computer environment.

Group Policy affects only Windows 2000 and later computers. Computers running pre-Windows 2000 operating systems do not support Group Policy.

Understanding Group Policy

Group Policy is as a set of rules that you can apply to help you manage users and computers. Active Directory defines two distinct sets of policies:

Computer policies
: Applied to computers that are stored under Computer Configuration in Group Policy

User policies
: Applied to users that are stored under User Configuration in Group Policy

Use Computer Configuration settings to configure policy on a per-computer basis. Use User Configuration settings to configure policy on a per-user basis.

The way Group Policy is processed depends on the type of policy. When a computer is started and the network connection is initialized, computer policy settings are applied and a history of the registry-based settings that were applied is written to *%AllUsersProfile%\Ntuser.pol*. When a user logs on to a computer, user policy settings are applied, and a history of the registry-based settings that were applied is written to *%UserProfile%\Ntuser.pol*.

Once applied, Group Policy settings are automatically refreshed to keep settings current and to reflect any changes. By default, Group Policy is refreshed every 5 minutes on domain controllers and every 90 to 120 minutes on other computers. Group Policy is refreshed every 16 hours in full. Slow link and policy-processing settings can affect when refresh occurs.

You can use Group Policy to manage settings on all workstations and servers running Windows 2000 or later. You can't use Group Policy to manage Windows NT, Windows 95, Windows 98, Windows Me, or Windows XP Home Edition.

Group Policy is applied using Group Policy Objects (GPOs). GPOs contain settings that are applied according to the Active Directory structure in place. Sites, domains, and organizational units all have related Group Policy Objects. The settings of top-level GPOs are inherited by lower-level GPOs.

For local environments, a subset of Group Policy called Local Group Policy is available that allows you to manage policy settings that affect everyone who logs on to a local machine. Local Group Policy is managed through the Local Group Policy Object (LGPO). All computers have an LGPO. Its settings have the least precedence and can be superseded by site, domain, and OU settings. Although domain controllers have LGPOs, Group Policy for domain controllers should be managed through the Default Domain Controllers Policy.

Using Group Policy

Manage Group Policy by configuring policy settings. Policy settings can be enabled, disabled, or not configured. Enabled policy settings are active and applied. Disabled policy settings are inactive and not applied or enforced. Not configured policy settings are not being used.

Inheritance and blocking can affect the meaning of these states. If inherited policy settings are enforced, you cannot override them and the inherited policy setting is applied as per the configured state. If inherited policy settings are blocked and inheritance is not enforced, the inherited policy setting is overridden and does not apply.

Each GPO has a specific inheritance precedence. Everyone who logs on to the local machine is affected by Local Group Policy. Active Directory–based policy settings are applied in this basic order: site, domain, OU. By default, when policy is set at one level, the setting applies to all objects at that level and all objects in the levels below due to inheritance.

Unless it is blocked, here's how inheritance works:

- A policy setting applied at the site level affects all users and computers located within domains and OUs that are part of the site.
- A policy setting applied at the domain level affects all users and computers located within OUs that are part of the domain.
- A policy setting applied at the OU level affects all users and computers defined within the OU as well to child OUs.

Understanding GPO Links and Default GPOs

Before you can move on to more advanced Group Policy topics, you must understand two fundamental concepts: GPO links and default GPOs. *GPO links* affect the way policy is applied. *Default GPOs* are special-purpose policy objects that Active Directory depends on to establish baseline security settings for domain controllers and domains.

In Active Directory, all GPOs are stored in the Group Policy Objects container. This container is replicated to all domain controllers in a domain. The link between a domain, site, or OU is what makes a GPO active and applicable to that domain, site, or OU. You can link a GPO to a specific site, domain, or OU. You can also link a GPO to multiple levels, such as to a site and a domain. If you unlink a GPO from a site, domain, or OU, you remove the association between the GPO and that site, domain, or OU.

You can work with Group Policy in a variety of ways. For managing Local Group Policy, you can use the Local Security Policy tool. For managing Active Directory Group Policy, you can use the Group Policy Object Editor (GPOE), which is included with a standard installation of Windows Server 2003, or the Group Policy Management Console (GPMC), which is available as a free download from the Microsoft Download Center (*http://www.microsoft.com/downloads*).

When you create a domain, two GPOs are created by default:

Default Domain Controllers Policy GPO
: This is the default GPO created for and linked to the Domain Controllers OU. It is applied to all domain controllers in a domain (as long as they aren't moved from the Domain Controllers OU). Use this GPO to manage security settings for domain controllers in a domain.

Default Domain Policy GPO
: This is the default GPO created for and linked to the domain within Active Directory. It is used to establish policy settings that apply to all users and computers in a domain.

These default GPOs are essential for processing of Group Policy. By default, the Default Domain Controllers Policy GPO has the highest precedence among GPOs linked to the Domain Controllers OU, and the Default Domain Policy GPO has the highest precedence among GPOs linked to the domain.

You should edit the Default Domain Policy GPO only to manage the default Account Policies settings for:

- Password Policy
- Account Lockout Policy
- Kerberos Policy

You should manage other areas of domain policy by creating a new GPO and linking it to the domain or an appropriate OU within the domain.

You should also manage these *Computer Configuration\Windows Settings\Security Settings\Local Policies\Security* options using the Default Domain Policy GPO:

Accounts: Rename Administrator Account
: Renames the built-in Administrator account on all computers throughout the domain.

Accounts: Rename Guest Account
: Renames the built-in Guest account on all computers throughout the domain.

Network Security: Force Logoff When Logon Hours Expire
: Forces users to log off from the domain when logon hours expire.

Network Access: Allow Anonymous SID/Name Translation
: Determines whether an anonymous user can request security identifier (SID) attributes for another user. This setting should only be enabled for backward compatibility with Windows NT applications that require this feature.

In the GPMC, the Default Domain Policy GPO is listed when you click the domain name in the console tree. Right-click the Default Domain Policy node and select Edit to get full access to the Default Domain Policy GPO. If you want only to work with security settings in the Default Domain Policy GPO, you can use the Domain Security Policy console on the Administrative Tools menu.

Use the Default Domain Controllers Policy GPO to ensure that all domain controllers in a specified domain have the same security settings. In the GPMC, the Default Domain Controllers Policy GPO is listed when you click the Domain Controllers node in the console tree. Right-click the Default Domain Controllers Policy and select Edit to get full access to the Default Domain Controllers Policy GPO. If you want only to work with security settings in the Default Domain Controllers Policy GPO, you can use the Domain Security Policy console on the Administrative Tools menu.

By default, all domain controllers are placed in the Domain Controllers OU. This means any policy setting changes you make to the Default Domain Controllers Policy GPO will apply to all domain controllers by default. Microsoft recommends that you edit the Default Domain Controllers Policy GPO only to configure User Rights Assignment and Audit Policy. You may also want to set Security Options and event log settings.

Working with Group Policy

As an administrator, you'll work with both Local Group Policy and Active Directory Group Policy. Local Group Policy applies only to a local machine, and there is only one Local GPO per local machine. With Active Directory Group Policy, each site, domain, and OU can have its own GPOs. To work with Active Directory Group Policy, you can the Group Policy Object Editor (GPOE) or the Group Policy Management Console (GPMC). Figure 11-32 shows Group Policy being accessed in the Group Policy Object Editor.

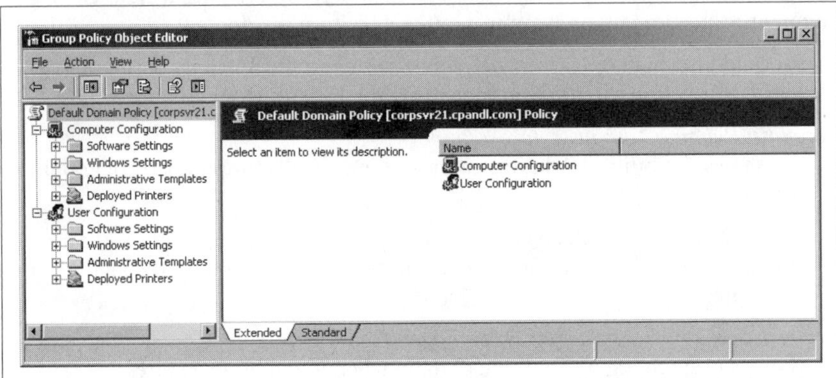

Figure 11-32. Accessing Group Policy.

Group Policy applies only to users and computers. Group Policy settings are divided into two categories:

Computer Configuration
: This contains settings that apply to computers.

User Configuration
: This contains settings that apply to user accounts.

These two categories are divided further into several major classes of settings, including:

Software Settings
: Provides settings for automating deployment of new software and software upgrades, and for uninstalling software.

Windows Settings
: Provides settings for managing Windows settings for both computers and users. For computers, you can manage security settings and startup/shutdown scripts. For users, you can also manage Remote Installation Services, Folder Redirection, Internet Explorer maintenance, security settings, and logon/logoff scripts.

Administrative Templates
: Provides settings for managing registry settings that configure the operating system, Windows components, and applications.

Implementing Group Policy

Manage Group Policy on a local machine using Local Group Policy. Manage Group Policy for Active Directory using the Active Directory Group Policy. Whenever you work with Active Directory Group Policy, any changes you make to policy settings are made first on the domain controller acting as the PDC Emulator if it is available. In this way, replication of changes is simplified because there is one central point of contact. If the PDC Emulator is unavailable when you try to edit policy settings, you are able to choose the domain controller on which changes should be made.

Managing Local Group Policy

To work with Local Group Policy, you must use an administrator account. You can access Local Group Policy by typing:

```
gpedit.msc /gpcomputer:"%computername%"
```

where *%computername%* is an environment variable that sets the name of the local computer and must be enclosed in double quotation marks.

Or by typing:

```
gpedit.msc /gpcomputer:"RemoteComputer"
```

where *RemoteComputer* is the name of a remote computer enclosed in double quotation marks, such as:

```
gpedit.msc /gpcomputer:"engsvr25"
```

You can also access Local Group Policy by completing the following steps:

1. At a command prompt, type `mmc`.
2. Click File → Add/Remove Snap-In.
3. In the Add/Remove Snap-In dialog box, click Add.
4. In the Add Standalone Snap-In dialog box, click Group Policy Object Editor, and then choose Add.
5. The Select Group Policy Object page is displayed with the Local Computer selected as the Group Policy Object target. Click Finish.
6. In the Add Standalone Snap-In dialog box, click Close.
7. In the Add/Remove Snap-In dialog box, click OK.

If you want only to work with security settings in Local Group Policy, you can use the Local Security Policy console. Click Start → Programs → Administrative Tools → Local Security Policy. Local Security Policy is not available if you are working on a domain controller.

In Group Policy Object Editor and Local Security Policy, you can configure security settings that apply to users and the local computer itself. Any policy changes you make are applied to that computer the next time Group Policy is refreshed.

You configure Local Group Policy in the same way that you configure Active Directory–based group policy. To apply a policy, you enable it, and then configure any additional or optional values as necessary. An enabled policy setting is turned on and active. If don't want a policy to apply, you can disable it. A disabled policy setting is turned off and inactive. The enforcement or blocking of inheritance can change this behavior.

Managing Active Directory Group Policy

Domain Admins and Enterprise Admins can work with Active Directory Group Policy. With Active Directory Group Policy, creating and linking objects are separate actions. You can create a GPO and later link it to a site, domain, or OU. Or you can create a GPO and simultaneously link it to a site, domain, or OU.

The way you create and manage GPOs depends on whether you want to work with a site GPO, a domain GPO, or an OU GPO:

- To create and manage a site's GPOs, open Active Directory Sites And Services. In the console tree, right-click the site you want to work with, and then select Properties. In the Properties dialog box, click the Group Policy tab.
- To create and manage a domain's GPOs, open Active Directory Users And Computers. In the console tree, right-click the domain you want to work with, and then select Properties. In the Properties dialog box, click the Group Policy tab.
- To create and manage an OU's GPOs, open Active Directory Users And Computers. In the console tree, right-click the OU you want to work with, and then select Properties. In the Properties dialog box, click the Group Policy tab.

You can then use the New, Add, Edit, and Delete options on the Group Policy tab to create and manage GPOs for the selected site, domain, or OU. Follow these procedures:

Creating and linking a GPO
: On the Group Policy tab, click New to create a new GPO that will be linked to the currently selected site, domain, or OU. Because the GPO is linked to the site, domain, or OU, any policy settings you define will be applied to the selected site, domain, or OU according to the inheritance and preference options used by Active Directory. After you create the GPO by clicking New, an entry is added to the Group Policy Object Links list with the name highlighted, as shown in Figure 11-33. Type in a name, and then press Enter. Use the Up and Down buttons to change the preference order of the GPO as necessary.

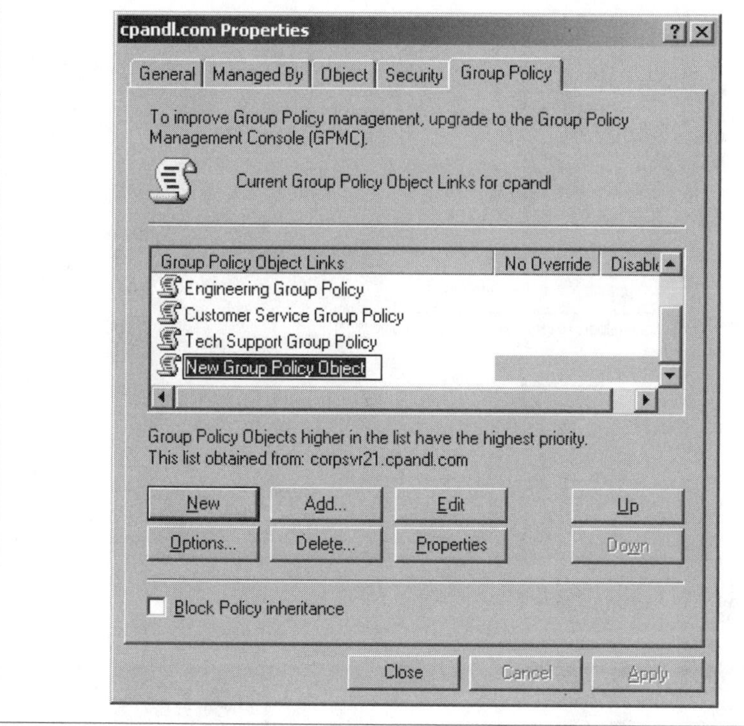

Figure 11-33. Creating a GPO.

Editing a GPO

On the Group Policy tab, you can edit an existing GPO linked to the selected container by selecting it, and then clicking Edit. This displays the Group Policy Object Editor dialog box. You can then make changes to Group Policy as necessary; these changes are applied the next time Active Directory is refreshed. To edit a policy, double-click it to display a properties dialog box similar to the one shown in Figure 11-34, and then configure the policy as appropriate.

Linking to an existing GPO

In the Group Policy tab, you can link to an existing GPO by clicking Add. This displays the Add A Group Object Link dialog box, as shown in Figure 11-35. Select the All tab to see all the GPOs that are available. Select the one you want to which you want to link, and then click OK. The linked policy is applied the next time Active Directory is refreshed.

Deleting a GPO

In the Group Policy tab, you can remove an existing GPO by selecting it, and then clicking Delete. As Figure 11-36 shows, you can then Remove The Link From The List so that the GPO no longer applies to the container, or you can Remove The Link And Delete so the GPO no longer applies and is deleted permanently.

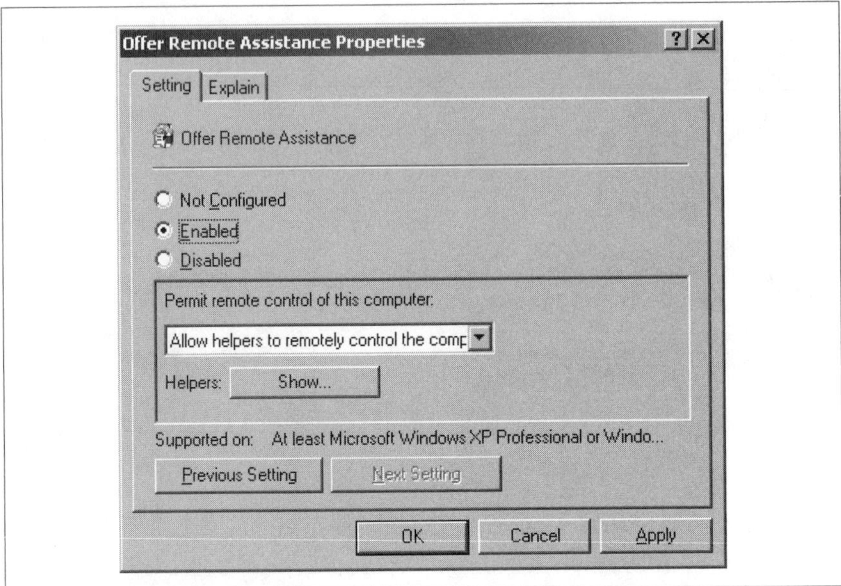

Figure 11-34. Configuring a policy.

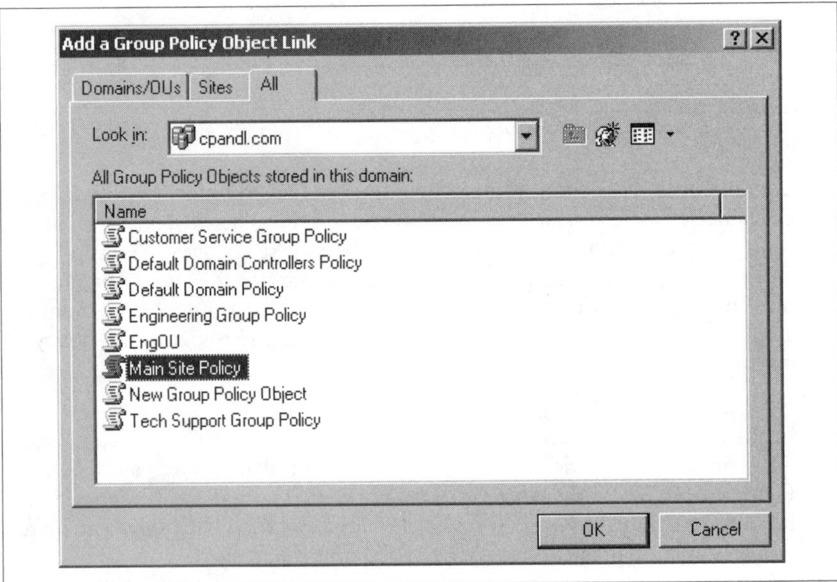

Figure 11-35. Linking to an existing GPO.

Configuring Administrative Templates

Administrative Templates are used to manage the Windows graphical user interface (GUI). You can use Administrative Templates to manage:

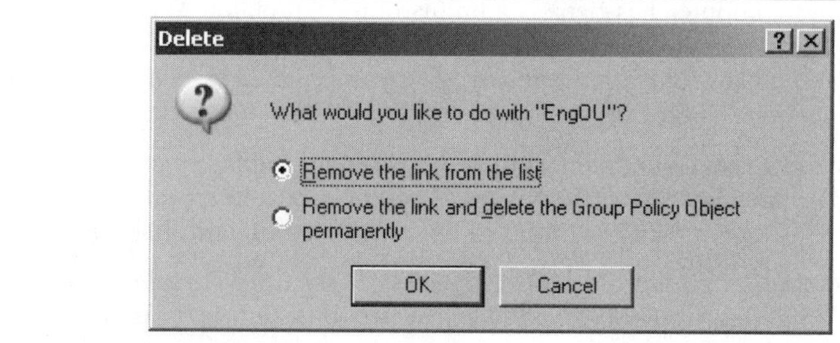

Figure 11-36. Deleting a GPO.

Exam 70-294 Study Guide

Control Panel
: These settings determine how the Control Panel and Control Panel utilities can be used.

Desktop
: These settings are used to configure the Windows desktop and the available options from the desktop.

Network
: These settings are used to configure networking and network client options for offline files, DNS clients, and network connections.

Printers
: These settings are used to configure printer settings, browsing, spooling, and directory options.

Shared folders
: These settings are used to allow publishing of shared folders and Distributed File System (DFS) roots.

Start Menu and Taskbar
: These settings determine the available options and configuration of the Start Menu and taskbar.

System
: These settings are used to configure system settings for disk quotas, user profiles, user logon, system restore, error reporting, etc.

Windows Components
: These settings determine the available options and configuration of various Windows components, including Event Viewer, Internet Explorer, Task Scheduler, Windows Installer, and Windows Updates.

Administrative Templates policy settings are registry-based, meaning changes you make to these settings affect actual registry settings. Each set of Administrative Templates is defined using an administrative template (*.adm*) file. Administrative template files do not affect the processing of policy. Instead, they are used to display the settings that can be configured. If a *.adm* file is removed from a GPO, the settings are not displayed in the Group Policy Object Editor. However, the settings will continue to be applied because the setting details are stored in the *Registry.pol* file associated with the GPO.

Every Windows computer has default administrative templates. With Windows XP Professional with Service Pack 1 or later and Windows Server 2003, the default administrative templates include *Conf.adm*, *Inetres.adm*, *System.adm*, *Wmplayer.adm*, and *Wuau.adm*. These files are stored in the *%Windir%\inf* folder.

When you create a new GPO, the default administrative templates on your system generally determine the default templates that are available initially and then stored with the GPO. Two GPO settings can be used to modify this behavior:

Turn Off Automatic Updates Of ADM Files under User Configuration\Administrative Templates\System\Group Policy. When this setting is enabled and you edit a GPO, the *.adm* files on your computer are compared with those stored in the GPO. If any *.adm* files on your computer have a newer timestamp, those files are written to the GPO.

Always Use Local ADM Files For Group Policy Editor under Computer Configuration\Administrative Templates\System\Group Policy. When this setting is enabled and you edit a GPO, the *.adm* files on your computer are used to determine the Administrative Templates options.

You can edit a GPO and determine which *.adm* files are being in the GPO by completing the following steps:

1. Open Active Directory Users and Computers.
2. In the console tree, right-click the domain or OU you want to work with, and then select Properties. In the Properties dialog box, click the Group Policy tab.
3. On the Group Policy tab, you can edit an existing GPO linked to the selected container by selecting it, and then clicking Edit.
4. In the Group Policy Object Editor dialog box, expand the User Configuration node.
5. Right-click Administrative Templates, and then select Add/Remove Templates.
6. As shown in Figure 11-37, the current templates are listed by name, size, and date modified.

When the Add/Remove Templates dialog box is displayed, you can import additional templates into the GPO, such as custom templates you've created or those for Microsoft Office. To do this, complete the following steps:

1. Click Add.
2. In the Policy Templates dialog box, select the *.adm* files you want to add, and then click Open.
3. The selected templates are added to the GPO for your use.

Managing policy inheritance and processing

With Active Directory Group Policy, GPOs can be linked to sites, domains, and OUs. When you create and link a GPO to a site, domain, or OU, the GPO is applied to the user and computer objects in that site, domain, or OU according to the current inheritance and preference options.

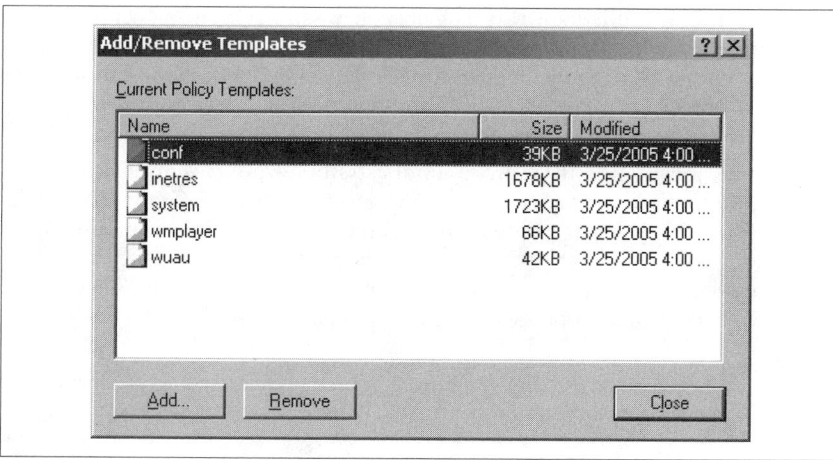

Figure 11-37. Viewing the .adm files for a GPO.

By default, Group Policy settings are inherited from top-level containers by lower-level containers (unless inheritance is blocked or overridden). Because of this, a setting in a top-level GPO can affect every user and computer throughout the enterprise. The end result of inheritance and policy processing is referred to as the Resultant Set of Policy (RSoP).

The order in which policies are applied determines which policy settings take effect if multiple policies modify the same settings. When multiple policies are in place, the policies are applied in the following order:

Local computer policy → Site policy → Domain policy → OU policy

If there are conflicts among the policy settings, the settings applied later have precedence by default. This means they overwrite previously applied settings.

Most policies have three configuration options: Not Configured, Enabled, and Disabled. The default state of most policies is Not Configured, meaning the policy setting is not configured and does not apply. If a policy is set to Enabled, the policy is enforced and does apply to users and computers that are subject to the GPO. If a policy is set to Disabled, the policy is not enforced and does not apply to users and computers that are subject to the GPO.

You can change inheritance in several ways:

- You can override a policy setting that is enabled in a higher-level container by disabling it in a lower-level policy. In Active Directory Users And Computers, right-click the domain or OU you want to work with, and then select Properties. In the Properties dialog box, click the Group Policy tab, select the GPO you want to work with, and then click Edit. After you locate the policy setting to override, double-click it, select Disabled, and then click OK.
- You can override a policy setting that is disabled in a higher-level container by enabling it in a lower-level policy. In Active Directory Users And Computers, right-click the domain or OU you want to work with, and then select Properties. In the Properties dialog box, click the Group Policy tab, select the GPO you want to work with, and then click Edit. After you locate the policy setting to override, double-click it, select Enabled, and then click OK.

- You can block inheritance so that no policy settings from higher-level containers are applied. In Active Directory Users and Computers, block inheritance by right-clicking the domain or OU that should not inherit settings from higher-level containers and selecting Properties. In the Group Policy tab of the Properties dialog box, select Block Policy Inheritance, and then click OK.
- Enforce inheritance to prevent administrators who have been delegated authority over a container from overriding the inherited Group Policy settings. In Active Directory Users And Computers, enforce inheritance by right-clicking the domain or OU that should be required to inherit settings from higher-level containers and selecting Properties. In the Group Policy tab of the Properties dialog box, select No Override, and then click OK.

For Exam 70-294, you'll need a strong understanding of inheritance and how it can be enforced, blocked, or overridden.

By default, the policy settings applied to a GPO apply to all users and computers in the container to which the GPO is linked. The GPO applies to all users and computers because the default settings of GPOs specify that Authenticated Users have Read permission as well as Apply Group Policy permission. Since both user accounts and computer accounts are considered to be types of authentication users, all users and computers with accounts in the domain are affected by the policy.

By default, Computer Configuration settings are applied during startup of the operating system, and User Configuration settings are applied when a user logs on to a computer. You can modify Group Policy processing by disabling a policy in whole or in part. In Active Directory Users And Computers, you can enable and disable policies partially or entirely by completing the following steps:

1. In Active Directory Users And Computers, right-click the domain or OU you want to work with, and then select Properties.
2. In the Properties dialog box, click the Group Policy tab, select the GPO you want to work with, and then click Edit.
3. To disable a GPO entirely, select the GPO, and then click Options. In the Options dialog box, shown in Figure 11-38, select Disabled. When prompted to confirm the action, click Yes, and then click OK. To later enable the GPO, you would repeat this process and clear the Disabled checkbox.
4. To disable a GPO partially, select the GPO, and then click Properties. In the Properties dialog box, shown in Figure 11-39, select or clear Disable Computer Configuration Settings and Disable User Configuration Settings as necessary.

Planning Group Policy Application Using Resultant Set Of Policy

Resultant Set Of Policy (RSoP) can be used for planning and logging purposes. Using RSoP Planning mode is discussed in this section. Using RSoP Logging mode is discussed in the section of this chapter titled, "Troubleshooting the application of Group Policy security settings."

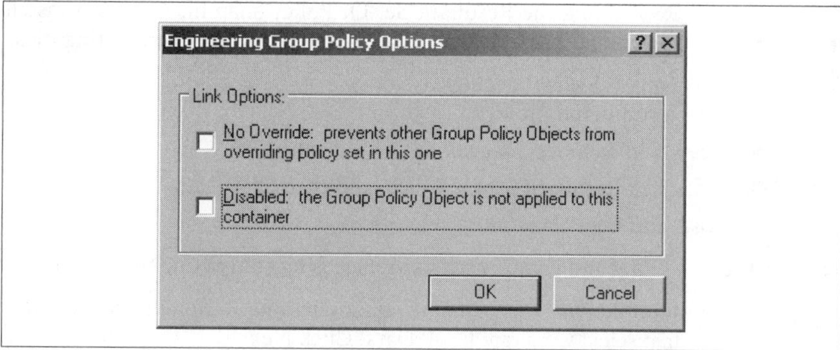

Figure 11-38. Disabling a GPO.

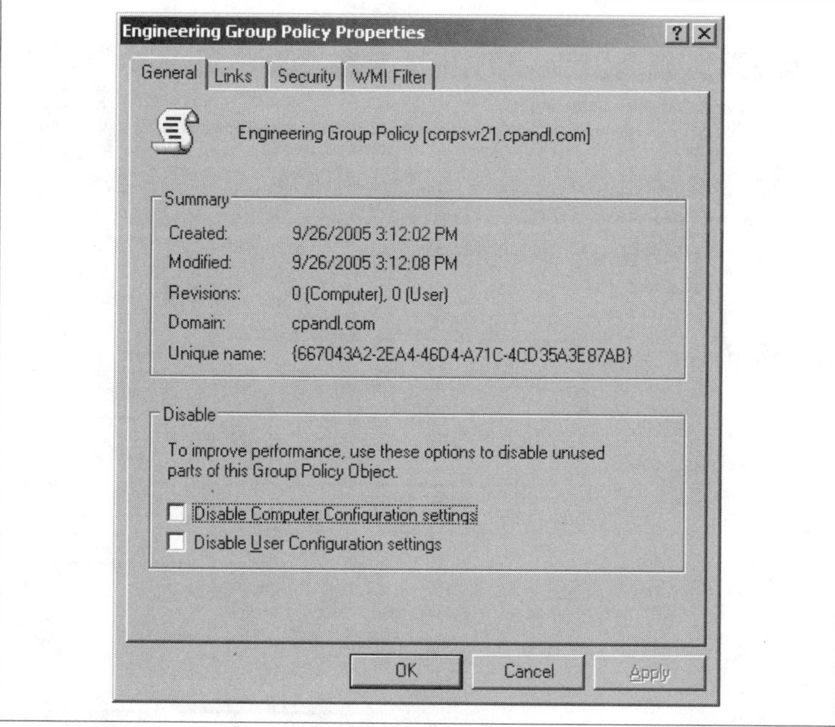

Figure 11-39. Disabling computer or user settings.

In Planning mode, RSoP can be used for testing different scenarios for modifying Computer Configuration and User Configuration settings. Using Planning mode, you can model the effects of:

- Modifying policy settings
- Moving a user or computer to another container in Active Directory
- Adding a user or computer to an additional security group

You work with RSoP using the Resultant Set Of Policy snap-in. After you install the AdminPak, you can add this snap-in to a custom console by completing these steps:

1. Type mmc at a command prompt.
2. Click File → Add/Remove Snap-in.
3. Click Add. Click Resultant Set Of Policy, and then click Add.
4. Click Close, and then click OK.

You can start planning and testing various scenarios by completing these steps:

1. In the Resultant Set Of Policy snap-in, right-click the Resultant Set Of Policy node, and then select Generate RSoP Data. Click Next.
2. Select Planning Mode, and then click Next to display the User And Computer Selection page, as shown in Figure 11-40.

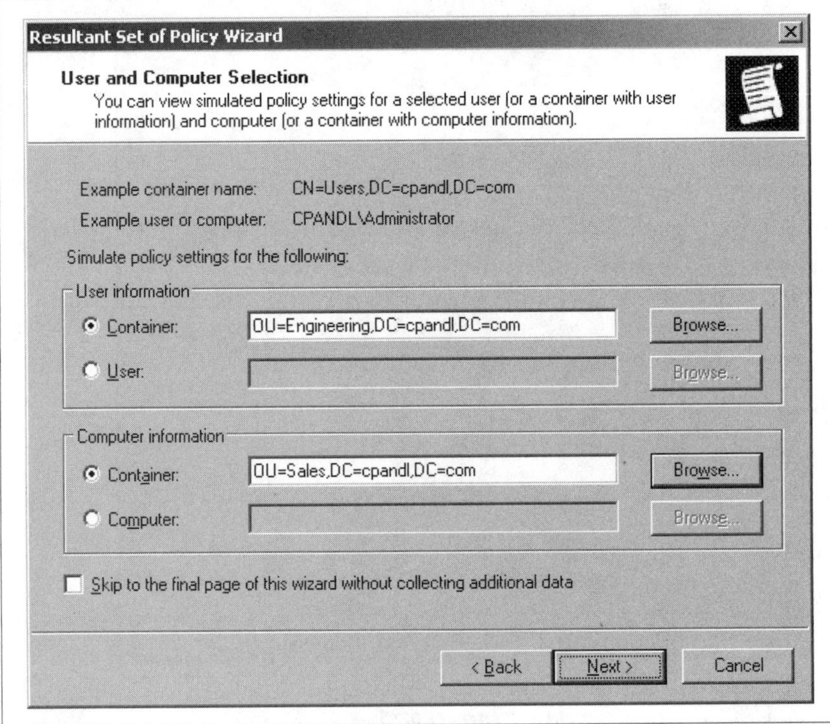

Figure 11-40. Select the user and computer containers.

3. Under User Information, select Container, and then click Browse to display the Choose User Container dialog box, which you can use to choose any of the available user containers in the selected domain.
4. Under Computer Information, select Container, and then click Browse to display the Choose Computer Container dialog box, which you can use to choose any of the available computer containers in the selected domain.

5. Click Next. On the Advanced Simulation Options page, select any advanced options for slow network connections, loopback processing, and sites as necessary, and then click Next.
6. On the User Security Groups page, shown in Figure 11-41, you can simulate changes to security group membership to model the results on Group Policy. Any changes you make to group membership affect the previously selected user container. For example, if you want to see what would happen if a user in the designated user container is a member of the Administrators group, you could add this group to the Security Groups list. Click Next.

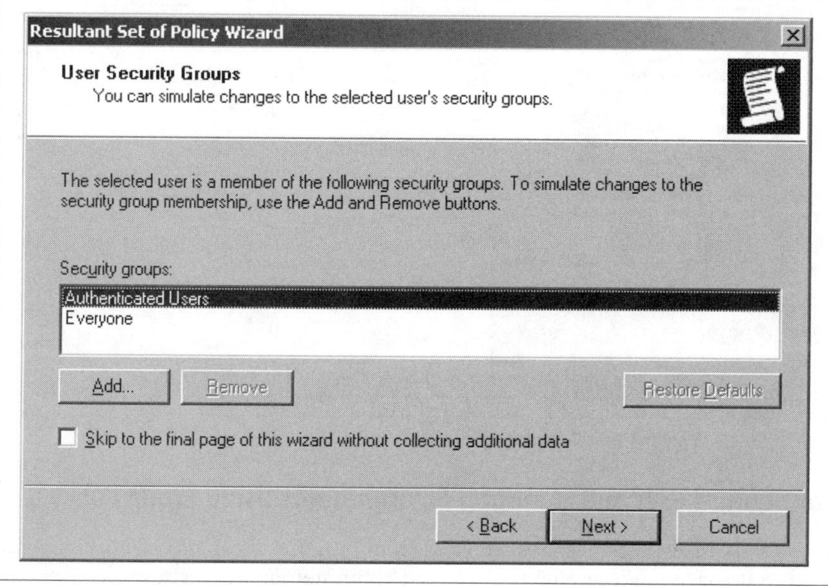

Figure 11-41. Simulating security group changes.

7. On the Computer Security Groups page, you can simulate changes to security group membership to model the results on Group Policy. Any changes you make to group membership affect the previously selected computer container. For example, if you want to see what would happen if a computer in the designated computer container is a member of the Domain Controllers group, you could add this group to the Security Groups list. Click Next.
8. WMI filters can be linked to Group Policy Objects. By default, the selected users and computers are assumed to meet all the WMI filter requirements, which is want you want in most cases for planning purposes. Click Next twice to accept the default options.
9. Click Next. The wizard gathers policy information. Click Finish.
10. When the wizard finishes generating the report, expand the report nodes in the left pane to see results in the right pane.

11. Computer and user policy information is listed separately. Computer policy information is listed under Computer Configuration. User policy information is listed under User Configuration Summary.
12. You can determine the settings that would be applied by browsing the report (see Figure 11-42).

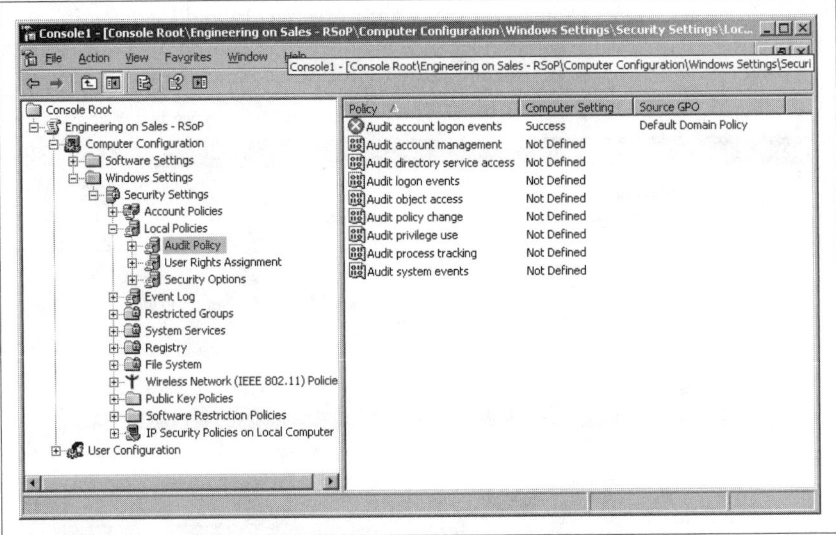

Figure 11-42. Viewing the planning results.

Configuring User and Computer Environments Using Group Policy

The User Configuration and Computer Configuration areas of Group Policy are used to manage the user environment and computer environment respectively. In previous sections, I've discussed how to create and manage GPOs, how to configure policy settings, and how to use Administrative Templates. Now let's look at specific areas of policy that you can configure, including:

- Computer and user certificate enrollment
- Computer and user scripts
- Folder redirection
- Software installation
- Automatic Updates configuration

Working with each of these areas of policies is discussed in the sections that follow.

Enrolling computer and user certificates by using Group Policy

Public Key Infrastructure (PKI) provides the components and services necessary to use public and private keys with digital certificates. Computers and users can use certificates for authentication and encryption. In Windows Server 2003, Microsoft

Certificate Services provide the necessary components for issuing and managing digital certificates.

A server designated as a certificate authority (CA) is responsible for issuing digital certificates and managing certificate revocation lists (CRLs). Servers running Windows Server 2003 can be configured as CAs by installing Microsoft Certificate Services. A CA used for autoenrollment must be configured as an enterprise root CA or an enterprise subordinate CA. Autoenrollment is a feature of Microsoft Certificate Services that can only be used when Active Directory is available to provide information required for validating the identity of users and computers.

Establish an enterprise CA hierarchy by installing an enterprise root CA and installing one or more levels of enterprise subordinate CAs. There can be only one root CA in an enterprise. All other CAs in the hierarchy must be enterprise subordinate CAs.

In an enterprise configuration, certificate servers are configured for automatic enrollment by default. This means authorized users and computers can request a certificate, and the CA can automatically process the certificate request so that the user and computers can immediately install the certificate.

Windows 2000 Active Directory supported autoenrollment of computer certificates using version 1 certificate templates. Windows XP Professional and Windows Server 2003 support autoenrollment of both user and computer certificates using version 2 certificate templates.

The way autoenrollment works is controlled by Group Policy. When you install enterprise CAs, autoenrollment policies for users and computers are enabled automatically. The policy for users is Autoenrollment Settings under *User Configuration\Windows Settings\Security Settings\Public Key Policies*. The policy for computers is Autoenrollment Settings under *Computer Configuration\Windows Settings\Security Settings\Public Key Policies*.

You can edit a GPO and access the Autoenrollment Settings policy by completing the following steps:

1. Open Active Directory Users And Computers.
2. In the console tree, right-click the domain or OU you want to work with, and then select Properties. In the Properties dialog box, click the Group Policy tab.
3. On the Group Policy tab, you can edit an existing GPO linked to the selected container by selecting it, and then clicking Edit.
4. In the Group Policy Object Editor dialog box, expand either *User Configuration\Windows Settings\Security Settings\Public Key Policies* or *Computer Configuration\Windows Settings\Security Settings\Public Key Policies* as appropriate for the type of policy you want to review.
5. Double-click Autoenrollment Settings to display the properties dialog box shown in Figure 11-43.

6. By default, once you've configured enterprise CAs, Enroll Certificates Automatically is selected.
7. If you want to automatically renew expired certificates, update pending certificates, and remove revoked certificates, select the related checkbox.
8. To ensure version 2 certificate templates are requested and used, you can select the Update Certificates That Use Certificate Templates checkbox.
9. Click OK.

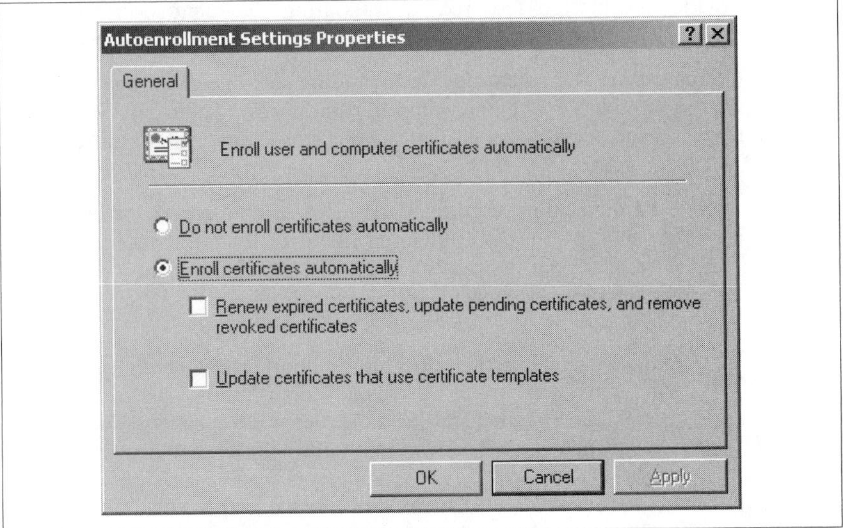

Figure 11-43. Viewing autoenrollment settings.

Configuring computer and user scripts by using Group Policy

With Group Policy, you can configure computers scripts that are executed during startup or shutdown, and user scripts that are executed during logon or logoff. These scripts can be written as command-shell batch scripts ending with the *.bat* or *.cmd* extension, or as Windows Script Host scripts written in a scripting language, such as VBScript.

With computer startup and shutdown scripts, you assign scripts to the GPO in which computer objects that should execute the scripts are located. To get started, you should copy the scripts you want to use to the *Machine\Scripts\Startup* or *Machine\Scripts\Shutdown* folder for the related policy. Policies are stored in the *%SystemRoot%\Sysvol\Domain\Policies* folder on domain controllers.

You can assign a computer startup or shutdown script to use by completing the following steps:

1. Open Active Directory Users and Computers.
2. In the console tree, right-click the domain or OU you want to work with, and then select Properties. In the Properties dialog box, click the Group Policy tab.

3. On the Group Policy tab, you can edit an existing GPO linked to the selected container by selecting it, and then clicking Edit.
4. In the Group Policy Object Editor dialog box, expand *Computer Configuration\Windows Settings\Scripts*.
5. To work with startup scripts, right-click Startup, and then select Properties.
6. To work with shutdown scripts, right-click Shutdown, and then select Properties.
7. Click Add to assign a script.
8. In the Add A Script dialog box, click Browse. If you copied the computer script to the correct location in the policies folder, you should see the script in the default folder.
9. Click the script, and then click Open. In the Script Parameters field, enter any command-line arguments to pass to the script.
10. Click OK to close the Add A Script dialog box.
11. During startup or shutdown, scripts are executed in the order in which they're listed in the properties dialog box. Use the Up or Down button to reposition scripts as necessary.
12. Click OK to close the Startup or Shutdown Properties dialog box.

With user logon scripts, you assign scripts to the GPO in which user objects that should execute the scripts are located. To get started, you should copy the scripts you want to use to the *User\Scripts\Logon* or the *User\Scripts\Logoff* folder for the related policy. Policies are stored in the *%System-Root%\Sysvol\Domain\Policies* folder on domain controllers.

You can assign a user logon or logoff script to use by completing the following steps:

1. Open Active Directory Users and Computers.
2. In the console tree, right-click the domain or OU you want to work with, and then select Properties. In the Properties dialog box, click the Group Policy tab.
3. On the Group Policy tab, you can edit an existing GPO linked to the selected container by selecting it, and then clicking Edit.
4. In the Group Policy Object Editor dialog box, expand *User Configuration\Windows Settings\Scripts*.
5. To work with logon scripts, right-click Logon, and then select Properties.
6. To work with logoff scripts, right-click Logoff, and then select Properties.
7. Click Add to assign a script.
8. In the Add A Script dialog box, click Browse. If you copied the user script to the correct location in the policies folder, you should see the script in the default folder.
9. Click the script, and then click Open. In the Script Parameters field, enter any command-line arguments to pass to the script.
10. Click OK to close the Add A Script dialog box.

11. During logon or logoff, scripts are executed in the order in which they're listed in the properties dialog box. Use the Up or Down button to reposition scripts as necessary.
12. Click OK to close the Logon or Logoff Properties dialog box.

Redirecting folders by using Group Policy

Folder redirection allows you to redirect special folders to a central network location instead of using default locations on a user's computer. This ensures that administrators have a central location for backing up and maintaining user data. It also ensures that users have consistent access to their data regardless of where they log on.

When you redirect the following special folders:

- Application Data
- Desktop
- My Documents
- My Pictures

a copy of the user's current special folder is made in the designated location, and from then on, the special folder is accessed from the designated location. When configuring redirection, you have two options:

- Redirect a special folder to the same network location for all users.
- Redirect a special folder based on a user's security group membership.

The network location to which you redirect folders must be configured as a shared folder. By default, folder redirection settings configure permissions on the redirected folder so that users have exclusive access to their folders (in most cases). The key exception is for Start Menu redirection, which works differently from redirection of other folders. Start Menu redirection does not copy the contents of a user's local Start Menu. Instead, users are redirected to a previously created, standard Start Menu.

You can redirect a special folder to a single location by completing the following steps:

1. Open Active Directory Users and Computers.
2. In the console tree, right-click the domain or OU you want to work with, and then select Properties. In the Properties dialog box, click the Group Policy tab.
3. On the Group Policy tab, you can edit an existing GPO linked to the selected container by selecting it, and then clicking Edit.
4. In the Group Policy Object Editor dialog box, expand *User Configuration node\Windows Settings\Folder Redirection*.
5. Right-click the special folder you want to redirect, and then select Properties.
6. In the properties dialog box, similar to the one shown in Figure 11-44, the Target tab is selected by default.

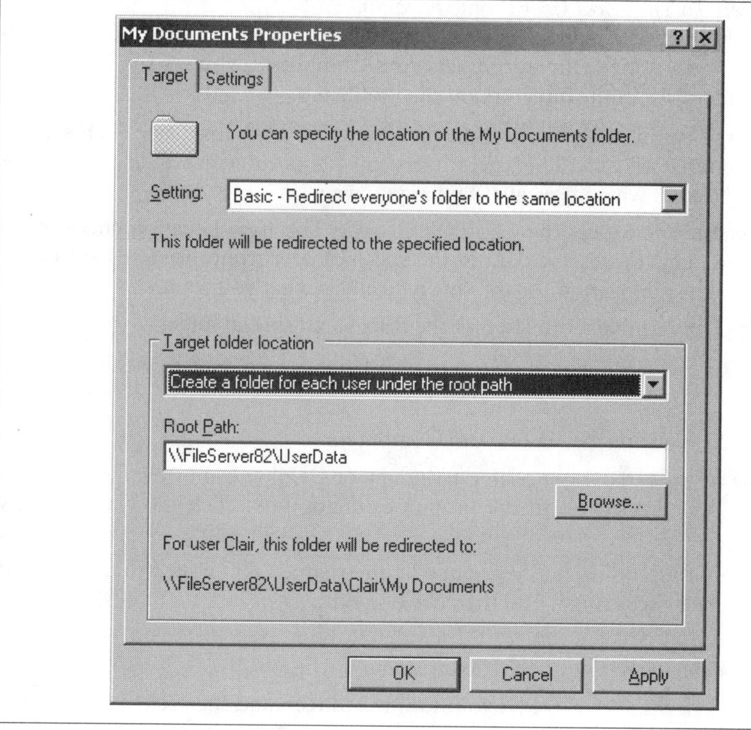

Figure 11-44. Configuring basic folder redirection.

7. Choose Basic-Redirect Everyone's Folder To The Same Location on the Setting selection list.
8. Use the Target Folder Location list options to specify how redirection should work. The options include:

   Redirect To The User's Home Directory
   : The folder is redirected to a subdirectory within the user's home directory. In Active Directory Users And Computers, you set the location of the user's home directory on the Profile tab.

   Create A Folder For Each User Under The Root Path
   : A folder is created for each user at the location you enter in the Root Path field. The folder name is the user logon name as specified by the `%UserName%` environment variable.

   Redirect To The Following Location
   : The folder is redirected to the exact location you enter in the Root Path field. Be sure to use an environment variable to customize the folder location for each user, such as *\\FileServer82\UserData\%UserName%\mydocs*.

Exam 70-294 Study Guide

Redirect To The Local User Profile Location

The folder is redirected to a subdirectory within the user profile directory. In Active Directory Users And Computers, you set the location of the user's profile directory on the Profile tab.

9. Click the Settings tab. By default, the Grant The User Exclusive Rights To... checkbox is selected. This gives users full rights to access their data in the special folder, which typically is what you want.
10. By default, the Move The Contents Of...To The New Location checkbox is selected. This moves the data in the special folder from the user's system to the designated location. Again, this typically is what you want.
11. Click OK to enable redirection of the designated special folder.

Redirect a special folder based on group membership by completing the following steps:

1. Open Active Directory Users And Computers.
2. In the console tree, right-click the domain or OU you want to work with, and then select Properties. In the Properties dialog box, click the Group Policy tab.
3. On the Group Policy tab, you can edit an existing GPO linked to the selected container by selecting it and then clicking Edit.
4. In the Group Policy Object Editor dialog box, expand *User Configuration node\Windows Settings\Folder Redirection.*
5. Right-click the special folder you want to redirect, and then select Properties.
6. In the properties dialog box, the Target tab is selected by default.
7. Choose Advanced – Specify Locations For Various User Groups on the Setting selection list.
8. As shown in Figure 11-45, a Security Group Membership panel is added to the properties dialog box. You configure redirection separately for each security group.
9. Click Add to specify the redirection settings for the first security group. In the Specify Group And Location dialog box, shown in Figure 11-46, click Browse. Use the Select Group dialog box to find a security group to add.
10. Configure the Target Folder Location list options as discussed previously.
11. Set a Root Path as necessary for the type of redirection.
12. Click OK to close the Specify Group And Location dialog box.
13. Repeat Steps 9–12 as necessary to configure redirection for other security groups.
14. Click the Settings tab. By default, the Grant The User Exclusive Rights To... checkbox is selected. This gives users full rights to access their data in the special folder, which typically is what you want.
15. By default, the Move The Contents Of...To The New Location checkbox is selected. This moves the data in the special folder from the user's system to the designated location. Again, this typically is what you want.
16. Click OK to enable redirection of the designated special folder.

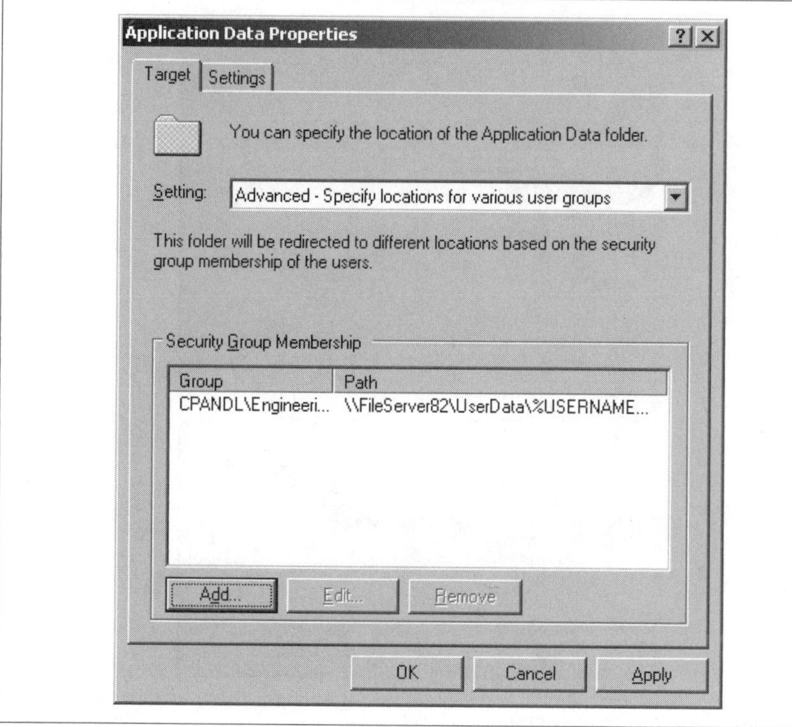

Figure 11-45. Configuring advanced folder redirection.

Exam 70-294 Study Guide

If you need to remove redirection, you can do so by completing the following steps:

1. Open Active Directory Users And Computers.
2. In the console tree, right-click the domain or OU you want to work with, and then select Properties. In the Properties dialog box, click the Group Policy tab.
3. On the Group Policy tab, you can edit an existing GPO linked to the selected container by selecting it, and then clicking Edit.
4. In the Group Policy Object Editor dialog box, expand *User Configuration node\Windows Settings\Folder Redirection*.
5. Right-click the special folder you want to redirect, and then select Properties.
6. In the properties dialog box, the Target tab is selected by default.
7. On the Settings tab, review the Policy Removal options. Two options are available:

   Leave The Folder In The New Location When Policy Is Removed
   : The folder and its contents remain at the redirected location and current users are still permitted to access the folder and its contents at this location.

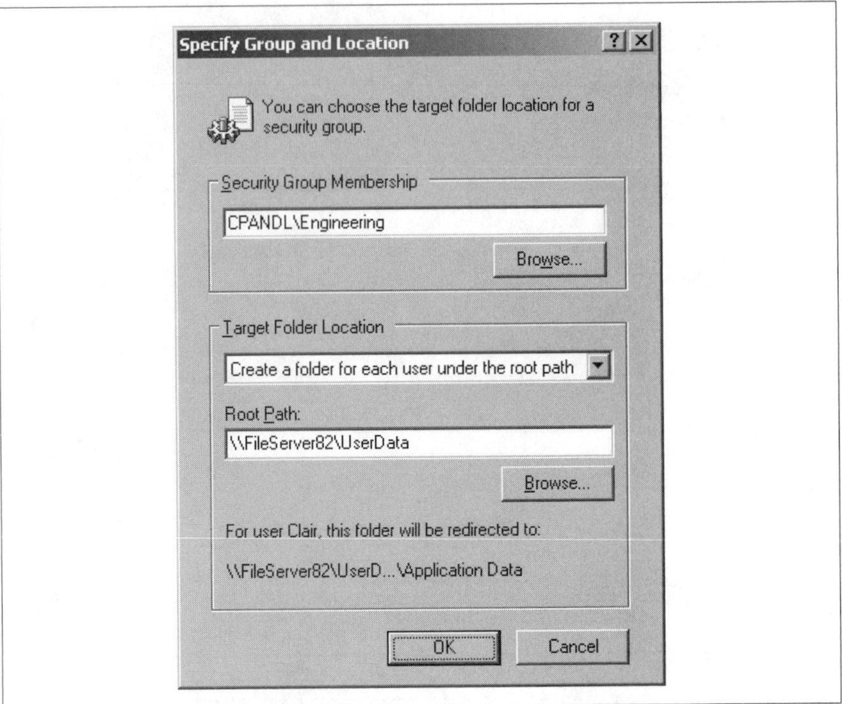

Figure 11-46. Setting a security group's redirection options.

Redirect The Folder Back To The Local Userprofile Location When Policy Is Removed
: The folder and its contents are copied back to the original location. The contents aren't deleted from the previous location, however.

8. If you changed the Policy Removal options, click Apply.
9. Select the Target tab.
10. To remove all redirection definitions for the special folder, use the Setting selection list to choose Not Configured.
11. To remove redirection for a particular security group, select the security group in the Security Group Membership panel, and then click Remove.
12. Click OK.

Distributing software by using Group Policy

Group Policy provides a limited solution for deploying software called Software Installation policy. Software Installation policy is not designed to replace enterprise solutions, such as Systems Management Server (SMS), but it can be used to automate the deployment and maintenance of software. Only computers running Windows 2000 and Windows XP Professional or later can use Software Installation policy. Server versions of Windows don't use it.

Understanding software deployment. Software deployed through Group Policy is referred to as managed software. In Group Policy, Software Installation policy can be configured through *Computer Configuration\Software Settings\Software Installation* and *User Configuration\Software Settings\Software Installation*. This allows you to deploy software on a per-computer basis, a per-user basis, or both. Per-computer applications are available to all users of a computer. Per-user applications are available to individual users.

Non-Windows Installer files can only be installed on a per-user basis.

Before you deploy software through policy, you should set up a distribution point. A *distribution point* is a shared folder that is available to the computers, users, or both to which you are deploying software. With basic applications, copy the installer package file and all required application files to the share and configure permissions so these files can be accessed. With other applications, such as Microsoft Office, perform administrative installations to the share by running the application's Setup program with the `/a` parameter and designate the share as the install location. Administrative installs can be patched and redeployed through Software Installation policy.

In most cases, when you configure Software Installation policy, you will not want to use existing GPOs. Instead, you will want to create GPOs that configure software installation, and then link these GPOs to the appropriate containers in Group Policy. This makes it must easier to redeploy software and apply patches.

You can deploy software in three key ways:

Computer assignment
: You can assign the software to client computers so it is installed when a client computer starts. This technique requires no user intervention, but does require a restart to install software. Installed software is available to all users on a computer. (Not available with Non-Windows Installer files.)

User assignment
: You can assign the software to users so it is installed when a user logs on. This technique requires no user intervention, but does require the user to log on to install or advertise software. The software is associated with the user only. (Not available with Non-Windows Installer files.)

User publishing
: You can publish the application so users can install it manually through Add Or Remove Programs. This technique requires the user to explicitly install software or activate the install. The software is associated with the user only.

When you use user assignment or user publishing, you can advertise the software so a computer can install the software when it is first used. With advertisements, the software can be installed automatically in several situations: when the user accesses a document that requires the software; when a user opens a shortcut to the application; or when another application requires a component of the software.

You can update applications deployed through Software Installation policy in two key ways:

- By using a patch or service pack
- By deploying a new version of the application

Each task is performed in a slightly different way.

Deploying software. Software Installation policy uses either Windows Installer Packages (*.msi*) or ZAW Down-level Application Packages (*.zap*) files. File permissions on these application installer packages must be set so the appropriate computer accounts, the appropriate user accounts, or both, have Read access.

Software Installation policy is applied only during foreground processing of policy settings. This means per-computer application deployments are processed at startup and per-user application deployments are processed at logon.

You can customize installation using transform (*.mst*) files. Transform files modify the installation process according to the settings you've defined, and in this way, allow you to configure applications for various types of computers and users.

Once you have your Windows Installer file and have copied all the necessary files to a network share, you can configure software installation through Group Policy by completing the following steps:

1. Open Active Directory Users And Computers.
2. In the console tree, right-click the domain or OU you want to work with, and then select Properties. In the Properties dialog box, click the Group Policy tab.
3. On the Group Policy tab, you can edit an existing GPO linked to the selected container by selecting it and then clicking Edit.
4. For a per-computer software deployment, access *Computer Configuration\Software Settings\Software Installation*. For a per-user software deployment, access *User Configuration\Software Settings\Software Installation*.
5. Right-click Software Installation and choose New → Package.
6. In the Open dialog box, type the path to the network share where your package is located or navigate to the package and select it.
7. Click Open.
8. In the Deploy Software dialog box, shown in Figure 11-47, select one of the following deployment methods, and then click OK:
    - Published to publish the application without modifications
    - Assigned to assign the application without modifications
    - Advanced to deploy the application using advanced configuration options

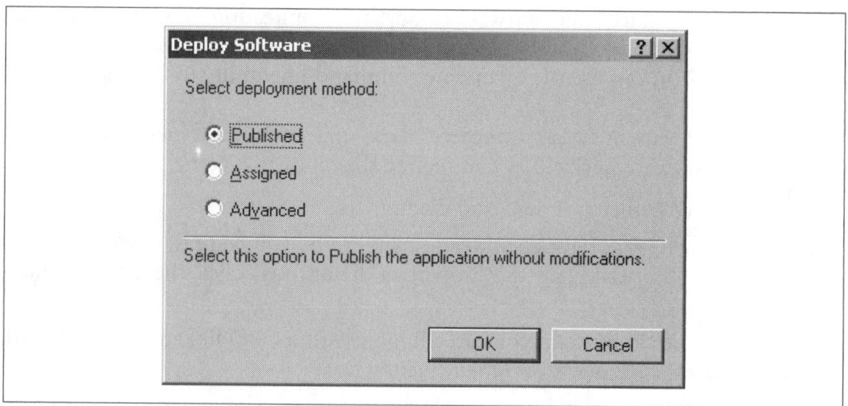

Figure 11-47. Choosing the type of deployment.

Once you've configured the software policy, the application will be deployed to all computers or users as appropriate. By default, per-computer software packages are made available when a computer starts up, and per-user software packages are made available when a user logs on. You can use the Gpupdate command-line utility to force restart or logoff.

Once you have your ZAP file and have copied all the necessary files to a network share, you can configure software installation through Group Policy by completing the following steps:

1. Open Active Directory Users And Computers.
2. In the console tree, right-click the domain or OU you want to work with, and then select Properties. In the Properties dialog box, click the Group Policy tab.
3. On the Group Policy tab, you can edit an existing GPO linked to the selected container by selecting it, and then clicking Edit.
4. Non–Windows Installer files can be installed only on a per-user basis. Access Software Installation under *User Configuration\Software Settings\Software Installation*.
5. Right-click Software Installation and choose New → Package.
6. In the Open dialog box, type the path to the network share where your package is located or navigate to the package and select it.
7. In the Files of Type list, select ZAW Down-Level Applications Packages (**.zap*) as the file type.
8. Click Open.
9. In the Deploy Software dialog box, select one of the following deployment methods, and then click OK:
   - Published to publish the application without modifications
   - Advanced to deploy the application using advanced configuration options

Once you've configured the software policy, the application is advertised to all users as appropriate. By default, per-use software packages are applied only when a user logs on. You can use the Gpupdate command-line utility to force logoff.

Viewing and setting software deployment options. You can view and set the general options for a software package by completing the following steps:

1. Open Active Directory Users And Computers.
2. In the console tree, right-click the domain or OU you want to work with, and then select Properties. In the Properties dialog box, click the Group Policy tab.
3. On the Group Policy tab, you can edit an existing GPO linked to the selected container by selecting it, and then clicking Edit.
4. For a per-computer software deployment, access *Computer Configuration\Software Settings\Software Installation*. For a per-user software deployment, access *User Configuration\Software Settings\Software Installation*.
5. Right-click the package you want to work with and select Properties.
6. Using the properties dialog box, you can now review or modify software deployment options (see Figure 11-48).

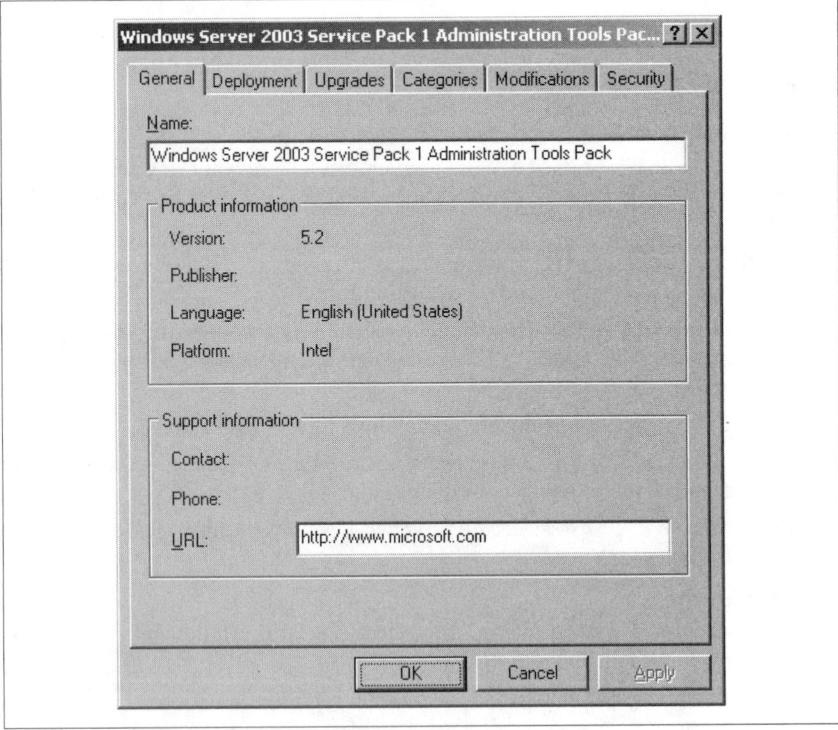

Figure 11-48. Viewing the configured software deployment options.

7. On the Deployment tab, shown in Figure 11-49, you can change the deployment type and configure the following deployment and installation options:

   Auto-Install This Application By File Extension Activation
   : Advertises any file extensions associated with this package for install-on-first-use deployment. This option is selected by default.

   Uninstall This Application When It Falls Out Of The Scope Of Management
   : Removes the application if it no longer applies to the user.

   Do Not Display This Package In The Add/Remove Programs Control Panel
   : Prevents the application from appearing in Add/Remove Programs, which prevents a user from uninstalling an application.

   Install This Application At Logon
   : Configures full installation, rather than advertisement, of an application when the user logs on. This option cannot be set when you publish a package for users.

   Installation User Interface Options
   : The default setting, Maximum, ensures that the user sees all setup screens and messages during installation. With the Basic option, the user sees only error and completion messages during installation.

8. Click OK.

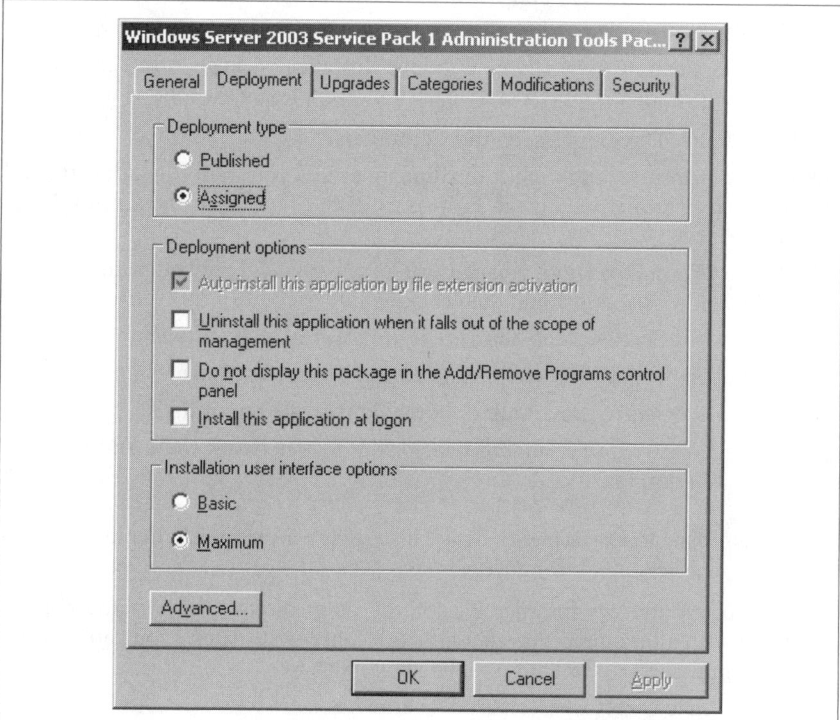

Figure 11-49. Changing deployment options.

Applying patches and service packs to deployed software. When an application uses a Windows Installer package, you can patch a deployed application or apply a service pack by completing the following steps:

1. Obtain an *.msi* file or *.msp* (patch) file containing the patch or service pack to be applied.
2. Copy the *.msi* or *.msp* file and any new installation files to the folder containing the original *.msi* file. Overwrite any duplicate files as necessary.
3. Open Active Directory Users And Computers.
4. In the console tree, right-click the domain or OU you want to work with, and then select Properties. In the Properties dialog box, click the Group Policy tab.
5. On the Group Policy tab, you can edit an existing GPO linked to the selected container by selecting it, and then clicking Edit.
6. For a per-computer software deployment, access *Computer Configuration\Software Settings\Software Installation*. For a per-user software deployment, access *User Configuration\Software Settings\Software Installation*.
7. Right-click the package you want to work with, and then select All Tasks → Redeploy Application.
8. When prompted to confirm the action, click Yes. The application is then redeployed to all users and computers as appropriate for the GPO you are working with.

When an application uses a Non-Windows Installer package, you can patch a deployed application or apply a service pack by completing the following steps:

1. Open Active Directory Users And Computers.
2. In the console tree, right-click the domain or OU you want to work with, and then select Properties. In the Properties dialog box, click the Group Policy tab.
3. On the Group Policy tab, you can edit an existing GPO linked to the selected container by selecting it and then clicking Edit.
4. Access *User Configuration\Software Settings\Software Installation*.
5. Right-click the package, and then select All Tasks → Remove.
6. Click OK to accept the default option of immediate removal.
7. Copy the new *.zap* file and all related files to a network share and redeploy the application.

Upgrading previously deployed software. You can upgrade a previously deployed application to a new version by completing these steps:

1. Obtain a Windows Installer file for the new software version and copy it along with all required files to a network share. Alternately, you can perform an administrative installation to the network share.
2. Open Active Directory Users And Computers.

3. In the console tree, right-click the domain or OU you want to work with, and then select Properties. In the Properties dialog box, click the Group Policy tab.
4. On the Group Policy tab, you can edit an existing GPO linked to the selected container by selecting it, and then clicking Edit.
5. For a per-computer software deployment, access *Computer Configuration\Software Settings\Software Installation*. For a per-user software deployment, access *User Configuration\Software Settings\Software Installation*.
6. Right-click Software Installation and choose New → Package. Create an assigned or published application using the Windows Installer file for the new software version.
7. After you've created the software installation policy for the upgrade, right-click the upgrade package, and then select Properties.
8. Click Add on the Upgrades tab.
9. Establish an upgrade relationship between the current application and the previously deployed application. You have two choices:
   - If both applications are in the current GPO, you'll be able to select the previously deployed application in the Package To Upgrade list.
   - If you want to establish a relationship with a package in a different GPO, select A Specific GPO, click Browse, and then use the Browse For A Group Policy Object dialog box to select the GPO. Then select the previously deployed application in the Package To Upgrade list.
10. Choose an upgrade option:

    Uninstall The Existing Package, Then Install The Upgrade Package
    This option completely reinstalls the application with the new version.

    Package Can Upgrade Over The Existing Package
    This option performs an in-place upgrade over the existing installation.
11. Click OK to close the Add Upgrade Package dialog box.
12. If you want to make this a required upgrade, select the Required Upgrade For Existing Packages checkbox.
13. Click OK.

Configuring automatic updates for network clients by using Group Policy

Computers running Windows 2000 or later can use Automatic Updates to maintain the operating system. Automatic Updates is an automatic distribution and installation mechanism for critical updates, security updates, update rollups, and service packs. Policy settings for Automatic Updates are found under *Computer Configuration\Administrative Templates\Windows Components\Windows Update* and under *User Configuration\Administrative Templates\Windows Components\Windows Update*.

Using Group Policy to manage Automatic Updates allows you to configure settings for all computers that apply a particular GPO or all users that apply a particular GPO. This allows you to have a standard Automatic Updates configuration for all computers and users in a site, domain, or OU.

To specify how Automatic Updates works for computers, follow these steps:

1. Open Active Directory Users And Computers.
2. In the console tree, right-click the domain or OU you want to work with, and then select Properties. In the Properties dialog box, click the Group Policy tab.
3. On the Group Policy tab, you can edit an existing GPO linked to the selected container by selecting it, and then clicking Edit.
4. In the Group Policy Object Editor dialog box, expand *Computer Configuration\Administrative Templates\Windows Components\Windows Update*.
5. Double-click Configure Automatic Updates.
6. Use the Disabled or Enabled settings to either prevent or allow the use of Automatic Updates for the computers affected by the current GPO.
7. If you enable Automatic Updates, you have additional configuration options, as shown in Figure 11-50. The options are used as follows:

   2 - Notify For Download And Notify For Install
   : Windows notifies the current user before retrieving any updates and then notifies the user again prior to installing.

   3 - Auto Download And Notify For Install
   : Windows automatically retrieves all updates according to the detection frequency and notifies users to install.

   4 - Auto Download And Schedule For Install
   : Windows automatically downloads updates according to the detection frequency and schedules the installation according to a specific schedule.

   5 - Allow Local Admin To Choose Setting
   : This option allows the local administrators to configure Automatic Updates using the Automatic Updates tab of the System utility. Local administrators are unable, however, to disable Automatic Updates through the System utility.

8. Set a schedule as necessary.
9. Click OK.

Most Automatic Updates are installed only when the system is shut down and restarted. However, some Automatic Updates can be installed immediately without interrupting system services or requiring system restart. To ensure the latter type of updates are immediately installed, complete the following steps:

1. Open Active Directory Users And Computers.
2. In the console tree, right-click the domain or OU you want to work with, and then select Properties. In the Properties dialog box, click the Group Policy tab.
3. On the Group Policy tab, you can edit an existing GPO linked to the selected container by selecting it, and then clicking Edit.
4. In the Group Policy Object Editor dialog box, expand *Computer Configuration\Administrative Templates\Windows Components\Windows Update*.
5. Double-click Allow Automatic Updates Immediate Installation.
6. Select Enabled, and then click OK.

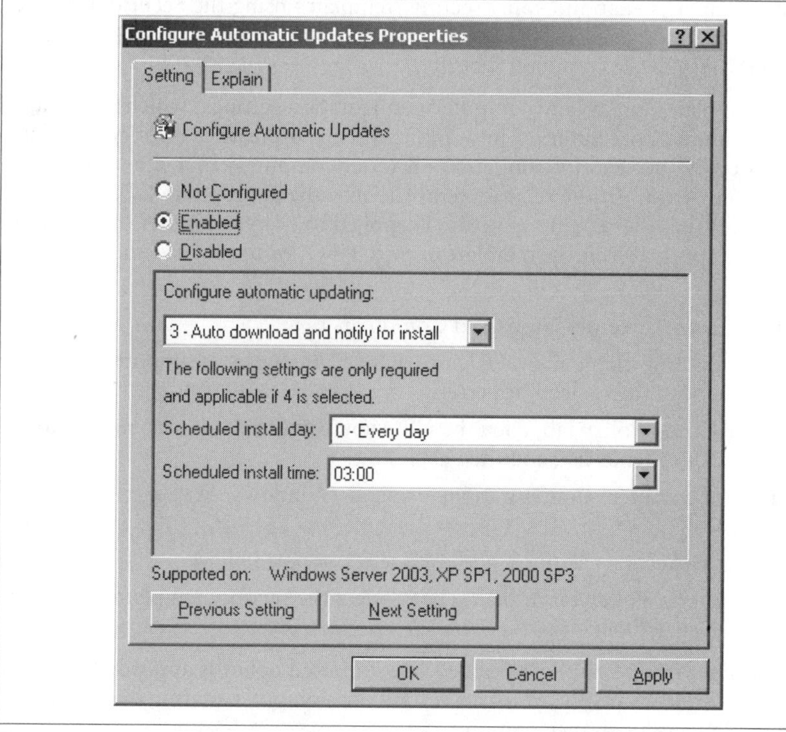

Figure 11-50. Configuring Automatic Updates through Group Policy.

By default, only users with local administrator privileges receive update notification. You can allow any user logged on to a computer to receive update notifications by completing the steps:

1. Open Active Directory Users and Computers.
2. In the console tree, right-click the domain or OU you want to work with, and then select Properties. In the Properties dialog box, click the Group Policy tab.
3. On the Group Policy tab, you can edit an existing GPO linked to the selected container by selecting it, and then clicking Edit.
4. In the Group Policy Object Editor dialog box, expand *Computer Configuration\Administrative Templates\Windows Components\Windows Update.*
5. Double-click Allow Non-Administrators To Receive Update Notifications.
6. Select Enabled, and then click OK.

Configuring Computer Security Settings Using Group Policy

As discussed in the section of Chapter 5 titled, "Implementing Secure Network Administration Procedures," security templates can be used to configure computer security settings. Create and configure security templates using the

Security Templates snap-in. Apply security templates using the Security Configuration And Analysis snap-in. The Security Configuration And Analysis snap-in can also be used to analyze computer security.

Security templates affect only computer configuration settings, which are located under Computer Configuration in a GPO. After you create a security template, you can deploy the security configuration to all computers in a site, domain, or OU. To do this, import the security template into the appropriate GPO, which is what ensures that the security template is applied to every computer object in the GPO. To import a security template into a GPO, you can use the following technique:

1. Open Active Directory Users And Computers.
2. Right-click the domain or OU into which you want to import a security template, and then select Properties.
3. On the Group Policy tab, click the GPO you want to work with in the Group Policy Object Links list, and then click Edit.
4. Under Computer Configuration, expand Windows Settings → Security Settings.
5. Right-click Security Settings, and then select Import Policy.
6. In the Import Policy From dialog box, select the security template to import, and then click Open.

The next time Group Policy is refreshed, the imported policy is applied. To force a computer to refresh policy, you can restart the computer or run the Gpupdate command-line utility on the computer.

To prepare for Exam 70-294, you should review the section of Chapter 5 titled, "Implementing Secure Network Administration Procedures."

Troubleshooting Group Policy and Group Policy Objects

Many problems with Group Policy are due to the way policy is inherited and processed. As discussed previously, in "Managing Policy Inheritance and Processing," administrators can use a variety of techniques to modify the way inheritance works and policy is processed, which can lead to unanticipated results when Group Policy is applied.

Troubleshooting the application of Group Policy security settings

When you are trying to determine why policy is not being applied as expected, one of the first things you should do is examine the Resultant Set of Policy for the user, computer, or both experiencing problems with policy settings. In the Resultant Set Of Policy snap-in, you can determine the GPO from which a setting is applied for the purposes of troubleshooting using Logging Mode. To determine applicable GPOs and last refresh, you can run the Resultant Set Of Policy Wizard by following these steps:

1. Type `mmc` at a command prompt.
2. Click File → Add/Remove Snap-in.
3. Click Add. Click Resultant Set Of Policy, and then click Add.
4. Click Close, and then click OK.
5. In the Resultant Set Of Policy snap-in, right-click the Resultant Set Of Policy node, and then select Generate RSoP Data. Click Next. Select Logging Mode, and then click Next.
6. On the Computer Selection page, shown in Figure 11-51, select This Computer to view information for the local computer. To view information for a remote computer, select Another Computer, and then click Browse. In the Select Computer dialog box, type the name of the computer, and then click Check Names. Once the correct computer account is selected, click OK.

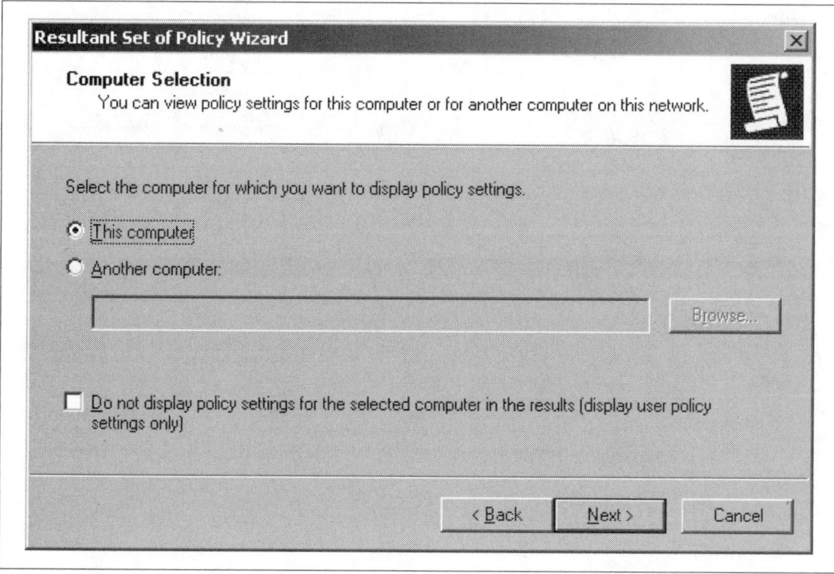

Figure 11-51. Select the computer to review.

7. On the User Selection page, shown in Figure 11-52, select the user whose policy information you want to view. You can view policy information for any user that has logged on to the computer. Click Next.
8. Click Next. The wizard gathers policy information. Click Finish.
9. When the wizard finishes generating the report, expand the report nodes in the left pane to see results in the right pane.
10. Computer and user policy information is listed separately. Computer policy information is listed under Computer Configuration. User policy information is listed under User Configuration Summary.
11. You can determine the settings being applied by browsing the report (see Figure 11-53).

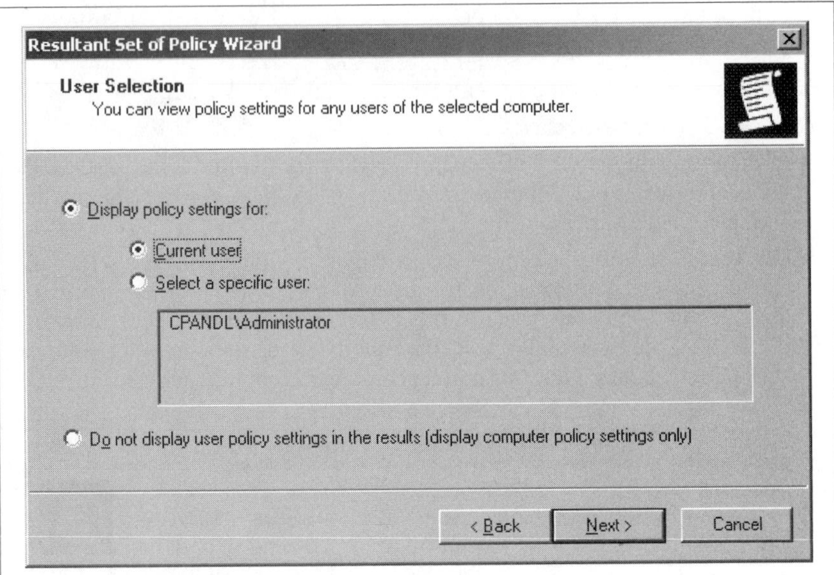

Figure 11-52. Select the user to review.

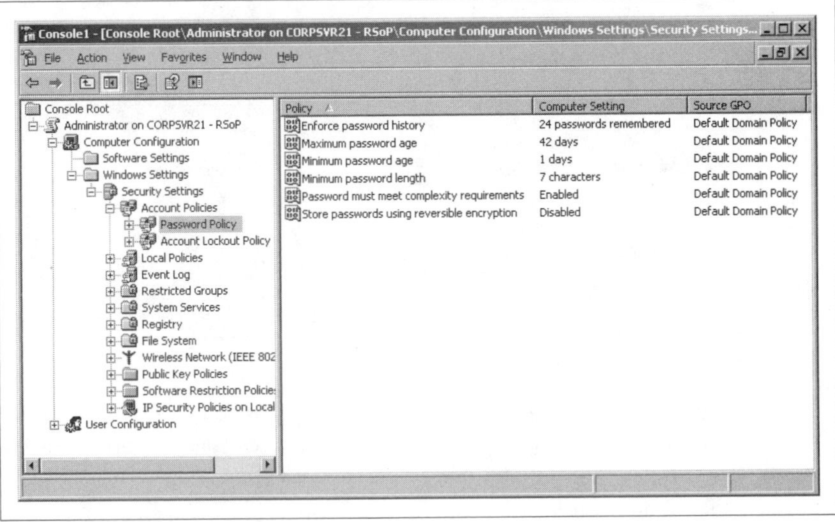

Figure 11-53. Viewing resultant set of policy.

If you add the Resultant Set Of Policy snap-in to a new console and run the Resultant Set Of Policy Wizard again in planning mode to view how settings should be applied based on the container in which a user, computer, or both are located. You can compare the settings between the planning and logging mode to see whether there are discrepancies between how you think policy is being applied and how it is actually being applied.

Using the Gpresult command-line utility, you can view resultant set of policy as well. Gpresult provides details on:

- The last time Group Policy was applied
- The domain controller from which the policy was applied
- The complete list of applied GPOs
- The complete list of GPOs not applied due to filters
- The security group memberships for the computer and user
- Details on special settings applied for folder redirection, software installation, disk quota, IPSec, and scripts

The basic syntax for Gpresult is:

```
gpresult /s ComputerName /user Domain\UserName
```

where *ComputerName* is the name of the remote computer for which you want to log policy results and *Domain\UserName* indicates the remote user for which you want to log policy results. For example, to view the RSoP for techpc34 and the user wrstanek in the CPANDL domain, you would type the following command:

```
gpresult /s techpc34 /user cpandl\wrstanek
```

You can view more detailed output using one of the two verbose options:

- `/v` turns on verbose output and result are displayed for policy settings in effect only.
- `/z` turns on verbose output with settings for policy settings in effect and all other GPOs that have the policy set.

Because Gpresult output can be fairly long, you should direct the output to a file, as shown in this example:

```
gpresult /s techpc34 /user cpandl\wrstanek /z > rsopsave.log
```

Restoring the Default Domain Policy and Default Domain Controller Policy GPOs

If the Default Domain Policy or Default Domain Controller Policy GPO becomes corrupted, Group Policy does not function properly. You can resolve this problem by using Dcgpofix to restore the default GPOs to their original, default state. Only Domain Admins or Enterprise Admins can run Dcgpofix.

By default, Dcgpofix restores both the Default Domain Policy and Default Domain Controller Policy GPOs. This means you will lose most changes made to these GPOs as a result of the restore process.

The only exceptions are for Remote Installation Services (RIS), Security Settings, and Encrypting File System (EFS), which are maintained separately and not affected by the restore operation. Nondefault Security Settings are not maintained, however, such as security settings configured by Microsoft Exchange, security settings configured as a result of a migration from Windows NT to Windows 2000, and security settings configured through Systems Management Server (SMS).

To restore the Default Domain Policy and Default Domain Controller Policy GPOs, follow these steps:

1. Log on to a domain controller in the domain in which you want to fix default Group Policy.
2. Type `dcgpofix` at the command prompt.

You can also restore only the Default Domain Policy or the Default Domain Controller Policy GPO. To restore only the Default Domain Policy, type `dcgpofix /target: domain`. To restore only the Default Domain Controller Policy, type `dcgpofix /target: dc`.

Refreshing Group Policy manually

Group Policy is refreshed automatically at a specific interval. On domain controllers, Group Policy is refreshed every five minutes by default. On member servers and workstations, Group Policy is refreshed every 90 to 120 minutes by default. You can refresh Group Policy manually using Gpupdate. Gpupdate replaces the SECEDIT /refreshpolicy tool provided in Windows 2000.

You can refresh both the Computer Configuration settings and the User Configuration settings in Group Policy on the local computer by typing `gpupdate` at a command prompt. By default, only policy settings that have changed are processed and applied. You can change this behavior by adding the `/Force` parameter. This forces a refresh of all policy settings.

Another way to use Gpupdate is to selectively refresh Group Policy:

- To refresh only Computer Configuration settings, type `gpupdate/target:computer` at the command prompt.
- To refresh only User Configuration settings, type `gpupdate /target:user` at the command prompt.

Gpupdate can also be used to log off a user or restart a computer after Group Policy is refreshed. This is useful because some group policies are applied only when a user logs on or when a computer starts up. To log off a user after a refresh, add the `/Logoff` parameter. To restart a computer after a refresh, add the `/Boot` parameter.

Troubleshooting GPOs and the Sysvol

The Windows Server 2003 Resource Kit includes a Group Policy verification tool called Gpotool. You can use it to troubleshooting problems with the server-side health of Group Policy. By default, if you type `gpotool` at a command prompt, Gpotool verifies the consistency, permissions and version numbers of all GPOs in the current logon domain. If any problems are found, a verbose listing of the GPO in question is provided, along with the specific issues and errors. Discrepancies found may be due to problems with File Replication Service (FRS), which is responsible for replicating the Sysvol files on domain controllers.

You can use Gpotool to check permissions on the Sysvol using the `/checkacl` option, such as:

```
gpotool /checkacl
```

Gpotool doesn't check permissions on subfolders within the Sysvol. Gpotool checks only the permissions on the Sysvol folder itself.

You can use Gpotool to check the state of a GPO on specified domain controllers. This is useful for determining the status of a GPO stored on particular domain controllers.

The syntax for checking the state of a GPO on specified domain controllers follows:

```
gpotool /gpo:"GPOName" /domain:DomainName /dc:DomainControllers /verbose
```

where *GPOName* is the name of the GPO to check, *DomainName* is the name of the domain, and *DomainControllers* is a comma-separated lists of DCs to check, such as:

```
gpotool /gpo:"Default Domain Policy" /domain:cpandl.com
/dc:corpsvr01,corpsvr02 /verbose
```

If the GPOs are found to have no problems, an OK status is returned. If there are problems, the results show the errors or discrepancies.

12

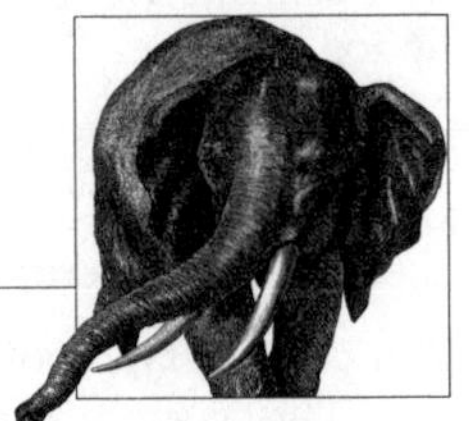

Exam 70-294 Prep and Practice

The material in this chapter is designed to help you prepare and practice for *Exam 70-294: Planning, Implementing, and Maintaining a Microsoft Windows Server 2003 Active Directory Infrastructure*. The chapter is organized into four sections:

Preparing for Exam 70-294
: This section provides an overview of the types of questions on the exam. Reviewing this section will help you understand how the actual exam works.

Exam 70-294 Suggested Exercises
: This section provides a numbered list of exercises that you can follow to gain experience in the exam's subject areas. Performing the exercises in this section will help ensure that you have hands-on experience with all areas of the exam.

Exam 70-294 Highlighters Index
: This section provides a compilation of the facts within the exam's subject areas that you are most likely to need another look at—in other words, the areas of study that you might have highlighted while reading the Study Guide. Studying the highlights is useful as a final review before the exam.

Exam 70-294 Practice Questions
: This section provides a comprehensive set of practice questions to assess your knowledge of the exam. The questions are similar in format to the exam. After you've reviewed the Study Guide, performed the Suggested Exercises, and studied the Highlighters Index, read the questions and see whether you can answer them correctly.

Before you take Exam 70-294, review the exam overview, perform the suggested exercises, and go through the practice questions provided. Many online sites provide practice tests for the exam. Duplicating the depth and scope of these practice exams in a printed book isn't possible. Visit Microsoft's Certification site for pointers to online practice tests (*http://www.microsoft.com/learning/mcpexams/prepare/practicetests.asp*).

Preparing for Exam 70-294

Exam 70-294 is a computer-generated exam. The exam is timed, and the amount of time remaining on the exam is displayed by an onscreen timer clock. Most questions on the exam are multiple choice. Multiple choice questions are either:

Multiple-choice, single answer
: A radio button allows you to select a single answer only.

Multiple-choice, multiple answer
: A checkbox allows you to select multiple answers. Usually the number of correct answers is indicated in the question itself.

Typically, the test environment will have Previous/Next and Mark For Review options. You can navigate through the test using the Previous/Next buttons. You can click the Mark For Review checkbox to flag a question for later review. At the bottom of the screen is a calculator button. You may need to use the calculator in scientific mode to calculate IP addresses, subnet masks, and subnet numbers.

Other formats for questions are used as well, including:

List prioritization
: Pick the choices that answer the question and arrange the list in a specified order. Lists initially appear on the right side, and you have to click << ADD to add them in the correct order to the list on the left side. For example, you might have to list the steps for changing an operations master role in priority order.

Hot area
: Indicate the correct answer by clicking one or more areas of the screen or dialog box provided with the question. For example, you might see a dialog box for a schema attribute and be asked to click the options that will ensure the attribute is replicated and indexed.

Select and Place
: Using drag-and-drop, pick answers from given set of choices and place them in an appropriate spot in a dialog box or diagram.

Active screen
: Use the dialog box provided to configure the options correctly or perform the required procedure. For example, you might see the New Object – Subnet dialog box and have to configure a new subnet for use with a particular site.

Simulation
: Use the simulated desktop environment provided to perform a specific task or troubleshoot. For example, you might be asked to create an organizational unit.

With the exception of multiple-choice, single-answer questions, all of the other questions can have multiple answers or multiple required procedures to obtain full credit. If all of the expected answers or procedures are not performed, you will only get partial credit for the answer.

While many of the questions on Exam 70-294 are multiple choice, others such as hot area, select and place, active screen, and simulation questions are being used increasingly to ensure that the testing process more accurately reflects actual hands-on knowledge rather than rote memorization. Individuals with adequate hands-on administration experience who have reviewed the study guide, performed the practice exercises, memorized the essentials, and taken practice tests should do well on this type of exam. Individuals who lack adequate hands-on experience and have not prepared appropriately will do poorly on this type of exam.

Exam 70-294 Suggested Exercises

Exam 70-294 expects you to know how to plan, implement, manage, and maintain Active Directory infrastructure for Windows Server 2003. You'll need plenty of hands-on previous experience to pass the exam. You'll need to review the study guide closely and review closely any areas with which you are unfamiliar. This section provides a numbered list of exercises that you can follow to gain experience in the exam's subject areas. Performing the exercises will be useful for help to ensure that you have hands-on experience with all areas of the exam.

For this exam, I recommend setting up a three-computer test network with two servers running Windows Server 2003 and one workstation running Windows XP Professional. One of your servers should be configured as a domain controller with DNS. The other should be configured as your DHCP server and as your Routing and Remote Access Server (RRAS). The workstation will need to be used in several roles. You'll need to configure it to be a member of the domain when you test TCP/IP, DHCP, and DNS client configurations. When you test RRAS, you'll want to configure the workstation as a RRAS client.

To help prepare for this exam, I recommend setting up a test environment that creates a forest root domain and a child domain with four servers running Windows Server 2003. In the forest root domain, install two domain controllers to handle the forest and parent domain roles. In a child domain, install two domain controllers to handle child domain roles. This configuration should help ensure that you can practice all the management and maintenance tasks measured by the exam.

In addition to performing the exercises below, you should also have experience using each of the Windows Server 2003 administrative tools described in the Study Guide.

Perform the exercises in this section in an isolated test environment. Do not perform these exercises on your organization's network.

Creating a Forest and Domain Plan

1. Create a plan for deploying a new forest using a dedicated root.
2. Create a plan for deploying a new forest using a nondedicated root.
3. Plan the placement of DNS servers.
4. Plan the placement of operations masters.
5. Plan the placement of global catalogs.
6. Plan the placement of bridgehead servers.

Installing an Active Directory Domain Controller

1. Prepare a test environment.
2. Install an Active Director domain controller in a new forest.
3. Add an additional domain controller to the forest.
4. Use DCPROMO /ADV promote a DC from backup.
5. Install a child domain in a new forest.
6. Install an additional domain controller to the child domain.
7. Demote one of the domain controllers in the child domain by uninstalling Active Directory.
8. Install an application data partition on one of the domain controllers.
9. Configure an application partition replica on another domain controller.
10. Remove the application partition replica.
11. Remove the application partition.

Setting Forest and Domain Functional Levels

1. View the current forest functional level.
2. Based on the server operating systems being used, determine whether you can raise the forest functional level.
3. View the current domain functional level.
4. Based on the server operating systems being used, determine whether you can raise the domain functional level.

Optimizing the Active Directory Infrastructure

1. Prepare a test environment.
2. Configure the UPN suffix for all users.
3. Update replication settings so the `wWWHomePage` attribute is replicated.
4. Update replication settings so the `wWWHomePage` attribute is indexed for searches.
5. Enable universal group membership caching.
6. Designate a global catalog server.

Transferring Operations Master Roles

1. Prepare a test environment.
2. Locate the current operations masters for all roles.
3. Transfer the schema master role to a new owner.
4. Transfer the PDC emulator master role to a new owner.

Creating Organizational Units

1. Prepare a test environment.
2. Create a new domain.
3. Create organizational units for each business unit in the company.
4. Modify the OU hierarchy so the top-level OU is for enterprise administration.
5. Create user and computer accounts and move these accounts to an OU.
6. Delegate control over an OU so a user can create, delete, and manage accounts in the OU.

Creating and Configuring Sites

1. Prepare a test environment.
2. Create two sites.
3. Create one or more subnets and associate them with each site.
4. Link one site to other site using site links.
5. Associate a domain controller with each site.
6. Specify a site license server for each site.

Configuring Intersite Replication

1. Prepare a test environment.
2. Create the site links for connecting two or more sites.
3. Configure site link properties for replication cost, interval, and schedule as appropriate.
4. Disable site link transitivity for IP and SMTP.
5. Create a site link bridges between sites.
6. Enable site link transitivity for IP and SMTP.
7. Determine a site's Inter-Site Topology Generator.
8. Determine a site's bridgehead servers.
9. Specify preferred bridgehead servers.

Configuring Trust Relationships

1. Prepare a test environment.
2. Examine the current trust relationships for all domains in a forest.
3. List the types of trusts, the trusting domains, and the trusted domains.
4. Establish a shortcut trust between two child domains in separate domain trees.

Monitoring Active Directory

1. Prepare a test environment.
2. Ensure that the dependent services are running.

3. Examine firewalls to ensure that TCP and UDP ports are open as appropriate for Active Directory.
4. Use Repadmin to examine all aspects of replication.
5. Use Replmon to synchronize a domain controller's domain partition with all other domain controllers in a domain.
6. Use Replmon to search for replication errors.
7. Use the Performance console to monitor the Directory Replication Agent in Active Directory.
8. Use the Performance console to monitor FRS.
9. Check the event logs for Active Directory errors.
10. Check the event logs for FRS errors.

Backing up and Restoring Active Directory

1. Prepare a test environment.
2. Back up a domain controller.
3. Perform a nonauthoritative restore of a domain controller.
4. Perform an authoritative restore of a domain controller.
5. Perform a primary restore of the Sysvol.

Planning Security Groups

1. Create a security group plan for a new network with 5,000 users.
2. Create a security group hierarchy that encompasses all resources and includes universal groups.
3. Create a distribution group hierarchy for users and includes universal groups.

Planning an Authentication Strategy That Uses Smart Cards and Group Policy

1. Prepare a test environment.
2. Configure an enterprise CA hierarchy.
3. Enable autoenrollment in Group Policy.
4. Configure user accounts to require smart cards for log on and authentication.
5. Configure remote access to require Extensible Authentication Protocol (EAP).
6. Configure domain-wide account password and account lockout policies in Group Policy.
7. Configure domain-wide policy for renaming the Administrator and Guest accounts.

Working with Local Group Policy

1. Prepare a test environment.
2. Access local group policy on a local computer.

3. Enable Automatic Updates policy on the local computer.
4. Access local group policy on a remote computer.
5. Enable Automatic Updates policy on the remote computer.

Managing Active Directory Group Policy

1. Prepare a test environment.
2. Create a GPO and link it to a site.
3. Configure the site GPO so that its setting cannot be overridden.
4. Edit the site GPO and configure policy settings.
5. Create a GPO and link it to a domain.
6. Configure the domain GPO to block inheritance.
7. Edit the domain GPO and configure policy settings.
8. Create a GPO and link it to an OU.
9. Configure the OU's GPO so user settings are disabled.

Configuring User and Computer Environments Using Group Policy

1. Prepare a test environment.
2. Create a GPO and link it to an OU.
3. Configure a startup script for computers in the OU.
4. Configure a logon script for users in the OU.
5. Configure folder redirection for AppData and My Documents.

Distributing Software by Using Group Policy

1. Prepare a test environment.
2. Deploy software using user publishing. *Adminpak.msi* is in the *%SystemRoot%\System32* folder on the servers.
3. Deploy a new version of the deployed software. If you've deployed the *Adminpak.msi* for Windows Server 2003, you can try deploying the *Adminpak.msi* for Windows Server 2003 Service Pack 1 as an update.

Troubleshooting the Application of Group Policy Security Settings

1. Prepare a test environment.
2. Use the Resultant Set Of Policy in planning mode to determine settings for a user and computer in a new OU.
3. Move the user and computer to the new OU.
4. Refresh Group Policy using `gpupdate`.
5. Use the Resultant Set Of Policy in logging mode to determine the applied policy settings.
6. Use Gpresult to determine the complete list of GPOs applied to a user and computer.

7. Use Gpresult to determine the security groups of which a user and computer are members.
8. Use Gpresult in verbose mode and store the results in a text file.

Restoring the Default Domain Policy and Default Domain Controller Policy GPOs

1. Prepare a test environment.
2. Examine the Default Domain Policy and the Default Domain Controller Policy for a domain.
3. Configure Account Lockout Policy and Password Policy in the Default Domain Policy in a nonstandard way.
4. Configure Audit Policy in the Default Domain Controller Policy in a nonstandard way.
5. Use Dcgpofix to restore the Default Domain Policy and the Default Domain Controller Policy for a domain.
6. Examine the Default Domain Policy and the Default Domain Controller Policy for the domain.

Exam 70-294 Highlighters Index

In this section, I've attempted to compile the facts within the exam's subject areas that you are most likely to need another look at—in other words, the areas of study that you might have highlighted while reading the Study Guide. The title of each highlighted element corresponds to the heading title in the Exam 70-294 Study Guide. In this way, if you have a question about a highlight, you can refer back to the corresponding section in the study guide. For the most part, the entries under a heading are organized as term lists with a Windows Server 2003 feature, component, or administration tool as the term and the key details for this feature, component, or administration tool listed next.

Planning an Active Directory Forest and Domain Structure

Summary of highlights from the "Planning an Active Directory Forest and Domain Structure" section of the Exam 70-294 Study Guide.

Active Directory infrastructure

- Forests, domain trees, and domains are the logical components of Active Directory.
- Sites and subnets are the physical components of Active Directory.

Active Directory domains

- Domains are logical groupings of objects that allow central management and control.
- A domain is implemented when Active Directory is installed on the first domain controller.

Active Directory domain trees

- Domain trees are groups of domains that share the same namespace.
- Every domain tree has a root domain, which is at the top of the domain tree.
- Domains in a domain tree have two-way transitive trusts between them.

Active Directory forests

- Forests are groups of domain trees that are grouped together to share resources.
- Every forest has a forest root domain, which is the first domain created in the forest.
- Domain trees in a forest have two-way transitive trusts between them.

Active Directory data

- Active Directory represents data stored in the database as objects.
- An object's common name is the name assigned when the object is created with the `CN=` designator.
- An object's distinguished name describes its place in the directory according to the series of containers in which it is stored.
- No two objects in the directory will have the same distinguished name.

Active Directory root

- All objects in the directory have parents except for the root of the directory tree.
- The rootDSE represents the top of the logical namespace for a directory.
- Below the rootDSE is the root domain, which is established when you create the first domain.
- Once established, the forest root domain never changes.

Forest-wide containers

- Forest Root Domain container is the container for objects in the forest root domain.
- Configuration container is the container for the default configuration and all policy information.
- Schema container is the container for all objects classes, attributes and syntaxes.
- The forest root domain, configuration, and schema containers are defined within like-named partitions:

Active Directory partitions

- Active Directory uses partitions to logically divide up the directory.
- Partitions are the largest logical category of objects in the directory.
- All directory partitions are created as instances of the domainDNS object class.
- When you create a new domain, you create a new container object for the domain in the directory tree.
- All domain controllers store at least one domain directory partition and two forest-wide data partitions.

Domain-wide data

- Domain-wide data is replicated to every domain controller in a domain as a writeable replica.
- Global catalogs maintain a partial replica of domain-wide data from all domains in a forest.

Forest-wide data

- Forest-wide data is replicated to every domain controller in a forest.
- The configuration partition is replicated as a writable replica.
- The schema partition is replicated as a read-only replica, except on the schema operations master.
- Application partition data is replicated on a forest-wide, domain-wide or other basis.

Creating the forest root domain

- Create a forest root domain by installing Active Directory on the first domain controller in a forest.
- Once you've established the forest root domain, you can add new domains to the forest.
- Any domains in a different namespace as the forest root establish a root domain for a new domain tree.

Forest root domains

- A dedicated root is used as a placeholder.
- A nondedicated root is used as a normal part of the directory.

Domains in a forest

- All domain controllers share the same configuration container.
- All domains in a forest trust all the other domains in that forest.
- All domains in a forest have the same global catalog.
- All domain controllers in a forest have the same schema.
- All domains in a forest have Enterprise Admins and Schema Admins as top-level administrators.

Working with domains

- Use domains to logically group objects for central management and control.
- Domains set the replication boundary for the domain directory partition and for domain policy information. Domain boundaries are also boundaries for resource access and administration.
- Group Policy settings that apply to one domain are independent from those applied to other domains.

Domain controllers

- DNS servers must be installed on the network prior to installing Active Directory.
- To designate a server as a domain controller, use Dcpromo to install the Active Directory.

- To demote a domain controller, use Dcpromo to uninstall the Active Directory.
- Configuring a domain controller in a new domain allows you to create:
  - — A new domain in a new forest
  - — A child domain in an existing domain tree
  - — A domain tree in an existing forest

Domain functional levels

- Windows 2000 mixed mode, the default mode, supports Windows Server 2003, Windows 2000, and Windows NT domains.
- Windows 2000 native mode supports Windows Server 2003 and Windows 2000 domains only.
- Windows Server 2003 interim mode supports Windows Server 2003 and Windows NT domains only.
- Windows Server 2003 mode supports Windows Server 2003 domains only.
- Only Windows Server 2003 mode supports group nesting, group type conversion, universal groups, easy domain controller renaming, update logon timestamps, migration of security principals, and Kerberos KDC key version numbers.
- Domain functional level can be raised, but not lowered. It is a one-way process.

Forest functional levels

- Windows 2000, the default mode, supports domain controllers running Windows Server 2003, Windows 2000, and Windows NT.
- Windows Server 2003 interim mode supports Windows Server 2003 and Windows NT only.
- Windows Server 2003 mode supports Windows Server 2003 domain controllers only.
- Only Windows Server 2003 mode supports extended two-way trusts between forests, domain rename, domain restructure using renaming, and global catalog replication enhancements.
- Forest functional level can be raised, but not lowered. It is a one-way process.

Using UPN suffixes

- Every user account has a User Principal Name (UPN).
- The UPN is the User Logon Name combined with @ and a UPN suffix.
- The names of the current domain and the root domain are set as the default UPN suffix.
- You can specify an alternate UPN suffix to use to simplify logon or provide additional logon security.

Planning and Implementing a Strategy for Placing Global Catalog Servers

Summary of highlights from the "Planning and Implementing a Strategy for Placing Global Catalog Servers" section of the Exam 70-294 Study Guide.

Global catalog servers

- A global catalog contains a full copy of all objects in host domain.
- A global catalog contains a partial, read-only replica of objects in all other domains.
- The global catalog enables logon by providing universal group membership information.
- The global catalog enables finding directory information throughout the forest.
- The global catalog helps to resolve User Principal Names beyond the current domain.
- By default, the first domain controller installed in a domain is the global catalog server.

Placing global catalog servers

- Queries to global catalog servers are done over TCP port 3268 and TCP port 3269.
- Each site should have at least one global catalog to ensure availability and optimal response time.
- Exchange Server mailbox names are resolved through queries to the global catalog server.

Designating replication attributes

- Each object has attributes that are designated for replication.
- Global catalog servers use the replication details.
- Schema administrators can designate additional attributes to be replicated.
- Use the Active Directory Schema snap-in.

Universal group membership caching

- Once caching is enabled, domain controllers store universal group membership information in a cache.
- The cache is maintained indefinitely and updated every eight hours by default.
- Up to 500 universal group memberships can be updated at once.
- Universal group caching allows faster logon, reduces bandwidth usage and reduces resource usage.

Planning Flexible Operations Master Role Placement

Summary of highlights from the "Planning Flexible Operations Master Role Placement" section of the Exam 70-294 Study Guide.

Operations masters

- A designated operations master has a flexible single-master operations (FSMO) role.
- Operations performed by an operations master can only occur at one place at the same time.

Prep and Practice

Forest roles

- The schema master and domain-naming master roles are assigned on a per-forest basis.
- There is only one schema master and only one domain-naming master in a forest.

Domain roles

- The RID master, infrastructure master and PDC emulator are assigned on a per-domain basis.
- Each domain in a forest has only one RID master, infrastructure master, and PDC emulator.

Schema master

- The schema master maintains the only writeable copy of the schema container.
- The schema master is the only domain controller in the forest on which you can change schema.

Domain-naming master

- The domain-naming master is responsible for adding or removing domains from the forest.
- If the domain-naming master cannot be contacted, you will not be able to add or remove the domain.

Relative ID (RID)

- The relative ID (RID) master allocates blocks of relative IDs.
- Every domain controller in a domain is issued a block of relative IDs by the RID master.
- RIDs are used to build the security IDs that uniquely identify security principals in a domain.
- If a domain controller cannot contact RID master and runs out of RIDs, no objects can be created.

PDC emulator

- The PDC emulator master acts as the PDC for Windows NT 4.0 BDCs.
- The PDC emulator master is responsible for processing password changes.

Infrastructure master

- The infrastructure master updates group-to-user references across domains.
- The infrastructure master compares its directory data with that of a global catalog.

Operations master role placement

- The first domain controller in a forest has all five roles are assigned to it.
- The first domain controller in a domain is the RID master, infrastructure master, and PDC emulator.
- Forest-wide roles—the schema master and domain-naming master—should be on same domain controller.

- The RID master and PDC emulator master roles should be on the same domain controller.
- Except for a single or multidomain forest with all DCs as global catalogs, the infrastructure master should not be placed on a DC that is also a global catalog.

Locating and transferring the operations master roles

- You can determine the current operations masters using `netdom query fsmo`.
- You can transfer domain-wide roles by using Active Directory Users And Computers.
- You can transfer domain-naming master using Active Directory Domains And Trusts.
- You can transfer schema master using the Active Directory Schema snap-in.

Seizing operations master roles

- When operations master fails and is not coming back, you can seize the role to forcibly transfer.
- Use `repadmin /showutdvec` *`DomainControllerName NamingContext`* to check USNs.
- Use `ntdsutil` to seize the role.

Planning and Implementing Organizational Unit Structure

Summary of highlights from the "Planning and Implementing Organizational Unit Structure" section of the Exam 70-294 Study Guide.

Understanding organizational units

- Within a domain, organizational units are used to:
  - Delegate administrator privileges while limiting administrative access
  - Create hierarchies that mirror business structure or functions
  - Manage groups of objects as a single unit through Group Policy
- Organizational units are represented as container objects that are part of a designated domain.
- Organizational units are not a part of DNS structure.

Organizing OU hierarchies

- Division or business unit OU hierarchies reflect the department structure within the organization.
- Geographic or business location OU hierarchies reflect the actual physical location of units.
- Areas of administrative control OU hierarchies reflect the way resources and accounts are managed.

Delegate administrative rights for OUs

- Delegate rights to assign a user full administrative control.
- Delegate rights to assign a user a specific set of administrative permissions.

Group Policy Objects

- Every site, domain, and OU has an associated Group Policy Object (GPO).
- Using Group Policy, you can specify a set of rules for computer and user configuration.
- Manage policy settings using Group Policy Object Editor or the Group Policy Management console.
- You can use Group Policy to:
  - Define default options for configuration and security settings
  - Limit options for changing configuration and security settings
  - Prevent changing certain configuration and security settings

Creating OUs

- Each domain has its own OU hierarchy.
- To create an OU, you must be a member of the Administrators group in the domain.
- You can create an OU using Active Directory Users And Computers or DSADD.

Moving Objects within an OU

- You can move existing objects from one OU to another using drag-and-drop.
- You can move existing objects from one OU to another using right-click → Move or DSMOVE.
- You cannot move objects between domains.
- To move objects between domains, you must use the *Movetree.exe* utility.

Planning and Implementing an Administrative Delegation Strategy

Summary of highlights from the "Planning and Implementing an Administrative Delegation Strategy" section of the Exam 70-294 Study Guide.

Planning for delegation

- Delegation can be used at the domain level and at the organizational unit level.
- You can:
  - Grant full control over an OU.
  - Grant full control over specific types of objects in an OU or domain.
  - Grant rights to perform specific tasks in a domain or OU.

Effects of delegation

- Any user that has designated as an administrator for a domain automatically has full control over the domain.
- Any user that has delegated permissions at the domain level has those permissions for all OUs in the domain.
- Any user delegated permissions in a top-level OU has those permissions for all OUs within the top-level OU.

Delegating administration

- You can delegate administration in Active Directory Users And Computers.
- Right-click the OU, and then select Delegate Control.

Planning and Managing Active Directory Sites

Summary of highlights from the "Planning and Managing Active Directory Sites" section of the Exam 70-294 Study Guide.

Understanding sites

- Every Active Directory implementation has at least one site.
- A *site* is a group of IP subnets that are connected by reliable, high-speed links.
- A *subnet* is a subdivision of an IP network. Sites are connected to each other via site links.
- A *site link* is a logical, transitive connection between two or more sites.
- Site structure reflects the physical environment and is separate from the logical representation.

Site boundaries

- Domain and site boundaries are separate.
- A single site can contain resources from multiple domains.
- A single domain can extend across multiple sites.
- A single site can have multiple subnets, but a single subnet can only be a part of one site.

Using sites

- Key reasons to create additional sites are to control replication traffic and isolate logon traffic.
- Each site should have at least one domain controller and one global catalog.
- Each site should have at least one DNS server and one DHCP server.
- Each site may also need local file servers, messaging servers, and certificate authorities.

Understanding replication

- Replication within a site is referred to as *intrasite replication*.
- Replication between sites is referred to as *intersite replication*.

How sites isolate logon traffic

- If a user logs in to their home domain, a DC within the local site authenticates the logon.
- If a user logs in to another domain, a DC in the local site forwards the logon request to a DC in the user's home domain.

Intrasite replication

- Replication data is not compressed, which reduces processor and memory usage.
- Replication partners notify when changes need to be replicated, allowing partners to request changes.

- Replication partners poll each other periodically to determine whether there are updates.
- Remote Procedure Call (RPC) over IP is used.

Intersite replication

- Replication data is compressed by default to reduce network bandwidth usage.
- Replication partners do not notify each other when changes need to be replicated.
- Replication partners poll each other at specified intervals, but only during scheduled periods.
- RPC over IP or Simple Mail Transport Protocol (SMTP) is used.
- Use of SMTP is limited to DCs in different domains. DCs in the same domains must use RPC over IP.

Knowledge Consistency Checker (KCC)

- The KCC runs on each DC.
- The KCC performs monitoring intrasite replication.

Inter-Site Topology Generator (ISTG)

- The ISTG runs on a designated DC.
- The ISTG performs monitoring for intersite replication.
- The ISTG designates a bridgehead server.
- You can also designate a preferred bridgehead server.
- When used, multiple preferred bridgehead servers should be specified.

Establishing sites

- When you install the first DC in a site, Dcpromo creates a default site and a default site link.
- The default site is named Default-First-Site-Name.
- The default site link is called DEFAULTIPSITELINK.

Configuring sites

1. Create the site.
2. Create one or more subnets and associate them with the site.
3. Link the site to other sites using site links.
4. Associating a domain controller with a site.
5. Specify a site license server for the site.

Creating sites

- You can create sites using Active Directory Sites And Services.
- Right-click the Sites container and select New Site.

Creating subnets

- Any computer with an IP address on a network segment associated with a site is in the site.
- Each subnet can be associated only with one site.

- You can create a subnet using Active Directory Sites And Services.
- Right-click the Subnets container in the console tree and select New Subnet.

Associating domain controllers with sites

- Each site should have at least one domain controller associated with it.
- To provide fault tolerance and redundancy, you should have at least two DC in each site.
- After associating a subnet with a site, any DCs you install on that subnet will be located in the site, and any existing DCs must be moved to the site.
- You can move a DC to a site using Active Directory Sites And Services.
- Right-click the domain controller object, and then select Move.

Specifying a site license server for a site

- Every site must have a site license server associated with it.
- For the default site, the default site license server is the first domain controller created in the site.
- You can determine the site-licensing server using Active Directory Sites And Services.

Configuring intersite replication

- To configure and maintain intersite replication, you must:
    1. Create the required site links.
    2. Configure site link properties for replication cost, interval, and schedule as appropriate.
    3. Optionally, create site link bridges.
    4. Optionally, determine and monitor the Inter-Site Topology Generator.
    5. Optionally, determine and monitor bridgehead servers.
    6. Optionally, specify preferred bridgehead servers.

Creating site links

- Site links are used over WAN links.
- By default, replication is 24 hours a day, 7 days a week, at an interval of at least 180 minutes.
- Prioritize links using link cost. The default link cost is set to 100.
- With site links, you can use RPC over IP for reliable links and SMTP for unreliable links.
- You can create a site link between two or more sites using Active Directory Sites And Services.
- Right-click the transport protocol, either IP or SMTP, and select New Site Link.

Site link bridges

- By default, site link transitivity is enabled.
- When more than two sites are linked for replication and use the same transport, sites links are bridged.
- The link path is determined by the site link bridge cost.

- The site link bridge cost is the sum of all the links included in the bridge.
- The path with the lowest total site link bridge cost is used.

Configuring site link transitivity

- With an Active Directory forest, site link transitivity can be set on a per-transport protocol basis.
- You can enable or disable transitivity using Active Directory Sites and Services.
- Right-click the transport protocol, and then select Properties.
- To enable site link transitivity, select Bridge All Site Links.
- If you disable transitive links, you can manually create site link bridges.

Determining the Inter-Site Topology Generator

- The Inter-Site Topology Generator (ISTG) in a site generates intersite replication topology.
- Operating as the ISTG adds considerable workload.
- You can determine the ISTG using Active Directory Sites And Services.
- Use the site's NTDS Site Settings.

Site bridgehead servers

- Replication between sites is performed by bridgehead servers.
- A bridgehead server is a domain controller designated by the ISTG to perform intersite replication.
- The ISTG configures a bridgehead server for each Active Directory partition that needs to be replicated.
- Operating as a bridgehead server adds to the workload of the domain controller.
- You can list the bridgehead servers in a site using `repadmin /bridgeheads site:`*`SiteName`*.

Using preferred bridgehead servers

- Once you designate preferred bridgehead servers for a site, the ISTG will use only them.
- You must configure a bridgehead server for each partition that needs to be replicated.
- If the preferred bridgehead servers are unavailable, intersite replication will stop.

Recovering from preferred bridgehead failure

- Remove failed servers as preferred bridgeheads, and then specify different preferred bridgeheads.
- Or remove all servers as preferred bridgehead servers and then allow the ISTG to select bridgeheads.

Configuring preferred bridgeheads

- You can configure preferred bridgeheads using Active Directory Sites and Services.
- Right-click the server you want to designate as a preferred bridgehead, and then select Properties.
- Add preferred transports to the Transports Available For list.

Maintaining Active Directory Infrastructure

Summary of highlights from the "Maintaining Active Directory Infrastructure" section of the Exam 70-294 Study Guide.

Two-way transitivity trust relationships

- All domains in a forest have automatic two-way transitive trusts between parent and child domains.
- Because trusts are automatic, you do not need to create them.
- Because trusts are two-way, a user in any domain in a forest can access resources in any other domain in the forest.
- Because trusts are transitive, users can access resources across any consecutive series of domains in a forest.

Establishing trusts

- Windows Server 2003 uses Kerberos or NT LM for authentication and establishment of trusts.
- Kerberos is used with Windows 2000 or later clients and servers.
- NT LM is used with pre-Windows 2000 clients and servers.

Trust trees

- When a user attempts to access a resource in another domain, a trust tree is used.
- The user's request passes through one DC in each domain between the user and the resource.
- The request is then authenticated in the domain where the resource resides.

Using the trust tree

- Authentication requests from the source domain pass through parent-child trusts to the tree-root.
- From the tree root, they pass through parent-child trusts to the destination domain.

Shortcut trusts

- Establish a shortcut trust between the domains to establish an authentication shortcut.
- The DC in the first domain can forward authentication requests directly to a DC in the second domain.
- You need two accounts: one that is a member of Domain Admins in the first domain, and one that is a member of Domain Admins in the second domain.

External trusts

- External trusts are nontransitive trusts that must be explicitly established by administrators.
- An external trust can be one-way or two-way.
- An external trust is applicable only to the domains for which the trust is established.
- Users in other domains cannot make use of the trust because it is nontransitive.
- External trusts are provided for backward compatibility with Windows NT domains.

Forest trusts

- Forest trusts are one-way or two-way transitive trusts between forest root domains.
- Forest trusts must be explicitly established by administrators.
- Forest trusts are used to share resources and to authenticate users between forests.
- All DCs in all domains of both forests must be upgraded to Windows Server 2003.
- Forest trusts are transitive between two forests only.
- You need two accounts: one that is a member of Enterprise Admins in the first forest, and one that is a member of Enterprise Admins in the second forest.

Realm trusts

- Realm trusts are trusts between Windows domains and Kerberos realms.
- Realm trusts must be explicitly established by administrators.
- Realm trusts can be nontransitive, transitive, two-way, or one-way.
- You need to establish the trust separately for the Windows domain and the Kerberos realm.

Viewing current trust relationships

- Using Active Directory Domains And Trusts, you can view available domains and existing trusts.
- To view the existing trusts for a domain, right-click the domain node and select Properties.
- Click the Trust tab.

Understanding trust relationships

- When a new domain is added to a new domain tree within a forest, the default trust is a tree-root trust.
- When a new domain is a subdomain of a root domain, the default trust is a parent-child trust.
- All default trusts are established as two-way, transitive trusts.
- For all trusts there are two sides: an incoming trust and an outgoing trust.
- To establish a trust, you must configure both sides of the trust.

Establishing trust relationships

- You can establish an explicit trust relationship using Active Directory Domains And Trusts.
- Right-click the domain for which you want to establish an explicit trust, and then select Properties.
- For a forest trust, this must be the forest root domain in one of the participating forests.
- In the domain's Properties dialog box, click the Trust tab and click the New Trust button.

Troubleshooting trusts

- Windows Server 2003 validates all incoming trusts automatically.
- If the credentials used to establish the trust are no longer valid, the trust fails verification.
- Failure of the trust means that users are not able to access resources.
- You can re-validate the trust by providing new credentials or by specifying that incoming trusts should not be validated.
- You can re-validate and reset a trust relationship using Active Directory Domains And Trusts.

Active Directory service dependencies

- LDAP
- Domain Name System (DNS)
- Kerberos v5 Authentication
- Remote Procedure Call (RPC)

Sysvol replication dependencies

- File Replication Service (FRS)
- NTFS and share permissions on the Sysvol

Troubleshooting Active Directory

- Use Replication Administrator (Repadmin) and Replication Monitor (Replmon).
- Use the NTDS performance object in the Performance console.
- Use performance logging and alerts.
- Review the Directory Service log on the domain controller.

Troubleshooting FRS

- Use the `FileReplicaConn` and `FileReplicatSet` performance objects in the Performance console.
- Use performance logging and alerts.
- Review the File Replication Service log on the domain controller.
- Review the Sysvol permissions.

Restoring Active Directory

- Back up the System State on domain controllers whenever you perform Normal backups.
- The System State of a domain controller can only be restored using Directory Services Restore Mode.
- Press F8 during boot up, and then selecting Directory Services Restore Mode as the startup option.

Authoritative Restore

- Use when you need to recover Active Directory and no other domain controller has the correct data.
- You must restore the System State, making sure not to reboot the computer, and then use NTDSUTIL to perform authoritative restore.
- Sysvol is not restored authoritatively unless you do a primary restore of the Sysvol.

Nonauthoritative Restore

- Use when you need to restore a DC and allow it to get any necessary updates from other DCs.
- You must restore the System State, and then reboot the domain controller.
- The restored DC gets updates of Active Directory and Sysvol from other DCs.
- You have the option of doing a primary restore of the Sysvol.

Performing a primary restore on Sysvol

- The Sysvol folder is backed up as part of the System State.
- If you restore a DC, the Sysvol data on the restored DC is overwritten with data from other DCs.
- You must perform a primary restore of the Sysvol to ensure the restored Sysvol is the master.
- Start by restoring System State using either authoritative or nonauthoritative restore.
- During the restore, do not accept the default restore settings.
- Instead, on the Completing The Restore Wizard page, click the Advanced button.
- Select When Restoring Replicated Data Sets, Mark The Restored Data As The Primary Data For All Replicas.

Planning and Implementing User, Computer, and Group Strategies

Summary of highlights from the "Planning and Implementing User, Computer, and Group Strategies" section of the Exam 70-294 Study Guide.

Groups

- Distribution groups are used for email distribution lists; they do not have security descriptors.
- Security groups are used to assign access permissions; they have security descriptors.

Domain local groups

- Used primarily to assign access permissions to resources within a single domain.
- Can include members from any domain in the forest and from trusted domains in other forests.
- Typically, global and universal groups are members of domain local groups.

Global groups

- Used primarily for users or computers in the same domain that share a similar role, function, or job.
- Can include only accounts and groups from domain in which they are defined, including other global groups.

Universal groups

- Used primarily to define sets of users or computers that should have wide permissions throughout a domain or forest.
- Can include accounts and groups from any domain in the forest, including other universal groups and global groups.

Using groups in Windows 2000 Mixed, Windows Server 2003 Interim domain functional level

- Domain local groups can contain accounts and global groups from any domain.
- Global groups can contain accounts from the same domain only.
- Universal security groups can't be created.

Using groups in Windows 2000 Native, Windows Server 2003 domain functional level

- Domain local groups can contain accounts and global groups from any domain. Domain local groups from the same domain only.
- Global groups can contain accounts and other global groups from the same domain only.
- Universal groups can contain accounts from any domain. Global and universal groups from any domain.

Changing group scope

- Domain local groups can be changed to universal groups; no member can have domain local scope.
- Global groups can be changed to universal groups; no member can have global scope.
- Universal groups can be changed to domain local or global groups; no member can have global scope for global.

Planning authentication using smart cards

- Smart cards store digital certificates used in logon authentication.
- Extensible Authentication Protocol (EAP) is used with remote access and smart cards.
- Require users to use smart cards for authentication using Active Directory Users And Computers.

- On the Account tab, select Smart Card Is Required For Interactive Logon.
- You must install smart card reader devices on computers and set up a smart card to use for user logon.
- With smart cards, enterprise CAs only can be used because they store certificates in Active Directory.

Planning, Implementing, and Maintaining Group Policy

Summary of highlights from the "Planning, Implementing, and Maintaining Group Policy" section of the Exam 70-294 Study Guide.

Group Policy

- Group Policy is as a set of rules that you can apply to help you manage users and computers.
- Active Directory defines computer policies and user policies.
- You can use Group Policy with all workstations and servers running Windows 2000 or later.

Computer policies

- Are applied to computers and are stored under Computer Configuration.
- You use Computer Configuration settings to configure policy on a per-computer basis.
- When a computer is started, computer policy settings are applied.
- A history of the registry-based settings that were applied is written to *%AllUsersProfile%\Ntuser.pol.*

User policies

- Are applied to users and are stored under User Configuration.
- Use User Configuration settings to configure policy on a per-user basis.
- When a user logs on, user policy settings are applied.
- A history of the registry-based settings that were applied is written to *%UserProfile%\Ntuser.pol.*

Group Policy refresh

- Group Policy settings are automatically refreshed to keep settings current.
- By default, Group Policy is refreshed every 5 minutes on DCs and every 90 to 120 minutes on other computers.
- Group Policy is refreshed every 16 hours in full.
- Slow link and policy processing settings can affect when refresh occurs.
- Use Gpupdate to manually refresh policy from the command line.

Group Policy Objects

- Group Policy is applied using Group Policy Objects (GPOs).
- Sites, domains, and organizational units all have related Group Policy Objects.
- The settings of top-level GPOs are inherited by lower-level GPOs.

Local Group Policy

- For local environments, a subset of Group Policy called Local Group Policy is available.
- This policy allows you to manage policy settings for those who log on to a local machine.
- Local Group Policy is managed through the Local Group Policy Object (LGPO).
- All computers have an LGPO.
- Although DCs have LGPOs, Group Policy for DCs should be managed through Default Domain Controllers Policy.

Group Policy settings

- Manage Group Policy by configuring policy settings.
- Policy settings can be enabled, disabled, or not configured.
- Enabled policy settings are active and applied.
- Disabled policy settings are inactive and not applied or enforced.
- Not configured policy settings are not being used.

Inheritance and blocking

- Inheritance and blocking can affect the meaning of these states.
- If inherited settings are enforced, you cannot override them.
- If inherited settings are blocked and inheritance is not enforced, the inherited setting does not apply.

Inheritance precedence order

- Everyone who logs on to the local machine is affected by Local Group Policy.
- LGPO settings have the least precedence and can be superseded by site, domain, and OU settings.
- Active Directory–based policy settings are applied in this order: site, domain, OU.

Inheritance without blocking

- Site policy affects all users and computers located within domains and OUs that are part of the site.
- Domain policy affects all users and computers located within OUs that are part of the domain.
- OU policy affects all users and computers defined within the OU as well in child OUs.

GPOs in Active Directory

- All GPOs are stored in the Group Policy Objects container.
- The link between a domain, site, or OU makes a GPO active.
- You can link a GPO to a specific level or to multiple levels.

Default Domain Controllers Policy GPO

- This is the default GPO created for and linked to the Domain Controllers OU.
- It is applied to all domain controllers in a domain by default.
- Use this GPO to manage security settings for domain controllers in a domain.
- Use only to configure User Rights Assignment And Audit Policy.
- You may also want to set Security Options and event log settings.
- Manage other areas of DC policy by creating a new GPO and linking as appropriate.

Default Domain Policy GPO

- This is the default GPO created for and linked to the domain within Active Directory.
- It is used to establish policy settings that apply to all users and computers in a domain.
- Use only to manage Password Policy, Account Lockout Policy, and Kerberos Policy.
- Manage other areas of domain policy by creating a new GPO and linking as appropriate.

Group Policy settings

- Two major categories of settings: Computer Configuration and User Configuration.
- These categories are divided into several major classes.
- Software Settings provide settings for automating deployment of software.
- Windows Settings provide settings for managing Windows settings for both computers and users.
- Administrative Templates provide settings for managing registry-based settings.

Managing Local Group Policy

- To work with Local Group Policy, you must use an administrator account.
- Use `gpedit.msc /gpcomputer:"%computername%"`
- Use `gpedit.msc /gpcomputer:"RemoteComputer"`

Managing Active Directory Group Policy

- Any changes you make are made first on the PDC Emulator if it is available
- Domain Admins and Enterprise Admins can work with Active Directory Group Policy.
- With Active Directory Group Policy, creating and linking objects are separate actions.
- You can create a GPO and later link it to a site, domain or OU.
- Or you can create a GPO and simultaneously link it to a site, domain or OU.
- Manage site GPOs using Active Directory Sites And Services.
- Manage domain and OU GPOs using Active Directory Users And Computers.

Administrative Templates

- Administrative Templates are used to manage registry-based settings.
- Each set of Administrative Templates is defined using an administrative template (*.adm*) file.
- Administrative template files do not affect the processing of policy.
- Administrative template files are used to display the settings that can be configured.
- Settings are stored in the *Registry.pol* file associated with the GPO.

Default Administrative Templates

- Every Windows computer has default administrative templates.
- These files are stored in the *%Windir%\inf* folder.
- The default templates on your system determine the templates used and stored in a new GPO.
- Turn Off Automatic Updates Of ADM Files forces comparison of local templates and stored templates to determine whether the stored templates should be updated.
- Always Use Local ADM Files For Group Policy Editor forces use of local templates instead of templates stored in GPO.

Viewing Administrative Templates

- You can edit a GPO and determine which *.adm* files are being used.
- Right-click Administrative Templates, and then select Add/Remove Templates.

Using Resultant Set Of Policy for planning

- Resultant Set Of Policy (RSoP) can be used for testing different scenarios.
- You can model the effects of modifying policy settings, moving a user or computer and adding groups.
- In the Resultant Set Of Policy snap-in, right-click Resultant Set Of Policy and select Generate RSoP Data.
- Select Planning Mode.

Autoenrollment using Group Policy

- Public Key Infrastructure (PKI) provides components for digital certificates.
- Computers and users can use certificates for authentication and encryption.
- Microsoft Certificate Services provide the necessary components for certificates.
- A server designated as a certificate authority (CA) issues certificates.
- A CA used for autoenrollment must be an enterprise root CA or an enterprise subordinate CA.

- When you install enterprise CAs, autoenrollment policies are enabled automatically through the following:
  - *User Configuration\Windows Settings\Security Settings\Public Key Policies\Autoenrollment Settings*
  - *Computer Configuration\Windows Settings\Security Settings\Public Key Policies\Autoenrollment Settings*

Computer scripts using Group Policy

- Computers scripts can run during startup or shutdown.
- Use Startup or Shutdown under *Computer Configuration\Windows Settings\Scripts*.

User scripts using Group Policy

- User scripts can run during logon or logoff.
- Use Logon or Logoff under *Computer Configuration\Windows Settings\Scripts*.

Redirecting folders using Group Policy

- Folder redirection allows you to redirect special folders to a central network location.
- You can redirect Application Data, Desktop, My Documents, and My Pictures.
- A copy of the user's current special folder is made in the designated location.
- You can redirect based on security group membership if desired.
- The network location to which you redirect folders must be configured as a shared folder.
- Configure redirection using *User Configuration node\Windows Settings\Folder Redirection*.

Start menu redirection

- Start Menu redirection works differently from redirection of other folders.
- Start Menu redirection does not copy the contents of a user's local Start Menu.
- Instead, users are redirected to a previously created, standard Start Menu.

Understanding software deployment

- Software deployed through Group Policy is referred to as managed software.
- You can deploy software on a per-computer basis, a per-user basis, or both.
- Per-computer applications are available to all users of a computer.
- Per-user applications are available to individual users.
- Non-Windows Installer files can only be installed on a per-user basis.

Using distribution points

- Before you deploy software through policy, you should set up a distribution point.
- A distribution point is a shared folder available to the computers/users for which you are deploying software.

Deploying software

- Copy the installer package file and all required application files to the distribution point.
- Perform an administrative installation to the distribution point using `Setup /a`.
- Administrative installs can be patched and redeployed through Software Installation policy.
- Create special GPOs that configure software installation, and then link these GPOs as appropriate.
- Software can be deployed using computer assignment, user assignment, or user publishing.

Computer assignment

- You can assign the software to client computers so it is installed when a client computer starts.
- Requires no user intervention, but does require a restart to install software.
- Installed software is available to all users on a computer.
- Not available with non-Windows Installer files.

User assignment

- You can assign the software to users so it is installed when a user logs on.
- Requires no user intervention, but does require the user to logon to install or advertise software.
- The software is associated with the user only.
- Not available with non-Windows Installer files.

User publishing

- You can publish the application so users can install it manually through Add Or Remove Programs.
- Requires the user to explicitly install software or activate the install.
- The software is associated with the user only.

Advertised software can be installed

- When the user accesses a document that requires the software
- When a user opens a short cut to the application
- When another application requires a component of the software

Updating deployed software

- You can update deployed software using a patch or service pack.
- You can update deployed software by deploying a new version of the application.

Deploying software

- Use Windows Installer Packages (*.msi*) or ZAW Down-level Application Packages (*.zap*) files.
- File permissions on these application installer packages must be set for Read access.

- Software Installation policy is applied only during foreground processing of policy settings.
- Per-computer application deployments are processed at startup.
- Per-user application deployments are processed at logon.
- You can customize installation using transform (*.mst*) files.
- For per-computer deployment, use *Computer Configuration\Software Settings\Software Installation*.
- For per-user software deployment, access *User Configuration\Software Settings\Software Installation*.

Applying patches and service packs for Windows Installer package

- Copy updates to the folder containing the original *.msi* file. Overwrite any duplicate files as necessary.
- Right-click the package you want to work with, and then select All Tasks → Redeploy Application.

Applying patches and service packs for Non-Windows Installer package

- Right-click the package, and then select All Tasks → Remove.
- Copy the new *.zap* file and all related files to a network share and redeploy the application.

Upgrading previously deployed Software

- Copy upgrade to share.
- Create a package for upgrade in Group Policy.
- Right-click the upgrade package, and then select Properties.
- Click Add on the Upgrades tab.

Configuring Automatic Updates using Group Policy

- Windows 2000 or later can use Automatic Updates to maintain the operating system.
- Automatic Updates is for critical updates, security updates, update rollups, and service packs.
- For per-computer, use Automatic Updates under *Computer Configuration\Administrative Templates\Windows Components\Windows Update*.
- For per-user, use Automatic Updates under *User Configuration\Administrative Templates\Windows Components\Windows Update*.
- Select the option 4 - Auto Download And Schedule For Install to fully automate.
- Most Automatic Updates are installed only when the system is shut down and restarted.
- Some Automatic Updates can be installed immediately if you enable Allow Automatic Updates Immediate Installation.
- By default, only users with local administrator privileges receive update notification.
- You can allow others to receive update notifications by enabling Allow Non-Administrators To Receive Update Notifications.

Troubleshooting the Application of group policy

- Use the Resultant Set of Policy snap-in in Logging Mode.
- Use the Gpresult command-line utility.

Restoring the default GPOs

- Use Dcgpofix to restore the default GPOs to their original, default state.
- Only Domain Admins or Enterprise Admins can run Dcgpofix.
- You lose changes made to these GPOs as a result of the restore process.

Refreshing Group Policy manually

- Group Policy is refreshed automatically.
- You can refresh Group Policy manually using Gpupdate.
- Gpupdate replaces the SECEDIT /refreshpolicy tool provided in Windows 2000.

Troubleshooting GPOs and the Sysvol

- Use Gpotool to troubleshooting GPOs and Sysvol.
- Check permissions on the Sysvol using the `/checkacl` option.

Exam 70-294 Practice Questions

1. John is a network administrator for a growing organization. While the company used to have only a single domain, they now have multiple domains. Users are having problems with logon, and John is looking for a way to simplify logon while retaining the current domain structure. What is the easiest way to resolve this problem?

   ❍ A. Assign all domains a common name (CN).

   ❍ B. Configure Active Directory to use DNS names.

   ❍ C. Specify an alternate user principal name (UPN).

   ❍ D. Reorganize the domain structure and use OUs instead.

   Answer C is correct. You can specify an alternate UPN suffix to simplify logon or provide additional logon security. This name is used only within the forest and does not have to be a valid DNS name.

2. Mary is installing a new domain controller. She wants the domain controller to be in a separate domain that is not part of an existing forest. What type of domain should Mary install?

   ❍ A. A forest root domain

   ❍ B. A parent domain

   ❍ C. A child domain

   ❍ D. A domain in a new domain tree in the existing forest

   Answer A is correct. If you want to create a domain that is not part of an existing forest, you must install a forest root domain. Every forest has a forest root domain, which is the first domain created in the forest.

3. Your organization is upgrading from Windows NT to Windows Server. You are planning the network strategy for Active Directory. On the current network, you have multiple user and resource domains. The SERVICE domain has over 1,500 users and computers from the Customer Service, Help Desk, and Technical Support departments. The MAIN domain is for over 5,000 users and computers from all departments located at the company's main office except for the service departments. The RESOURCE domain has all servers, printers, and other shared resources. There are also domains for each remote office, including SEATTLE, TACOMA, and PORTLAND domains. Users in the remote office are part of the Sales, Customer Service, Help Desk, or Technical Support departments. Which of the following documents will best help you determine where to place global catalog servers?

   ❍ A. An organization chart

   ❍ B. A spreadsheet with users organized by department, manager, and location

   ❍ C. A diagram of the local area network topology

   ❍ D. A diagram of the wide area network topology and traffic analysis

   Answer D is correct. To determine where to place global catalog servers, you need to understand the types of WAN connections used and details on current network traffic.

4. The organization has a central office and 18 remote offices. Remote offices are connected over a 256 Kbps link to the central office. You are installing a domain controller in each remote office and want to be sure remote users can always log on. Which of the following provides the best solution while reducing replication traffic?

   ❍ A. Configuring remote office domain controllers as global catalog servers

   ❍ B. Enabling universal group caching on remote office domain controllers

   ❍ C. Granting remote office administrators full control over domain controllers

   ❍ D. Installing redundant site links for each site

   Answer B is correct. On a domain with domain controllers running Windows Server 2003, universal group membership caching can be enabled. Once caching is enabled, domain controllers no longer need to access global catalogs to obtain universal group membership details.

5. What type of forest root domain should you configure if you want to use the forest root as a placeholder rather than as a normal part of the directory?

   ❍ A. A parent-child root

   ❍ B. A tree root

   ❍ C. A dedicated root

   ❍ D. A nondedicated root

   Answer C is correct. A dedicated root is used as a placeholder to start the directory and has no accounts associated with it other than those created when the forest root is installed; except those that are needed to manage the forest. It is not used to assign access to resources.

6. Which of the following is the default domain functional level when you are not upgrading from Windows NT 4?

   ❍ A. Windows 2000 mixed mode

   ❍ B. Windows 2000 native mode

   ❍ C. Windows Server 2003 interim mode

   ❍ D. Windows Server 2003 mode

   Answer A is correct. Windows 2000 mixed mode is the default domain functional level unless you're upgrading from Windows NT 4.0.

7. Which of the following are the forest-wide operations master roles?

   ❑ A. Schema master

   ❑ B. Domain naming master

   ❑ C. Relative ID (RID) master

   ❑ D. PDC emulator

   ❑ E. Infrastructure master

   Answers A and B are correct. The schema master and domain-naming master roles are assigned on a per-forest basis. There is only one schema master and only one domain-naming master in a forest.

8. You've recently completed an enterprise-wide upgrade. All domain controllers in all domains in the forest are running Windows Server 2003. After the upgrade, the help desk has received sporadic complaints about users not being able to log on after they've changed their password. What is the most likely cause of the problem?

   ❍ A. Account lockout policy is causing the users to get locked out and the accounts need to be reset.

   ❍ B. Password policy is set so users cannot reuse old passwords.

   ❍ C. The PDC emulator master is malfunctioning or unavailable.

   ❍ D. Password policy is set so users can only change their password after seven days.

   Answer C is correct. The PDC emulator master is responsible for processing password changes. When a user tries to log on to the network but provides an incorrect password, the logon domain controller checks the PDC emulator to see whether there is a recent password change for the user's account. If so, the domain controller retries the logon authentication on the PDC emulator.

9. Your organization just merged with another company. You want to ensure that users in either forest can access resources in the other forest. You also want to ensure that users can log on in either forest. What type of trust should you create between the forests?

   ❍ A. One-way transitive forest trust

   ❍ B. Two-way transitive forest trust

   ❍ C. One-way nontransitive forest trust

   ❍ D. Two-way nontransitive forest trust

Answer B is correct. Forest trusts are one-way or two-way transitive trusts between forest root domains that must be explicitly established by administrators. If you want users in both forests to be able to use and access resources in the other forest, you should establish a two-way transitive trust.

10. Your organization is restructuring its domains. You've been asked to install a new domain in a new domain tree and three child domains in that domain tree. The root domain for the new tree is *seattle.local*. The child domains are *tech.seattle.local*, *eng.seattle.local*, and *support.seattle.local*. You install the root domain and the first two child domains with no problems. However, before you can install the third child domain, one of the domain controllers in the *seattle.local* domain has an unrecoverable hardware problem and goes offline permanently. When you try to install the *support.seattle.local*, you are unable to. What can you do to resolve this problem?

    ❍ A. Transfer the infrastructure master role in the seattle.local domain to a new domain controller.

    ❍ B. Configure a domain controller in the seattle.local domain as a global catalog server.

    ❍ C. Configure a domain controller in the seattle.local domain as a preferred bridgehead server.

    ❍ D. Seize the domain-naming master role in the seattle.local domain and transfer it to a new domain controller.

    Answer D is correct. The domain-naming master is responsible for adding or removing domains from the forest. If the domain-naming master cannot be contacted when you are trying to add or remove a domain, you will not be able to add or remove the domain.

11. Which of the following is used to install Active Directory and establish a server as a domain controller?

    ❍ A. Ntdsutil

    ❍ B. Dcpromo

    ❍ C. Gpotool

    ❍ D. Gpresult

    Answer B is correct. Use the Active Directory Installation Wizard (*DCPROMO.EXE*) to install the Active Directory directory service.

12. Which of the following is used to uninstall Active Directory and demote a domain controller?

    ❍ A. Ntdsutil

    ❍ B. Dcpromo

    ❍ C. Gpotool

    ❍ D. Gpresult

    Answer B is correct. Use the Active Directory Installation Wizard (*DCPROMO.EXE*) to uninstall the Active Directory directory service and demote domain controllers.

13. Your company has merged with another company. You want to merge the forest structures of the two companies using an extended two-way forest trust, and you need to restructure some of the domains. What are the requirements to do these tasks?

   ❍ A. The forest functional level must be set to Windows 2000. The domain controllers must be running Windows 2000 or later.

   ❍ B. The forest functional level must be set to Windows Server 2003 interim mode. The domain controllers must be running Windows 2000 or later.

   ❍ C. The forest functional level must be set to Windows Server 2003 mode. The domain controllers must be running Windows 2000 or later.

   ❍ D. The forest functional level must be set to Windows Server 2003 mode. The domain controllers must be running Windows Server 2003.

   Answer D is correct. Forests operating in Windows Server 2003 mode can use many Active Directory features, including extended two-way trusts between forests, domain rename, domain restructure using renaming, and global catalog replication enhancements. In this mode, only Windows Server 2003 domain controllers are supported.

14. You organization has a central office and remote office locations in Seattle, New York, Memphis, and Los Angeles. The central office is has separate 512 Kbps WAN connections to each remote office. The Seattle and New York offices have a 256 Kbps WAN connection between them. The Memphis and Los Angeles offices have a 256 Kbps WAN connection between them. What is the best way to configure sites for these locations?

   ❍ A. Create a single site for the entire network and have each office location on a separate subnet.

   ❍ B. Create a separate site for each location and have each office location on separate subnets.

   ❍ C. Create a separate site for each location, connect the sites with site links, and have each office location on separate subnets as appropriate for the related sites.

   ❍ D. Create a separate site for each location and connect the sites using two-way trusts.

   ❍ E. Create a single site for the entire network and connect the subnets using two-way trusts.

   Answer B is correct. When office locations are connected over relatively slow links, individual sites should represent the individual LANs within an organization, and the WAN links between locations should mark site boundaries.

15. You organization has a central office in Austin, Texas and remote office locations in Dallas, Houston, and San Antonio. The central office has separate, dedicated 512 Kbps WAN connections to each remote office. The Dallas and Houston offices have a dedicated 256 Kbps WAN connection between them. The Houston and San Antonio offices have a dedicated 256 Kbps WAN connection between them. What is the best way to configure site links for these locations?

❍ A. Configure site links between the central office and remote office using SMTP; configure remote office to remote office links using SMTP.

❍ B. Configure site links between the central office and remote office using SMTP; configure remote office to remote office links using RPC over IP.

❍ C. Configure site links between the central office and remote office using RPC over IP; configure remote office to remote office links using SMTP.

❍ D. Configure site links between the central office and remote office using RPC over IP; configure remote office to remote office links using RPC over IP.

Answer D is correct. All WAN connections are dedicated. RPC over IP should be used when there are reliable, dedicated connections between sites.

16. For the site link configuration discussed in Question 14, you want to ensure that replication traffic between the Dallas and Houston office goes over the dedicated 256 Kbps WAN connection between the offices whenever possible. How can you do this?

❍ A. By configuring the Dallas-Houston site link so it has the lowest link cost.

❍ B. By setting the replication schedule for the Dallas-Houston site link to 24 hours a day, 7 days a week.

❍ C. By reducing the replication schedule for the Dallas-Houston site link, allowing replication to occur every 30 minutes.

❍ D. By using RPC over IP rather than SMTP as the transport protocol fro the Dallas-Houston site link.

Answer A is correct. If there are multiple possible routes to a site, the route with the lowest site link cost is used first.

17. You work for an organizational with global operations in 17 countries. The central office in the United States is connected to the central office in the United Kingdom over a dedicated, high-speed WAN link. You notice that this link is being saturated with replication traffic. You investigate the issue and find almost all replication traffic is passing over the U.S.-U.K. link multiple times. What is a possible cause of this problem and how can this problem be resolved?

❍ A. By default, replication is scheduled to occur over the site link 24 hours a day, 7 days a week, at an interval of at least 180 minutes. If you have limited bandwidth, you can alter the schedule to allow user traffic to have priority during peak usage times.

❍ B. By default, intersite replication topology is optimized for a maximum of three hops. You can resolve this problem by disabling site link transitivity and configuring site link bridges.

❍ C. By default, intersite replication does not use compression, and replication partners do not notify each other when Active Directory changes need to be replicated. You can resolve this problem by enabling compression and configuring replication partners to notify each other of changes.

❍ D. By default, intersite replication uses RPC over IP. You can resolve this problem by configuring site links to use SMTP as the transport.

Answer B is correct. By default, intersite replication topology is optimized for a maximum of three hops. In large site configuration, this can have unintended consequences, such as the same replication traffic going over the same link several times. In this case, you want to disable automatic site link bridging and manually configure site link bridges.

18. You work for an organization with a very large extended network. The organization has three central offices, which are each connected over T-1 WAN links. Each central office has up to eight remote offices to which it is connected. Central offices and remote offices are connected over 512 Kbps WAN links. You've noticed a recurring problem with high latency. In some cases, changes to the directory are not replicated throughout the enterprise for days. At the same time, much of the network is being restructured, and you notice that the bridgehead servers at most locations have 100 percent processor utilization at all times. To resolve this problem, you configured one preferred bridgehead server on each site. However, this made the problem worse, and now most changes to Active Directory are not being replicated to other sites. Users have also reported problems with DNS. What is the best way to resolve this problem?

❍ A. Remove all servers as preferred bridgehead servers, and then allow the ISTG to select the bridgehead servers that should be used.

❍ B. For each site, configure a preferred bridgehead server for each Active Directory partition that needs to be replicated.

❍ C. For each site, configure a preferred bridgehead server for each Active Directory and DNS partition that needs to be replicated.

❍ D. Upgrade the domain controller hosting the Inter-Site Topology Generator (ISTG) in each site.

Answer C is correct. You must configure a preferred bridgehead server for each partition that needs to be replicated. This means you must configure at least one domain controller with a replica of each directory partition as a preferred bridgehead server.

19. You are a network administrator for a company setting up a new network. You've been asked to plan the domain structure. The company has two office locations: an office in London, England and an office in Paris, France. The organization has three administrative groups: IT Admins, which are responsible for administration throughout the enterprise, Desktop Support, which is responsible for user support at all levels, and Help Desk, which is responsible for level 1 support. Members of the Help Desk team need to be able to reset user passwords for all users. What is the best way to configure the domain structure?

❍ A. Create a forest with a London domain and a Paris domain. Make all IT Admins members of the Enterprise Admins group. Make all Desktop Support members of the Domain Admins group. Make all Help Desk members of the Administrators group.

❍ B. Create a forest with a dedicated root domain. Create two additional domains: one for London and one for Paris. Make all IT Admins members of the Enterprise Admins group. Make all Desktop Support members of the Domain Admins group. Make all Help Desk members of the Administrators group.

❍ C. Create a single domain. Create a top-level OU within the domain called IT. Create second-level OUs called London and Paris. Make the IT administrators members of the Domain Admins group. Grant Desktop Support administrators full control over the London and Paris OUs. Grant Help Desk administrators the right to reset passwords in the London and Paris OUs.

❍ D. Create a forest with a dedicated root domain. Create two additional domains: one for London and one for Paris. Create a top-level OU within each domain called IT. Create second-level OUs called London and Paris within each domain. Make the IT administrators members of the Enterprise Admins group. Grant Desktop Support administrators full control over the London and Paris OUs in each domain. Grant Help Desk administrators the right to reset passwords in the London and Paris OUs in each domain.

Answer C is correct. There is no requirement to create a dedicated root domain. In this case, a single domain with a top-level OU called IT and second-level OUs for London and Paris meets all requirements.

20. You work for a large enterprise with 3 regional headquarters and 25 additional office locations. Each office location has its own domain and supports 1,000 to 5,000 users on average. The organization uses a dedicated root domain, which is named domain.local. Domains are structured so the regional offices are the top-level domains and all additional offices are configured as child domains of one of the regional office domains. As an example, the Midwest United States regional office is in Chicago, and the domain in Chicago is named *chicago.domain.local*. The domain in the Springfield office, also in the Midwest United States, is named *springfield.chicago.domain.local*. Due to a new business alliance, users in the Springfield and Newark offices recently have started working very closely together. The Newark office is located under the Northeast United States regional office in New York and has a domain name of *newark.newyork.domain.local*. When users from Springfield visit the Newark office or try to access file servers at the Newark office, they have problems and often have to wait several minutes to be authenticated. Sometimes authentication fails. The same is true when users from Newark visit the Springfield office or try to access file servers at the Springfield office. What is the best way to speed up the authentication process and make it easier for these offices to work together?

❍ A. Configure a domain controller at each office to act as a global catalog server and enable universal group caching.

❍ B. Configure a preferred bridgehead at each office location, and then configure the site links so that the Newark to New York, New York to Chicago, Chicago to Springfield route has the lowest link cost.

❍ C. Create a shortcut trust between the springfield.chicago.domain.local domain and the *newark.newyork.domain.local* domain.

❍ D. Configure a new domain for the Springfield and Newark users and resources, and move all the related objects to this domain.

Answer B is correct. While configuring a domain controller at each office to act as a global catalog server and enable universal group caching can help improve performance by allowing for faster logon authentication and searching, it doesn't resolve the problem with the large trust tree that must be navigated. You can streamline the authentication process by creating a shortcut trust between the domains.

21. You are a network administrator for a medium-sized business. The company has 535 users. The domain structure for the network is organized into a single domain with multiple OUs. One of the domain controllers has had a hard disk fail. This domain controller is backed up every day, and you have a current backup available. What must you do to restore the server as a domain controller?

❍ A. Replace the failed hard disk and perform a nonauthoritative restore.

❍ B. Replace the failed hard disk and perform an authoritative restore.

❍ C. Replace the failed hard disk and perform a primary restore of the Sysvol.

❍ D. The domain controller cannot be recovered. Install a new domain controller.

Answer A is correct. To restore Active Directory on a domain controller and have the domain controller get directory updates from other domain controllers, you should repair the server, replacing an failed hardware as necessary, and then perform a nonauthoritative restore. A nonauthoritative restore allows the domain controller to come back online, and then get replication updates from other domain controllers.

22. You are a network administrator for a medium-sized business. The company has 817 users. When you arrive at work, the office is in a panic. No one can access resources on any of the office's file servers. You check the file servers and find no apparent problems. Later, one of the new administrators says he deleted security groups called FSUsers, FSManagers, FSSales, and FSTechs because he thought they weren't being used after the organization's latest restructure. These groups, however, were the primary groups through which file server permissions were assigned. What is the best way to resolve this problem?

❍ A. Recreate the security groups, and make the appropriate users members of the appropriate groups.

❍ B. Recreate the security groups, make the appropriate users members of the appropriate groups, and configure file shares on the file servers to use these groups as appropriate.

❍ C. Perform an authoritative restore of Active Directory and restore only the deleted security groups.

❍ D. Perform an authoritative restore of Active Directory and restore the entire database.

Answer C is correct. To recover the security groups, you can perform an authoritative restore of Active Directory and restore only the deleted security groups.

23. You are a network administrator at a large company. The company has a single domain spread across five sites. The organization has 17 OUs with the top-level OU as Operations. You've created a separate GPO for the Software Installation policy and want to configure Software Installation policy to deploy an application to all users, with no user intervention required. What is the best way to deploy the software?

❍ A. Deploy the application using computer assignment and link the Software Installation policy GPO to the domain.

❍ B. Deploy the application using user assignment and link the Software Installation policy GPO to the domain.

❍ C. Deploy the application using user publishing and link the Software Installation policy GPO to the domain.

❍ D. Deploy the application using computer assignment and link the Software Installation policy GPO to each site separately.

❍ E. Deploy the application using user assignment and link the Software Installation policy GPO to each site separately.

❍ F. Deploy the application using user publishing and link the Software Installation policy GPO to each OU separately.

❍ G. Deploy the application using computer assignment and link the Software Installation policy GPO to each OU separately.

❍ H. Deploy the application using user assignment and link the Software Installation policy GPO to each OU separately.

Answer A is correct. Since all users in the company should get the application, create a GPO for the Software Installation Policy and link it to the domain. Using computer assignment, you can assign the software to client computers so it is installed when a client computer starts automatically and is available to all users on a computer.

24. Mary is a network administrator at a small company. The organization has an OU named Sales. Accounts for all sales team members are within the Sales OU. She's created a new GPO to configure folder redirection and linked it to the Sales OU. Since she doesn't want the GPO to apply to anyone except the sales team, she removed rights for Authenticated Users from the GPO. Later, she discovered none of the sales team members are using redirected folders. What is the best way to resolve this problem?

- ❍ A. Enforce policy inheritance for the GPO in the Sales OU.
- ❍ B. Block policy inheritance from the domain for the GPO in the Sales OU.
- ❍ C. Link the GPO to the domain instead.
- ❍ D. Create a group for the sales team, add the team as members, and grant the group the right to Read and Apply GPOs for the GPO.

Answer D is correct. By default, the policy settings applied to a GPO apply to all users and computers in the container to which the GPO is linked. The GPO applies to all users and computers because the default settings of GPOs specify that Authenticated Users have Read permission as well as Apply Group Policy permission. If you remove permissions for Authenticated Users, you must grant these permissions to the security groups that should process the GPO.

Prep and Practice

25. You are a network administrator at a company that is about to have its first major reorganization. You've been asked to identify possible problems due to the reorganization from an administrative perspective. While you will not be creating new domain structures or OUs, user accounts will be moved according to the realignment. What is the best way to test the effects of moving various user accounts to new OUs?

- ❍ A. Use RSoP in planning mode to simulate the effects of moving user accounts to new OUs.
- ❍ B. Use RSoP in logging mode to simulate the effects of moving user accounts to new OUs.
- ❍ C. Move a sample of user accounts to new OUs and use Gpresult to determine the applied security settings.
- ❍ D. Move a sample of user accounts to new OUs and use RSoP in planning mode to determine the applied security settings.

Answer A is correct. When you use RSoP in planning mode, you can simulate the effects of moving user and computer accounts. You do not need to actually move accounts to perform testing. You do not use logging mode for testing.

26. John is a network administrator at a large company with global operations. He works at the Denver office. At the Phoenix office, the organization has an OU named ProfServices. Accounts for all professional services team members are within the ProfServices OU. He's created a new GPO to configure logon scripts and linked it to the ProfServices OU. He waited for Group Policy to refresh. When he asked a user to log off and then log back on, he discovered the logon script was not being used. In fact, none of the professional services team members were getting the logon script. John checked the GPO and found no problems with permissions. What is the probable cause of this problem?

- ❍ A. Active Directory replication has failed.
- ❍ B. FRS has failed.
- ❍ C. The infrastructure master has failed.
- ❍ D. The bridgehead server connecting the site links between offices has failed.

Answer B is correct. The most likely problem is the File Replication Service (FRS) has failed. FRS is responsible for replicating Sysvol files, which includes logon, logoff, shutdown, and startup scripts.

27. You are installing smart cards for using in the domain. You install an enterprise certificate authority to issue certificates and create smarts cards for all users. Smart cards are loaded with the digital certificates for users. After installing smart card readers and distributing smart cards, you find out users are able to log on without using smart cards. What is the most likely cause of this problem?

   ❍ A. Autoenrollment is disabled.

   ❍ B. The CA is not validating certificates.

   ❍ C. Remote users aren't using EAP for authentication.

   ❍ D. The Smart Card Is Required For Interactive Logon option is not selected in user account properties.

   Answer D is correct. After you install an enterprise certificate authority and configure smart cards for use, you must also require the use of smart cards for interactive logon. You do this through the Account tab in the user account properties in Active Directory Users And Computers.

28. Which tool or command-line utility do you use to determine the applied Group Policy settings, security group membership, and the domain controller from which policy was applied?

   ❍ A. Group Policy Object Editor

   ❍ B. Gpresult

   ❍ C. Gpotool

   ❍ D. Gpupdate

   Answer B is correct. Gpresult provides details on many aspects of Group Policy and can be used in `/v` and `/z` verbose modes to get more detail.

29. You've made changes to User Configuration settings in Group Policy. You do not want to wait for automatic refresh to test these settings. What should you do?

   ❍ A. Type `gpotool` at a command prompt.

   ❍ B. Type `gpotool /checkacl` at a command prompt.

   ❍ C. Type `gpupdate /target:user` at a command prompt.

   ❍ D. Type `gpupdate /target:computer` at a command prompt.

   Answer C is correct. To refresh only User Configuration settings, type `gpupdate /target:user` at the command prompt.

30. You have applied the hisecws security template to all users in the Sales OU by creating a GPO, importing the template into the GPO, and then linking the GPO to the Sales OU. You later made changes to the GPO settings. These changes caused undesirable results, and you want to change the settings back to the default settings for the hisecws security template. You do not have a backup of the GPO available. What is the fastest way to make this change?

❍ A. Import the hisecws security template into the GPO a second time.

❍ B. Edit the policy settings in the GPO.

❍ C. Use Dcgpofix to restore the default GPOs.

❍ D. Delete the existing GPO. Create a new GPO, import the template into it, and link it to the Sales OU.

Answer D is correct. Without a backup of a GPO, the fastest and most reliable way to ensure that you get back to the default settings in a security template is to create a new GPO, import the template into it, and link it to the Sales OU.

Index

Symbols

A

We'd like to hear your suggestions for improving our indexes. Send email to *index@oreilly.com*.

D

E

H

I

K

L

M

N

Q

R

S

T

U

V

W

X

Z

About the Author

William R. Stanek has over 20 years of hands-on experience with advanced programming and development. He has written 61 books, including: *Microsoft Windows Server 2003 Administrator's Pocket Consultant*, *Windows Server 2003 Inside Out*, *Microsoft Exchange Server 2003 Administrator's Pocket Consultant*, and *Microsoft IIS 6.0 Administrator's Pocket Consultant*. These are currently the best sellers in their respective markets. Mr. Stanek has an MS degree in Information Systems with distinction, and a BS degree in Computer Science magna cum laude. He served in the Persian Gulf War as a combat crew member on an electronic warfare aircraft. He flew on numerous combat missions into Iraq and was awarded nine medals for his wartime service, including one of the United States of America's highest honors, the Air Force Distinguished Flying Cross. Currently, he resides in the Pacific Northwest with his wife and children.

Colophon

The animal on the cover of *MCSE Core Required Exams in a Nutshell,* Third Edition, is an African elephant (*Elephas maximus*). Elephants are the world's largest terrestrial animals, striking not only for their great size (4 tons) but also their trunk. The trunk is used for both smell and touch, as well as for picking things up and as a snorkel when swimming. The most important use of the trunk is obtaining food and water. Another distinguishing feature is the tusks, modified incisors of durable ivory, for which man has hunted the elephant nearly to extinction. Like right- or lefthanded people, elephants favor one tusk.

Elephants spend most of their day—up to 17 hours—preparing and eating their food, which consists of several hundred pounds per day of bamboo, bark, grass, roots, wood, and other vegetation. They generally sleep standing up for short periods. Elephants also take frequent baths in water or mud, and, when the weather is hot, fan themselves with their ears. They can trumpet loudly and also often make a kind of relaxed purring or rumbling noise.

The lifespan of an elephant is about 40 to 50 years, though a few live into their sixties. They have keen hearing and can learn verbal commands, increasing their popularity as circus stars and beasts of burden. Elephants have also been used in war, most notably by the Carthaginian general Hannibal.

Elephant cemeteries, where old and sick elephants congregate to die, are a myth. Experiments have proved that they are not afraid of mice, but do fear rabbits and some dogs. They have no natural enemies apart from man.

The cover image is from *The Illustrated Natural History: Mammalia*. The cover font is Adobe ITC Garamond. The text font is Linotype Birka; the heading font is Adobe Myriad Condensed; and the code font is LucasFont's TheSans Mono Condensed.

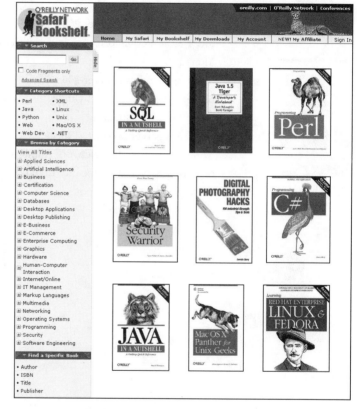

Related Titles from O'Reilly

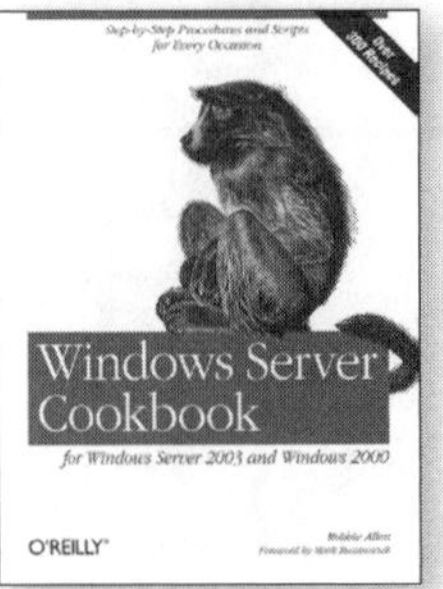

Windows Administration

Active Directory Cookbook, *2nd Edition*

Active Directory, *3rd Edition*

DNS on Windows Server 2003

Essential Microsoft Operations Manager

Essential SharePoint

Exchange Server Cookbook

Learning Windows Server 2003, *2nd Edition*

MCSE Core Required Exams in a Nutshell, *3rd Edition*

Monad

Securing Windows Server 2003

SharePoint Office Pocket Guide

SharePoint User's Guide

Windows Server 2003 in a Nutshell

Windows Server 2003 Network Administration

Windows Server 2003 Security Cookbook

Windows Server Cookbook

Windows Server Hacks

Windows XP Cookbook